J

MOON

PENNSYLVANIA

ANNA DUBROVSKY

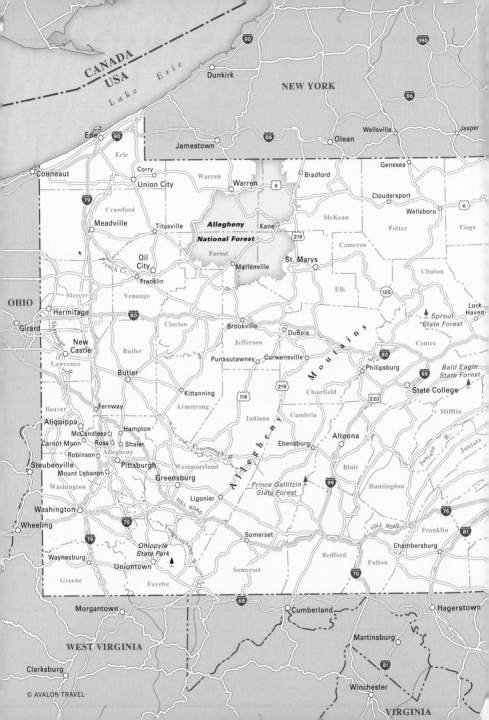

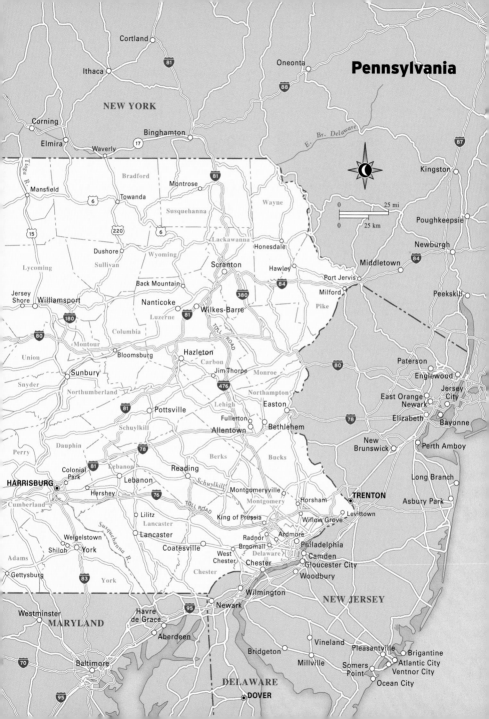

Contents

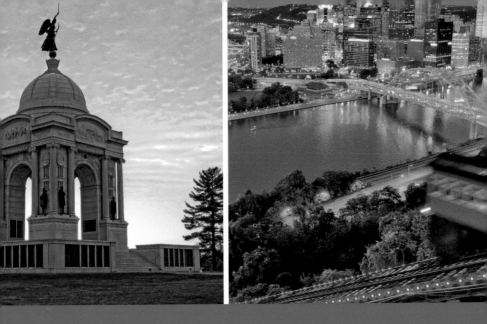

DISCOVER
Pennsylvania

If there's one thing Pennsylvania's founder insisted on, it's that everyone feel welcome. Centuries before New York's Greenwich Village and San Francisco's Haight-Ashbury district gained fame as centers of counterculture, William Penn's colony was the place where people could let their freak flags fly. It's thanks to Billy that Pennsylvania is home to the oldest Amish community in the world. It's thanks to him that today's visitor can, in less than 90 minutes, go from one of the largest cities in the country to a place where horse-drawn buggies share the road. "Something for everyone" may be the most tired phrase in destination marketing, but Pennsylvania really means it.

The state that goes by "PA" is a magnet for history buffs, art enthusiasts, and nature lovers. It's where the nation's founders came up with "life, liberty, and the pursuit of happiness." It's where four score and seven years later, President Abraham Lincoln delivered the timeless speech that began: "Four score and seven years ago our fathers brought forth on this continent a new nation." Pennsylvania is where Andy Warhol first touched a drawing pencil and where Andrew Wyeth painted his whole life. It's where you'll find the only U.S. museum dedicated to hiking and the largest herd of free-roaming elk east of the Rockies.

Clockwise from top left: the Pennsylvania Memorial in Gettysburg National Military Park; the Pittsburgh skyline; the Capitol Complex in Harrisburg; a whitetail deer in winter; pretzels in Pennsylvania Dutch country; the Liberty Bell.

Pennsylvania is a wide expanse of mostly wilderness and farmlands flanked by two cosmopolitan cities. In the southeast corner: Philadelphia, the nation's birthplace. In the southwest corner: Pittsburgh, the manufacturing powerhouse turned cultural hub. The places in between jockey for distinction: "The Sweetest Place on Earth" (Hershey), the "Factory Tour Capital of the World" (York County), "Antiques Capital USA" (Adamstown), and a borough made famous by a groundhog (Punxsutawney), to name a few.

Pennsylvania is a study in the art of the comeback. Pittsburgh, described by one 19th-century writer as "hell with the lid off," topped Forbes.com's list of "America's most livable cities" in 2010. In the Lehigh Valley, a cultural center and casino resort have risen on the site of a shuttered steel works. Forests depleted by logging have regrown. Abandoned railroad lines have morphed into multiuse trails. For visitors, too, Pennsylvania is a place of renewal.

It's safe to say that William Penn would be pleased at the shape his land has taken. Welcome.

Clockwise from top left: penguin ice sculptures in Pittsburgh; stone bridge over a creek in Adams County; apple harvest; bird's eye view of Harrisburg.

Planning Your Trip

Where to Go

Philadelphia

The state's largest city is rich in **historic and cultural attractions.** A thorough exploration of **Independence National Historical Park** is a better primer on the founding of this nation than any textbook, and the city's **art museums** are too numerous to see in a day. Known for **cheesesteaks** and **rabid sports fans,** the City of Brotherly Love has reached new heights of hipness in recent years, with galleries and eateries sprouting in the unlikeliest places. Idyllic towns such as **Kennett Square** and **New Hope** lure Philadelphians past the city limits.

Pennsylvania Dutch Country

With its **Germanic heritage,** fabled cuisine (pass the shoofly pie), and unmatched concentration of **Amish,** this region ranks as Pennsylvania's most unique. **Gettysburg,** site of the Civil War's bloodiest battle, reels in school groups and history buffs, while **Hershey** defends its title as "The Sweetest Place on Earth."

Pocono Mountains

Pennsylvania's **winter sports** capital holds as much appeal during the warmer months, thanks to its **rivers, lakes, waterfalls,** and **trails.** Let's not forget its many **resorts,** where there's never a dull moment. Though most are geared toward families, the champagne glass whirlpool is alive and well in the Poconos.

Pittsburgh

Once known as the Smoky City, the Burgh has

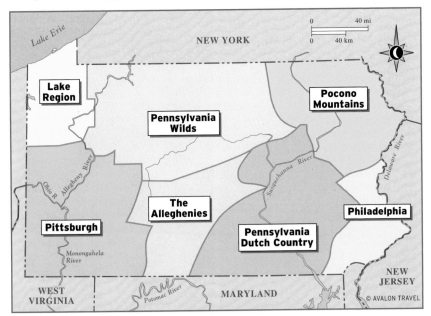

If You Have...

- **A WEEKEND:** Get to know the City of Brotherly Love.

- **A LONG WEEKEND:** Add a day trip to the Brandywine Valley.

- **5 DAYS:** Unwind in Amish country, where time seems to slow down.

- **10 DAYS:** Continue in a clockwise loop through the state, taking in Gettysburg, Pittsburgh, and Presque Isle.

the Betsy Ross House in Philadelphia

risen from the ashes to become a **cultural hotbed.** It boasts the world's largest single-artist museum and the state's largest history museum, not to mention the NFL's winningest **football team. Fallingwater,** the world-renowned work of architecture, is one of many reasons to explore its surrounds.

The Alleghenies

Rail fans flock to this mountainous region to drink in the famous **Horseshoe Curve,** walk through the nation's **first railroad tunnel,** and tour a **19th-century roundhouse.** Motorcyclists flood the so-called **Flood City** in June, and **football fever** strikes State College in the fall.

Lake Region

Pennsylvania's northwest corner shines in the summer months, when **Erie's natural harbor** teems with pleasure boats and the sandy beaches of **Presque Isle** are open for business. Families pack swim gear and stale bread for their pilgrimage to **Pymatuning Lake,** where fish and waterfowl compete for crumbs. As the birthplace of the modern oil industry, this region also attracts **history buffs.**

Pennsylvania Wilds

Home to the largest herd of **free-roaming elk** east of the Rockies, a national forest, and the so-called **Grand Canyon of Pennsylvania,** this nature lover's wonderland is also home to a major celebrity: **Punxsutawney Phil.**

summertime in York County

When to Go

Like the rest of the northeastern United States, Pennsylvania experiences **all four seasons.** There's no best or worst time to visit because the state has plenty to offer year-round, but some areas are better at certain times than others.

Summer is the season to take advantage of Pennsylvania's lakes: Loll on the beaches of Presque Isle, feed the ducks at Pymatuning, sail Lake Arthur in Moraine State Park, pilot a houseboat around Raystown Lake, or zoom around Lake Wallenpaupack. It's also a great time to visit Hershey, where a chocolate empire has given rise to an amusement park and zoo, among other family-friendly attractions.

It's not called Pennsylvania, as in "Penn's woods," for nothing. This is a tree-blanketed state, which makes **fall** a fabulous time to visit. Head to the northern half of the state—Allegheny National Forest, Pine Creek Gorge, or the Pocono Mountains—for landscapes ablaze in color. While you're there, be sure to visit Benezette, the

autumn in Kinzua Bridge State Park

winter in rural Pennsylvania

epicenter of Pennsylvania elk country. September and October are when the elk get it on, and they're apt to do it in the open.

Speaking of wildlife, fall is the best time to visit Hawk Mountain Sanctuary, which lies in the flight path of thousands of migrating raptors. 'Tis also the season to cruise the farmlands of Pennsylvania, stopping to pick apples, stomp grapes, and take a hayride. If possible, head to Lancaster County, where Amish farmers rely on horsepower of the four-legged variety to work their fields.

Ah, **winter.** Love it or hate it, the season of snow and ice brings unique opportunities. Pennsylvania's top snow sports destinations are in opposite corners of the state: the Pocono Mountains in the northeast and the Laurel Highlands in the southwest. In early February, head to Punxsutawney to join the Groundhog Day hubbub.

Rainfall and melting snow and ice make **springtime** ideal for hitting the rivers. Lehigh Gorge State Park in the Poconos and Ohiopyle State Park in the Laurel Highlands are popular for white-water rafting and kayaking. Spring is also a swell time to visit the state's largest city, Philadelphia, which gets hot and crowded in summer.

springtime in Harrisburg

The Best of Pennsylvania

Pennsylvania is a large state, and few visitors set out to see east, west, north, and south in one go. To pull it off, you'll need 10 days, a car, and a copy of *Moon Pennsylvania* (but of course). The following itinerary assumes travel during the warmer months, when the bulk of attractions are open and the roads are more inviting.

Day 1

It only makes sense to begin in the nation's birth-place: **Philadelphia.** Pick up a timed ticket to **Independence Hall** at the Independence Visitor Center, loading up on maps and brochures while you're at it. Make your way to the **Liberty Bell,** and if there's still time before your Independence Hall tour, take a constitutional through the **Rose Garden** and **Magnolia Garden** or **Franklin Square.** After your tour, try a Supreme Court robe on for size at the **National Constitution Center.** Come sundown, head to the neon-lit, Cheez Whiz-stained intersection of 9th Street and Passyunk Avenue in South Philly, home to **rival cheesesteakeries** Pat's King of Steaks and Geno's Steaks.

Day 2

Do some time at **Eastern State Penitentiary** before sprinting up the so-called **Rocky steps** and getting lost in the period rooms of the **Philadelphia Museum of Art.** Then take a stroll along the picturesque Benjamin Franklin Parkway and your pick of museums: the **Barnes Foundation, Rodin Museum, Franklin Institute** science museum, or **Academy of Natural Sciences.** Finally, treat your culturally enriched self to a show on the **Avenue of the Arts** and a cocktail at **The Ritz-Carlton.**

Day 3

Head south on Route 1 to the **Brandywine River Museum,** home to works by three generations of Wyeths. Down the road you'll find **Chaddsford**

Geno's Steaks in Philadelphia

a buggy ride in Lancaster County

springtime at Longwood Gardens

Winery, Pennsylvania's largest maker of grown-up grape juice, and then stunning **Longwood Gardens.**

Day 4

It's time for Intercourse (go ahead, snigger away), one of several Lancaster County burgs with an eyebrow-raising name. Taste your way through **Kitchen Kettle Village,** then drive west on Route 340 to **Plain & Fancy Farm,** where you can learn all about Amish life and eat your weight in Pennsylvania Dutch-style foods. After a **buggy ride** through the Amish countryside, shop your heart out at the Rockvale and Tanger **outlet malls.**

Day 5

Head west on Route 30 to **Gettysburg,** site of the Civil War's bloodiest battle. Take your pick of battlefield tours—horseback and Segway are two ways to go—and don't leave Gettysburg National Military Park without seeing the **cyclorama** in the visitors center. For dinner, indulge

in colonial-style chow at the **Dobbin House Tavern.** Bed down among (friendly) ghosts at the **Best Western Gettysburg Hotel.**

Day 6

Get an early start. Today's destination is the **Laurel Highlands,** home to Frank Lloyd Wright's **Fallingwater.** On your way to the architectural masterpiece, pay your respects to victims of the 9/11 attacks at the **Flight 93 National Memorial.**

Day 7

Start your day in Pittsburgh with a visit to the **Andy Warhol Museum,** then head to the **Mattress Factory** for more jaw-dropping art or the **National Aviary** for something to tweet about. Make your way to **Station Square** and dine at the Grand Concourse before ascending Mount Washington via the **Monongahela Incline.** When you're done oohing and aahing over the view, report to party central: the South Side's **East Carson Street.**

a hayride in the Poconos

Day 8

Set out on I-79 north for **Erie.** Stop at the **Tom Ridge Environmental Center** as you enter **Presque Isle State Park,** home to the finest beaches in the state. Ride a coaster or two at **Waldameer,** order an "orange vanilla twist" cone at nearby **Sara's,** and call it an early night. You'll need plenty of shut-eye for day 9.

Day 9

The bad news: You'll spend about four hours behind the wheel on your eastward journey to the so-called **Grand Canyon of Pennsylvania.** The good news: Route 6 winds through gorgeous country, including **Allegheny National Forest.** Stretch your legs on the trails of **Leonard Harrison State Park** before watching the sun set over the "Grand Canyon," appropriately known as **Pine Creek Gorge.**

Day 10

Devote the last day to outdoor adventure in the **Pocono Mountains,** where the options are virtually endless.

Sara's, near the entrance of Presque Isle State Park

Kennett Square, the "Mushroom Capital of the World"

Weekend Getaways

You don't have to hit up your boss for vacation time to get to know Pennsylvania. Seeing it bit by bit is a good way to go, and the state has no shortage of juicy bits. Here are some two-day itineraries to get you started.

From Philadelphia

While walking and public transportation are the easiest ways to get around Philly, you'll need a car for the following escapes.

WYETH COUNTRY

Wake up early and drive to **Nemours Mansion & Gardens,** 30 miles southwest of Philly, in time for the first tour of the day. (Reservations are strongly recommended. If you're traveling January-April, when the magnificent French-style estate is closed to the public, head to nearby **Winterthur Museum & Country Estate** instead.) After your tour, cross back into Pennsylvania and have lunch at **Talula's Table** in historic **Kennett Square,** the "Mushroom Capital of the World." Devote the afternoon to the horticultural wonderland that is **Longwood Gardens.** The next day, visit the **Brandywine River Museum,** home to a remarkable collection of works by three generations of Wyeths. If you're there April-November, take advantage of the opportunity to tour **Kuerner Farm,** which inspired nearly 1,000 works by Andrew Wyeth, one of the most celebrated artists of the 20th century. Treat yourself to a tasting at **Chaddsford Winery** before returning to the big city.

BUCKS COUNTY

Drive to Doylestown, 25 miles north of Philly, to marvel at the **Mercer Museum** and **Fonthill,** concrete castles built by one incorrigible collector. Then follow Route 202 north to **New Hope** (10 miles), stopping to browse the specialty shops of **Peddler's Village** along the way. After checking into a B&B in the New Hope area, head to **Marsha Brown** for New Orleans-style fine dining. (It's not a bad idea to book a table in advance.)

Outdoor Adventure

Ricketts Glen State Park

Pennsylvania is packed with mountains, forests, lakes, and rivers, so you never have to look far for outdoor adventure. The state parks alone number 117, and there's no fee for entry. Not sure where to start? Here are some ideas:

HIKING

- Twenty-one waterfalls along a 7.2-mile trail? No wonder **Ricketts Glen State Park** is one of northeast Pennsylvania's main attractions. The tallest falls is an impressive 94 feet.

- Pennsylvania is home to 230 miles of the famed **Appalachian Trail,** which passes through 14 states, and the **Appalachian Trail Museum.** The nation's first museum dedicated to hiking is located near the midpoint of the 2,180-mile footpath.

- Climb **Mount Nittany** for a bird's-eye view of Penn State, which borrowed the mountain's name for its mascot, the Nittany Lion.

- With trees as old as 450 years, **Cook Forest State Park** will have you craning your neck. Choose from 29 miles of trails.

BIKING

- *Outside* magazine lauded the 26-mile **Lehigh Gorge Trail** in Lehigh Gorge State Park as one of "America's sweetest rides." It's especially alluring in October, at the peak of fall foliage.

- Completed in 2013, the 150-mile **Great Allegheny Passage** stretches from Downtown Pittsburgh to Cumberland, Maryland, where it meets another trail that continues all the way to Washington DC. Ohiopyle State Park contains 27 miles of the GAP, the first trail inducted into the Rails-to-Trails Conservancy's Rail-Trail Hall of Fame.

- Designed by the International Mountain Bicycling Association, the 33-mile **Allegrippis Trail System** attracts mountain bikers from around the world. You'll find two trailheads at Seven Points Recreation Area.

- Take a ride on the wild side on the 60-mile **Pine Creek Rail Trail,** which leads through woods inhabited by coyotes, black bears, and even bald eagles.

WATER SPORTS

- Beloved by canoeists for its 40 miles of calm river, **Delaware Water Gap National Recreation Area** is one of the 10 most visited sites in the National Park System.

- **Ohiopyle State Park** features the most popular section of white water east of the Mississippi. Guides are available for less experienced paddlers.

- You can rent a houseboat—complete with hot tub—at **Raystown Lake,** the largest lake entirely within Pennsylvania.

- **Presque Isle,** a peninsula jutting into Lake Erie, offers ocean-style beaches, vistas, and activities, including surfing, windsurfing, kayaking, paddleboarding, and scuba diving.

WINTER SPORTS

- With seven major ski areas, the **Pocono Mountains** are a popular destination for skiing, snowboarding, and tubing. At Blue Mountain, you can even give luging a go. The **Laurel Highlands** region is home to Pennsylvania's largest ski resort, Seven Springs, which has been featured on the cover of *Snowboarder* magazine.

WILDLIFE WATCHING

- At **Hawk Mountain Sanctuary,** enjoy eye-level views of migrating hawks, eagles, and falcons. This is one of the best places in the country for spotting birds of prey.

- **Pymatuning Lake** is beloved by birders. Families flock to the **Pymatuning spillway,** where ducks walk on the backs of fish in a mad scramble for bread crumbs.

- The remote village of **Benezette** is the capital of Pennsylvania elk country. Mating season, in September and October, is the best time to visit.

URBAN ESCAPES

- The outdoors are in reach even in Pennsylvania's largest cities. **Philadelphia** has thousands of acres of parkland, from tree-lined **Rittenhouse Square** to untamed **Wissahickon Valley Park.** Breathtaking **Longwood Gardens** is a short drive from the city.

- **Pittsburgh** also boasts a horticultural hotspot: **Phipps Conservatory and Botanical Gardens. Moraine State Park,** which lies north of the city, offers boating, swimming, hiking, and more.

Hawk Mountain Sanctuary

A Weekend With the Kids

Hersheypark

These weekend excursions are designed for summertime, when kids are out of school and amusement parks are open.

HERSHEY
- **Day 1:** The so-called Sweetest Place on Earth is packed with attractions, so go easy on day 1 to avoid burnout by day 2. Start at **The Hershey Story,** which tells the story of Milton Hershey and his eponymous chocolate company and town. Children as young as four can experiment in the museum's Chocolate Lab. Then head to **Hershey's Chocolate World,** where singing cows (of the animatronic breed) lend insights into the field-to-factory process of making chocolate. Treat yourself—and the kids, of course—to a chocolate milkshake before you leave. In the late afternoon, stroll through the **Hershey Gardens,** which has a popular butterfly exhibit, and **The Hotel Hershey,** home to a sweets shop known for its cupcakes. Spend the night at the more affordable **Hershey Lodge,** which offers such activities as poolside movies and family bingo.
- **Day 2:** Romp through **Hersheypark** and **ZooAmerica.**

LANCASTER COUNTY
- **Day 1:** Spend today at **Dutch Wonderland,** being sure to catch a high-dive show. Bed down at the adjacent **Old Mill Stream Campground** or at **Verdant View Farm B&B,** where the kids can give milking a go in the morning.
- **Day 2:** Get lost in the Amazing Maize Maze at **Cherry Crest Adventure Farm** and your fill of whoopie pies at **Hershey Farm Restaurant.**

BUCKS COUNTY AND THE LEHIGH VALLEY
- **Day 1:** Visit Easton's **Crayola Experience** and **National Canal Museum,** where the kids can make like Picasso and build a bridge, respectively. In the evening, take in a double feature at **Becky's Drive-In,** dining on hot dogs, fresh-cut fries, and funnel cake. Spend the night in Easton or Bethlehem.
- **Day 2:** Wake up ready to tackle **Sesame Place** or **Dorney Park & Wildwater Kingdom,** the former being best suited to kids still young enough to idolize Elmo.

Devote the next day to exploring the boutiques and galleries of New Hope and its across-the-Delaware neighbor, **Lambertville.** To return to Philly, take Route 29 south to I-95 south.

AMISH COUNTRY

Drive to the **Strasburg Rail Road,** about 60 miles west of Philly, to ride a steam train through Amish farmlands. Enjoy a light lunch, a decadent dessert, and a view of the horse-and-buggy traffic through Strasburg's main intersection at the **Strasburg Country Store & Creamery.** Then make your way to Intercourse (9 miles) via Route 896 north and Route 340 east to sample the likes of pepper jam and chow-chow at **Kitchen Kettle Village.** Check out some **quilt shops** before checking into **AmishView Inn & Suites,** midway between Intercourse and Bird-in-Hand on Route 340. For dinner, pig out at **Shady Maple Smorgasbord** (11 miles). Devote the next day to the **Plain & Fancy Farm** complex, learning about the Amish way of life, experiencing a family-style meal at the on-site restaurant, and clip-clopping through the countryside with **Aaron and Jessica's Buggy Rides.**

From Pittsburgh

Pittsburgh's surroundings are particularly appealing to outdoorsy types, and the following itineraries are weather dependent.

MORAINE AND MCCONNELLS MILL

In the heat of summer, pack the makings of a cookout, drive 40 miles north to **Moraine State Park,** rent a pontoon boat and gas grill, and while away the day on **Lake Arthur.** After a night under the stars at **Bear Run Campground,** hit the trails of **McConnells Mill State Park** (5 miles). Chow down at **North Country Brewing Co.** before heading back to the Burgh.

WRIGHT AWAY

Drive to fabulous **Fallingwater,** 60 miles southeast of Pittsburgh, and learn how much over budget architect Frank Lloyd Wright went. In the afternoon, tour **Kentuck Knob,** one of his lesser-known creations, taking time to explore the sculpture-studded grounds. (Reservations are recommended for both Wright houses.) Rough it at a tent site in

patio dining at North Country Brewing Co.

Visitors to the Flight 93 National Memorial leave tributes.

Ohiopyle State Park or do the opposite at **Nemacolin Woodlands Resort.** In the morning, rent a bike in Ohiopyle and pedal part of the **Great Allegheny Passage** before finding your way to the moving **Flight 93 National Memorial** (45 miles).

COOK FOREST

Drive to **Cook Forest State Park,** 90 miles north of Pittsburgh, to size up the towering pines and hemlocks of the "Forest Cathedral." Spend the night at **Gateway Lodge** and paddle the **Clarion River** in the morning.

Ready, Aim, Fire!

A great deal of blood was shed in Pennsylvania during the 18th and 19th centuries, and war history buffs have been drawn here ever since. The **French and Indian War** (1754-1763), a power struggle between Great Britain and France that snowballed into the global **Seven Years' War,** began in present-day Pennsylvania. The **Revolutionary War** (1775-1783), which ended British rule in America, came to Philadelphia in 1777, forcing the Founding Fathers to flee to a more westerly Pennsylvania town. And the most harrowing battle of the **Civil War** (1861-1865) was fought on Pennsylvania soil. Books can teach us a lot about military history, but they're no substitute for standing on hallowed ground. Because war-related sites tend to be clustered, you can see a lot in just two days. Wear comfortable shoes that you won't mind getting dirty, as many sites call for walking on natural terrain.

French and Indian War

This war began over control of the "forks of the Ohio River" in present-day Pittsburgh, so it only makes sense to begin your tour there. The **Fort Pitt Museum** marks the contested spot. Up next: the Senator John Heinz History Center, where the ***Clash of Empires*** exhibit

Gettysburg reenactment

tells the story of the protracted war. The following day, drive 60 miles south to **Fort Necessity National Battlefield,** where a young George Washington fought his first battle—and surrendered for the first and last time. Don't dawdle too long because the museum at **Fort Ligonier,** about 40 miles away, is a must-see. If possible, time your trip to coincide with October's Fort Ligonier Days, featuring reenactments of a dramatic 1758 battle.

Revolutionary War

Start the morning at **Independence National Historical Park** in Philadelphia, where on July 4, 1776, representatives of the 13 colonies adopted the Declaration of Independence. Pay your respects to the Revolutionary War's fallen at the **Tomb of the Unknown Soldier,** pop by the **Betsy Ross House,** and quaff a beer based on Ben Franklin's fave recipe at **City Tavern.** Get an early start to day 2 and drive north to **Washington Crossing Historic Park,** commemorating the site from which General George Washington and his men crossed the Delaware

River on Christmas night 1776. Leave plenty of daylight for **Valley Forge National Historical Park,** where Washington's army suffered through the winter of 1777-1778. If you don't mind the cold, plan your trip around the annual reenactment of the Delaware crossing, held on Christmas Day.

Civil War

Devote the first day to **Gettysburg National Military Park,** site of the bloodiest battle between North and South, and if time permits, visit the **Shriver House Museum** to learn about the civilian experience. Come evening, tiptoe around town with a lantern-toting guide on a **Ghosts of Gettysburg** tour. The next day, head north on Route 15 to Harrisburg and pay a visit to the singular **National Civil War Museum** and the **John Harris-Simon Cameron Mansion,** whose porch served as a reviewing stand for a parade of the Union's African American soldiers. If you don't mind crowds, consider visiting Gettysburg during the annual reenactment of the July 1-3 battle.

Ride the Rails

Pennsylvania is a rail fan mecca, with multiple museums dedicated to trains and trolleys, motels made of railroad cars, B&Bs boasting prime views of active tracks, and tourist railroads in every region. Here are a dozen places where you can ride the rails.

PHILADELPHIA
New Hope & Ivyland Railroad: Soak in beautiful Bucks County from the comfort of an antique passenger coach or bar car.

DUTCH COUNTRY
Strasburg Rail Road: Based across from the Railroad Museum of Pennsylvania, America's oldest operating short-line railroad chugs through Amish farmlands.

Hawk Mountain Line: Proximity to the awesome Hawk Mountain Sanctuary gives this tourist railroad its name.

Steam Into History: Pennsylvania's newest tourist railroad features a faithful replica of the steam locomotive that carried President Abraham Lincoln to Gettysburg in 1863.

Steamtown National Historic Site

POCONO MOUNTAINS
Lehigh Gorge Scenic Railway: The open-air car is *the* place to be on the journey from Jim Thorpe.

Steamtown National Historic Site: Take advantage of the rare opportunity to ride in the cab of an operating steam engine. Located on the grounds of Steamtown, the **Electric City Trolley Museum** offers excursions to PNC Field, home of the Scranton/Wilkes-Barre RailRiders.

PITTSBURGH
Duquesne and Monongahela Inclines: Views of Pittsburgh's spectacular skyline await at the top of these 19th-century funiculars.

Pennsylvania Trolley Museum: Admission to this Washington County museum includes unlimited trolley rides.

THE ALLEGHENIES
Johnstown Inclined Plane: Built in the aftermath of the Great Johnstown Flood of 1889, the world's steepest vehicular inclined plane carried people to safety during subsequent floods.

Rockhill Trolley Museum: Take a ride through the countryside on a meticulously restored trolley.

LAKE REGION
Oil Creek & Titusville Railroad: You'll learn about Pennsylvania's important place in oil history during your trip through "the valley that changed the world."

THE WILDS
Tioga Central Railroad: Dining aboard the Tioga Central is a trip back in time.

Philadelphia

Look for ★ to find recommended
sights, activities, dining, and lodging.

Highlights

★ **Independence Hall:** It's here that the Founding Fathers debated and drafted the Declaration of Independence and later the Constitution. Timed tickets go fast during peak tourist periods (page 33).

★ **National Constitution Center:** Learn about the nation's supreme law and pose with life-size statues of its framers at this expansive museum (page 34).

★ **Philadelphia Museum of Art:** The nation's third-largest art museum is home to more than 225,000 objects, including a bronze statue of fictional boxer Rocky Balboa. Don't forget to sprint up the "Rocky steps" (page 45).

★ **Eastern State Penitentiary:** Opened in 1829, this sprawling prison served as a model for hundreds around the world, horrified Charles Dickens, and hosted Al "Scarface" Capone. It's a tourist attraction now, but it hasn't lost its eerie edge (page 46).

★ **City Hall:** Philadelphia's elaborately adorned seat of government is the largest municipal building in the country, and the view from its observation deck is tops (page 50).

★ **Masonic Temple:** The mother ship of Pennsylvania Masonry offers a smorgasbord of architectural styles under one roof (page 52).

★ **Reading Terminal Market:** In business since 1892, this indoor farmers market is a great place to grab lunch and people-watch (page 54).

★ **Longwood Gardens:** This Brandywine Valley treasure is quite simply one of the nation's premier horticultural attractions (page 92).

Pennsylvania's largest city hardly needs introduction. Anyone with a basic knowledge of U.S. history—or a DVD collection that includes the *Rocky* saga, for that matter—knows a thing or two about Philadelphia. It's where the Founding Fathers wrestled with the wording of the Declaration of Independence and the U.S. Constitution. It's where Ben Franklin came up with so many bright ideas.

Philadelphia was founded by William Penn in 1682, not long after King Charles II of England granted him a colony as payment for a debt owed to his late father. It was the monarch who named the colony Pennsylvania, meaning "Penn's woods," in honor of Penn's papa. But "Philadelphia" was Penn's idea. As a Quaker, Penn was no stranger to persecution, and he wanted his colony to be a live-and-let-live sort of place. He derived the name for his capital city from the Greek *philos,* or "love," and *adelphos,* or "brother." In part because of Penn's insistence on religious freedom, the City of Brotherly Love grew into the largest city in the colonies and the second largest in the British Empire after London.

Fast-forward to 1774. The 13 American colonies aren't so jazzed about British policies. Delegates from 12 meet in Philadelphia, the geographic center of the colonies, and send King George III a message: Ease up or else—or something to that effect. The king doesn't pay much heed to the First Continental Congress, and in May 1775, the Second Continental Congress convenes in Philadelphia. By now, the colonies and Great Britain are at war. The delegates get down to business, creating the Continental Army and appointing George Washington as commanding general. On July 4, 1776, they approve the Declaration of Independence, formally cutting ties with the British Empire. The following year, as British troops occupy Philadelphia, the Congress relocates to York, Pennsylvania. But Philadelphia's role in early American history is far from over.

To tell you what happened next would take some of the fun out of exploring Philadelphia and its surrounds. Find out for yourself at Independence Hall, where the Founding

---

Previous: the Liberty Bell; Rocky sculpture at the Philadelphia Museum of Art; Independence Hall. **Above:** Ben Franklin statue in The Franklin Institute.

Philadelphia

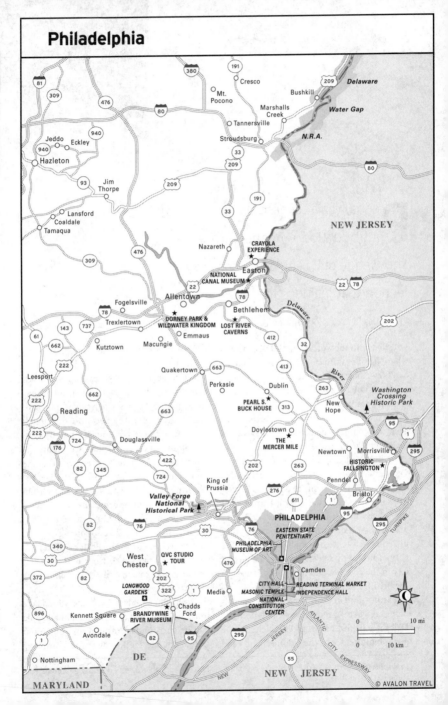

© AVALON TRAVEL

Fathers made so many important decisions; at Valley Forge, where Washington and his troops spent the winter of 1777-1778, after Philadelphia fell to the British; at the National Constitution Center, which tells the story of the nation's supreme law; and at dozens of other historic sites and museums.

If Philly had nothing but its historical significance going for it, it would still attract enough tourists to support fleets of open-top buses, faux trolleys, and horse-drawn carriages. It has much more going for it. It's an arts town—home to the nation's third-largest art museum, more Auguste Rodin sculptures than any place outside of Paris, an astounding number of outdoor murals and sculptures, and theaters both historic and thoroughly modern. It's a sports town, with teams in all four major leagues. And it's a food town. The cheesesteak may be its most famous dish, but Philadelphia is increasingly recognized for its profusion of BYOBs (bring-your-own-bottle restaurants) and gastropubs (bars with superb food). A growing number of celebrity restaurateurs are extending their culinary tentacles into the city. "Philadelphia's evolution from day trip to destination city is such that you can spend a long weekend there without visiting any 18th-century sites, and not even miss them," *The New York Times* asserted recently.

Several areas around the city are also worthy of a long weekend. To its west is the Brandywine Valley, home to stunning Longwood Gardens and other former estates of the uber-wealthy du Pont clan. To its north is Bucks County, known for its concrete castles and boutique shopping. Farther north is the Lehigh Valley, where you can catch two movies for $9 at the nation's oldest drive-in theater. New Jersey, to the east and south of Philadelphia, is a subject for another book.

PLANNING YOUR TIME

William Penn designed Philadelphia as a rectangular gridiron sandwiched between two rivers: the Delaware in the east and the Schuylkill in the west. Though the city has expanded far beyond his rectangle, most tourist attractions lie within it. The area is blessedly compact—roughly 25 blocks from river to river—and easy to navigate by foot. Most historic sites are concentrated near the Delaware, and while it would take three or more days of morn-to-eve sightseeing to experience them all, it's possible to hit the highlights in one day. First order of business: Get a timed ticket

a horse-drawn carriage tour in Old City

for Independence Hall at the Independence Visitor Center.

Many of Philadelphia's art and science museums are conveniently clustered around the Benjamin Franklin Parkway, close to the Schuylkill, so visiting two or even three in one day isn't out of the question. After museum hours, soak in the scenery, boathouses, and sculptures along Kelly Drive. If you're traveling with children, set aside a day to explore the Philadelphia Zoo, across the Schuylkill, or Adventure Aquarium, across the Delaware in Camden, New Jersey. If, on the other hand, you're traveling with your better half, book a B&B in the winery-rich Brandywine Valley or Bucks County.

Sights

Philadelphia is rich in historic and cultural attractions, some of which can be enjoyed at little or no cost. Admission to Independence Hall and the Liberty Bell Center, two major tourist draws, doesn't cost a cent. You can stroll down the nation's oldest residential street, Elfreth's Alley, for free and see where Betsy Ross sewed so many flags for just $5. If you're an art lover on a tight budget, you're going to love this city. It's home to more than 3,600 murals and, according to the Smithsonian Institution, more outdoor sculptures than any other U.S. city. And while guided tours of the city can cost a pretty penny, an all-day pass to ride the Phlash—a purple road trolley that stops at more than 25 key locations—is just $12.

If you plan on seeing several higher cost attractions, consider investing in a CityPass or Philadelphia Pass. A **CityPass** (888/330-5008, www.citypass.com/philadelphia, $59 per person, children 2-12 $39) is a booklet of tickets good for admission to four attractions and 24 hours of hop-on, hop-off privileges with Philadelphia Trolley Works and The Big Bus Company. It's valid for nine days and cuts the cost of all that sightseeing by almost half. A **Philadelphia Pass** (877/714-1999, www.philadelphiapass.com, $49-115 per person, children 2-12 $39-95) is a smart card good for admission to about 35 attractions in and around the city. The cost of the pass depends on how long it's valid. One-day, two-day, three-day, and five-day passes are available, and the more attractions you hit, the more you save. One of the best things about both passes is that you don't have to wait in line at some attractions. They're to Philadelphia sightseeing what first-class tickets are to air travel.

HISTORIC DISTRICT

The section of Philadelphia now known as the Historic District was, for a while there, the center of America. It's here that delegates from the American colonies debated and adopted the U.S. Declaration of Independence, a silver-tongued "buh-bye" to Great Britain, in 1776. It's here that another enduring document, the U.S. Constitution, was approved in 1787. The young nation's leaders met here from 1790 to 1800, while Washington DC was taking shape. Quite a few of the buildings where the Founding Fathers conducted their business, clinked glasses, or crawled into bed are still standing, which is why the area is often called "America's most historic square mile." Millions of people visit each year to walk in their footsteps.

Walking is, in fact, the best way to experience the Historic District, which is compact and dense with museums and monuments. It comprises two neighborhoods adjacent to the Delaware River: Old City and Society Hill to its south. Contrary to its name, Old City is a magnet for the young and hip of Philadelphia. Once teeming with industry, it's now peppered with galleries and boutiques. There's no better time to visit than the first Friday of the month, when many stay open as late as 9pm as part of **First Fridays in Old City**

Historic District

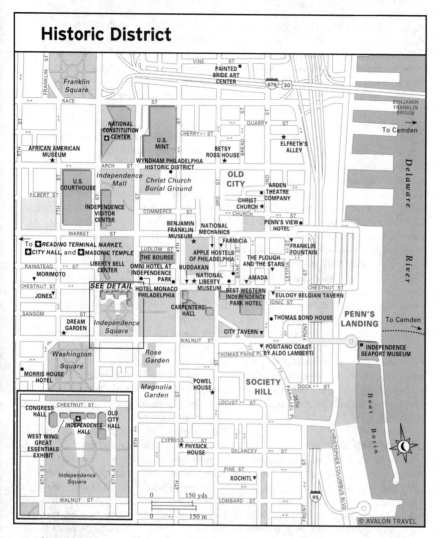

(215/625-9200, www.oldcityarts.org). Society Hill was home to many politicians and power brokers during Philadelphia's tenure as the nation's capital but eventually went to pot. In the 1950s the city undertook a revitalization of the crime-ridden slum, acquiring colonial houses and selling them to people on the condition that they be restored. Today it's one of the poshest neighborhoods in Philly.

Its upscale shopping and dining attract the moneyed, but the Historic District is also a magnet for travelers on a tight budget. It's home to one of only a handful of hostels in Pennsylvania. Many of its major attractions are part of **Independence National Historical Park** (215/965-2305, www.nps.gov/inde), and admission to most park sites is free. Guided tours are a great way to experience historic Philadelphia, but if you're there on a summer day and short on cash, look for teak benches marked "Once Upon a Nation." They're staffed by "storytellers" who dispense information about the area and America's birth—for free.

It's best to start your visit at the **Independence Visitor Center** (6th and Market Streets, 800/537-7676, www.phlvisitorcenter.com, 8:30am-6pm daily, open until 7pm June-Aug.), a large modern building sandwiched between the Liberty Bell Center and the National Constitution Center, two can't-miss sights. As the official visitors center for Philadelphia and its environs, it's stocked with maps and brochures and staffed by helpful sorts—some of them conspicuous in 18th- or 19th-century attire. Exhibits and free films help the orientation process. Tickets for a variety of tours and area attractions are sold here. If you're visiting March-December and plan to tour Independence Hall—and you should—you'll need a free timed-entrance ticket. Day-of tickets are distributed at the Visitor Center. Early birds get the greatest choice of times; it's not unusual for tickets to be gone by 1pm during peak tourist periods (namely summer and holidays). To ensure that tickets will be waiting for you, reserve them by phone or online (877/444-6777, www.recreation.gov, $1.50 per ticket surcharge). Tickets aren't required to tour Independence Hall in January or February.

Liberty Bell Center

Like New York's Statue of Liberty, the much-photographed Liberty Bell is an international icon of escape from oppression. How it came to symbolize freedom, justice, and all that good stuff is the subject of exhibits in its home since 2003, the **Liberty Bell Center** (Market Street between 5th and 6th Streets, 215/965-2305, www.nps.gov/inde, hours vary by season but generally open 9am-5pm daily, free admission). The fact that it's been mute for more than 150 years and still speaks to so many people is curious indeed.

Its history begins in 1751, when the Pennsylvania Assembly ordered a new bell for the State House (now Independence Hall) from a London foundry. The splurge was occasioned by the 50th anniversary of the Pennsylvania Charter of Privileges, which codified William Penn's ideals of religious toleration and political rights. The speaker of the Assembly chose an apt Bible quotation to be inscribed on the bell: "Proclaim liberty throughout all the land unto all the inhabitants thereof." No sooner was it hung than the bell cracked. Two local craftsmen, John Pass and John Stow, were tasked with melting and recasting it. They took the liberty of putting their surnames on the bell—and a lot of flak for its tone.

Anyone agitated by its E-flat strike note would have been frequently agitated. The bell was rung to call lawmakers together, to summon the citizenry for announcements, and to mark important occasions. It's often said that the bell tolled for the first public reading of the Declaration of Independence in 1776, but historians pooh-pooh that because the State House steeple was in shabby condition at that time.

Eventually the bell suffered a thin crack, which was purposely widened to keep the edges from vibrating against each other. When the bell tolled in celebration of the late George Washington's birthday in February 1846, the crack expanded something awful. "It received a sort of compound fracture in a zig-zag direction through one of its sides which put it completely out of tune and left it a mere wreck of what it was," reported the *Public Ledger*, a daily newspaper of the time.

By then the bell had achieved iconic status, thanks to abolitionists who had adopted it as a symbol of their cause. After the Civil War, the fatally cracked bell traveled the country, serving as a reminder of days when Americans were united in their quest for independence. Pass and Stow's 2,080-pound bell came home to Philadelphia in 1915, but a replica forged that year was used to promote women's suffrage. It appeared in different cities with its clapper chained to its side, a metaphor for the silencing of women, and was finally rung when they won the right to vote in 1920. To this day, oppressed groups evoke the image of the Liberty Bell. That its evocative power

Rose Garden, Magnolia Garden, and *Dream Garden*

There are plenty of ways to kill time while waiting for a tour of Independence Hall. The Historic District is packed with museums and other attractions. Some, of course, can take hours to explore. If half an hour is all you've got and it's a beautiful warm day, head to the **Rose Garden,** centerpiece of a landscaped area between Locust and Walnut Streets and 4th and 5th Streets. Planted by the Daughters of the American Revolution in honor of the men who penned the Declaration of Independence, the garden features antique roses. Among the 90-some varieties are "Old Blush" and the unusual green rose. Most flower only once a year, peaking in June. The cobblestone-paved entrance to the garden was once the courtyard of a stable. If you still have time, cross Locust Street to admire the smaller **Magnolia Garden,** a tribute to the nation's founders by the Garden Club of America. The 13 hybrid magnolias around its walled perimeter represent the original colonies. They bloom in early spring.

In the colder months, you can pass the time gazing at the *Dream Garden* (Curtis Center, Walnut and 6th Streets), a dazzling glass mosaic in the lobby of a somber 19th-century office building. Measuring 15 feet high and 49 feet wide, the leafy landscape was designed by Philadelphia-born artist Maxfield Parrish and executed by stained glass guru Louis Comfort Tiffany in 1916. It comprises more than 100,000 pieces of Favrile glass in 260 colors.

transcends nationality is evidenced by the variety of languages that mingle in the glass-walled Liberty Bell Center. The bell itself is cleverly displayed at the southern end of the building, where Independence Hall serves as backdrop.

★ Independence Hall

If Philadelphia is the nation's birthplace, then **Independence Hall** (Chestnut St. between 5th and 6th Streets, 215/965-2305, www.nps.gov/inde, hours vary by season but generally open 9am-5pm daily, free tours, timed ticket required Mar.-Dec.) can well be thought of as the womb. Within its walls, the Founding Fathers debated and drafted the Declaration of Independence and later the Constitution. George Washington himself presided over the Constitutional Convention, and the mahogany armchair in

Independence Hall

which he sat is among the furnishings visitors see today.

There's no charge for tours of Independence Hall, but tickets are required March-December. Day-of tickets are available at **Independence Visitor Center** (6th and Market Streets, 800/537-7676, www.phlvisitorcenter.com, 8:30am-6pm daily, open until 7pm June-Aug.) starting at 8:30am. It's a good idea to get there early; it's not unusual for tickets to be gone by 1pm during peak tourist periods (namely summer and holidays). To ensure that tickets will be waiting for you, reserve them by phone or online (877/444-6777, www.recreation.gov, $1.50 per ticket surcharge).

Independence Hall was built as the State House while Pennsylvania was still a British colony. Construction began in 1732 and continued for two decades. The legislature began meeting in the Assembly Room long before the ambitious building project was completed. (Even unfinished, the State House was a more dignified meeting place than private homes and taverns.) When tensions between American colonists and Great Britain erupted into war in 1775, the Second Continental Congress began meeting in the Assembly Room. Composed of delegates from the 13 colonies, including Benjamin Franklin and Thomas Jefferson, the Congress made one history-making decision after another in that room. It appointed Washington as commander in chief of the Continental Army (1775), adopted the Declaration of Independence (July 4, 1776), and settled on the design of the American flag (1777).

In September 1777 the Congress fled to York, Pennsylvania, as British forces occupied Philadelphia. During the occupation, which lasted until the following summer, the State House served as a hospital, prison, and barracks. There was much remodeling after Washington's troops regained control of the city and the Congress returned. In 1783, as the Revolutionary War drew to a close, the nation's governing body relocated from Philly. Pennsylvania's legislature reoccupied its chamber, only to surrender it to the framers of the Constitution in May 1787. The nation's supreme law was signed on September 17, and the State House reverted to its intended use until 1799, when the Pennsylvania capital was moved to Lancaster.

The building saw many alterations and uses in the 19th century. At one point it housed a museum of natural history. At another, its basement served as the city's dog pound. Since the creation of Independence National Historical Park in 1948, it has been returned to its late-18th-century appearance. Tours start in the East Wing, attached to the main building by a colonnade. Be sure to visit the West Wing, which is not part of the tour. It's home to the **Great Essentials Exhibit** (9am-5pm daily, free admission), which displays surviving copies of the Declaration of Independence, Articles of Confederation (the nation's first constitution), and the Constitution. There's also a silver inkstand said to have been used during the signing of the Declaration and Constitution.

Flanking Independence Hall are two park sites worth a quick peek. Constructed in the 1780s as the county courthouse, **Congress Hall** (Chestnut and 6th Streets, hours vary by season, free admission) is so named because the newly formed U.S. Congress met there during Philadelphia's 1790-1800 tenure as the nation's capital. Almost all the chairs on the second floor, which was occupied by the Senate, are authentic. Note the "spitting boxes" near the fireplaces. (Chewing tobacco didn't carry warning labels back then.) **Old City Hall** (Chestnut and 5th Streets, hours vary by season, free admission), which is so named because it was built as Philadelphia's second city hall, was home to the U.S. Supreme Court from its completion in 1791 to 1800, when the federal government moved to Washington DC.

★ National Constitution Center

The first museum dedicated to the U.S. Constitution, the **National Constitution Center** (525 Arch St., 215/409-6600, www.

constitutioncenter.org, 9:30am-5pm Mon.-Fri., 9:30am-6pm Sat., noon-5pm Sun., admission $14.50, seniors, students, and children 13-18 $13, children 4-12 $8) opened on July 4, 2003, a day that marked the adoption of another formulated-in-Philly document, the Declaration of Independence. It's one of the flashier sights in town—not surprising given its $185 million price tag. The visitor experience begins with *Freedom Rising*, a multimedia presentation in a star-shaped theater with a 360-degree screen. It's a stirring introduction to the Constitution's main themes. Anyone interested in the nitty-gritty can spend the better part of a day at the museum, which presents the story of the nation's supreme law through more than 100 exhibits. But an hour or two is enough to hit the highlights, including Signers' Hall, featuring life-size bronze statues of the 39 men who signed the Constitution and three dissenters.

Be sure to check the calendar of events, available on the museum's website. The Constitution Center serves as a sort of town hall, regularly hosting prominent lawmakers, scholars, authors, and other expert sorts. In March 2008 then-Senator Barack Obama delivered his seminal speech on race ("I am the son of a black man from Kenya and a white woman from Kansas . . .") there. The following month the museum hosted the final debate between the presidential hopeful and his Democratic primary rival, Hillary Clinton.

The Constitution Center's glass-enclosed Delegates' Café is a good place to fuel up for more sightseeing.

Franklin Square

Visitors to the Historic District run a real risk of information overload. To the rescue: **Franklin Square** (6th and Race Streets, 215/629-4026, www.historicphiladelphia.org), a lovely park within skipping distance of the Constitution Center. It's arguably the most kid-friendly spot in the area, with a distinctive playground, old-fashioned carousel, and Philadelphia-themed mini golf course. On the 18th hole, players putt through the crack in the Liberty Bell.

It's not a bad idea to come hungry. In 2009 the city's most prolific restaurateur, Stephen Starr, opened **SquareBurger** on the 7.5-acre green. It offers burgers (including a veggie version), hot dogs, root beer floats, shakes, and sundaes—all for under $7. SquareBurger's "Cake Shake," made with vanilla ice cream and Tastykake snacks, is an utterly unique indulgence.

the National Constitution Center

Franklin Square is one of five squares included in William Penn's original plan for the city. Initially known as Northeast Square, it served as a cattle pasture, burial ground, and military drill site before the city reclaimed it as a park in 1837, erecting an elegant marble fountain. By the turn of this century, the park was in sorry shape. A 2006 facelift transformed the desolate square block into a swell family destination. The original fountain remains its centerpiece.

African American Museum in Philadelphia

Founded in 1976, less than a decade after the assassination of Martin Luther King Jr. and the ensuing riots, the **African American Museum in Philadelphia** (701 Arch St., 215/574-0380, www.aampmuseum.org, 10am-5pm Wed.-Sat., noon-5pm Sun., admission $14, seniors, students, and children 4-12 $10) was the first institution of its kind to be funded by a major city. Its large collection of art and artifacts documents the history and culture of the African diaspora. In 2009 the Smithsonian affiliate unveiled a new core exhibition with a high-tech twist. *Audacious Freedom: African Americans in Philadelphia 1776-1876* brings unsung heroes to life by way of video projections. When approached by a visitor, each trailblazer sounds off about life during the time period. Think of it as a cross-era cocktail party.

Carpenters' Hall

Most visitors to historic Philadelphia quickly learn that Independence Hall was the meeting place of the Second Continental Congress, the esteemed assemblage responsible for the Declaration of Independence. Fewer come to appreciate that nearby **Carpenters' Hall** (Chestnut St. between 3rd and 4th Streets, 215/925-0167, www.carpentershall.org, 10am-4pm Tues.-Sun. Mar.-Dec. and Wed.-Sun. Jan.-Feb., free admission) hosted the First Continental Congress, which convened in the fall of 1774 to coordinate resistance to a series of heavy-handed laws imposed by

Britain. Composed of delegates from 12 of the 13 colonies, the Congress organized a boycott of British goods, petitioned King George III to redress colonists' grievances, and resolved that a second Congress would meet if the monarch turned a deaf ear. The monarch turned a deaf ear.

Among the exhibits in Carpenters' Hall is a room furnished as it might have been in 1774. You'll also find a parade float built to celebrate ratification of the Constitution, a banner carried in the parade, a remarkably detailed model illustrating the hall's construction, and early carpentry tools.

The Georgian-style gem was constructed from 1770 to 1774 as a meeting hall for the Carpenters' Company, a trade guild whose members built much of colonial Philadelphia. Practical men, they immediately began renting out space in their new headquarters. The list of tenants is long and includes the nation's first lending library and the American Philosophical Society, both founded by Benjamin Franklin. In 1798 the hall was leased to the Bank of Pennsylvania and later that year became the target of America's first bank robbery. (The inside job netted $162,821, which was returned in exchange for a pardon.) The Carpenters' Company, founded in 1724, still holds regular meetings, making it the oldest trade guild in the country.

Benjamin Franklin Museum

Author and printer, politician and diplomat, scientist and inventor, Benjamin Franklin (1706-1790) gets a lot of props in his adopted hometown of Philadelphia. A river-spanning bridge, a public square, a science museum, a scenic boulevard, and even an ice cream shop bear the name of the Boston-born brainiac, whose formal schooling ended when he was a preteen. Philadelphia is also home to the only museum in the world dedicated to Franklin's life and times. The **Benjamin Franklin Museum** (Franklin Court, entries on Market and Chestnut Streets between 3rd and 4th Streets, 215/965-2305, www.nps.gov/inde, 9am-5pm daily, admission $5, children

4-16 $2), which reopened in 2013 following a two-year overhaul, is designed to appeal to both kids and adults. It covers topics as wide ranging as the armonica, a musical instrument Franklin invented, to his stance on slavery.

The museum is housed underground, beneath the site of Franklin's home during the last few years of his life. His three-story house is long gone, but it's represented by a steel "ghost structure" erected in 1976 in celebration of the nation's bicentennial. Franklin Court, as the site is called, also features the only active post office in the country that doesn't fly an American flag—because there wasn't one when Franklin became the first Postmaster General of the United States in 1775.

The Founding Father's passing at the ripe age of 84 was mourned throughout America and France, its Revolutionary War ally. An estimated 20,000 people gathered for his funeral at **Christ Church Burial Ground** (Arch St. between 4th and 5th Streets, 215/922-1695, www.christchurchphila.org, 10am-4pm Mon.-Sat. and noon-4pm Sun. Mar.-Nov., noon-4pm Fri.-Sat. in Dec., closed Jan.-Feb., admission $2, children $1, guided tour $3, children $1), which is a short walk from Franklin Court and worth a visit. Almost 300 years old, the graveyard is peppered with 1,400 markers. Franklin is one of five Declaration of Independence signers interred there, along with a host of other colonial- and Revolutionary-era bigwigs. Some visitors believe that tossing a penny on Franklin's gravestone brings good luck. Keep in mind that the thrifty Renaissance man coined the phrase "A penny saved is a penny earned."

National Liberty Museum

A paean to heroism, the **National Liberty Museum** (321 Chestnut St., 215/925-2800, www.libertymuseum.org, 10am-5pm Tues.-Sat., noon-6pm Sun., open daily Memorial Day-Labor Day, admission $7, seniors $6, students $5, children 5-17 $2) tells the stories of courageous people from throughout the ages, including biblical figures, Anne Frank, Nelson Mandela, and the astronauts of the ill-fated space shuttle *Columbia*. A three-story exhibit through its center pays tribute to the heroes of 9/11. The point of it all is to foster "good character, civic responsibility, and respect for all people." And while some exhibits come off as sensitivity training on steroids—witness the paper shredder that allows visitors to symbolically destroy negative words—others are mesmerizing. Particularly yummy is an installation sculpture featuring two life-size children made of jellybeans.

The museum also houses an impressive collection of contemporary glass art, including Dale Chihuly's 21-foot *Flame of Liberty*. Why glass art? Because, like freedom, it's both beautiful and fragile.

Betsy Ross House

Betsy Ross, one of the most famous figures in American history, is known for one thing: sewing the nation's first flag. Whether she did that one thing has long been a matter of debate. Witness the measured wording on the historic marker near the **Betsy Ross House** (239 Arch St., 215/629-4026, www.historicphiladelphia.org, 10am-5pm daily, closed Mon. Dec.-Feb., admission $5, seniors, students, and children $4, admission and audio tour $7, seniors, students, and children $6), where she supposedly lived when she supposedly stitched the flag in 1776: "Credited with making the first stars and stripes flag, Ross was a successful upholsterer." The dearth of evidence doesn't stop hundreds of thousands of people from visiting the circa 1740 townhouse every year. After all, the version of events sworn to by Betsy's family hasn't been *discredited*. And there's no debating that she was a gutsy patriot, a working mother who produced flags for the government for half a century.

It doesn't take long to explore the little house, which is furnished with period antiques and some reproductions. Several items

Take a Tour

As one of America's largest and most historic cities, Philadelphia has no shortage of tour operators. Choosing one is a matter of preference—and budget. Would you rather walk or cover more ground by bike, bus, or other vehicle? Are you hungry for history, scenery, or a good cheesesteak? Here are some tour options worth considering.

GET THE LAY OF THE LAND

As cities go, Philadelphia is supremely walkable. But the quickest way to get a feel for its main attractions is to hop on a tourist bus. **Philadelphia Trolley Works** (215/389-8687, www.phillytour. com, daily year-round except for Christmas and New Year's Day, 24-hour pass $27, children 4-12 $10) offers sightseeing tours 363 days a year, weather permitting. The company operates road trolleys and double-decker buses (marked "The Big Bus Company"), and tickets are good for both vehicle types. They depart from the northeast corner of 5th and Market Streets in Old City, but you can hop on or off at any of their 21 stops, including Chinatown, City Hall, Eastern State Penitentiary, the Philadelphia Museum of Art, the Philadelphia Zoo, and Penn's Landing. Tickets can be purchased on board, online, at the Independence Visitor Center, and at many hotel concierge desks. Philadelphia Trolley Works offers a variety of other tours, including a **Philly by Night** bus tour and **horse-drawn carriage rides** through the Historic District. Check the website for details.

In the warmer months, Segway and bike tours are a fun way to get to know Philly. **DeTours** (267/324-5408, www.detourstouring.com, daily Apr.-Sept., Fri.-Mon. in Oct., Fri.-Sun. in Nov.) offers several Segway tours, including a 90-minute Center City tour ($65) and a **cheesesteak tour** ($85) complete with tastings. You must weigh 90-275 pounds to ride a Segway. **Philadelphia Bike Tours** (215/514-3124, www.philadelphiabiketour.com, year-round) offers three-hour river-to-river tours ($68) as well as customized tours for groups of four or more. If you prefer to explore on your own, you can have a bike, helmet, and lock delivered to your hotel ($57/day).

GET EDUCATED (AND MAYBE A LITTLE TIPSY)

A walking tour in the Historic District is a great way to learn about Philadelphia's role in American history. The 75-minute **Constitutional Walking Tour** (215/525-1776, www.theconstitutional.com, daily Apr.-Nov., $17.50 per person, children 3-12 $12.50, family of four $55) stops at more than 20 sites in and around Independence National Historical Park, including the Betsy Ross House, Franklin Court, and Christ Church Burial Ground. Tours meet outside the main entrance to the National Constitution Center (525 Arch St.). If you prefer to go at your own pace, you can download the **Constitutional Audio Tour** for $14.99.

In the summer months, volunteers for the nonprofit **Friends of Independence National Historical Park** (215/861-4971, www.friendsofindependence.org) lead free **Twilight Tours** (6pm daily mid-June-Labor Day) of the park. The tours begin at the Independence Visitor Center and last about an hour.

that belonged to the thrice-widowed tradeswoman are on display. Visitors can learn about the "life and times of the remarkable woman behind the legend" via a 25-minute audio tour. The highlight of the museum is its first-floor upholstery shop, where an actress portraying Betsy welcomes visitors as if they were potential customers. She fields questions about everything from making draperies to her acquaintance with George Washington, so ask away.

Elfreth's Alley

Popularly known as the nation's oldest residential street, **Elfreth's Alley** (off 2nd St., between Arch and Race Streets, www.elfrethsalley.org) is a charming swatch of the city. The 30-some houses that line it were built between the 1720s and 1830s and have been so meticulously restored that the block feels like a movie set—or a time warp. Here's a horse post. There's a shoe scrape. Up there: That's a "busybody," a set of mirrors that allow

Historic Philadelphia Inc. (Historic Philadelphia Center, 6th and Chestnut Streets, 215/629-4026, www.historicphiladelphia.org), which operates the Betsy Ross House and other attractions in the Historic District, offers two evening tours with unique twists. On the **Tippler's Tour** (Thurs. Apr.-Jan., $40, seniors and students $35), participants visit four watering holes, where they enjoy drinks and snacks while learning about 18th-century taverns and drinking traditions. Prepare to be carded when purchasing tickets for the two-hour tour. It may be pricey, but **Independence After Hours** (select days Apr.-Oct., $85, seniors and students $80, children 12 and under $55) features a three-course dinner at the famed City Tavern and an exclusive opportunity to visit Independence Hall after it's closed to the public. Actors playing a variety of 18th-century Philadelphians enhance the experience. The tour lasts about two and a half hours. Reservations are strongly recommended. Arrive at Historic Philadelphia's headquarters at least half an hour before your tour to catch a showing of **Liberty 360** (daily year-round, $6, seniors and students $5, children 12 and under $5, family of four $20), a 3-D film that explores iconic American symbols such as the Liberty Bell and the bald eagle. The 15-minute film is shown every 20 minutes.

GET SPOOKED

Philadelphia may be as haunted as it is historic. You don't need an electromagnetic field meter to get acquainted with the ghosts said to inhabit Independence Hall and other Historic District sites. Just reserve a spot on one of several ghost-themed tours. Created by the company behind The Constitutional Walking Tour, the **Spirits of '76 Ghost Tour** (215/525-1776, www.spiritsof76.com, nightly July-Aug. and Oct., select nights Apr.-June, Sept., and Nov., $17.50, children 3-12 $12.50, family of four $55) visits more than 20 sites, from paranormal hot spots to filming locations used in *The Sixth Sense* and other thrillers. The 75-minute walking tour departs from the Così restaurant at 4th and Chestnut Streets. Those who prefer to go it alone can download the **Spirits of '76 Ghost Tour Audio Adventure** for $17.50.

Ghost Tour of Philadelphia (215/413-1997, www.ghosttour.com), the city's original and much-heralded ghost tour operator, offers several regular tours, plus special events like its New Year's Eve "Toast with a Ghost." Its year-round **Candlelight Walking Tour** (nightly Mar.-Oct., select nights Nov.-Feb., $17, children 4-12 $10) has been featured in *USA Today* and was named one of the country's top 15 attractions for anyone under 15 by *Budget Travel*. If your tootsies need a rest after a day of sightseeing, opt for the **Haunted Trolley Tour** (Sat. July-Aug., $30, children 4-12 $20), which covers more ground. Ghost Tour of Philadelphia also offers a **Ghost Hunting Tour** (select days, $22) that includes a look inside the Physick House or Powel House, both said to be haunted. Electromagnetic field meters are provided. All three tours last 75-90 minutes. The walking and ghost-hunting tours begin at Signers Garden at 5th and Chestnut Streets. The trolley tour begins and ends at 5th and Market Streets.

a person on the second floor to see who's knocking on the front door.

Like the cobblestone street, the houses are tiny by today's standards. They weren't built for the city's nabobs. In the 18th and early 19th centuries, Elfreth's Alley was the address of numerous artisans and craftsmen, many of whom conducted business out of their homes. Opportunity-seeking immigrants from Germany, Ireland, and other parts of Europe flooded the neighborhood in the 19th century. By the start of the Great Depression, this had become a blighted block. Its present prettiness—and very existence—owes much to the Elfreth's Alley Association, founded in the 1930s to rescue buildings from the wrecking ball. The organization operates the **Elfreth's Alley Museum** (Houses 124 and 126, 215/574-0560, 10am-5pm Tues.-Sat. and noon-5pm Sun. Apr.-Dec., 11am-5pm Thurs.-Sun. Jan.-Mar., guided tour $5, children 6-12 $2, family $12), which focuses on the lives of

Elfreth's Alley

working people. It's located in the only two houses open to the public. Most of the others are private homes. Many residents throw open their doors during two annual fundraisers for preservation programs: **Fete Day,** a celebration of colonial history usually held on the first or second Saturday in June, and **Deck the Alley** in early December.

Physick and Powel Houses

The narrow houses along Elfreth's Alley reflect the lifestyles of early Philadelphia's blue-collar citizens. To see how the other half lived, head south to Society Hill, where two elegant 18th-century townhouses are open for tours noon-4pm Thursday-Saturday and 1pm-4pm Sunday from late February through December. The Physick and Powel Houses, as they're known, are rented for special events, so call ahead to avoid crashing a party.

Built in 1765, the **Powel House** (244 S. 3rd St., 215/627-0364, www.philalandmarks.org) was home to Philadelphia's last mayor under British rule and first mayor after the creation of the United States, one of its wealthiest citizens. Samuel Powel wasn't a self-made man. His grandfather, an orphan, had arrived in the colonies in 1685, worked hard, married well, and amassed a fortune, the bulk of which Powel inherited upon turning 18. The scion

purchased the Georgian-style brick mansion in 1769. He and his wife entertained frequently, welcoming the likes of George and Martha Washington, John Adams, and Benjamin Franklin. A thank-you note from the nation's first president is on display. The house museum's collection also includes a lock of Washington's hair and wood from his coffin.

In the early 20th century, the now-dilapidated building was slated for demolition. The Philadelphia Society for the Preservation of Landmarks, which manages the Physick and Powel Houses, was formed to save it. Today the house looks much as it did during Powel's residency, which is to say absolutely fabulous.

The 1786 **Physick House** (321 S. 4th St., 215/925-7866, www.philalandmarks.org) is named for Dr. Philip Syng Physick, often referred to as the "father of American surgery." Physick was one of the few doctors who remained in Philadelphia during the yellow fever epidemic of 1793, which killed several thousand people (including Powel). He moved into the four-story, 32-room townhouse in 1815, while undergoing a messy divorce, and lived there until his death in 1837. It's notable as the only freestanding Federal-style townhouse remaining in Society Hill and for its unusually large city garden, adorned with classical statuary and plants popular in the 19th century. Inside, you'll find excellent examples of neoclassic furnishings in one period room after another. The second floor serves as a museum devoted to Physick's medical career. The surgeon, who was so grossed out by boiling cadavers that he almost dropped out of med school, invented a number of surgical instruments and techniques. He also created America's first carbonated beverage, which he used to treat patients with gastric disorders.

General admission to each house is $5. Seniors and students pay $4, and families enjoy a discounted rate of $12.

Penn's Landing and Camden Waterfront

Philadelphia's Delaware River waterfront has been a hot topic among developers and city planners for decades. In 2008 the mayor griped that the waterfront had "been the target of big ideas that went nowhere" for too long and appointed a new board to oversee it. Bottom line: It's an area in flux. But there's plenty to see and do in the section known as Penn's Landing and across the river in Camden, New Jersey.

A mecca for maritime history buffs, Penn's Landing is home to the **Independence Seaport Museum** (211 S. Columbus Blvd. and Walnut St., 215/413-8655, www.phillyseaport.org, 10am-5pm daily, admission $13.50, seniors, students, and children $10) and several storied ships. The museum covers everything from the science of buoyancy to the immigrant experience to the history of undersea exploration. A boatload of interactive exhibits makes it fun for kids. They can play at unloading cargo using a miniature crane, stretch out on a hard bunk in steerage, and crawl through a full-size replica of a 19th-century boat used to fish for shad. The 22-foot skiff was built in the museum's boatbuilding and restoration shop, Workshop on the Water, which offers occasional classes.

Admission includes tours of two former U.S. Navy vessels docked beside the museum. The *Becuna,* a 307-foot submarine

launched in 1944, prowled the Pacific Ocean for Japanese ships during World War II, eavesdropped on Soviet submarines in the Atlantic during the Cold War, and served in the Korean and Vietnam Wars before she was decommissioned in 1969. Launched in 1892, the *Olympia* made a name for herself during the Spanish-American War. She's the sole surviving naval ship of that 1898 conflict and the oldest steel warship afloat in the world.

Penn's Landing is also home to a venerable tall ship. The *Gazela,* a wooden barkentine built in Portugal more than a century ago, still sails. When she's not off visiting other ports, you'll find her at the northern end of Penn's Landing, near the Market Street footbridge across I-95. She's lovingly maintained by members of the **Philadelphia Ship Preservation Guild** (215/238-0280, www.gazela.org), who will show you around if you ask nicely. The nonprofit group doesn't charge for tours of *Gazela* or *Jupiter,* a 1902 iron tugboat under its care, but donations are always welcome.

You can't hitch a ride on the vintage vessels, but pleasure trips from Penn's Landing are available. The three-deck *Spirit of Philadelphia* (401 S. Columbus Blvd., 866/455-3866, www.spiritofphiladelphia.com) cruises the Delaware year-round. With its all-you-can-eat buffets, full-service bars, dance floors, and DJs, the ship offers a taste of the Carnival Cruise life. Fair warning: The waitstaff sometimes break into song. Tickets aren't cheap, ranging from $37 for a two-hour late-night cruise to upwards of $100 for a dinner cruise on 4th of July weekend.

Another way to get a boat's-eye view of Philadelphia is to hop aboard the **RiverLink Ferry** (215/925-5465, www.riverlinkferry.org, service daily Memorial Day-Labor Day and weekends in May and Sept., ferry service $7, seniors and children $6, children 3 and under free), which shuttles between Penn's Landing and Camden's waterfront. The ferry departs from its terminal near the Seaport Museum every hour on the hour starting at 10am, arriving in New Jersey 12-15 minutes later. It makes its last run from Camden at 5:30 or 6:30pm. The RiverLink Ferry also offers specialty cruises.

With a population of roughly 80,000, the city of Camden is quite small relative to Philadelphia. But it has something its neighbor doesn't: an aquarium. The RiverLink Ferry pulls right up to **Adventure Aquarium** (1 Riverside Dr., Camden, 856/365-3300, www. adventureaquarium.com, 10am-5pm daily, admission $24.95, children 2-12 $18.95), a watery wonderland complete with 3,000-pound hippos. Its shark-petting pool is a huge hit with kids. Tickets are steep, and there's a lot to see, so come at least three hours before closing. Adjacent to the aquarium is the **Camden Children's Garden** (3 Riverside Dr., Camden, 856/365-8733, www.camden-childrensgarden.org, 10am-4pm Fri.-Sun., call for winter schedule, admission $6, children 2 and under free, admission from aquarium $4), a four-acre "horticultural playground" operated by the nonprofit Camden City Garden Club. Its buds and butterflies are no match for the aquarium's razzle-dazzle, but it's far less crowded and more affordable.

A visit to Camden isn't complete without a tour of the **Battleship *New Jersey*** (100 Clinton St., Camden, 866/877-6262, www. battleshipnewjersey.org, open weekends Feb.-Mar., daily Apr.-early Nov., weekends early Nov.-Dec., hours vary, admission $21.95, seniors and children 5-11 $17), one of the biggest battleships ever. The 45,000-ton behemoth was built in Philadelphia and launched in 1942, a year to the date after the Japanese attack on Pearl Harbor. *New Jersey* racked up so many service stars over the next five decades that she's considered America's most decorated battleship. Visitors get to peer into her nooks and crannies.

Philadelphia's Magic Gardens

South Street, which forms the border between posh Society Hill and gritty South Philly, is one of those rare roads with an identity all its own. Like L.A.'s Hollywood Boulevard, New York's Broadway, and New Orleans's Bourbon Street, South Street is more a destination than a route from here to there. It's Philadelphia's center of counterculture, nightlife capital, and most eclectic shopping district. It's also Isaiah Zagar's canvas. Since the late 1960s, the artist has been plastering the South Street area with mosaic murals that make you stop in your tracks. They're shimmering collages of mirrors, tiles, colored glass, and found objects. In a city awash with public art, Zagar's 100-plus creations are unmistakable. **Philadelphia's Magic Gardens** (1020 South St., 215/733-0390, www.philadelphiamagicgardens.org, 11am-6pm Sun.-Thurs. and 11am-8pm Fri.-Sat. Apr.-Oct., 11am-5pm Sun.-Thurs. and 11am-6pm Fri.-Sat. Nov.-Mar., admission $7, seniors and students $5, children 6-12 $3) is his most ambitious creation—his "opus," as he calls it. As colorful and textured as a coral reef, it consists of a fully mosaiced gallery and a maze-like outdoor installation covering half a block. Disfigured bicycle wheels, bottles, Christmas ornaments, folk art from far-flung places, pottery shards, and perseverance went into its making. When Zagar began the project in 1994, his canvas was a vacant lot. Eight years later, his work still in progress and South Street property values on the rise, the owner of the lot decided to sell. Monies were raised and a nonprofit formed to save the Magic Gardens from the bulldozer.

Guided tours ($10, children 6-12 $6, children 5 and under $3, prices include admission) are offered on weekends. From April through October, guides take visitors on a walk through the neighborhood, explaining Zagar's approach and the personal and community stories depicted in his murals. If you don't catch a walking tour, be sure to pick up a brochure that lists the addresses of more than 60 murals. During the colder months, guided tours are limited to the Magic Gardens and nearby Zagar-zapped properties. Two-day mosaic workshops with Zagar himself ($350, alumni $100) are offered monthly from April through October. The gray-haired artist, whose studio overlooks his opus, teaches the fundamentals of breaking tile, cutting mirror, gluing, and grouting—then gives participants a go at a mural.

PARKWAY MUSEUM DISTRICT AND FAIRMOUNT PARK

Examine a Philadelphia map and you can't help but think: *One of these things is not like the others.* Per William Penn's 17th-century plan, Philly is a city of parallel lines and right angles. Bucking the trend—daring to be diagonal—is the Benjamin Franklin Parkway. Penn was long dead by the time construction of the mile-long Parkway began in 1917. Designed by landscape architect Jacques Gréber and inspired by the Champs-Élysées in his hometown of Paris, the road starts near City Hall, carves a circle through Logan Square, and terminates at the magnificent Philadelphia Museum of Art, known simply as the Art Museum. Trees, sculptures, and flags representing some 90 nations line the grand boulevard. (Looking for a particular flag? With a few exceptions, they're hung alphabetically.) Like Center City's Avenue of the Arts, the Parkway is a cultural mecca. In addition to the Art Museum, it's home to the nation's oldest natural history museum, a splendid science museum, the largest collection of Auguste Rodin sculptures outside Paris, and the Barnes Foundation, renowned for its extensive holdings of works by the likes of Picasso, Matisse, Cézanne, and Renoir.

At roughly 4,200 acres, Fairmount Park is one of the largest municipal parks in the country. (For comparison's sake, New York's Central Park covers an area of 843 acres.) It stretches north from the Philadelphia Museum of Art, hugging both sides of the Schuylkill River. The portion east of the river is sometimes called East Fairmount Park and the portion west of it—you guessed it— West Fairmount Park. Winding through East Fairmount Park is the spectacularly scenic Kelly Drive, named for a former city councilman, Olympic rower, and brother of actress-turned-princess Grace Kelly. There are so many statues along Kelly Drive that it's better experienced by foot or bicycle than by car. West Park is home to the nation's oldest zoo, the city's children's museum, and its premier outdoor concert venue, the Mann Center for the Performing Arts.

Academy of Natural Sciences

Founded in 1812, the **Academy of Natural Sciences** (1900 Benjamin Franklin Parkway, 215/299-1000, www.ansp.org, 10am-4:30pm

Fairmount Park

Mon.-Fri., 10am-5pm Sat.-Sun., admission $15, seniors, students, and children 3-12 $13) is the oldest natural history museum in the Western Hemisphere. As in most natural history museums, visitors spend a good deal of time looking at dead things. Critters from around the world strike permanent poses in 37 dioramas, most of which were created in the 1920s and '30s, before television brought the animal kingdom into people's living rooms. The skeletal remains of prehistoric beasts fill Dinosaur Hall. But living, breathing beings also have a place in this museum. Its Live Animal Center is home to more than 100 birds, reptiles, amphibians, and other animals, all of which are injured or were born in captivity and wouldn't make it in the wild. They take turns starring in daily naturalist shows and delighting children in the museum's hands-on discovery center. The academy also boasts a live butterfly exhibit.

The Franklin Institute

It's no surprise that Philadelphia's science museum is named for favorite son Ben Franklin, whose 18th-century discoveries are still remembered. Founded in 1824, **The Franklin Institute** (222 N. 20th St., 215/448-1200, www.fi.edu, 9:30am-5pm daily, admission $16.50, children 3-11 $12.50, additional charges for IMAX and Franklin theaters) became a venue for showcasing new technologies. In 1893 Nikola Tesla demonstrated the principle of wireless telegraphy at the institute. The first public demonstration of an all-electronic television system took place there in 1934, the same year the institute moved to its current home and opened to the public. A 20-foot-high marble statue of a seated Ben Franklin dominates its dramatic rotunda, which was modeled after Rome's Pantheon. The Founding Father's presence is also felt in an exhibit devoted to electricity, which features an electronic version of his book *Experiments and Observations on Electricity,* along with a dance floor that generates power as visitors bust a move. The museum's bioscience exhibit, with its giant walk-through model of a human heart, is a perennial favorite. (Cool factoid: The two-story heart would fit nicely inside a 220-foot-tall person.) If you're the queasy sort, steer clear of the exhibit's full-size re-creation of a surgery room, where the "patient" is forever undergoing open-heart surgery. The aviation exhibit offers would-be pilots a chance to climb into a flight simulator and pull maneuvers including a 360-degree roll.

The museum has three state-of-the-art theaters: a digital projection planetarium, an IMAX theater, and the Franklin Theater, which specializes in 3-D films. Museum admission includes one planetarium show.

Barnes Foundation

The **Barnes Foundation** (2025 Benjamin Franklin Parkway, 215/278-7000, www. barnesfoundation.org, 10am-6pm Mon. and Wed.-Thurs., 10am-10pm Fri., 10am-6pm Sat.-Sun., admission $22, seniors $20, students and children 6-18 $10) is new to the Benjamin Franklin Parkway but hardly a new name in the art world. Founded in the 1920s by pharmaceutical magnate Albert C. Barnes, the Barnes boasts a legendary collection of Impressionist, post-Impressionist, and early Modern paintings, including more than 180 works by Pierre-Auguste Renoir, 67 by Paul Cézanne, and 59 by Henri Matisse. In 2012, after a decade of legal wrangling, the masterpieces were moved from the suburban gallery Barnes built for them to a brand-new building on the Parkway. It's easier to get to but not necessarily easy to get *into.* Due to high demand, the Barnes strongly recommends purchasing tickets in advance.

Try to catch a free guided tour of the collection. They're offered several times on most days. To get the biggest bang for your buck, visit on a Friday, when the Barnes stays open until 10pm and offers special programming.

Rodin Museum

The **Rodin Museum** (2151 Benjamin Franklin Parkway, 215/763-8100, www.rodin-museum.org, 10am-5pm daily except Tues., suggested admission $8, seniors $7, students and children 13-18 $6) is home to more than 120 works by its namesake sculptor, including a bronze cast of **The Thinker,** perhaps the most famous sculpture in the world. You'd have to go to Paris to find a larger collection of the Frenchman's masterpieces. The museum, which opened its Paris-made gates in 1929, was a gift to the city from movie theater magnate Jules Mastbaum. He began collecting all things Auguste Rodin in 1923 and died three years later, just as his museum project was getting underway.

It's best to visit on a temperate, rainless day, as some sculptures are displayed in the museum's formal gardens and other outdoor spaces. Among them is a bronze cast of the unfinished but incredible **Gates of Hell,** which the artist worked on from 1880 until his death in 1917. The museum has a "pay what you wish" admission policy, and the suggested prices are quite reasonable. Take advantage of its free guided tours, offered at 1:30pm daily.

★ Philadelphia Museum of Art

Little needs to be said about the **Philadelphia Museum of Art** (2600 Benjamin Franklin Parkway, 215/763-8100, www.philamuseum. org, 10am-5pm Tues.-Sun., open until 8:45pm Wed. and Fri., admission $20, seniors $18, students and children 13-18 $14), which is quite simply one of the preeminent cultural institutions in the country. Since its founding in 1876, the museum has amassed more than 225,000 objects representing 2,000 years of creative expression. It's worth a visit whether your passion is medieval armor, modern sculpture, or the movie character Rocky Balboa (more on that later). Architecture and decorative arts buffs are particularly well served. The museum, which is in itself an architectural gem, contains about 80 period rooms, including entire furnished rooms from historic houses. One can meander through a French cloister, a Chinese palace hall, a Japanese teahouse, and a stone temple straight from India in the space of 10 minutes. The nation's third-largest art museum has more than 200 galleries, so if you're dead set on seeing the whole thing, arrive while the neoclassical temple of art is still bathed in morning light. Better yet, come on a Wednesday or Friday, when it stays open until 8:45pm. If money is tight, visit after 5pm on a Wednesday or the first Sunday of the month, when the price of admission is up to you.

Having long outgrown the home built for it in the 1920s, the museum expanded into an

the Philadelphia Museum of Art

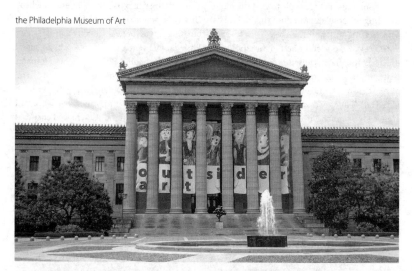

the Rocky steps

Art Deco landmark across the way in 2007. The **Perelman Building** (2525 Pennsylvania Ave., 10am-5pm Tues.-Sun.) showcases some of the museum's more cutting-edge collections. Admission prices include two consecutive days of access to the main building, the Perelman Building, the Rodin Museum, and two historic houses in Fairmount Park. The museum offers complimentary shuttle service between the main building, the Perelman Building, and the Rodin Museum.

It's not unusual for people to visit the main building without stepping foot inside. It sits on a granite hill, and the view from its east entranceway is one of the best in the city. Dead ahead is the plaza known as **Eakins Oval,** featuring a statue of a uniformed George Washington astride a horse, and beyond it, City Hall. The broad steps leading to the entrance are as much a tourist attraction as any in town, having appeared in an iconic scene in *Rocky,* the 1976 sleeper hit starring Sylvester Stallone as a fictional Philly boxer who takes on a heavyweight champ. Not everyone has the stamina to sprint up the steps à la Rocky, but almost every first-time visitor has an "Italian Stallion" moment at the top, posing with arms outstretched for a camera-wielding friend. A bronze statue of the movie character, commissioned by Stallone for a scene in *Rocky*

III, can be found near the base of the so-called **Rocky steps.**

★ Eastern State Penitentiary

When **Eastern State Penitentiary** (2027 Fairmount Ave., 215/236-3300, www.easternstate.org, 10am-5pm daily, admission $14, seniors $12, students and children $10) opened in 1829, it was unlike any other prison in the world. For one thing, it was architecturally ingenious, with long cell blocks radiating from a surveillance hub like the spokes of a wheel. In an era when the White House had coal-burning stoves for heat and no running water, Philadelphia's pricey new prison had central heat and flush toilets. Its treatment of inmates was also a radical departure from the norm. Rather than pen them up like cattle, Eastern State assigned each prisoner a private cell complete with skylight. It eschewed corporal punishment, adhering to a Quaker-influenced formula for reforming criminals: strict isolation plus labor. The prison was so serious about curbing interaction that inmates were hooded when it was necessary to move them. Left alone with their thoughts and a Bible, criminals would come to realize the error of their ways and become genuinely penitent—or so thought proponents of the "penitentiary."

Charles Dickens thought otherwise. "I hold

Eastern State Penitentiary

On select evenings from mid-September to early November, the already eerie site moonlights as a massive haunted attraction. **Terror Behind the Walls** is too terror-ific for kids under the age of seven (and even some grown-ups). It's recommended that families with children 7-12 visit on "family nights" (Sundays before 7:30pm), when actors are on the lookout for kids who may be too scared. Ticket prices vary but are always cheaper online.

Philadelphia Zoo

America's oldest **zoo** (3400 W. Girard Ave., 215/243-1100, www.philadelphiazoo.org, 9:30am-5pm daily Mar.-Oct., 9:30am-4pm daily Nov.-Feb., in-season admission $20, children 2-11 $18, off-season admission $16) packs a lot into its 42 manicured acres. It's home to more than 1,300 animals representing some 300 species and subspecies: lions, tigers, and bears, of course, but also a host of critters that only an Animal Planet addict would recognize. You won't soon forget the wrinkled mug of naked mole rats in the Rare Animal Conservation Center, the wide-eyed Coquerel's sifakas in the PECO Primate Reserve, or the aquatic acrobatics of the giant river otters in Carnivore Kingdom. Also unforgettable: hovering high above the treetops in the **Channel 6 Zooballoon** (Apr.-Nov. weather permitting, $15 per person, $50 per family of four), the region's only passenger-carrying helium balloon.

The Philadelphia Zoo received its charter in 1859 but didn't open its gates until 1874, after the Civil War. The oldest building on the grounds, **The Solitude,** predates the zoo. Built in 1784 by John Penn, grandson of Pennsylvania founder William Penn, it's the only surviving American residence once owned by a Penn family member. Penn named his elegant manor house after the Duke of Württemberg's La Solitude in Stuttgart's sylvan environs.

Fair warning: Unless you're a zoo member, parking will set you back $15. It is possible to get there via SEPTA, Philly's public

this slow and daily tampering with the mysteries of the brain to be immeasurably worse than any torture of the body," he wrote after an 1842 visit. Some 300 prisons around the world emulated Eastern State's design and system of solitary confinement, but detractors like Dickens eventually prevailed. By the time Al "Scarface" Capone was booked into the prison in 1929, inmates lived two or three to a cell, worked alongside each other in the weaving shops and kitchens, exercised together, and ate together.

After 142 years of use, the prison closed in 1971. In 1994 the National Historic Landmark opened its doors to the public. The *Voices of Eastern State* audio tour, available April-November, covers everything from intake procedures to escape attempts. It's narrated by actor Steve Buscemi and punctuated with firsthand accounts from former wardens, guards, and inmates. From December through March, guides lead one-hour tours of the complex. It's not heated, so be sure to bundle up.

a cheetah at the Philadelphia Zoo

transit system, but an easier way to travel between Center City and the zoo is by **Phlash trolley** (800/537-7676, www.phillyphlash.com, single ride $2, all-day pass $12, seniors and children 4 and under free), operating May-October. Phlash trolleys (actually buses in disguise) also stop at the nearby Please Touch Museum, where parking for nonmembers is $8.

Please Touch Museum

The **Please Touch Museum** (Memorial Hall, 4231 Ave. of the Republic, 215/581-3181, www.pleasetouchmuseum.org, 9am-5pm Mon.-Sat., 11am-5pm Sun., admission $16, children under 1 free) answers a question for the ages: where to take the kids on a rainy day? Designed for the seven and under set, it offers several hours' worth of learning experiences disguised as fun. Kids can push a cart through a supermarket, fill up a tank at a gas station, race sailboats, take a spin on a hamster wheel, and enter the magical world of *Alice in Wonderland.* On most days, they can also catch an original theater performance by a cast that includes puppets.

The museum has moved several times since opening in 1976. It settled into its current home, West Fairmount Park's historic Memorial Hall, in 2008. Memorial Hall was one of about 200 buildings erected for the 1876 Centennial Exposition, the first World's Fair held in America, and it's the only major one still standing. The beaux-arts-style building served as the city's art museum until the Philadelphia Museum of Art opened in 1928. Please Touch Museum's *Centennial Exploration* exhibit gives kids a taste of the atmosphere at the World's Fair, where inventions including the telephone, the typewriter, and root beer were revealed. Its centerpiece, a 20-by-30-foot scale model of the fairgrounds, was first unveiled in 1889.

CENTER CITY

Center City is Philadelphia's downtown, its business and governmental center. It's generally regarded as the area between the Delaware and Schuylkill Rivers to the east and west, Vine Street to the north, and South Street to the south—the portion of Philadelphia that once comprised the whole city. At the center of this rectangular area is City Hall, a dramatic building made more dramatic by elaborate nighttime lighting. Broad Street, the north-south thoroughfare interrupted by City Hall, divides Center City into Center City East and Center City West.

In addition to being a business and governmental center, Center City is a cultural mecca.

Mural, Mural on the Wall

Philadelphia Muses by Meg Saligman, 13th & Locust Streets, Center City

With more than 3,600 murals, Philadelphia has been called the world's largest outdoor art gallery. The colorful, larger-than-life artworks brighten schools, community centers, businesses, and homes from Center City to outlying neighborhoods that most tourists never see.

Philadelphia's **Mural Arts Program** (215/685-0750, www.muralarts.org) traces its roots to the mid-1980s, when the city was plastered with graffiti. Muralist and community activist Jane Golden was hired to redirect the energies of graffitists into mural painting. She still runs the program, which has not only alleviated much of the graffiti problem but also empowered thousands of at-risk youths and contributed to neighborhood revitalization in many parts of the city.

While the works of art speak for themselves, a guided tour is the best way to experience them. The Mural Arts Program offers trolley, walking, biking, and even train tours. Most tours leave from **Mural Arts at The Gallery** (The Gallery at Market East, 901 Market St., level 2, 10am-4pm Wed.-Fri., 9am-4pm Sat., noon-5pm Sun.), a gift shop and painting studio, and last an hour and a half to two hours. It's not unusual for tours to sell out, so advance ticket purchase is strongly advised. You can buy tickets at the gift shop, through the Mural Arts Program website, or by calling 215/925-3633.

Trolley tours ($30, seniors $28, children 3-12 $20) of various neighborhoods are offered April-November. The **Mural Mile walking tour** ($20), also offered April-November, covers two miles and 15 murals in Center City. You can experience them at your own pace with the **self-guided audio tour** ($10). **Bike tours** ($25) are offered on the second and fourth Saturday of each month May-October. The mural program's most unique offering may be its **train tour of *Love Letter*** ($20), a public art project consisting of 50 rooftop murals in West Philadelphia. Participants take in the murals from SEPTA's elevated train and several train platforms. The tour is offered weekends April-December.

Be sure to check the website for a full schedule of tours and special events, as the Mural Arts Program is constantly adding more murals and more ways to experience them.

—*Contributed by Karrie Gavin, author of* Moon Philadelphia

Center City

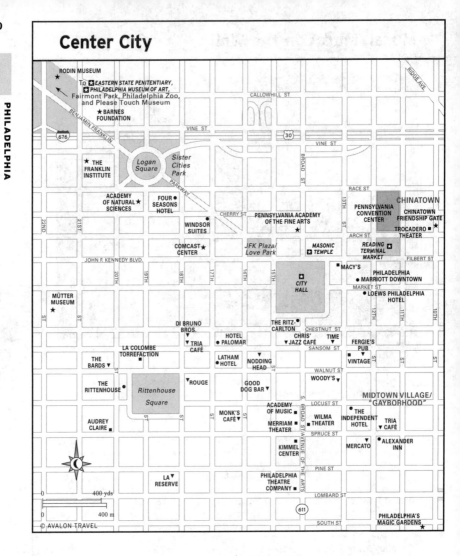

The portion of Broad Street south of City Hall is known as Avenue of the Arts because it's flanked by concert halls and theaters. The scenic Benjamin Franklin Parkway, which starts near City Hall, is flanked by museums.

The Parkway Museum District and the Historic District, the easternmost part of Center City, are described in previous pages. This section deals with sights in the rest of Center City.

★ City Hall

City Hall (Broad and Market Streets, tour office room 121, 215/686-2840, www.phila. gov/virtualch, observation deck access noon-4:15pm Mon.-Fri., guided tour 12:30pm Mon.-Fri.) is a building of many distinctions. When construction began in 1871, it was to be the tallest building in the world. The project dragged on for so long that by the time of its completion in 1901, the Washington

Monument and Eiffel Tower stood higher. Still, City Hall had bragging rights as the tallest *habitable* building in the world—for a few years anyway. At 37 feet, the bronze statue of city founder William Penn that crowns its central tower is the tallest statue atop any building. Long after skyscrapers twice its height dotted the globe, City Hall remained Philadelphia's tallest thanks to a gentleman's agreement that no building would tower over Billy Penn's head. The agreement was broken in the mid-1980s, when One Liberty Place went up, and today City Hall barely makes the top 10. But it hangs on to several distinctions: world's tallest occupied masonry structure, America's largest (and most expensive) municipal building, and one of the continent's finest examples of Second Empire architecture. It's such a fine example, in fact, that a tourist could snap some pics and convince folks back home that he'd been to Paris.

There's plenty to see without stepping foot inside the building, including some 250 sculptures and motifs by Alexander Milne Calder, the Scottish-born son of a tombstone carver and grandfather of the Calder renowned for his sculptural mobiles. He devoted two decades to City Hall's ornamentation. In addition to the colossal Penn statue, Calder's crowning work (literally and figuratively), the central tower is adorned with bronze statues depicting Native American and Swedish settlers. An eagle with a wingspan of 15 feet is perched above each face of the tower's four-faced clock. The many sculptures closer to eye level include representations of continents, various arts and sciences, commerce, agriculture, and justice. Be sure to check out the courtyard's western entrance, though it's the smallest and least ornate of the four. With its carvings of thorns, thistles, and menacing serpents, it's hardly inviting. But Calder knew what he was doing: The portal was used by horse-drawn vans carrying accused criminals.

City Hall isn't nearly as ornate inside as it is outside. Its more lavish spaces are the focus of 90-minute tours ($12, seniors and students $8, children 3 and under free) that depart from room 121 at 12:30pm weekdays. The tours conclude with an elevator ride to an observation deck below the Penn statue. You don't have to take the tour to enjoy the panoramic view. The elevator ferries visitors to the observation deck 9:30am-4:15pm weekdays. It only fits four, and the view is fantastic, so it's not unusual for timed tickets ($6, seniors and students $4, children 3 and under free) to sell out by noon.

Masonic Temple (left) and City Hall

★ Masonic Temple

Philadelphia's **Masonic Temple** (1 N. Broad St., 215/988-1917, www.pagrandlodge.org, tours Tues.-Sat., admission $10, students $6, seniors and children 12 and under $5, family $25), just across the street from City Hall, is easily mistaken for a church. It's imposing, topped with turrets and spires, and clearly not of this century or the last. Divine: yes. Ecclesiastical: no. Dedicated in 1873, the temple is the mother ship of Pennsylvania Masonry. Though its origins are obscure, Masonry is considered the world's oldest fraternal organization. Some of the fraternity's practices are as shrouded in secrecy as an Apple product launch, but you don't have to whisper a password to pass through the temple's grand entrance gate. Guided tours are offered at 10am, 11am, 1pm, 2pm, and 3pm Tuesday-Friday and 10am, 11am, and noon Saturday.

The place is an architectural wonderland, with each of seven resplendent meeting halls paying tribute to a different style. The Grecian-themed Corinthian Hall shares the second floor with Egyptian Hall, Ionic Hall, and rooms decorated in the Italian Renaissance and Rhenish Romanesque styles. Groin vaults, pointed arches, and pinnacles abound in the third-floor Gothic Hall, with its hand-carved furniture. Oriental Hall, located on the first floor, is not what its name suggests. It's patterned after the Alhambra, the exquisite Moorish-style palace complex in Granada, Spain. Be sure to check out its ceiling, which is divided into thousands of panels of various shapes.

You don't have to tour the building to visit the **Masonic Library and Museum** (9am-5pm Tues.-Fri., 9am-noon Sat., admission $5), which displays the Masonic apron presented to George Washington by the Marquis de Lafayette, the French aristocrat who served in Washington's Continental Army during the Revolutionary War. Washington is one of more than a dozen U.S. presidents on the Masonry's long list of "brothers." Other notable pieces in the collection include a reverse glass painting of Washington being lifted into the heavens, Benjamin Franklin's circa 1779 Masonic sash, and the Masonic apron of General Tom Thumb, the dwarf whose circus performances made him an international celebrity in the mid-1800s.

Comcast Center

At 975 feet, the **Comcast Center** (17th and Arch Streets) is Pennsylvania's tallest building. Its opening in 2008 bumped One Liberty Place, the skyscraper that ended City Hall's reign as the tallest building in town, out of the top slot. Most office buildings don't hold much interest for anyone who doesn't work in them, but the 58-story Comcast Center, headquarters to the largest U.S. cable company, is something of a tourist attraction. That's because of the colossal LED wall in its main lobby. **The Comcast Experience,** as it's called, is 83.3 feet wide, 25.4 feet high, and packed with 10 million pixels for phenomenal picture quality. You can think of it as a high-definition TV on steroids. Or you can think of it as installation art.

From 6am to midnight, the video wall pulses with ever-changing images of everything from Philly's historic sites to outer space. Nature footage might follow an artsy dance sequence. At times the visual mimics the lobby's wood paneling, blending in like a bullfrog on a pebbled shore. You never know what you'll see because a virtual "video jockey" selects from thousands of hours of content.

Pennsylvania Academy of the Fine Arts

In a lesser city, a museum as impressive as the **Pennsylvania Academy of the Fine Arts** (118 and 128 N. Broad St., 215/972-7600, www.pafa.org, 10am-5pm Tues.-Sat., 11am-5pm Sun., admission $15, seniors and students $12, children 13-18 $8) could well top the list of cultural attractions. But Philadelphia offers art lovers a veritable buffet, and PAFA

The Curse of Billy Penn

If you believe a broken mirror brings seven years' bad luck, rub a rabbit's foot with regularity, or stay in bed on Friday the 13th, you'll probably believe in the Curse of Billy Penn. Billy Penn—that's Philadelphia founder William Penn if you're not from these parts—has neither confirmed nor denied the existence of said curse, which may have something to do with the fact that he's been dead for almost 200 years. Anyhow, we digress. The story of the curse goes something like this.

For more than 80 years after its completion in 1901, City Hall stood taller than any other building in Philadelphia. It's not that developers couldn't build taller. By 1980, buildings two times and even three times its height had risen in New York and Chicago. The technology was there. In Philadelphia, however, a gentleman's agreement dictated that the statue of Billy Penn at the tippy-top of City Hall remain the highest point in the city. The agreement was finally cast aside in the mid-1980s, and a 61-floor skyscraper sprouted two blocks from City Hall. Soon it was joined by other soaring towers.

the statue of William Penn at the top of City Hall

As the city's skyline changed, so did the luck of its sports teams. Between the mid-1970s and early '80s, the Philadelphia Flyers had won two Stanley Cups (1974 and 1975), the Phillies had won a World Series (1980), the 76ers had won an NBA championship (1983), and the Eagles had reached the Super Bowl (1981). But the two decades starting in the mid-'80s were trying times for Philly sports fans. The four major sports teams had close-but-no-cigar seasons. It didn't escape notice that the streak of championships ended around the time that the gentleman's agreement was breached.

Had the breach unleashed a curse? Lots of people talked about it. Few would admit to believing it. But when the Comcast Center marked its near-completion with a "topping out" ceremony in 2007, a statue of William Penn sat on the beam hoisted to the highest point of Philadelphia's newest tallest skyscraper. Just to be safe.

The following year, the Philadelphia Phillies defeated the Tampa Bay Rays for their second World Series title. The curse—if there was one—was broken.

is often passed up for meatier fare like the Philadelphia Museum of Art and the Barnes Foundation. It's a shame, because its collection of 19th- and 20th-century American art is really quite something. Among the artists represented are Winslow Homer, John Singer Sargent, and Edward Hopper. PAFA is an art school as well as a museum—the oldest in the nation in both respects—and its collection abounds with works by its founders, faculty, and alumni, including Charles Willson Peale, William Rush, Thomas Eakins, Mary Cassatt, and Violet Oakley. The museum doesn't shun

modern and contemporary American artists. You can expect to see a fairly even mix of historical and contemporary art.

Two strikingly different buildings make up the PAFA campus, and you'll find galleries in both. The older of the two is known as the Historic Landmark Building and dates to 1876. It's considered one of the premier examples of Victorian Gothic architecture in the country. PAFA opened the adjacent Samuel M. V. Hamilton Building in 2005 as part of its 200th anniversary celebration. Built as an automobile showroom and storage facility in the early 1900s, the ingeniously repurposed building is used for most traveling exhibitions.

Docent-led tours of the permanent collection are generally offered at 1 and 2pm Tuesday-Sunday. They're free with admission.

★ Reading Terminal Market

The Reading Railroad was forced into bankruptcy several decades ago, but the indoor farmers market that bears its name pulses with activity seven days a week. **Reading Terminal Market** (12th and Arch Streets, 215/922-2317, www.readingterminalmarket.org, 8am-6pm Mon.-Sat., 9am-5pm Sun.) is a regular stop for local chefs and other gastronomes foraging for fresh produce, eggs, dairy products, meats, seafood, and specialty foods. More than a third of its 80-some stands are eateries, making the market an extremely popular lunchtime destination. The dizzying array of options—from spicy Cajun fare to savory crepes to caviar—can breed indecision. If you're a fan of Pennsylvania Dutch cuisine, come Tuesday-Saturday, when Amish and Mennonite vendors fill out the northwest corner of the market house. Top off a meal at the excellent **Dutch Eating Place** with hand-dipped ice cream straight from Lancaster County at **Miller's Twist.** Handcrafted jewelry, new and used books, housewares, bath products, and other nonedibles are also on offer.

The market opened its doors in 1892 as part of the Reading Railroad's new train depot and company headquarters. In an age before refrigerated trucks, its location couldn't have been more ideal for shipping and receiving goods. At one point, a free service made it possible for a suburban housewife to "shop" at the market without venturing into the city. Her grocery order would be placed on a train bound for her town and held at the station until she came for it. The market's continued existence was threatened by the demise of the Reading Railroad in the 1970s and the subsequent decision to incorporate the terminal into the design of a new convention center.

Philadelphians demanded that the venerable market be preserved, and preserved it was. Meeting facilities replaced train tracks and platforms above the street-level market.

The area is well served by public transportation, but if you must drive, park in the garage at 12th and Filbert or 11th and Arch. Any merchant will validate the ticket with a purchase of $10 or more, entitling you to two hours of parking for a flat rate of $4. Regular garage rates apply after two hours.

Chinatown

Philadelphia's **Chinatown** (9th St. to 11th St. between Arch and Vine Streets) doesn't approach New York's or San Francisco's in scale or sales of knockoff handbags and Rolexes. But if you're in the market for canned shark fin soup, roasted eel, dried squid, or porcelain dragons, the compact enclave just east of the Pennsylvania Convention Center won't disappoint. It's packed with restaurants and stores of the Asian variety. (Vietnamese, Burmese, Malaysian, Thai, and Japanese eateries have sprung up among the Chinese businesses, but "Asiatown" doesn't have the same ring as "Chinatown," does it?) A plaque marks the Race Street site of the district's first Chinese restaurant, which opened in 1870.

The landmark most associated with Chinatown is of fairly recent vintage. **Chinatown Friendship Gate** (10th St. near Arch St.), a symbol of friendship between Philadelphia and its sister city of Tianjin, China, was dedicated in 1984 by officials from both cities. Artisans from China had a hand in the creation of the colorful portal, which stands 40 feet tall and proclaims "Philadelphia Chinatown" in large Chinese characters. The temptation to stand beneath it for a photo op is strong but, given the nature of Center City traffic, best resisted.

If you're curious about Chinatown's history and food, hook up with local chef and media darling Joseph Poon. His **Wok 'N Walk Tour** (Chef Kitchen, 1010 Cherry St., 2nd floor, 215/928-9333, www.josephpoon.com,

Philadelphia's Chinatown Friendship Gate

$60) includes a Tai Chi demonstration, visits to a fortune cookie factory and a Chinese herbal medicine shop, and a four-course lunch or dinner.

Mütter Museum

Best visited on an empty stomach, the **Mütter Museum** (19 S. 22nd St., 215/563-3737, www.collphyphil.org, 10am-5pm daily, admission $15, seniors $13, students and children 6-17 $10) houses an unforgettable collection of what physicians of yore called "nature's books." We call them body parts. Its treasures are truly one of a kind. They include bladder stones removed from U.S. Chief Justice John Marshall, tissue from the thorax of President Abraham Lincoln's assassin, and a tumor taken from President Grover Cleveland's jaw during a secret surgery aboard a private yacht. The museum is home to the tallest skeleton on display in North America and a wax model of a human head that sprouted a horn. Perhaps most disturbing is the preserved colon of a man so constipated that he was carrying some 40 pounds of feces when he died at the age of 29. Giant doesn't begin to describe the swollen organ.

The Mütter is part of the College of Physicians of Philadelphia, a professional medical organization founded in 1787. Members started the museum in the mid-1800s to help educate future doctors about the human body and its myriad afflictions. Like library books, its specimens were borrowed and studied. The 1874 autopsy of conjoined twins Chang and Eng—the original "Siamese twins"—was performed in the museum. Their bodies were returned to their adopted home of North Carolina, where they'd married sisters and fathered 21 children, but the Mütter was allowed to keep their fused livers. They're on display beneath a plaster cast of the twins' torsos, which were connected by a band of skin and cartilage.

The small gift shop is guaranteed to turn exhibit-induced grimaces into smiles. Its inventory includes plush toys of deadly microbes, syringe-shaped pens, skull-shaped beads, gummy maggots, and, of course, the game Operation. Still queasy? Get some air in the college's lovely garden, which is planted with more than 50 medicinal herbs and dotted with benches.

GREATER PHILADELPHIA
Valley Forge National Historical Park

On September 26, 1777, British troops marched into Philadelphia. If Britain

wood cabin at Valley Forge National Historical Park

thought that capturing the capital of its rebellious colonies would put an end to the Revolutionary War, Britain thought wrong. That winter, George Washington and his battle-weary army set up camp in the small community of Valley Forge, 20 miles northwest of Philadelphia. The soldiers built a city of 2,000-some huts, miles of trenches, and five earthen forts. In February, a former Prussian officer with an epic name arrived in camp. The charismatic Baron Friedrich Wilhelm Augustus von Steuben whipped the Continental Army into a finely tuned marching machine. The war for independence would continue for several years, but the six-month encampment at Valley Forge would be remembered as a turning point. In came ready-to-quit rebels. Out went warriors.

The visitors center at **Valley Forge National Historical Park** (Rte. 23 and N. Gulph Rd., Valley Forge, 610/783-1099, www.nps.gov/vafo, grounds open 7am-dark daily, visitors center open 9am-5pm daily and until 6pm in summer, free admission) offers a good introduction to this chapter of history. The 18-minute film *Valley Forge: A Winter Encampment* plays every half hour, and exhibits round out the picture. A map with a suggested auto tour of historic sites is available in several languages. Among the historic sites is Washington's Headquarters, the small building that General George Washington and his military staff called home during the encampment. The soldiers' huts often seen in photos of the national park are reproductions; the hastily built originals are long gone. During the warmer months, the visitors center is the starting point for 40-minute walking tours, 90-minute trolley tours, and two-hour biking tours. Rental bikes are available.

As one of the largest open spaces in southeastern Pennsylvania, the park is as much a destination for outdoor recreation as historical edification. Almost 30 miles of hiking, biking, and horseback riding trails carve through its 3,500 acres. The Horseshoe Trail, which begins near Washington's Headquarters, connects to the legendary Appalachian Trail.

Entertainment and Events

BARS AND LOUNGES
Historic District

Before the construction of Independence Hall, it wasn't unusual for men of state to hold meetings in Philadelphia's taverns. Watering holes served as unofficial places of business even after buildings of government and commerce rose in the burgeoning city. So it's only fitting that the Historic District has a good number of bars. For an 18th-century-style libation, head to **City Tavern** (138 S. 2nd St., 215/413-1443, www.citytavern. com, lunch from 11:30am daily, dinner from 4pm Mon.-Sat. and 3pm Sun., lunch $10-20, dinner $18-33), a replica of a favorite haunt of the Founding Fathers. There's a small bar area and a cozy sitting room on the first floor of the restaurant, which teamed with locally based Yards Brewing Company to create a line of beers based on recipes endorsed by George Washington, Thomas Jefferson, and Ben Franklin. Try the Tavern Porter, a rich molasses-based brew like the kind General Washington served to his thirsty field officers.

Thirsting for Belgian-style suds? Old City has just the place. **Eulogy Belgian Tavern** (136 Chestnut St., 215/413-1918, www.eulogybar.com, 5pm-2am Mon.-Wed., 11am-2am Thurs.-Sun., kitchen closes at 10:30pm Mon.-Wed. and 1:30am Thurs.-Sun., food $8-22) offers more than 300 craft brews, including Eulogy's Busty Blonde, brewed in Belgium exclusively for its Philly namesake. Housed in a 19th-century townhouse, the Belgian-owned pub is known for its plump mussels, juicy burgers, twice-fried *frietjes,* and second-floor "coffin room," where caskets serve as tables.

One of Philly's most popular Irish-style joints is **The Plough and the Stars** (2nd St. between Market and Chestnut Streets, 215/733-0300, www.ploughstars.com, 11:30am-2am Mon.-Fri., 10:30am-2am Sat.-Sun., food $7-24). With its soaring ceilings, Corinthian columns, and 16-foot windows, the Plough is a far cry from the typical breed of Irish pub. And its menu has just a smattering of Irish specialties. But Guinness drinkers claim it pours the perfect pint, and the level of joviality reaches St. Patty's Day proportions on a fairly regular basis. Weekend brunches are a big draw, and Sunday evenings feature a traditional Irish music session.

A do-it-yourself Bloody Mary bar is a hallmark of weekend brunches at **National Mechanics** (22 S. 3rd St., 215/701-4883, www. nationalmechanics.com, 5pm-2am Mon., 11am-2am Tues.-Sun., food $9-15), which occupies an imposing Greek Revival building that once served as a bank for the hardworking mechanics of the Industrial Revolution. Mechanical doodads, homemade lighting fixtures, and stained glass windows embellish a space far cozier than the facade suggests. The bar features 30-odd varieties of beer, including some from very near and some from very far. Food options range from corn dogs to crab cakes. Servers speak of the veggie burger with a reverential tone usually reserved for meaty fare.

South Philadelphia

The neighborhoods below South Street are unpretentious and largely tourist-free and, for the most part, so are the bars. On the divey end of the spectrum are **Bob & Barbara's** (1509 South St., 215/545-4511, www.bobandbarbaras.com, 3pm-2am daily) and **Tattooed Mom** (530 South St., 215/238-9880, www.tattooedmomphilly.com, noon-2am daily, food under $10). Getting sloppy drunk at the hipster havens is cheaper than going to the movies. The throngs chug cans of Pabst Blue Ribbon as if it were holy water. Indeed, B&B's is something of a shrine to the historic brew, plastered as it is with Pabst memorabilia. At Tattooed Mom, the walls are awash in graffiti. Gang turf? Yeah, it's a great place to bring the whole gang, sink into a ratty couch, and have a Scrabble throw-down. Tattooed Mom serves $1 tacos (beef or vegetarian) on Tuesdays and $0.50 pierogies on Thursdays. If you enjoy a good drag show, B&B's is the place to be on Thursday nights.

Red-walled and dimly lit, the **Royal Tavern** (937 E. Passyunk Ave., 215/389-6694, www.royaltavern.com, 11:30am-2am Mon.-Fri., 10am-2am Sat.-Sun., food $6-16) is a couple of notches above "dive" and firmly entrenched in the "gastropub" category. Most people come here with food on their minds. The Royal's specialty: gussied-up comfort food. Its grilled cheese sandwich is a gooey marriage of smoked gouda, sharp provolone, goat cheese, and rustic French bread. The much-trumpeted burger features bacon, caramelized onions, and smoked gouda. And the popcorn—oh, the popcorn—is freshly popped and drizzled with truffle butter. The Royal does right by vegans with a meat-free sloppy joe and grilled tempeh sandwich complete with vegan bacon. In spite of all the chewing, the long, narrow space tends to get loud.

Deciding whether to put **Southwark** (701 S. 4th St., 215/238-1888, www.southwarkrestaurant.com, 5pm-2am Tues.-Sun., dinner until 10pm, late-night menu 10pm-midnight, dinner $19-25) in the restaurant or bar section of this book was a tough call. It excels as a farm-to-table eatery, even breaking into *Philadelphia* magazine's list of top 50 restaurants in 2009. But locavores wouldn't go hungry if it closed its doors tomorrow; the Slow Food movement is sweeping this city. If Southwark shut down, its cocktails would be missed most of all. Since opening in 2004, the gentlemanly Queen Village joint has carved out a niche by eschewing newfangled libations and nailing classics like the Sazerac, sidecar, and Tom Collins. Its Manhattan is said to be the best in the city, and few bars can match its gin and rye collection. To boot, its beer selection outshines that of many beer-centric establishments.

Northern Liberties

NoLibs, as the neighborhood north of Old City is known, has starred in something of a Cinderella story in recent years. Publicans, restaurateurs, and developers have played the fairy godmother, transforming a bedraggled and unappreciated area into the belle of the ball. **Standard Tap** (901 N. 2nd St., 215/238-0630, www.standardtap.com, 4pm-2am daily, kitchen closes at 1am, brunch 11am-3pm Sat.-Sun., food $15-40) led the charge, setting a high bar when it opened in 1999. Widely regarded as Philadelphia's original gastropub, the Tap looks no further than Pennsylvania and neighboring states for its draft-only beer selection. Asking for a Heineken brands you an outsider. So does asking for a food menu. Chef Carolynn Angle switches things up so frequently that chalkboards have a clear advantage over ink and paper. Servers make no excuses when listed dishes are sold out; that's the way the cookie crumbles when a buy-fresh ethos prevails. Mussels and sausage, duck confit salad, and crispy smelts consistently find their way onto the chalkboards. The first-floor jukebox contains a preponderance of punk and indie rock. Seat yourself upstairs for a quieter good time.

North 3rd (801 N. 3rd St., 215/413-3666, www.norththird.com, 4pm-2am Mon.-Fri., 10am-2am Sat.-Sun., dinner 5pm-midnight Sun.-Wed. and 5pm-1am Thurs.-Sat., brunch 10am-3:30pm Sat.-Sun., food $8-19) is also known for top-notch food, especially its customizable burger. The selection of draft beers is small but well edited. Signature cocktails like the mojito martini and Stoli Doli taste best at a sidewalk table, but be sure to have a look around inside, where it's wall-to-wall artwork and tchotchkes. It's a particularly artsy scene every other Tuesday night, when aspiring filmmakers share their short masterpieces with a sauced-up audience.

Nobody has done more to reshape Northern Liberties than developer Bart Blatstein, who gathered up 28 (largely derelict) acres at the start of the millennium and has been dolling them up ever since. His marquee projects include Liberties Walk, a four-block pedestrian strip framed by new townhouses with boutiques and eateries at street level and high-end apartments above, and The Piazza at Schmidts, an enormous open-air plaza surrounded by large mixed-use buildings. Forming the eastern gateway to Liberties Walk are **Bar Ferdinand** (1030 N. 2nd St., 215/923-1313, www.barferdinand.com, 4:30pm-midnight Mon.-Thurs., 4:30pm-2am Fri., 11am-2am Sat., 11am-midnight Sun., brunch 11am-3pm Sat.-Sun., food $10-35) and **El Camino Real** (1040 N. 2nd St., 215/925-1110, www.elcaminophilly.com, 11am-2am Mon.-Fri., 10am-2am Sat.-Sun., kitchen closes at 1am, food $8-20). The former is a stylish tapas bar with an exceptional selection of Spanish wines and a way with fruity drinks. Try the clericot, a refreshing *bebida* of white wine, melons, berries, and citrus fruit, if you're seated outside on a summer day, or the Sol de Cádiz, a pilsner and OJ combo, if you're there for brunch. Dried roses dangle over the wraparound bar, which is plenty wide for an assortment of small plates. Amble over to El Camino Real for a Texas-size tequila list. The bar at the faux rustic Tex-Mex joint also stocks dozens of whiskeys, daring beers like Rogue's chipotle-infused ale as well as Corona, Tecate, and other south-of-the-border staples, and everything it takes to make a jalapeño margarita.

The Piazza at Schmidts is home to **P.Y.T.** (1050 N. Hancock St., 215/964-9009, www.pytphilly.org, 11am-2am Mon.-Fri., 10:30am-2am Sat.-Sun., food $9-15), a much-hyped bar specializing in burgers and booze-infused ice cream shakes. Yeah, you read that right. The "adult shakes" taste great with P.Y.T.'s sensational onion rings. Burger options include The Doh! Nut, which features chocolate-covered bacon and a glazed donut bun.

Center City East

The half of Center City east of Broad Street is home to drinking establishments of every stripe, including most of Philadelphia's queer bars. For the laid-back beer drinker, there's **Fergie's Pub** (1214 Sansom St., 215/928-8118, www.fergies.com, 11am-2am Mon.-Sat., 4pm-2am Sun., food $6-15). Irish-born owner Fergus Carey is Philly's favorite publican, a former bartender whose beer-soaked ventures include Monk's Café and Nodding Head in Center City West and Grace Tavern just off South Street. His namesake bar has his conviviality and good taste in beer and offers some form of entertainment most every night. Its Tuesday and Thursday Quizzo games vie for liveliest in the city. Monday night's open mic draws a talented crowd, and traditional Irish music is a Saturday afternoon staple.

Vintage (129 S. 13th St., 215/922-3095, www.vintage-philadelphia.com, 4pm-2am Mon.-Fri., 2pm-2am Sat.-Sun., kitchen closes at midnight, food $6-18) is a mellow little wine bar invitingly outfitted in exposed brick, artfully arranged wine corks, a chandelier crafted of iron and wine bottles, and flickering votive candles. It offers more than 60 wines by the glass. A nearby sister establishment, **Time** (1315 Sansom St., 215/985-4800, www.timerestaurant.net, 5pm-2am daily, kitchen closes at 1am Sun.-Thurs. and 11pm Fri.-Sat., bar menu $5-13, dinner $16-23), boasts a whiskey selection that's nearly 200 strong. It also specializes in absinthe, the storied herbal liqueur that was banned in the United States until 2007. You don't have to be a whiskey or absinthe lover to appreciate Time, which offers 20 seasonal drafts, a seasonal menu featuring local ingredients, housemade bread and desserts, and live music seven nights a week. DJs spin in its second-floor lounge on Friday and Saturday nights.

The swatch of Center City approximately bounded by Walnut, Pine, 11th, and Broad Streets is known as the "Gayborhood." Gone are the gay bathhouses and other red-light establishments that characterized the area in the 1970s. But a good time can still be had here. The up-and-coming nabe with the rainbow-emblazoned street signs is dotted with gay bars and clubs. Named one of the 50 greatest gay bars in the world by *Out* magazine, **Woody's** (202 S. 13th St., 215/545-1893, www.woodysbar.com, 4pm-2am daily) is the unofficial capital of the Gayborhood.

It's huge—big enough to call itself a "nightlife complex"—with several bars and two dance floors. Themed nights and special events give it broad appeal. Thursday nights feature Latin-flavored beats, and Friday evenings are geared toward the country-western crowd. Wednesday college nights attract posses of out-and-proud Penn, Drexel, and Temple students.

"Hanging out" takes on a whole new meaning on jockstrap Mondays and underwear Wednesdays at **The Bike Stop** (206 S. Quince St., 215/627-1662, www.thebikestop. com, 4pm-2am Mon.-Fri., 2pm-2am Sat.-Sun.), a longtime gathering spot for Philly's leather-loving gays and lesbians.

Center City West

It's easy as pie to find a watering hole west of Broad Street, especially in the area around Rittenhouse Square. Among the standouts is **Tria Café** (123 S. 18th St., 215/972-8742, www.triacafe.com, noon-late night daily, food under $10), which pays homage to the "tasty threesome of fermentation": wine, beer, and cheese. If you have a taste for wine and a date who prefers microbrews, it's the place to go. It's also the place to go if you don't know chardonnay from shiraz or cheddar from chèvre but want to learn. Servers are knowledgeable and anything but snooty, and the menus helpfully group each day's offerings under layman's descriptors like "approachable," "stinky," and "extreme." Toothsome small bites, salads, and sandwiches round out the experience for those who come hungry. The concept proved so popular in the Rittenhouse neighborhood that a second **Tria Café** (1137 Spruce St., 215/629-9200, noon-late night daily) opened in Center City East. Both locations slash the price of one unique wine, beer, and cheese every Sunday.

Center City West has perhaps the highest concentration of gastropubs—bars even a teetotaler can love—in the Philadelphia region. A mecca for beer aficionados from well outside the region, **Monk's Café** (264 S. 16th St., 215/545-7005, www.monkscafe. com, 11:30am-2am daily, kitchen closes at 1am, food $8-30) could do a brisk business even if its food menu consisted of peanuts and Fritos. The beer emporium has one of the most impressive bottle selections on the East Coast and a much-ballyhooed array of Belgians on draft. It was the only U.S. bar in the top 10 on *All About Beer Magazine*'s list of "125 Places to Have a Beer Before You Die." But Monk's doesn't rest on its sudsy laurels. Its far-from-standard menu includes frog legs, lightly smoked trout, an ever-popular duck salad, mussels, mussels, and more mussels.

If you're craving mussels and pommes frites but can't stomach the wait at Monk's, foot it to **Nodding Head Brewery & Restaurant** (1516 Sansom St., 2nd floor, 215/569-9525, www.noddinghead.com, 11:30am-2am Mon.-Sat., 11am-2am Sun., kitchen closes at midnight Mon.-Sat. and 11pm Sun., food $10-23), a sibling establishment. Not long after it opened its doors in 2000, a customer returned from vacation bearing a small animal figurine with a bobbing head. The brewpub's staff put it on display—and opened the floodgates. Patrons have donated enough bobbleheads to fill a large display case, decorate the back bar, and relegate hundreds more to storage. Like the doll collection, which includes Ozzy Osbourne, Hello Kitty, and disgraced state senator Vincent Fumo, the brews are wideranging. Sample as many as you like before committing to a pint, or order a flight and savor them all. Nodding Head offers seven or eight of its creations daily. The chef knows his way around a meat smoker. Nod your head yes to anything spicy, jerked, or pulled.

Patrons of **Good Dog Bar** (224 S. 15th St., 215/985-9600, www.gooddogbar.com, 11:30am-2am daily, kitchen closes at 1am, food $9-18) also had a hand in its decor. Framed black-and-white photos of their pooches adorn the walls of the three-level bar and restaurant, which bills itself as "a cozy alternative to the ultra-trendy" newcomers to Philly's bar scene. Good Dog's signature burger is something to bark about: molten roquefort cheese erupts from the meat upon first bite. Head to the third floor for pool, darts, and retro arcade games.

Center City has no shortage of Irish pubs, but few have as faithful a following as **The Bards** (2013 Walnut St., 215/569-9585, www.bardsirishbar.com, 11am-2am Mon.-Fri., 10am-2am Sat.-Sun., kitchen closes at 1am, food $9-15). Irish owned and operated since its opening in 1995, The Bards pulls off an Irish literary theme without straying into theme-y territory and pours a good Guinness. Irish dishes share the menu with flatbreads, mussels, burgers, and more.

NIGHTCLUBS

Silk City (435 Spring Garden St., 215/592-8838, www.silkcityphilly.com, 4pm-2am daily, dinner 5pm-1am daily, brunch 10am-3:45pm Sat.-Sun., food $8-18) is a strange and wonderful beast: a classic diner car that opens to a nightclub complete with disco ball chandeliers. Once frequented by truckers, the neon-lit diner now fills with 20- and 30-somethings hungry for a good time—or just plain hungry. In the warmer months, the party spills into the 3,000-square-foot beer garden. Like owner Mark Bee's other Northern Liberties haunt, North 3rd, Silk City is known for satisfying eats. The kitchen injects pizzazz into diner standards like meatloaf, fried chicken, and mac and cheese, and the fact that you can wash them down with a Hoegaarden or strawberry martini is icing on the cake. The club side hosts a DJ-driven dance party most nights of the week.

South Philly's **L'Etage** (624 S. 6th St., 215/592-0656, www.creperie-beaumonde.com, 7pm-2am Fri.-Sat., 7:30pm-1am Sun. and Tues.-Thurs., cover varies) fancies itself a French cabaret. The club upstairs from the lovely crepe café Beau Monde books DJs on Fridays and Saturdays. Live music, film screenings, burlesque, and other diversions round out the calendar.

LIVE MUSIC
Rock
The **Wells Fargo Center** (3601 S. Broad St., event hotline 215/336-3600, box office 800/298-4200, www.wellsfargocenterphilly.com) may be one of the hardest-working arenas in the country. Home to Philadelphia's professional basketball, hockey, and lacrosse teams, it's also the largest concert venue in the region. Acts as varied as Hannah Montana, Metallica, and Barbra Streisand have brought down the house since it opened in 1996. Billy Joel and Bruce Springsteen have sold out so many concerts in the 20,000-seat arena and its predecessor that banners honoring them hang from the rafters.

Venues offering a more intimate live music experience are scattered around town. Best of the bunch is **World Cafe Live** (3025 Walnut St., 215/222-1400, www.worldcafelive.com) in the University City neighborhood, home to the University of Pennsylvania and Drexel University. One expects certain things from a music venue in a collegiate setting: frat boys on the prowl, shooter specials, and sticky floors, for starters. World Cafe Live is not what one expects. It's a grown-up sort of place with two performance spaces. Designed for major acts, Downstairs Live is a three-tiered music hall that's usually furnished with tables and chairs for 300 but can hold as many as 650 for standing-room-only events. (Be aware that a food and beverage minimum applies during seated shows. Fortunately, the grub is quite good.) Upstairs Live is a full-service restaurant open for lunch and dinner on weekdays and dinner on weekends. It lures 9-to-5ers with happy-hour specials and serves up live music most evenings. World Cafe Live shares a converted factory building with public radio station WXPN, which produces the nationally syndicated *World Cafe* with David Dye.

Several of Philadelphia's best-known music venues can be found in the neighborhoods north of Old City. The largest, **Electric Factory** (421 N. 7th St., 215/627-1332, www.electricfactory.info), can pack in about 3,000 people and caters to all musical tastes. Shows are open to all ages unless otherwise specified. Expect to be patted down before entering.

Fishtown institution **Johnny Brenda's**

(1201 N. Frankford Ave., 215/739-9684, www.johnnybrendas.com, kitchen open 11am-1am daily) is a triple threat: bar, restaurant, and music venue. Its owners also own Standard Tap, a locally legendary gastropub, and they're so serious about serving foods made with fresh, seasonal ingredients that they don't bother printing menus. Look for strategically hung chalkboards if you want to know what's cooking. The beer list consists entirely of locally brewed drafts. "Local" doesn't rule the day in the upstairs performance space, which is strictly off limits to the underage. A stone's throw away is **The M Room** (15 W. Girard Ave., 215/739-5577, www.mroomphilly.com, 4pm-2am Mon.-Fri., noon-2am Sat.-Sun.), which reinvented itself as a bar-cum-music-venue in 2005 after more than three decades as a diner. Its food menu is heavy on Greek specialties like stuffed grape leaves, spana-kopita, and moussaka. In 2008 the nabe welcomed yet another watering hole with a soft spot for indie bands. The curiously named **Kung Fu Necktie** (1250 N. Front St., 215/291-4919, www.kungfunecktie.com, 5pm-2am daily) boasts tables crafted from bowling lanes and bathrooms marked "balls" and "boobs."

A longtime presence on a street synonymous with nightlife, **Theatre of the Living Arts** (334 South St., 215/922-2599, www.tlaphilly.com) has hosted heavyweights such as the Red Hot Chili Peppers, Dave Matthews Band, Bob Dylan, Paul Simon, Jane's Addiction, Radiohead, Nickelback, Norah Jones, John Mayer, and Patti Smith. Vintage concert posters and newspaper clippings decorate the onetime movie theater.

Center City's preeminent rock venue, the **Trocadero Theatre** (1003 Arch St., 215/922-6888, www.thetroc.com), was also a cinema at one point. At other points in its long life—it first opened in 1870 as the Arch Street Opera House—the Victorian theater hosted traveling minstrel shows, vaudeville, and burlesque. It did time as a dance club in the 1980s. The Troc, as the concert hall in the heart of Chinatown is known, can accommodate 1,200 people for shows on its main stage. The Balcony, an intimate venue within the venue, has a capacity of 250. It's used for screenings of recently released films and classics like *Ghostbusters* on "Movie Monday," a regular event for the 21-plus set. Most concerts are all-ages.

Center City's most unusual temple of music is an active church. Built by a large and prosperous congregation in the 1880s, the **First Unitarian Church of Philadelphia** (2125 Chestnut St.) responded to a shrinking urban population a century later not by closing its doors, as many churches did, but by opening them for nonchurch events. Philly-based concert promoter R5 Productions has been staging rock shows in the historic house of worship since the mid-1990s. Visit www.r5productions.com for a concert calendar.

About half a mile north of the Art Museum in the Fairmount neighborhood, **North Star Bar & Restaurant** (2639 Poplar St., 215/787-0488, www.northstarbar.com, 5pm-1am Sun.-Thurs., 5pm-2am Fri.-Sat.) compensates for its off-the-beaten-path location by putting bands on its stage almost nightly. Ticket prices rarely top $15, and North Star resists the temptation to overcharge for food.

Jazz

Philly certainly has a place in the annals of jazz. Legendary saxophonist Stan Getz was born in this city. John Coltrane, another tenor master, lived and played here. So did trumpeter John Birks Gillespie, who picked up the nickname "Dizzy" while in town. But Philly has few jazz clubs today. Zanzibar Blue, whose stage was graced by the likes of Maynard Ferguson, Arturo Sandoval, Harry Connick Jr., and Diana Krall, closed in 2007. Ortlieb's Jazzhaus, named one of the top 10 jazz clubs in the country by *Playboy* magazine, closed in 2010 after more than 20 years of showcasing local and visiting talent. Philly's jazz enthusiasts are—how to put it—kind of blue. But they're not high and dry. There's still **Chris' Jazz Cafe** (1421 Sansom St., 215/568-3131, www.chrisjazzcafe.com), which serves up live music every day but Sunday. And then there's the **Philadelphia Clef Club of Jazz & Performing Arts** (738 S. Broad St., 215/893-9912, www.clefclubofjazz.org). Founded in 1966 as a social club for members of a black musicians union, it counted Coltrane, Gillespie, Nina Simone, and Grover Washington Jr. among its members. Today it's a nonprofit institution dedicated to the promotion and preservation of jazz music. Its event calendar is regrettably sparse but worth keeping an eye on. Also worth a gander: www. phillyjazz.org. Maintained by jazz enthusiast and middling saxophonist Jan Klincewicz, the website features a calendar of live jazz events.

CASINOS

Opened in 2010, **SugarHouse Casino** (1001 N. Delaware Ave., 877/477-3715, www.sugarhousecasino.com, open 24 hours) boasts 1,600 slots, 50-some table games, and waterfront dining. The city's first and only casino is located along the Delaware River in the Fishtown neighborhood.

PERFORMING ARTS
Avenue of the Arts

South Broad Street is so crowded with performing arts venues that it's rightly known as the Avenue of the Arts. The venues are a mix of old and new. The most striking is the **Kimmel Center for the Performing Arts** (Broad and Spruce Streets, 215/893-1999, www.kimmelcenter.org), which opened in 2001. Described by architect Rafael Viñoly as "two jewels inside a glass box," it consists of two freestanding performance halls beneath a vaulted glass ceiling. The larger Verizon Hall, which seats 2,500, features acoustics designed specifically for the illustrious **Philadelphia Orchestra** (www.philorch. org). The Kimmel Center's resident companies also include the **Philly Pops** (www. phillypops.com) and the Philadelphia Dance Company, better known as **PHILADANCO** (www.philadanco.org). The performing arts complex is open 10am to 6pm daily, so take a look around if you're passing by. You might catch a free performance on its lobby stage,

and you won't believe the views from its glass-enclosed rooftop garden.

One block closer to City Hall is the historic **Academy of Music** (Broad and Locust Streets, 215/893-1999, www.academyofmusic.org), the oldest grand opera house in the country still used for its original purpose. The long list of renowned artists who have performed at the academy since its opening in 1857 includes Pyotr Ilyich Tchaikovsky, Sergei Rachmaninoff, Anna Pavlova, Maria Callas, and Luciano Pavarotti. U.S. President Ulysses S. Grant was nominated for his second term here in 1872. The National Historic Landmark rarely gets a rest. It hosts the **Opera Company of Philadelphia** (www.operaphila.org) and the **Pennsylvania Ballet** (www. paballet.org), plus Broadway shows and other touring productions. The adjacent **Merriam Theater** (Broad and Spruce Streets, 215/893-1999, www.merriam-theater.com), which dates to 1918, is now part of Philadelphia's University of the Arts. Students have the privilege of performing on a stage graced by John Barrymore, Katharine Hepburn, Sir Laurence Olivier, and Sammy Davis Jr. The university has a number of smaller performance spaces, including the **Arts Bank** at Broad and South Streets. Once a bank, the building now houses a 230-seat main stage and a cabaret theater.

Across from the Merriam is the **Wilma Theater** (Broad and Spruce Streets, 215/546-7824, www.wilmatheater.org), which has racked up dozens of Barrymore Awards—the local equivalent of Tony Awards—for its superbly crafted plays. "Dedicated to presenting theater as an art form," the Wilma moved into its 296-seat Avenue of the Arts digs in 1996, after packing smaller houses for 20-some seasons. Serious theater lovers seriously love the theater's tradition of postshow discussions with members of the artistic team. In 2007 the Avenue became home to **Philadelphia Theatre Company** (Suzanne Roberts Theatre, Broad and Lombard Streets, 215/985-0420, www.philadelphiatheatrecompany.org), a highly respected cradle of contemporary works. Founded in 1974, PTC has presented more than 140 world and Philadelphia premieres, including Terrence McNally's Tony Award-winning *Master Class*. Its 365-seat theater is named for actress/benefactor Suzanne Roberts.

Other Center City Theaters

Philadelphia is home to America's oldest art museum, oldest natural history museum, oldest zoo, and oldest residential street. Perhaps not surprisingly, it's also home to America's oldest theater. The **Walnut Street Theatre** (825 Walnut St., 215/574-3550, www.walnutstreettheatre.org) opened in 1809 as an equestrian circus, of all things. By 1812, the horses had been canned and the building converted to a bona fide theater. President Thomas Jefferson was in attendance at the first theatrical production. In 1863 the Walnut was purchased by Edwin Booth, a member of a prominent theatrical family. His actor brother would soon tarnish the family name—and etch his in the history books—by assassinating President Abe Lincoln. The Shubert Organization snapped up the theater in the 1940s and used it as a pre-Broadway testing ground for productions including *A Streetcar Named Desire* starring Marlon Brando and *A Raisin in the Sun* featuring Sidney Poitier. These days the Walnut is a nonprofit regional theater company that generally serves up light fare: *Dirty Rotten Scoundrels, Hairspray,* Neil Simon's *The Odd Couple,* and the like. It also offers an annual series designed for kids in grades K-6.

Unlike the Walnut, the **Forrest Theatre** (1114 Walnut St., 800/447-7400, www.forresttheatre.com) doesn't produce shows. It's what folks in the biz call a road house—a venue for touring companies. Owned by the Shubert Organization, Broadway's biggest bigwig, since it was built in the 1920s, the Forrest gets little use these days. The Academy of Music is the Philly venue of choice for most traveling Broadway productions.

The **Adrienne Theatre** (2030 Sansom St., 215/567-2848, www.adriennelive.org) is the venue of choice for many of Philadelphia's small theater companies. Home to the Wilma Theatre before its 1996 move to the Avenue of the Arts, it has three performance spaces that seat between 55 and 120 people. Its most established resident, **InterAct Theatre Company** (www.interacttheatre.org), wouldn't touch a zany caper with a 10-foot pole. Founded in 1988, InterAct has a stated mission of stirring things up and a fondness for never-before-seen plays. A few doors down from the Adrienne is the **Philadelphia Shakespeare Theatre** (2111 Sansom St., 215/496-8001, www.phillyshakespeare.org), devoted to the prolific playwright's works since 1996.

Thanks to the **Curtis Institute of Music** (1726 Locust St., 215/893-7902, www.curtis.edu) and its "learn by doing" philosophy, Philly's classical music junkies can get a fix without paying a cent. The prestigious conservatory presents free recitals several times a week throughout the school year. Most take place in Field Concert Hall, a 240-seat auditorium in the institute's main building on Rittenhouse Square. No tickets are required, and seating is on a first-come, first-served basis. Call the student recital hotline at 215/893-5261 for the lowdown on each week's programs. Curtis has about 165 students, all of whom show such artistic promise that they get a full ride. (Leonard Bernstein is an alumnus.)

Historic District

Old City's transformation from abandoned industrial area to hip nabe was helped by the arrival of two arts organizations in the 1980s and '90s. Founded in 1969 as a cooperative art gallery on South Street, the **Painted Bride Art Center** (230 Vine St., 215/925-9914, www.paintedbride.org) relocated to Old City in 1982 and is now better known as a performance space. The Bride, as locals call the mosaic-wrapped building, showcases world and jazz music, dance, theater, and poetry. Its commitment to nurturing emerging artists is unquestioned, but it certainly doesn't discriminate against established ones. The long list of past performers includes rocker Carlos

Santana, magicians Penn and Teller, and storyteller Spalding Gray.

"Dedicated to bringing to life the greatest stories by the greatest storytellers of all time," **Arden Theatre Company** (40 N. 2nd St., 215/922-1122, www.ardentheatre.org) serves up a mix of popular plays and musicals, new works, and new spins on popular works. The professional company's interpretation of Thornton Wilder's *Our Town* found the audience walking to historic Christ Church for the second act.

Fairmount Park

With covered seating for about 5,000, outdoor seating for 4,500 more, and a 4,000-person lawn, the **Mann Center for the Performing Arts** (52nd St. and Parkside Ave., 215/878-0400, www.manncenter.org) is one of the nation's largest outdoor amphitheaters. Named for a local businessman who championed its construction in the 1970s, the Mann is best known as the summer home of the fabulous Philadelphia Orchestra. In 2010 the orchestra's six-week series included a performance featuring Aretha Franklin on vocals and former Secretary of State Condoleezza Rice on piano. The amphitheater in West Fairmount Park also hosts an incredible variety of traveling acts, from cellist Yo-Yo Ma to rock band Cheap Trick. Picnicking on the lawn is a Philly tradition.

FESTIVALS AND EVENTS
Summer

Philadelphians are treated to a host of free concerts and festivals in the summer months. They take place throughout the city, but **Penn's Landing** in particular is a hive of activity. The nonprofit Delaware River Waterfront Corporation (DRWC), which oversees development of the riverfront, brings all sorts of free entertainment to the Great Plaza at Penn's Landing (Columbus Blvd. at Chestnut St.) from May through September. Movies are screened Thursday evenings in July and August. Friday evenings in August

are set aside for smooth jazz. Festivals celebrating the diverse cultures that converge in Philly take place on weekends throughout the summer. A complete schedule of DRWC-produced events is available at www.delawareriverevents.com or by calling 215/922-2386.

Center City's Rittenhouse Square is always a social hub but especially so on Wednesday evenings in August, when it hosts *Philadelphia Weekly*'s **Concerts in the Park** (www.philadelphiaweekly.com). The free concerts start at 7pm; arrive early to claim a prime picnicking spot.

Beer festivals are a summertime tradition in towns across the country, typically involving a couple of party tents, a cadre of craft brewers, and a day or two of mingling and tasting. **Philly Beer Week** (215/985-2106, www.phillybeerweek.org, June, free and paid events) puts them to shame. Inaugurated in 2008, the 10-day celebration features hundreds of beer-soaked events throughout the city and its suburbs. It's one of the reasons *Maxim* magazine handed the City of Brotherly Love the "crown of Best Beer Town" in 2010. Philadelphia has been a beer-loving town for more than 300 years—let's not forget that the nation's forefathers did a lot of their best work in its taverns—and its craft brewers are heralded at the national and international level. With its list of participating venues, the Beer Week website is a great resource for beer lovers visiting the city at any time.

A Philly tradition since 1975, the **Odunde Festival** (23rd and South Streets and surrounding area, 215/732-8510, www.odundefestival.org, second Sun. of June, free) is one of the largest African American street festivals in the country. Named for a Nigerian expression for "happy new year," it kicks off with a colorful procession to the Schuylkill River and an offering of fruits, flowers, and prayers. Back at Odunde central, musicians and dancers entertain on two stages while tens of thousands of festivalgoers browse a marketplace with vendors from various African nations, the Caribbean, and Brazil.

In the city where the Declaration of

Independence was signed, Independence Day warrants several days of festivities. **Wawa Welcome America** (various locations, 215/683-2200, www.welcomeamerica.com, free) traditions include spectacular fireworks, an all-you-can-eat ice cream festival, a three-day food-tasting event, a *Rocky* screening at the Philadelphia Museum of Art's "Rocky steps," and what's billed as the largest free concert in America.

Fall

The end of summer is a period of transition in Pennsylvania's largest city. Tourism tapers off, and the city's resident population rebounds with the return of the Jersey Shore set. Just as the weather is starting to cool, the **Fringe Festival** (various locations, 215/413-9006, www.fringearts.com, Sept., free and paid events) causes a spike in the city's cultural temperature. Performing artists from Philly and around the globe stage more than 150 shows over 18 days. Traditional venues can't contain the smorgasbord of artistic expression, which spills into galleries, bars, churches, and even vacant storefronts.

Designers get a chance to show off their talents the following month. Billed as the largest U.S. event of its kind, **DesignPhiladelphia** (various locations, 215/569-3186, www.designphiladelphia.org, Oct., free and paid events) spotlights the work of hundreds of creative folks in a wide variety of disciplines, from fashion design to product design to urban planning.

Winter

The Macy's Thanksgiving Day Parade in New York City may be better known, but Philadelphia's **Thanksgiving Day Parade** (www.6abc.com, free) holds the distinction of being the oldest Thanksgiving parade in the country. The holiday tradition was started in 1920 by the Gimbel Brothers department store chain. When Gimbels went out of business in the 1980s, local television station 6abc picked up the torch, and more

recently, Dunkin' Donuts signed on as title sponsor. That's why the extravaganza is properly known as the 6abc Dunkin' Donuts Thanksgiving Day Parade.

The annual **Wing Bowl** (Wells Fargo Center, 800/298-4200, http://wingbowl.cbslocal.com, admission charged) is a newer Philly tradition. Cooked up by a local sports radio station in 1993, the wing-eating showdown packs Philadelphia's 20,000-seat indoor arena. Soused spectators and scantily clad "Wingettes" cheer on contestants vying for the title of wing king (or queen). The bacchanalia is usually held on the Friday before the Super Bowl.

Spring

Spring is a fertile time for festivals. Among the standouts is the **Subaru Cherry Blossom Festival** (various locations, 215/790-3810, www.subarucherryblossom.org, Mar.-Apr., free and paid events). The celebration of Japanese culture lasts for several weeks—sometimes outlasting the cherry blossoms, or *sakura,* themselves. Organized by the Japan America Society of Greater Philadelphia, the festival features drumming and dance performances, traditional tea ceremonies, Japanese movie screenings, and demonstrations of everything from sushi making to swordsmanship. Japan's government presented Philadelphia with a gift of cherry trees on America's 150th birthday in 1926. The ephemeral blossoms can be seen along East Fairmount Park's Kelly Drive and near **Shofuso** (Lansdowne and Horticultural Drives, 215/878-5097, www.shofuso.com, 11am-5pm weekends in Apr., 10am-4pm Wed.-Fri. and 11am-5pm Sat.-Sun. May-Sept., 11am-5pm weekends in Oct., admission $6, seniors, students, and children 3-17 $4), a 17th-century-style Japanese house and garden in West Fairmount Park.

Formerly known as PrideFest, **Equality Forum** (various locations, 215/732-3378, www.equalityforum.com, late Apr.-early May,

Nothing Quite Like a Philly New Year's

Few cities welcome the new year with as much pomp as Philadelphia. On New Year's Eve, revelers gather at Penn's Landing for a fireworks spectacular. The following day brings an even bigger show: the **Mummers Parade,** a ritual so unique that it landed a *National Geographic* spread in 2001. More razzle-dazzle than many people see in a lifetime, the parade is the culmination of a year's worth of planning by 40-odd clubs whose express purpose is to make the first of the year a magical day. To that end, they create costumes so fantastical that club members—Mummers, as they're called—resemble cartoon characters more than humans as they strut and twirl up Broad Street to City Hall. Such a volume of glitter, sequins, and feathers is rarely seen outside Vegas. It's worth noting that Philadelphia's Mummers are not, for the most part, performers by trade. They're notaries and nurses, postal workers and plumbers, real estate agents and retirees. On the first day of the current millennium, then-mayor Ed Rendell gave mummery a go, donning a dress, a wig, and golden slippers. (Wearing drag didn't hurt the political career of the outgoing mayor, who became Pennsylvania governor three years later.)

The origins of mummery are rather obscure. Some trace its roots to ancient Rome, where laborers ushered in the festival of Saturnalia by donning masks, swapping gifts, and satirizing current affairs. Some credit Swedes who settled in the area in the 1600s. We do know that Philadelphia's first official Mummers Parade was held on January 1, 1901. Like cheesesteaks, the parade has become synonymous with the City of Brotherly Love.

Dress warmly if you're parking yourself on the parade route. The pageantry lasts hours and hours. **MummersFest,** usually held at the Pennsylvania Convention Center in the days leading up to the parade, offers a temperature-controlled taste of what's in store. On New Year's Day, Mummers clubs known as Fancy Brigades put on two elaborate shows at the convention center. Tickets for the Fancy Brigade shows, MummersFest, and grandstand seating at the parade can be purchased at the Independence Visitor Center at 6th and Market Streets or by calling 800/537-7676.

Costumes of Mummers Parades past can be seen any time of year at the **Mummers Museum** (1100 S. 2nd St., 215/336-3050, www.mummersmuseum.com, 9:30am-4pm Wed.-Sat., admission $3.50, seniors, students, and children under 12 $2.50), located in the South Philly neighborhood that many Mummers clubs call home. On Thursday evenings May-September, the museum hosts free concerts by clubs in the String Bands division of Mummers.

free and paid events) is a week of panel discussions, parties, film screenings, and other events geared toward the gay, lesbian, bisexual, and transgender community. Philly's LGBT citizenry also looks forward to the **PrideDay** parade each June and the **OutFest** block party each October, both organized by the volunteer organization Philly Pride Presents (215/875-9288, www.phillypride.org).

The tony Rittenhouse Square neighborhood welcomes spring with an uncommonly chic street festival. The **Rittenhouse Row Spring Festival** (Walnut St. between Broad and 19th Streets, www.rittenhouserow.org, May, free) features gourmet food, wine and cocktail tastings, and open-air shopping for designer duds.

Collegiate rowing teams from across North America converge on Philadelphia for the **Dad Vail Regatta** (215/542-1443, www.dadvail.org, early May), two days of racing on the Schuylkill River. Named for Harry Emerson "Dad" Vail, who coached University of Wisconsin rowers in the early 1900s, the nation's largest collegiate regatta is a beautiful sight. Grandstands in East Fairmount Park afford the best views of the finish line. Kelly Drive is closed to regular traffic during the regatta, but the grandstands can be reached by shuttle bus from the Art Museum and Boathouse Row, a set of Victorian boathouses along the southern end of Kelly Drive.

Shopping

HISTORIC DISTRICT

If you're looking for mainstream retailers—J.Crew, H&M, Ann Taylor, and the like—head to the Rittenhouse Square area. If you're looking to adorn your person or your abode with rare finds, Old City has you covered. Philadelphia's most historic neighborhood is peppered with chic boutiques and art galleries beloved by young, hip (and relatively well-off) shoppers. Wandering aimlessly is as good a strategy as any for exploring the neighborhood's retail offerings. If time is of the essence, concentrate on the square blocks bounded by Front and 3rd Streets and Market and Race Streets. The first Friday of every month is a particularly good day for an Old City excursion because dozens of shops and galleries stay open as late as 9pm.

Among the area's gems is **Vagabond Boutique** (37 N. 3rd St., 267/671-0737, www.vagabondboutique.com, open daily). Owners Mary Clark and Megan Murphy deal in hand-knit sweaters by Mary, hand-sewn pieces by Megan, and threads by other creative sorts, some of them local. Head to the back room for yarn, children's clothing, accessories, housewares, and art exhibitions.

Sugarcube (124 N. 3rd St., 215/238-0825, www.sugarcube.us, open daily) makes life a little sweeter with its carefully curated collection of men's and women's fashions by indie designers. Bicycles and canine friends are welcome inside. If you haven't maxed out the plastic, try **Third Street Habit** (153 N. 3rd St., 215/925-5455, www.thirdstreethabit.com, open daily), named best women's boutique by *Philadelphia* magazine soon after its 2004 opening. If of-the-moment labels like Earnest Sewn, Ella Moss, Graham & Spencer, and Rag & Bone make your heart pitter-patter, then shopping here could easily become a habit. Vagabond, Sugarcube, and Third Street Habit all carry select vintage duds.

SOUTH PHILADELPHIA

South Philly's northern boundary, **South Street,** is a retail melting pot. Sex shops share the corridor with Starbucks. Tattoo parlors coexist with darling boutiques. Foot Locker is just steps from a store specializing in pimp-worthy shoes made of exotic skins (alligator, stingray, lizard, and the like). The street stretches from the Delaware River in the east to the Schuylkill River in the west, but most of the action is concentrated between Front and 10th Streets. The action spills over to some surrounding blocks. South 4th Street, also known as Fabric Row, is especially colorful—the place to go for a body piercing or a bolt of fabric.

East Passyunk Avenue, which runs diagonally across South Philly, is coming into its own as a shopping destination. **Metro Mens Clothing** (1615 E. Passyunk Ave., 267/324-5172, metromensclothing.com, open daily), which sells exactly what its name suggests, and **Green Aisle Grocery** (1618 E. Passyunk Ave., 215/465-1411, www.greenaislegrocery.com, open daily), a self-described "boutique" market co-owned by food critic Adam Erace, are part of the renaissance.

Fabric Row

To the Yiddish-speaking Jews who populated Philadelphia's southern outskirts a century ago, what's now called Fabric Row (S. 4th St. between South and Catharine Streets) was known as "Der Ferder" (The Fourth). In the early 1900s it was chockablock with pushcarts and stands loaded with fabrics, produce, and other goods. The city outlawed pushcarts in the 1950s, but by then, many of the fabric merchants had acquired storefronts and a reputation that attracted tailors and dressmakers from all over Philadelphia. It's still home to more than a dozen fabric-related businesses.

Marmelstein's (760 S. 4th St., 215/925-9862, open Mon.-Sat.), whose founders sold thread, needles, thimbles, and such from a stand, specializes in fabrics and trims for window treatments and upholstery. For cut-to-size foam cushions, come into **Adler's Fabrics** (742 S. 4th St., 215/925-8984, www.adlersfabricsonline.com, open Mon.-Sat.), which also custom makes bedspreads, duvets, shams, and bedskirts. **Albert Zoll Inc.** (744 S. 4th St., 215/922-0589, www.albertzoll.com, open Mon.-Sat.) is heaven for the home sewer. Family owned and operated for three generations, it carries everything from scissors and chalk to Swarovski crystals and exotic buttons. Brides-to-be flock there for custom veils.

Sprinkled among the fabric establishments are bars and eateries and an eclectic mix of shops, including **Bus Stop** (727 S. 4th St., 215/627-2357, www.busstopboutique.com, open daily), a must-stop for ladies who love unique designer shoes, and the highly regarded **Bicycle Revolutions** (756 S. 4th St., 215/629-2453, www.bicyclerevolutions.com, open Mon.-Sat.) bike shop.

Italian Market

Age hasn't slowed down South Philly's **Italian Market** (S. 9th St. between Wharton and Fitzwater Streets, www.italianmarketphilly.org), which throbs with activity seven days a week. The outdoor market, said to be the oldest in the country, traces its history to the 1880s, when an Italian immigrant opened a boarding house for his countrymen. Food stalls sprang up to serve the influx of immigrants, and then came butcher shops, cheese shops, bakeries, and restaurants. Some never left. Produce purveyor **P&F Giordano** and meat-centric **Cannuli's,** where you can pick up a whole roasted pig, date to the 1920s. You'll find both along 9th Street between Washington Avenue and Christian Street, the busiest stretch of the market. Across the street from Cannuli's is the gourmet grocery **Di Bruno Bros.,** which opened in 1939. In recent years Di Bruno has set up shop in the ritzy Rittenhouse Square area and in the Comcast Center, Philly's tallest skyscraper, but the unpolished original has an inimitable

old-world charm. The Italian Market has of late made room for merchants of other ethnic backgrounds. Mexican eateries and bodegas are prevalent. Korean barbecue and Vietnamese *pho* (noodle soup) are as easy to come by as a slice of pizza.

Be aware that some street vendors and shop owners take Mondays off. If you're averse to crowds, it's a great day to come. Steel yourself for thick crowds and impossibly tempting foods if you come during the **Italian Market Festival** (www.italianmarketfestival.com) in mid-May.

CENTER CITY
Macy's

The venerable department store chain's Center City **emporium** (1300 Market St., 215/241-9000, www.visitmacysphiladelphia.com, open daily) holds as much appeal for architecture and history buffs as it does for fashionistas. It occupies a stately tower built a century ago as the flagship of Philadelphia native John Wanamaker's retailing empire. No less a dignitary than U.S. President William Howard Taft dedicated the department store, which bore the Wanamaker name until a buyout in the 1990s, then went by several others before opening as a Macy's in 2006. Tours of the National Historic Landmark leave from the first-floor visitors center at 3:30pm Monday-Friday. The building's soaring atrium features a pipe organ that Wanamaker purchased in 1909 and enlarged to its current glory. With nearly 28,500 pipes and the prowess of three symphony orchestras, it's said to be the largest playable instrument in the world. Macy's shoppers are treated to 45-minute recitals twice daily Monday-Saturday. The marble-clad atrium is especially magical in March and April, when it's filled with flowers and topiaries from around the world, and during the holiday season, when a Christmas-themed light show runs every hour on the hour. The store offers more than 150,000 square feet of fashion and home decor—enough to overwhelm an unseasoned shopper. Fortunately, an appointment with a Macy's personal shopper (800/343-0121) costs nothing at all.

Midtown Village

Ask a Philly native to point you to Midtown Village, and you're liable to get a "What's dat?" There was no "Midtown Village" in William Penn's 17th-century plan for the city or, for that matter, a couple decades ago. It's what merchants and restaurateurs in an up-and-coming area better known as the Gayborhood have taken to calling their pocket of Center City. And why shouldn't they get to call it what they please? Where most saw shuttered storefronts and transvestite prostitutes, they saw potential. The heart of the newly hip area is the stretch of South 13th Street between Chestnut and Walnut Streets. Here you'll find **Open House** (107 S. 13th St., 215/922-1415, www.openhouseliving.com, open daily) with its ever-changing collection of modern housewares. Valerie Safran and chef Marcie Turney, the couple who opened it in 2002, have since started multiple other businesses on the same block. Their empire includes several restaurants, a gourmet market named Grocery, and **Verde** (108 S. 13th St., 215/546-8700, www.verdephiladelphia.com, open daily), a boutique specializing in women's jewelry and accessories.

Nearby **Duross & Langel** (117 S. 13th St., 215/592-7627, www.durossandlangel.com, open daily) is an olfactory delight. It's stocked with its own brand of face, body, and hair care products and offers custom-blended balms for whatever ails you.

Jewelers' Row

Philadelphia's diamond district is the oldest in America and second in magnitude only to New York's. Dozens of jewelry stores compete for business along the brick-paved stretch of Sansom Street between 7th and 8th Streets as well as 8th Street between Chestnut and Walnut Streets. Located a (precious) stone's throw from Independence National Historical Park, the area has been bling central since the second half of the 19th century.

With goldsmiths and diamond setters on premises, **Campbell & Company** (702 Sansom St., 215/627-4996, www.campbelljewelers.com, open Mon.-Sat.) is a must-stop for anyone interested in a custom-made sparkler. **Unclaimed Diamonds** (113 S. 8th St., 215/923-3210, www.unclaimeddiamonds.com, open daily) offers deals on engagement rings, wedding bands, watches, and other valuables that people put on layaway and never claimed.

Rittenhouse Row

The area around leafy Rittenhouse Square is a fashion plate's Eden, a destination for everything from mass-produced tees to haute couture frocks. Walnut and Chestnut Streets are especially crowded with stores. The former is home to Gap, Juicy Couture, Kiehl's, Ann Taylor, American Apparel, Aerosoles, Zara, Armani Exchange, Brooks Brothers, Banana Republic, Club Monaco, Cole Haan, Esprit, Guess, Kenneth Cole, Lucky Brand, Talbots, and more.

At the corner of Broad and Walnut Streets stands **The Bellevue** (215/875-8350, www.bellevuephiladelphia.com, open daily), a 1904 Beaux Arts building that houses a luxury hotel and stores to match, including Tiffany & Co., Polo Ralph Lauren, and Williams-Sonoma. In 2009 Walnut Street welcomed Pennsylvania's first **Barneys CO-OP** (1811 Walnut St., 215/563-5333, www.barneys.com, open daily), much to the delight of Philly's Carrie Bradshaw wannabes.

Chestnut Street boasts a Sephora and **The Shops at Liberty Place** (1625 Chestnut St., 215/851-9055, www.shopsatliberty.com, open daily), an indoor mall with about 30 stores, including J.Crew, Victoria's Secret, and Aveda.

It's not all chains in this pocket of Center City, dubbed "Rittenhouse Row." Tucked among the nationally recognized stores are gems found nowhere else. **Boyds** (1818 Chestnut St., 215/564-9000, www.boydsphila.com, open Mon.-Sat.), family owned since its founding in 1938, stocks luxury fashions by the likes of Armani, Escada, Gucci, and Dolce & Gabbana, employs an army of tailors, and offers free valet parking. Jewelry mavens flock to **Tselaine** (1927 Walnut St., 215/301-4752, open daily) for the sort of baubles seen on starlets and in the pages of *Elle*.

GREATER PHILADELPHIA
King of Prussia Mall

With more than 400 stores and eateries, including seven department stores, **King of Prussia** (160 N. Gulph Rd., King of Prussia, 610/265-5727, www.kingofprussiamall.com, 10am-9pm Mon.-Sat., 11am-6pm Sun.) is the East Coast's largest shopping mall. According to mall management, its footprint could accommodate five Great Pyramids or two Louisiana Superdomes. In other words,

you'd be wise to wear your comfiest shoes. If money isn't an object, toss your keys to the valets at Neiman Marcus and save your tootsies the trouble of walking from one of 13,000 parking spaces. What's notable about the shopping complex—besides its size—is that it's home to both garden-variety chains (Gap, Old Navy, Victoria's Secret) and luxury retailers (Thomas Pink, Ralph Lauren, Lilly Pulitzer, Hermes). Five of its department stores—Nordstrom, Neiman Marcus, Lord & Taylor, Sears, and JCPenney—frame a building known as The Plaza. Macy's and Bloomingdales occupy the neighboring Court building. If you've traveled far to get your shop on, consider budgeting time for a visit to Valley Forge National Historical Park, just a few minutes away.

Sports and Recreation

Philadelphia sports fans have it good: The city has a bushel of professional teams. The Phillies brought home a World Series championship as recently as 2008. But packing stadiums and tailgating aren't the only forms of recreation in Rocky Balboa's hometown. There are parks to explore, rivers to row, and trails to hike and bike, not to mention museum steps to conquer.

PARKS

Philadelphia boasts more than 10,000 acres of parkland, from small urban oases like Rittenhouse Square to unmanicured areas large enough to get lost in, e.g. Wissahickon Valley Park. If you have time for just one outdoorsy activity while in town, go for a bike ride on the Schuylkill River Trail, which runs through East Fairmount Park.

Rittenhouse Square

One of five public squares included in William Penn's 1680s plan for Philadelphia, **Rittenhouse Square** (between 18th and 19th Streets and Walnut and Locust Streets)

has been called the heart of the city. When the weather is nice, you'll find children at play, senior citizens warming the benches, office workers enjoying their lunches, and fat squirrels soliciting handouts. An address near the tree-lined park is a mark of status. Rittenhouse was known as Southwest Square until 1825, when it was renamed for 18th-century astronomer and clockmaker David Rittenhouse. The present layout, with its diagonal walkways and reflecting pool, dates to 1913, when architect Paul Philippe Cret was recruited to spruce it up. Cret would go on to design the Benjamin Franklin Bridge connecting Philadelphia and Camden, New Jersey, and the Rodin Museum, among other memorable structures.

Washington Square

Originally called Southeast Square, **Washington Square** (Walnut St. between 6th and 7th Streets) is another of Philadelphia's five original squares. It's less trafficked than Rittenhouse despite its proximity to the major historic attractions. Used as a mass graveyard for casualties of the Revolutionary War and for victims of the yellow fever epidemics of the 1790s, it was renamed for the nation's first commander-in-chief and president in 1825. The **Tomb of the Unknown Soldier,** featuring a bronze sculpture of George Washington and an eternal flame, was erected in the 1950s.

Wissahickon Valley Park

Less than 30 minutes north of Center City, Wissahickon Valley Park offers more than 50 miles of trails, a stocked trout stream, and some of the region's best leaf-peeping. Stretching seven miles from Chestnut Hill in the north to Manayunk in the southwest, it's one of the largest parks in the Philly region. Wissahickon Creek, which runs through it, was once lined with water-powered mills and taverns. The only remaining example is the **Valley Green Inn** (Valley Green Rd. at Wissahickon, 215/247-1730, www.valleygreeninn.com, lunch noon-4pm Mon.-Fri. and 11am-4pm Sat., brunch 10am-3pm Sun., dinner 5pm-9pm Mon.-Thurs., 5pm-10pm Fri.-Sat., 4pm-8pm Sun., lunch $10-18, brunch $19-23, dinner $20-32), built in 1850. Originally known as Edward Rinker's Temperance Tavern, it now serves new American cuisine in a cozy and romantic setting. Hitching posts are still found out front.

There are multiple entry points to the 1,800-acre park, but if you're unfamiliar with the area, you're best off parking near the restaurant. Use the public restrooms, then set out on Forbidden Drive, the wide and flat gravel road that parallels the creek. You'll find plenty of opportunities to hop on more rugged trails. The nonprofit **Friends of the Wissahickon** (8708 Germantown Ave., 215/247-0417, ww.fow. org) publishes a detailed map of the park. You can purchase it through the website and at locations including the Valley Green Inn.

SCHUYLKILL RIVER TRAIL

The Philadelphia region boasts hundreds of miles of trails that range from paved to rocky, flat to steep, and crowded to rarely trodden. None are so popular as the multiuse **Schuylkill River Trail** (484/945-0200, www. schuylkillrivertrail.com), a work in progress expected to grow to nearly 130 miles. It's already possible to travel from Center City to Valley Forge National Historical Park, a distance of about 20 miles, via the riverside trail. The Philadelphia section, which hugs the Schuylkill River's east bank, stretches north from Locust Street, passes the Philadelphia Museum of Art and Boathouse Row, and continues through the charming Manayunk neighborhood. It's accessible via ramps from Market and Chestnut Streets, stairs from Walnut Street, and street-level crossings at Locust and Race Streets, among other places.

The trailhead near **Lloyd Hall** (1 Boathouse Row on Kelly Dr., 215/685-3936), a community rec center just north of the Art Museum, is particularly popular because of the availability of parking, restrooms, drinking water, and **bike and inline skate rentals** (215/568-6002, www.breakaway-bikes.com, 10am-7pm Sat. during trail season). You can also rent a bike at Manayunk's **Human Zoom** (4159 Main St., 215/487-7433, www.humanzoom.com, 11am-7pm Mon.-Fri., 10am-5pm Sat., 11am-4pm Sun.).

WATER ACTIVITIES

Philadelphia is known as a center for rowing, and the set of boathouses sandwiched between Kelly Drive and the Schuylkill River just north of the Art Museum is one of the most recognizable sights in the city. But unless you belong to a local rowing club, boating opportunities are quite limited. Your best bet is to call or check the website of the **Schuylkill River Development Corporation** (215/222-6030, www.schuylkillbanks.org), which offers kayak and riverboat tours of the river.

If you've always wanted to give rowing a go, register for a **PA Rowing Camps** (267/971-9073, www.parowing.com) course, open to anyone age 13 and older. You don't need to have any knowledge of the sport or any equipment, but you must know how to swim.

SPECTATOR SPORTS

Philadelphia is one of about a dozen U.S. cities with teams in all four major sports leagues: Major League Baseball, the National Hockey League, the National Football League, and the National Basketball Association. In 2010 the Philly area welcomed a Major League Soccer franchise. Sports addicts can also get their fix from minor league baseball, professional indoor football, professional indoor lacrosse, and professional team tennis. A discussion of the sports scene isn't complete without mention of the fierce hoops rivalries between local colleges.

Baseball

In 2007 the **Philadelphia Phillies** (Citizens Bank Park, 1 Citizens Bank Way, 215/463-1000, www.phillies.com) became the first American professional sports franchise to lose 10,000 games. So you can imagine the city's elation when the team beat the Tampa Bay Rays in the 2008 World Series. Founded in 1883, the franchise had captured baseball's highest prize only once before, in 1980. The Phillies made it back to the World Series in 2009 but fell to the New York Yankees four games to two.

Their current home, the 43,651-seat Citizens Bank Park, opened in 2004. While some die-hard fans decried the move from Veterans Stadium, demolished that same year, "The Bank" has proved a hit. The open outfield affords a scenic view of the Center City skyline, and the food is said to be the best in baseball. People for the Ethical Treatment of Animals, or PETA, has crowned it the most vegetarian-conscious ballpark.

For minor league baseball and the joy it brings, cross the Delaware River into New Jersey. The **Camden Riversharks** (Campbell's Field, 401 N. Delaware Ave., Camden, NJ, 866/742-7579, www.riversharks.com) play in the Atlantic League of Professional Baseball, which isn't affiliated with MLB. The view of the Benjamin Franklin Bridge and Philadelphia from their riverfront ballpark is worth the ticket price alone. Built

in time for the franchise's first season in 2001, Campbell's Field seats 6,400 and features family-friendly amenities such as a rock-climbing wall and a carousel.

Basketball

The **Philadelphia 76ers** (Wells Fargo Center, 3601 S. Broad St., 215/339-7676, www.nba.com/sixers) have been very good and very bad. Since moving to the city in 1963, the pro basketball franchise has won two NBA championships—one in 1967 and the other in 1983. In between, it set a league record for fewest wins in a season, finishing the 1972-73 season with a 9-73 record. What the Sixers lack in consistency they make up for in star power. The roster has included some of the greatest players in basketball history: Wilt Chamberlain, Julius "Dr. J" Erving, Moses Malone, Charles Barkley, and Allen Iverson. Sixers management has riled fans by letting superstars slip through its fingers. Chamberlain was traded to Los Angeles, Malone to Washington, and Barkley to Phoenix. Iverson, who was sent to Denver in 2006 after 10 successful years with the Sixers, returned in 2009, giving fans hope that disadvantageous trades were a thing of the past. The home arena, known by several names since its 1996 opening, was rechristened the Wells Fargo Center in 2010.

Local basketball fans also relish the intense rivalries between five area universities—the University of Pennsylvania, La Salle, Saint Joseph's, Temple, and Villanova—known as the **Big 5** (215/898-4747, www.philadelphiabig5.org).

Football

In a passionate sports town, no team inspires more passion than the **Philadelphia Eagles** (Lincoln Financial Field, 1 Lincoln Financial Field Way, 215/463-5500, www.philadelphiaeagles.com). The club's popularity—and the scarcity of tickets—can't be explained by Super Bowl trophies. Established in 1933, the Eagles have not a one. (To be fair, they did win three NFL championships before the Super

Bowl was first played in 1967.) "Da Iggles" have been perennial contenders since 2000, playing in five conference championship games and advancing to the Super Bowl once. Despite exciting games and a roster stocked with high-profile players, the team's failure to bring home the ultimate prize looms large over the city. Fans grow crankier with each passing year, turning Lincoln Financial Field into a cauldron of noise, heightened emotions, and the occasional drunken brawl. Be warned: If you show up at the stadium (or a sports bar) wearing the opposing team's jersey, you *will* catch heat—or worse.

If you need a football fix and Eagles tickets are out of reach, you're not out of luck. Philadelphia's Arena Football League team captured its second straight American Conference championship in 2013. The **Philadelphia Soul** (Wells Fargo Center, 3601 S. Broad St., 215/253-4900, www.philadelphiasoul.com) are named for a style of soul music associated with Philadelphia.

Hockey

The "Broad Street Bullies," as the **Philadelphia Flyers** (Wells Fargo Center, 3601 S. Broad St., 800/298-4200, http://flyers.nhl.com) are known, are arguably the most successful of the city's pro franchises. Added to the NHL in 1967, the Flyers won back-to-back Stanley Cups in 1973-74 and 1974-1975, earning their nickname along the way. They have appeared in the play-offs 36 times, more than all but one other expansion team. Do home games sell out? You bet.

The bruising style that worked for them in the 1970s made the Flyers local heroes and one of the most reviled teams in the league. Fans still eat up the rough-and-tumble approach. A crunching check or violent confrontation between two enforcers can get the Philly crowd

more juiced than a wicked pass or sweet goal. Hockey tends to take a back seat to the other three major sports in terms of overall effect on the city, but when the Flyers are doing well, fair-weather fans come out in droves.

Soccer

In 2010 Major League Soccer awarded Philadelphia an expansion team. An 18,500-seat soccer stadium rose in the satellite city of Chester, and the **Philadelphia Union** (PPL Park, One Stadium Dr., Chester, 877/218-6466, www.philadelphiaunion.com) began play in March 2010. By the time their riverfront stadium celebrated its grand opening that June, season tickets had sold out. The team's name alludes to the union of the 13 American colonies in the Revolutionary period, when Philadelphia was the de facto capital. Players wear navy blue and gold—just like soldiers in George Washington's Continental Army.

Other Spectator Sports

The National Lacrosse League's **Philadelphia Wings** (Wells Fargo Center, 3601 S. Broad St., 215/389-9464, www.wingslax.com) are famous for their rabid fans, who have turned heckling of opposing players into an art form. If you leave a game without a hoarse throat, you've missed half the fun.

Heckling during a **Philadelphia Freedoms** (The Pavilion at Villanova University, Villanova, 215/667-8132, www.philadelphiafreedoms.com) match will get you the boot. One of eight teams in the Mylan World TeamTennis professional league, the Freedoms counted Andy Roddick among their ranks in 2010. World TeamTennis is a coed sport. Each match consists of five sets: men's and women's singles, men's and women's doubles, and mixed doubles.

Accommodations

Philadelphia has a wide range of lodging options, from hostels to bed-and-breakfasts to luxury hotels like The Ritz-Carlton and the Four Seasons. The city has experienced a hotel boom in recent years. Among the newest properties are The Independent, Hotel Palomar, and Hotel Monaco—all of which took up residence in historic buildings. Boom notwithstanding, it can be hard to get a room at the last minute. Book well in advance if you're visiting during summer or a holiday, when tourism is high.

If you're coming by car—and even if you're not—the **Visit Philly Overnight Hotel Package** may be a wise choice. The two-night package includes free parking, which is no small perk in a city whose parking garages charge upwards of $25 per day. (Hotel valet parking can exceed $50 per day.) Go to www.visitphilly.com for a list of participating hotels and information on other hotel packages.

HISTORIC DISTRICT
Under $100

A short walk from the Liberty Bell Center, Independence Hall, and other marquee attractions, **Apple Hostels of Philadelphia** (32 S. Bank St., 215/922-0222, www.applehostels.com, $35-100) is as cheap as it gets in Old City. It's not open to everyone; guests must provide a foreign passport, Canadian driver's license, college ID, or Hostelling International membership card upon check-in. College students and Hostelling International members must also show proof that they don't live within 100 miles of Philadelphia. The neighborhood's only hostel offers female-only, male-only, and couples-only dorms, plus private and semiprivate rooms. Rates include bed linens, wireless Internet, weekly pub crawls, laundry detergent, and all the coffee and tea you can drink.

$100-250

Don't let "Best Western" fool you. With its grand staircase, high ceilings, and period-style furnishings, the **Best Western Independence Park Hotel** (235 Chestnut St., 215/922-4443, www.independenceparkhotel.com, $130-200) is no ordinary franchise. More than 150 years old, the five-floor Italianate building was designed by an architect better known for churches and served as both a brewery and dry goods store before opening as a hotel in the 1980s. Book well in advance; the National Register of Historic Places property has just 36 guest rooms and a prime location.

You can't throw a rock from the roof of the 364-room **Wyndham Philadelphia Historic District** (400 Arch St., 215/923-8660, www.wyndham.com, $170-400) without hitting a historic something or other. It's that centrally located. The roof, incidentally, features a nice little swimming pool. You couldn't ask for a better amenity on a hot summer day, especially if you're traveling with kids. Hotel parking is $35 per night.

The **Sheraton Society Hill Hotel** (2nd and Walnut Streets, 215/238-6000, www.sheratonphiladelphiasocietyhill.com, $140-270), with 364 recently renovated guest rooms and suites, is a recommendable option in the Penn's Landing area.

Be sure to ask for a room with a river view at the **Holiday Inn Express Philadelphia E Penn's Landing** (100 N. Christopher Columbus Blvd., 215/627-7900, www.hiepennslanding.com, $99-369), a stone's throw from the Ben Franklin Bridge. I-95 stands between the 184-room hotel and Old City's historic attractions, but guests needn't worry about navigating. The hotel offers free shuttle service to sights including Independence Hall, Reading Terminal Market, and the Barnes Foundation. Breakfast and wireless Internet access are also on the house. Hotel parking is $25 per night.

It's not all chains in the Historic District.

Take the **Thomas Bond House** (129 S. 2nd St., 215/923-8523, www.thomasbondhouse-bandb.com, $125-190), a charming B&B across from the famed City Tavern restaurant. Built in 1769, the townhouse is named for its first tenant, an acclaimed surgeon and friend of Ben Franklin, with whom he founded the nation's first public hospital. Its 12 guest rooms feature period furnishings and private baths, some with whirlpool tubs. Bear in mind that the four-story house doesn't have an elevator. Rates include wireless Internet access, local phone calls, a continental breakfast on weekdays, a full breakfast on weekends, and a nightly wine and cheese hour.

A National Historic Landmark, the ★ **Morris House Hotel** (225 S. 8th St., 215/922-2446, www.morrishousehotel.com, $160-430) was built in 1787 as a home for one of Philadelphia's most prominent families. It boasts an idyllic private garden and 15 guest rooms and suites decorated in a variety of styles, from Victorian to contemporary. Rates include a continental breakfast, afternoon tea complete with house-baked cookies, and a glass of wine in the late afternoon. The on-site **M Restaurant** (215/625-6666, www.mrestaurantphilly.com) offers live jazz every Wednesday and Friday evening.

Opened in 1990 in what used to be a shipping warehouse, the **Penn's View Hotel** (Front and Market Streets, 215/922-7600, www.pennsviewhotel.com, $165-350) has since expanded into two adjacent buildings on North Front Street. Its success is no surprise. The hotel is owned and operated by the Sena family, who honed their hospitality skills at nearby La Famiglia Ristorante, a local favorite since 1976. Some rooms feature balconies and others whirlpool tubs. The on-site **Ristorante Panorama** (215/922-7800) is known for its extensive selection of wines by the glass, made possible by a custom-built 120-bottle wine dispensing system. Wine flights and three-ounce pours give you the chance to taste very expensive vintages without shelling out for a glass or bottle.

Over $250

Smack-dab in the heart of the Historic District, the **Omni Hotel at Independence Park** (401 Chestnut St., 215/925-0000, www.omnihotels.com, $230-460) is what you'd expect from the brand: luxurious. Readers of *Travel + Leisure* have ranked it among the 500 best hotels in the world. The smallest of its 150 guest rooms and suites is a generous 375 square feet. Treat yourself to an aromatherapy massage at the on-site spa, and don't forget to pack a swimsuit. Parking at the nearby Bourse Garage is $27 per 24-hour period, with no in-and-out privileges. If you plan on getting around by car, the hotel's valet service ($37 per 24 hours with unlimited access) may be a better deal.

Opened in 2012 in a building erected more than a century earlier, **Hotel Monaco Philadelphia** (433 Chestnut St., 215/925-2111, www.monaco-philadelphia.com, $205-550) is the city's second Kimpton property. (The boutique hotel company opened a Hotel Palomar in the Rittenhouse Square neighborhood three years earlier.) The 268-room hotel is typical Kimpton, which is to say that it's largely unique. Its look is bold and modern; animal-print bathrobes help guests feel at home. Kimpton guest rooms come standard with yoga mats, and in Ben Franklin's old stomping ground, they also come with kites. The hotel's most notable feature may be its rooftop lounge, a rarity in Philadelphia. Stop by for cocktails if you can. **Stratus** (215/925-2889, www.stratuslounge.com), as the hot spot is called, is open year-round thanks to movable walls.

CENTER CITY
$100-250

With 1,400-plus guest rooms and suites on 23 floors, the **Philadelphia Marriott Downtown** (1201 Market St., 215/625-2900, www.marriott.com, $180-330) isn't just the largest hotel in town. It's the largest in the state. Attached to the Pennsylvania Convention Center via skybridge, the recently renovated colossus is one of three Marriotts just steps from City Hall. The **Courtyard Philadelphia Downtown** (21 N. Juniper St., 215/496-3200, www.marriott.com, $120-380) opened in 1999 in what had been the City Hall Annex. Its 498 guest rooms and suites boast 11-foot ceilings and 42-inch LCD TVs. Request a room with a view of City Hall, which looks especially enchanting after sundown. Rounding out the Marriott triumvirate is the **Residence Inn Philadelphia Center City** (1 E. Penn Square, 215/557-0005, www.marriott.com, $140-350), designed for extended stays. Its 290 suites have fully equipped kitchens, and guests can avail themselves of a grocery shopping service.

If you plan to spend a lot of time exploring the museums along the Benjamin Franklin Parkway, the **Windsor Suites** (1700 Benjamin Franklin Parkway, 215/981-5678, www.windsorhotel.com, $110-300) is a fine choice. The hotel is right on the tree-lined Parkway and boasts a rooftop pool. Its apartment-style accommodations add up to big savings for travelers who do their own cooking. Request an upper-floor room for the best views. Also convenient to the Parkway museums, the **Best Western Center City** (501 N. 22nd St., 215/568-8300, www.bestwesternpa.com, $130-200) is a rare breed of Philadelphia hotel: It doesn't charge a cent for parking. Add to that its reasonable room rates and you're looking at one of the best lodging deals in town. The hotel is otherwise unremarkable. Amenities include a fitness center, outdoor swimming pool, and sports bar. Did we mention the free parking?

Prefer boutique hotels or B&Bs? You'll find plenty of both in the tony Rittenhouse Square neighborhood. The **Latham Hotel** (135 S. 17th St., 215/563-7474, www.lathamhotelphiladelphia.com, $130-350) completed a multimillion-dollar renovation in 2012, trading a Victorian aesthetic for a modern one. The century-old building has 135 guest rooms and four suites. Dogs weighing 30 pounds or less are welcome to stay for $30 per day. The Latham stands out from the pack by offering

complimentary chauffeur service in a fully loaded Audi A8.

Hotel Palomar Philadelphia (117 S. 17th St., 215/563-5006, www.hotelpalomar-philadelphia.com, $160-400), another boutique hotel in the Rittenhouse area, doesn't discriminate against plus-size pooches. Guests can bring any number of pets, of any size or weight, for no extra charge. Opened in 2009, the 230-room hotel was the first Kimpton property in Philly. (The boutique hotel company has since opened a Hotel Monaco in the Historic District.) It's true to the Kimpton brand: stylish and service-oriented, with outside-the-box amenities like custom-designed bikes for guests to borrow and a yoga mat in every room. Valet parking is $42 per night with in-and-out privileges.

Three blocks south of Rittenhouse Square, ★ **La Reserve** (1804-1806 Pine St., 215/735-1137, www.lareservebandb.com, $90-185) is a great value. The B&B consists of two 1850s townhouses with a combined 12 guest rooms and suites. The executive suites, with their kitchenettes and separate living rooms, were designed with extended stays in mind. Guests are welcome to tickle the ivories of the vintage Steinway in the sunny parlor, and breakfast is made to order.

The "Gayborhood," aka Midtown Village, is another neighborhood with a good number of boutique hotels and B&Bs. A colorful 30-foot-tall mural of Independence Hall greets guests in the lobby of **The Independent Hotel** (1234 Locust St., 215/772-1440, www.theindependenthotel.com, $160-270), which opened in 2008 in a restored Georgian Revival building. Its 24 guest rooms feature hardwood floors, 32-inch HDTVs, microwaves and refrigerators, and bathrooms with tin ceiling tiles. Some have fireplaces, others exposed brick walls or lofts. Breakfast is not only complimentary but delivered right to your room. A few doors away, **Uncle's Upstairs Inn** (1220 Locust St., 215/546-6660, www.ubarphilly.com/the-inn, $125-150) offers six bargain-priced rooms above a low-key gay bar. Another Gayborhood option: the 48-room

Alexander Inn (12th and Spruce Streets, 215/923-3535, www.alexanderinn.com, $120-170), which takes its design cues from Deco-era cruise ships. Rates include a buffet breakfast and access to an always-stocked snack bar. The hotel is popular among return visitors, so booking well in advance is advised.

Located on a quiet, tree-lined street, **Clinton Street Bed & Breakfast** (1024 Clinton St., 215/802-1334, www.1024clintonstreetbb.com, $125-200) has seven spacious suites with galley or full kitchens, which the innkeeper stocks with eggs, yogurt, cereals, and other breakfast foods. The 1836 townhouse is equipped with satellite TV and wireless Internet.

Over $250

The domed lobby of ★ **The Ritz-Carlton, Philadelphia** (10 Avenue of the Arts, 215/523-8000, www.ritzcarlton.com from $300) is worth a visit even if a room there is entirely out of your price range. Modeled on Rome's Pantheon, it's one of the grandest spaces in Center City. Stop by between 5 and 7pm if you can for $5 appetizers and glasses of wine in the **10 Arts Lounge** (215/523-8273, www.10arts.com). The landmark hotel, a bank in a previous incarnation, has 299 guest rooms and suites ranging 280-1,900 square feet. Housekeeping visits twice daily, and room service is available around the clock. Fancy a bath strewn with rose petals? A butler will be happy to oblige.

Popular among visiting b-ballers for its extra-long beds, the **Four Seasons Hotel Philadelphia** (1 Logan Square, 215/963-1500, www.fourseasons.com/philadelphia, from $400) is one of three AAA five-diamond hotels in the City of Brotherly Love. (The Ritz-Carlton and The Rittenhouse are the others.) A so-called moderate room measures 500 square feet. Appropriately enough, the Philadelphia branch of the luxury chain pays tribute to the Federal period, when America was in its infancy, in its design aesthetic. It's home to the French-influenced **Fountain Restaurant,** Philadelphia's *only*

AAA five-diamond restaurant, and a spa with a palm-flanked lap pool. It's the Four Seasons. Enough said.

Count on **Loews Philadelphia Hotel** (1200 Market St., 215/627-1200, www.loewshotels.com, from $170) for sleek, modern digs. Built in 1932 as the headquarters for the Philadelphia Savings Fund Society, Philly's first modern skyscraper has 581 guest rooms and suites and a 15,000-square-foot wellness center complete with lap pool. A 27-foot-high "PSFS" sign still graces its roof. Another deluxe option in the center of town: the **Westin Philadelphia** (99 S. 17th St., 215/563-1600, www.westinphiladelphiahotel.com, from $200), with 294 guest rooms and 19 suites. Call ahead if you're bringing a canine friend. The hotel will prepare a dog-friendly version of its signature Heavenly Bed.

For lodging near Philadelphia's favorite public square, you can't beat **The Rittenhouse** (210 W. Rittenhouse Square, 215/546-9000, www.rittenhousehotel.com, from $600). A AAA five-diamond winner since 1991, it's been rated the number one hotel in Pennsylvania and among the 100 best in the world. The on-site **Lacroix** (215/790-2533, www.lacroixrestaurant.com) was hailed as the nation's best new restaurant when it opened in 2003. Its Sunday brunch is a $69 spectacular complete with chocolate fountains, house-cured charcuterie, and build-your-own Bloody Marys. The independent hotel has 116 oversized guest rooms and suites, some commanding upwards of $3,000 per night. Four-legged guests receive house-baked treats upon arrival.

Just off Rittenhouse Square is a more intimate alternative: the 23-room **Rittenhouse 1715** (1715 Rittenhouse Square St., 215/546-6500, www.rittenhouse1715.com, from $260).

FAIRMOUNT PARK
Under $100

Philadelphia isn't off limits to penny-pinching globetrotters thanks to **Chamounix Mansion** (3250 Chamounix Dr., 215/878-3676, www.philahostel.org, $20-23 per person, children 16 and under $8), which isn't nearly as opulent as its name suggests. Built in 1802 as a country retreat for a wealthy Philadelphia merchant, it was saved from demolition in the mid-1900s by community members who agitated for its conversion to a youth hostel. There are 80 beds between the mansion and carriage house, most in dorm-style rooms. The awesomely low rates include linens, as sleeping bags are prohibited. Billed as the nation's first urban youth hostel, Chamounix is actually in West Fairmount Park, across the Schuylkill and well north of Center City. But with free bikes at their disposal and public transportation nearby, guests have no excuse for staying in. In fact, they must leave the hostel by 11am each day and return no earlier than 4:30pm.

Food

Philadelphia's food scene has matured into one of the best, most talked-about in the country. Decades-old mom-and-pops share the streets with stylish destination restaurants helmed by renowned chefs. Cozy neighborhood BYOBs boast loyal followings. And gastropub dining is more appealing than ever thanks to a smoking ban passed in 2007.

It goes without saying that the food scene extends far beyond cheesesteaks. That said, unless you're a vegetarian, there is no excuse for not sampling Philly's signature sandwich while you're here. They're just not the same anywhere else. Philly's other culinary trademarks include soft pretzels, hoagies (elsewhere known as sub sandwiches), and water ice (the frozen dessert most Americans know as Italian ice). And no visit to Philadelphia is complete without a stop at Reading Terminal Market or the Italian Market, both of which offer a wide selection of delectable eats and a unique atmosphere.

The availability of healthy options has also improved in recent years, with many restaurants focusing on fresh, locally grown ingredients—which isn't hard considering the wealth of farms around the city.

HISTORIC DISTRICT
Asian
Few people have played a bigger role in Philadelphia's culinary renaissance than Stephen Starr, who has opened more than a dozen restaurants since the mid-1990s.

Perhaps the most famous is **Buddakan** (325 Chestnut St., 215/574-9440, www.buddakan. com, lunch 11:30am-2:30pm Mon.-Fri., dinner 5pm-11pm Mon.-Thurs., 5pm-midnight Fri.-Sat., 4pm-10pm Sun., $15-40), offering "modern Asian cuisine" in a low-lit space presided over by a massive Buddha statue. The decor is over the top (if not cheesy), and there are certainly more authentically Asian restaurants in town. But Buddakan can be counted on for a night-on-the-town vibe, delicious drinks, and undeniably tasty, creative dishes, which are designed to be shared. Starr joined forces with Masaharu Morimoto of *Iron Chef* fame to open **Morimoto** (723 Chestnut St., 215/413-9070, www.morimotorestaurant.com, lunch 11:30am-2pm Mon.-Fri., dinner 5pm-10pm Sun.-Thurs., 5pm-midnight Fri.-Sat., sushi rolls $8-12, lunch sets $16-38, dinner entrées $26-44) in 2001. Though the Japanese-born chef now spends most of his time in New York, his first American restaurant is still a jewel. Guests are treated to something of a light show in the ultramodern dining room. But the real treat is the food: exquisitely prepared sushi, entrées like "Morimoto surf and turf" (kobe filet and hamachi ribbons), and several eat-till-you-die *omakase* (chef's choice) options.

Colonial American
City Tavern (138 S. 2nd St., 215/413-1443, www.citytavern.com, lunch from 11:30am daily, dinner from 4pm Mon.-Sat. and 3pm

Sun., lunch $10-20, dinner $18-33) looks older than its years, which is exactly what its builders had in mind. Completed in time for the U.S. bicentennial in 1976, the restaurant is a historically accurate reconstruction of the original City Tavern, built in 1773 and frequented by the likes of George Washington, Benjamin Franklin, John Adams, and Thomas Jefferson. Chef-proprietor Walter Staib, host of the Emmy-winning PBS series *A Taste of History*, also strives for historical accuracy. Waiters in 18th century garb serve up braised rabbit legs, medallions of venison, Martha Washington-style turkey pot pie, and other foods inspired by olden days. The commendable children's menu includes "meat and cheese pie," billed as a colonial version of lasagna. Don't miss the sweet potato and pecan biscuits, said to have been a favorite of Thomas Jefferson.

Italian

Designed to evoke the feel of a seaside holiday in Italy, **Positano Coast by Aldo Lamberti** (212 Walnut St., 215/238-0499, www.positano-coast.net, 11:30am-10:30pm Mon.-Thurs., 11:30am-11pm Fri., noon-11pm Sat., 12:30pm-10:30pm Sun., lunch $8-17, dinner $14-23) is awash in whites and blues. Request outdoor seating for the full away-from-it-all effect. Appropriately enough, the restaurant specializes in fish and seafood, including *crudo*, or Italian-style sashimi. Its extensive wine and cocktail lists also deserve mention. You can save big during happy hour (4pm-7pm Mon.-Fri. and 12:30pm-6pm Sun.), featuring $4 beers, $5 wines, and $6 cocktails.

Mexican

Xochitl (408 S. 2nd St., 215/238-7280, www.xochitlphilly.com, 5pm-10pm Sun.-Thurs., 5pm-midnight Fri.-Sat., bar open until 2am daily, $16-26) offers upscale, creative twists on Mexican fare in a cozy setting. Start with the delicious guacamole, prepared tableside and served with house-made tortilla chips, or one of the ceviches. Finish with the churros, which are out of this world. Xochitl (pronounced so-cheet) boasts an extensive list of tequilas, available by the shot or flight.

New American

Farmicia (15 S. 3rd St., 215/627-6274, www.farmiciarestaurant.com, breakfast 8:30am-10am Sat.-Sun., brunch 10am-3pm Sat.-Sun., lunch 11:30am-3pm Tues.-Fri., dinner 5:30pm-10pm Tues.-Thurs., 5:30pm-11pm Fri.-Sat., 5pm-9pm Sun., breakfast/brunch/lunch under $15, dinner $17-29) is fairly atypical as Old City spots go. Its farm-fresh cuisine and friendly, relaxed atmosphere are a refreshing departure from the look-at-me approach taken by some of its neighbors. The menu emphasizes local, seasonal ingredients and always includes several vegetarian options. Farmicia boasts a full bar, but you can bring your own wine at no charge.

Part of Stephen Starr's ever-expanding gastronomic empire, **Jones** (700 Chestnut St., 215/223-5663, www.jones-restaurant.com, 11:30am-11pm Mon.-Thurs., 11:30am-midnight Fri., 10am-3pm and 5pm-midnight Sat., 10am-3pm and 4pm-11pm Sun., bar open until 1am Mon.-Thurs., 2am Fri.-Sat., midnight Sun., $10-22) takes its design cues from the Brady Bunch era. But don't let the shag carpeting fool you; it wouldn't be a Starr restaurant without some contemporary twists. The focus here is comfort foods: fried chicken and waffles, grilled cheese, meat loaf with whipped potatoes, beef brisket, and even matzo ball soup. It's more vegetarian-friendly than you might expect, offering baked mac and cheese, "Buf-Faux-Lo" tofu wings, and a meatless burger. Like most Starr establishments, Jones has a great selection of tasty if overpriced drinks.

Spanish

Chef Jose Garces is threatening to overtake Stephen Starr as Philly's most prolific restaurateur. The "Latin Emeril," as he's known, has opened more than half a dozen restaurants in the City of Brotherly Love since 2005. ★ **Amada** (217-219 Chestnut St., 215/625-2450, www.amadarestaurant.com, lunch

11:30am-2:30pm Mon.-Fri., brunch 11:30am-2:30pm Sat.-Sun., dinner 5pm-10pm Sun.-Thurs., 5pm-11pm Fri.-Sat., tapas $5-19) was the very first and an immediate hit. It specializes in authentic Spanish tapas—from artisanal olives and aged Manchego to lamb meatballs and grilled baby squid. The vibe is always stylish, fun, and energetic.

Coffee and Sweets

Opened in 2004 by brothers with a passion for history and an eye for antiques, **The Franklin Fountain** (116 Market St., 215/627-1899, www.franklinfountain.com, 11am-midnight daily) is part ice cream parlor, part time machine. Don't be surprised if "Gee whiz!" rolls off your tongue when you step inside; the place is a dead ringer for a turn-of-the-century soda fountain, complete with soda jerks in period attire. Order a soda or phosphate and they'll reach for the silver-plated spigots of a 1905 draft tower, believed to be the oldest operating soda fountain in the country. Don't be shy about asking for samples of the handmade ice cream, and do try the teaberry, a tribute to Clark's Teaberry chewing gum. Hardly old-timey, prices for signature sundaes like the Stock Market Crunch (rocky road ice cream with peanut butter sauce and crumbled pretzels) range from $8-15—and only cash is accepted. Not a bad deal for time travel.

SOUTH PHILADELPHIA
Brunch

Thoughts of ★ **Sabrina's Café** (910 Christian St., 215/574-1599, www.sabrinascafe.com, 8am-5pm daily, under $15) propel many a hungover local out of bed. Quite simply the best brunch spot in Philadelphia, Sabrina's offers standard breakfast fare along with showstoppers like challah French toast stuffed with cream cheese and bananas. Expect a long wait on weekends. That's worth repeating: Expect a long wait. The cozy BYOB doesn't accept reservations, but you can ring before you arrive to put your name on the waiting list. Sabrina's has expanded to two other locations: **Sabrina's**

Cafe & Spencer's Too (1804 Callowhill St., 215/636-9061, 8am-10pm Tues.-Sat., 8am-4pm Sun.-Mon.) near the Philadelphia Museum of Art and **Sabrina's Café @ Powelton** (227 N. 34th St., 215/222-1022, 8am-9pm Tues.-Thurs., 8am-10pm Fri.-Sat., 8am-4pm Sun.-Mon.), which occupies a Victorian manse in University City. You can bring your own bottle to the former but not the latter. Both serve dinner ($14-19), which the original does not.

If the line at Sabrina's is simply unbearable, mosey over to **Sam's Morning Glory Diner** (10th and Fitzwater Streets, 215/413-3999, www.themorningglorydiner.com, 7am-4pm Mon.-Fri., 8am-3pm Sat.-Sun., under $15), where the wait might be marginally shorter. Check your diet at the door of the hipster-filled joint, and tuck into a frittata or the French toast stuffed with caramelized bananas and mangos. House-made ketchup adds an unusual zing to things.

Moroccan

Tucked away in an alley off South Street, **Marrakesh** (517 S. Leithgow St., 215/925-5929, www.marrakesheastcoast.com, 5:30pm-11pm Sun.-Thurs., 5:30pm-midnight Fri.-Sat.) is worth searching out. Its mazelike interior is dimly lit and eminently romantic. Waiters in traditional Moroccan garb serve a lovely multicourse meal (about $30 per person) that you eat with your hands. Make a reservation, come hungry, and pace yourself. Each course is more delicious than the last. Marrakesh has a short wine list, but you're welcome to bring your own.

Seafood

It can take upwards of an hour to get a table at **Dmitri's** (795 S. 3rd St., 215/625-0556, www.dmitrisrestaurant.com, 5:30pm-10pm Mon.-Thurs., 5:30pm-11pm Fri.-Sat., 5pm-10pm Sun., $10-19), a tiny corner BYOB that doesn't accept reservations. But the Mediterranean-inspired seafood will turn your wait-induced frown upside down. Don't pass up the perfect hummus in your rush toward the clams, mussels, smelts, and squid. Dmitri's also has

Cheesesteaks 101

As much as I'd love to give you a definitive answer to the question of where to get the best cheesesteak in Philly, there just isn't one. The argument will never be settled because it's truly a matter of personal preference. Some like the roll toasted and crispy, while others prefer it soft and chewy. Some like a cheesesteak dripping with grease, while others complain that too much grease makes the roll soggy. Some like the meat diced as thinly as possible, while others prefer slightly larger slices or even small chunks. Some love yellow Cheez Whiz, but most opt for American or provolone cheese. The one indisputable fact is that cheesesteaks are just not the same anywhere else. The closest I've come to a perfect cheesesteak outside of Philly is at the New Jersey shore, and not surprisingly, it turned out the chef hailed from Philly. While it's a fact that locals eat cheesesteaks regularly, we try to keep our consumption in check. Let's be honest, they're not exactly health food.

HOW TO ORDER

While not everyone is hardcore about ordering correctly, in South Philly or anywhere there is a long line, it's best to know what you're doing. First, don't *ever* order a "Philly cheesesteak." You're in Philly, so that part goes without saying. The basic rule of thumb is to minimize the words you need to convey what you want. "Whiz wit" means Cheez Whiz with fried onions, and "prov without" means—yes, you guessed it—provolone cheese without fried onions. These rules are most strictly observed at **Pat's King of Steaks** (215/468-1546, www.patskingofsteaks.com) and **Geno's Steaks** (215/389-0659, www.genosteaks.com), the famous dueling spots at the intersection of 9th Street and Passyunk Avenue in South Philly. Of the two, I prefer Pat's to the neon-bedazzled Geno's, in part because the meat at Pat's is chopped more finely and in part because of the questionable sign at Geno's that reads: "This is America, when ordering please speak English." While there are certainly better cheesesteaks out there, this corner offers a worthwhile cultural experience. Perhaps best of all, it is the only place where you can find cheesesteaks (and cheese fries if you really want to go all out) 24 hours a day.

locations near **Rittenhouse Square** (2227 Pine St., 215/985-3680) and in **Northern Liberties** (944 N. 2nd St., 215/592-4550). The former has a full bar, while the latter is a BYOB.

NORTHERN LIBERTIES
Brunch

Honey's Sit 'n Eat (800 N. 4th St., 215/925-1150, www.honeyssitneat.com, 7am-4pm Mon.-Fri., 7am-5pm Sat.-Sun., under $15) is a strange and wonderful beast. Popular with hipsters, it pays tribute to Jewish and Southern cuisines in equal measure. That's right: nova lox on the same menu as biscuits and sausage gravy. The menu also includes ethnically ambiguous fare like giant buttermilk pancakes and a deep-fried banana split. Don't overlook the long list of specials, where dishes like fried green tomatoes and lobster mac and cheese make appearances. In 2013, Honey's

opened a long-awaited second location near Rittenhouse Square. **Honey's South** (2101 South St., 215/732-5130, 7am-10pm Mon.-Sat., 7am-5pm Sun.) has dinner hours, unlike the original. Neither takes reservations, and both accept cash only. Feel free to bring your own booze.

CENTER CITY EAST

The half of Center City east of Broad Street is packed with restaurants, with the greatest concentrations in Chinatown, along the Avenue of the Arts, and in the area known as Midtown Village, or the Gayborhood.

Asian

Raw Sushi & Sake Lounge (1225 Sansom St., 215/238-1903, www.rawlounge.net, lunch noon-3pm Mon.-Sat., dinner 5pm-10pm Mon.-Tues., 5pm-11pm Wed.-Sat., 3pm-9pm Sun., lunch $10-19, dinner $15-40) offers a

Be sure to check out the autographed photos of celebs at both eateries—everyone from Justin Timberlake to Oprah has been here.

WHERE TO GO

You're never far from a great cheesesteak in Philly. They're served in every neighborhood, at diners and in bars, out of food trucks and storefront windows, and even in restaurants serving upscale twists on the classic sandwich. Here are a few of my faves, but if you find yourself wanting a cheesesteak and not in close range of any of these spots, just ask a local to point you in the right direction. Almost as famous as Pat's and Geno's, and far superior, is **Jim's Steaks** (400 South St., 215/928-1911, www.jimssteaks.com, 10am-1am Mon.-Thurs., 10am-3am Fri.-Sat., 11am-10pm Sun.), which has locations in West and Northeast Philly as well as on South Street.

Other great spots include **Sonny's Famous Steaks** (228 Market St., 215/629-5760, 11am-10pm Sun.-Thurs., 11am-3am Fri.-Sat.) in Old City; **Tony Luke's** (39 E. Oregon Ave., 215/551-5725, www.tonylukes.com, 6am-midnight Mon.-Thurs., 6am-2am Fri.-Sat., 11am-8pm Sun.) in South Philly; and **John's Roast Pork** (14 E. Snyder Ave., 215/463-1951, www.johnsroastpork.com, 6:45am-3pm Mon.-Fri., 9am-4pm Sat.), also in South Philly.

Geno's Steaks

—Contributed by Karrie Gavin, author of Moon Philadelphia

---

lounge-like atmosphere with its red walls, bamboo ceiling, and high-backed booths, plus a courtyard for al fresco dining. Its salads, small plates, and traditional dishes don't disappoint, but it does sushi better than anything else. Raw is also known for its sake selection. You can sample four for $18.

Italian

Mercato (1216 Spruce St., 215/985-2962, www.mercatobyob.com, 5pm-10:30pm Mon.-Thurs., 5pm-11pm Fri.-Sat., 5pm-10pm Sun., $16-29), a tiny, cash-only BYOB, is always noisy and crowded. The culprits: close tables, an open kitchen, and the restaurant's immense popularity. Start with bread, artisan cheeses, and an olive oil tasting. You can't go wrong with anything on the menu, but standouts include the whole grilled artichoke appetizer and pan-seared diver scallops over risotto. The desserts are also excellent.

Mercato doesn't take reservations, so you can expect a wait, especially on weekends.

Vietnamese

Located in the heart of Chinatown, the warm and inviting **Vietnam Restaurant** (221 N. 11th St., 215/592-1163, www.eatatvietnam.com, 11am-9:30pm Sun.-Thurs., 11am-10:30pm Fri.-Sat., under $15) is one of Philly's most popular ethnic eateries. You can't go wrong with anything on the reasonably priced menu. The crispy spring rolls and delicate rice-paper rolls are top-notch. If you're unfamiliar with Vietnamese cuisine, take your pick of the clay-pot dishes or vermicelli noodle bowls. You may have to wait for a table on weekends; the bar's strong specialty drinks help pass the time. If the wait is too long for your tastes, defect to Vietnam's main competitor, **Vietnam Palace** (222 N. 11th St., 215/592-9596, www.vietnampalace.

net, 11am-9:30pm Sun.-Thurs., 11am-10pm Fri.-Sat., $9-16), just across the street. And if you happen to be in University City when a Vietnamese food craving hits, head to Vietnam's stylish sister, **Vietnam Café** (816 S. 47th St., 215/729-0260, www.eatatvietnam. com, 11:30am-9pm Mon.-Thurs., 11:30am-9:30pm Fri., noon-9:30pm Sat., noon-9pm Sun., under $15).

Coffee and Sweets

Capogiro Gelato Artisans (119 S. 13th St., 215/351-0900, www.capogirogelato.com, 7:30am-11:30pm Mon.-Thurs., 7:30am-1am Fri., 9am-1am Sat., 10am-11:30pm Sun.) serves deliciously dense Italian-style ice cream in countless flavors that change with the seasons. In addition to traditional flavors like chocolate and hazelnut, you'll find creations like pear with Wild Turkey bourbon, pineapple with mint, and lemon and ginger with rum. Ideal for a sweet ending to a date or a break in a day of shopping, Capogiro now has four Philadelphia locations (the others are at 117 S. 20th St., 3925 Walnut St., and 1625 E. Passyunk Ave.). A small cone will set you back almost $5, but it's worth every cent.

CENTER CITY WEST

The western half of Center City is home to many of Philly's most elegant restaurants, but you can find a meal in any price range. The section of Walnut Street between Broad and 18th Streets is lined with restaurants, with additional options on side streets.

Markets

Di Bruno Bros. (1730 Chestnut St., 215/665-9220, www.dibruno.com, 9am-8:30pm Mon.-Fri., 9am-8pm Sat., 9am-7pm Sun., coffee/espresso bar opens at 7am daily), Philadelphia's answer to Dean & DeLuca, began in 1939 as a small grocery store in the Italian Market. The original store (930 S. 9th St., 215/922-2876, 9am-5pm Mon., 8am-6pm Tues.-Sat., 8am-4pm Sun.) still does a brisk business, but its selection of gourmet foods pales in comparison to that of the Chestnut

Street store, which opened in 2004. The two-level gourmet emporium is a popular lunch spot. Its upstairs café (11:30am-3pm Mon.-Fri., 11:30am-4pm Sat., 10:30am-3pm Sun.) offers salads, sushi, deli sandwiches, and hot entrées. Both stores set out so many samples that it's possible to sate your hunger without spending a cent.

Mexican

Tequilas (1602 Locust St., 215/546-0181, www.tequilasphilly.com, 11:30am-10pm Mon.-Thurs., 11:30am-11pm Fri., 5pm-11pm Sat., 5pm-10pm Sun., lunch $10-22, dinner $22-28) offers authentic Mexican fare in the elegant setting of a converted brownstone. You'll find high ceilings, dim lighting, and a grand bar stocked with more than 90 varieties of tequila. Start with the limey ceviche or divine guacamole and proceed to the finely tuned entrées. Wash it all down with a rose-infused margarita. And be sure to let the staff know if you're celebrating a birthday; they'll serenade you in Spanish and treat you to a shot of sweet tequila.

New American

Open since 1996, **Audrey Claire** (276 S. 20th St., 215/731-1222, www.audreyclaire.com, 5pm-10pm Sun.-Thurs., 5pm-11pm Fri.-Sat., $17-27) remains immensely popular. The cash-only BYOB near Rittenhouse Square—a spec of a space—serves up Mediterranean-inspired fare. Its seared brussels sprouts are unlike anything your mother tried to feed you. Owner Audrey Claire Taichman is also responsible for **Twenty Manning Grill** (261 S. 20th St., 215/731-0900, www.twentymanning.com, 5pm-10pm Sun.-Mon., 5pm-11pm Tues.-Thurs., 5pm-midnight Fri.-Sat., bar open until 2am Tues.-Sat. and midnight Sun.-Mon., $11-27) across the street. Completely revamped in 2010, it has made a host of new fans with its upscale comfort foods. Unlike its older sister restaurant, Twenty Manning serves alcohol. Both boast sidewalk seating.

One of the few restaurants directly on Rittenhouse Square, **Rouge** (205 S. 18th

St., 215/732-6622, www.rouge98.com, 11:30am-10pm Mon.-Tues., 11:30am-11pm Wed.-Thurs., 11:30am-midnight Fri., 10am-midnight Sat., 10am-10pm Sun., bar open as late as 2am daily, lunch/brunch $9-23, dinner $16-35) is always packed—usually with yuppies letting their highlighted hair down. Snagging a table from happy hour onward can be difficult, especially when the weather allows for sidewalk seating, but you can enjoy a drink at the elegant bar while you wait. It affords an excellent view of the square. Prices reflect the prime location. Fortunately the food—American with a French flair—is quite good.

Coffee and Sweets

The flagship café of coffee roaster **La Colombe Torrefaction** (130 S. 19th St., 215/563-0860, www.lacolombe.com, 7am-7pm Mon.-Fri., 8am-7pm Sat.-Sun.), which supplies beans to some of the chicest restaurants and hotels in the country, is just off Rittenhouse Square. Don't be daunted by the line to the register, which has a tendency to stretch out the door. There's no menu overhead, coffee and espresso drinks come in one size only, and pastry offerings are few, all of which makes for speedy service. For a wide selection of sweets, stroll to **Metropolitan Bakery** (262 S. 19th St., 215/545-6655, www.metropolitanbakery.com, 7:30am-7pm Mon.-Fri., 8am-6pm Sat.-Sun.) on the opposite side of the square. It's a wee wonderland of artisanal breads, handsome desserts, and treats that straddle the line, like a chewy loaf made with sour cherries and bittersweet chocolate. The millet muffins and French berry rolls are particularly beloved. Founded in 1993 by two alumni of the celebrated White Dog Café, Metropolitan now boasts half a dozen locations.

WEST PHILADELPHIA

It's a shame that so many visitors to the city never cross the Schuylkill River. West Philly, especially the section known as University City, has a wide variety of restaurants, many of which can be enjoyed on a student's budget.

New American

The oldest continually operating BYOB in the city, **Marigold Kitchen** (501 S. 45th St., 215/222-3699, www.marigoldkitchenbyob.com, 6pm-9pm Tues.-Sat., $85) has seen chefs come and go and reinvented itself again and again. The cozy atmosphere in the converted row home remains a constant. Under the direction of Robert Halpern, its owner and executive chef since 2009, the restaurant landed in the number two spot on *Philadelphia Magazine*'s 2013 best restaurants list. Needless to say, reservations are a must. Prepare to be dazzled. Dinner is a gastronomic journey through 15-odd dishes of the chef's choosing.

The one-of-a-kind ★ **White Dog Café** (3420 Sansom St., 215/386-9224, www.whitedog.com, 11:30am-11pm Mon.-Fri., 10am-11pm Sat., 10am-9pm Sun., lunch/brunch $12-19, dinner $17-35, bar menu $10-12) owes its success to longtime community activist Judy Wicks, who opened it in 1983 and went on to prove that progressive and socially conscious business models can work. Local farmers deliver organic produce and humanely raised meats to the restaurant, which composts in its backyard to reduce waste. Wicks sold her baby in 2009 but remains involved in its management. Housed in three adjacent Victorian brownstones, the restaurant can still be counted on for inspired contemporary American cuisine. If you're on a budget, have a seat in the bar and order a burger, truffle parmesan fries, and Leg Lifter Lager (the White Dog's private label beer).

Information

Located in the heart of the Historic District, the airy **Independence Visitor Center** (6th and Market Streets, 800/537-7676, www.phlvisitorcenter.com, 8:30am-6pm daily, open until 7pm June-Aug.) is a gold mine of information about what to do in Philadelphia and its environs. It also boasts one of the largest gift shops in the region. You'll also find visitors centers in **City Hall** (Broad and Market Streets, room 121, 215/686-2840, 9am-5pm Mon.-Fri.); nearby **Love Park** (16th St. and JFK Blvd., 215/683-0246, 10am-5pm Mon.-Sat.), so called because it's home to Robert Indiana's iconic *LOVE* statue; and **Sister Cities Park** (18th St. and Benjamin Franklin Parkway, 800/537-7676, 9:30am-5:30pm daily May-Oct.), which is convenient to the museums along the Benjamin Franklin Parkway.

If you're driving to Philadelphia via I-95 north, you can load up on brochures at the state-run **welcome center** a half mile north of the Pennsylvania-Delaware line.

Personalized travel counseling is available 7am-7pm daily.

The website of Visit Philadelphia, **visitphilly.com,** is a great source of information for visitors. In addition to descriptions of countless attractions, restaurants, hotels, and shops, it offers an events calendar and more than 40 suggested itineraries, including one inspired by the award-winning blockbuster *Silver Linings Playbook.*

Philadelphia has two major dailies: *The Philadelphia Inquirer* and the *Philadelphia Daily News,* which have been owned by the same company since 2006 and share the website philly.com. When it comes to planning their leisure time, many young Philadelphians reach for the free weeklies *PW* (www.philadelphiaweekly.com) and *City Paper* (www.citypaper.net). The former is distributed on Wednesdays and the latter on Thursdays. Both keep a trained eye on the city's food, arts, and entertainment landscape.

Transportation

GETTING THERE
Car
Philadelphia is an easy drive from several major cities: about 95 miles southwest of New York via I-95, 105 miles northeast of Baltimore via I-95, and 300 miles east of Pittsburgh via the Pennsylvania Turnpike. All told, about a quarter of the U.S. population lives within a half-day's drive of the City of Brotherly Love. While road trips can be fun, parking in Philly isn't. So even if you live within driving distance, consider taking public transportation.

Bus and Rail
30th Street Station (2955 Market St.), located just across the Schuylkill River from Center City, is one of the nation's busiest

intercity passenger rail stations. It's a stop along several **Amtrak** (800/872-7245, www.amtrak.com) routes, including the Northeast Regional, which connects Boston, New York, Baltimore, and Washington DC, among other cities; the Pennsylvanian, which runs between New York and Pittsburgh; and the Cardinal, running between New York and Chicago. New Jersey's public transportation system, **NJ Transit** (973/275-5555, www.njtransit.com), has a commuter rail line between Atlantic City, New Jersey, and 30th Street Station. Its bus route network also extends into Philly.

The Southeastern Pennsylvania Transportation Authority, or **SEPTA** (215/580-7800, www.septa.org), provides service to Philadelphia from countless suburban towns, Philadelphia International Airport, New Jersey's capital of Trenton, and Wilmington, Delaware. It's an uncommonly versatile public transit agency, offering bus, trolley, trackless trolley, subway, and commuter rail services.

Thanks to competition among intercity bus companies, traveling to Philly can be dirt cheap. **Greyhound** (800/231-2222, www.greyhound.com) buses collect Philly-bound travelers from all over the country and deposit them at Filbert and 10th Streets in Center City. **Megabus** (877/462-6342, www.megabus.com) offers service to Philadelphia from about a dozen cities, including Pittsburgh, Boston, New York, Baltimore, Washington DC, and Toronto. Its main stop in Philadelphia is on JFK Boulevard near North 30th Street, a stone's throw from 30th Street Station. **YO! Bus** (855/669-6287, www.yobus.com) provides nonstop service between Philadelphia and New York City. It operates out of Philly's Greyhound terminal at Filbert and 10th Streets.

Air

Philadelphia International Airport (PHL, 215/937-6937, www.phl.org) boasts seven terminals, four runways, and daily departures to more than 120 cities. It's served by about 30 airlines, including budget carriers Southwest, AirTran, and Frontier. Among its amenities: free Wi-Fi, children's play areas in terminals A and D, a full-service postal facility, Travelex currency exchange booths, and more than 150 stores and eateries, including duty-free shops for international passengers.

Located seven miles southwest of Center City, the airport offers the usual array of ground transportation options, including rental cars, taxis, and shared-ride vans. Taxis charge a flat rate of $28.50 between the airport and the "Center City zone," defined as the area bounded by Fairmount Avenue in the north, South Street in the south, the Delaware River in the east, and the Schuylkill River in the west, plus a portion of West Philly between the Schuylkill and 38th Street. If you're heading anywhere else, metered rates apply: $2.70 when your tush hits the seat, $0.23 for each 0.1 mile, and $0.23 for each 37.6 seconds of wait time. Trips from the airport are subject to an $11 minimum. A tip of 15-20 percent is customary. All taxis accept credit cards.

SEPTA offers rail service from the airport to Center City. The fare is $8. Trains depart every half hour from shortly after 5am to shortly after midnight.

30th Street Station

The airport website (www.phl.org) has a directory of ground transportation providers. Call 215/937-6958 to chat with a ground transportation specialist.

Ferry

Philadelphia, as we all know, isn't a coastal city. But it is a port city, and arriving by boat is possible in the warmer months. The **RiverLink Ferry** (215/925-5465, www.riverlinkferry.org, service daily Memorial Day-Labor Day and weekends in May and Sept., fare $7, seniors and children $6, children 3 and under free) shuttles between Philly and its New Jersey neighbor, Camden. Sadly, the scenic trip across the Delaware River lasts just 12-15 minutes.

GETTING AROUND

A car is entirely unnecessary for getting around Center City. In fact, having one can be a downright pain. Street parking is a competitive sport, and parking garages are pricey. If you're able-bodied and not in a hurry, walking is the best way to explore the heart of Philly. You can flag a cab when your tootsies get tired. The extensive public transportation network can be intimidating, but studying it is worthwhile if you're in town for more than a couple of days.

A car is advisable if you plan to spend much time outside of Center City. Good luck getting to gorgeous Wissahickon Valley Park without one.

On Foot

Center City is eminently walkable. For one thing, it's compact. Just 25 blocks separate the rivers that serve as its eastern and western boundaries. For another, it's easy to navigate. Founder William Penn is largely to thank for that, having called for a grid street plan. Most north-south streets are numbered. If the numbers are getting lower, you're heading east, toward the Delaware River. If they're getting higher, you're on your way to the Schuylkill. (It's worth noting that there's no 1st Street or 14th Street. What would be 1st is named

Front Street, and what would be 14th is Broad Street.) A preponderance of east-west streets have tree names, as in Chestnut, Walnut, Spruce, and Pine. East-west Market Street separates Center City roughly in half. Addresses with an "S" prefix, as in 99 S. 17th Street, are south of Market, and addresses with an "N" prefix are north of it.

A number of Philly outfits offer suggested walking tours. **The Constitutional Walking Tour of Philadelphia** (215/525-1776, www.theconstitutional.com), which offers guided tours of the Historic District April-November, publishes a self-guided tour brochure with information on 30-plus sites. You can print it from the website or pick it up at the Independence Visitor Center at 6th and Market Streets. The nonprofit **Preservation Alliance** (215/546-1146, www.preservation-alliance.com), whose volunteers lead architectural walking tours of neighborhoods throughout the city May-October, offers several self-guided tours on its website.

Car

If you choose to drive to Center City, be prepared to spend a good amount of time looking for street parking or a good amount of money for off-street parking. It's worthwhile to look for street parking if you're only leaving your vehicle for an hour or two. Read parking regulation signs *very carefully* to make sure you don't need a permit and don't overstay your welcome. Some blocks permit parking during certain hours but prohibit it during periods of heavy traffic. This may be the City of Brotherly Love, but its meter maids are merciless.

Meter parking is generally $2 per hour. Some blocks have individual meters that take coins or prepaid SmartCards, which can be purchased through the website of the **Philadelphia Parking Authority** (888/591-3636, www.philapark.org) and at many convenience stores, newsstands, and other retailers. Other blocks have pay stations that accept bills and credit cards in addition to coins and SmartCards.

Getting There in a Phlash

One of the cheapest and easiest ways to travel between Philadelphia's major attractions is aboard a purple road trolley called the **Phlash** (800/537-7676, www.phillyphlash.com, 10am-6pm daily Memorial Day-Labor Day and Fri.-Sun. in May, Sept., and Oct.). A single ride is just $2, and an all-day pass is $12. Passes are sold at the Independence Visitor Center at 6th and Market Streets and other visitors centers. Seniors and children four and under ride for free.

The Phlash route stretches from Penn's Landing in the east to the Philadelphia Zoo and Please Touch Museum in the west, with 19 stops in all. Service is about every 15 minutes. Stops include:

6th and Market Streets
Independence Visitor Center, Liberty Bell Center, Independence Hall

12th and Market Streets
Reading Terminal Market, Chinatown, City Hall

22nd Street and the Benjamin Franklin Parkway
Barnes Foundation, Rodin Museum

Philadelphia Museum of Art

You can eliminate the risk of getting a parking ticket—or worse yet, having your vehicle towed—by parking in a garage or lot. Be prepared to spend upwards of $20 per day. The website of the Philadelphia Parking Authority has a handy "parking locator" feature that will find and compare parking options near your destination.

Taxi

Taxis prowl the streets of Center City at all hours. In less trafficked parts of town, you can call for a cab. Taxi companies include **PHL Taxi** (215/232-2000, www.phl-taxi.net), **Quaker City Cab** (215/726-6000, www.quakercitycab.com), and **Yellow Cab** (215/333-8294, www.ridewithpride.com). Trips between the airport and the "Center City zone" are $28.50. For all other trips, metered rates apply. The meter reads $2.70 to start, and the fare climbs by $0.23 with each 0.1 mile or 37.6 seconds of wait time. Rates are regulated by the Philadelphia Parking Authority and must be posted in all cabs. It's customary to tip drivers $1 or $2 for rides within Center City and 15-20 percent of the fare for longer trips. Need a fancier ride?

Call **Astro Limousine** (267/228-7943, www.astrolimoservice.com).

Public Transportation

Mastering Philadelphia's public transit system, commonly known as **SEPTA** (215/580-7800, www.septa.org), is no small thing. The multimodal system, which serves a five-county, 2,202-square-mile area, consists of almost 150 fixed routes. More than 100 of those are bus routes. SEPTA also offers trolley, trackless trolley, subway, and commuter rail (known locally as Regional Rail) services.

Trip planning is a cinch if you have Internet access. Simply enter your starting location and destination in the Trip Planner feature on SEPTA's website. The resulting itinerary spells out how to get there, how long the trip will take, and how much it will cost. The cash fare for bus, subway, and trolley service is $2.25. Exact fare must be used. Regular riders save time and money by purchasing packs of tokens, which cost $1.80 apiece, or weekly or monthly passes. Transfers are $1. Regional Rail fares are a different animal. A one-way ticket can cost anywhere from $3.75 to $10 depending on where you're going, when

a SEPTA bus

you're traveling, and whether you pay in advance or on the train. Senior citizens don't pay a cent to ride buses, subways, or trolleys and pay just $1 for Regional Rail travel within Pennsylvania. Up to two children age four and under can ride for free with a fare-paying adult. Discounts are available for riders with disabilities.

SEPTA offers two one-day passes custom-made for tourists. Priced at $8, the **Convenience Pass** is good for eight trips by bus, subway, or trolley. The **Independence Pass,** valid for unlimited travel on all SEPTA lines and Phlash, is $12 per person or $29 for a family of up to five people. Passes can be purchased at many locations, including SEPTA headquarters at 1234 Market Street, the Independence Visitor Center at 6th and Market Streets, major newsstands, and online at shop.septa.org.

Brandywine Valley

As it winds its way from southeastern Pennsylvania to the northern Delaware city of Wilmington, Brandywine Creek crosses what geologists refer to as a fall line. In layman's terms, it takes a nosedive. That nosedive made the Brandywine Valley attractive to water-powered industries—flour mills, cotton mills, and the like—in days of yore. In 1802 a French immigrant by the name of Eleuthère Irénée (E. I.) du Pont began construction of a gunpowder works along the creek, often referred to as the Brandywine River. It wasn't long before his company was the nation's largest gunpowder producer, and the du Ponts grew wildly wealthy. The Brandywine Valley's present popularity as a tourist destination has much to do with their wealth. It was a du Pont who created Longwood Gardens, one of the nation's premier horticultural attractions. It was a du Pont who built the magnificent Nemours Mansion and its garden, one of the finest examples of a formal French garden outside of France. And it was a du Pont who turned Winterthur, another family estate, into a showplace for American decorative arts. You'll hear a lot about the du Ponts if you pay the region a visit.

You'll also hear a lot about the Wyeths, often called America's first family of art.

Brandywine Valley

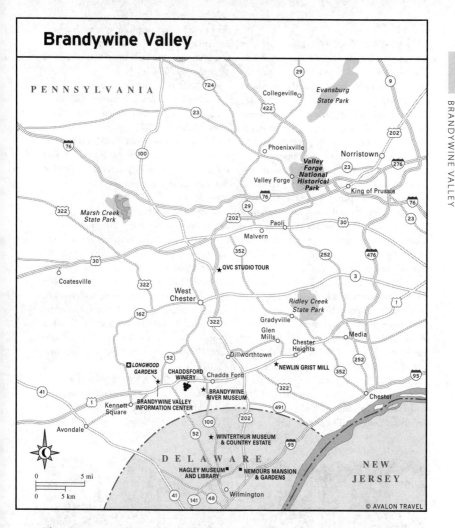

Three generations of Wyeth artists have lived and painted in the Brandywine region, capturing its people and landscapes on canvas. The Brandywine River Museum boasts a renowned collection of works by members of the uber-talented clan, including Andrew Wyeth, one of the most celebrated and influential artists of the 20th century.

The region boasts some cute-as-a-button towns, including West Chester, which brazenly bills itself as "the perfect town," and Kennett Square, the so-called Mushroom Capital of the World. More than 60 percent of the mushrooms consumed in the United States are grown in the Kennett Square area. The annual Mushroom Festival, held the weekend after Labor Day, showcases mushrooms in every imaginable form, including ice cream. In recent years the Brandywine Valley has become associated with another crop: wine grapes. It's home to more than a dozen wineries, including Pennsylvania's largest.

SIGHTS
★ Longwood Gardens

Longwood Gardens (1001 Longwood Rd., Kennett Square, 610/388-1000, www.longwoodgardens.org, 9am-6pm daily, open until 10pm during holiday season, admission $18-25, seniors $15-22, children 5-18 and students $8-11) is one of Pennsylvania's most exquisite spots, the sort of place people come back to again and again. It's unusual among horticultural showplaces in the Northeast in that it's open 365 days a year. In fact, Longwood is busiest not in spring or summer but from Thanksgiving through early January, when fountains dance to holiday music and ice dancers perform under the stars. Its 1,050 acres of gardens, woodlands, and meadows were shaped by many hands, but the greatest credit is due to Pierre S. du Pont (1870-1954), whose French-born great-grandfather founded the DuPont chemical company.

In 1906, Pierre purchased a property of about 200 acres from a Quaker family by the name of Peirce. The Peirces' 1730 farmhouse became his weekend residence, and the creation of Longwood Gardens began. Pierre drew inspiration from Italian villas and French chateaux but had a tendency to supersize. Longwood's Italian Water Garden, for example, was inspired by a garden near Florence. But where the original had only a few fountains, the Longwood version boasts 18 pools and 600 jets.

Budget at least an hour to take in the 20-plus outdoor gardens, including the otherworldly Topiary Garden and the 600-foot-long Flower Garden Walk, whose beds are replanted with more than 120,000 spring bulbs every October. You'll need at least two hours for the Longwood Conservatory, which houses everything from cacti to a colossal pipe organ.

Longwood's **Terrace** restaurant, famous for its mushroom soup, offers both casual and fine dining. Reservations are strongly recommended for the fine dining room, named **1906** (11:30am-3:30pm daily, open until 7:30pm during holiday season, $14-35) after the year Pierre purchased the grounds. Alternatively, bring a cooler of food and a bottle of wine. Longwood's picnic area, located a short drive from the main parking lot, features 70 tables, grills, and restroom facilities.

Delaware's du Pont Sights

Longwood's creator wasn't the only du Pont with lavish tastes. The Wilmington, Delaware, area boasts three du Pont

Longwood Gardens

estates-turned-museums, each good for several hours of oohs and aahs. Just six miles south of Longwood on Route 52 is **Winterthur Museum & Country Estate** (5105 Kennett Pike, Winterthur, DE, 302/888-4600, www.winterthur.org, 10am-5pm Tues.-Sun., admission $18, seniors and students $16, children 2-11 $5), home to a vast collection of Americana and a splendid naturalistic garden. E. I. du Pont, who founded the company that made his family one of the wealthiest in America, purchased the land that would become Winterthur in the 1810s. But it wasn't until his great-grandson Henry Francis du Pont (1880-1969) got his hands on the property a century later that it evolved into the extraordinary estate it is today.

Henry doubled the size of the existing mansion, installing historical architectural interiors and filling the rooms with his burgeoning collection of American decorative arts. By the time the mansion opened as a museum in 1951, he had created 175 period rooms. First Lady Jacqueline Kennedy was so wowed during a 1961 visit that she invited Henry to head the committee overseeing the restoration of the White House. General admission includes an introductory tour of the mansion, admittance to galleries displaying highlights from Winterthur's collection of more than 85,000 objects made or used in America from 1640 to 1860, and free rein of the Winterthur Garden. A tram tour of the 60-acre garden is offered when weather permits. The last house tour begins at 3:30pm. Winterthur (pronounced "winter-tour") also offers one- and two-hour in-depth tours that cost an additional $12 and $22, respectively. Reservations are strongly recommended for in-depth tours.

While Henry amassed all things American, another great-grandson of E. I. du Pont lived in French-style splendor a few miles away. Alfred I. du Pont (1864-1935) built **Nemours Mansion & Gardens** (Rte. 141 and Alapocas Rd., Wilmington, DE, 302/651-6912, www.nemoursmansion.org, open Tues.-Sun. May-Dec., admission $15) to please his second wife, a Francophile who also happened to be his cousin. The spectacular Louis XVI-style mansion and formal French gardens, modeled after those at Versailles's Petit Trianon, reopened in 2008 after a three-year renovation to the tune of $39 million. Tours depart three times a day Tuesday through Saturday and twice on Sundays, lasting 2.5-3 hours. Reservations are strongly recommended. Nemours is closed January through April.

Wondering how the du Ponts earned all that dough? Head to **Hagley Museum and Library** (200 Hagley Rd., Wilmington, DE, 302/658-2400, www.hagley.org, museum open 9:30am-4:30pm daily, admission $14, seniors and students $10, children 6-14 $5), located on the site of the gunpowder works E. I. du Pont established in 1802, three years after fleeing France amid the turmoil and bloodshed of the French Revolution. In time, the company established a virtual monopoly on the U.S. gunpowder industry, raking in more than $1 billion during World War I. Spanning 235 acres along the Brandywine River, Hagley features restored gunpowder mills, the remains of a workers' community, and the first du Pont home in America. Exhibits in the visitors center tell the story of the DuPont company, which evolved from America's largest explosives manufacturer into its largest chemical company.

Brandywine River Museum

Museums with an emphasis on regional art rarely enjoy international renown. The **Brandywine River Museum** (1 Hoffman's Mill Rd., Chadds Ford, 610/388-2700, www.brandywinemuseum.org, 9:30am-4:30pm daily, extended hours for several days after Christmas, admission $12, seniors $8, children 6-12 and students $6) is an exception, thanks in large part to one family with a surfeit of talent. Opened in 1971 in a converted Civil War-era gristmill, the museum on the banks of the Brandywine is home to an unparalleled collection of works by three generations of Wyeths. Patriarch N. C. Wyeth (1882-1945) moved to the Brandywine region in 1902 to study with famed illustrator Howard Pyle. He became Pyle's star pupil and one of America's foremost commercial artists, painting advertisements for the likes of Coca-Cola and Cream of Wheat and illustrating such literary classics as *Treasure Island, Robin Hood, The Last of the Mohicans,* and *Robinson Crusoe.*

Three of his five children also became artists, including daughters Henriette and Carolyn, who are well represented in the museum's collection. But it was his youngest child who made the greatest mark. Realist painter Andrew Wyeth (1917-2009) was the first artist awarded the Presidential Medal of Freedom, the nation's highest civilian honor; the first living artist to have an exhibition at the White House; and the first living American artist to have an exhibition at London's Royal Academy of Arts. His 1948 painting *Christina's World,* part of the permanent collection of the Museum of Modern Art in New York, is one of the best-known images of the 20th century. Born in 1946, son Jamie Wyeth was only 20 when his first one-man show opened in New York and less than 30 at his first retrospective. He's known for portraits of larger-than-life figures such as John F. Kennedy, Rudolf Nureyev, and Andy Warhol, as well as large-scale animal portraits. Hundreds of other artists, including Pyle and many of his students, are represented in the museum's collection of more than 3,000 works.

For even more insight into America's first family of art, tour the **N.C. Wyeth House and Studio,** where N. C. raised his uber-talented brood; the **Andrew Wyeth Studio,** where Andrew painted from 1940 to 2008; or the **Kuerner Farm,** which inspired so many of Andrew's works. The historic properties are open for tours from April to late November. Tickets cost $8 in addition to museum admission. A complimentary shuttle bus provides transportation from the museum.

Brandywine Valley Wine Trail

The Brandywine region boasts nearly a dozen wineries, including Pennsylvania's largest.

Most band together under the **Brandywine Valley Wine Trail** (610/444-3842, www.bvwinetrail.com) banner, and the website is a good first stop on your wine-tasting journey. You'll find directions to participating wineries, their hours, and information on concerts, picnics, and other winery happenings. **Chaddsford Winery** (632 Baltimore Pike, Chadds Ford, 610/388-6221, www.chaddsford.com, 10am-6pm Tues.-Sat., noon-6pm Sun., tastings noon-5:45pm, tasting fee $5) is a good second stop. Though it's the largest of Pennsylvania's 100-plus wineries, Chaddsford is hardly the large and impersonal operation that the distinction implies. Founded in 1982 by a husband-and-wife team, the winery occupies a renovated barn along Route 1, midway between Longwood Gardens and the Brandywine River Museum. It produces roughly 40,000 cases a year of dry reds, dry whites, and sweet wines. The Spiced Apple wine—aka "apple pie in a glass"—is a hot seller in the fall. About five miles away is the vineyard and tasting room of **Penns Woods Winery** (124 Beaver Valley Rd., Chadds Ford, 610/459-0808, www.pennswoodsevents.com, noon-5pm Mon. and Thurs., 11am-7pm Fri.-Sat., 11am-5pm Sun., tasting fee $8), known for its Traminette, a hybrid white wine, and Ameritage Reserve, a blend of many grapes. Its off-site winery is not open to the public.

Paradocx Vineyard (1833 Flint Hill Rd., Landenberg, 610/255-5684, www.paradocx.com, noon-6pm Fri.-Sun., tasting fee $8) grows grapes and produces wines on one picturesque property. It's owned by two couples, all practicing physicians (hence its name, a play on "pair of docs"). The tasting room at the vineyard and winery has limited hours, but you can sample the full line of wines any day but Monday at **Paradocx's Kennett Square location** (The Market at Liberty Place, 148 W. State St., Kennett Square, 11am-9pm Tues.-Thurs., 11am-10pm Fri.-Sat., 11am-8pm Sun.). **Kreutz Creek Vineyards** (553 S. Guernsey Rd., West Grove, 610/869-4412, www.kreutzcreekvineyards.com, 11am-6pm Sat.-Sun., tasting fee $7), which serves wine slushies at its summer concerts, is just four miles from Paradocx's Landenberg location.

Members of the Brandywine Valley Wine Trail collaborate on two "passport" events: the **Harvest Festival** (late Sept./early Oct.), a grape-stomping good time, and **Barrels on the Brandywine** (weekends in Mar.), a celebration of the newest vintages. Passports, which can be purchased online or at the wineries, are good for tastings at multiple wineries.

No longer a wine trail member but an absolute must for oenophiles: **Va La Vineyards** (8820 Gap Newport Pike, Avondale, 610/268-2702, www.valavineyards.com, noon-5:30pm Fri., noon-6pm Sat.-Sun., call ahead to verify hours, tasting fee $20), which relies almost exclusively on its 6.73 acres of grapes to produce four distinctive wines.

QVC Studio Tour

A tour of **QVC's world headquarters** (1200 Wilson Dr., West Chester, 800/600-9900, www.qvctours.com, tours at 10:30am, noon, 1pm, 2:30pm, and 4pm daily, admission $7.50, children 6-12 $5) is to fans of home shopping what Universal Studios Hollywood is to movie buffs: a peek behind the curtain. Guided walking tours begin with a short video introduction to the TV retailer, founded in 1986 with the goal of providing "Quality, Value, and Convenience," and culminate in a bird's-eye view of the sprawling studio from a perch within earshot of the producer's booth. QVC broadcasts live 24 hours a day, 364 days a year in the United States, so the odds of seeing a program in progress are overwhelming. In addition to the regular tour, which lasts 60-75 minutes, QVC offers a three-hour "all access tour" once or twice a week. Reservations are required for the $75-per-person tour, which includes lunch in the corporate cafeteria. Don't underestimate QVC's popularity; it's not unusual for the pricey tour to sell out. The QVC Studio Store, open 10am-5:30pm daily, offers an ever-changing selection of beauty products, jewelry, kitchenware, home decor, and other products.

Newlin Grist Mill

Set within a 150-acre park, the **Newlin Grist Mill** (219 Cheyney Rd., Glen Mills, 610/459-2359, www.newlingristmill.org, visitors center open 9am-4pm daily, park open until dusk) is the only working 18th-century gristmill in Pennsylvania. The water-powered mill was built in 1704 and operated commercially until 1941, grinding wheat, corn, oats, buckwheat, and rye. Today it grinds corn into cornmeal that can be purchased in the visitors center, a former railroad station and post office. Adjacent to the mill is a two-story stone house built in 1739 for the miller. Admission to the park is free, but tours of the mill and miller's house are $5 per person. They're offered at 11am and 2pm daily and last about an hour. On weekends tours are also offered at 10am and 1pm. There's no charge for tours during the **Fall Harvest Festival** (first Sat. in Oct., free), featuring demonstrations of period crafts, pumpkin decorating, hayrides, and other family-friendly fun.

The park attracts nature lovers as well as history buffs. Eight miles of hiking trails and the West Branch of Chester Creek, a popular trout stream, run through it. Stream fishing is reserved for fly fishers with a seasonal park pass. Pond fishing (9am-4pm weekends Apr.-Oct., $5 per person plus $4 per fish caught) is open to all visitors.

ENTERTAINMENT AND EVENTS
Festivals and Events

The Brandywine Valley is horse country, and many of its main spring and summer events fall in the equestrian category. The equestrian season opens with **Point-to-Point** (302/888-4600, www.winterthur.org, early May, admission charged), a day of steeplechase racing and tailgate picnicking amid the splendor of Henry Francis du Pont's Winterthur estate in Delaware. Almost as impressive as the racehorses are the antique Rolls-Royces, Bentleys, steam autos, and horse-drawn carriages rolled out for the occasion. Proceeds from the **Radnor Hunt Races** (Malvern,

610/388-8383, www.radnorhuntraces.org, third Sat. in May, admission charged), another steeplechase event, benefit the Brandywine Conservancy, the Chadds Ford-based nonprofit that operates the Brandywine River Museum. Admission passes must be purchased in advance.

Started in 1896, when horses were still a primary mode of transportation, the **Devon Horse Show and Country Fair** (Devon, 610/688-2554, www.devonhorseshow.net, late May/early June, admission charged) is the oldest and largest outdoor multibreed horse competition in the country. The event, which has grown from one day to 11, has raised more than $14 million for Bryn Mawr Hospital in suburban Philadelphia.

Other equine-centric traditions include **Ludwig's Corner Horse Show and Country Fair** (Glenmoore, 610/458-3344, www.ludwigshorseshow.org, Labor Day weekend, admission charged) and Sunday afternoon matches at the **Brandywine Polo Club** (232 Polo Rd., Toughkenamon, 610/268-8692, www.brandywinepolo.com, admission charged).

The region's wineries host a wide variety of events in the warmer months, from free concerts to running races to outdoor yoga classes. Visit the website of the **Brandywine Valley Wine Trail** (610/444-3842, www.bvwinetrail. com) for a schedule.

The two-day **Chester County Balloon Festival** (Unionville, 855/451-9002, www. ccballoonfest.com, June, admission $10 per car) is a chance to take flight or simply delight in the sight of mass balloon ascensions and fireworks. Balloon rides ($200 per person) must be reserved in advance.

It's not unusual for hundreds of people to run out of Phoenixville's Colonial Theatre screaming at the top of their lungs. It's tradition. Built in 1903, the theater provided the setting for a memorable scene in 1958's *The Blob,* and reenacting it is part of the town's annual homage to the sci-fi flick starring Steve McQueen. Started in 2000, **BlobFest** (227 Bridge St., Phoenixville, 610/917-1228, www.

thecolonialtheatre.com, July, free and ticketed events) also features a street fair and screenings of horror classics.

Nearly 200 vendors hawk everything from mushroom-shaped jewelry to mushroom ice cream during the **Mushroom Festival** (610/925-3373, www.mushroomfestival.org, weekend after Labor Day, admission $2, children under 12 free), Kennett Square's annual celebration of its number one cash crop. The fungi-themed fete features mushroom soup cook-offs, mushroom growing and cooking demos, an antique and classic car show, and a community parade. Buses whisk festivalgoers to local mushroom farms for behind-the-scenes tours.

ACCOMMODATIONS
Bed-and-Breakfasts

As befitting a region known for mansions and gardens, wineries and horse farms, the Brandywine Valley has a healthy stock of elegant B&Bs. Fairest of them all is the ★ **Fairville Inn** (506 Kennett Pike, Chadds Ford, 610/388-5900, www.fairvilleinn.com, $175-310), with 15 rooms and suites spread between three buildings on five bucolic acres. It's conveniently located between Longwood Gardens and Winterthur on Route 52, but guests have been known to forgo sightseeing in favor of an afternoon on their private deck, by their in-room fire, or in their canopied bed. Breakfast features a buffet of fresh fruit, yogurt, cereal, and house-baked breads and muffins, plus your choice of three hot entrées.

Set on 50 acres, **Sweetwater Farm Bed & Breakfast** (50 Sweetwater Rd., Glen Mills, 610/459-4711, www.gracewinery.com, $150-395) offers the ultimate country retreat. Choose from seven rooms in the manor house, with one wing dating to 1734 and the other to 1815, and eight guest cottages. The Greenhouse Cottage, which has two bedrooms, a living room with panoramic pasture views, and a full kitchen, can easily accommodate two couples or a family. Five of the cottages are pet-friendly. Amenities include an outdoor pool, a golf green, a fitness center, and a massage room. Owned by Grace Kelly's nephew, Chris Le Vine, and his wife, painter Vicky Le Vine, Sweetwater Farm also boasts a five-acre vineyard and boutique winery.

For closer-to-town digs, **Faunbrook Bed & Breakfast** (699 W. Rosedale Ave., West Chester, 610/436-5788, www.faunbrook.com, $135-209) is an excellent choice. Less than two miles from the heart of West Chester, the 1860 manse has seven antique-filled guest rooms and grand common areas. Once home to a U.S. congressman, it still has a dignified air about it. Breakfast is served by candlelight.

Hotels

Bed-and-breakfasts aren't for everyone, and the Brandywine Valley is not without recommendable hotels. Opened in 2012, the 80-room **Hotel Warner** (120 N. High St., West Chester, 610/692-6920, www.hotelwarner. com, $140-190) is the only hotel in downtown West Chester, the region's most happening burg. It's a great choice if you want to be within walking distance of restaurants, shops, and galleries. Amenities include free Wi-Fi, an indoor pool, and a complimentary continental breakfast.

The **Inn at Mendenhall** (323 Kennett Pike, Mendenhall, 610/388-1181, www.mendenhallinn.com, $118-209) has an old-world charm, even though it only dates to 1990. It's on Route 52, just minutes from Longwood Gardens to its north and Winterthur to its south. Each spacious room and suite is equipped with a microwave, refrigerator, coffeemaker, safe, and flat-screen TV. The hotel's sundry shop, fitness center, and business center are accessible 24/7. Rates include wireless Internet access and a breakfast buffet complete with omelet station. Fine dining is available in the on-site **Mendenhall Inn,** known for its over-the-top Sunday brunch (10am-2pm, $28.50, children 12 and under $12).

FOOD
Chadds Ford

Two noteworthy restaurants can be found near the intersection of Route 1 (Baltimore Pike) and Creek Road, convenient to the Brandywine River Museum. A humble establishment, **Hank's Place** (1410 Baltimore Pike, 610/388-7061, www.hanks-place.net, 6am-3pm Mon., 6am-7pm Tues.-Sat., 7am-3pm Sun., $2-16) is known for better-than-average diner food, including Greek specialties like gyros and spanakopita. Renowned painter Andrew Wyeth, who died in 2009, was a regular.

Chadds Ford's favorite son was also spotted at the upscale **Brandywine Prime** (1617 Baltimore Pike, 610/388-8088, www.brandywineprime.com, lunch noon-4pm Sat., brunch 10am-2pm Sun., dinner 5pm-10pm Mon.-Sat. and 4pm-9pm Sun., dinner $18-44), a seafood and steak restaurant with a superb Sunday brunch ($19.95, children 4-12 $10.95). Can't afford a meal of butter-poached lobster tail or grass-fed New York strip steak? You're not out of luck. A bar menu with burgers and sandwiches in the $12-16 range is available from 5pm Monday-Thursday and noon Friday-Sunday. Burgers are half-price on Friday evenings.

Kennett Square

You need a reservation to eat dinner at ★ **Talula's Table** (102 W. State St., 610/444-8255, www.talulastable.com, market 7am-7pm daily, dinner 7pm-11pm daily), and that's no small matter. The foodie heaven in the heart of Kennett Square accepts just one reservation a day—for that date *the following year*. Fortunately, you don't need foresight to enjoy breakfast or lunch at Talula's, a gourmet market by day. Burgundy snails, artisanal preserves from Armenia, and other delicacies from afar compete for attention with house-made foods, which run the gamut from breads and pastries to barbecue sauce and spiced salts. Talula's even makes its own sausages, bacon, and other charcuterie with locally raised meat. Seating is sparse, so you may want to avoid the lunch rush.

The **Half Moon Restaurant & Saloon** (108 W. State St., 610/444-7232, www. halfmoonrestaurant.com, 11:30am-10pm

Mon.-Sat., $8-32) specializes in wild game and Belgian beers. Its rooftop atrium is one of the most delightful dining spots in the region.

West Chester

The county seat of Chester County has become something of a dining destination in recent years. More than 50 eateries representing a wide variety of cuisines can be found within its 1.8 square miles. The main intersection of Gay and High Streets is home to an **Iron Hill Brewery & Restaurant** (3 W. Gay St., 610/738-9600, www.ironhillbrewery.com/westchester, 11am-close daily, $9-25), one of about 10 that have sprouted in Pennsylvania, Delaware, and New Jersey since 1996. Even people who detest beer dine here. The food is that good.

Foodies have good reason to venture off Gay Street. Chief among them is **Carlino's** (128 W. Market St., 610/696-3788, www.carlinosmarket.com, 9am-7pm Mon.-Fri., 9am-6pm Sat., 9am-4pm Sun.), a gourmet market with a mind-blowing selection of cheeses. Belly up to the Brie Bar for a custom-made hunk. Load up on cured delicacies at the olive bar and fresh greens at the salad bar, order a deli sandwich or something hot—a pasta dish or hearth-fired pizza, perhaps—and take your bounty to the **Kreutz Creek Vineyards tasting room** (44 E. Gay St., 610/436-5006, www.kreutzcreekvineyards.com, 11am-8pm Tues.-Thurs., 11am-11pm Fri.-Sat., tasting fee $7), a BYOF (bring your own food) establishment that serves up live music on Friday and Saturday evenings. For a truly decadent dining experience, drop by **Éclat Chocolate** (24 S. High St., 610/692-5206, www.eclatchocolate.com, 10am-6pm Mon.-Fri., 10am-4pm Sat.-Sun.) en route and pick up some single-origin mendiants (melt-in-your-mouth chocolate disks) or rose-infused caramels. Owner and master chocolatier Christopher Curtin was the first American to be awarded the honor of German Master Pastry Chef and Chocolatier after nailing a five-day exam in Cologne, Germany.

A few miles south of downtown is the incomparable ★ **Dilworthtown Inn** (1390 Old Wilmington Pike, 610/399-1390, www.dilworthtown.com, 5:30pm-9pm Mon.-Fri., 5pm-9pm Sat., 5pm-8pm Sun., $25-50), offering inspired American cuisine and a stellar wine list in a colonial setting. The original section of the three-floor restaurant, which boasts 15 dining rooms and walk-in fireplaces, dates to 1754. The ruins of an old stone stable provide the setting for outdoor dining when weather permits. Candlelight and dishes like wild Burgundy escargot and chateaubriand for two—carved tableside—make the Dilworthtown a romantic choice. Its wine cellar is one of Pennsylvania's largest and a perennial winner of *Wine Spectator*'s Award of Excellence. Looking to improve your wine IQ? There's a class for you at **The Inn Keeper's Kitchen,** a state-of-the-art demonstration kitchen across from the inn. A course calendar is available on the restaurant's website.

INFORMATION AND SERVICES

You'll find hundreds of free brochures at the **Brandywine Valley Information Center** (300 Greenwood Rd., Kennett Square, 484/770-8550, www.brandywinevalley.com, 11am-5pm Mon.-Sat., noon-5pm Sun.), adjacent to Longwood Gardens' main entrance. The **Greater Wilmington Convention & Visitors Bureau** (100 W. 10th St., Ste. 20, Wilmington, DE, 800/489-6664, www.visitwilmingtonde.com, 9am-5pm Mon.-Thurs., 8:30am-4:30pm Fri.) represents Delaware's largest city and its surrounds, where the Nemours Mansion and Winterthur Museum are found.

GETTING THERE AND AROUND

Longwood Gardens, the Brandywine River Museum, and Chaddsford Winery, located within a few miles of each other along Route 1, are about 30 miles west from the heart of Philadelphia. They're even closer to **Philadelphia International Airport** (PHL, 215/937-6937, www.phl.org), which is about seven miles southwest of Center City. Although the Southeastern Pennsylvania Transportation Authority, or **SEPTA** (215/580-7800, www.septa.org), connects Philadelphia to West Chester, Phoenixville, and other Brandywine towns, exploring the region without a vehicle of your own is tough. If you're dead set against driving, familiarize yourself with the services of the **Transportation Management Association of Chester County** (TMACC, 610/993-0911, www.tmacc.org) and **DART First State** (302/652-3278, www.dartfirststate.com), Delaware's public transportation system.

Bucks County

Like the Brandywine Valley, Bucks County offers a unique blend of bucolic beauty and a bustling arts and culture scene. Popular destinations include Peddler's Village, an old-timey shopping, dining, and entertainment complex, and the lovely towns of New Hope and Doylestown. All three lie along a 10-mile stretch of Route 202, about an hour's drive from Center City Philadelphia.

SIGHTS
New Hope
The village of New Hope boasts nearly 200 independently owned shops and galleries, a relatively vibrant nightlife, and a thriving gay culture. It's the sort of place that attracts art-collecting socialites and leather-clad bikers alike. Just across the Delaware River, the New Jersey town of Lambertville tries hard to keep up with its hip neighbor, so be sure to cross the auto/pedestrian bridge that connects them. There's no need to move your car to and fro: The toll-free bridge is less than a quarter-mile long, and the best parts of both burgs are within strolling distance of the river.

If you're a first-time visitor, get your bearings at the **New Hope Visitors Center** (Main and Mechanic Streets, 215/862-5030, www.newhopevisitorscenter.org, open daily from 10 or 11am to between 4 and 7pm), built in 1839 as the first town hall. Then pop by the **Bucks County Playhouse** (70 S. Main St., 215/862-2121, www.buckscountyplayhouse.com) to see what's showing.

the Bucks County Playhouse

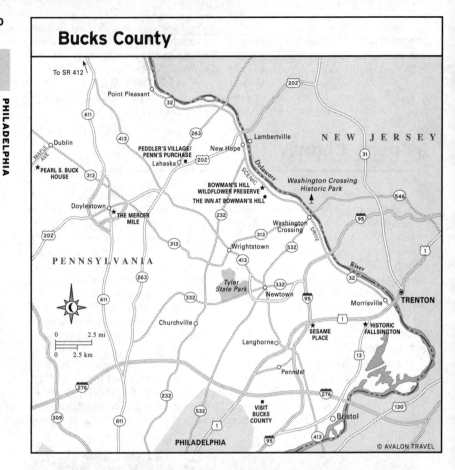

Bucks County

To SR 412

Point Pleasant

611

32

263

413

PEDDLER'S VILLAGE/
PENN'S PURCHASE

Dublin

MAPLE AVE

★ PEARL S. BUCK
HOUSE

313

Lahaska

202

New Hope

Lambertville

N E W   J E R S E Y

31

202

Delaware

SCENIC

BOWMAN'S HILL
WILDFLOWER PRESERVE
THE INN AT BOWMAN'S HILL

Washington Crossing
Historic Park

546

95

Doylestown

★ THE MERCER
MILE

232

Washington
Crossing

313

DRIVE

1

202

313

Wrightstown

413

532

River

32

PENNSYLVANIA

263

Tyler
State Park

332

TRENTON

611

332

Newtown

332

95

Morrisville

1

0   2.5 mi

Churchville

Langhorne

SESAME
PLACE

★ HISTORIC
FALLSINGTON

0   2.5 km

Penndel

13

276

232

VISIT
BUCKS
COUNTY

276

130

309

611

532

1

Bristol

413

PHILADELPHIA

95

© AVALON TRAVEL

Opened in 1939 in a renovated gristmill, the theater quickly became known as a place to catch premieres of shows that would later open on Broadway. Grace Kelly, Bea Arthur, Liza Minnelli, and Merv Griffin have graced its stage.

Should you tire of exploring on foot, take a scenic cruise aboard the **Wells Ferry** (behind The Landing Restaurant, 22 N. Main St., 215/205-1140, www.newhopeboatrides.com, May-Oct., fare $12, children 2-12 $8) or **Coryell's Ferry** (22 S. Main St., 215/862-2050, www.coryellsferry.com, May-Sept., fare $10, children 2-12 $5, children under 2 $2). You'll learn a bit about the history of New Hope—which was known as Wells Ferry in

the early 1700s and Coryell's Ferry during the Revolutionary period—aboard the pontoon boats.

Alternatively, take a ride on the **New Hope & Ivyland Railroad** (32 W. Bridge St., 215/862-2332, www.newhoperailroad.com, hourly excursions $18.95-25.90, children 2-11 $16.95-23.90, children under 2 $3.95, call or check website for special event fares). The tourist railroad has an authentic steam locomotive as well as historic diesel engines, 1920s passenger coaches, and an antique bar car. Hourly excursions give you the option of disembarking near Peddler's Village, a popular shopping destination, and taking a later train back.

The Mercer Mile

The quantity and quality of museums in Doylestown, population 8,200, is remarkable for a town its size. Four are concentrated in an area known as the Mercer Mile. Get an early start if you plan to hit them all, and wear comfortable shoes so you can walk between them. You'll find charming shops and eateries along the way.

Three of the museums owe their existence to one local genius: Henry Chapman Mercer (1856-1930), a lawyer by schooling, an archaeologist and maker of architectural tiles by profession, and an artifact hoarder by passion. In his 50s, Mercer poured his talents into constructing three edifices entirely of reinforced concrete. The first was his dream home, a 44-room castle with 10 bathrooms, 18 fireplaces, 32 stairwells, and more than 200 windows of various shape and size. He named it **Fonthill** (E. Court St. and Rte. 313, 215/348-9461, www.fonthill-museum.org, 10am-5pm Mon.-Sat., noon-5pm Sun., last tour at 4pm, admission $12, seniors $10, children 6-17 $6). The National Historic Landmark is elaborately adorned with Mercer's own tiles as well as the Persian, Chinese, Spanish, and Dutch tiles he collected. Access is by guided tour only, and reservations are strongly advised.

Next to his home he built a tile factory. A leading figure in the Arts and Crafts movement, Mercer produced handmade tiles for thousands of private and public buildings, including the state capitol in Harrisburg and Grauman's Chinese Theatre in Hollywood. Reminiscent of a Spanish mission, his **Moravian Pottery & Tile Works** (130 Swamp Rd., 215/348-6098, www.buckscounty.org/government/moravianpotterytileworks, 10am-4:45pm daily, last tour at 4pm, admission $5, seniors $4, children 7-17 $3) is now maintained as a "working history" museum by the Bucks County Department of Parks and Recreation. Tours, offered every half hour, consist of a 17-minute video and a self-guided walk through the facility, where ceramicists press and glaze tiles in a manner similar to Mercer's. The gift shop carries reissues of tiles and mosaics in the Arts and Crafts tradition.

The polymath built his final concrete masterpiece, the **Mercer Museum** (84 S. Pine St., 215/345-0210, www.mercermuseum.org, 10am-5pm Mon.-Sat., noon-5pm Sun., admission $12, seniors $10, children 6-17 $6), to showcase his enormous collection of early American artifacts. Determined to preserve the handmade goods being discarded in favor of machine-made versions, Mercer amassed more than 30,000 objects, from Native American implements dating to 8,000 BC and tiny clock-making tools to horse-drawn vehicles and a whaleboat. The collection, which has grown considerably since his death, is regarded as the most complete of its kind. Heads up: The museum isn't heated or cooled, so dress accordingly. Fonthill and the Mercer Museum are administered by the Bucks County Historical Society, which offers a reduced rate ($20, children 6-17 $12) for admission to both.

A stone's throw from the Mercer Museum is the **James A. Michener Art Museum** (138 S. Pine St., 215/340-9800, www.michenermuseum.org, 10am-4:30pm Tues.-Fri., 10am-5pm Sat., noon-5pm Sun., extended hours late Oct.-late Jan., admission $18, seniors $17, college students $16, children 6-18 $8), known for its extensive collection of Pennsylvania Impressionist paintings. It also hosts nationally touring exhibits and showcases important regional artists. A permanent exhibit celebrates the career of its namesake, a Doylestown native who rose to fame as an author, snagging a Pulitzer Prize for 1947's *Tales of the South Pacific* and a Presidential Medal of Freedom in 1977. The museum opened in 1988, about a decade before Michener's death, in a building that served as the county jail for more than a century.

Pearl S. Buck House

James Michener wasn't the only prolific, Pulitzer Prize-winning author who called the region home. Raised in China by missionary parents, Pearl S. Buck (1892-1973) settled on a Bucks County farm several years after winning the esteemed award for 1931's *The Good Earth*. There she raised seven adopted children and several foster children and started an international adoption agency that continues today. Now open to the public, the 68-acre **Pearl S. Buck House estate** (520 Dublin Rd., Perkasie, 215/249-0100, www.psbi.org, tours at 11am, 1pm, and 2pm Mon.-Sat., 1pm and 2pm Sun., admission $12, seniors $10, students $6) features an 1835 stone farmhouse filled with Buck's belongings, including the Pulitzer, a subsequent Nobel Prize in Literature, and a silk wall hanging from the Dalai Lama. It's surrounded by gardens, greenhouses, and outbuildings including an 1827 barn. You'll find Asian giftware and some of Buck's 50-plus books in the gift shop.

Washington Crossing Historic Park

On December 25, 1776, General George Washington and his ragged troops crossed the ice-choked Delaware River from Pennsylvania to New Jersey. **Washington Crossing Historic Park** (Rte. 32, between Rte. 532 and Aquetong Rd., 215/493-4076, www.ushistory.org/washingtoncrossing, visitors center open 10am-4pm Tues.-Sun. mid-Mar.-Dec., free admission, tours $6 per site, combination ticket for 3 tours $11, children 5-11 $6), which preserves their put-in site, consists of two sections several miles apart. The lower section, near the intersection of Routes 32 and 532, features a visitors center, an 18th-century inn that served as a guard post during the encampment preceding the river crossing, several 19th-century structures, and a 20th-century boathouse with replicas of the type of craft used by Washington and his men. The boats are used every Christmas Day in a reenactment of the crossing that changed the course of history. Guided tours of Lower Park and the Thompson-Neely House, where wounded or sick soldiers were treated, are offered Thursday-Sunday.

At the upper section, you'll find more historic structures, graves of soldiers who died during the winter encampment, and a 125-foot tower completed in 1931 to commemorate the Revolution. The tower is open for self-guided tours Tuesday-Sunday. It offers a swell view of the river and surrounding countryside.

Sesame Place

Sesame Place (100 Sesame Rd., Langhorne, 215/752-7070, www.sesameplace.com, open

a Christmas Day reenactment at Washington Crossing Historic Park

daily late May-Labor Day and select other days, admission $60.99, children 23 months and younger free, rates discounted online) is the nation's only theme park based entirely on the enduring children's television show starring Big Bird, Elmo, and Cookie Monster. Kids can hobnob with their favorite *Sesame Street* characters in the 14-acre park, designed with the show's demographic in mind. Attractions include Cookie Mountain, a vinyl cone for pint-size mountaineers, and Ernie's Bed Bounce, a giant air mattress for aspiring moonwalkers. Bring swimwear and a towel for wet attractions such as The Count's Splash Castle, a multilevel play area featuring a 1,000-gallon tipping bucket, and the adult-friendly Big Bird's Rambling River. Admission is pricey (and parking will set you back another $17-30), but tickets are good for a second visit in the same season. The park opens at 10am and closes between 6 and 9pm.

Historic Fallsington

Billed as "the village that time forgot," **Historic Fallsington** (4 Yardley Ave., Fallsington, 215/295-6567, www.historic-fallsington.org, 10:30am-3:30pm Tues.-Sat. mid-May-mid-Oct., by appt. Tues.-Fri. mid-Oct.-mid-May, admission $6, seniors $5, children $3) consists of more than 90 buildings dating from the 1600s to early 1900s. The village formed around a Quaker meetinghouse built in 1690. Pennsylvania founder William Penn worshiped and preached there while living at Pennsbury Manor, several miles to the south. Guided walking tours, offered every half hour during the regular season, visit three preserved buildings, including a 1760s log house. You're welcome to stroll through the historic district on your own (be sure to grab a pamphlet describing about 20 structures), but don't go turning any doorknobs. Most of the buildings are privately owned.

SHOPPING

Boutique shopping is one of Bucks County's biggest draws. New Hope, Doylestown, and Newtown are great places to stroll and spend

disposable income. New Hope has a particularly eclectic mix of stores. You'll find everything from antiques to motorcycle leathers to Wiccan supplies along its Main Street. About four miles west of New Hope is the ever-popular **Peddler's Village** (Routes 202 and 263, Lahaska, 215/794-4000, www.peddlersvillage.com, open daily, hours vary), a 42-acre complex with about 70 specialty shops, several restaurants, a 70-room inn, and a family entertainment area featuring an antique carousel. Designed to evoke colonial America, the "village" hosts nearly a dozen annual festivals and events, including the popular **Apple Festival** (first weekend in Nov., free) and a gingerbread house display during the holiday season.

Across from Peddler's Village is an outlet center, **Penn's Purchase** (5861 York Rd., Lahaska, 215/794-2806, www.pennspurchase.com, open daily, hours vary by season), with stores including Coach, Brooks Brothers, Gymboree, and Jones New York.

Flea market enthusiasts can also find their bliss in the region. **Rice's Sale & Country Market** (6326 Greenhill Rd., New Hope, 215/297-5993, www.ricesmarket.com, 7am-1pm Tues. and Sat.), a 30-acre open-air market, hosts as many as 400 vendors. The indoor/outdoor **Golden Nugget Antique and Flea Market** (1850 River Rd., Lambertville, 609/397-0811, www.gnmarket.com, 6am-4pm Wed. and Sat.-Sun.), across the Delaware River in New Jersey, is another gem.

ACCOMMODATIONS

You'll have no trouble finding distinctive accommodations in Bucks County, especially in and around New Hope. At the top of the heap: ★ **The Inn at Bowman's Hill** (518 Lurgan Rd., New Hope, 215/862-8090, www.theinnatbowmanshill.com, $405-625), set on five idyllic acres on New Hope's outskirts. The romantic B&B was named best "weekend hideaway" in *Philadelphia* magazine's 2010 Best of Philly issue, and it's the only AAA four-diamond lodging in the county. Its six guest rooms and suites feature king-size featherbeds, fireplaces, and bathrooms with all the bells and whistles. Want a massage in the privacy of your room? No problem. Want breakfast in bed? No problem. Want to collect your own organic eggs from the resident hens? Feel free. The 134-acre **Bowman's Hill Wildflower Preserve** (1635 River Rd., New Hope, 215/862-2924, www.bhwp.org, grounds open 8:30am-sunset daily, visitors center open 9am-5pm Tues.-Sun., admission $5, seniors and students $3, children 4-14 $2), home to 800 species of plants native to Pennsylvania, is a stone's throw away.

The **Logan Inn** (10 W. Ferry St., New Hope, 215/862-2300, www.loganinn.com, $120-220) is an excellent, more affordable choice. Opened in the 1720s, it's the oldest continuously run inn in Bucks County and one of the oldest in the United States. It's no coincidence that lantern-lit **Ghost Tours of New Hope** (215/343-5564, www.ghosttoursofnewhope.com, 8pm Sat. June-late Nov. and Fri. Sept.-Oct., $10 per person) begin outside its doors: the 16-room inn is said to be extremely haunted. Good luck booking the legendary Room 6 in October, when paranormal investigators flock to town. With two restaurants, the Logan Inn is also known for good food. The casual **Logan Terrace**

features fresh seafood and a wide variety of Belgian beers. Its patio is one of the best people-watching spots in town. **Nikólas** offers a Mediterranean-inspired prix-fixe experience.

Wedgwood Inn (111 W. Bridge St., New Hope, 215/862-2570, www.wedgwoodinn.com, $95-295) owners Nadine and Carl Glassman are so good at what they do that they run training programs for aspiring innkeepers. The couple offers 18 rooms and suites spread between three 19th-century houses a short walk from the heart of New Hope and the bridge to Lambertville. Guests enjoy a continental-plus breakfast and a tot of housemade almond liqueur when it's time to turn in.

A few miles west of New Hope and only a minute from Peddler's Village, **Ash Mill Farm Bed & Breakfast** (5358 York Rd., Holicong, 215/794-5373, www.ashmillfarm.com, $145-295) offers spacious accommodations on a working sheep farm. Feeding the sheep and pygmy goats is permitted, but unlike some farm B&Bs, Ash Mill doesn't market itself to families with young kids (children 13 and older are welcome). So count on peace and quiet as you enjoy a massage in the cleverly named spa barn, The New Ewe. Children of all ages are welcome at the **Golden Plough Inn**

The Inn at Bowman's Hill

(Rte. 202 and Street Rd., Lahaska, 215/794-4004, www.goldenploughinn.com, $159-369), with 70 rooms situated throughout Peddler's Village. Many feature gas fireplaces and two-person whirlpools. Rates include a voucher toward breakfast in a Peddler's Village restaurant.

Just minutes from the heart of Doylestown, the three-story **Highland Farm Bed & Breakfast** (70 East Rd., Doylestown, 215/345-6767, www.highlandfarmbb.com, $170-300) was once home to Oscar Hammerstein II—as in half of the famous Rodgers and Hammerstein songwriting duo. Hammerstein (1895-1960) worked on the lyrics to *Oklahoma* on its wraparound porch and entertained such guests as Stephen Sondheim in its grand living room. Today the living room is the setting for wine and cheese receptions for guests of the four-room B&B.

Visit the website of the **Bucks County Bed and Breakfast Association** (www.visitbucks.com) for more options.

FOOD

New Hope and its across-the-Delaware neighbor, Lambertville, have several top-notch restaurants. A true original, ★ **Marsha Brown** (15 S. Main St., New Hope, 215/862-7044, www.marshabrownrestaurant.com, lunch 11:30am-4pm daily, dinner 5pm-10pm Mon.-Thurs., 5pm-11pm Fri.-Sat., 4:30pm-9pm Sun., lunch $10-18, dinner $25-48) offers New Orleans-style cuisine and Southern hospitality in a former church complete with stained glass windows. The menu features upscale versions of Creole classics like gumbo ya ya and jambalaya, a raw bar, and Maine lobster.

Housed in a restored 19th-century train station on the banks of the Delaware, **Lambertville Station** (11 Bridge St., Lambertville, 609/397-8300, www.lambertvillestation.com, 11:30am-10pm Mon.-Thurs., 11:30am-11pm Fri.-Sat., 10:30am-10pm Sun., lunch $9-20, dinner $17-36) is a superb choice any time of year but especially in the warmer months, when its outdoor dining area is open and the on-site herb garden is in full bloom.

Specialties include Chesapeake-style crab cakes and roasted rack of lamb. The Sunday brunch buffet (10:30am-3pm, $28.95, children 3-10 $16.95), served in the ballroom of the 45-room **Inn at Lambertville Station** (609/397-4400, $150-195), is a worthy splurge. An à la carte brunch menu ($11-21) is available.

In Doylestown, try the **Pennsylvania Soup & Seafood House** (22 S. Main St., Doylestown, 215/230-9490, www.pasoupandseafood.com, 11am-3pm Mon., 11am-7pm Tues., 11am-8pm Wed.-Thurs., 11am-9pm Fri.-Sat., $6-25). Head chef Keith Blalock is known around town as "the soup guy." His lobster bisque, Tuscan onion, and mulligatawny make it easy to stick to a liquid diet.

INFORMATION AND SERVICES

Visit Bucks County (800/836-2825, www.visitbuckscounty.com) is a great source of information about the region. Its main visitors center (3207 Street Rd., Bensalem, 215/639-0300, 9am-5pm daily) features an orientation theater, a large gift shop, and an interactive exhibit on the region's arts heritage. The tourism promotion agency also has visitors centers in downtown New Hope (1 W. Mechanic St., 215/862-5030, open daily, hours vary by season) and Quakertown (21 N. Main St., 215/536-3211, 9am-4pm Mon.-Fri.).

GETTING THERE AND AROUND

Central Bucks County, where New Hope, Doylestown, and Peddler's Village are found, is less than an hour north of Philadelphia and an hour and a half southwest of New York City. To reach New Hope from Philadelphia, head north on I-95, then Route 29. From New York, head west on I-78, then south on I-278 and Route 202. The nearest major airports are **Philadelphia International Airport** (PHL, 215/937-6937, www.phl.org) and **Lehigh Valley International Airport** (ABE, 800/359-5842, www.lvia.org). **Newark Liberty International Airport** (EWR,

973/961-6000, www.panynj.gov) isn't much farther away. **Amtrak** (800/872-7245, www. amtrak.com) can get you to Trenton, New Jersey, 17 miles southeast of New Hope. The Southeastern Pennsylvania Transportation Authority, or **SEPTA** (215/580-7800, www. septa.org), provides regional rail service between Philadelphia and Doylestown, and **Trans-Bridge Lines** (610/868-6001, www. transbridgelines.com) offers bus service between New York City and New Hope, Doylestown, and Peddler's Village.

While you can certainly make do without a car in these popular destinations, you'll want one for traveling between them and exploring the surrounding countryside. If you're fit, of course, a bicycle will do. **New Hope Cyclery** (404 York Rd., New Hope, 215/862-6888, www.newhopecyclery.com, 10am-6pm Mon.-Wed., 10am-8pm Thurs., 10am-6pm Fri.-Sat., 10am-4pm Sun.), which rents mountain bikes, tandems, and child trailers, is a stone's throw from Trans-Bridge's New Hope stop.

Lehigh Valley

About an hour north of Philadelphia, the Lehigh Valley is better known for what it was than what it is. Home to the cities of Allentown, Bethlehem, and Easton, the region used to be a cradle of industry. Most anyone who owned a radio in the early 1980s knows about the erosion of its manufacturing base, memorialized in Billy Joel's "Allentown" *(Well we're living here in Allentown / And they're closing all the factories down / Out in Bethlehem they're killing time / Filling out forms / Standing in line).* When Bethlehem Steel, once the second-largest steel producer in the United States after Pittsburgh-based U.S. Steel, made its last cast in November 1995, the hard job of redefining the valley began.

Today the shuttered steelworks is a shining example of redevelopment, home to a sprawling casino/hotel/shopping complex and a 10-acre cultural campus with indoor and outdoor concert venues. That's part of the "new" Lehigh Valley. But much of what's attractive about the region is really quite old. Bethlehem, founded in 1741 by Moravian missionaries, boasts more 18th-century buildings than Virginia's Colonial Williamsburg. It's home to the oldest continually operated bookstore in the world, the Moravian Book Shop, and the oldest Bach choir in the country. Martin guitars, beloved by musicians from Johnny Cash to John Mayer, have been

made in nearby Nazareth since the 1830s. The Martin Guitar Museum is a must-see for music lovers. (Alas, it's not open on weekends, so plan accordingly.) Crayola has been making crayons in Easton since the early 1900s. Its Crayola Experience attraction is a must-stop for pint-size Picassos. Allentown, Pennsylvania's third-largest city, boasts one of the oldest fairs in the United States. The country's oldest drive-in theater is a 15-minute drive from town.

SIGHTS
Dorney Park & Wildwater Kingdom

One of the most popular amusement parks on the East Coast, **Dorney Park** (3830 Dorney Park Rd., Allentown, 610/395-3724, www. dorneypark.com, open daily Memorial Day weekend-Labor Day and select other days, admission $49.99, seniors and children under 48 inches tall $29.99, children 2 and under free, rates discounted online) boasts more than 50 rides, games galore, and a 600-seat theater used for ice shows as well as song and dance revues. Among its rides is the Talon, the tallest and longest inverted roller coaster in the Northeast. One of its newest attractions, Dinosaur's Alive! ($5 with park admission) features more than 30 life-size animatronic dinosaurs. Prefer tamer attractions? Dorney

Dorney Park & Wildwater Kingdom

Park has plenty. Camp Snoopy, a two-acre play area themed around the Peanuts comic strip, is home to about a dozen tyke-friendly rides, some of which are scaled-down versions of park favorites.

Dorney Park traces its history to 1860, when Solomon Dorney opened a fish hatchery and several picnic groves along Cedar Creek. By the end of the 19th century, Dorney's Trout Ponds and Summer Resort had grown to include a hotel and restaurant, a Ferris wheel and other mechanical rides, a bowling alley, and a swimming pool. The Whip, a mild ride added in 1920, and a wooden coaster built in 1923 remain in service today. **Wildwater Kingdom,** which opened in 1985, has two wave pools, two winding rivers, and dozens of slides. Access to the water park is included in regular admission. Unless you have a season pass, expect to drop $15 on parking.

Drive-In Theaters

Opened in 1934, **Shankweiler's** (4540 Shankweiler Rd., Orefield, 610/481-0800, www.shankweilers.com, double feature $9, children 3-12 $5) is the oldest drive-in movie theater in America. Movie prices hark back to the good old days, and they don't sock it to you at the snack bar. A cheeseburger and funnel cake will set you back less than $5. About 15 minutes northwest of Allentown, the theater is generally open weekends in April and May and daily June through Labor Day. Weekends in September aren't out of the question.

About 10 miles farther north, **Becky's Drive-In** (4548 Lehigh Dr., Walnutport, 610/767-2249, www.beckysdi.com, double feature $9, children 3-12 $5) has been in continuous operation since 1946. The theater makes a point of showing child-appropriate movies on Fridays and Saturdays and offers pony rides to boot.

Sands Casino Resort Bethlehem

In 2009 Bethlehem joined the growing list of Pennsylvania casino towns. The **Sands Casino Resort Bethlehem** (77 Sands Blvd., Bethlehem, 877/726-3777, www.pasands.com, open 24 hours) represents one of the most ambitious brownfield redevelopment projects in the United States. Built on the site of the shuttered Bethlehem Steel mill, it pays tribute to the onetime industrial giant with design elements such as brick walls and exposed steel beams. Crystal chandeliers hang from large "gears" in a swanky lounge named Molten. Owned by Las Vegas Sands, whose portfolio includes The Venetian and The Palazzo on the Las Vegas Strip, the casino boasts thousands of slot machines, more than 180 table games, and a poker room with 36 tables.

The casino is part of a sprawling complex that also includes a 302-room hotel, about 30 outlet stores, and the **Sands Bethlehem Event Center** (610/297-7400, www.sandseventcenter.com), which hosts concerts by the likes of Weezer and Diana Krall, big-name comedians, and even mixed martial arts tournaments.

Dining options include an Irish pub, an outpost of New York's famous Carnegie

Deli, and three restaurants from celebrity chef Emeril Lagasse: **Burgers and More by Emeril,** his first burger joint; **Emeril's Italian Table** (4pm-10pm Sun.-Thurs., 4pm-11pm Fri.-Sat., $10-27), his first Italian restaurant; and the upscale **Emeril's Chop House** (5pm-10pm Sun.-Thurs., 5pm-11pm Fri.-Sat., $28-56).

Lost River Caverns

Lost River Caverns (726 Durham St., Hellertown, 610/838-8767, www.lostcave. com, 9am-6pm daily Memorial Day weekend-Labor Day, 9am-5pm daily rest of year, admission $12, children 3-12 $7.50), a panoply of stalactites, stalagmites, helictites, and other crystal formations, is just off Route 412 about five miles south of Bethlehem. Thirty-minute tours of the limestone cavern, discovered in 1883 during a quarrying operation, are offered at frequent intervals. One of its five chambers was dedicated as a nonsectarian chapel in 1949, and more than 80 couples have said "I do" there. It's a constant 52 degrees underground, so dress accordingly. The on-site Gilman Museum houses fossils, minerals, gems, and a collection of antique weapons. There's no charge for trailer camping or picnicking on the grounds.

Crayola Experience

The Lehigh Valley is home to Crayola's world headquarters and two of its major factories. The factories aren't open to the public, but you can learn how crayons are made at the **Crayola Experience** (30 Centre Square, Easton, 610/515-8000, www.crayolaexperience.com, 10am-6pm daily Memorial Day weekend-Labor Day, 9:30am-4pm Tues.-Fri. and 10am-6pm Sat.-Sun. remainder of year, admission $16.99, seniors $14.99, children under 2 free), a children's museum of sorts with three floors of attractions. Kids can personalize a crayon label, make a multicolor marker, paint with melted wax, and more. Completely redesigned in 2013, the Crayola Experience also features a café and a store with the world's largest selection of Crayola products. Don't miss the world's largest crayon in the café seating area. Measuring 15 feet long and weighing 1,500 pounds, the colossus was made with crayon nubs sent by children from around the country.

National Canal Museum

The **National Canal Museum** (2750 Hugh Moore Park Rd., Easton, 610/923-3548, www. canals.org, noon-5pm Wed.-Sun. early June-Labor Day and weekends in Sept., admission

the Crayola Experience

$11.75, seniors $10.50, children 3-15 $9) is the only museum dedicated to America's towpath canals, the highways of yesterday. Created with kids in mind, it's packed with interactive exhibits. Visitors can float a boat down a 90-foot-long model canal complete with locks and incline planes, learn how to harness a mule, and build a bridge. Admission includes a mule-drawn boat ride on a restored section of the Lehigh Canal. The boat departs on the hour 1pm-4pm.

Martin Guitar Museum and Factory Tour

The Martin Guitar Company is as rare as an original Martin D-45, which sells for as much as $1 million on eBay. For one thing, it's more than 175 years old. The company properly known as C. F. Martin & Co. traces its history to 1833, when Christian Frederick Martin emigrated from his native Germany, opened a music shop in lower Manhattan, and began making guitars in the back room. Five years later he relocated to the tiny Pennsylvania town of Nazareth, where Martin guitars have been made ever since. The fact that most Martins are still built in the United States distinguishes the company from so many manufacturers. Dynastic leadership also sets

it apart. The **Martin Guitar Museum** (510 Sycamore St., Nazareth, 610/759-2837, www. martinguitar.com, 8am-5pm Mon.-Fri., free admission), located at the company's main facility, tells its unique story. Home to more than 170 rare guitars, the museum also offers snapshots of music history. The list of seminal musicians who have played a Martin includes Elvis and Eric Clapton, Jimmy Buffet and Johnny Cash, Paul Simon and Sting, Buddy Guy and Beck. Visitors can get their hands on high-end and limited-edition models in the Pickin' Parlor or test out Martin's top-selling guitars and new offerings in the 1833 Shop, which also carries branded apparel, souvenirs, and collectibles.

Factory tours are offered at regular intervals 11am-2:30pm weekdays. Guides give an overview of the 300-plus steps required to turn rough lumber into a Martin. The free tours, available on a first-come, first-served basis, last about an hour. Anyone with more than an idle curiosity in the art of guitar-making should pay a visit to the **Guitarmaker's Connection** (10 W. North St., Nazareth, 610/759-2837, 9am-4pm Mon.-Fri.), located in the original Martin factory. The store offers a unique collection of luthier tools, guitar parts, and kits.

Martin Guitar Museum

ENTERTAINMENT AND EVENTS
Festivals and Events

Founded in 1898, The Bach Choir of Bethlehem is the oldest American choir dedicated to the works of Johann Sebastian Bach. It performs throughout the year, but its signature event is the **Bethlehem Bach Festival** (Lehigh University, Bethlehem, 610/866-4382, www.bach.org, ticketed and free events), held over two weekends in May. In addition to multiple concerts, the festival features a distinguished scholar lecture and a dinner.

More than a million people pour into Bethlehem over 10 days starting the first Friday in August. The draw: **Musikfest** (610/332-1300, www.musikfest.org). First held in 1984, the (mostly) outdoor festival features more than 300 (mostly) free performances on upwards of a dozen stages, dubbed "platzes" in honor of the city's Germanic heritage. Just about every music genre is represented, from Afrobeat to jazz to pop to zydeco. Musikfest is perhaps as famous for its official beer mugs as its music lineup. Mug holders enjoy cheap refills at beer tents and bars.

A tradition dating to 1852, **The Great Allentown Fair** (Allentown Fairgrounds, 302 N. 17th St., Allentown, 610/433-7541, www.allentownfairpa.org, week ending on Labor Day, admission charged) is unique among agricultural showcases in its track record of lassoing big-name entertainers. In 2013 the weeklong extravaganza featured singer-songwriter John Mayer, country superstar Toby Keith, and comedian Jeff Dunham, among others.

Inspired by the open-air markets held throughout Germany during the Christmas season, **Christkindlmarkt Bethlehem** (PNC Plaza at SteelStacks, 645 E. First St., Bethlehem, 610/332-1300, www.christmascity.org, Nov./Dec., admission charged) is a chance to stock up on holiday ornaments and handcrafted gifts, listen to live Christmas music, sample German fare, and watch ice carvers and other artisans at work. *Travel + Leisure* magazine named it one of the top holiday markets in the world.

SPORTS AND RECREATION
Bear Creek Mountain Resort & Conference Center

About 15 miles southwest of Allentown, **Bear Creek Mountain Resort** (101 Doe Mountain Ln., Macungie, 866/754-2822, www.bcmountainresort.com, all-day lift ticket $47-62,

The Great Allentown Fair

seniors 62-69 and youths 6-21 $40-53, seniors 70 and over and children 5 and under free, all-day ski or snowboard rental $35, snow tubing $24-29) offers snow sports in the winter and diversions such as boating, disc golfing, and mountain biking in the off-season. Steps from the chairlifts, the rustic-chic **Hotel at Bear Creek** (610/641-7101, from $160) features 118 rooms and suites, indoor and outdoor pools and hot tubs, and a ski rental shop reserved for guests. **The Spa at Bear Creek** (610/641-7174) is open to guests and nonguests alike.

Dutch Springs

As scuba destinations go, Pennsylvania is no Cozumel. But it is lucky enough to have **Dutch Springs** (4733 Hanoverville Rd., Bethlehem, 610/759-2270, www.dutchsprings.com, general admission $16-28, children 5-9 $12-18, scuba diving $37 per day), one of the largest freshwater scuba diving facilities in the country. The 50-acre lake, a flooded former quarry, is as deep as 100 feet in some areas and boasts 20- to 30-foot visibility. It's filled with sunken treasures: boats, trucks, a school bus, a Cessna plane, a Sikorsky H-37 helicopter, and more. Divers and snorkelers also encounter a variety of aquatic life, including koi, large-mouth bass, bluegills, and zebra mussels. The

diving season begins in April and stretches into November. Dutch Springs offers air and nitrox fills and rents tanks and weights. Divers must bring all other necessary equipment. A wetsuit no thinner than seven millimeters, a hood, and gloves are advisable even in the summer, as temperatures at the bottom of the lake hover in the 40s year-round.

Nondivers can have a good time, too. Dutch Springs rents ocean kayaks and paddleboats. The Aqua Park at Dutch Springs, a cordoned section of the lake, features a water trampoline and inflatable waterslides. For landlubbers, there's Sky Challenge, a combination rock-climbing wall and ropes course.

Tent and RV camping are permitted on Friday and Saturday nights (and holiday Sundays) May through October and Saturday nights in April and November. Campers can avail themselves of two bathhouses with heated showers and toilets. Utility hookups aren't available, and alcohol is prohibited. The camping fee is $10 per person per night, or $5 for children 5-9, plus the next day's admission. No reservations needed.

Spectator Sports

In 2008 the Lehigh Valley welcomed its first Major League-affiliated baseball team since

Bear Creek Mountain Resort & Conference Center

the Allentown Red Sox relocated to western Pennsylvania nearly 50 years earlier. The **Lehigh Valley IronPigs** (Coca-Cola Park, 1050 IronPigs Way, Allentown, 610/841-7447, www.ironpigsbaseball.com) are the AAA affiliate of the Philadelphia Phillies, which made the World Series in 2008 and 2009, winning the first year and losing the second. The team's name, an homage to the region's steelmaking heritage, was derived from the term *pig iron,* which refers to ingots of crude iron that can be used to produce steel. Mascot Ferrous and his sidekick, FeFe, owe their monikers to the chemical name for iron.

The **Valley Preferred Cycling Center** (1151 Mosser Rd., Breinigsville, 610/395-7000, www.thevelodrome.com) has been bringing the world's best track cyclists to rural Lehigh County since the mid-1970s. The velodrome hosts races most Tuesdays, Fridays, and Saturdays during the summer. Racing legends including Marty Nothstein, Greg LeMond, and Bobby Julich have been known to show up at its cycling-specific flea markets, held each spring and fall.

ACCOMMODATIONS

The Lehigh Valley's hotels and motels are mostly of the chain variety, but unique accommodations aren't impossible to find. The ★ **Historic Hotel Bethlehem** (437 Main St., Bethlehem, 800/607-2384, www.hotelbethlehem.com, $159-475) fits the bill. Built in the Roaring Twenties to cater to clients of the mammoth Bethlehem Steel Corporation, the 128-room hotel features old-school grandeur, modern amenities, and a few friendly ghosts—or so it's said. It sits on the site of the first house built by Bethlehem's Moravian settlers, where on Christmas Eve of 1741 the missionaries named their community after the birthplace of Jesus Christ. The hotel's fine dining restaurant, **1741 on the Terrace,** boasts some of the best food in the Lehigh Valley, while the casual **Tap Room** specializes in comfort dishes. If you're not staying or dining at the Hotel Bethlehem, at least stop in to see the set of murals commissioned from artist George Gray in the 1930s. Hung in the aptly named Mural Ballroom, they chronicle Bethlehem's evolution from religious settlement to industrial center.

The **Grand Eastonian Suites Hotel** (140 Northampton St., Easton, 610/258-6350, www.grandeastoniansuiteshotel.com, $104-169), overlooking the Delaware and Lehigh Rivers, has a similarly long and rich history. Opened in 1927 as The Hotel Easton, it hosted the likes

Historic Hotel Bethlehem

of Eleanor Roosevelt, heavyweight champion Jack Dempsey, musician Tiny Tim, and John F. Kennedy before running into hard times in the 1980s and closing its doors. When a New York-based nonprofit dedicated to sustainable development purchased it in 2000, there were still unfinished drinks on the bar and unmade beds in the rooms. In the ensuing renovation, which preserved the brick and limestone facade and the original entrance, 140 guest rooms were transformed into 30 condos—just in time for a major downturn in real estate. With more than two-thirds of the units still unsold in 2008, the building returned to its roots as a hotel. Its suites boast handsome wood floors, kitchens with slate countertops and stainless steel appliances, spa tubs, fireplaces, flat-screen TVs, and free high-speed Internet. An indoor pool, a fitness center, and free parking round out the amenities.

For a romantic getaway, the **Glasbern Country Inn** (2141 Pack House Rd., Fogelsville, 610/285-4723, www.glasbern.com, $150-400) is unrivaled in the region. Located on a 100-acre working farm just west of Allentown, it features 38 rooms and suites in seven renovated farm buildings. The former stables house loft suites with cathedral ceilings, spiral staircases, and whirlpools. Rates include a hearty breakfast complete with house-made granola and bread. By evening the dining room transforms into a fine dining restaurant featuring farm-to-table cuisine.

FOOD

The sting of Bethlehem Steel's demise was still fresh when the **Bethlehem Brew Works** (569 Main St., Bethlehem, 610/882-1300, www.thebrewworks.com, 11am-11pm Sun.-Wed., 11am-midnight Thurs.-Sat., bar open until 2am daily, $8-29) opened in 1998. So it was only fitting that the brewpub pay tribute to the region's steelmaking heritage. Brick walls, exposed ducts, and furnishings accented with textured sheet metal contribute to an industrial vibe. A mural of Bethlehem Steel's once-mighty blast furnaces flanks gleaming beer tanks, where brews such as Steelworker's Oatmeal Stout and Blastberry Wheat mature. The food is respectable. Specialties include the Foundry Bratwurst, a locally made sausage topped with sauerkraut soaked in the Brew Works' own Valley Golden Ale, and a pulled-pork sandwich with beer-infused barbecue sauce.

In 2007 an abandoned furniture store building in downtown Allentown was reborn as the **Allentown Brew Works** (812 W. Hamilton St., Allentown, 610/433-7777, 11am-11pm Sun.-Thurs., 11am-midnight Fri.-Sat., bar open until midnight Sun.-Thurs. and 2am Fri.-Sat.). The steel theme of the Bethlehem original wasn't carried over, but the menu is largely the same. The place is massive. Mingle with mostly professional 20- to 50-somethings on the ground floor or enjoy a bird's-eye view from a table on the mezzanine.

For contemporary Italian cuisine and a little shopping on the side, head to **Melt** (2805 Center Valley Parkway, Center Valley, 610/798-9000, www.meltgrill.com, 11am-10pm Mon.-Thurs., 11am-11pm Fri.-Sat., 11am-9pm Sun., lunch $9-24, dinner $13-40). Located at The Promenade Shops at Saucon Valley, an upscale "lifestyle center" between Allentown and Bethlehem, the 350-seat restaurant offers the likes of bresaola (air-cured beef), osso bucco, and *spiedini* (skewers of mixed seafood). With its floor-to-ceiling wine wall, curved banquettes, and cylindrical chandeliers, it wouldn't be out of place in L.A. or Las Vegas. Its rooftop lounge, **Level 3** (5pm-2am Fri.-Sat. weather permitting), is as swanky as it gets in the Lehigh Valley. Melt is not to be confused with Bethlehem's **Melting Pot** (1 E. Broad St., Bethlehem, 484/241-4939, www.meltingpot.com, 5pm-10pm Mon.-Thurs., 5pm-11pm Fri., 4pm-11pm Sat., 4pm-9pm Sun., $15-42) franchise, which specializes in fondue.

For Italian in an intimate setting, it doesn't get better than **Sette Luna** (219 Ferry St., Easton, 610/253-8888, www.setteluna.com, 11:30am-9:30pm Mon.-Thurs., 11:30am-10:30pm Fri.-Sat., 10:30am-9pm Sun., $8-24). The trattoria in Easton's historic district is known for its crispy pizzas, house-made desserts, and Sunday jazz brunch.

INFORMATION AND SERVICES

Discover Lehigh Valley (610/882-9200, www.discoverlehighvalley.com), the region's tourism promotion agency, is a great source of information. Visit the website to request free brochures or page through a digital version of the *Official Visitors Guide*. If you're already in the area, you can load up on brochures at more than half a dozen visitors centers, including the **Historic Bethlehem Visitor Center** (505 Main St., Bethlehem, 610/691-6055, 10am-5pm Tues.-Sat., 11am-4pm Sun.).

GETTING THERE AND AROUND

Allentown, the largest city in the Lehigh Valley, is about 60 miles north of Philadelphia via I-476 and 90 miles east of New York City via I-78. **Lehigh Valley International Airport** (ABE, 800/359-5842, www.lvia. org) is less than 10 miles from downtown Allentown and Bethlehem. Intercity bus service to the area is available through **Greyhound** (800/231-2222, www.greyhound.com) and its interline partners. Local bus service is provided by the **Lehigh and Northampton Transportation Authority** (610/776-7433, www.lantabus.com), or LANTA.

Pennsylvania Dutch Country

Look for ★ to find recommended
sights, activities, dining, and lodging.

Highlights

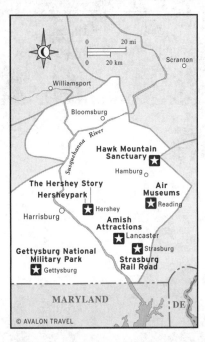

★ **Amish Attractions:** If you learned every-thing you know about the Amish from the movie *Witness*, you've got a lot to learn. Get schooled at Plain & Fancy Farm, the Amish Farm and House, or the Mennonite Information Center (page 121).

★ **Strasburg Rail Road:** Take a trip to Paradise on the nation's oldest operating short-line railroad (page 128).

★ **Air Museums:** Take to the skies in an antique plane, or take a trip back in time during World War II Weekend (page 151).

★ **Hawk Mountain Sanctuary:** Some 20,000 hawks, eagles, and falcons soar past this rap-tor sanctuary on their southward journey. The sight is awe-inspiring and the hiking terrific (page 153).

★ **The Hershey Story:** One of Pennsylvania's newest museums, The Hershey Story offers hands-on experience in chocolate-making (page 161).

★ **Hersheypark:** Hershey's century-old amusement park has been adding coasters like they're going out of style (page 163).

★ **Gettysburg National Military Park:** Site of the Civil War's most hellish battle, this national park is heaven for history buffs (page 192).

South-central Pennsylvania has no blockbuster cities. Its largest, Reading, has fewer than 90,000 residents. And yet, tourism is a multibillion-dollar industry here. Part of the reason is the public's fascination with the Amish, whose way of life is in

sharp contrast to the average American's. Lancaster County, the most popular destination in Dutch country, boasts the largest concentration of Amish in the world. Their use of horse-drawn buggies, adherence to strict dress codes, and rejection of technologies including television and computers makes them exotic. A casual drive through Lancaster County's fertile farmlands has a safari-esque quality. ("Look, honey, buggy at three o'clock!") Unlike giraffes and elephants, the Amish take offense to being photographed, so resist the temptation to aim your camera at the farmer working his fields with mule-drawn equipment, the children driving a pony cart, or the women selling their pies and preserves at a market stand.

There's more to the region's allure than the Amish experience. Less than 40 miles from the heart of Amish country is the town of Hershey, the product of one chocolatier's expansive vision. Few places offer as high a concentration of family-friendly attractions as "The Sweetest Place on Earth." In the southern part of Pennsylvania Dutch country is the town of Gettysburg, site of the Civil War's bloodiest battle and President Abraham Lincoln's most memorable speech. The place throbs with history—and not just on days when it's awash with musket-toting reenactors. The region is also home to the state capital, Harrisburg, and York County, the self-proclaimed "Factory Tour Capital of the World."

Travelers unfamiliar with the term *Pennsylvania Dutch* may wonder what south-central Pennsylvania has to do with the Netherlands. The answer is: nada. "Dutch," in this case, is generally regarded as a corruption of the word *Deutsch*, the German word for "German." Tens of thousands of German-speaking Europeans immigrated to Pennsylvania in the 18th century (before Germany as we know it existed). They, their descendants, and their English-influenced

Previous: Gettysburg; Amish buggy; Countries of Origin Chocolate Tasting at The Hershey Story. **Above:** the dome of the State Capitol.

Pennsylvania Dutch Country

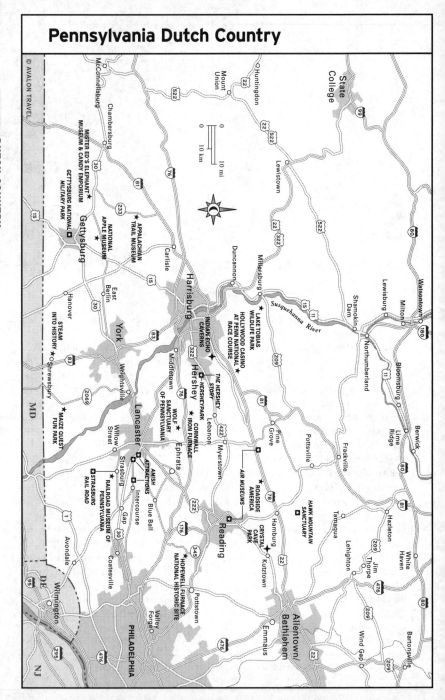

© AVALON TRAVEL

0   10 mi
0   10 km

State College

Mount Union
Huntingdon
Lewistown
Duncannon
Millersburg
Susquehanna River
Lewisburg
Milton
Watsontown
Shamokin Dam
Northumberland
Bloomsburg
Lime Ridge
Berwick

McConnellsburg
Chambersburg
MISTER ED'S ELEPHANT MUSEUM & CANDY EMPORIUM ★
GETTYSBURG NATIONAL MILITARY PARK ♦
Gettysburg
APPALACHIAN TRAIL MUSEUM ★
NATIONAL APPLE MUSEUM ♦
Carlisle
East Berlin
Hanover
STEAM INTO HISTORY ★
Shrewsbury
York
Wrightsville

Harrisburg
INDIAN ECHO CAVERNS ★
LAKE TOBIAS WILDLIFE PARK ★
HOLLYWOOD CASINO AT PENN NATIONAL RACE COURSE ★
THE HERSHEY STORY ★
HERSHEYPARK ★
Hershey
Middletown
WOLF SANCTUARY OF PENNSYLVANIA
Lebanon
CORNWALL IRON FURNACE ★
Myerstown
Pine Grove
Pottsville
Frackville
Tamaqua
Hazleton
White Haven

Willow Street
Lancaster
Strasburg
AMISH ATTRACTIONS ★
RAILROAD MUSEUM OF PENNSYLVANIA ♦
STRASBURG RAIL ROAD ★
Intercourse
Blue Ball
Gap
Ephrata
AIR MUSEUMS
ROADSIDE AMERICA ♦
CRYSTAL CAVE PARK ♦
Hamburg
Kutztown
Lehighton
Jim Thorpe
Wind Gap
Bartonsville

MAIZE QUEST FUN PARK ★
Avondale
Coatesville
HOPEWELL FURNACE NATIONAL HISTORIC SITE ★
Reading
Pottstown
Valley Forge
Emmaus
Allentown/ Bethlehem

Wilmington
PHILADELPHIA

MD
DE
NJ

HAWK MOUNTAIN SANCTUARY ♦

dialect came to be called Pennsylvania German, or Pennsylvania Dutch. A common misconception is that "Pennsylvania Dutch" is synonymous with "Amish." In fact, the Amish made up a very small percentage of the Germanic settlers. The overwhelming majority were affiliated with Lutheran or Reformed churches. But the Amish and a handful of related "plain" groups have emerged as the guardians of the Pennsylvania Dutch dialect. They speak it at home and among friends. Amish children learn English as part of their formal education, which typically takes place in a one-room schoolhouse (think *Little House on the Prairie*) and ends after the eighth grade. *Wilkom* to Pennsylvania Dutch country.

PLANNING YOUR TIME

You could spend weeks exploring the small, smaller, and smallest towns of Pennsylvania Dutch country, but three or four days is sufficient time to hit the highlights. Plan to spend at least a day tootling around Lancaster County's Amish countryside, sharing the roads with horse-drawn buggies and buying direct from farmers and bakers, quilters and furniture makers. Keep in mind that the Amish and their "plain" cousins don't do business on Sundays. See to it that you eat at a restaurant serving Pennsylvania Dutch fare, preferably one that offers family-style dining. If your agenda also includes outlet shopping, save it for the evening. The Rockvale and Tanger outlets, just minutes apart along Lancaster County's main east-west thoroughfare, are open until 9pm every day but Sunday. Anyone into antiques should plan to spend Sunday in Adamstown, aka "Antiques Capital USA," about 20 miles northeast of Lancaster city.

The Lancaster area is a good base of operations for exploring other parts of Pennsylvania Dutch country. Reading is about 30 miles to Lancaster's northeast, Hershey and Harrisburg are 30-40 miles to its northwest, and Gettysburg is 55 miles to its southwest. There was a time when demand for rooms in Lancaster County far exceeded supply. Some visitors slept in their cars; others settled for hotels and motels as far as an hour away. The local chamber of commerce beseeched residents with spare rooms to open their doors to Amish-obsessed tourists, and many answered the call. Today the county boasts more than 150 B&Bs.

If you have kids, a visit to Hershey is nonnegotiable. You'll run yourself ragged trying to hit all the attractions in one day, so set aside two. A day is generally enough for Gettysburg, but ardent history buffs and ghost hunters can keep busy for several.

Your trip through rural Lancaster County may take you over a covered bridge.

Lancaster County

In January 1955, *Plain and Fancy* opened on Broadway. The musical comedy is the story of two New Yorkers who travel to Bird-in-Hand, Pennsylvania—a real-life village amid Lancaster County's Amish farmlands—to sell a piece of property they've inherited. There, just a few hours from home, they encounter a way of life completely foreign to them. The Amish, or "plain," lifestyle was completely foreign to most playgoers, too. A modest success on Broadway, the show sparked enormous interest in its setting. Before *Plain and Fancy*, Lancaster County was lucky to get 25,000 visitors a year. After, the number rocketed to more than two million. Tourists traipsed through farm fields, knocked on doors, and peered through windows in their quest for a close encounter of the Amish kind. Today there's no need to trespass. Lancaster County, which now welcomes upwards of 10 million visitors annually, is flush with information centers, attractions, and tour operators offering an Amish 101 curriculum.

About 282,000 Amish live in North America, according to the Young Center for Anabaptist and Pietist Studies at Lancaster County's Elizabethtown College. Though the church originated in Europe, it's extinct there. Lancaster County is home to about 33,000 Amish—roughly half of Pennsylvania's Amish—and is neck and neck with Ohio's Holmes County for the distinction of having the world's largest Amish settlement. It also holds the distinction of having the oldest surviving Amish settlement in the world. The first ship carrying a significant group of Amish from their homelands in central Europe to the New World docked in Philadelphia in 1737. Some of the Amish passengers made their home in Lancaster County; a larger number settled 20-odd miles away in present-day Berks County. While the Amish all but disappeared from Berks County by the early 1800s, Lancaster County had six congregations (known as church districts) at the close of the century. Their numbers have soared since then, more than doubling between 1980 and 2000 and climbing more than 30 percent in the first decade of this century. Large families have

Bird-in-Hand

Lancaster County

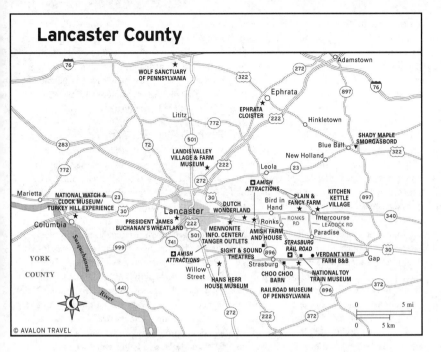

© AVALON TRAVEL

a lot to do with the vigorous growth: most Amish couples have five or more children. And while many Amish teens are allowed a period of *rumspringa,* or "running around," during which they decide whether to join the church, very few leave the fold. Given the chance to drive cars and dress how they please, about 85 percent ultimately choose the horse and buggy as their mode of transport and the distinctive garb that sets them apart from the "English," i.e., everyone else.

As you explore the region, keep in mind that not all traditionally dressed people are Amish. Some conservative Mennonite and Brethren groups also practice "plain" dress. You may not be able to tell them apart, but each has distinguishing characteristics.

There's more to Lancaster County than its Amish population. The county seat, Lancaster city, boasts a thriving arts scene. Rail fans will find an abundance of train-related attractions in and around the town of Strasburg. Antiques enthusiasts will fall in love with Adamstown, aka "Antiques Capital USA." Bargain hunters

can get their fix at a pair of outlet malls along Route 30. Anyone fascinated by the Amish and their strict codes of conduct will likely be fascinated by the towns of Lititz and Ephrata. The former began as an experiment in utopia by members of a Protestant denomination that prohibited everything from dancing to changing professions without approval from church elders. The latter was home to a religious group so disdainful of worldly pleasures that its members slept on wooden pillows. Other Lancaster County communities are remarkable for their names: Intercourse, Paradise, Blue Ball, Fertility, and, of course, Bird-in-Hand.

★ AMISH ATTRACTIONS

If you're visiting Lancaster County for the number one reason people visit Lancaster County—to see the Amish—you may be at a loss as to where to start. Unlike malls and museums, amusement parks and ski resorts, the Amish are an attraction without an address. You can't punch "Amish" into your GPS and get turn-by-turn directions. They're people living their lives—people who don't necessarily appreciate being the focus of tourists' attention. And while it's not hard to catch sight of them living their lives, you'll shortchange yourself if you don't garner some understanding of why they live the way they do.

Plain & Fancy Farm, the Amish Farm and House, and the Mennonite Information Center are great places to acquaint yourself with the ways of the Amish. Visiting one is quite enough. Each offers a hearty menu of get-to-know-the-Amish options. Choosing between the attractions is a matter of taste. Plain & Fancy is smack-dab in the heart of Amish country, while the other two are located along Route 30, a major east-west thoroughfare. It's the only one that offers buggy rides through Amish countryside and the opportunity to visit an Amish family in their home, but it's also the priciest of the three. The Amish Farm and House is your best bet if you're traveling with kids. It's crawling with animals and offers a variety of children's activities, including pony rides, a corn maze, and "Buttercup," a life-size fiberglass cow always ready to be milked. While all three offer driving tours of the countryside, the Mennonite Information Center is unique in that it doesn't operate tour buses. Instead, a guide will climb into your car and lead you on a personal tour. It's the way to go if you tend to ask loads of questions. It's also a great value: just $49 for a vehicle carrying as many as seven people. On the downside, the Mennonite Information Center is closed on Sundays.

Plain & Fancy Farm

In 1958, a few years after *Plain and Fancy* hit the Broadway stage, a man named Walter Smith built an Amish-style house and barn along Route 340, midway between the villages of Bird-in-Hand and Intercourse, with the intent of giving house tours and holding barn dances. Shrewdly, he named the property after the Broadway musical that ignited so much interest in Amish country. Half a century later, **Plain & Fancy Farm** (3121 Old Philadelphia Pike, Bird-in-Hand, www.plainandfancyfarm.com) offers everything a tourist could want: food, lodging, souvenirs, and an excellent orientation to the Amish way of life.

A good place to begin your orientation: the **Amish Experience Theater** (717/768-8400, ext. 210, www.amishexperience.com, open daily mid-Mar.-Nov. and select days in Dec., shows on the hour 10am-5pm, admission $10.95, children 4-12 $7.95). This is not

a one-room schoolhouse at the Amish Farm and House

your garden-variety movie theater. Designed to look like a barn, it features five screens, a fog machine, and other bells and whistles that produce three-dimensional effects. *Jacob's Choice*, the film for which the theater was built, packs some 400 years of history into 40 minutes. It's the contemporary story of an Old Order Amish family and the teenage son torn between joining the church and leaving the fold for a modern life. As the title character learns about the persecution his religious ancestors faced in Europe and their journey to the New World, so does the audience. Filmed locally in 1995, *Jacob's Choice* doesn't dwell on the blood and gore, but a burning-at-the-stake scene could rattle children.

The Amish-style house Mr. Smith built back in 1958 is still open for tours. Tickets can be purchased at the Amish Experience Theater box office. Now known as the **Amish Country Homestead** (open daily mid-Mar.-late Nov. and select days in Dec., admission $10.95, children 4-12 $7.95), the nine-room house is continually updated to reflect changes in the Amish lifestyle. (Contrary to popular belief, the Amish don't live just as they did centuries ago.) Guides explain such head-scratchers as why the Amish eschew electricity but use refrigerators and other appliances powered by propane gas. The tour takes about 45 minutes. Combo tickets for the theater and house tour are available.

Several minibus tours depart from the theater. The most popular is the **Amish Farmlands Tour** (daily mid-Mar.-Nov. and select days in Dec., $27.95, children 12 and under $15.95), a 90-minute cruise through the surrounding countryside. Guides are well-versed in the Amish way of life. A "SuperSaver Package" is available for those who wish to experience *Jacob's Choice*, the house tour, and the Farmlands Tour.

Other tours include the **Visit-in-Person Tour** (June-Nov., $49.95), which gives visitors the opportunity to interact with Amish locals. Participants visit an Amish dairy farm during milking time and then an Amish craftsperson. The three-hour excursion culminates in a sit-down chat at an Amish home. It often sells out, so it's a good idea to purchase tickets in advance. Harrison Ford fans may opt for the **Witness Tour** (May-Oct., $49.95), featuring a visit to the farm where he filmed the 1985 thriller *Witness*.

The bus tours are top-notch, but if you're short on time or traveling with kids, a buggy ride is the way to go. **Aaron and Jessica's Buggy Rides** (9am-dusk Mon.-Sat. and 10am-5pm Sun. Apr.-Nov., 9am-4:30pm Mon.-Sat. Dec.-Mar., 717/768-8828, www.amishbuggyrides.com) depart from Plain & Fancy Farm on a regular basis. Trips range from 20 minutes to more than an hour, with prices starting at $10 for adults and $5 for children 3-12. Aaron and Jessica's—named for owner Jack Meyer's oldest daughter and her first horse—bills itself as Lancaster County's only buggy tour operator staffed entirely by "plain" people (except on Sundays, which they set aside for worship).

Plain & Fancy Farm's main attraction is its restaurant, famous for its family-style meals. The on-site AmishView Inn & Suites makes Plain & Fancy Farm a 24-hour attraction.

The Amish Farm and House

The easiest way to find the **Amish Farm and House** (2395 Lincoln Hwy. East, Lancaster, 717/394-6185, www.amishfarmandhouse.com, 10am-4pm daily Jan.-Mar., 9am-5pm daily Apr.-May, 9am-6pm daily June-Aug., 9am-5pm daily Sept.-Oct., 10am-4pm daily Nov.-Dec., admission $8.95, seniors $7.95, children 5-11 $5.95) is to look for its neighbor, a Target. The store opened in 2005 on property carved from the hundreds-year-old farm, and its bull's-eye logo is easier to spot than the barn, silo, and windmill that once dominated the skyline. Their juxtaposition is emblematic of the Amish community's insoluble dilemma: modernity.

Opened to the public in July 1955, the Amish Farm and House bills itself as the first tourist attraction in Lancaster County and the first Amish attraction in the United States. The operating farm has since shrunk from 25 acres to 15 (making room for Target, PetSmart, Panera, etc.), but there's more to see than ever. Start with a guided tour of the farmhouse, included in general admission. Built in 1805 of limestone quarried on the property, the house has counted Quakers, Mennonites, and Amish as residents. Today it's furnished in the manner of a typical Amish home. The front room features wooden benches arranged in preparation for a church service, opening the door for a discussion of why the Amish worship in their homes and other aspects of their religion. Their manner of dress is explained in the bedrooms. After the 45-minute tour, explore the farm at your own pace. Children love the chicken house and the 1803 barn with its cows, horses, and pigs. A goat playground makes for great photo ops with the frisky ruminants. Kids (we're talking humans now, not goats) also enjoy the corn maze, up and running mid-July through October, and tootling around on Amish scooters when weather permits. The farm also has an original tobacco shed, one of the few remaining lime kilns in Lancaster County, a working waterwheel, a circa 1855 covered bridge, and a one-room Amish schoolhouse built specifically for tourists in 2006.

The Amish Farm and House offers 90-minute **Countryside Tours** ($19.95, children 5-11 $12.95, children 4 and under $4.95) year-round. Reservations are recommended, especially in the warmer months. The minibus tours usually stop at an Amish roadside stand or two (except on Sundays, when the Amish don't conduct business). Combo tickets for the house, farm, and bus tour are available.

Mennonite Information Center

Don't be put off by its name. You *will* learn about the Amish at the **Mennonite Information Center** (2209 Millstream Rd., Lancaster, 717/299-0954, www.mennoniteinfoctr.com, 8am-5pm Mon.-Sat. Apr.-Oct., 8:30am-4:30pm Mon.-Sat. Nov.-Mar.), located next to Tanger Outlets. Start by watching the three-screen feature *Who Are the Amish?* (on the hour 9am-4pm, $6, children 6-16 $4). It answers such questions as: How many are there? Why do they dress that way? Why do they drive buggies? And what do they have against electricity? The images are beautiful and the narration intelligent, but at 30 minutes long, the movie won't necessarily hold the attention of young children. Also showing: *Postcards From a Heritage of Faith,* which elucidates the similarities and differences between the Amish and

A buggy ride is a great way to see the countryside.

Mennonites, both of whom trace their roots to the Anabaptist movement in 16th-century Europe. (Anabaptists rejected infant baptism and advocated for separation of church and state, for which they faced severe persecution.) There's no charge to see the 17-minute film, shown on the half hour. Admission to the center's exhibits on Anabaptist life is also free.

Movies and exhibits are nice, but what sets the Mennonite Information Center apart are its **personal tours of Amish country.** For about the cost of two seats on other countryside tours, a guide will hop in your vehicle and point the way to Amish farms, one-room schoolhouses, quilt shops, covered bridges, etc. All guides have a Mennonite or Amish heritage. The rate for a vehicle with 1-7 people is $49 for two hours, $16 for each additional hour. Call ahead to arrange for a tour at a specified time or just show up and request one. The wait for a guide is rarely longer than 30 minutes. Another great service from the Mennonite Information Center is its list of **Mennonite guest homes,** available on its website and in pamphlet form at the center.

The center is home to a life-size reproduction of the portable place of worship described in the biblical book of Exodus. A wax figure of the high priest sports a breastplate of gold and precious stones. The **Biblical Tabernacle Reproduction** (admission $7.50, children 6-16 $5) can only be seen by guided tour, offered at regular intervals year-round. The reproduction has no real connection to Lancaster County's Anabaptist communities. It was constructed in the 1940s by a Baptist minister in St. Petersburg, Florida, purchased by Mennonites in the 1950s, and installed in its current home in the 1970s.

The information center sells a variety of tabernacle model kits, fair-trade handicrafts from around the world, and a wide selection of books about Anabaptist history and faith.

Next door to the center is the headquarters of the **Lancaster Mennonite Historical Society** (2215 Millstream Rd., 717/393-9745, www.lmhs.org, 8:30am-4:30pm Tues.-Sat.), which also boasts a fantastic bookstore. It has a museum (admission $5, seniors $4.50, students $3) that showcases Pennsylvania German artifacts.

DOWNTOWN LANCASTER

It's not unusual for tourists to come and go from Lancaster County without stepping foot in downtown Lancaster. Many are entirely unaware that the county has an urban center. It's hard to blame them. Lancaster County's countryside and quaint towns have gotten all the press for decades. It doesn't help that its major east-west thoroughfare, Route 30, bypasses downtown Lancaster altogether. Well, downtown's museums and merchants have had just about enough of being ignored. Revitalization efforts in recent years have given downtown a fresh look and its boosters more cred. Now, in addition to boasting the oldest continuously operated farmers market and theater in the United States, downtown boasts a new convention center and adjoining 19-floor hotel. New restaurants, stores, and galleries add to its promotional arsenal. Plan on devoting a day to downtown. Make it a Tuesday, Friday, or Saturday, when the farmers market is open. Ideally, make it the first or third Friday of any given month, when many galleries, boutiques, and other businesses extend their hours. **First Fridays** (5pm-9pm, 717/291-4758, www.lancasterarts.com) feature special exhibitions, artist receptions, and other arts-related events. Live music wafts from one doorway after another on third Fridays, known as **Music Fridays** (717/291-4758, www.lancastercityevents.com).

Walking Tour

The city of Lancaster is so steeped in history—it was capital of the 13 colonies for one day during the American Revolution and capital of Pennsylvania for 13 years—that a guided tour is a good idea. Led by a volunteer guide in 18th- or 19th-century garb, the **Historic Lancaster Walking Tour** (Lancaster Visitors Center, 5 W. King St., 717/392-1776, www.historiclancasterwalkingtour.com, $7, seniors $6, college students $4, children 6-18 $1) visits dozens of sites. Allow about 90 minutes for the tour, which begins with a DVD presentation. It's offered at 1pm daily April-October. On Tuesdays, Fridays, and Saturdays, when nearby Central Market is open, tours depart at 10am as well as 1pm.

Central Market

Central Market (23 N. Market St., 717/735-6890, www.centralmarketlancaster.com, 6am-4pm Tues. and Fri., 6am-2pm Sat.) is the pulsing heart of the city. Granted, the indoor farmers market pulses just three days a week, but given its advanced age, it's incredible that it pulses at all. Central Market is the oldest continually operated farmers market in the country. When Lancaster was laid out in the 1730s, a lot adjacent to the town square was designated as a public marketplace in perpetuity. In its early years, the market was simply an open space where farmers and others could sell their wares. The current market house, an eye-catching Romanesque Revival structure with two towers and ornate brick and stone work, was built in 1889. Many of the 60-some market stalls have been operated by multiple generations of the same family. The Stoner's vegetable stall, famous for its arugula, has been around for more than a century. Fresh produce isn't the half of it. Central Market is one-stop shopping for everything from hand-stitched Amish quilts to foie gras. There's beef, poultry, and fish; milk and cheeses; breads and pastries; coffees and teas; candies and candles; preserves and prepared foods. There's even a stall devoted to horseradish. Come on the early side for the best selection. On Tuesdays and Fridays, some vendors call it quits at 3pm, an hour before the market closes.

Art Museums and Galleries

Lancaster has a thriving arts scene, with several dozen galleries, artist studios, fine craft stores, and art museums. It has an art college and even an art-themed hotel. The **Lancaster City Arts** (717/291-4758, www.lancasterarts.com) website is a good resource for visitors who wish to explore the scene. There's no better place to start than **Gallery Row,** roughly defined as the section of Prince Street between Walnut Street and King Street to its south. Notable tenants include the **Red Raven Art Company** (138 N. Prince St., 717/299-4400, www.redravenartcompany.com, 10am-5pm Tues. and Thurs.-Sat., open until 8:30pm First Fridays), which showcases a diverse array of fine art. If you're partial to folk art, you'll dig **CityFolk** (146 N. Prince St., 717/393-8807,

a bird's-eye view of downtown Lancaster

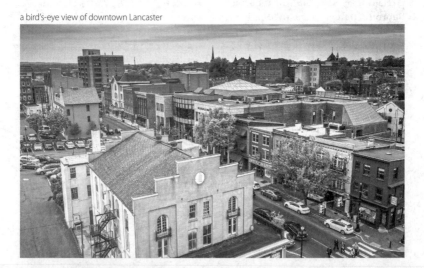

www.cityfolkonprince.com, 10am-4pm Tues.-Sat., open until 9pm First Fridays) with its ever-changing galleries of furniture, paintings, carvings, pottery, and other works.

A couple of blocks east of Gallery Row is the onetime home of Lancaster's most acclaimed artist, the Modernist painter Charles Demuth. It's now open to the public as the **Demuth Museum** (120 E. King St., 717/299-9940, www.demuth.org, 10am-4pm Tues.-Sat., 1pm-4pm Sun., closed Jan., free admission). Demuth was born in Lancaster in 1883 and died there in 1935 but moved in avant-garde circles in places as far-flung as Paris, New York, and Bermuda. He was very much appreciated during his lifetime, earning a place in the permanent collection of New York's Metropolitan Museum of Art by his 40s. Rotating exhibits showcase works by Demuth's contemporaries or artists with a thematic or stylistic connection to him.

Not to be forgotten is the **Lancaster Museum of Art** (135 N. Lime St., 717/394-3497, www.lmapa.org, 10am-4pm Tues.-Sat., noon-4pm Sun., free admission), home to an extensive collection of works by contemporary regional artists. The museum building is a remarkably intact example of Greek Revival-style domestic architecture. The Grubb Mansion, as it's called, was built in the 1840s for an iron master with an eye for art.

Lancaster Science Factory

Geared toward children 7-13, the **Lancaster Science Factory** (454 New Holland Ave., 717/509-6363, www.lancastersciencefactory. org, 10am-5pm Tues.-Sat., noon-5pm Sun., open Mon. Memorial Day-Labor Day, admission $8, seniors $7, children 3-15 $6.50) features dozens of interactive exhibits that help visitors—even those well over 13—understand such things as electricity, magnetism, acoustics, and fluid dynamics. If your kids like blowing bubbles, they'll love the *Minimal Surfaces* exhibit. Budding Beethovens can experiment with the "bongophone," a bongo/xylophone. The Fac, which opened in 2008 after five years in the making, isn't the only

science museum in Lancaster. Less than two miles away is the **North Museum of Natural History & Science** (400 College Ave., 717/291-3941, www.northmuseum.org, 10am-5pm Tues.-Sat., noon-5pm Sun., admission $7.50, seniors and children 3-17 $6.50, museum and planetarium admission $10, seniors and children $9), which boasts a dinosaur gallery, live animal room, and planetarium.

"TRAIN TOWN USA"

The town of **Strasburg,** some nine miles southwest of downtown Lancaster, bills itself as "the real Lancaster County." Which is to say that it has changed little in the last couple of centuries. Buggies clip-clop through the town square at the intersection of Routes 741 and 896. Families stream in and out of the old-timey **Strasburg Country Store & Creamery** (1 W. Main St., Strasburg, 717/687-0766, www.strasburg.com, open daily), where scoops of homemade ice cream are pressed into just-made waffle cones. Much of *Witness,* the 1985 romantic thriller that did more for tourism to Amish country than any marketing campaign, was filmed on a farm nearby.

But what brings tourists here by the busload is train mania. There are half a dozen train-related attractions within two miles of the square, including the **Red Caboose Motel and Restaurant** (312 Paradise Ln., Ronks, 717/687-5000, www.redcaboosemotel. com, accommodations $70-160, food $4-17), where rail fans bed down and chow down in refurbished train cars and cabooses. The Strasburg area is such a magnet for "foamers," as the most zealous of rail fans are known, that it's sometimes called "Train Town USA" (not to be confused with "Railroad City," aka Altoona, three hours away). The oldest of the attractions and a good place to start is the Strasburg Rail Road. Don't leave town without a visit to the Choo Choo Barn, where you can see the historic railroad and much more in miniature.

From the town square, head east on Route 741 (Main Street). You'll see the Choo Choo Barn on your right after half a mile. Half a mile later, you'll arrive at the Strasburg Rail Road and Railroad Museum of Pennsylvania, located on opposite sides of Route 741. Continue to the next intersection and turn left onto Paradise Lane to check into the Red Caboose or check out the National Toy Train Museum.

★ Strasburg Rail Road

Incorporated in 1832, the **Strasburg Rail Road** (300 Gap Rd., Ronks, 866/725-9666, www.strasburgrailroad.com) is America's oldest operating short-line railroad. It was almost abandoned in the late 1950s, after an upsurge in the use of highways for freight transportation and a series of storms that destroyed parts of its 4.5-mile track. But rail fans came to its rescue, turning it into a tourist attraction and time capsule of early-1900s railroading. The Strasburg Rail Road offers trips to Paradise and back—as in Paradise, Pennsylvania—every month but January. Steam locomotives pull painstakingly restored passenger cars past farm fields plowed by horses and mules. Amish buggies wait at railroad crossings.

Ticket prices vary widely, depending on the type of excursion and your choice of passenger car. In addition to standard rides, which depart hourly on most operating days, the Strasburg Rail Road offers a wide variety of themed trips, from murder mystery dinners to "The Great Train Robbery" to "Santa's Paradise Express." On select days each June, September, and November, fans of Thomas the Tank Engine can ride behind a steam locomotive based on the storybook character. **"Day Out With Thomas"** and other themed trips sometimes sell out, so it's a good idea to purchase tickets in advance.

The round-trip takes just 45 minutes, but train buffs and families with young children should plan to spend a couple of hours at the home station. A guided tour of the railroad's mechanical shop ($18) is offered at noon on most operating days. It's limited to 25 people and often sells out. Kids can operate a vintage pump car along a short track or ride in a circa 1920 miniature steam train. A train-themed play area was added in 2013. The station also features gift shops geared toward train lovers, a toy store with a large selection of Thomas the Tank Engine merchandise, and a café. Consider packing a picnic basket or buying a box lunch at the station and disembarking the train at one of two picnic groves. Groff's Grove is popular with families because it has vintage playground equipment and is convenient to Cherry Crest Adventure Farm. (The

Strasburg Rail Road

Strasburg Rail Road sells discounted Cherry Crest tickets.) Leaman Place Grove, at the end of the line, appeals to rail fans because it's adjacent to active Amtrak lines. Just don't miss the last train back.

Combo passes good for a train ride and admission to the nearby Railroad Museum of Pennsylvania are available.

Railroad Museum of Pennsylvania

Directly across the street from the Strasburg Rail Road, the **Railroad Museum of Pennsylvania** (300 Gap Rd., Ronks, 717/687-8628, www.rrmuseumpa.org, 9am-5pm Mon.-Sat., noon-5pm Sun., closed Mon. Nov.-Mar., admission $10, seniors $9, children 3-11 $8) boasts a world-class collection of railroad artifacts, including many last-of-their-kind locomotives. Its 100,000-square-foot exhibit hall holds some 50 locomotives and rail cars. Dozens of others reside in the restoration yard, which is open to visitors when weather and staffing permit. The museum offers daily tours of its restoration shop, normally closed to the public for safety reasons. The $10 tour fee directly benefits the museum's efforts to rescue historic railroad equipment from extinction.

Rail fans hoping to find a rare "Big Boy" steam locomotive will be disappointed. The museum, which opened in 1975, is owned and operated by the Pennsylvania Historical and Museum Commission and endeavors to preserve objects relating to the history of railroading in Pennsylvania. The legendary Big Boys didn't ply Pennsylvania's rails. With its 195-ton engine, Pennsylvania Railroad "Mountain" No. 6755 is the largest and heaviest steam locomotive in the museum's collection.

National Toy Train Museum

Real trains are well and good, but there's something enchanting about their much-shrunken kin. Which makes the **National Toy Train Museum** (300 Paradise Ln., Strasburg, 717/687-8976, www.nttmuseum. org, hours vary by season, admission $7, seniors $6, children 6-12 $4) an exceptionally enchanting place. It houses one of the most extensive collections of toy trains in the world. More than 100 different manufacturers are represented in the museum's collection, which includes some of the earliest and rarest toy trains. It also includes some model trains. The museum, which aspires to look like a Victorian-era station, has five large train layouts.

The museum is operated by the Train Collectors Association, which has its national headquarters there. Those new to "the world's greatest hobby," as the TCA calls it, can learn the ropes via video presentations in the museum. Seasoned collectors can bury their noses in repair guides, trade catalogs, and other materials in the reference library.

Choo Choo Barn

Model train enthusiasts can also find nirvana at the **Choo Choo Barn** (226 Gap Rd., Strasburg, 717/687-7911, www.choochoobarn. com, 10am-5pm daily mid-Mar.-Dec. and select days in Jan., admission $7, children 3-12 $4), which predates the National Toy Train Museum. The family-owned attraction has just one layout: a massive, marvelous display featuring 22 operating trains and more than 150 animated figures and vehicles. Local landmarks including the Strasburg Rail Road and Dutch Wonderland amusement park are represented.

Located next to the Choo Choo Barn, the **Strasburg Train Shop** (717/687-0464, www. etrainshop.com, 10am-5pm daily) caters to the layout builder. It's known as the place to go for uncommon things such as garbage cans.

OTHER SIGHTS
President James Buchanan's Wheatland

The only U.S. president from Pennsylvania lived—and died—on a handsome estate west of downtown Lancaster. James Buchanan, the only bachelor to lead the nation, was secretary of state when he moved to **Wheatland** (230

N. President Ave., Lancaster, 717/392-4633, www.lancasterhistory.org, tours on the hour 10am-3pm Mon.-Sat. Apr.-Oct., hours vary Nov.-Mar., admission $10, seniors $8, children 10 and under free, Yuletide at Wheatland admission $12, children 6-13 $6) in 1848. He announced his 1856 presidential campaign on the front porch of the Federal-style mansion. Reviled for his wishy-washiness on slavery and his handling of the secession crisis, the 15th president penned a defensive memoir after retiring to Wheatland in 1861. His writing desk is among the many artifacts displayed throughout the manse today. The collection includes everything from his White House china to his bathing tub and even a bottle of 1827 Madeira, now half evaporated, from his wine cellar. Buchanan died at his beloved Wheatland in 1868 and is buried at Woodward Hill Cemetery in Lancaster.

Wheatland is part of the campus of LancasterHistory.org, a nonprofit historical organization formed by the 2009 merger of the Lancaster County Historical Society and the James Buchanan Foundation for the Preservation of Wheatland. The campus is also home to an arboretum with more than 100 species of trees. The newly redesigned and expanded **LancasterHistory.org** headquarters (9:30am-5pm Mon., Wed., and Fri.-Sat., 9:30am-8pm Tues. and Thurs.) has several galleries, which are worth visiting if you're interested in Lancaster County's unique history. Gallery admission is $7 for adults, $5 for seniors and students 11-17. A discount applies when combined with a tour of Wheatland.

Dutch Wonderland

Dutch Wonderland (2249 Lincoln Hwy. E., Lancaster, 717/291-1888, www.dutchwonderland.com) doesn't boast of adrenaline-pumping rides like many amusement parks. Its coaster count has stood at two for more than a decade, and you wouldn't call them hair-raising. The 48-acre park, fronted by a castle facade visible from Route 30, bills itself as "A Kingdom for Kids." In addition to 30-some rides, it offers a variety of live shows daily. They're all quite delightful but none so much as the high-dive shows at Herr's Aqua Stadium. Performers twist, somersault, and splash their way through Disneyesque storylines. Bring swimsuits for Duke's Lagoon, the park's water play area.

Dutch Wonderland is open daily from late May through Labor Day and some weekends before and after that period. Gates open at

President James Buchanan's Wheatland

10am. A variety of admission plans are available. One-day admission is $36.75 for guests ages 3-59, $31.75 for adults 60-69, $23.75 for those 70 and older. Hang on to your ticket stub in case you decide to come back the next day; consecutive-day admission is $28.75. A two-day flex pass, good for visits on any two days during the season, is $52 for anyone 3 or older. If your summer plans also include Hersheypark in nearby Hershey, ask about combo tickets. Hershey Entertainment & Resorts acquired Dutch Wonderland in 2001.

Cherry Crest Adventure Farm

Dutch Wonderland isn't the only must-stop attraction for pint-size visitors to Lancaster County. There's also **Cherry Crest Adventure Farm** (150 Cherry Hill Rd., Ronks, 717/687-6843, www.cherrycrestfarm.com), where every summer a five-acre cornfield is transformed into the Amazing Maize Maze. This maze is no cakewalk. It takes most visitors about an hour to find the exit. But there's no danger of getting hopelessly lost—or bored for that matter. Helpful "Maze Masters" are always on hand, and the paths are peppered with clues and diversions. Open from the week of July 4 though early November, the maze isn't the only attraction on the working farm. Kids can crawl through a hay tunnel, slide down a hay chute on a burlap sack, or hurl pumpkins with giant slingshots. They can ride pedal karts or a tractor-pulled wagon. They can even watch chicks hatch and hold the little fuzzballs. Now that's agritainment.

Cherry Crest is open Saturdays starting Memorial Day weekend; Tuesday-Saturday from the week of July 4 to Labor Day; select days in September; and Thursday-Saturday in October and early November. Admission is $10 before the maze opens and $15-18 afterward, with no charge for children two and under. Cherry Crest, which is not an Amish farm, is just east of Strasburg, less than three miles from the Strasburg Rail Road. In fact, the excursion trains stop at Cherry Crest to pick up and drop off passengers. Cherry Crest sells discounted Strasburg Rail Road tickets.

Kitchen Kettle Village

What started as a home-based jelly-making business has grown into **Kitchen Kettle Village** (3529 Old Philadelphia Pike, Intercourse, 717/768-8261, www.kitchenkettle.com, 9am-6pm Mon.-Sat. May-Oct., 9am-5pm Mon.-Sat. Nov.-Apr.), home to about 40 specialty shops, a pair of restaurants, and a handful of kid-centric attractions. To call it a mall would fail to convey its quaintness. Think of it as a mall in a fairy tale—the sort of place where Snow White would buy ribbons for her hair. The canning kitchen is still the heart of it all. Its repertoire has grown to include not just jellies, jams, and preserves but also relishes, pickles, mustards, salad dressings, grilling sauces, and salsas. All products are made by hand in small batches, and visitors get a front-seat view. (Because the kitchen is staffed by Amish women, photos aren't permitted.) Plenty of visitors have discovered a taste for pickled beets or pepper jam in the **Jam & Relish Kitchen,** which abounds with samples. An attached bakery fills the air with the smells of shoofly pie, whoopie pies, molasses snaps, snickerdoodle cookies, and other local favorites.

Many of the village shops feature locally made foods or goods, including ice cream from a dairy farm just a few miles away, fudge and kettle corn made on-site, fabric bags, quilts, and pottery. The popular **Kling House Restaurant** (8am-3pm Mon.-Thurs., 8am-4pm Fri.-Sat., breakfast $4-9, lunch $8-15) serves the likes of cinnamon-raisin French toast and baked oatmeal for breakfast, a variety of sandwiches, flatbread pizzas, and entrées for lunch, and a killer coconut cream pie. There's also a cafeteria-style restaurant.

The village is home base to **AAA Buggy Rides** (717/989-2829, www.aaabuggyrides.com, 9am-6pm Mon.-Sat. May-Oct., 9am-5pm Mon.-Sat. in Apr. and Nov.), which offers a 35-minute ride ($14, children 3-12 $7) through Amish countryside and a 55-minute ride ($18, children 3-12 $9) that passes over a covered bridge. Other village attractions include pony rides, a petting zoo, and a playground.

Want to stick around after dark? Scattered throughout the village are guest rooms and suites collectively known as **The Inn at Kitchen Kettle Village** ($110-200). Rates include breakfast at the Kling House Restaurant every day except Sunday. Book well in advance if you're coming for the **Rhubarb Festival** (third weekend in May) or another of the village's annual events.

Landis Valley Village & Farm Museum

Born two years apart in the 1860s, brothers Henry and George Landis had a lot in common. Both became engineers. Neither married. They were the kind of people who never threw anything away—the kind who collected things other people regarded as valueless. By 1925 the brothers had amassed so many objects reflective of Pennsylvania German rural life that they opened a small museum on their homestead a few miles north of downtown Lancaster, charging visitors 25 cents apiece. They died a year apart in the 1950s, but the **Landis Valley Village & Farm Museum** (2451 Kissel Hill Rd., Lancaster, 717/569-0401, www.landisvalleymuseum.org, 9am-5pm Mon.-Sat., noon-5pm Sun., admission $12, seniors $10, children 3-11 $8) lives on. Owned by the state since 1953, it has grown into an assemblage of 30-plus historic and re-created buildings housing a collection of more than 100,000 farm, trade, and household artifacts. While some historic buildings are original to the site, including the Landis brothers' 1870s house, many were relocated here over the years. They include a blacksmith shop, a circa 1800 log building that houses exhibits on early printing and leatherworking, and a late 1800s schoolhouse complete with authentic furnishings. Rather than a time capsule of a particular era, Landis Valley is a repository for all things illustrative of Pennsylvania Dutch village and farm life from the mid-1700s to

mid-1900s. Costumed interpreters are often on hand to demonstrate skills such as open-hearth cooking, horse-drawn plowing, tin-smithing, wood carving, and weaving. Heirloom gardens and heritage breed farm animals help bring the past to life. Be sure to stop by the museum store, which features traditional handicrafts.

Landis Valley shares a parking lot with **Hands-on House** (721 Landis Valley Rd., Lancaster, 717/569-5437, www.handson-house.org, 10am-5pm Mon.-Thurs. and Sat., 10am-8pm Fri., noon-5pm Sun. Memorial Day-Labor Day, 11am-4pm Tues.-Thurs., 11am-8pm Fri., 10am-5pm Sat., noon-5pm Sun. Labor Day-Memorial Day, admission $8.50), a museum designed for children 2-10.

Hans Herr House Museum

Built in 1719, the **Hans Herr House** (1849 Hans Herr Dr., Willow Street, 717/464-4438, www.hansherr.org, 9am-4pm Mon.-Sat. Apr.-Nov.) is the oldest structure in Lancaster County and the oldest Mennonite meeting-house in the Western Hemisphere. Though named for the Mennonite bishop whose flock established the first permanent European settlement in present-day Lancaster County, the stone house was actually built by his son Christian. Today it's the centerpiece of a museum complex that also includes two 19th-century Pennsylvania German farmhouses, several barns and other outbuildings, and a collection of farm equipment spanning three centuries. In 2013 the museum unveiled a replica of a Native American longhouse. The 62-foot-long structure was modeled on remnants of a longhouse excavated locally in 1969. It's one of the country's few replica longhouses—multifamily homes made of logs, saplings, and tree bark.

You can explore the grounds at your own pace—for free—but the Herr House and longhouse can only be seen by guided tour. A 45-minute tour of either structure is $8 for adults, $4 for children 7-12. A combined tour is $15 for adults, $7 for children. Tours begin on the hour. Aficionados of 20th-century

the National Watch & Clock Museum

bowls of water, candles, oil lamps, and incense were used to measure the passage of time.

Perhaps its most impressive holding is a so-called monumental clock made in Hazleton, Pennsylvania, by one Stephen Engle. Designed to awe and amuse audiences, monumental clocks had their heyday in the late 19th century, touring the United States and Europe like so many modern rock stars. Engle spent more than 20 years crafting his 11-foot-tall clock, which has 48 moving figurines and displays such information as month, day of the week, and moon phase along with time. Finishing it around 1878, he entrusted it to promoters who touted it as "The Eighth Wonder of the World" as they hauled it around the eastern United States, charging people to see it. In 1951, after an appearance at the Ohio State Fair, the clock vanished. Members of the National Association of Watch and Clock Collectors spent years hunting for it, finally discovering it in a barn in 1988.

Turkey Hill Experience

Like The Hershey Story in Hershey and the Crayola Experience in Easton, the **Turkey Hill Experience** (301 Linden St., Columbia, 888/986-8784, www.turkeyhillexperience.com, admission $9.95, seniors $8.95, children 5-17 $7.95) is a family attraction centered on a consumer brand. Opened in 2011, it tells the story of Turkey Hill Dairy, a Lancaster County-based producer of ice cream and iced tea. It's packed with interactive exhibits. Kids get a huge kick out of milking the mechanical cows and creating their own virtual ice cream flavor. The Taste Lab exhibit, added in 2013, gives visitors the opportunity to turn their virtual ice cream recipe into actual ice cream. The Taste Lab costs an additional $4.55 per person, and reservations are required.

There's no actual production at the Turkey Hill Experience, which occupies a former silk mill in the borough of Columbia, a few blocks from the National Watch & Clock Museum.

Lititz

In a county studded with lovely little towns,

American art may recognize the 1719 house. The great Andrew Wyeth, a descendant of Hans Herr, captured it on canvas before its restoration.

National Watch & Clock Museum

The largest and most comprehensive horological collection in North America can be found in the river town of Columbia, about 10 miles west of Lancaster. Horology is the science of measuring time. Sounds like staid stuff, but a visit to the **National Watch & Clock Museum** (514 Poplar St., Columbia, 717/684-8261, www.nawcc.org, 10am-4pm Tues.-Sat. Dec.-Mar., 10am-5pm Tues.-Sat. and noon-4pm Sun. Apr.-Nov., also open Mon. Memorial Day-Labor Day, admission $8, seniors $7, children 5-16 $4, family $20) will convince you otherwise. Located in the world headquarters of the National Association of Watch and Clock Collectors, the museum traces the history of timekeeping from ancient times to present day. Learn how

Lititz is generally regarded as the loveliest one of all. Validation came in 2013, when Lititz was named America's Coolest Small Town by *Budget Travel*. The clip-clop of Amish buggies that contributes so much to the appeal of Bird-in-Hand, Intercourse, Strasburg, and other communities west of Lancaster is rarely heard in Lititz. What draws visitors to the borough nine miles north of downtown Lancaster is a combination of historical ambience, boutique shopping, and a busy calendar of events. It doesn't hurt that the smell of chocolate wafts through the streets.

Most of the shops, galleries, eateries, and landmarks lie along East Main Street (Route 772) or Broad Street (Route 501), which meet in the center of town. Be aware that many are closed on Sundays. The second Friday of the month is a great day to visit because merchants pull out all the stops for **Lovin' Lititz Every 2nd** (717/626-6332, www.lititzpa.com, 5pm-9pm), featuring free entertainment and free parking throughout town. Lititz is also a great place to be on Independence Day. First held in 1818, the **4th of July Celebration** (717/626-8981, www.lititzspringspark.org, admission charged) in Lititz Springs Park is the oldest continuous observance of the national holiday. The daylong festivities conclude with

the lighting of thousands of candles and a fireworks show.

Lititz boasts a unique history. It was founded in 1756 by members of the Moravian Church, an evangelical Protestant denomination that originated in the modern-day Czech Republic. For almost 100 years, only Moravians were permitted to live in the village. A group of strict church elders oversaw all aspects of day-to-day life, calling the shots in economic as well as religious matters. After opening its doors to outsiders in the 1850s, Lititz became a stop on the Reading and Columbia Railroad and a summer resort area. Lititz Springs Park and the limestone springs that give it its name were the main attraction. A replica of the passenger depot that stood at the entrance to the park from 1884 to 1957 houses the **Lititz Welcome Center** (18 N. Broad St., 717/626-8981, www.lititzspringspark.org, 10am-4pm Mon.-Sat. and until 8pm on the second Fri. of the month). On the opposite side of the train tracks, which are still used for moving freight, is the **Wilbur Chocolate Company** (48 N. Broad St., 717/626-3249, www.wilbur-buds.com, store and museum open 10am-5pm Mon.-Sat., free admission). Founded in 1884 in Philadelphia, based in Lititz since

the Wilbur Chocolate Company

the 1930s, and owned by agribusiness conglomerate Cargill since 1992, Wilbur manufactures chocolate and other ingredients for the baking, candy, and dairy industries. It's best known to consumers for chocolates that resemble a flower bud. (Wilbur Buds also bear a striking resemblance to Hershey's Kisses, which at more than 100 years old aren't quite as old as the squatter Buds.) The factory store offers free samples of the signature confection and a wide selection of other goodies, including fudge, marshmallows, almond bark, and peanut butter meltaways made on the spot. The attached Candy Americana Museum showcases antique candy machinery, cocoa tins, chocolate molds and boxes, marble slabs and rolling pins, and more than 150 porcelain chocolate pots from around the world.

Lititz is also home to a chocolate-centric eatery. **Café Chocolate of Lititz** (40 E. Main St., 717/626-0123, www.chocolatelititz.com, 10:30am-5pm Mon.-Thurs., 9am-9pm Fri.-Sat., 9am-5pm Sun., $6-10) is all about dark chocolate, eschewing varieties with less than 50 percent cocoa solids. The menu draws inspiration from around the globe, which presents a challenge when choosing a bottle to bring to the BYOB. What pairs well with mulligatawny soup, West African peanut chowder, *and* "chili con chocolate" topped with vegan sausage? A chocolate fountain in the front window reminds passersby of the house specialty: dark chocolate fondue.

The food lover's tour of Lititz doesn't end there. Just a couple of blocks from Café Chocolate is the **Julius Sturgis Pretzel Bakery** (219 E. Main St., 717/626-4354, www.juliussturgis.com, 10am-4pm Mon.-Fri. and 9am-5pm Sat. Jan.-mid-Mar., 9am-5pm Mon.-Sat. mid-Mar.-Dec., tour $3.50, children $2.50). Established in 1861, it's regarded as America's first pretzel bakery. Tours include a hands-on lesson in pretzel twisting. The bakery, with its original brick ovens, doesn't do a whole lot of baking these days. Soft pretzels are made in-house, but the many varieties of hard pretzels available in the store come from

Tom Sturgis Pretzels, a Reading-area bakery founded by Julius's grandson.

The sturdy stone house that Julius turned into a pretzel bakery was built in 1784. It's one of more than a dozen 18th-century buildings still in use on East Main Street. Another houses the **Lititz Museum** (145 E. Main St., 717/627-4636, www.lititzhistoricalfoundation. com, 10am-4pm Mon.-Sat. Memorial Day-last Sat. in Oct. and Fri.-Sat. Nov.-Sat. before Christmas, free admission), the place to go for a primer on the town's history. The Lititz Historical Foundation operates the museum and the neighboring **Johannes Mueller House,** which is open for tours ($5, seniors $4, high school students $3) from Memorial Day through the last Saturday in October. Built in 1792, the stone house remains practically unchanged and is furnished with hundreds of artifacts from the late 1700s and early 1800s. The 45-minute tours are led by costumed guides.

Wolf Sanctuary of Pennsylvania

Despite its official-sounding name, the **Wolf Sanctuary** (465 Speedwell Forge Rd., Lititz, 717/626-4617, www.wolfsancpa.com) is not a state facility. It's the pet project of one Lancaster County family, the Darlingtons, with a lot of land and a love for the animal portrayed so harshly in fairy tales. The Darlingtons began taking in wolves and wolf hybrids in the 1980s, after the state forbade keeping them as house pets. Today more than 40 onetime pets—who can't be released into the wild because they rely on humans for food—roam 20-odd acres of the family's property. Walking tours of the fenced refuge are offered Tuesdays, Thursdays, Saturdays, and Sundays. Reservations are required for the weekday tours, which start at 10am and cost $15 for adults, $14 for seniors, and $13 for children 12 and under. You can just show up for weekend tours, offered at 10am June-September and noon October-May. They're $12 for adults, $11 for seniors, and $10 for children. Once a month, on the Saturday closest to the full moon, the sanctuary offers an evening tour (7:30pm, $20, must be 16 or older) complete with campfire and some form of entertainment. Private tours are available by appointment and cost $25 per person. It's best to visit during cold weather, which wolves prefer. On hot days the sanctuary's furry residents are loath to emerge from holes they dig beneath their shelters.

If you're interested in spending hours or even days with the wolves, you're in luck. In 2005 the Darlingtons opened a B&B on their 100-plus acre property, which was the site of an iron forge from the 1760s to 1850s. **Speedwell Forge B&B** (717/626-1760, www.speedwellforge.com, $135-300) offers three guest rooms in what used to be the ironmaster's mansion and three private cottages. The Paymaster's Office cottage, so named because it's where forge employees were paid, is a honeymoon-worthy retreat complete with vaulted ceiling, massive brick fireplace, king-size bed, and in-room whirlpool bath.

Ephrata Cloister

The town of Ephrata, about 15 miles north of downtown Lancaster, is best known as the onetime home of a religious community whose faithful ate meager rations and slept on wooden benches with blocks of wood for pillows. The **Ephrata Cloister** (632 W. Main St., Ephrata, 717/733-6600, www.ephratacloister.org, 9am-5pm Wed.-Sat. and noon-5pm Sun. Jan.-Feb., 9am-5pm Tues.-Sat. and noon-5pm Sun. Mar., 9am-5pm Mon.-Sat. and noon-5pm Sun. Apr.-Oct., 9am-5pm Tues.-Sat. and noon-5pm Sun. Nov.-Dec., admission $10, seniors $9, children 3-11 $6) was the hub of their community and home to members who chose a celibate life. The buildings where white-robed Brothers and Sisters lived, worked, and prayed in the 1700s are now open to the public. At its zenith in the mid-1800s, the community consisted of about 80 celibate members and 200 "householders" who lived on farms around the cloister. The community became known for its Germanic calligraphy, publishing center, and original a cappella music.

Their leader, Conrad Beissel, prescribed a special diet for members of the choir, who sang at an otherworldly high pitch. Today the music composed by Beissel and crew is performed by the Ephrata Cloister Chorus at occasional concerts.

Beissel died in 1768 and was buried in a graveyard on the cloister grounds. His successor wasn't married to the idea of monastic life. After the death of the last celibate member in 1813, householders formed the German Seventh Day Baptist Church. The congregation disbanded in 1934, and several years later the state purchased the cloister property, now a National Historic Landmark. Some of the original buildings, including a worship hall known as the saal, can only be viewed during guided tours, which are offered daily. You can explore other structures on your own.

ENTERTAINMENT AND EVENTS
Performing Arts

Downtown Lancaster is home to one of the oldest theaters in the country. Built in 1852 on the foundation of a pre-Revolutionary prison, the **Fulton Theatre** (12 N. Prince St., Lancaster, 717/397-7425, www.thefulton.org) hosted lectures by Mark Twain and Horace Greeley, performances by Sarah Bernhardt and W. C. Fields, a production of *Ben-Hur* featuring live horses in a spectacular chariot-racing scene (fistfights broke out at the box office when tickets went on sale), and burlesque in its first 100 years. In the 1950s and '60s it served primarily as a movie house. Since then the Fulton has reinvented itself as a producer of professional theater. Productions range from small-cast plays such as *Doubt* to beloved musicals such as *Les Misérables* and *Hello, Dolly!* Each season features a handful of shows designed for pint-size theatergoers. The auditorium, which seats about 700, was restored to its original Victorian splendor in 1995. It's one of a dwindling number still using sandbags and hemp ropes to move scenery. Named for a Lancaster County native credited with developing the first commercially successful steamboat, the Fulton is the primary venue of the **Lancaster Symphony Orchestra** (717/397-7425, www.lancastersymphony.org).

Lancaster County has not one but two dinner theaters. In business since 1984, **Rainbow Dinner Theatre** (3065 Lincoln Highway East, Paradise, 717/687-4300, www.rainbowdinnertheatre.com) bills itself as America's only all-comedy dinner theater. It produces several knee-slappers per year, including a Christmas show. The **Dutch Apple Dinner Theatre** (510 Centerville Rd., Lancaster, 717/898-1900, www.dutchapple.com) serves up more shows, and its menu includes dramatic fare such as *Rent*. Both theaters are set back from the road and easily missed. Rainbow is behind the Best Western Plus Revere Inn & Suites on Route 30, about three miles east of the Rockvale Outlets. The Dutch Apple shares a driveway with the Heritage Hotel—Lancaster, just off the Centerville exit of Route 30.

Sight & Sound Theatres

With a theater in Lancaster County and a second in Branson, Missouri, **Sight & Sound Theatres** (800/377-1277, www.sight-sound.com) is the nation's largest Christian theatrical company. Founded in the 1970s by a Lancaster County native, it pulls out all the stops to dramatize biblical stories such as Noah's wet and wild journey, Joseph's journey from slavery to power, and the birth of Jesus. Think elaborate sets and special effects, professional actors and live animals. The Lancaster County **theater** (300 Hartman Bridge Rd., Strasburg) is a vision inside and out. The sprawling, pastel-hued palace features three exterior domes (representing the Trinity), a wraparound stage double the size of Radio City Music Hall's, and one of the largest moving light systems on the East Coast. Four-legged cast members amble to their spots—and "dressing rooms"—via specially designed passageways under the theater floor.

Festivals and Events

What started in 1980 as a jousting demo to draw attention to a new winery has grown into one of Pennsylvania Dutch country's marquee attractions. Jousting is just the tip of the lance at the **Pennsylvania Renaissance Faire** (Mount Hope Estate, 2775 Lebanon Rd., Manheim, 717/665-7021, www.parenfaire.com, admission charged), held weekends August-October. Transported to Elizabethan England, Faire-goers party

the Fulton Theatre

like it's 1589 alongside sword swallowers and fire-breathers, magicians and musicians, jugglers and jesters. The Ren Faire features more than 70 shows per day, including performances of Shakespeare's plays in a three-story replica of London's Globe Theatre. Human pawns, knights, and bishops battle it out on a massive chessboard. Merchants in period costumes demonstrate glassblowing, pottery throwing, leatherworking, bow and arrow making, and more. Even the food vendors wear the clothes and talk the talk of Shakespeare's day as they serve up everything from gelato to giant turkey legs. Though best known for the Ren Faire, Mount Hope Estate hosts a variety of events throughout the year, including murder mystery dinners, a beer festival, and a Celtic festival. Located 15 miles north of Lancaster, the National Register-listed property was home to a prominent iron-making family in the 19th century.

Lancaster's **Long's Park** (1441 Harrisburg Pike, Lancaster, 717/735-8883, www.longspark.org) is another site of much merrymaking. The city park just off Route 30 is a poultry-lover's paradise on the third Saturday of May, when the Sertoma Club of Lancaster holds its annual fundraiser for the park. Members of the civic organization serve more than 25,000 chicken dinners over the course of eight hours. The **Sertoma Chicken BBQ** (717/354-7259, www.lancastersertomabbq.com, admission charged), a tradition since 1953, held the Guinness World Record for most meat consumed at an outdoor event for more than a decade, losing it to a Paraguayan shindig in 2008. June marks the start of the **Long's Park Summer Music Series** (7:30pm Sun. June-Aug.), another decades-old tradition. Bring blankets, lawn chairs, and nibbles for the free concerts. Alcohol isn't permitted in the 80-acre park. The music series is funded in part by proceeds from the **Long's Park Art & Craft Festival** (Labor Day weekend, admission charged), which showcases 200 artists from across the country.

SHOPPING
Outlet Malls

Lancaster County's two outlet malls are just a couple of minutes apart on Route 30. **Rockvale Outlets** (35 S. Willowdale Dr., Lancaster, 717/293-9595, www.rockvaleoutletslancaster.com, 9:30am-9pm Mon.-Sat., 11am-5pm Sun.) features about 100 stores, including Lane Bryant, Jones New York, Pendleton, Casual Male XL, Izod, Gymboree, and Disney Store. It's a great place to shop for the home, counting Pottery Barn, Lenox, and Corningware Corelle Revere among its tenants.

Tanger Outlets (311 Stanley K. Tanger Blvd., Lancaster, 717/392-7260, www.tangeroutlet.com, 9am-9pm Mon.-Sat., 10am-6pm Sun.), located across Route 30 from Dutch Wonderland amusement park, is smaller but chicer, offering designer brands such as Polo Ralph Lauren, Kenneth Cole, Calvin Klein, Brooks Brothers, Coach, and Movado.

"Antiques Capital USA"

Located just off exit 286 of the Pennsylvania Turnpike, the little burg of Adamstown has made a big name for itself in antiquing circles. It's crowded with antiques shops, malls, and markets, most of which can be found along North Reading Road (Route 272). Sundays are a big day in "Antiques Capital USA." That's when **Renninger's Antiques Market** and the **Black Angus Antiques Mall** are open. The former (2500 N. Reading Rd., Denver, 717/336-2177, www.renningers.com, indoor market 7:30am-4pm Sun., outdoor market opens at 5am) features 375 dealers indoors and, weather permitting, hundreds more outdoors. Bring a flashlight to get in on the early morning action.

The 70,000-square-foot **Black Angus Antiques Mall** (2800 N. Reading Rd., Adamstown, 717/484-4386, www.stoudts.com, mall 7:30am-4pm Sun., outdoor pavilions 5:30am-noon) is part of a sprawling complex of attractions operated by husband and wife Ed and Carol Stoudt. More than 300 dealers set up shop inside the mall, selling everything from fine art and early American furniture to tools and small collectibles. About 100 more can be found outside. At 1pm, take a break from shopping for a free tour of **Stoudt's Brewing Company.** Frequent visitors to Europe, the Stoudts established the microbrewery in 1987 with the goal of making an authentic German-style beer. And they succeeded: Gold Lager and Pils, the brewery's German-style flagship beers, have racked up awards and accolades. Brewery tours, also offered at 3pm Saturdays, meet in the lobby of the adjacent **Black Angus Restaurant & Pub,** which specializes in steaks. Its breads are made in the **Wonderful Good Market** (9am-4pm Fri.-Sun.), the Stoudts' bakery, creamery, and specialty foods store.

Adamstown offers plenty of antiquing on days other than Sunday. **Heritage Antique Center** (2750 N. Reading Rd., Adamstown, 717/484-4646, www.heritageantiquecenter. com), one of the area's oldest antiques stores, and the **Antiques Showcase & German Trading Post** (2152 N. Reading Rd., Denver, 717/336-8847, www.blackhorselodge.com), with nearly 300 showcases full of fine antiques and collectibles, are open seven days a week. Not to be missed: **The Country French Collection** (2887 N. Reading Rd., Adamstown, 717/484-0200, www.country-frenchantiques.com, noon-5pm Sat.-Sun. and by appointment), which imports 18th- and 19th-century antiques from France and England and restores them to pristine condition.

Adamstown's antiquing scene goes into overdrive during **Antique Extravaganza** (www.antiquescapital.com), held each April, June, and September. Outside markets mushroom and inside markets keep longer hours during the four-day event, which attracts dealers from across the country.

Mud Sales

Held at fire companies throughout Lancaster County, "mud sales" are a chance to get dirt-cheap prices on everything from antiques to aluminum siding, lawn equipment to livestock, homemade food to horse carriages. Teeming as they are with Amish and Mennonite buyers and sellers, these fundraising sales/auctions are also a cultural immersion experience. Why are they called mud sales? Because many take place in the spring, when the ground is thawing—though it's not unusual for fire companies to hold mud sales in summer or fall. Visit www.padutchcountry.com or call 717/299-8901 for a schedule of mud sales.

Black Angus Antiques Mall

Quilts and Fabrics

Mud sales are great places to buy locally crafted quilts, but if your visit to Lancaster County doesn't coincide with one, you're not out of luck. Quilt shops are more common than stoplights in the Amish countryside. Most sell a variety of handicrafts. (This author's fave: the ingenious pillow-blanket hybrid known as the "quillow.") Many are home-based businesses, allowing shoppers a glimpse into the everyday lives of locals. Just about all quilt shops are closed on Sundays. The **Quilt Shop at Miller's** (2811 Lincoln Highway East, Ronks, 717/687-8439, www.quiltshopatmillers.com, open Wed.-Sun. Jan.-Feb., daily Mar.-Dec.) is an exception. It's right next to the popular Miller's Smorgasbord on Route 30, about a mile and a half east of Route 896.

Intercourse is a good place to start a quilt shopping spree. The village along Route 340 (Old Philadelphia Pike) is home to **The Old Country Store** (800/828-8218, www.theoldcountrystore.com, open Mon.-Sat.), stocked with thousands of items made by local craftspeople, most of them Amish or Mennonite. In addition to hundreds of quilts, it carries potholders and pottery, Christmas ornaments and cornhusk bunnies, faceless Amish dolls and darling stuffed bears, pillows of various sizes and paper cuttings known as *scherenschnitte*. With its selection of more than 6,000 bolts of fabric, the store is as much a starting point for needlecraft projects as a showplace for finished products. Quilt books, color-coordinated fabric packs, and pattern kits are also on offer. There's a quilt museum on the second floor of the store. It's best known for showcasing antique Amish and Mennonite quilts but has also mounted exhibitions of contemporary quilts, African American quilts, and antebellum album quilts.

In the complex of shops known as Kitchen Kettle Village is the airy **Village Quilts** (3529 Old Philadelphia Pike, Intercourse, 717/768-2787, www.kitchenkettle.com/quilts, open Mon.-Sat.), which commissions works from a select group of home quilters. Each

masterpiece is signed and dated and comes with a certificate for insurance purposes. The shop offers one-on-one quilting instruction ($80 for 90 minutes) by appointment.

A few minutes east of Intercourse along Route 340 is **Esh's Handmade Quilts** (3829 Old Philadelphia Pike, Gordonville, 717/768-8435, open Mon.-Sat.), an Amish-owned shop on an operating dairy farm. And a few minutes west of Intercourse is **The Quilt & Fabric Shack** (3137 Old Philadelphia Pike, Bird-In-Hand, 717/768-0338, www.thequiltandfabricshack.com, open Mon.-Sat.), boasting four rooms of fabrics. Its "bargain room" has hundreds of bolts priced at $4-5 per yard. Just northwest of Intercourse along Route 772, **Family Farm Quilts** (3511 W. Newport Rd., 717/768-8375, www.familyfarmquilts.com, open Mon.-Sat.) counts more than 200 local women among its quilt suppliers. Its selection of handicrafts includes purses made of antique quilts, place mats, chair pads, children's toys, and baskets.

Witmer Quilt Shop (1076 W. Main St., New Holland, 717/656-9526, open Mon.-Tues. and Thurs.-Sat.), located five miles north of Intercourse along Route 23, is remarkable for its selection of lovingly restored antique quilts. Emma Witmer's shop/home is also stocked with more than 100 new quilts, many in patterns she herself designed. Give her a few months and she'll give you a custom quilt.

As you make your way between quilt shops, keep your eyes peeled for handmade "quilts sold here" signs inviting you to pull into a drive and knock on the door.

Susquehanna Glass Factory Outlet and Tour

Founded in 1910, **Susquehanna Glass** (731 Ave. H, Columbia, 717/684-2155, www.susquehannaglass.com, store open 9am-5pm Tues.-Sat., tours 10:30am and 1pm Tues. and Thurs., reservations required) counts retailers Williams-Sonoma, Restoration Hardware, and David's Bridal among its customers. The glass decorator best known for personalized products offers everything from storage jars to lead crystal bowls at its factory store, located half a mile from the National Watch & Clock Museum in the Susquehanna River town of Columbia. Tours of the factory, where glass is still cut by hand, are offered year-round except when temps creep into the 90s. The tours are free and last 30-45 minutes.

ACCOMMODATIONS

Lancaster County has lodging options aplenty. Its hotels and motels run the gamut from major brands such as Holiday Inn, Comfort Inn, and Travelodge to unique independents such as the **Red Caboose** (312 Paradise Ln., Ronks, 717/687-5000, www.redcaboosemotel.com, $70-160), a motel made of historic train cars and cabooses, and the 97-room **Fulton Steamboat Inn** (Routes 30 and 896, Lancaster, 717/299-9999, www.fultonsteamboatinn.com, $80-180), built to resemble a steamboat and named for a Lancaster County native who pioneered steam-powered shipping. Travelers who prefer bed-and-breakfasts can take their pick of more than 150. Indeed, Lancaster County has more B&Bs than any place on the East Coast except Cape Cod. They're a diverse bunch: Bed down in an 18th-century stone house, an elegant Victorian manse, or on a working farm. If you travel with young children, you probably eschew B&Bs, but a farm stay is a different animal (hardy har har). It's lodging, education, and entertainment rolled into one—assuming you find gathering eggs and bottle-feeding calves entertaining. A list of Lancaster County farms that offer overnight accommodations is available at www.afarmstay.com.

The **Pennsylvania Dutch Convention & Visitors Bureau** (717/299-8901, www.padutchcountry.com) is a good source of information about lodging options. Its website allows for searches by lodging type and price range. The **Mennonite Information Center** (2209 Millstream Rd., Lancaster, 717/299-0954, www.mennoniteinfoctr.com) maintains a list of Mennonite-owned guesthouses, available at the center and on its website.

Under $100

Located next to Dutch Wonderland amusement park, **Old Mill Stream Campground** (2249 Lincoln Hwy. E., Lancaster, 717/299-2314, www.oldmillstreamcampground.com, campsite $37-49, mobile home rental $100-180, open Apr.-Dec.) makes a great home base for families with young children. The 15-acre campground has more than 160 tent and RV sites, a game room, a country store, laundry rooms, and free wireless Internet access.

The **Carriage House Motor Inn** (144 E. Main St., Strasburg, 717/687-7651, www.carriagehousemotorinn.net, $60-110) is a good noncamping option in this price range. It's walking distance from the Railroad Museum of Pennsylvania and the Strasburg Rail Road, which makes it appealing to rail fans. Families will appreciate its three-room suite. Rates include a continental breakfast. For about the same price, you can spend the night at nearby **Rayba Acres Farm** (183 Black Horse Rd., Paradise, 717/687-6729, www.raybaacres.com, $85-90) or **Neffdale Farm** (604 Strasburg Rd., Paradise, 717/687-7837, www.neffdalefarm.com, $80), both Mennonite-owned.

$100-150

Located just off Route 30 west of Lancaster city, the **Heritage Hotel—Lancaster** (500 Centerville Rd., Lancaster, 800/223-8963, www.heritagelancaster.com, $90-180) is a great choice for nightlife-loving travelers. **Loxley's** (717/898-2431), its restaurant and bar, attracts locals and hotel guests alike. Named for Robin of Loxley, the archer and outlaw better known as Robin Hood, it boasts a two-level deck that looks like a giant tree house. The hotel has 166 standard-looking guest rooms, a business center, a fitness room, and an outdoor pool. The Dutch Apple Dinner Theatre is right next door.

Sleep under handmade quilts and awake to the clip-clop of Amish buggies at **The Inn at Kitchen Kettle Village** (3529 Old Philadelphia Pike, Intercourse, 717/768-8261, www.kitchenkettle.com, $110-200). Scattered throughout the uber-quaint village, accommodations range from standard rooms to two-bedroom suites that sleep up to six. Guests enjoy a free breakfast at the on-site Kling House Restaurant Monday-Saturday.

Breakfast at ★ **Verdant View Farm B&B** (429 Strasburg Rd., Paradise, 717/687-7353, www.verdantview.com, $70-120), one mile east of Strasburg on Route 741, begins with a joining of hands and a rendition of the Johnny Appleseed song (*Oh, the Lord's been good to me . . .*). It's not unusual for two, three, or even four generations of the Ranck family, which has operated the 118-acre dairy and crop farm for almost a century, to join guests around the table, set with pitchers of raw milk, platters of farm-fresh meat and eggs, and homemade pies. Breakfast isn't the first thing on the menu at Verdant View. Guests can begin the day with a farm tour, complete with opportunities to milk a cow, frolic with kittens, and feed calves, goats, bunnies, and other animals. Verdant View also offers tractor-pulled wagon rides and "farmer's apprentice" programs in topics as diverse as making cheese and artificially inseminating cows. (Breakfast and some farm experiences aren't offered on Sundays, when the Rancks attend their Mennonite church.) The nine guest rooms, spread between an 1896 farmhouse and the "little white house" down the lane, are nothing fancy. But what it lacks in frills the B&B more than makes up for in hospitality.

The charming town of Lititz has several recommendable accommodations in this price range. Chief among them is the **General Sutter Inn** (14 E. Main St., Lititz, 717/626-2115, www.generalsutterinn.com, $70-225), which offers 16 rooms and suites in two radically different styles. Ten are decorated in a Victorian style. The third floor, known as the Rock Lititz Penthouse, features edgy, rock-inspired décor, including curtain rods fashioned from microphone stands and a signed poster from singer Roger Daltrey of The Who. More than 200 years old, the inn took its present name in the 1930s to honor John Augustus Sutter, who established a settlement in California in the 1840s, saw it overrun by gold-seekers, and lived his final years in Lititz. Guests enjoy a complimentary continental breakfast. The **Alden House Bed & Breakfast** (62 E. Main St., Lititz, 717/627-3363, www.aldenhouse.com, $110-160), with seven guest rooms and suites, is another fine choice in the center of town. Its breakfast is a multicourse affair.

Over $150

Visitors to downtown Lancaster may find it hard to believe that the **Lancaster Marriott at Penn Square** (25 S. Queen St., Lancaster, 717/239-1600, www.lancastermarriott.com, $150-300) and adjoining Lancaster County Convention Center opened in 2009. The 19-floor hotel smack-dab in the center of town looks mighty historical. That's because developers incorporated the Beaux Arts facade of a shuttered century-old department store into its design. A contemporary aesthetic takes over in the soaring lobby and spacious rooms. The hotel boasts an indoor pool and a spa (717/207-4076, www.mandarinrosespa.com). The on-site **Penn Square Grille and Rendezvous Lounge** (717/207-4033, www.pennsquaregrille.com) offer contemporary American cuisine and 30 wines by the glass. Central Market, the Fulton Theatre, the Demuth Museum, and other downtown attractions are just a skip and a jump away. On the downside: On-site parking is $18 per day ($30 if you go the valet route), and in-room Internet access will set you back $12.95 per day.

With its brick walls and wood beams, locally crafted furnishings and flat-screen TVs, art gallery and all-natural restaurant, the ★ **Lancaster Arts Hotel** (300 Harrisburg Ave., 717/299-3000, www.lancasterartshotel.com, $180-360) is the city's hippest lodging property by a mile. "Hip" implies new, but the building itself dates to the late 1800s. Built as a tobacco warehouse, it found a new life as a boutique hotel in 2006. Original works by area artists adorn each of 63 guest rooms and suites, some of which boast in-room whirlpools. Amenities include 24-hour business and fitness centers, bicycle rentals, and free parking. Internet access and a continental breakfast are also on the house. **John J. Jeffries** (717/431-3307, www.johnjjeffries. com), the on-site restaurant and lounge, bills itself as the leading consumer of local organic meats and vegetables in central Pennsylvania. Happy hour is 4pm-6pm daily.

Located midway between the villages of Intercourse and Bird-in-Hand on Route 340, ★ **AmishView Inn & Suites** (3125 Old Philadelphia Pike, Bird-in-Hand, 866/735-1600, www.amishviewinn.com, $125-350) is right in the heart of Amish country. Rooms on the backside of the hotel boast farmland views, and it's not unusual to spot a farmer working his fields with horse-drawn equipment or Amish children heading to school. That's not the only thing it has going for it. AmishView has an indoor pool and whirlpool, a fitness center, an arcade room, and a guest laundry. Its 50 guest rooms and suites feature mahogany furniture, kitchenettes, DVD players, and free high-speed Internet access. Suites have fireplaces and/or whirlpools. A complimentary country breakfast complete with made-to-order omelets and waffles is served every morning. Plain & Fancy Farm Restaurant, one of the region's most popular Pennsylvania Dutch eateries, is just outside the doors.

FOOD

Leave your diet at the Lancaster County line. Visiting this corner of the globe without indulging in a Pennsylvania Dutch-style meal is like visiting Disney World and not riding the rides. The cuisine is anything but light, and unless you seek out a restaurant with an à la carte menu (wussy), you're looking at an all-you-can-eat experience. Approach it with the abandon you bring to Thanksgiving dinner. If you don't stuff yourself silly, you're sort of missing the point. This is the food of hardworking farm families. This is no time to turn down seconds.

It would be unwise to fill up on Pennsylvania Dutch foods meal after meal, not only because of the effect on your waistline but because Lancaster County has some excellent non-Deutsch eateries. You can find everything from crepes to authentic Cajun cuisine within its borders. The city of Lancaster, in particular, is undergoing a restaurant boom.

Pennsylvania Dutch Fare

If you're new to Pennsylvania Dutch cuisine, you should know a few things. Around here, **chicken pot pie** isn't a pie at all. It's a stew with square-cut egg noodles. A **whoopie pie** isn't a pie either. Think of it as a dessert burger: creamy icing pressed between two bun-shaped cakes. Chocolate cake with white icing is most common, but you'll also encounter variations such as pumpkin cake with cream cheese icing. The annual **Whoopie Pie Festival** (Hershey Farm Restaurant & Inn, Rte. 896, Strasburg, 717/687-8635, www.whoopiepiefestival.com, early Sept., free) features more than 100 varieties. Pennsylvania Dutch country's most iconic dessert, the **shoofly pie,** is, in fact, a pie with a crumb crust. But it's nothing like the fruit or cream pies served at diners throughout the country. Packed with molasses and brown sugar, the joltingly sweet treat comes in "wet bottom" and "dry bottom" varieties. A wet-bottomed shoofly pie is more gooey and molasses-y than its dry-bottomed cousin. Other regional specialties include egg noodles with browned butter, **chow-chow** (a pickled vegetable relish), **scrapple** (a breakfast food made with pork scraps), and **schnitz un knepp** (a dish consisting of dried apples, dumplings, and ham).

Lancaster County's most popular Pennsylvania Dutch restaurants generally fall into one of two categories: smorgasbord and family-style. With seating for 1,200 and a seemingly endless array of dishes, ★ **Shady Maple Smorgasbord** (129 Toddy Dr., East Earl, 717/354-8222, www.shady-maple.com/smorgasbord, 5am-8pm Mon.-Sat.) is the behemoth of the bunch. Don't be surprised to find a waiting line. On Saturday evenings it can take upwards of an hour to get seated. You really need to see this place to appreciate its enormity. Lunch and dinner buffets feature everything from Pennsylvania Dutch dishes to pizza to fajitas. Save room for dozens of dessert options. Lunch is $13 on weekdays, $19 on Saturday. Dinner is $18-24, depending on the day's specials. Seniors enjoy a 10 percent discount, and children 4-10 eat for half price. (Anyone who has recently undergone a gastric bypass operation also gets a discount.) Shady Maple's breakfast buffet ($10 weekdays, $12 Saturday) gets high marks from scrapple fans. A breakfast menu (under $10) is available on weekdays.

Bird-in-Hand Family Restaurant & Smorgasbord (2760 Old Philadelphia Pike, Bird-in-Hand, 717/768-1500, www.bird-in-hand.com, 6am-8pm Mon.-Sat., breakfast buffet $9, lunch buffet $12-14, dinner buffet $16-19, age-based pricing for children 4-12) offers both menu and smorgasbord dining for breakfast, lunch, and dinner. Its kids buffet is designed to look like Noah's Ark, complete with stuffed animals peering through the portholes. If you enjoy the baked goods, stop by the **Bird-in-Hand Bakery** (2715 Old Philadelphia Pike, Bird-in-Hand, 800/524-3429, www.bird-in-hand.com, 6am-6pm Mon.-Fri., 6am-5pm Sat.) and take some home. It's just down the road. Specialties include soft potato rolls, red velvet cake, and apple dumplings.

Hershey Farm Restaurant (240 Hartman Bridge Rd., Ronks, 717/687-8635, www.hersheyfarm.com, 8am-8pm Mon.-Fri. and 7am-8pm Sat.-Sun., closed Sun. evenings and Mon. Nov.-Apr., breakfast buffet $11, lunch/dinner buffet $17-26, age-based pricing for children 4-12) also offers a choice of menu or smorgasbord dining. The on-site bakery is known for its whoopie pies (Hershey Farm hosts the Whoopie Pie Festival) and triple-layer chocolate cake. A chocolate fountain graces the dessert bar on evenings and weekends. **Miller's Smorgasbord** (2811 Lincoln Hwy. East, Ronks, 717/687-6621, www.millerssmorgasbord.com, breakfast 7:30am-10:30am Sat.-Sun. year-round, lunch/dinner

from 11:30am daily early Mar.-Dec., dinner from 4pm Mon.-Thurs. and lunch/dinner from 11:30am Fri.-Sun. Jan.-early Mar., breakfast buffet $11, lunch/dinner buffet $24, age-based pricing for children 4-12) is unusual in that it serves alcohol, including cocktails made with its own shoofly liqueur. Menu dining is available during lunch and dinner.

★ **Plain & Fancy Farm Restaurant** (3121 Old Philadelphia Pike, Bird-in-Hand, 717/768-4400, www.plainandfancyfarm.com, lunch/dinner from 11:30am daily Mar.-Dec., closed Jan.-Feb.) is Lancaster County's oldest and arguably best destination for family-style dining. Most family-style restaurants in Pennsylvania Dutch country follow a similar recipe: guests are seated—often at tables with other parties—and brought platters of food, which are replenished until everyone is sated. Plain & Fancy's "Amish farm feast" ($20 per person, children 4-12 $10) features made-from-scratch fried chicken, baked sausage, chicken pot pie with homemade noodles, real mashed potatoes, and more. The restaurant, which opened in 1959, also offers an à la carte menu. Its signature dessert, sour cream apple crumb pie, is out of this world. Though it seats 700, you'd be wise to make a reservation. It's more popular than ever after being featured in an episode of the Travel Channel's *Man v. Food Nation*.

Lancaster

With a wide variety of cuisines represented under one roof, **Central Market** (23 N. Market St., 717/735-6890, www.centralmarketlancaster.com, 6am-4pm Tues. and Fri., 6am-2pm Sat.) is one of downtown Lancaster's most popular lunch spots. You'll find vendors selling everything from made-to-order salads to homemade rice pudding. Ethnic options include Narai Exotic Thai Cuisine (get there early for the hot-selling fresh spring rolls) and Saife's Middle Eastern Food. The downsides: Central Market is open just three days a week, and seating is limited.

More upscale dining options abound. Lancaster County native Tim Carr lent his culinary talents to area country clubs before putting his name to a restaurant. Spitting distance from Central Market, **Carr's Restaurant** (50 W. Grant St., 717/299-7090, www.carrsrestaurant.com, lunch 11:30am-2:30pm Tues.-Sat., brunch 11:30am-2:30pm Sun., dinner 5:30pm-9:30pm Tues.-Thurs. and 5:30pm-10pm Fri.-Sat., lunch/brunch $9-20, dinner $14-32) puts a sophisticated spin on comfort foods, e.g., mac and cheese loaded with Maine lobster chunks. Request a table near the back of the basement-level restaurant, where a glass wall affords a view of the wine cellar. You're welcome to bring your own bottle (a $15 corkage fee applies), but the selection here is one of the best in town. In 2009 Carr opened **Crush Wine Bar** (4:30pm-9:30pm Tues.-Thurs., 4:30pm-10pm Fri.-Sat.) above his restaurant. On offer: 20-odd wines by the glass and half glass, a carefully curated assortment of beers, several kinds of absinthe, and creative tapas.

A short stroll away, German-born chef Gunter Backhaus presides over **The Loft** (201 W. Orange St., 717/299-0661, www.theloftlancaster.com, lunch 11:30am-2pm Mon.-Fri., dinner 5:30pm-9pm Mon.-Sat., lunch $9-14, dinner $16-34), locally famous for its jumbo shrimp cocktail. Backhaus doesn't shy away from the likes of frog legs, snails, and alligator tails, but timid palates needn't fear. The menu also features rosemary roasted free-range chicken, filet mignon, and lobster. Cozy and unpretentious, the restaurant gets its name from the open-beam ceiling in one of two dining rooms.

It's not just dieters who sup on salad at the **Belvedere Inn** (402 N. Queen St., 717/394-2422, www.belvederelancaster.com, lunch 11am-2pm Mon.-Fri., dinner 5pm-11pm Sun.-Thurs. and 5pm-midnight Fri.-Sat., bar open until 2am daily, lunch $7-14, dinner $12-32). The grilled Caesar salad at this elegant restaurant is a thing of legend. Have it plain or choose from toppings including tenderloin tips, sautéed scallops, and grilled salmon. A petite version is available at dinnertime, when entrées such as wild boar Bolognese

and gnocchi with Maine lobster vie for attention. **Crazy Shirley's** (7pm-2am Wed.-Thurs., 5pm-2am Fri.-Sat.), a piano bar and lounge on the second floor of the Belvedere, hosts karaoke every Wednesday and DJs Thursday-Saturday.

The classic and seasonal cocktails at **Checkers Bistro** (300 W. James St., 717/509-1069, www.checkersbistro.com, 11:30am-2:30pm and 4:30pm-10pm Tues.-Fri., 11:30am-10pm Sat., 4pm-9pm Sun., lunch $9-17, dinner $20-34) bode well for the meal ahead. "Classic and seasonal" also describe the food menu, which includes fish-and-chips, steak frites, and grilled pizzas with toppings such as lobster, pine nuts, prosciutto, and fig. The small plates menu is particularly appealing, with options both common (chicken wings) and singular (Peking duck tacos).

Like Checkers, ★ **FENZ Restaurant & Latenight** (398 Harrisburg Ave., Ste. 100, 717/735-6999, www.fenzrestaurant.com, dinner from 5pm Mon.-Sat., lounge opens at 4pm, $14-28) excels in cocktails and small plates. Give the pickle fries a chance: the tempura-battered kosher dill spears are positively addictive. Stylishly appointed with a clientele to match, FENZ has two levels with a bar on each. The upstairs has a livelier, more youthful vibe. Take a seat at the downstairs bar to watch the chef at work. The menu is mindful of vegetarians and vegans. FENZ is housed in a 19th-century foundry. Don't waste time searching for street parking. There's a lot behind the building, accessible from Charlotte Street.

A discussion of Lancaster's fine dining scene wouldn't be complete without words of praise for **Gibraltar** (931 Harrisburg Ave., 717/397-2790, www.kearesrestaurants.com/gibraltar, lunch 11:30am-2:30pm Mon.-Fri., dinner 5pm-10pm Mon.-Thurs., 5pm-10:30pm Fri.-Sat., 5pm-9:30pm Sun., bar open as late as 2am, lunch $8-19, dinner $19-34), with its Mediterranean-influenced cuisine, *Wine Spectator*-lauded wine list, and gracious service. The seafood is simply phenomenal.

Start off with selections from the raw bar or an order of steamed mussels and proceed to entrées like whole Adriatic Sea branzino (European sea bass), rainbow trout stuffed with crab, and Moroccan spiced colossal shrimp. A tapas menu is available for those in the sharing spirit. Save room for a house-made pastry.

Strasburg

Strasburg, with its train-related attractions and proximity to the Sight & Sound theater, sees large numbers of tourists. But its restaurants feel refreshingly untouristy. Smack-dab in the center of town, the **Strasburg Country Store & Creamery** (1 W. Main St., 717/687-0766, www.strasburg.com, open daily, hours vary) is best known as a destination for dessert and a dose of nostalgia. But it also offers deli fare, including Reuben sandwiches, cheeseburgers, and hot dogs—all served with locally made potato chips. Cross your fingers that the day's specials include a bread bowl filled with Pennsylvania Dutch-style chicken corn soup. As for dessert, choose from 20-plus flavors of ice cream and mix-ins such as M&M's and granola. A wide variety of chocolate-covered goodies vie for attention with fudge, peanut brittle, and caramel corn. Have a seat inside to soak in the old-timey touches, from vintage Cream of Wheat posters to a 19th-century marble soda fountain. Have a seat outside to watch horse-drawn buggies negotiating the intersection of Routes 741 and 896.

Purchased in 2003 by a couple with no experience in food service, ★ **The Iron Horse Inn** (135 E. Main St., 717/687-6362, www.ironhorsepa.com, noon-9pm Mon. and Wed., noon-10pm Thurs.-Sat., noon-7pm Sun., lunch $7-10, dinner $9-42) has emerged as one of those rare restaurants that pair fine food with a casual ambience. Denise Waller, one-half of the ownership team and a nurse by training, buys broccoli, squash, potatoes, and other produce directly from local Amish farmers, shrinking the field-to-table timeline to a few hours in some cases. Lunch at the Iron Horse (a Native American term for trains) can be as simple as a grilled ham and cheddar sandwich or as sophisticated as crepes stuffed with lump crabmeat. The asparagus fries—that's right: deep-fried spears of asparagus—go well with any dish. Dinner options range from the "Strasburger" to German/Austrian specialties to vegetable stir-fry. The lineup of draft beers features local brews along with German imports, and the wine list includes

the Strasburg Country Store & Creamery

selections from Twin Brook Winery, about 10 miles east of Strasburg.

Just east of town on Route 741 is an outpost of regional chain **Isaac's Restaurant & Deli** (226 Gap Rd., 717/687-7699, www.isaacsdeli.com, 10am-9pm Mon.-Thurs., 10am-10pm Fri.-Sat., 11am-9pm Sun., call for winter hours, $6-12). The Strasburg location, which shares an address with the Choo Choo Barn, a model railroader's mecca, boasts a dining area decked out like a train car. Its repertoire of made-from-scratch soups is 200 strong, but only the delicious creamy pepperjack tomato is available every day. The long list of sandwiches includes half a dozen veggie options. Pretzel sandwiches like the Salty Eagle (grilled ham, Swiss cheese, mustard) and Mallard (roast beef, bacon, mushrooms, melted cheddar, mild horseradish sauce) are particularly popular. You'll also find Isaac's in downtown Lancaster (25 N. Queen St., 717/394-5544), Lititz (4 Crosswinds Rd., 717/625-1181), and Ephrata (120 N. Reading Rd., 717/733-7777), among other places.

Lititz

The historic **General Sutter Inn** (14 E. Main St., 717/626-2115, www.generalsutterinn. com), located at the junction of Route 501 and East Main Street in the heart of Lititz, offers dining as well as accommodations. The elegant restaurant (11am-3pm Mon., 11am-3pm and 5pm-9pm Tues.-Thurs., 11am-3pm and 5pm-9:30pm Fri., 8am-9:30pm Sat., 11am-9pm Sun., $10-33) isn't as pricey as its white tablecloths suggest. Its menu includes burgers and sandwiches as well as loftier fare such as filet mignon and roasted half duck. The crab cakes sell like hotcakes. Alfresco dining is available during the warmer months. In 2010 the inn unveiled a British-style pub, **Bulls Head Public House** (11:30am-11pm Sun.-Thurs., 11:30am-midnight Fri.-Sat., kitchen closes at 9:30pm Sun.-Thurs. and 10pm Fri.-Sat.), which offers the same menu. Beer lovers are bonkers for the place, which boasts more than a dozen rotating drafts and 80-plus bottles.

Columbia

Order the whoopie pie at ★ **Prudhomme's Lost Cajun Kitchen** (50 Lancaster Ave., 717/684-1706, www.lostcajunkitchen.com, 4:30pm-11pm Mon., 11am-11pm Tues.-Thurs., 11am-midnight Fri.-Sat., 11am-9pm Sun., $4-22) and what you'll get is a far cry from the classic Pennsylvania Dutch dessert. In place of the mound-shaped cakes: homemade cornbread. In place of the icing center: tender crabmeat. Served with a side of creamy mushroom sauce, the appetizer is a Lost Cajun original. Owners David and Sharon Prudhomme—he of Louisiana, she of New Jersey—brought their brand of Cajun cooking to Pennsylvania Dutch country in 1992. The name Prudhomme should not be unfamiliar to foodies. David's uncle, Paul Prudhomme, owner of K-Paul's Louisiana Kitchen in New Orleans, is widely credited with popularizing Cajun cuisine. David learned the ropes in the restaurant his uncle opened in 1979. He makes just about everything from scratch—from salad dressings to the turkey andouille sausage that flavors his jambalaya—and still finds time to work the front of the house, where Sharon presides. Adventurous eaters delight in the menu, which includes turtle soup, alligator tail, and deep-fried bison testicles. But what Lost Cajun does best is blackened catfish. Try the melt-in-your-mouth catfish nuggets or the Cajun-meets-Mexican catfish fajita. The casual, playfully decorated restaurant and bar is also famous for its oversized onion rings. You'll need a knife and fork to attack these bad boys.

Mount Joy

Bube's Brewery (102 N. Market St., 717/653-2056, www.bubesbrewery.com) is reason enough to visit the town of Mount Joy, which at 14 miles northwest of Lancaster isn't particularly close to major tourist attractions. The one-of-a-kind Bube's is many things. For starters, it's a trip back in time. Listed in the National Register of Historic Places, the large brewery/restaurant complex looks much as it did in the late 1800s, when German immigrant Alois Bube produced lager beers there. Bube died in 1908, and the buildings were largely untouched until 1968, when restoration work began. Today they house a microbrewery, several restaurants, a gift shop, and an art gallery. Occupying the original bottling plant is the **Bottling Works** (lunch from 11am Mon.-Sat. and noon Sun., dinner from 5pm daily, $6-29), most casual of the restaurants. Its menu is typical of brewpubs: plenty of deep-fried munchies, soups and salads, burgers and sandwiches, and a selection of hearty entrées. Open-air dining is available in the adjacent **Biergarten,** where you'll find the huge boiler that created steam to power Mr. Bube's brewery.

It's best to make a reservation if you're keen on dining more than 40 feet below ground in the **Catacombs** (dinner from 5:30pm weekdays and 5pm weekends, $22-45). The fine dining restaurant in the original brewery's stone-walled cellars offers the likes of roast duckling, crabmeat-stuffed lobster tail, and filet mignon amid candlelight. On most Sundays it serves a themed feast with a heaping side of theatrics. Bawdy medieval-themed feasts are most common, but its repertoire also includes Roman-, pirate-, and fairy-themed feasts, Halloween-themed feasts in October, and Christmas-themed feasts in December. Feast tickets must be purchased in advance.

Bube's also offers murder mystery dinners ($45) and ghost tours ($10, restaurant guests $5).

INFORMATION

The **Pennsylvania Dutch Convention & Visitors Bureau** (717/299-8901, www.padutchcountry.com) is an excellent source of information about Lancaster County. Visit the website to request a free "getaway guide" or flip through a digital version. At the CVB's main visitors center (501 Greenfield Rd., Lancaster, 9am-5pm Mon.-Sat. and 10am-4pm Sun. Memorial Day weekend-Oct., 10am-4pm daily Nov.-Memorial Day weekend), located just off Route 30 at the Greenfield Road exit, you can watch a brief film, load up on maps and brochures, and chat with travel consultants. Ninety-minute tours of the Amish countryside depart from the visitors center from Memorial Day through October. The CVB also operates a visitors center in downtown Lancaster (5 W. King St., 717/735-0823, open Tues. and Fri.-Sun. Jan.-Mar., daily Apr.-Dec., hours vary by season).

GETTING THERE AND AROUND

The city of Lancaster is about 70 miles west of Philadelphia via Route 30 and 80 miles northeast of Baltimore via I-83 north and Route 30 east. The Pennsylvania Turnpike (I-76) passes through the northern part of Lancaster County, but many of the main attractions lie along or near Route 30, which traverses the central part.

Lancaster Airport (LNS, 717/569-1221, www.lancasterairport.com) is served by just one airline, Sun Air International. The larger **Harrisburg International Airport** (MDT, 888/235-9442, www.flyhia.com) is about 30 miles from Lancaster city. **Amtrak** (800/872-7245, www.amtrak.com) provides rail service to the city. Lancaster's Amtrak station (53 E. McGovern Ave.), which also serves as an intercity bus terminal, was built in 1929 by the Pennsylvania Railroad. Bus service is available through **Greyhound** (800/231-2222, www.greyhound.com) and its interline partners.

For getting around Lancaster County, it's best to have your own wheels, but public transportation is available. **Red Rose Transit Authority** (717/397-5613, www.redrosetransit.com) operates 17 bus routes throughout the county. It also has a tourist trolley that plies the streets of Lancaster city on weekdays. Trolley stops include the Amtrak station and the Downtown Lancaster Visitors Center.

Reading and Vicinity

With a population of 88,000, Reading is the largest city in Pennsylvania Dutch country. It was laid out in 1748 by sons of Pennsylvania founder William Penn and named the seat of Berks County several years later. By then the area was already home to an Amish community, one of the first in the country. Most Amish left Berks County in the latter part of the 1700s and early 1800s for reasons that may have included their pacifism. Reading was a military base during the French and Indian War, and its ironworks helped supply George Washington's troops with ammunition during the Revolutionary War. After Washington famously crossed the icy Delaware River in December 1776 and captured hundreds of Hessian soldiers garrisoned in Trenton, New Jersey, Reading hosted a prisoner-of-war camp.

The construction of the Reading Railroad in the 19th century ushered in the region's economic heyday. Built in the 1830s and '40s, the original mainline stretched south from the coal-mining town of Pottsville to Reading and then on to Philadelphia, a journey of less than 100 miles. Over the next century, the Reading grew into a many-tentacled transportation system with more than 1,000 miles of track. Heavily invested in Pennsylvania's anthracite coal industry, it reigned as one of the world's most prosperous corporations at the turn of the 20th century. Within a few decades, anthracite coal and rail transportation had both fallen out of favor. The railroad filed for bankruptcy and was absorbed by Conrail in the 1970s. But it lives on in the form of a property in the standard version of the board game Monopoly. One of Berks County's 30-plus historical museums and sites is dedicated to the railroad.

Historical attractions notwithstanding, the county is best known as a shopping destination. It's home to an outlet mall and the only Cabela's outdoor megastore in Pennsylvania. It also has much to offer antiques lovers.

By the way, it's pronounced "RED-ing," not "REED-ing."

SIGHTS
The Pagoda

Reading's most prominent landmark is a building of the sort rarely seen outside the Far East. Perched atop Mount Penn, 886 feet above downtown, the **Pagoda** (Duryea Dr., 610/655-6271, www.readingpagoda.com, noon-4pm Fri.-Sun. in summer and Sat.-Sun. rest of year, suggested donation $1) has become a symbol of the city. You'll see it in the logos of businesses and civic organizations and on a shoulder patch worn by the men and women of the Reading Police Department. More than a century old, it's believed to be one of only three pagodas of its scale in the country and the only one in the world with a fireplace and chimney. The story of how the multitiered tower came to be is as interesting as the structure itself. "Reading to Have Japanese Pagoda," read a headline in the August 10, 1906, issue of the *Reading Eagle*. The man behind the plan was local businessman William Abbott Witman, who had made himself very unpopular by starting a stone quarrying operation on the western slope of Mount Penn. The Pagoda would cover the mess he'd left on the mountainside. Moreover, it would serve as a luxury resort.

The exotic building was completed in 1908, but Witman's plan to operate it as a mountain retreat was dealt a fatal blow: his application for a liquor license was denied. By 1910, the property was in foreclosure. To save the bank from a loss, local merchant and bank director Jonathan Mould purchased the Pagoda and presented it to the city as a gift. Before radios came into common use, the seven-story structure served as a sort of public announcement system. Lights installed on its roof flashed Morse code to direct firemen and relay baseball scores, political outcomes, and

Reading's Pagoda

other information. Today the temple of stone and terra-cotta tiles is a popular tourist stop. Visitors can climb 87 solid oak steps to a lookout offering a view for 30-plus miles. There's a small café and gift shop on the first floor. The Pagoda is quite a sight at night, when it's aglow with red LED lights.

Reading Railroad Heritage Museum

Opened in 2008 in a former Pennsylvania Steel foundry complex, the **Reading Railroad Heritage Museum** (500 S. 3rd St., Hamburg, 610/562-5513, www.readingrailroad.org, 10am-4pm Sat., noon-4pm Sun., admission $5, seniors $4, children 5-12 $3) tells the story of the profound impact the railroad had on the communities it served. It's operated by the Reading Company Technical & Historical Society, which began rounding up locomotives and freight and passenger cars several years after the railroad's 1971 bankruptcy filing. The all-volunteer nonprofit is now the proud owner of the nation's largest collection of rolling stock dedicated to a single railroad.

Reading Public Museum

The **Reading Public Museum** (500 Museum Rd., Reading, 610/371-5850, www.readingpublicmuseum.org, 11am-5pm daily, admission $10, seniors, students, and children 4-17 $6, planetarium show $8, seniors, students, and children 4-17 $6) is part art museum, part natural history museum, and part anthropological museum. Founded in 1904 by a local teacher, the museum even has a gallery devoted to its own history. Its fine art collection is particularly strong in oil paintings and includes works by John Singer Sargent, Edgar Degas, Winslow Homer, N. C. Wyeth, George Bellows, Milton Avery, and Berks County native Keith Haring. Among the highlights of its natural history collection are the fossilized footprints of reptiles that roamed the immediate area some 200 million years ago. They were found just a few miles away. The anthropological and historical collections include everything from an Egyptian mummy to 16th-century samurai armor to Pennsylvania German folk art. As if that weren't enough, the museum boasts a 25-acre arboretum and a full-dome planetarium.

GoggleWorks Center for the Arts

Like other cities wrestling with the erosion of their industrial base, Reading has rolled out

Have a Lager

If Pennsylvania had an official state beer, it would have to be **Yuengling Traditional Lager.** It's so ubiquitous and popular that asking for it by name is oftentimes unnecessary. Most bartenders translate "I'll have a lager" as "Pour me a Yuengling." Pronounced properly (YING-ling), the brand sounds like an import from the Far East. But the brewing company more properly known as D.G. Yuengling & Son has been based in Pottsville, Pennsylvania, since its 1829 founding. Yeah, about its age: Yuengling is America's oldest brewery, a fact stamped on every bottle. It survived Prohibition by producing "near beers"—now known as nonalcoholic beers—and celebrated the 1933 repeal of the 18th Amendment by shipping a truckload of real beer to the White House. We don't know how then-president Franklin Roosevelt felt about the suds, but Barack Obama is a fan. When he lost a friendly wager on the outcome of the U.S.-Canada battle for ice hockey gold at the 2010 Winter Olympics, he sent a case of "lager" (as in Yuengling) to the Canadian prime minister.

About 35 miles north of Reading, Pottsville lies in Pennsylvania's coal region, home to the largest fields of anthracite in the country. The city is still recovering from the demise of the anthracite industry after World War II. Yuengling also had it rough in the post-war decades, as the full-flavored products of regional breweries lost favor to lighter national brands. But the company has more than recovered since Richard L. Yuengling Jr. became its fifth-generation owner in 1985. According to a 2013 report by the Boulder, Colorado-based Brewers Association, Yuengling is the fourth largest brewing company in the country. Only Anheuser-Busch, MillerCoors, and Pabst sell more suds. Its rapid growth has much to do with the popularity of "lager," introduced in 1987. Yuengling produces half a dozen other beers but sells more lager than all the rest combined.

Free tours of the Pottsville **brewery** (5th and Mahantongo Streets, 570/628-4890, www.yuengling. com, gift shop open 9am-4pm Mon.-Fri. year-round and 10am-3pm Sat. Apr.-Dec.) are offered at 10am and 1:30pm weekdays year-round and from 11am to 1pm on Saturdays April-December. They include a visit to the "caves" where beer was fermented in years past, and end with free samples. You don't have to be of drinking age to take a tour, but you do have to wear closed shoes. Built in 1831, the facility isn't handicapped accessible.

While in Pottsville, you may want to pay a visit to **Jerry's Classic Cars and Collectibles Museum** (394 S. Center St., 570/628-2266, www.jerrysmuseum.com, noon-5pm Fri.-Sun. May-Oct., admission $8, seniors $6, children 6 and under free), a tribute to the 1950s and '60s.

---

the red carpet for artists and cultural organizations. In 2005 an abandoned factory in Reading's urban core was transformed into the **GoggleWorks Center for the Arts** (201 Washington St., Reading, 610/374-4600, www.goggleworks.org, 11am-7pm daily, free admission). So named because the factory manufactured safety goggles, the arts center boasts several galleries, a film theater, a café, dozens of artist studios, a wood shop, a ceramics studio, a jewelry studio, a glassblowing facility, dance and music studios, and more. The best time to visit is on the **second Sunday** of the month, when most of the artists are in their studios. Held 11am-4pm, the open house features live music and walk-in workshops.

The **GoggleWorks Store** (11am-7pm Mon.-Fri., 11am-5pm Sat.-Sun.) offers unique handcrafted items. GoggleWorks is also home to the **Greater Reading Visitors Center** (610/375-4085, www.gogreaterreading.com), where you can load up on maps and brochures.

★ Air Museums

Berks County is home to not one but two museums dedicated to the history of aviation. Both offer thrill-of-a-lifetime rides in antique planes. Larger and older, the **Mid-Atlantic Air Museum (MAAM)** (11 Museum Dr., Reading, 610/372-7333, www.maam.org, 9:30am-4pm daily, admission $8, seniors $6, children 6-12 $3) at Reading Regional Airport is home to more than 60 aircraft built from 1928 to the early 1980s. Among them is a Northrop P-61 Black Widow—one of only four in existence. In January 1945, the night fighter crashed into a mountainside on the South Pacific Island of New Guinea. World War II veteran Eugene "Pappy" Strine and his son established the air museum in 1980 for the purpose of recovering the rare aircraft, which had logged only 10 flight hours before stalling and crashing during a proficiency check. Green-lighted by the Indonesian government in 1984, the recovery project took seven years. Other highlights of the collection include a North American B-25 Mitchell, a World War II bomber that appeared in half a dozen movies before she was donated to the museum in 1981, and a Douglas R4D-6 Skytrain, which delivered supplies and specialist personnel to combat zones during the war. MAAM's impressive holding of vintage military aircraft and annual **World War II Weekend** have given it a reputation as a "warbird" museum, but in fact, about two-thirds of its flying machines were built for civilians.

Reading's airport was used as a military training airfield during World War II, and for three days each summer, it takes on the look and feel of that era. Held the first full weekend in June, WWII Weekend features air and military vehicle shows, battle re-creations, troop encampments, a militaria flea market, and 1940s entertainment, including big band dances.

The **Golden Age Air Museum** (Grimes Airfield, 371 Airport Rd., Bethel, 717/933-9566, www.goldenageair.org, 10am-4pm Sat. and 11am-4pm Sun. May-Oct., self-guided tour $5, children 6-12 $3, guided tour $8, children 6-12 $3), about 20 miles away, was established in 1997. True to its name, it concentrates on the so-called golden age of aviation: the years between the two World Wars. More than 20 of its 30-some aircraft were built in the late 1910s, '20s, and '30s. The museum is also home to a handful of antique automobiles, including a 1930 Ford Model A roadster. Its **"Flying Circus" air shows,** held twice yearly, pay tribute to barnstorming, a popular form of entertainment in the 1920s.

MAAM offers rides in a pair of 1940s aircraft, including an open-cockpit biplane trainer, on the second weekend of May and July-October, as well as during the WWII extravaganza. The cost of the flight, which lasts about 20-25 minutes, is $225. Reservations are required. Golden Age Air Museum offers rides in an open-cockpit 1929 biplane year-round by appointment. A 15-minute flight costs $99 for one person, $119 for two. One or

World War II reenactment at the Mid-Atlantic Air Museum

two people can fly for 30 minutes for $199 or 60 minutes for $379.

Hopewell Furnace National Historic Site

If you ask Pennsylvanians about the state's iron and steel heritage, they'll probably tell you about the fire-breathing plants that brought renown to cities such as Pittsburgh, Johnstown, and Bethlehem. Most people don't associate the industry with rural Pennsylvania. They haven't been to **Hopewell Furnace National Historic Site** (2 Mark Bird Ln., Elverson, 610/582-8773, www.nps. gov/hofu, 9am-5pm daily in summer and Wed.-Sun. in other seasons, free admission), which features the restored remains of an iron furnace and the village that grew around it. Established in 1771, Hopewell Furnace was one of dozens of "iron plantations" operating in southeastern Pennsylvania by the time the American colonies declared their independence from Great Britain. It supplied cannons, shot, and shells for patriot troops during the Revolutionary War. During the first half of the 19th century, the charcoal-fired furnace produced a wide variety of iron products, including pots, kettles, flatirons, and hammers, gaining fame for its stoves. Even Joseph Bonaparte, elder brother of Napoleon, ordered a Hopewell stove in 1822. After 112 years of operation, the outdated furnace closed in 1883. The workers and their families packed up and left.

Purchased by the federal government in 1935, the Hopewell Furnace property has been restored to the way it looked during its heyday in the 1830s and '40s. Visitors still have to use their imaginations: The National Park Service lacks the wizardry to re-create the billows of charcoal dust, noises, and stench that emanated from the active furnace. Exhibits in the visitors center and occasional living history programs help the imagination. The core of the Hopewell Furnace experience is strolling through the frozen-in-time village, popping into open buildings, so it's best to visit when the weather is nice. Early September through October is a particularly good time because the park's apple orchard, which includes historic varieties you won't find in the supermarket, is open for picking. The apples are sold by the pound. Hiking enthusiasts should plan to stay a while. More than 40 miles of trails traverse the 848-acre historic site and neighboring **French Creek State Park** (843 Park Rd., Elverson, 610/582-9680, www.visit-paparks.com).

Roadside America

Billed as "the world's greatest indoor miniature village," **Roadside America** (109 Roadside Dr., Shartlesville, 610/488-6241, www.roadsideamericainc.com, 9am-6:30pm weekdays and 9am-7pm weekends July-Labor Day, 10am-5pm weekdays and 10am-6pm weekends Sept.-June, admission $6.75, children 6-11 $3.75) ranks among the most unique attractions in Pennsylvania. The massive display features more than 300 miniature structures, 4,000 miniature people, and 10,000 miniature trees. There are horse-drawn carriages and muscle cars, trollies and trains, construction crews and a coal mine. There's even an animated circus. Started in the 1930s by a local carpenter, the masterpiece depicts rural life from pioneer days to the present. In addition to Roadside America, the small town of Shartlesville offers Pennsylvania Dutch food and quaint shops. It's in northern Berks County, about 20 miles northwest of Reading.

★ Hawk Mountain Sanctuary

Located 25 miles north of Reading, **Hawk Mountain Sanctuary** (1700 Hawk Mountain Rd., Kempton, 610/756-6000, www.hawkmountain.org, trails open dawn to dusk daily except during deer season in Dec., visitors center open 8am-5pm daily Sept.-Nov., 9am-5pm Dec.-Aug.) is one of the best places in the country to watch migrating hawks, eagles, falcons, and other winged predators. During the fall migration, counters may record upwards of 1,000 birds in one day. That's because of the sanctuary's location on the Blue Mountain (aka Kittatinny) ridge, part of the

Appalachian range. In the fall, the topography and prevailing northwesterly winds conspire to create updrafts that allow raptors to glide, soar, and save energy on their southward journeys. Lookouts at Hawk Mountain allow for eye-level views of the majestic birds. Some fly so close that you can't help but duck. The migration begins in mid-August and continues into December, peaking September through November. The very best time to visit is two or three days after a cold front passes. Sightings are considerably less frequent during the northbound migration, when prevailing easterlies push raptors west of the sanctuary. Still, it's possible to spot as many as 300 on a day in April or early May.

Founded in 1934 to stop hunters from shooting the migrants, Hawk Mountain is the world's oldest refuge for birds of prey. The nonprofit charges a fee for use of its eight-mile trail system, which connects to the epic Appalachian Trail. The fee is $6 for adults, $5 for seniors, and $3 for children 6-12 except on national holidays and autumn weekends, when adults and seniors pay $8 and children $4. The most popular path winds past a series of lookouts and is known, appropriately enough, as the Lookout Trail. The first lookout is only a couple hundred yards from the trailhead and is accessible by all-terrain wheelchair, available at the visitors center. The trail becomes rocky and uneven after the first few overlooks, but soldier on and you'll reap just rewards. At the end of the mile-long trail is the famed **North Lookout,** site of the sanctuary's official hawk count. It's hard to tear yourself away from the panoramic view from 1,490 feet above sea level, so consider bringing a cushion and something to eat or drink. Definitely pack food and water if you plan to tackle longer trails like the four-mile River of Rocks loop, which drops into a valley and skirts an ice-age boulder field. Trail maps are available on the sanctuary's website and in the visitors center.

If you're new to bird-watching, browse the visitors center's educational displays before starting your hike. A bit of time in the Wings of Wonder Gallery, featuring life-size wood carvings of each migrating raptor, will do wonders for your ability to identify the real deal. You'll more than likely meet longtime visitors as you explore the sanctuary, many of whom can chirp up a storm about spotting and identifying birds. Educators are stationed at some lookouts during busy periods.

North Lookout at Hawk Mountain Sanctuary

Hawk Mountain Line

Known as the Hawk Mountain Line because of its proximity to the bird sanctuary, the **Wanamaker, Kempton & Southern** (home station 42 Community Center Dr., Kempton, 610/756-6469, www.kemptontrain.com, regular ticket $10, children 3-11 $5) is a tourist railroad consisting of several miles of track purchased from the Reading Railroad in the 1960s and a collection of rolling stock that includes both steam and diesel-electric locomotives. The Reading began pulling up tracks in the 1970s, leaving the WK&S with two dead ends. Regular and themed train rides are offered on weekends March-December.

The home station is off Route 737 in Kempton, an itty-bitty community about 30 miles north of Reading. From I-78, take exit 35 for Route 143 north or exit 40 for Route 737 north and continue about five miles to Kempton, where signs point the way to the station. Originally part of the vast Reading Railroad network, the station was moved from the southern tip of Berks County to its present location at the northern tip in 1963.

Crystal Cave Park

Discovered in 1871, **Crystal Cave** (963 Crystal Cave Rd., Kutztown, 610/683-6765, www.crystalcavepa.com, opens at 9am daily Mar.-Nov., closes between 5 and 7pm, tour $12.50, children 4-11 $8.50) is the oldest operating show cave in Pennsylvania. Guides who know their stalagmites from their stalactites lead visitors along concrete pathways, pointing out the "prairie dogs," the "totem pole," the "ear of corn," and other exquisite formations. Tours last 40-50 minutes and include a short video presentation on cave geology. It's a constant 54 degrees inside, so dress accordingly.

There's quite a bit to keep visitors entertained outside the cave, including an 18-hole miniature golf course ($4.50), a panning-for-gemstones attraction, and an ice cream parlor and restaurant open daily in July and August and weekends in June and September. Amish buggy rides and use of the picnic facilities are included in the price of admission.

ENTERTAINMENT AND EVENTS
Concert Venues

Home to Reading's professional ice hockey, indoor soccer, and indoor football teams, the **Santander Arena** (700 Penn St., Reading, 610/898-7469, tickets 800/745-3000, www.santander-arena.com) also hosts concerts, professional wrestling, conventions, and other events. Previous performers include Neil Diamond, Kenny Chesney, Cher, Elton John, and Sting. Opened in 2001, the arena seats 7,200 for hockey and 8,800 for concerts. It's sometimes converted into a smaller, more intimate venue known as the **Reading Eagle Theater.**

Performing Arts

In 2000 the Berks County Convention Center Authority purchased Reading's only surviving movie palace and sank $7 million into renovations. Now known as the **Santander Performing Arts Center** (136 N. 6th St., Reading, 610/898-7469, www.santander-arena.com), the 1,700-seat theater is home to the **Reading Symphony Orchestra** (www.readingsymphony.org). It also hosts touring Broadway productions, popular music concerts, and other events.

The **Miller Center for the Arts** (4 N. 2nd St., Reading, 610/607-6270, www.racc.edu/MillerCenter) also welcomes a wide array of touring acts—from modern dance to classical marionette theater. The glass-walled theater on the campus of Reading Area Community College seats about 500.

Festivals and Events

First held in 1991, **Berks Jazz Fest** (various venues, tickets 800/745-3000, www.berksjazzfest.com, Mar.) has grown bigger and bigger over the years. Famed trumpeter Wynton Marsalis, who played at the inaugural fest, returned in 2010 with his Jazz at Lincoln Center Orchestra. Other past performers include Béla

Fleck and the Flecktones, the Count Basie Orchestra, and Kurt Elling. The 10-day festival is presented by the Berks Arts Council, which is also to thank for a series of free concerts held on Friday evenings in the summer. These **Bandshell Concerts** (City Park, 1261 Hill Rd., Reading, 610/898-1930, www.berksarts.org) showcase various musical genres, including blues, doo-wop, and bluegrass.

Berks County's premier event is the **Kutztown Folk Festival** (Kutztown Fairgrounds, 225 N. White Oak St., Kutztown, 888/674-6136, www.kutztownfestival.com, late June/early July, admission charged, free for children 12 and under), a nine-day celebration of Pennsylvania Dutch culture. Founded in 1950, it's said to be the oldest continuously operated folklife festival in the country. To call it a unique event is an understatement. Where else can you see a reenactment of a 19th-century hanging, watch a Mennonite wedding, take a seminar on the Pennsylvania Dutch dialect, *and* buy bread baked in an early 1800s oven? The festival also features one of the largest quilt sales in the country. More than 2,500 locally handmade quilts are available for purchase; collectors from around the world attend an auction of the prizewinners. Demonstrations of quilting and other traditional crafts are a hallmark of the event. The words *Pennsylvania Dutch* are practically synonymous with *pig-out,* and the Kutztown extravaganza does nothing to dispel that association. All-you-can-eat ham and chicken dinners are a festival tradition, as is roasting a 1,200-pound ox over a bed of coals. The borough of Kutztown is about 20 miles northeast of Reading.

Folks who like it hot descend on an itty-bitty community four miles south of Kutztown for the **Chile Pepper Festival** (William Delong Park, 233 Bowers Rd., Bowers, www.pepperfestival.com, Sept., admission by donation). The two-day event features a jalapeño-eating contest, a salsa contest, and excursions to a local chili pepper field.

Winter's main event is a Christmas display on steroids. **Koziar's Christmas Village** (782 Christmas Village Rd., Bernville, 610/488-1110, www.koziarschristmasvillage. com, first weekend of Nov. to Jan. 1, admission charged) traces its history to 1948, when William M. Koziar strung lights around his house and barn in rural Berks County to the delight of his wife and four children. Each year, he stepped up his game, decorating more and more of his property. The increasingly elaborate display began attracting people from nearby and then people from not-so-nearby. These days more than half a million Christmas lights go into the creation of the winter wonderland. A reflective lake doubles the wow factor. There's more to Koziar's than twinkling lights. It also offers large dioramas of scenes such as "Christmas Beneath the Sea" and "Santa's Post Office," extensive model train layouts, and shops selling ornaments, souvenirs, toys, and other gifts. Santa's on-site, of course.

SHOPPING
VF Outlet Center
One of greater Reading's most popular tourist destinations, the **VF Outlet Center** (801 Hill Ave., Wyomissing, 610/378-0408, www. vfoutletcenter.com, 9:30am-9pm Mon.-Sat., 10am-6pm Sun., call for winter hours) has a rich history. For most of the 20th century, its buildings comprised the Berkshire Knitting Mills. The Berkie, as locals called it, was the world's largest manufacturer of hosiery in the early decades of the century, before seamless nylons became all the rage. In 1969 it was purchased by VF Corporation, which opened a factory store in one end of a manufacturing building. A drop cloth separated the retail and manufacturing areas. The mill ceased operations several years later, but the store remained. Today the VF Outlet store sells brands including Wrangler, Lee, JanSport, and Nautica. Other stores in the mill-turned-mall include Timberland, Reebok, OshKosh B'gosh, and Dooney & Bourke.

Cabela's
The 2003 opening of a **Cabela's** (100 Cabela Dr., Hamburg, 610/929-7000, www.cabelas.

com, 8am-9pm Mon.-Sat., 9am-8pm Sun., call for winter hours) store less than 20 miles north of Reading warranted a story in *The New York Times* travel section. After all, it was the first Cabela's outpost on the East Coast. The revered retailer of outdoor gear has since expanded into Connecticut and Maine, but the Pennsylvania store still reels in millions of hunting and fishing enthusiasts a year. The 250,000-square-foot showplace just off I-78 features shooting and archery ranges, massive aquariums, life-size wildlife dioramas that put many natural history museums to shame, and a restaurant offering sandwiches stuffed with your choice of meats—the choices including elk, wild boar, bison, and ostrich. And then there's the merchandise. The dizzying selection includes everything from guns to outdoor-inspired home decor. Live bait is available for anglers heading to nearby waters. Also available: kennels for shoppers who bring their canine friends, a corral for those who bring their equine friends, and a dump station for those arriving by RV.

Antiques

Antiques lovers can find plenty of what they're looking for in the Reading area. Just 10 miles southwest of Reading, straddling Berks and Lancaster Counties, is the borough of Adamstown, also known as "Antiques Capital USA." See the *Lancaster County* section for the lowdown on Adamstown. Twenty miles northeast of Reading is another antiquing destination: Kutztown's **Renninger's** (740 Noble St., Kutztown, 610/683-6848, www.renningers.com, antiques and flea markets 8am-4pm Sat., farmers market 10am-7pm Fri. and 8am-4pm Sat.). With locations in Adamstown and Florida as well as Kutztown, Renninger's is a big name in antiquing circles. The Kutztown location is open Saturdays and the Adamstown location Sundays, so it's not unusual for treasure hunters to hit both in one weekend. The Kutztown location offers more than antiques; it also boasts a flea market and year-round farmers market. What's for sale? Everything from Indian artifacts and early farm tools to neon beer signs and Pez dispensers. The farmers market has a strong Pennsylvania Dutch flavor. You'll find produce, fresh and smoked meats, baked goods, handmade candies, gourmet coffees and teas, and french fries to die for.

ACCOMMODATIONS
Reading

Though it's the cultural, governmental, and business capital of Berks County, downtown Reading has few lodging options. Its only hotel is the historic ★ **Abraham Lincoln** (100 N. 5th St., 610/372-3700, www.wyndham-readinghotel.com, $120-160), a Wyndham property since 2005. Conveniently located within three blocks of the GoggleWorks Center for the Arts, the Santander Arena, and the Santander Performing Arts Center, the recently renovated hotel has 104 guest rooms, two restaurants, a 24-hour gift shop, and free shuttle service to area businesses and attractions. Abraham Lincoln never slept here. The hotel, which opened in 1930, is named for the nation's 16th president because his great-grandfather lived nearby. Music fans and marines will be interested to know that John Philip Sousa, the famed composer of military marches, suffered a heart attack while rehearsing in the area in 1932 and died in his 14th-floor room at the Abraham Lincoln. With its original chandeliers, stately pillars, and brass and wrought iron railings, the hotel lobby is worth a peek even if you're just passing by.

The great stone mansion now known as the **Stirling Guest Hotel** (1120 Centre Ave., 610/373-1522, www.stirlingguesthotel.net, $150-275) was built in the early 1890s in what was then considered a far suburb of Reading. It's a mere mile north of the city center. Designed in the Châteauesque style for a local iron and steel magnate and named for a castle in Scotland, the mansion has nine sumptuously decorated guest suites. A large Tudor-style carriage house offers six more.

Less than a mile north of the VF Outlet Center, **The Inn at Reading** (1040 N. Park

Rd., Wyomissing, 610/372-7811, www.inna-treading.com, $100-150) has 170 tradition-ally furnished rooms and suites. Amenities include a large outdoor pool open May-September, a half-court basketball court, an exercise facility, and a restaurant modeled on a traditional English pub. Breakfast is on the house Monday-Friday.

Northern Berks County

Pheasants, quail, and chukar, oh my! **Wing Pointe** (1414 Moselem Springs Rd., Hamburg, 610/562-6962, www.wingpt.com) is a resort custom-made for sport-shooting enthusiasts. From September through March, shotgun-toting guests hunt game birds released onto the grounds. Rental dogs and guides are avail-able. The resort, 15 minutes from outdoor me-gastore Cabela's, also offers skeet and sporting clays shooting. Its main lodge features four guest suites ($145-191), a common room with a fireplace and large-screen TV, and an out-door pool and whirlpool. Parties of up to nine people can rent a five-bedroom retreat ($550 for four guests, $83 per additional guest) with plush furnishings, a large modern kitchen, a formal dining room, and its own pool and whirlpool.

For those who venture to these parts to aim binoculars rather than shotguns at birds, there's ★ **Pamela's Forget Me Not B&B** (33 Hawk Mountain Rd., Kempton, 610/756-3398, www.pamelasforgetmenot.com, $115-170). A short drive from the famed Hawk Mountain Sanctuary and the Appalachian Trail, the B&B is as charming as its name. It offers three suites complete with whirlpool tubs and one room with a shared bath. Made for romance, the Cottage Suite features a handcrafted four-poster bed, gas fireplace, and private deck. (The couple that purchased the B&B in 2006 stayed here as guests on the night of their 1999 engage-ment.) The comfy Carriage House Suite, which sleeps up to six people, is perfect for families. The remaining suite and guest room are in the main house, dating to 1879 and Victorian in decor.

FOOD
Reading

Most of Reading's recommendable restau-rants are concentrated in the gritty down-town area. The most famous, thanks to its longevity and a 2008 visit from the Travel Channel, is **Jimmie Kramer's Peanut Bar** (332 Penn St., 610/376-8500, www.peanutbar.com, 11am-11pm Mon.-Thurs., 11am-mid-night Fri., noon-midnight Sat., $7-25). At the "bar food paradise," as the Travel Channel dubbed it, patrons are welcomed with a bowl of peanuts and encouraged to toss the shells on the floor. The casual joint is also known for its hot wings, seafood, house-made des-serts, and draft beer blends. Opened in 1933 as Jimmie Kramer's Olde Central Cafe, the bar and restaurant originally plied patrons with pretzels. When the pretzels ran out one day in 1935, Jimmie sent someone to a peanut roaster across the street, and the shell-tossing tradition was born. Renamed for the humble legume in 1958, the restaurant is now run by Jimmie's grandson.

One block south of the Peanut Bar is a cluster of three eateries owned by local chef Judy Henry. **Judy's on Cherry** (332 Cherry St., 610/374-8511, www.judysoncherry.com, open for lunch Tues.-Fri. and dinner Tues.-Sat., lunch $8-14, dinner $9-30) offers Mediterranean-style fare, most of it cooked in a 6,000-pound hearth-stone oven. The lunch menu features salads, sandwiches, and pasta dishes. Dinnertime selections include the likes of pan-seared golden sea bass and half rack of lamb. Elegant small plates and crispy pizzas are always on offer, and warm focaccia is free with every meal. The adjoining **Speckled Hen Cottage Pub & Alehouse** (30 S. 4th St., 610/685-8511, www.speckledhenpub.com, 4:30pm-midnight Wed.-Sat., $10-23) offers an altogether different dining experience. Henry transformed downtown Reading's oldest building—a log house built in the 1780s—into the sort of pub you'd find in the countryside of England or Ireland. With its working fire-places and comfort cuisine (chicken pot pie, bangers and mashed potatoes, baked mac and cheese, and such), the Speckled Hen hits the spot on a wintry day. On a warm day, make a beeline for **Plein Air** (610/374-8511, open for lunch Tues.-Fri. and dinner Tues.-Sat. mid-May-Sept., $8-18), an outdoor café accessible from either Judy's or the Speckled Hen. The fare is light and summery, and the featured cocktails are delish.

Just outside the downtown area is the lovely **Abigail's Tea Room** (1441 Perkiomen Ave., 610/376-6050, www.abigailstearoom.com, 11am-3pm Wed.-Sat., open Sun. in Dec. with reservation), which offers a simple lunch menu (under $10) as well as high tea experiences ($19-22). For the latter, be sure to make a reservation at least a day in advance. Abigail's is Victorian through and through, from its setting—an 1883 manse outfitted with period furnishings and crystal chandeliers—to its delicate floral china. Lady Gaga has been photographed with exquisite teacups purchased from the owner's website.

In 2012 downtown's chicest dining establishment relocated to a 200-year-old inn a few miles south of town. ★ **Dans at Green Hills** (2444 Morgantown Rd., 610/777-9611, www.dansatgreenhills.com, 4pm-9pm Tues.-Sat., $19-36) is no longer owned by the two Dans who opened it in 1989 but carries on their mission of providing "a contemporary alternative to the traditional Berks County dining scene." If it's fine dining you seek, look no further.

Northern Berks County

With a name like **Deitsch Eck** (87 Penn St., Lenhartsville, 610/562-8520, www.deitscheck.com, 4pm-8pm Wed.-Fri., 11:30am-8pm Sat., 11:30am-7pm Sun., $4-15), it has to be Pennsylvania Dutch. Chef-owner Steve Stetzler began working in the corner restaurant (*Deitsch Eck* means "Dutch Corner") when he was 15 and bought it nine years later in 1997. His mother and sister are among the staff. In addition to heaping portions of Pennsylvania Dutch cooking, they serve a wide variety of burgers and sandwiches and Italian favorites like veal parmigiana. A meat market in their quaint country town provides the ground beef, hams, pork chops, and sausages.

INFORMATION AND SERVICES

The **Greater Reading Convention & Visitors Bureau** (610/375-4085, www.gogreaterreading.com) is a good source of information about the area. Visit the website to request a free copy of its official visitors guide or peruse a digital version. The guide and some 300 brochures are available at the CVB's visitors center in the **GoggleWorks Center for the Arts** (201 Washington St., Reading, 11am-7pm daily).

GETTING THERE AND AROUND

Located about 60 miles northwest of Philadelphia via I-76 west and I-176 north and 30 miles northeast of Lancaster, Reading is primarily a drive-to destination. There's no scheduled service to Reading Regional Airport, home to the Mid-Atlantic Air Museum. **Lehigh Valley International Airport** (ABE, 800/359-5842, www.flyvia.com), served by airlines including Delta and United, is 40 miles from Reading. **Harrisburg International Airport** (MDT, 888/235-9442, www.flyhia.com) and **Philadelphia International Airport** (PHL, 215/937-6937, www.phl.org) are about 60 miles away.

Intercity bus service to Reading is available through **Greyhound** (20 N. 3rd St., 800/231-2222, www.greyhound.com) and its interline partners. Local bus service is provided by the Berks Area Reading Transportation Authority, or **BARTA** (610/921-0601, www.bartabus.com). Call **Reading Metro Taxi** (610/374-5111) if you need a lift.

Hershey and Vicinity

Hershey is a town built on chocolate as surely as if cocoa were used in place of concrete. It owes its name and existence to Milton S. Hershey, founder of the largest chocolate company in North America. Milton Hershey was born in 1857 in a small central Pennsylvania community. His family moved frequently while his father pursued a series of get-rich schemes, and as a consequence, he never advanced past the fourth grade. At 14, he began a four-year apprenticeship with a Lancaster confectioner—and found his calling. But the young candy maker wasn't immediately successful. His first candy business, in Philadelphia, collapsed after six years. In 1883 he opened a candy shop in New York. Again, his venture failed. Penniless, he returned to Lancaster and gave it a third try, making caramels by day and selling them from a pushcart in the evenings. A large order from a British candy importer and a loan from a local bank marked a turning point for the persistent entrepreneur. His Lancaster Caramel Company soon became one of the leading caramel manufacturers in the country, and he became a very rich man.

At the Chicago World's Fair in 1893, Mr. Hershey was transfixed by an exhibit of German chocolate-making equipment. He purchased the machinery and had it installed in the east wing of his caramel factory. The Hershey Chocolate Company was born.

Back then, milk chocolate was a Swiss luxury product. Mr. Hershey was determined to develop a formula for affordable milk chocolate, and by the dawn of the new century, he had succeeded. He sold the Lancaster Caramel Company for $1 million, retaining his chocolate-making machinery, and in 1903 broke ground on a new, larger factory. The site: a cornfield in Derry Township, Pennsylvania, about a mile from his birthplace. It wasn't simply nostalgia that brought him back. Mr. Hershey needed fresh milk for his milk chocolate, and the area was rich in dairy farms. There was a railroad line and turnpike nearby. The absence of housing and other infrastructure for future employees didn't faze him. He was bent on building not only a manufacturing plant but also a model town.

The intersection of two dirt roads a short

the town of Hershey at night

distance from the factory became the center of his town. He named one Chocolate Avenue and the other Cocoa Avenue. A trolley system was up and running even before the factory was completed. As Americans fell in love with his chocolate, homes for workers and executives were built on streets named after cocoa-growing regions: Trinidad, Java, Ceylon, and such. Mr. Hershey saw to it that builders used a variety of designs so that the community wouldn't look like a company town. It wasn't long before his eponymous town had a fire company, barber shop, blacksmith shop, gas station, service garage, and weekly newspaper. He had set aside land for a park, and by 1910 it boasted a band shell, swimming pool, zoo, and bowling alley. Today Hersheypark boasts more than 60 rides and attractions, including a dozen roller coasters. Sales of Hershey's chocolates grew even during the Great Depression, and so did the town. Taking advantage of low-cost materials, the chocolate magnate launched a massive building campaign that employed hundreds of people. Among the town's Depression-era landmarks are the grand Hotel Hershey and Hersheypark Arena, home to the Hershey Bears hockey team (originally named the Hershey B'ars) until 2002 and site of a massive

surprise party on Mr. Hershey's 80th birthday. He died in 1945 at the age of 88.

The Hershey Company, as it's now named, does business all over the world. But the company founded by Milton Hershey is still based in the town built by Milton Hershey—a town with streetlights shaped like Hershey's Kisses. It still makes chocolate there. You can smell it in the air. "The Sweetest Place on Earth," as Hershey is called, attracts several million visitors a year. Factory tours are no longer given, but it's still possible to learn a world about chocolate and the man who brought it to the masses. Start at The Hershey Story, one of the newest attractions, for an excellent overview. Of course, if you have kids in tow, as a great deal of visitors do, they'll probably insist on starting at Hersheypark. Wherever you start, pace yourself. This place is right up there with Disney World in its concentration of attractions.

SIGHTS
★ The Hershey Story

The Hershey Story (63 W. Chocolate Ave., Hershey, 717/534-3439, www.hersheystory. org, hours vary but generally open 9am-5pm daily) opened in 2009, the first new landmark building on Chocolate Avenue in 75 years. It

The Hershey Story

Milton Hershey's Orphan Heirs

The mural *Community Builder* by William Cochran, located in the lobby of The Hershey Story, depicts Milton Hershey as if he were visiting modern-day Hershey to witness the growth of his legacy.

Married for 10 years and unable to have children, Milton Hershey and his wife, Catherine, established a boarding school for orphaned boys in 1909. The Hershey Industrial School, as it was called at the time, had an initial enrollment of 10. Catherine Hershey—"Kitty" to her adoring husband—wouldn't live to see its dramatic expansion. After a long and debilitating muscular illness, she died in 1915. Three years later, Milton Hershey transferred the bulk of his fortune, including his stock in the Hershey Chocolate Company, to the trust created to fund the school. Upon his death in 1945, townspeople streamed into the school's foyer, where his body lay in state. The funeral service was held in the auditorium, with eight boys from the senior class serving as pallbearers.

Renamed the **Milton Hershey School** (www.mhs-pa.org) in 1951, it began enrolling girls in the 1970s. Today more than 1,800 underprivileged children from prekindergarten through 12th grade live and learn on the 9,000-acre campus—at no cost to their families. Milton Hershey's endowment has grown in value to more than $7 billion. The school trust's assets include full ownership of Hershey Entertainment & Resorts, the company behind Hersheypark, ZooAmerica, The Hotel Hershey, the Giant Center, the Hershey Theatre, and other products of Milton Hershey's vision of a town rich in recreational and cultural resources.

delivers exactly what its name promises: the story of the man, the company, and the town named Hershey. The story unfolds on the museum's second floor, where visitors learn about Milton Hershey's childhood and rocky road to success, his chocolate-making innovations and creative promotion strategies, his model town, and his philanthropies. Among the artifacts displayed are a chocolate-mixing machine from the 1920s and a Hershey's Kisses-wrapping machine, both in working order. Admission to the exhibit area is $10 for adults, $9 for seniors, $7.50 for children 3-12.

The main floor features the Chocolate Lab, where visitors get hands-on experience in chocolate-making. Arrive early if you're interested. Classes can only be booked on the day of, and they fill quickly. They're $10 for adults, $9 for seniors, $7.50 for children 4-12. Children under 4 aren't permitted in the lab.

Combo tickets are available for visitors who want to take in the exhibits and take part in a class: $17.50 for adults, $16.50 for seniors, $14 for children.

Also on the main floor is Café Zooka, named after one of Milton Hershey's early chocolate novelties. You won't find his Chocolate Zooka Sticks on the menu (they were discontinued in 1904), but you will find a variety of sandwiches, salads, pizzas, and desserts. Leave room for the Countries of Origin Chocolate Tasting: six warm drinking chocolates, each representing a different chocolate-growing region, for $9.95.

★ Hersheypark

Even before his chocolate factory was built, Milton Hershey had laid out the plans for a town. He'd set aside 150 acres along Spring Creek for a park where his employees could picnic and paddle the day away. The park opened in the spring of 1907 and soon became a tourist attraction, with excursion trains and trolleys delivering fun-seekers from surrounding communities. Today **Hersheypark** (100 W. Hersheypark Dr., Hershey, 717/534-3900, www.hersheypark.com) lures people from across the state and beyond with more than 60 rides and attractions, including a dozen roller coasters. The historic park spends generously to stay current. Five of the coasters were installed in the 21st century, including Lightning Racer, the first wooden dueling coaster in the United States. Bring bathing suits to enjoy Hersheypark's water attractions, which include Tidal Force, one of the tallest splash-down rides in the world, and a 378,000-gallon wave pool. For those who prefer to stay firmly planted on the earth, Hersheypark offers shopping and a busy schedule of live entertainment.

The park is open daily from Memorial Day weekend through Labor Day and some weekends before and after that period. Gates open at 10am and close between 6pm and 11pm. One-day admission is $57.95 for guests ages 9-54, $36.95 for children 3-8 and adults 55-69,

$23.95 for those 70 and older. Hang on to your ticket stub in case you decide to come back the next day; consecutive-day admission is $35.50. The park also offers special "sunset" rates and flex passes good for admission to the park on any two or three days of the season. Hersheypark tickets are good for same-day admission to ZooAmerica.

The park opens several times outside its regular season. **Springtime in the Park** is a chance to preview what's in store for summer over several days in April. **Hersheypark in the Dark** offers Halloween-themed fun. The park is also open in late November and throughout December for **Hersheypark Christmas Candylane.** Meet Santa's reindeer and take in a light show set to holiday tunes at Hersheypark. Then hop in the car and crank up the heater for **Hershey Sweet Lights,** a drive-through spectacular located a few minutes from the amusement park.

ZooAmerica

In 1905, a couple from Lebanon, Pennsylvania, approached Milton Hershey with an idea. Several years earlier they'd emigrated from Germany, where they'd owned 12 prairie dogs and a bear cub. Alas, their yard in Lebanon couldn't accommodate their brood. They figured Mr. Hershey's proposed park could. **ZooAmerica** (30 Park Ave., Hershey, 717/534-3900, www.zooamerica.com, open year-round, hours vary, admission $10.50, seniors and children 3-8 $8.50, free admission with Hersheypark ticket) traces its history to their meeting with the chocolate magnate. The 11-acre zoo is home to more than 200 animals from five regions of North America. Visitors are never terribly far from the critters but have a rare opportunity to get even closer during behind-the-scenes tours ($45), offered Tuesday, Friday, and Sunday mornings and Wednesday and Saturday evenings. Preregistration is required for the two-hour tours. ZooAmerica is connected to Hersheypark by a walking bridge. It also an entrance on Park Avenue (Route 743).

Hershey's Chocolate World

When The Hershey Company ceased factory tours in the 1970s, it gave the public **Hershey's Chocolate World** (251 Park Blvd., Hershey, 717/534-4900, www.hersheys.com/chocolateworld, open year-round, hours vary). Adjacent to Hersheypark, Chocolate World is part mall, part interactive museum. Its shops sell anything and everything Hershey's, including pillows shaped like packets of Reese's Peanut Butter Cups, Twizzlers-shaped pens, and personalized chocolate bars. A primer on the chocolate-making process is available in the form of a slow-moving amusement ride. Passengers are transported from a tropical rainforest where cocoa beans flourish to a chocolate factory, encountering some singing cows along the way. The ride is free; other Chocolate World attractions have an admission fee. The *Hershey's Great Chocolate Factory Mystery in 4D,* which premiered in May 2013, is $7.95 for adults and $6.95 for children 12 and under. The show features animated characters controlled by professional puppeteers, and audience participation determines its outcome. For $14.95, visitors can create their own candy bar and design the package. Chocolate World also has a chocolate-tasting attraction ($9.95, seniors $9.45, children $6.95).

To fill up on something other than candy, head to the food court for sandwiches, soups, pizzas, and of course desserts. If you buy nothing else during your visit to Chocolate World, buy a chocolate milkshake. Worth every calorie.

Complimentary shuttle service is available between Chocolate World and Hersheypark. You can also hop aboard an old-fashioned trolley car for a fascinating tour of the town with a ham of a conductor. **Hershey Trolley Works** (717/533-3000, www.hersheytrolleyworks.com, fare $12.95, seniors $11.95, children 3-12 $7.95) tours depart Chocolate World daily rain or shine (but not in snow).

Hershey Gardens

When chocolate magnate and philanthropist Milton Hershey was asked to sponsor a national rosarium in Washington DC, he decided to create one in his eponymous town instead. "A nice garden of roses," as he called it, opened to the public in 1937 and within five years had blossomed into a 23-acre horticultural haven. Roses are still the specialty at **Hershey Gardens** (170 Hotel Rd., Hershey, 717/534-3492, www.hersheygardens.org, open daily late Mar.-Oct. and select days Nov.-Dec., hours vary, admission $10, seniors $9, children 3-12 $7.50), located across from The Hotel Hershey. More than 5,000 roses of 275 varieties bloom during the summer months. Springtime is pretty special, too. That's when 45,000 tulips of 100 varieties blanket the Seasonal Display Garden and daffodils light up the Perennial Garden. Bold-colored chrysanthemums steal the show in fall. But what most visitors go gaga over isn't roses or tulips or any flower for that matter. It's the Butterfly House, open late May to mid-September. Visitors can observe the entire life cycle of the ethereal insects. Also popular is the Children's Garden, filled with not only flora but also fun activities.

The Hotel Hershey

The Hotel Hershey (100 Hotel Rd., Hershey, 717/533-2171, www.thehotelhershey.com), a Mediterranean-style product of Milton Hershey's Depression-era building campaign, deserves a spot on your itinerary even if you're not staying there. Grand to begin with, the hotel is grander than ever on the heels of a $67 million renovation and expansion that was completed in 2009. Some amenities are exclusively for guests. But nonguests can still have a field day. For starters, they can sink into a chocolate milk bath at The Spa at The Hotel Hershey (717/520-5888, www.chocolatespa.com), better known by its nickname, the **"Chocolate Spa."** Other chocolate-inspired services include a Swedish massage with chocolate-scented oil and an exfoliating treatment with cocoa bean husks. The spa menu also pays homage to Cuba, where Milton Hershey spent much of his time after his wife's death in 1915, buying and building sugar mills. The Noche Azul Soak, for example, is a 15-minute dip in waters infused with Cuba's national flower. The three-story spa overlooks the hotel's formal gardens and reflecting pools.

The hotel's boutiques welcome the general public. Among them is a swimwear store with a particularly large selection of chocolate-brown pieces and a sweets shop known for its cupcakes. One of the oldest and most distinguished restaurants in central Pennsylvania calls the hotel home. **The Circular** owes its shape to Mr. Hershey, who noticed during his world travels that guests who tipped poorly were often seated in the corners of restaurants. "I don't want any corners," he reportedly said. He also saw to it that the restaurant had no pillars, having noticed that single diners were often seated at tables with obstructed views.

Not interested in spa treatments, shopping, or excellent food? Come to The Hotel Hershey for the view. Situated on a hilltop, it overlooks "The Sweetest Place on Earth."

Antique Auto Museum at Hershey

Home to the Lakeland bus used in the movie *Forrest Gump* and a green Cadillac Seville once owned by actress Betty White, the **Antique Auto Museum at Hershey** (161 Museum Dr., Hershey, 717/566-7100, www.aacamuseum.org, 9am-5pm daily, admission $10, seniors $9, children 4-12 $7) is one of the few attractions in town that have nothing to do with chocolate. An affiliate of the Smithsonian Institution, the museum has more than 150 cars, motorcycles, and buses. As many as 100 are displayed at any given time. You don't have to be an auto enthusiast to appreciate the elaborate dioramas depicting scenes such as a 1940s gas station and 1950s drive-in.

Indian Echo Caverns

Geological forces make for family entertainment at **Indian Echo Caverns** (368 Middletown Rd., Hummelstown, 717/566-8131, www.indianechocaverns.com, 9am-6pm daily Memorial Day-Labor Day, 10am-4pm rest of year, admission $14, seniors $12, children 3-11 $8), located four miles west of Hershey off Route 322. The first visitors to the limestone caverns were likely Susquehannock Indians seeking shelter from inclement weather. The caverns still do a brisk business on rainy days, when Hersheypark holds less than its usual appeal. Guides point out

the Antique Auto Museum at Hershey

spectacular formations and share cavern lore during 45-minute walking tours. It's always a cool 52 degrees inside, so dress accordingly. In summer, allot an extra hour if you're bringing kids. The grounds include a playground, a petting zoo, and Gem Mill Junction, where budding prospectors can search for amethyst, jasper, agate, and other treasures.

Hollywood Casino at Penn National Race Course

Not every attraction in the Hershey area was built with kids in mind. Nine miles north of chocolate central, grown-ups gamble on slots and horses at **Hollywood Casino at Penn National Race Course** (77 Hollywood Blvd., Grantville, 717/469-2211, www.hcpn. com, open 24 hours). Live thoroughbred races, a tradition since 1972, are held Wednesday-Saturday evenings throughout the year. The casino, which opened in 2008, is ding-dingding 24/7 with the occasional ka-ching! Dining options include the upscale **Final Cut Steakhouse** (717/469-3090, 5:30pm-10pm Wed.-Fri., 5pm-10pm Sat., 5pm-9pm Sun., $25-42) and a buffet restaurant open for lunch and dinner Wednesday-Sunday.

Cornwall Iron Furnace

Cornwall Iron Furnace (94 Rexmont Rd., Cornwall, 717/272-9711, www.cornwallironfurnace.org, 9am-5pm Thurs.-Sat., noon-5pm Sun., admission $8, seniors $7, children 3-11 $4) was retired from service more than a century ago, but it still has a job to do: teaching visitors about the fiery infancy of America's metals industry. Charcoal-fueled furnaces dotted the Pennsylvania countryside in the 18th and 19th centuries, but this one is unique in its intactness. Indeed, the blast furnace and related buildings are regarded as one of the best-preserved 19th-century iron-making complexes in the world.

What used to be the charcoal barn is now a visitors center with interpretive exhibits on mining, charcoal-making, and iron-making. Other surviving structures include a blacksmith shop, a building where wagons were built and repaired, and a darling Gothic Revival building that served as a butcher shop for the ironmaster's estate.

The iron ore mine, which continued to operate until 1973, is just south of the furnace site and visible from Boyd Street. The open pit mine was sensationally prolific, yielding more than 100 million tons before beginning to flood. Today it's filled with water. Houses built in the 19th century for miners and furnace workers still line Boyd Street.

ENTERTAINMENT AND EVENTS
Performance Venues

Best known as the home arena of the Hershey Bears hockey team, **Giant Center** (550 W. Hersheypark Dr., Hershey, 717/534-3911, www.giantcenter.com) hosts some of the flashiest performers to pass through Hershey. It opened in 2002 with a Cher concert. More recent guests have included 50 Cent, Kelly Clarkson, the Harlem Globetrotters, and the Ringling Bros. and Barnum & Bailey circus. Less-than-famous folks can hit the ice during occasional public skating sessions. The arena seats 10,000-12,500 depending on the nature of the event.

Hersheypark Stadium (100 W. Hersheypark Dr., Hershey, 717/534-3911, www.hersheyparkstadium.com) can accommodate 30,000 fans for concerts. The outdoor stadium has hosted the likes of The Who and U2. It's also the venue for sporting events such as the Big 33 Football Classic, an annual all-star game between high school players from Pennsylvania and Ohio. Built as part of Milton Hershey's Depression-era building campaign, the stadium at one point served as the summer home of the Philadelphia Eagles. The **Star Pavilion** opened at Hersheypark Stadium in 1996. It's a more intimate open-air venue with reserved and lawn seating for 8,000.

The spectacular **Hershey Theatre** (15 E. Caracas Ave., Hershey, 717/534-3405, www. hersheytheatre.com) went up during Mr. Hershey's "Great Building Campaign," which created jobs for an estimated 600 skilled workers. The lobby boasts a floor laid with polished Italian lava rock, soaring marble arches, and a ceiling adorned with bas-relief images of swans, war chariots, and more. An intricate lighting system creates the illusion of twinkling stars and floating clouds overhead. The 1,904-seat theater hosts touring Broadway shows, concerts, dance performances, and classic films.

For a list of events at Giant Center, Hersheypark Stadium, Star Pavilion, and Hershey Theatre, visit www.hersheyentertainment.com. If you catch a summer concert at any of these venues, you can visit Hersheypark the day before, day of, or day after the concert for a discounted admission price of $38.95. Present your ticket or ticket stub at Hersheypark's front gate to receive the discount.

Festivals and Events

With Hersheypark closed and temps that dip below freezing, February wouldn't seem like a good time to visit Hershey. If you're a bargain-hunting chocolate lover, it's an ideal time. Each day of **Chocolate-Covered February** (800/437-7439, www.chocolate-coveredfebruary.com) brings a host of chocolate-themed activities along with discounts on everything from museum tickets to spa treatments. The month-long celebration of Hershey's signature foodstuff features chocolate-inspired meals, chef demonstrations, and classes in topics such as truffle-making, chocolate martini mixology, and wine and chocolate pairing.

There's no shortage of entertainment in Hershey during the summer months, but fans of classical and jazz music may wish to head east, to Mount Gretna. The resort community about 12 miles from Hershey has long been known as a cultural mecca. It's home to the **Pennsylvania Chautauqua** (general information 717/964-3270, summer programs 717/964-1830, www.pachautauqua.org), which sponsors Thursday evening organ recitals, a Friday morning writers' series, and a host of other cultural and educational programs throughout the summer. **Music at Gretna** (717/361-1508, www.gretnamusic.org), a classical chamber music and jazz festival spanning several weeks, has welcomed the likes of jazz pianist Dave Brubeck and singer/guitarist John Pizzarelli.

Hershey draws thousands of antique automobile enthusiasts during the first full week of October. The **Antique Automobile Club of America's Eastern Division Fall Meet** (717/566-7720, www.aaca.org), held in Hershey since 1955, is one of the largest antique automobile shows and flea markets in the country.

SHOPPING

The **Tanger Outlets Hershey** (46 Outlet Square, Hershey, 717/520-1236, www.tanger-outlet.com, 9:30am-9pm Mon.-Sat., 11am-5pm Sun.) are just off Hershey Park Drive, within minutes of Hersheypark and other main attractions. Brooks Brothers, J.Crew, Calvin Klein, Tommy Hilfiger, and Polo Ralph Lauren are among the 60-some stores.

SPORTS AND RECREATION
Spectator Sports

The **Hershey Bears** (Giant Center, 550 W. Hersheypark Dr., Hershey, 717/508-2327, www.hersheybears.com) have competed in the professional American Hockey League without interruption since 1938. Amateur hockey came to Hershey even earlier, in 1931. The popularity of matches between college teams convinced chocolate czar Milton S. Hershey and his longtime chief of entertainment to sponsor a permanent team the following year. They called it the Hershey B'ars. Renamed the Hershey Bears in 1936, the team has brought home at least one Calder Cup, the AHL's ultimate prize, every decade since the 1940s. The Bears "draw more fans and inspire more passion than just about any team in minor league hockey," *The Washington Post* wrote of the Washington Capitals affiliate in 2009. Later that year, the Bears became the first team in league history to win 10 championships. They won their 11th Calder Cup in 2010.

ACCOMMODATIONS

Hershey Entertainment & Resorts

(800/437-7439, www.hersheypa.com), the company founded when Milton Hershey decided to separate his nonchocolate ventures from the business that made them all possible, controls not only most of the tourist attractions in town but also three lodging properties: the upscale Hotel Hershey, the more affordable Hershey Lodge, and Hersheypark Camping Resort. There are plenty of other places to bed down, but staying at a Hershey Resorts property has its privileges. Guests of The Hotel Hershey and Hershey Lodge get free admission to the Hershey Gardens and The Hershey Story, while campground guests get discounted admission. Other perks include discounted admission to Hersheypark and access to some rides before the gates officially open. Hershey Resorts guests also have the exclusive opportunity to purchase a **Hersheypark Sweet Access Pass** ($209-250, seniors and children 3-8 $125-150), which includes admission to Hersheypark, a meal voucher, various discounts, and best of all, front-of-the-line privileges at most rides.

For obvious reasons, most Hershey hotels charge a heckuva lot more in summer than the rest of the year.

Under $100

Open year-round, **Hersheypark Camping Resort** (1200 Sweet St., Hummelstown, reservations 800/437-7439, direct 717/534-8995, www.hersheyparkcampingresort.com, campsites $36-60, cabins $76-158) offers more than 300 tent and RV sites and cabins ranging from rustic to deluxe. The 55-acre campground is minutes from Hersheypark. Amenities include two swimming pools, a game room, basketball and volleyball courts, horseshoe pits, and a country store. Organized activities add to the fun in summer. Another good budget option: the family-run **Chocolatetown Motel** (1806 E. Chocolate Ave., Hershey, 717/533-2330, www.chocolatetownmotel.com, $54-140), which boasts an outdoor pool. Even during the busiest weeks of the busy season, rates start at just $89.

$100-300

With 665 guest rooms and suites and 100,000 square feet of function space, ★ **Hershey Lodge** (325 University Dr., Hershey, reservations 800/437-7439, direct 717/533-3311, www.hersheylodge.com, summer $260-320, off-season $160-280) is Pennsylvania's largest convention resort. Not surprisingly, it's quite often crawling with convention-goers. But it's also wildly popular with families, won over by amenities including a mini golf course, activities such as poolside movies and family bingo, and appearances by Hershey's product characters. (Who can resist a huggable Hershey's Kiss?) The chocolate theme extends to the decor of the guest rooms, which feature complimentary wireless Internet access, refrigerators, and flat-screen TVs. Guests can catch A&E Biography's *Milton Hershey: The Chocolate King* any time of day.

Hershey has several chain hotels in this price range. Closest to the action: **Days Inn Hershey** (350 W. Chocolate Ave., Hershey, 717/534-2162, www.daysinnhershey.com, summer $190-250, off-season $100-160). Owned and operated by a lifelong Hershey resident, the hotel has more to recommend it than convenience. The rooms are spacious and the staff gracious. Guests get all sorts of freebies: hotel-wide wireless Internet access, a hot breakfast, shuttle service to Hersheypark, 24-hour coffee and tea service, and use of the Gold's Gym less than two miles away. Plus, they get to bring their pets. Another fine choice is **SpringHill Suites Hershey** (115 Museum Dr., Hershey, 717/583-2222, www. springhillsuiteshershey.com, summer $250-260, off-season $125-160), where Internet access and breakfast are likewise free. It's next door to the Antique Auto Museum and freshly renovated. All guest rooms are studio-suites with a pull-out sofa in addition to one or two beds. Both the Days Inn and SpringHill Suites have an indoor pool and whirlpool, a fitness center, and guest laundry facilities.

For homier digs, head to the **1825 Inn Bed & Breakfast** (409 S. Lingle Ave., Palmyra, 717/838-8282, www.1825inn.com, $134-269). The main house has six country-style guest rooms with private baths. A pair of cottages with a more contemporary aesthetic, king-size beds, two-person whirlpool tubs, and private decks seem to have been designed with honeymooners in mind.

Some of the area's most elegant accommodations can be found on a picturesque horse farm. ★ **The Inn at Westwynd Farm** (1620 Sand Beach Rd., Hummelstown, 717/533-6764, www.westwyndfarminn.com, $109-275) is just 10 minutes north of Hershey but, as owners Carolyn and Frank Troxell are fond of saying, "a world apart." Their goal is simple: to pamper the heck out of guests. That means refreshments upon arrival, a bottomless cookie jar, and gourmet breakfasts that reflect the season, often flavored with herbs from their own garden. The Troxells are happy to point guests to good restaurants and even arrange for dinner at the home of an Amish family. Bringing your family? Ask for the carriage house with its full bath, living room, and space enough for six. The main house has nine en suite guest rooms, eight of which have fireplaces, five of which have whirlpool tubs, and all of which have charm in spades.

Over $300

Milton Hershey's plan to build a luxury hotel during the Great Depression met with ridicule. He poured $2 million into the project anyway. When he addressed the first guests of **The Hotel Hershey** (100 Hotel Rd., Hershey, reservations 800/437-7439, direct 717/533-2171, www.thehotelhershey.com, summer traditional room from $400, cottage room from $500, off-season traditional room from $280, cottage room from $380) on May 26, 1933, he also addressed his critics. "When we farmers go to the city, we are impressed by the fine hotels we see there," he said. "So I

thought I'd impress the city folks by building a fine hotel on one of our farms. I am of the opinion that there will be a need for this hotel someday, although the prospects do not look very encouraging at the present time." Mr. Hershey's 170-room hotel impressed folks, indeed. Renowned newsman Lowell Thomas, who visited the hotel in its first year, described it as "a palace that out-palaces the palaces of the Maharajahs of India." The Hotel Hershey is even more palatial now, having treated itself to a $67 million facelift and expansion on the occasion of its 75th anniversary. Among the new facilities is an outdoor swimming complex with an infinity-edge pool, whirlpool, and family pool with two large slides. The pool complex also has 14 swanky cabanas complete with flat-screen TVs, ceiling fans, and refrigerators, available to guests for $200 a day. (The hotel has an indoor pool, so guests can still get their swim on during the colder months.) Also added as part of the expansion: 10 luxury guest cottages. Bordering dense woods, the four- and six-bedroom cottages are the hotel's poshest accommodations. Guests can reserve individual bedrooms or an entire cottage. The latter affords them access to a great room with a fireplace, French doors opening to a porch, and other comforts. The hotel's main building has 228 guest rooms and suites, including the especially elegant Milton Hershey Suite with its veranda overlooking the town of Hershey.

FOOD

Some of Hershey's best restaurants are within The Hotel Hershey (100 Hotel Rd., Hershey). Finest of them all is ★ **The Circular** (717/534-8800, www.thecircular.com, breakfast 7am-10:30am daily, lunch noon-2pm Fri.-Sat., brunch noon-2:30pm Sun., dinner 5pm-9:30pm Mon.-Wed., 5pm-10pm Thurs.-Sat., 6pm-9:30pm Sun., breakfast $8-20, dinner $14-49), which dates to the 1930s. Milton Hershey insisted that the restaurant have no pillars or corners, noting that other restaurants seated single diners at tables with obstructed views and poor tippers in corners.

Previously called the Circular Dining Room, the restaurant was redesigned and rebranded in 2013. It's less formal—you can get away with denim—and livelier than its previous incarnation. A large central bar serves up cocktails inspired by the Prohibition era and Milton Hershey's pursuits and travels, several varieties of chocolate martini, and even chocolate-tinged beers. The Circular puts a sophisticated spin on all-you-can-eat dining, offering a daily breakfast buffet ($19.50, children 3-11 $9), a lunch buffet ($23, children $11.50) on Fridays and Saturdays, and a spectacular Sunday brunch buffet ($39.95, children $19.50) complete with seafood bar and carving station. Dinner showcases the restaurant's highly trained servers and ends with a salted caramel, a tribute to Mr. Hershey's first successful candy business. Make a reservation if you're coming for lunch, Sunday brunch, or dinner.

The Hotel Hershey's other restaurants include **Harvest** (717/534-8800, www.thehotelhershey.com, 11:30am-9pm Sun.-Thurs., 11:30am-10pm Fri.-Sat., lunch $12-29, dinner $13-48), which prides itself on using ingredients from nearby farms and purveyors. It's also rightly proud of its burgers and steaks. **Trevi 5** (717/534-8800, www.thehotelhershey.com, 11:30am-10pm daily, lunch $12-21, dinner $12-32), the hotel's newest restaurant, is an Italian grill. Delicious antipastos and meat and cheese platters threaten to sate your appetite before your main course.

Fenicci's of Hershey (102 W. Chocolate Ave., Hershey, 717/533-7159, www.feniccis.com, 11am-1am Mon.-Thurs., 11am-2am Fri.-Sat., noon-1am Sun., $11-27) is spitting distance from Hersheypark, The Hershey Story, and other main attractions, but don't mistake it for a tourist trap. The casual Italian eatery, which dates to 1935, is beloved by generations of locals. It's famous for its upside-down pizza—cheese on bottom, sauce on top—and its homemade meat, marinara, and mushroom sauces. The Italian wedding soup, made daily, is also a hit. The menu is extensive, with several risottos, six parms, and scores of variations on pasta. There's a kids menu, too. Grown-ups have the benefit of a full bar and late-night hours.

Also popular with locals, **Fire Alley** (1144 Cocoa Ave., Hershey, 717/533-3200, www.firealley.net, noon-10pm Mon.-Thurs., noon-midnight Fri.-Sat., 10am-10pm Sun., bar open until 2am nightly, $8-29) is an offshoot of Harrisburg's Fire House, which occupies a restored 19th-century firehouse. What Fire Alley lacks in historical value it makes up for in style. Inside the suburban eatery, murals, awnings, window boxes, and streetlights create the impression of an urban streetscape, complete with graffiti. Fire Alley's cleverest design element is banquette-styling seating at the bar: all the comfort of a booth with readier access to the bartender. It's the food, of course, that accounts for the large roster of regulars. The kitchen does wings, burgers, veal parmesan—stuff you'd expect from a casual eatery—but also lobster bisque, mussels steamed in Guinness, and seared tuna on seaweed salad. The meatloaf is swaddled in bacon, and the nachos fall in the seafood category. Drop by on a Thursday for $4 margaritas.

The curiously named **What If . . .** (845 E. Chocolate Ave., Hershey, 717/533-5858, www.whatifdining.com, 11am-10pm Mon.-Thurs., 11am-11pm Fri.-Sat., 4pm-10pm Sun., lunch $8-14, dinner $17-33) is in an off-putting location: below street level in the Howard Johnson Inn Hershey. But if you can overlook the lack of natural light, you'll be glad you came. Start with the crab martini and end with the profiterole du jour, made in-house along with every other dessert. In between, tuck into an entrée from the menu of continental cuisine. The extensive wine list is partial to California and the Pacific Northwest.

INFORMATION

The **Hershey Harrisburg Regional Visitors Bureau** (17 S. 2nd St., Harrisburg, 717/231-7788, www.visithersheyharrisburg.org, 9am-5pm Mon.-Fri. and 10am-3pm Sat., also open noon-3pm Sun. May-Oct.) has loads of information about attractions, lodging, and dining in and around Hershey. Visit the bureau's website to request a copy of its annual travel guide or peruse a digital version.

You can also find a lot of useful information on the website of **Hershey Entertainment & Resorts** (800/437-7439, www.hersheypa.com), the company behind Hersheypark, ZooAmerica, The Hotel Hershey, and Hershey Lodge, among other ventures.

GETTING THERE

Hershey is about 30 miles northwest of Lancaster via Routes 283 west and 743 north, and 15 miles east of Harrisburg via Route 322. **Harrisburg International Airport** (MDT,

888/235-9442, www.flyhia.com), about a 20-minute drive from Hershey, is served by several major airlines. Note that while locals refer to the airport as HIA, its Federal Aviation Administration booking code is MDT. That's because of its physical location in the borough of Middletown, about eight miles south of Harrisburg.

Harrisburg is served by **Amtrak** (800/872-7245, www.amtrak.com) and intercity bus companies. Once there, rent a car or hop in a cab to get to Hershey. You can also travel to Hershey from Harrisburg by **Capital Area Transit** (717/238-8304, www.cattransit.com) bus, which stops at Hersheypark and The Hotel Hershey.

Harrisburg and Vicinity

Like many state capitals, Harrisburg isn't much of a vacation destination. It's awfully close to one; Hershey, aka Chocolate Town, USA, is just 15 miles to its east. Most people come to Harrisburg because they have business there, and more often than not, it's government business. That's not to say there's nothing to see or do in the city, which lies on the east bank of the Susquehanna River. Harrisburg has some excellent museums, including the State Museum of Pennsylvania and the National Civil War Museum. It has a charming park along the river and another *on* the river. It has more minor league teams than you can imagine. In recent years the dining and nightlife scenes have improved to such a degree that it's not unusual for innkeepers in the Hershey area to point guests toward Harrisburg for dinner.

The city owes its name to John Harris, who emigrated from England in the late 17th century, built a home on the river near the present juncture of Paxton and Front Streets, and eventually established the first ferry across the Susquehanna. The ferry played an important role in the westward migration of other pioneers and later in the Revolutionary War,

carrying supplies to the Continental army west of the Susquehanna. After the war, John Harris Jr. made plans for a town on his father's land. Harrisburg was incorporated in 1791 and in 1812 replaced Lancaster as the state capital.

Over the next several decades, Harrisburg emerged as a transportation center, first as a linchpin of Pennsylvania's canal system and then as a railroad hub. During the Civil War, the rail yards teemed with Union soldiers. Hundreds of thousands of men received their instructions at Harrisburg's Camp Curtin. With its transportation arteries and trove of supplies, Harrisburg was a target for Confederate General Robert E. Lee. His troops might have captured the vulnerable capital in 1863—they made it as far as Camp Hill, just across the river—had they not received an urgent order to turn south. The Battle of Gettysburg was at hand.

More than a century later, the citizens of Harrisburg would feel threatened once again. In March 1979, the Three Mile Island nuclear power plant, about 15 miles south of the capital, suffered a partial meltdown. Tens of thousands of people fled their homes. The sight of the plant's cooling towers is still somewhat chilling.

It's best to visit Harrisburg during the warmer months, when the Susquehanna calls to boaters and anglers and the riverfront hosts one festival after another. If you have time to venture outside the city, take a trip on the only remaining ferry across the Susquehanna or a hike on the Appalachian Trail.

SIGHTS
Whitaker Center for Science and the Arts

Part science museum, part performing arts center, and part movie theater, the **Whitaker Center** (222 Market St., Harrisburg, 717/214-2787, www.whitakercenter.org, 9:30am-5pm Tues.-Sat., 11:30am-5pm Sun., admission Science Center only $16, children 3-17 $12.50) is downtown Harrisburg's cultural hub. The $53 million center, which opened in 1999, houses the Sunoco Performance Theater and an IMAX theater with an 80-foot-wide screen—the largest in central Pennsylvania. It's also home to the Harsco Science Center, three floors of exhibits about everything from weather systems to the physics of dance. Visitors can venture a hand into a writhing tornado, test their physical and mental fitness, build bridges, make their own animated video, and more. KidsPlace, a gallery for children five and under, features a miniature version of Harrisburg's Broad Street Market, the oldest continuously operated market house in the United States. Combo tickets for Science Center visitors who want to catch an IMAX documentary are $19.75 for adults and $16.75 for children 3-17. Hollywood movies shown on the giant screen are $13.75 for adults and $11.75 for children.

State Museum of Pennsylvania

Free for more than a century, the **State Museum of Pennsylvania** (300 North St., Harrisburg, 717/787-4980, www.statemuseumpa.org, 9am-5pm Wed.-Sat., noon-5pm Sun., admission $5, seniors and children 1-12 $4) implemented an admission fee in 2009, citing "budget considerations." But it's still a bargain. The four-story circular museum next to the State Capitol offers a well-rounded perspective on Pennsylvania's story. The Hall of Paleontology and Geology introduces visitors to earlier life forms, including a massive armored fish that prowled the seas of Pennsylvania and Ohio some 367 million years ago. Also popular is the Hall

a view of Harrisburg

of Mammals, a set of 13 life-size dioramas of native animals in their natural environments. The Civil War gallery features Peter Rothermel's famous painting of Pickett's Charge at the Battle of Gettysburg. Unveiled in 1870, the plus-size masterpiece (32 feet long and almost 17 feet high) toured the country, appearing at the World's Fair in Philadelphia in 1876. Though it garnered much praise, it also came under fire. Critics complained that the dying Union soldiers had angelic countenances while the rebels appeared wracked with guilt.

Access to Curiosity Connection, a play area designed for children ages 1-5, is included in general admission. Planetarium shows are $2 apiece.

Civil War Sights

Though enemy forces failed to reach it, Harrisburg was not untouched by the Civil War. Far from it. The city was a major transportation hub for the North's war effort. Only Baltimore and Washington had more soldiers pass through their railroad stations. It was also a strategic center. Harrisburg's **Camp Curtin,** which opened in April 1861, was the first and largest training facility in the North. Today a statue of then-Governor Andrew G.

Curtin stands in a small park one block north of the intersection of Maclay and North Sixth Streets, where soldiers entered the camp.

At the end of the war, tens of thousands of Union soldiers paraded through the streets of Washington DC toward a reviewing stand in front of the White House. Excluded from the Grand Review of the Armies were the regiments of the U.S. Colored Troops. In November 1865, a parade honoring them was held in Harrisburg. The veterans marched through town to the Front Street home of Simon Cameron, a longtime abolitionist who'd served in the U.S. Senate and, for a spell, as President Abraham Lincoln's secretary of war. He reviewed them from his front porch and delivered a speech in which he promised: "If you continue to conduct yourselves hereafter as you have in this struggle, you will have all the rights you ask for, all the rights that belong to human beings." No other state held such an event. Cameron's residence was donated to the Historical Society of Dauphin County in 1941 and is now known as the **John Harris-Simon Cameron Mansion** (219 S. Front St., Harrisburg, 717/233-3462, www.dauphin-countyhistory.org, tours at 1pm, 2pm, and 3pm Mon.-Thurs. and second Sun. of the month, $8, seniors $7, children 6-16 $6). The house

the Whitaker Center for Science and the Arts

has undergone many additions and renovations since it was built in the mid-1700s for John Harris Jr., who founded Harrisburg on land his father had settled. Cameron was responsible for its makeover into an Italianate-style Victorian, adding a grand staircase and solarium and lowering a floor to accommodate a pair of 14-foot-tall pier mirrors he'd found in France. Guided tours reveal what else he snapped up on his way to Russia, where he was sent as U.S. ambassador after his scandal-marred stint as war secretary.

Harrisburg's premier Civil War attraction opened in 2001. The **National Civil War Museum** (1 Lincoln Circle at Reservoir Park, Harrisburg, 717/260-1861, www.nationalcivilwarmuseum.org, 10am-5pm Mon.-Tues. and Thurs.-Sat., 10am-8pm Wed., noon-5pm Sun., admission $10, seniors $9, students $8) bills itself as a bias-free presentation of the Union and Confederate causes, "the only museum in the United States that portrays the entire story of the American Civil War." Its focus isn't on the famous—President Lincoln, General Robert E. Lee, and such—but on the common soldier and the men and women on the home front. Particular attention is paid to the African American experience. Lifelike mannequins star in depictions of a slave auction, soldier life at Camp Curtin, the amputation of a soldier's leg, and other facts of 19th-century life.

Pennsylvania State Capitol

Completed in 1906, the current **Capitol** (N. 3rd St., between North and Walnut Streets, 800/868-7672, www.pacapitol.com) was the tallest structure between Philadelphia and Pittsburgh for 80 years. It's still among the most ornate. The seat of state power features a spectacular vaulted dome inspired by Michelangelo's design for St. Peter's Basilica in Rome. Architect Joseph Huston incorporated elements of Greek, Roman, Renaissance, and Victorian design into the building, envisioning a "palace of arts." His vision cost a pretty penny, and Huston was sentenced to prison for overcharging the state. There's no charge for guided tours of the Capitol, part of a large complex of government buildings. They're offered every half hour 8:30am-4pm Monday-Friday and at 9am, 11am, 1pm, and 3pm on weekends and most holidays. Reservations are required for groups of 10 or

Pennsylvania State Capitol

more and recommended for smaller parties. A welcome center in the East Wing is open 8:30am-4:30pm weekdays. Its interactive exhibits explain how laws are made.

Other Harrisburg Sights

The **Broad Street Market** (1233 N. 3rd St., Harrisburg, 717/236-7923, 7am-2pm Wed., 7am-5pm Thurs.-Fri., 7am-4pm Sat.) is said to be the oldest continuously operating farmers market in the country. Founded in 1860, it's the sole survivor of six markets that once operated in the city. At its peak in the 1920s, the market just a few blocks north of the State Capitol had more than 725 vendors, many of whom leased space outside and waited years for an indoor stall. Today it has about 40. They hawk everything from hand-rolled soft pretzels to home decor.

One mile north of the Capitol, the **Pennsylvania National Fire Museum** (1820 N. 4th St., Harrisburg, 717/232-8915, www.pnfm.org, 10am-4pm Tues.-Sat., 1pm-4pm Sun., admission $6, seniors and students $5) has fascinating answers to questions you may not have thought to ask. Why were firehouses built with spiral staircases? To keep the horses from climbing them. Why the poles? Because spiral staircases slowed down the firemen. Housed in an 1899 Victorian firehouse, the museum traces the history of firefighting from the days of hand-drawn equipment to modern times.

Lake Tobias Wildlife Park

A little drool never hurt anyone. Bear that in mind as elk, oxen, llamas, and other beasts approach you for a snack at **Lake Tobias Wildlife Park** (760 Tobias Dr., Halifax, 717/362-9126, www.laketobias.com, open daily May-Labor Day and weekends Sept.-Oct., admission $6, safari tour $6, children under 3 free), about 20 miles north of Harrisburg off Route 225. Africa it's not, but the family-owned animal park offers a safari experience that visitors aren't soon to forget. Specially designed safari cruisers—think school buses with their top halves hacked off—ply 150 rolling acres home to some 500 animals. Among them are species rarely seen in these parts, including water buffalo, the ostrich-like rhea, and the zonkey, a zebra-donkey hybrid. The last safari tour departs one hour before closing. Come too late and you can still have a close encounter with residents of the petting zoo, including African pygmy goats, Patagonian cavies, camels, green monkeys, lemurs, and spotted sheep. Not-so-pettable creatures such as lions, tigers, and bears are exhibited in a zoo-like setting.

Millersburg Ferry and Ned Smith Center

Before bridges spanned the Susquehanna River, people and goods crossed it by ferry. John Harris, the first European to permanently settle in the wilderness that would later become Harrisburg, established the first ferry across the river. One survives. Now a nostalgic tourist attraction more than anything else, the **Millersburg Ferry** (717/692-2442, www.millersburgferry.org, operates May-mid-Oct., car $8, walk-on fare $3, round-trip walk-on fare $5) fleet consists of two wooden sternwheelers that accommodate several vehicles as well as about 50 passengers. The ferry service connects the quaint town of Millersburg, about 25 miles north of Harrisburg, to a modern campground (32 Ferry Ln., Liverpool, 717/444-3200, www.ferryboatcampsites.com, campsites $22-47, cabins $45) on the west bank of the river. It's available weekends and holidays in May, daily June through Labor Day, and then weekends and holidays until mid-October. Weekday hours are 11am-5pm, while weekend and holiday hours are 9am-dusk. To reach the Millersburg landing from Harrisburg, take Route 22/322 west to Route 147 north. Follow 147 into Millersburg and turn left onto North Street.

Just outside Millersburg is the **Ned Smith Center for Nature and Art** (176 Water Company Rd., Millersburg, 717/692-3699, www.nedsmithcenter.org, gallery and gift shop 10am-4pm Tues.-Sat. year-round and noon-4pm Sun. Memorial Day-Labor Day, gallery admission $7, seniors and students $2), which celebrates the life and works of a local boy turned nationally recognized wildlife artist. Ned Smith (1919-1985) painted almost 120 covers for the Pennsylvania Game Commission's magazine, created the state's first duck stamp, and illustrated 14 books. Original paintings now command upwards of $60,000. The Ned Smith Center is home to a $1.5 million collection of paintings, drawings, and manuscripts donated by Smith's widow. The center sits on 500 rustic acres crisscrossed by more than 12 miles of hiking, biking, horseback riding, and cross-country skiing trails. The trails are open to the public at no charge.

ENTERTAINMENT AND EVENTS
Performing Arts

The 600-plus-seat **Sunoco Performance Theater** within the Whitaker Center for Science and the Arts (222 Market St., Harrisburg, 717/214-2787, www.whitakercenter.org) hosts live theater, music, and dance by touring and local performers. Resident companies include **Theatre Harrisburg** (717/232-5501, www.theatreharrisburg.com), a community theater that dates to 1926.

Part of the Capitol Complex, **The Forum** (N. 5th and Walnut Streets, Harrisburg, 717/783-9100) is a 1,763-seat concert hall where "star-studded" refers to the architecture as well as some performances. Its ceiling is studded with hundreds of lights of varying levels of brilliance, arranged to depict constellations. Dedicated in 1931, The Forum is home to the **Harrisburg Symphony Orchestra** (717/545-5527, www.harrisburgsymphony.org).

A storm blew the roof off the **Allenberry Playhouse** (1559 Boiling Springs Rd., Boiling Springs, 717/258-3211, www.allenberry.com) during its dedication in 1949. Adhering to the adage that "the show must go on," the theater didn't let a soaked stage get in the way of its 10-week opening season. Today the season lasts more than 40 weeks, starting in March and running through December. The playhouse

on the grounds of Allenberry Resort, about 20 miles southwest of Harrisburg, stages musicals, comedies, and dramas with professional actors. Alumni include John Travolta, who sang and danced on the Allenberry stage in 1971, and Norman Fell, best known for his role as Mr. Roper on *Three's Company*.

Festivals and Events

Harrisburg kicks off each year with the largest indoor agricultural event in the nation, the **Pennsylvania Farm Show** (717/787-2905 during show, www.farmshow.state.pa.us, Jan., free). Some 6,000 animals and hundreds of thousands of people pass through the **Pennsylvania Farm Show Complex & Expo Center** (N. Cameron and Maclay Streets, Harrisburg, 717/787-5373, www.pafarmshowcomplex.com) during the weeklong event. Farmers from across the state show off the fruits of their labors—everything from pecans to powerful Percherons—in the hopes of taking home prize money and bragging rights. Come for an education in the state's number one industry, and come on an empty stomach. The Farm Show's best feature could very well be its food court, where a baked potato isn't a humdrum side but a tour de force. Food purchases feed the coffers of nonprofit commodity associations like Pennsylvania Co-Operative Potato Growers Inc. and the Pennsylvania Maple Syrup Producers Council. Though admission to the Farm Show is free, parking is $10.

Harrisburg's largest arts event, **The Patriot-News Artsfest** (717/238-1887, www.jumpstreet.org), brings artists and craftspeople from around the country to Harrisburg's Riverfront Park over Memorial Day weekend. The free festival has been named one of the top 100 arts events in the country by *Sunshine Artist* magazine.

Riverfront Park also provides the setting for the city's annual Independence Day and Labor Day celebrations. Previously known as the Harrisburg Jazz and Multicultural Festival, the multiday **Fourth of July Celebration** (717/255-3020, www.

Carlisle: Car Show Capital

If you love cars, you'll love Carlisle. The Cumberland County seat, about 20 miles southwest of Harrisburg, is named for a town in England, and locals usually emphasize its second syllable. But auto aficionados can't be blamed for thinking the "car" in "Carlisle" has something to do with engines and chrome. The town is the site of collector car, truck, and motorcycle events every season but winter.

Carlisle Events (1000 Bryn Mawr Rd., Carlisle, 717/243-7855, www.carlisleevents.com) rented the Carlisle Fairgrounds when it began producing car shows in the mid-1970s. By 1981 the gatherings had grown so popular that the company purchased the property. Today it produces more than a dozen annual events. Held in April, **Spring Carlisle** is the kickoff to the season and one of the largest automotive swap meets in the world. **Fall Carlisle,** which caps the season, is another opportunity to buy, sell, and celebrate all things automotive. Between them are specialty shows for Corvettes, Fords, GMs, Chryslers, trucks, imports, and tricked-out "performance and style" vehicles.

Car enthusiasts have even more reasons to love Cumberland County. Mechanicsburg, 10 miles east of Carlisle, is home to the **Rolls-Royce Foundation** (189 Hempt Rd., Mechanicsburg, 717/795-9400, www.rollsroycefoundation.org), which operates a research library and museum dedicated to Rolls-Royces and Bentleys. It's open to the public 10am-4pm Monday-Friday. Mechanicsburg—named for the mechanics of an earlier vehicle make, the Conestoga wagon—also has an automobile racetrack that dates to 1939. Motorsports legends including Ted Horn, A. J. Foyt, and Mario Andretti have raced at the **Williams Grove Speedway** (1 Speedway Dr., Mechanicsburg, 717/697-5000, www.williamsgrove.com). The half-mile track hosts weekly sprint car races March-October. Two other racetracks are within a half-hour drive: the **Quarter Aces Drag-O-Way** (1107 Petersburg Rd., Boiling Springs, 717/258-6287, www.quarteracesdragway.com) and the **Shippensburg Speedway** (178 Walnut Bottom Rd., Shippensburg, 717/532-8581, www.shippensburgspeedway.com).

harrisburgrec.com, free) still features a whole lot of music. There's also a lot to keep kids occupied, including amusement rides and video karaoke. **Kipona** (717/255-3020, www.harrisburgrec.com, free), held over Labor Day weekend, pays homage to the Susquehanna River. (*Kipona* means "bright, sparkling water" in the Delaware Indian tongue.) It's a blockbuster of a festival. You've got live entertainment on multiple stages, children's activities, fireworks, food, and more food. You've also got a chili cook-off—not just any chili cook-off but the Pennsylvania State Chili Cook-Off (www.chiefchili.com), a qualifying event for the International Chili Society's world championship. The perennial festival is also the occasion for a Native American encampment on City Island. The powwow, as it's called, features demonstrations of traditional dance, drumming, and arts and crafts. Some 150 artists and craftspeople from around the country sell their works at the southern end of Riverfront Park.

SPORTS AND RECREATION
City Island

Harrisburg's recreational hub is **City Island,** a mile-long island on the Susquehanna River. It's home to the city's minor league baseball team (717/231-4444, www.senatorsbaseball.com) and USL Pro soccer team (717/441-4625, www.cityislanders.com). Spectator sports aren't the half of it. The island boasts a beach, sand volleyball courts, **batting cages** (717/461-3223, www.cityislandfun.com), and an elaborate 18-hole **miniature golf course** (717/232-8533, www.watergolfcityisland.com). It also has several marinas. If you don't have a boat of your own, board the *Pride of the Susquehanna* (717/234-6500, www.harrisburgriverboat.com), an old-fashioned paddlewheeler that plies the river May-November. Alternatively, set off in a kayak or canoe from **Susquehanna Outfitters** (717/503-0066, www.susquehannaoutfitters.com), which also rents bicycles. Other City Island amenities

A Major Minor League Market

The Hershey-Harrisburg region doesn't have a single major league franchise, but its sports fans have plenty to cheer about. *SportsBusiness Journal* named it the top minor league market in the country in 2009 and again in 2011.

Best known of Harrisburg's franchises is the **Harrisburg Senators** (Metro Bank Park, City Island, Harrisburg, 717/231-4444, www.senatorsbaseball.com), the Class AA affiliate of the Washington Nationals. Formed in 1987, the baseball team won the Eastern League championship in its first season. It captured four consecutive championships from 1996 to 1999, becoming the first team in league history to do so. More than 200 of its players have been called up to the majors.

Hockey fans get their fix at **Hershey Bears** (Giant Center, 550 W. Hersheypark Dr., Hershey, 717/508-2327, www.hersheybears.com) games. Originally named the Hershey B'ars, the team has competed in the professional American Hockey League without interruption since 1938. The Bears "draw more fans and inspire more passion than just about any team in minor league hockey," *The Washington Post* wrote of the Washington Capitals affiliate in 2009. In 2010 the Bears became the first team in league history to win 11 championships.

The Bears share Giant Center with the **Harrisburg Stampede** (Giant Center, 550 W. Hersheypark Dr., Hershey, 717/534-3911, www.harrisburgstampede.com), who captured the American Indoor Football championship in 2013. The team moved to the Professional Indoor Football League shortly thereafter. Other area football teams include the **Central Penn Piranha** (717/385-9649, www.piranhafootball.net), which bills itself as the "winningest team in minor league football history."

The region is also home to **Harrisburg City Islanders** (Skyline Sports Complex, City Island, Harrisburg, 717/441-4625, www.cityislanders.com) soccer and **Harrisburg Horizon** (717/298-1083, www.harrisburghorizon.com) basketball.

include a playground, picnic pavilions, an antique carousel, and scaled-down versions of a Civil War-era steam train and San Francisco-style trolley.

You can walk or bike to the island from downtown Harrisburg via the Walnut Street Bridge, which was closed to cars after Hurricane Agnes in 1972. Cars access the island via the Market Street Bridge.

Appalachian Trail

The **Appalachian Trail Conservancy** (www.appalachiantrail.org), the volunteer-based organization charged with managing and protecting the famous footpath, has an information center about 15 miles southwest of Harrisburg. Located right on the A.T., the **Boiling Springs information center** (4 E. 1st St., Boiling Springs, 717/258-5771) is staffed 9am-5pm weekdays year-round. Weekend hours are based on volunteer availability. You can get answers to questions about short jaunts, thru-hikes, and everything in between, plus guidebooks, maps, postcards, and A.T. merchandise.

The A.T. crosses the Susquehanna River at Duncannon, about 15 miles north of the state capital. Duncannon's **Doyle Hotel** (7 N. Market St., 717/834-6789) is a legendary stop along the Georgia-to-Maine trail. It's a bit of a dive, but that's part of its charm. The hotel serves food and drink, accepts mail drops, and plasters its walls with photos of thru-hikers. Rooms are $25 per night.

Boating and Fishing

Almost a mile wide at Harrisburg, the Susquehanna River tempts outdoor lovers to float or fish the day away. Among the enablers: **Susquehanna Outfitters** (City Island, 717/503-0066, www.susquehannaoutfitters.com, open Tues.-Sun. during boating season) with its rental fleet of kayaks, canoes, and stand-up paddleboards. It offers guided floats and shuttle service to points upriver. Experienced paddlers can rent boats by the hour to paddle around City Island or the cluster of islands just upriver.

If you want to paddle for days, fishing in

The *Pride of the Susquehanna* paddles past the Capitol.

secluded coves and sleeping in riverfront campgrounds or primitive island campsites, you want to call **Blue Mountain Outfitters** (Rte. 11/15, 2 miles north of I-81 interchange, Marysville, 717/957-2413, www.bluemountain-outfitters.net, open Tues.-Sun. during boating season, Tues.-Sat. in winter). Located several miles north of Harrisburg on the west side of the Susquehanna, Blue Mountain is a full-service paddle sports store with a wide selection of canoes, kayaks, stand-up paddleboards, and accessories. Rentals are available during the warmer months. Paddlers can start at Blue Mountain and float downstream or hop on a shuttle to explore the river's more northerly stretches. The outfitter, housed in an erstwhile train station, offers lifts to put-ins upwards of 40 miles away for multiday trips. It also facilitates trips on the Juniata River, Sherman Creek, and other nearby waters. Novice paddlers and shutterbugs can leave the piloting to Blue Mountain's pros by booking a trip on the "war canoe"—a 22-foot vessel that can accommodate eight people. The ride is especially thrilling during high water.

The Harrisburg-area section of the Susquehanna is a top-notch smallmouth bass fishery. Anglers can also get bites from catfish, carp, panfish, and other swimmers. Short on poppers, plastic crayfish, or rubber worms? No worries. Harrisburg Mall is home to Pennsylvania's only **Bass Pro Shops** (3501 Paxton St., Harrisburg, 717/565-5200, www.basspro.com, 9am-9pm Mon.-Sat., 10am-6pm Sun.). The mammoth store is as much a spiritual experience as shopping experience for fishing and hunting fanatics. With its 60,000-gallon aquarium and wildlife dioramas, it's also a family attraction. The store boasts a rock-climbing wall, a NASCAR simulator, an archery range, and a boat showroom.

Yellow Breeches Creek, which flows through communities to Harrisburg's southwest and dumps into the Susquehanna three miles south of City Island, is among the most popular trout streams in the state. Anglers interested in the stocking program can visit the **Huntsdale State Fish Hatchery** (195 Lebo Rd., Carlisle, 717/486-3419, www.fish.state.pa.us, visitors center 8am-3:30pm daily), which produces brook trout, brown trout, rainbow trout, and golden rainbow trout, among other species. Fly fishers flock to a mile-long catch-and-release section in the town of Boiling Springs, which has an excellent fly shop, **Yellow Breeches Outfitters**

(2 E. 1st St., Boiling Springs, 717/258-6752, www.yellowbreechesoutfitters.com, open Tues.-Sun.). The shop sells a wide variety of rods, reels, waders, and other gear. It also offers fly-fishing instruction and guided fishing. **Allenberry Resort Inn and Playhouse** (1559 Boiling Springs Rd., Boiling Springs, 717/258-3211, www.allenberry.com), at the downstream end of the no-kill area, offers fly-fishing courses on select weekends.

ACCOMMODATIONS

If you're looking for a central location, look no further than the ★ **Hilton Harrisburg** (1 N. 2nd St., Harrisburg, 717/233-6000, www.hilton.com, $140-250). It's connected by an enclosed walkway to the Whitaker Center for Science and the Arts and a shopping center called Strawberry Square. The State Capitol Complex and City Island are a short walk away. The hotel is at the end of Harrisburg's Restaurant Row, but finding an excellent meal is easier than stepping outside. The Hilton is home to the **The Golden Sheaf** (717/237-6400, www.hiltonharrisburgdining.com, open for lunch Mon.-Fri. and dinner Mon.-Sat., lunch $10-17, dinner $22-48), Harrisburg's only AAA four-diamond restaurant, and **Raspberries** (717/237-6419, www.hiltonharrisburgdining.com, open for breakfast daily, lunch Mon.-Fri., brunch Sun., and dinner Mon.-Sat., $10-26), famous for its Sunday jazz brunch. The hotel's 300-plus guest rooms feature flat-screen TVs, refrigerators, Hilton's trademark Serenity beds, and free wireless Internet access.

Nestled on the west shore of the Susquehanna River, **Bridgeview Bed & Breakfast** (810 S. Main St., Marysville, 717/957-2438, www.bridgeviewbnb.com, $90-120) doesn't have antique furnishings, luxury linens, heaven-scented bath products, or even in-room televisions. Breakfast isn't what you'd call gourmet. It does have killer views of the river and the Rockville Bridge, famous for being the world's longest stone masonry arch railroad bridge. Built in the opening years of the 20th century by the Pennsylvania Railroad, the bridge still sees a good deal of train traffic—which makes the Bridgeview a magnet for train buffs. Formerly a sporting goods and tackle shop, the B&B has 10 en suite guest rooms, each named for a Pennsylvania river.

FOOD

Politicos don't have to venture far from the Capitol Complex to strategize or negotiate over a meal that receives bipartisan approval. Second Street in downtown Harrisburg has such a high concentration of restaurants and bars that it's known as Restaurant Row. Consider taking a walkabout before settling on a choice. One you won't regret: ★ **Café Fresco** (215 N. 2nd St., Harrisburg, 717/236-2599, www.cafefresco.com, 6:30am-11pm Mon.-Wed., 6:30am-1am Thurs.-Fri., 11am-1am Sat., breakfast and lunch under $10, dinner $10-36). By day, it's a chic but casual spot, offering pizza, burgers, sandwiches, and wraps. It glams up in the evening, becoming a destination for swishy cocktails and Asian-influenced cuisine, though casual fare such as pizzas and a Kobe burger are still on offer. After dinner, you can sashay upstairs to get your groove on. At **Level 2** (717/236-6600, www.level2.us, 8pm-2am Thurs.-Sat.), the dress code is "fashionable and fierce," and the DJs are tireless. Bottle service is available.

One of the newest additions to Restaurant Row, **The Federal Taphouse** (234 N. 2nd St., Harrisburg, 717/525-8077, www.federaltaphousehbg.com, 11:30am-2am Mon.-Fri., 11am-2am Sat., 10:30am-2am Sun., $9-28) boasts 100 craft beers on tap and a coal-fired oven. Customers nosh on fire-roasted olives and smoked pork belly while waiting for pork ribs, sausages, chicken skewers, and other hearty fare. The Taphouse also has a wood-fired oven that turns out crispy pizzas with toppings both common and exotic.

Ethnic options on Restaurant Row include **Miyako** (227 N. 2nd St., Harrisburg, 717/234-3250, www.pasushi.net, 11am-10pm Mon.-Thurs., 11am-11pm Fri., noon-11pm

Sat., $5-19), a sushi restaurant that also offers a variety of teriyaki, tempura, and hibachi dishes.

Not every noteworthy restaurant has a 2nd Street address. Third Street is home to the *muy excelente* **El Sol Mexican Restaurant** (18 S. 3rd St., Harrisburg, 717/901-5050, www.elsolmexicanrestaurant.net, 11am-10pm Mon.-Thurs., 11am-11pm Fri., 4pm-11pm Sat., 10am-3pm Sun., $8-23). Owners Juan and Lisa Garcia—he of the Guadalajara region of Mexico, she of Harrisburg—specialize in dishes from his home state, but they pull off burritos, fajitas, and other familiar fare with equal aplomb.

Across the street at ★ **Bricco** (31 S. 3rd St., Harrisburg, 717/724-0222, www.briccopa.com, lunch 11:30am-2:30pm Mon.-Fri., dinner 5:30pm-10pm Mon.-Sat. and 4:30pm-10pm Sun., lunch $11-19, dinner $14-36), chef Jason Viscount creates masterly Mediterranean dishes with the help of students from the Olewine School of Culinary Arts at Harrisburg Area Community College. Though inspired by Tuscan cuisine, Bricco sources Pennsylvania products whenever possible. Particularly popular are its raw-bar offerings and pizzas, baked in a stone oven and topped with delicacies such as fig jam, white truffle oil, and local feta. The restaurant boasts an extensive wine list and a daily changing menu of artisan cheese.

For barbecue connoisseurs, it doesn't get better than **MoMo's BBQ & Grill** (307 Market St., 717/230-1030, www.momosbbqandgrill.com, 11am-10pm Mon.-Thurs., 11am-11pm Fri.-Sat., 11am-9pm Sun., $7-22). Owner Mike Moran has won awards at barbecue battles around the country and created more than a dozen sauces. The mayo-based Alabama White is his personal favorite.

INFORMATION

The **Hershey Harrisburg Regional Visitors Bureau** (17 S. 2nd St., Harrisburg, 717/231-7788, www.visithersheyharrisburg.org, 9am-5pm Mon.-Fri. and 10am-3pm Sat., also open noon-3pm Sun. May-Oct.) is a good source of information about attractions, lodging, and dining in and around the state capital. Visit the bureau's website to request a copy of its current visitors guide or peruse a digital version.

GETTING THERE AND AROUND

Harrisburg is about 15 miles west of Hershey via Route 322 and 40 miles northwest of Lancaster via Route 283. **Harrisburg International Airport** (MDT, 888/235-9442, www.flyhia.com) is served by several major airlines. Note that while locals refer to the airport as HIA, its Federal Aviation Administration booking code is MDT. That's because of its physical location in the borough of Middletown, about eight miles south of Harrisburg.

Amtrak (800/872-7245, www.amtrak.com) provides rail service to the Harrisburg Transportation Center, located at 4th and Chestnut Streets. **Greyhound** (800/231-2222, www.greyhound.com) and other intercity bus operators also deliver travelers to the station.

Local bus service is provided by **Capital Area Transit** (717/238-8304, www.cattransit.com), or CAT. The base fare is $1.75. Call **Keystone Cab** (717/234-4400) for door-to-door service.

York County

Just west of Lancaster County, York County touts itself as the "Factory Tour Capital of the World." Indeed, more than 20 factories open their doors to visitors. Frugal families can live it up here; admission is free in almost every case. So many of the factories are dedicated to guilty pleasures that York County also claims the title of "Snack Food Capital of the World." I know what you're thinking: York Peppermint Patties. Alas, the brand born here in 1940 now belongs to Hershey Co., and the minty, chocolaty confections are made elsewhere. The biggest name on the factory circuit has nothing to do with mmmm-mmmm and everything to do with vroom-vroom. York's Harley-Davidson factory attracts bikers from across the United States and countries as far-flung as Turkey, China, and Australia.

Long before the county became the Factory Tour Capital, its only city, also named York, served as the capital of what would soon be known as the United States of America. The Continental Congress, that body of delegates who spoke for the colonies during the Revolutionary period, met in York for nine months in 1777 and 1778, adopting the Articles of Confederation. The York County Heritage Trust operates several museums and historic sites that offer a window into the past. Murals throughout downtown York also serve as a record of local history.

The county's greatest asset could be its location in the center of Pennsylvania Dutch country. Gettysburg and its Civil War battlefield are 30 miles west of York. Lancaster's Amish farmlands are about that distance to its east. The state capital, Harrisburg, is 25 miles north of the city, and Hershey, aka "The Sweetest Place on Earth," is just 10 miles farther. That makes York County a good base of operations for travelers who want to take in the more touristy areas without paying touristy lodging prices.

FACTORY TOURS

The "Factory Tour Capital of the World" has more factories than you can visit in a day—or even two. You'll find a comprehensive list at www.yorkpa.org, the website of the York County Convention & Visitors Bureau. Bear in mind that most factories don't offer tours on weekends.

The most famous name on the list is Harley-Davidson. The company has been producing its legendary motorcycles in York since 1973. Free tours of the **Harley-Davidson factory** (1425 Eden Rd., York, 877/883-1450, www.harley-davidson.com/experience, tour center and gift shop open 8am-4pm Mon.-Fri.) begin at regular intervals 9am-2pm Monday-Friday. They offer a limited view of the assembly line and last about an hour. Friday isn't the best day to visit because production may not be scheduled. For $35, you can have a two-hour tour that's more personalized and includes access to some "employee only" areas. The in-depth tour is offered at 9:30am and noon Monday-Thursday. It sells out quickly, so it's a good idea to book tickets by phone or online. Children under 12 aren't allowed on the factory floor, but they're welcome in the tour center, which has exhibits about assembly processes and motorcycles for the straddling.

If you're traveling with kids, put **Perrydell Farm Dairy** (90 Indian Rock Dam Rd., York, 717/741-3485, www.perrydellfarm. com, 7am-9pm Mon.-Sat. and noon-6pm Sun., self-guided tours free) on your itinerary. Depending on when you visit the family-owned farm, you might see cows being milked, calves being fed, or milk being bottled. The oh-so-fresh milk is sold on-site, along with ice cream, locally grown produce, and locally baked goods.

To see why York County bills itself as the "Snack Food Capital of the World," head to the borough of Hanover, 20 miles southwest of York. It's home to several munchies manufacturers. Best known for its pretzels, **Snyder's of Hanover** (1350 York St., Hanover, 800/233-7125 ext. 28592, www. snydersofhanover.com, store open 9am-6pm Mon.-Sat. and noon-5pm Sun.) offers free tours at 10am, 11am, and 1pm Tuesday-Thursday. Reservations are required. Snyder's snacks are sold around the world, so the half-hour tours are an education in large-scale manufacturing. You'll get to see the raw material warehouse, finished goods warehouse, packing room, and oven room. Tours start and end at the factory store, where you'll get a free bag of pretzels and bargains on everything from Old Tyme Pretzels, first made in 1909, to the popular flavored pretzel pieces, introduced some 80 years later.

Hanover is also home to **Utz Quality Foods** (900 High St., Hanover, 800/367-7629, www.utzsnacks.com), where you can watch raw spuds become crunchy chips from an observation gallery. The gallery is open 8am-4pm Monday-Thursday and select Fridays. Though famous for its potato chips—Rachael Ray talked up Utz Kettle Classics on her eponymous TV show—the company also makes pretzels, cheese curls, pork rinds, and more. Its outlet store (861 Carlisle St., Hanover,

8am-7pm Mon.-Sat., 11am-6pm Sun.) is two blocks from the plant.

Far smaller than Snyder's or Utz, **Revonah Pretzels** (507 Baltimore St., Hanover, 717/630-2883, www.revonahpretzel.com) takes its name from the town (Revonah is Hanover spelled backward) and its cues from the past. Pretzels are rolled and twisted by hand, hearth-baked, and slowly hardened in a kiln. Word has it that the Pittsburgh Steelers munch on these when they're on the road. Revonah offers free 20-minute tours 8am-1pm Tuesday-Thursday. Reservations are recommended. Visitors can sample a "greenie," a pretzel that's crunchy on the outside but still warm and soft on the inside.

Be sure to wear comfortable closed-toe shoes when you go factory hopping. Open-toe shoes and heels are prohibited in some areas.

OTHER SIGHTS
Central Market

York's public market house is a can't-miss if you're in town on a Tuesday, Thursday, or Saturday. Built in 1888, **Central Market** (34 W. Philadelphia St., York, 717/848-2243, www. centralmarketyork.com, 6am-2pm Tues., Thurs., and Sat.) is not just a showcase for area farmers but also a hopping lunch spot.

the Harley-Davidson factory

In fact, lunch counters outnumber produce stands by more than three to one. You'll find Greek, Filipino, Malaysian, and Caribbean foods. You'll find fresh-cut fries, homemade fudge, and craft-brewed beer. Busy Bee, run by a classically trained chef, serves inventive soups, salads, and sandwiches. Roburrito's, a popular local burrito joint, joined the vendor ranks in 2009. You can't miss its stand, which resembles a foil-wrapped burrito and serves up venison-stuffed burritos during deer season.

Heritage Sites

The **York County Heritage Trust** (250 E. Market St., 717/848-1587, www.yorkheritage.org, peak-season admission to all sites $15, children 6-18 $7, off-season admission $12, children $5) operates several museums and historic sites within walking distance of each other in downtown York. They include the **Colonial Complex** (157 W. Market St.), a set of four buildings that transport visitors to early York. Built in 1741, the Golden Plough Tavern is the oldest structure in town. Adjacent to it is the General Gates House, named for the Revolutionary War hero who occupied it during York's 1777-1778 tenure as capital of the American colonies. Some members of the Continental Congress were so impressed with General Horatio Gates that they plotted to have him replace General George Washington as commander of the Continental army. The Colonial Complex also features a reconstruction of the courthouse where congressional delegates met during their nine-month stay in York and an 1812 log house. The buildings can only be seen by guided tour. Tours are usually offered at 10am, 11am, 1pm, 2pm, and 3pm Tuesday-Saturday April-December, but call 717/848-1587 to confirm.

Other Heritage Trust sites include the **Agricultural and Industrial Museum** (217 W. Princess St., 10am-4pm Tues.-Sat.), which houses artifacts spanning three centuries. Exhibits cover topics as diverse as casket manufacturing, piano and organ manufacturing, and York's industrial contribution to World War II. The 12,000-square-foot transportation wing showcases automobiles made in York, a Conestoga wagon, and a 1937 Aeronca K airplane.

The **Fire Museum** (757 W. Market St., 10am-4pm Sat. Apr.-Nov.) displays artifacts such as horse-drawn fire carriages, vintage fire trucks, and old-fashioned alarm systems.

USA Weightlifting Hall of Fame

If you've ever done bicep curls or bench presses, "York" probably rings a bell. The name is emblazoned on barbells, dumbbells, and other weightlifting equipment made by York Barbell, founded in York in 1932. Its manufacturing operations have shifted to other parts of the world, but the company still has administrative offices just north of the city. They're home to the **Weightlifting Hall of Fame** (3300 Board Rd., York, 717/767-6481, www.yorkbarbell.com, 10am-5pm Mon.-Sat., free admission), a must-stop for fans of strength sports. The Hall of Fame is part history museum and part homage to company founder and weightlifting legend Bob Hoffman. Raised near Pittsburgh, Hoffman was a sickly kid. In 1919, after serving in World War I, he moved to York and co-founded an oil burner company. Determined to build not just his business but also his body, Hoffman bought a barbell. By the late 1920s, the now-buff businessman was training other lifters and hiring them to work in his factory, which he eventually transformed from York Oil Burner into York Barbell. In 1946, when the United States won its first weightlifting world championship, four of the six teammates worked for York Barbell. Hoffman coached the U.S. Olympic team from 1948 to 1964, and York came to be known as "Muscletown USA."

A 7.5-foot bronze statue of Hoffman guards the entrance to the Hall of Fame. Exhibits trace the evolution of strength sports, highlighting legendary strongmen such as Joe "The Mighty Atom" Greenstein, whose feats

USA Weightlifting Hall of Fame

of strength included biting nails in half. Highlights of the collection include a seven-foot Travis dumbbell weighing more than 1,600 pounds. Its lifter and namesake, Warren Lincoln Travis, weighed just 180 pounds during his zenith in the early 1900s.

Steam Into History

On November 18, 1863, President Abraham Lincoln traveled by train from Washington DC to Gettysburg to deliver the speech that came to be known as the Gettysburg Address. One hundred and fifty years later, in 2013, the nonprofit **Steam Into History** (2 W. Main St., New Freedom, 717/942-2370, www.steamintohistory.com) began operating an excursion train on the rail line that carried him to York County's Hanover Junction, where the lanky leader stretched his legs before continuing on to Gettysburg. (Seventeen months later, the same line carried his funeral train through York County.) The train is pulled by a replica

the Steam Into History excursion train

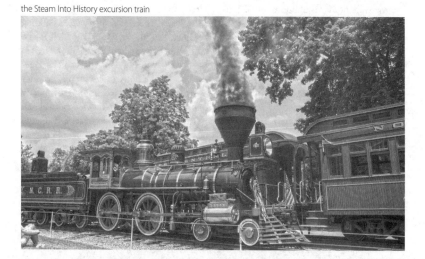

of an 1860s steam locomotive. Many excursions feature reenactors, raconteurs, or musicians who help bring the Civil War era to life. Steam Into History offers round-trips from its headquarters in New Freedom to Glen Rock and Hanover Junction, which last one hour and two and a half hours, respectively. The train runs Tuesday-Sunday in the summer and select days in other seasons.

Haines Shoe House

Worth a stop if you're tootling along Route 30 or Route 462 (aka the Lincoln Highway) in western York County is the **Haines Shoe House** (197 Shoe House Rd., Hellam, 717/840-8339, www.shoehouse.us, 11am-5pm Wed.-Sun. June-Aug., 11am-5pm Sat.-Sun. Sept.-Oct., by appointment Nov.-May, tour $4.50, children 4-12 $3). Built in 1948, the shoe-shaped house was an advertising gimmick by "Shoe Wizard" Mahlon Haines, whose shoe empire grew to more than 40 stores in central Pennsylvania and northern Maryland. At first, the eccentric millionaire invited elderly couples to spend an expense-free weekend in the three-bedroom, two-bath shoe house. In 1950 he extended the invitation to honeymooning couples from any town with a Haines shoe store. After his death in 1962, the house became an ice cream parlor. Today the roadside oddity is a museum dedicated to Haines, who staged safaris on his nearby "Wizard Ranch" and used to stop smokers on the streets of York, offering them cash if they promised to quit.

The shoe motif is ubiquitous throughout the property. You'll find it on the wooden fence that surrounds the house and in the stained glass windows. There's even a shoe-shaped doghouse. Guided tours reveal other novelties, including a curved eating booth in the kitchen, located in the heel of the shoe house. Ice cream and other snacks are sold on-site, along with kitschy gifts like shoe house lamps with lighted windows.

Maize Quest Fun Park

In 1997, Hugh McPherson carved a maze into a cornfield in southern York County. It proved such a hit that in 2000, the Penn State graduate added a straw bale maze, a fence maze, and a maze of living bamboo. Year after year, **Maize Quest Fun Park** (2885 New Park Rd., New Park, 866/935-6738, www.mazefunpark. com) unveiled new attractions. Today it boasts more than 20, including an 80-foot-long tube slide, a stone labyrinth, a pumpkin patch, and peddle karts. The signature cornfield maze reflects a different theme each year. Past themes include "Ice Age Adventure," "Space Explorers," and "The Vikings!"

Maize Quest is open Friday-Sunday and holidays in the fall. Admission is $10 for adults, $8 for children 2-12. On Saturdays in winter and spring, it offers an indoor play area for kids ages 2-8. Admission to the "fun barn" is $7.50 for kids; there's no charge for adults.

ENTERTAINMENT AND EVENTS
Performing Arts

Downtown York's **Strand-Capitol Performing Arts Center** (50 N. George St., York, 717/846-1111, www.strandcapitol.org) plays host to touring musicians, dance companies, and comedians. The **York Symphony Orchestra** (717/812-0717, www.yorksymphony.org), which has performed without interruption since the Depression, can also be seen there. "There" is actually a five-building complex that includes two historic theaters. What's now known as the Capitol Theatre opened in 1906 as a dance hall and later became a movie house. The larger, grander Strand Theatre opened in 1925 primarily for vaudeville and silent movies. Both closed in the late 1970s as suburbia sucked the life out of downtown. But a movement to reopen them quickly took shape, and the Strand and Capitol reopened their doors in 1980 and 1981, respectively. At 500 seats, the Capitol is less than half the size of the Strand, but it boasts a restored 1927 Mighty Wurlitzer. The organ is put to use before classic film showings, which sometimes involve audience participation (e.g., singing along to *The Sound of*

Music or dressing like the title character in *The Big Lebowski*). Contemporary independent and foreign films are also shown at the Capitol.

Festivals and Events

Thousands of gleaming vintage cars of every description roll into York for **Street Rod Nationals East** (901/452-4030, www.nsra-usa.com, early June, admission charged), one of about a dozen annual events hosted by the National Street Rod Association. The street rods—vintage vehicles that have been modernized with features such as air-conditioning and cruise control—congregate on the grounds of the **York Expo Center** (334 Carlisle Ave., York, 717/848-2596, www.yorkexpo.com), where auto enthusiasts can get a close look and chat up the owners. Spectators line the streets of York for a parade of the candy-colored cars.

The Expo Center's signature event is the 10-day **York Fair** (717/848-2596, www.yorkfair.org, opens Friday after Labor Day, admission charged). The fair dates to 1765—11 years before the nation was founded—and bills itself as America's first and oldest. It was interrupted during the Civil War, when the fairgrounds served as a hospital for wounded soldiers, and in 1918 due to a deadly influenza outbreak. But the fair hasn't taken a hiatus since, growing larger and longer with each passing decade. It even remained open in the days following the 9/11 attacks, in celebration of American culture and spirit.

One of the most happening spots in York County, **Moon Dancer Vineyards & Winery** (1282 Klines Run Rd., Wrightsville, 717/252-9463, www.moondancerwinery.com, noon-5pm Wed.-Thurs., noon-10pm Fri., 11am-6pm Sat.-Sun.) hosts live music on Fridays, Saturdays, and Sundays year-round and a series of music festivals each summer. In the warmer months, visitors can mingle on the patio or picnic on the grounds of the French chateau-like winery overlooking the Susquehanna River. In the colder ones, they can sip hot mulled wine by a fire.

SPORTS AND RECREATION
Boating

The **lower section of Pennsylvania's Susquehanna River Water Trail** (717/252-0229, www.susquehannawatertrail.org), which forms the eastern boundary of York County, is beloved by paddlers and birders. It's home to the Conejohela Flats, a series of small islands and mud flats that attract scores of migratory shorebirds in spring and fall. You can get everything you need to hit the water at **Shank's Mare Outfitters** (2092 Long Level Rd., Wrightsville, 717/252-1616, www.shanks-mare.com, open daily during boating season). Housed in an 1890s general store on the banks of the Susquehanna, the family-owned store sells and rents kayaks and stand-up paddleboards. On a calm day, it takes about 40 minutes to paddle from Shank's Mare to the Conejohela Flats. The store also offers guided paddle tours, kayaking and paddleboarding instruction, and guided hiking tours. The 193-mile **Mason-Dixon Trail** (www.mason-dixontrail.org) follows the west bank of the Susquehanna in York County, passing right by Shank's Mare.

Heritage Rail Trail

The 21-mile **Heritage Rail Trail** (717/840-7440, www.yorkcountyparks.org) stretches from York City to the Mason-Dixon line, where it connects to Maryland's 20-mile Northern Central Railroad Trail. It's open for hiking, bicycling, horseback riding, cross-country skiing, and snowshoeing. The parking lot for the York City trailhead is on Pershing Avenue near the Colonial Courthouse. Traversing the trail is part exercise, part history lesson. About six miles south of the reconstructed courthouse is the 370-foot Howard Tunnel, one of the oldest railroad tunnels in the country. The rail line adjacent to the Heritage Rail Trail was a vital link between Washington DC and points north in the 19th century. As such, it was a prime target for Confederate troops during the Civil War. After the Battle of Gettysburg in 1863,

President Lincoln traveled via these rails to deliver the Gettysburg Address, stretching his legs at York County's **Hanover Junction Station** (Rte. 616, Hanover Junction). The station at the midpoint of the Heritage Rail Trail has been restored to its 1863 appearance and houses a Civil War museum. There's another historic station near the southern end of the trail. The **New Freedom Station** (Front and Franklin Streets, New Freedom) has been restored to its 1940s appearance and houses a railroad museum. The museums are open on select days May-October. Check the York County Parks website for dates and times.

Four Springs Winery (50 Main St., Seven Valleys, 717/428-2610, www.foursprings winerypa.com, 1pm-6pm Wed.-Fri., 11am-6pm Sat., 1pm-6pm Sun.) is also adjacent to the rail trail. It's not unusual to see spandex-clad cyclists in the tasting room.

Roundtop Mountain Resort

About midway between York and Harrisburg, **Roundtop Mountain Resort** (925 Roundtop Rd., Lewisberry, 717/432-9631, www.skiroundtop.com) offers skiing, snowboarding, and snow tubing in the colder months and activities like zip-lining and bumper boating in the warmer ones. Homemade contraptions of cardboard, tape, and glue careen down the tubing runs during Roundtop's annual **Cardboard Derby** in January. In summer, the tubing area becomes the site of an even zanier activity: rolling downhill in a giant plastic ball known as an OGO. Each OGO accommodates as many as three people.

ACCOMMODATIONS

Built during the Roaring Twenties, the 121-room ★ **Yorktowne Hotel** (48 E. Market St., York, 717/848-1111, www.yorktowne.com, $100-300) is resplendent with high ceilings, brass and crystal chandeliers, and wood paneling. Just as impressive is the service; some of the staff have worked at the downtown landmark for upwards of 20 years. The Yorktowne is conveniently located within walking distance of the Colonial Complex, the northern terminus of the Heritage Rail Trail, Central Market, and the Strand-Capitol Performing Arts Center.

York County has no shortage of excellent B&Bs. Among them: **Lady Linden Bed and Breakfast** (505 Linden Ave., York, 717/843-2929, www.ladylindenbedandbreakfast.

downtown York

com, $139), a meticulously restored 1887 Queen Anne Victorian with two guest suites. Breakfast is a four-course affair. **The Beechmont** (315 Broadway, Hanover, 717/632-3013, www.thebeechmont.com, $159-184) is an excellent choice in southern York County. Owner Kathryn White has received the Pennsylvania Tourism & Lodging Association's Innkeeper of the Year Award. The seven-room inn is convenient to historic Gettysburg. Now an oasis of calm, the house witnessed the Battle of Hanover, which delayed a Confederate cavalry's arrival at the more famous Battle of Gettysburg. White is a font of information about Hanover's role in the Civil War—and a whiz in the kitchen. Exquisite breakfasts are served by candlelight; homemade cookies or other treats are offered each evening.

FOOD

York's **Central Market** (34 W. Philadelphia St., York, 717/848-2243, www.centralmarketyork.com, 6am-2pm Tues., Thurs., and Sat.) is a hopping lunch spot. It's perfect for dining companions with different tastes, offering everything from soups and sandwiches to Caribbean and Malaysian dishes. On the downside, it's closed four days of the week.

Located across the street from Central Market, **White Rose Bar and Grill** (48 N. Beaver St., York, 717/848-5369, www.whiterosebarandgrill.com, 11am-10pm Sun.-Thurs., 11am-11pm Fri.-Sat., bar open until 2am Mon.-Sat. and midnight Sun., $5-35) dates to the 1930s. Extensive renovations in recent years have given it a thoroughly modern feel. The appetizer menu includes little neck clams, seared sushi-grade tuna, and plenty of deep-fried goodies, but nothing compares to the soft pretzel sticks topped with crab dip and melted cheese. Main dishes range from a simple BLT to seafood paella. Order from the "hot rock menu" and your seafood or steak will arrive at the table on heated volcanic stones, continuing to cook while you dig in.

York's most impressive martini list can be found at ★ **The Left Bank** (120 N. George St., York, 717/843-8010, www.leftbankyork.com, lunch Tues.-Fri., dinner Mon.-Sat., lunch $10-25, dinner $19-35), a chef-owned fine dining restaurant with a big-city feel. This is where Yorkers come on special occasions. Don't think "Philly cheesesteak" and "fancy" belong in the same sentence? You haven't tried chef David Albright's cheesesteak appetizer, made with beef tenderloin, bruschetta, and basil aioli. The seafood entrées are outstanding, as is the service. Don't hesitate to ask the waitstaff for wine recommendations.

If your visit to York County includes a visit to Moon Dancer Vineyards & Winery or Shank's Mare Outfitters, plan on dining at the nearby **John Wright Restaurant** (234 N. Front St., Wrightsville, 717/252-0416, www.johnwrightrestaurant.com, 11am-3pm Mon.-Tues., 11am-3pm and 4pm-9pm Wed.-Fri., 8am-9pm Sat., 11am-3pm Sun., lunch $7-14, dinner $12-27), which occupies a restored warehouse along the Susquehanna River. Heck, plan on dining there if you're anywhere within a 20-mile radius. The casual atmosphere, comfort foods, and killer views make it worth a drive. (You can also kayak to it.) Come for the Sunday brunch buffet ($16.95, children 3-12 $7.95) if you get the chance. In the warmer months, you can choose between the main restaurant and an outdoor dining area known as The Patio, which specializes in wood-fired pizzas. If you have to wait for a table, you can kill time in the **John Wright Store** (717/252-2519, www.johnwrightstore.com, 10am-4pm Mon.-Wed., 10am-8pm Thurs.-Fri., 9am-8pm Sat., 11am-3:30pm Sun.), which sells cast iron products, Vera Bradley accessories, Dansko shoes, and more.

INFORMATION

If you're arriving in York County via I-83 north, look for the state-run **welcome center** 2.5 miles north of the Pennsylvania-Maryland line. Personalized travel counseling is available 7am-7pm daily.

Visit the website of the **York County**

Convention & Visitors Bureau (717/852-9675, www.yorkpa.org) to request a free visitors guide or peruse a digital version. The CVB operates a visitors center in downtown York (149 W. Market St., 717/852-9675, 9:30am-4pm daily) and another at the Harley-Davidson plant (1425 Eden Rd., York, 717/852-6006, 9am-5pm daily).

GETTING THERE AND AROUND

York County shares its southern border with Maryland. Its county seat and largest municipality, York, is about 50 miles north of Baltimore and 25 miles south of Harrisburg via I-83. Route 30 provides east-west access to the city, which is about 30 miles from Gettysburg to its west and Lancaster to its east.

Harrisburg International Airport (MDT, 888/235-9442, www.flyhia.com), about half an hour's drive from York, is served by several major airlines. **Baltimore/Washington International Thurgood Marshall Airport** (BWI, 800/435-9294, www.bwiairport.com) is farther—about an hour from York assuming minimal traffic—but considerably larger.

Intercity bus service to York is available through **Greyhound** (53 E. North St., 800/231-2222, www.greyhound.com) and its interline partners. York County's public bus system is **Rabbittransit** (800/632-9063, www.rabbittransit.org).

Gettysburg and Vicinity

Few places in America have the name recognition of Gettysburg. There's hardly an eighth grader who hasn't heard of the town, which has fewer than 8,000 residents. It earned its place in the history books in 1863, when it was the setting for the Civil War's bloodiest battle and President Abraham Lincoln's most famous speech. The former took place July 1-3, with more than 165,000 soldiers converging on the crossroads town. Under the command of General George G. Meade, the Union army desperately and successfully defended its home territory from General Robert E. Lee's Confederate army. The war would continue for almost two years, but the Confederacy's hopes for independence effectively died on the Gettysburg Battlefield. The hellish battle's human toll was astronomical: 51,000 soldiers were dead, wounded, or missing. Interestingly, only one of Gettysburg's 2,400 citizens was killed during the biggest battle ever fought on this continent. The casualty was a young woman named Jennie Wade, and the bullet-riddled house in which she died is now a museum.

In the aftermath of the battle, the townspeople dedicated themselves to caring for the wounded and burying the dead. A group of prominent residents convinced the state to help fund the purchase of a portion of the battlefield to serve as a final resting place for the Union's defenders. Gettysburg attorney David Wills was appointed to coordinate the establishment of the Soldiers' National Cemetery, and he invited President Lincoln to deliver "a few appropriate remarks" at the dedication ceremony on November 19, 1863. The lanky commander-in-chief arrived by train the previous day and strolled down Carlisle Street to Wills's stately home on the town square. There, in a second-floor bedroom, he polished his talk. The National Park Service acquired the house in 2004 and opened it as a museum in 2009. Lincoln's two-minute Gettysburg Address—so succinct that a photographer on the scene failed to snap a picture—is regarded as the rhetorical zenith of his career and one of the greatest speeches in history.

The four-year Civil War was fought on many battlegrounds, but none is as hallowed as Gettysburg's. Established in 1895,

Gettysburg National Military Park was the first historic site owned by the U.S. government. As the only major Civil War battlefield in a northern state and an easy trip from population centers such as Philadelphia and Baltimore, it attracted scores of veterans and other visitors. The battlefield's popularity as a tourist destination bred commercial development in the 20th century. At one point there was even a casino on what is now park property. In recent years, preservationists have gotten the upper hand. Commercial establishments have been given the boot. Billboards have vanished. The National Park Service is even removing trees from parts of the battlefield, planting them in others, and reconstructing long-gone farm lanes and roads so that the landscape looks more like it did in 1863. Bottom line: There hasn't been a better time to visit Gettysburg in the last century. The picture of what transpired there is getting clearer and clearer.

PLANNING YOUR TIME

When to visit? That depends on your interests and tolerance for crowds. The Gettysburg area is busiest in early July, during the annual battle reenactment, which is held not on the battlefield but on private land. The town swarms with tourists and rifle-toting reenactors, and the weather tends toward hot and humid. Visitation tapers off as the summer draws to a close, then picks up in October, when paranormal enthusiasts flock to what they believe is one of the most haunted places in the country. Mid-November brings scores of Lincoln scholars and admirers. They discuss his life and legacy at an annual symposium before joining in a town-wide celebration of his famous address. Winter is the slow season, an ideal time for hushed contemplation of the carnage and courage that shaped this country. Some Gettysburg attractions are closed during the coldest months, but the battlefield is open daily year-round. Things pick up in April with the arrival of busload after busload of schoolchildren. By June, tourism is in full swing.

The battlefield is certainly the area's biggest draw, but there are more than a dozen other sights of interest to history buffs. Downtown Gettysburg is itself a historical attraction: About 60 percent of its buildings predate the battle. One of the most popular tourist stops isn't about history at all. It's a museum housing one man's collection of

living history in downtown Gettysburg

Gettysburg Guides

It's easy to explore Gettysburg on your own, but if you're hazy on Civil War history, a tour can make for a richer experience. Tour operators are a dime a dozen. Which one is right for you depends on your preferred mode of transport and whether you're keen on a live guide or satisfied with recorded narration.

Many Gettysburg tours are led by members of the **Association of Licensed Battlefield Guides** (717/337-1709, www.gettysburgtourguides.org), who have spent years if not decades studying the Battle of Gettysburg. Licensure applicants first take a rigorous written exam; the highest scorers prove themselves further by passing an oral test. If you appreciate a lot of detail and ask a lot of questions, hire a licensed guide who will take the wheel of your car and show you around. Guides are available on a first-come, first-served basis at the **Gettysburg National Military Park Museum and Visitor Center** (1195 Baltimore Pike/Rte. 97, Gettysburg, 717/338-1243, reservations 717/334-2436, www.gettysburgfoundation.org, 8am-6pm daily Apr.-mid-Oct., 8am-5pm daily mid-Oct.-Mar.), but reservations are strongly recommended. A two-hour tour costs $65 per vehicle with 1-6 people, $90 per vehicle with 7-15. It's customary to tip your guide if you're satisfied. Bus tours with a licensed guide ($30, children 6-12 $18) also leave from the Museum and Visitor Center. Allow 2.5 hours for the bus tour.

Gettysburg Tours (778 Baltimore St., Gettysburg, 717/334-6296, www.gettysburgbattlefieldtours.com) offers two varieties of double-decker bus tours: one with a licensed guide ($30, children 6-12 $19) and another featuring recorded narration complete with cannon booms and rifle cracks ($26, children 6-12 $15). Both take about two hours. Gettysburg Tours operates several area attractions, including the Jennie Wade House and the Hall of Presidents & First Ladies. Combo packages are available.

You can feel like General Lee by touring the battlefield on horseback. **Artillery Ridge Campground** (610 Taneytown Rd., Gettysburg, 717/334-1288, www.artilleryridge.com), just across the street from the battlefield, offers one- and two-hour horseback tours ($50 and $80, respectively). Riding experience isn't necessary. Another option: gliding around the battlefield on a Segway.

---

elephants (man-made, not living). Another nonhistorical attraction, the Land of Little Horses (living, not man-made), scores big with kids.

★ GETTYSBURG NATIONAL MILITARY PARK

Expect to spend the better part of a day at **Gettysburg National Military Park** (717/334-1124, www.nps.gov/gett, 6am-10pm daily Apr.-Oct., 6am-7pm daily Nov.-Mar., free admission), site of the Civil War's biggest and bloodiest battle. The 6,000-acre park is not only one of the nation's most popular historical attractions but also one of the world's most extraordinary sculpture gardens. It's dotted with more than 1,300 monuments, markers, and memorials. They include equestrian bronzes of the battle's commanders, tributes to common soldiers, a statue of a civilian hero, and another of a priest who

gave absolution to Irish soldiers as they prepared for battle.

It's best to begin your visit at the **Museum and Visitor Center** (1195 Baltimore Pike/Rte. 97, Gettysburg, 717/338-1243, reservations 717/334-2436, www.gettysburgfoundation.org, 8am-6pm daily Apr.-mid-Oct., 8am-5pm daily mid-Oct.-Mar., admission to film/cyclorama/museum $12.50, seniors $11.50, children 6-12 $8.50), operated by the nonprofit Gettysburg Foundation. There you can orient yourself to the park and learn about the nightmarish clash of armies. Be sure to ask for a schedule of lectures, guided walks, and other special programs, which are especially frequent in the summer months. If you plan on touring the battlefield on your own, pick up the National Park Service map and guide (also available at www.nps.gov/gett). It outlines a 24-mile auto tour and briefly describes what transpired at each tour stop. For detailed descriptions of the three-day battle, you can

SegTours (22 Springs Ave., Gettysburg, 717/253-7987, www.segtours.com) offers a three-hour tour ($70) of the most famous battlefield sites and a two-hour tour ($50) to a lesser-known part of the battlefield, both with recorded narration. Live guides are available for an additional fee. Reservations are recommended for recorded tours and required for live guides. Tours depart on a regular schedule March-November. Off-season tours may be available by reservation.

Located in the bus parking lot at the Gettysburg National Military Park Museum and Visitor Center, **GettysBike** (1195 Baltimore Pike/Rte. 97, Gettysburg, 717/752-7752, www.gettysbike.com) offers bicycle tours of the battlefield and the town of Gettysburg. Led by licensed guides, the tours range from $51 to $71 per person. You can save $5 by bringing your own bike. GettysBike also offers bike rentals for those who want to explore on their own.

While most tours focus on the battlefield and the clashes of troops that culminated in a Union victory, the nonprofit **Main Street Gettysburg** (717/339-6161, www.mainstreetgettysburg.org) offers 90-minute walking tours of downtown that illumine the civilian experience. One need only to look at a map of Gettysburg National Military Park to realize that the town must have been deeply scarred. The battlefield enfolds the town—the last in America to be occupied by an invading army. Most walking tours ($16, seniors and children 6-18 $12) depart from the historic Gettysburg Hotel at 1 Lincoln Square.

Paranormal enthusiasts consider Gettysburg one of the most haunted places in the country. If you're not terribly squeamish, an evening ghost-themed tour may be for you. The original and most reputable operator is **Ghosts of Gettysburg** (271 Baltimore St., Gettysburg, 717/337-0445, www.ghostsofgettysburg.com, Mar.-Nov.) Its walking and bus tours, led by guides in period attire with candle lanterns in hand, are based on the books of historian, ghost hunter, and former National Park Service ranger Mark Nesbitt. Walking tours are $9.50-10 per person, free for children 7 and under. Bus tours are $18 per person, $16 for children 5-10, and off-limits to children under 5.

buy an audio tour CD in the museum bookstore or hire a federally licensed guide, who will get behind the wheel of your car and take you on a two-hour personalized tour ($65 per vehicle with 1-6 people). The highly knowledgeable guides are available on a first-come,

Gettysburg National Military Park

first-served basis as soon as the visitors center opens, but reservations are recommended. Bus tours with a licensed guide ($30, children 6-12 $18) are also offered.

The visitors center, which opened in 2008, is home to a colossal cyclorama depicting Pickett's Charge, a futile infantry assault ordered by Confederate General Robert E. Lee on the final day of battle. It's said that veterans wept at the sight of the 360-degree painting when it was unveiled in 1884. Measuring 42 feet high and 377 feet in circumference, the **Gettysburg Cyclorama** is the largest painting in the country. It's displayed with a diorama that gives the masterpiece a 3-D quality. A sound and light show amps up the drama. The cyclorama experience is preceded by a 22-minute film, *A New Birth of Freedom*, narrated by Morgan Freeman. Timed tickets are issued for the film and cyclorama. They include admission to the on-site **Gettysburg Museum of the American Civil War,** which explores the causes and consequences of the deadliest war in American history. Museum-only tickets are available.

The **Soldiers' National Cemetery,** where President Lincoln delivered his famous Gettysburg Address, is a short walk from the visitors center. It's open from dawn to sunset and closed to vehicular traffic. Walking tour brochures are available at the visitors center and online at www.nps.gov/gett. Work on the cemetery began soon after the bloodshed ended. Thousands of Union and Confederate dead had been hastily buried on or near the battlefield, many of them in shallow graves. Heavy rains would expose decaying bodies, a grisly sight that helped convince Pennsylvania governor Andrew Curtin to appropriate state funds for the cemetery project. About 3,500 Union soldiers were interred there. The Confederate dead remained in scattered graves until the 1870s, when they were relocated to cemeteries in the south. Today the Soldiers' National Cemetery is the final resting place for veterans from all of America's wars through Vietnam. It's the setting for several annual events, including a Memorial Day service and a commemoration of the Gettysburg Address held each November.

OTHER SIGHTS
Gettysburg Seminary Ridge Museum

The **Seminary Ridge Museum** (111 Seminary Ridge, Gettysburg, 717/339-1300, www.seminaryridgemuseum.org, 10am-5pm Fri.-Mon., admission $9, seniors and children

the Gettysburg Cyclorama

6-12 $7) opened July 1, 2013, exactly 150 years after the Battle of Gettysburg erupted. That first day of battle is one of the museum's main focuses. Built in 1832 for the Lutheran Theological Seminary at Gettysburg, the museum building was used as a field hospital during the 1863 battle. Appropriately enough, the new museum also places special emphasis on Civil War medicine and the moral and spiritual debates of that tumultuous era. It features four floors of exhibits, large-scale reproductions of 10 commissioned paintings by renowned historical artist Dale Gallon, interactive stations for children, and an outdoor interpretive trail. The building's cupola, which was used by Union General John Buford to survey the battlefield, is accessible by guided tour. You must be at least 13 years old and able to climb stairs to take the cupola tour ($29, seniors $27, includes museum admission).

Eisenhower National Historic Site

Located adjacent to the Gettysburg Battlefield, **Eisenhower National Historic Site** (717/338-9114, www.nps.gov/eise, admission $7.50, children 6-12 $5) preserves the onetime home and farm of President Dwight D. Eisenhower. The Texas-born Army general and 34th president first visited Gettysburg as a cadet at the U.S. Military Academy at West Point and returned during World War I to run a training camp. After commanding the Allied forces during the Second World War, "Ike" came to Gettysburg with his wife, Mamie, in search of a retirement home. The house has changed little since then. Furnishings include a coffee table given to the Eisenhowers by the first lady of South Korea, a rug from the shah of Iran, and a desk fashioned from old floorboards removed from the White House during a 1948 renovation. Visitors can also explore the grounds, which include a putting green, rose gardens, and a garage that still houses the Eisenhowers' jeep, golf carts, and station wagon. Due to limited on-site parking and space in the home, visitors must arrive by shuttle bus from the Museum and Visitor Center at Gettysburg National Military Park (1195 Baltimore Pike/Rte. 97, Gettysburg, 717/338-1243, reservations 717/334-2436, www.gettysburgfoundation.org). Shuttles depart every hour or half hour 9am-4pm during most times of the year.

Shriver and Jennie Wade Houses

These two house museums explore the civilian

Eisenhower National Historic Site

experience during the Civil War. Both feature tour guides in period attire.

The **Shriver House Museum** (309 Baltimore St., Gettysburg, 717/337-2800, www.shriverhouse.org, open daily Apr.-mid-Nov., call or check website for off-season hours, admission $8.50, seniors $8.25, children under 13 $6.35) tells the story of George Washington Shriver and his family. In 1860, Shriver paid $290 for what was then considered a double lot on the edge of town. He built a home for his family, opening a saloon in the cellar and a 10-pin bowling alley in an adjacent building. When the Civil War erupted in 1861, Shriver answered President Lincoln's call for troops. He was still away when the war came to Gettysburg in July 1863. While his wife and two young daughters hunkered down at her parents' farm about three miles away, Confederate soldiers occupied their home. Today visitors learn about life during the Civil War as they tour all four floors of the house, including the attic used by Confederate sharpshooters. Three live Civil War bullets and period medical supplies were discovered under floorboards when the house was under restoration in 1996. They're among the artifacts displayed in the museum shop next door.

The nearby **Jennie Wade House** (548 Baltimore St., Gettysburg, 717/334-4100, www.gettysburgbattlefieldtours.com, hours vary by season, admission $7.75, children 6-12 $4) is a shrine to the only civilian casualty of the Battle of Gettysburg. Jennie Wade was baking bread for Union soldiers when bullets ripped through the door of the house, taking her life. She was 20 years old and engaged to a childhood friend who'd been mustered into the service two years earlier. He died just nine days later of wounds sustained in a Virginia battle, never knowing of his sweetheart's fate.

General Lee's Headquarters Museum

On the first day of the Battle of Gettysburg, Confederate General Robert E. Lee established his personal headquarters in a stone house at the center and rear of his battle lines. There, he and his commanders pondered the problems of the great battle, which ended in a victory for the Union. Fifty-nine years after Lee escaped south, the house was opened to the public as a museum named for him. **General Lee's Headquarters Museum** (401 Buford Ave., Gettysburg, 717/334-3141, www.civilwar-headquarters.com, 9am-5pm mid-Mar.-Nov., extended summer hours, free admission) is one of the oldest museums in Gettysburg and unique in its focus on the Confederate cause. It's also unique in that visitors can spend a night upstairs. The **Quality Inn at General Lee's Headquarters** (717/334-3141, www.thegettysburgaddress.com, $65-250) has hosted such bigwigs as General George Patton and President Dwight Eisenhower as well as the last surviving Confederate widow.

Wax Museums

The little town of Gettysburg is home to not one but two wax museums. More than 300 life-size wax figures depict events of the nation's deadliest war at the **American Civil War Wax Museum** (297 Steinwehr Ave., Gettysburg, 717/334-6245, www.gettysburgmuseum.com, 9am-5pm daily Mar.-Dec., extended spring and summer hours, open weekends and holidays Jan.-Feb., admission $6.95, children 6-17 $3.95). Visitors learn about the economic, social, and political causes of the war, the assassination of President Abraham Lincoln, and everything in between. The sounds of bullets and battle cries echo in the Battle Auditorium, home to a life-size diorama of the Battle of Gettysburg. The **Gettysburg Gift Center,** located in the lobby of the museum, is one of the largest and best gift shops in town.

A stone's throw from the main entrance to Soldiers' National Cemetery, the **Hall of Presidents & First Ladies** (789 Baltimore St., Gettysburg, 717/334-5717, www.gettysburgbattlefieldtours.com, hours vary by season, admission $7.50, children 6-12 $3.50) features wax figures of every American president. Extra attention is paid to 34th President Dwight D. Eisenhower, who bought a home in Gettysburg before winning the presidency and lived out his days there. The museum also has a collection of doll-size first ladies in their inaugural gowns.

Land of Little Horses Farm Park

Admission isn't cheap, but the **Land of Little Horses** (125 Glenwood Dr., Gettysburg, 717/334-7259, www.landoflittlehorses.com, 10am-5pm Mon.-Sat. and noon-5pm Sun. May-late Aug., Sat.-Sun. only through Oct., admission $15.95, children 6-11 $13.95, children 2-5 $11.95) is a hit with little 'uns. Just a few miles west of downtown Gettysburg, the "performing animal theme park" is home to not only miniature horses but also goats, sheep, donkeys, emus, and other critters. Animal performances are held daily in the summer and on weekends in spring and fall. The park also offers pony rides and wagon rides at $5 a pop. (Alas, if you're over 70 pounds, no pony ride for you.)

Mister Ed's Elephant Museum & Candy Emporium

Ed Gotwalt's passion for all things pachyderm started on his wedding day more than 40 years ago, when he received an elephant knickknack as a good luck charm. By 1983 his elephant collection had grown so large that he opened a museum to showcase it. Miss Ellie Phant, a life-size talking elephant with animated eyes and ears, greets visitors at **Mister Ed's Elephant Museum** (6019 Chambersburg Rd., Orrtanna, 717/352-3792, www.mistereds.com, 10am-6pm Sun.-Thurs., 10am-8pm Fri.-Sat., free admission), located on Route 30 about 12 miles west of Gettysburg. It doesn't cost a cent to see Gotwalt's collection, which has ballooned to more than 12,000 elephants. After a 2010 fire claimed roughly 2,000 elephants, thousands more arrived from donors around the world. There are stone elephants, wood elephants, metal elephants, and plush elephants. There's an elephant potty chair and an elephant hair dryer. There are even elephant-embroidered pillowcases that once belonged to Cher.

Elephants aren't the only draw. The **Candy Emporium** features fresh roasted peanuts, more than 70 flavors of fudge, and old-time candy like wax bottles and Pez.

Appalachian Trail Museum

After 12 years in the making, the **Appalachian Trail Museum** (1120 Pine Grove Rd., Gardners, 717/486-8126, www.atmuseum.org, open spring-fall, hours vary by season, free admission) opened in 2010. Housed in a former gristmill in Pine Grove Furnace State Park, the museum pays tribute to pioneer hikers such as Earl Shaffer, the first person to thru-hike the trail, and "Grandma" Gatewood, who was 67 when she became the first female to complete the journey alone. There's even an exhibit on Ziggy, the first feline to conquer the Georgia-to-Maine trail. (To be fair, the cat spent most of the journey riding on the backpack of hiker Jim "the Geek" Adams, but he contributed much in the way of mice patrol at trail shelters.) Highlights of the collection include a trail shelter that Shaffer, a native of nearby York County, built about a decade after his 1948 history-making hike. The shelter was painstakingly dismantled at its original site and reassembled in the museum.

Visitors stand a good chance of rubbing shoulders with modern-day thru-hikers because the museum is just a few hundred yards off the Appalachian Trail. The midpoint of the 2,180-mile footpath is just south of **Pine Grove Furnace State Park** (1100 Pine Grove Rd., Gardners, 717/486-7174, www.visitpaparks.com), and tradition dictates that thru-hikers stop at the park's general store to face a test of mettle known as the "half-gallon challenge." Those who succeed, i.e., eat half a gallon of ice cream in one sitting, are rewarded with a commemorative wooden spoon. Word has it that chunky flavors are harder to finish.

The state park is named for an ironworks founded in 1764, and the charcoal iron furnace that operated until 1895 is still standing. A mansion built in 1829 for the ironmaster's family now serves as a hostel and event venue. The 696-acre park also features a campground and two small lakes with beaches and a boat rental. Pine Grove allows overnight parking for anyone who wants to hit the A.T., but registration at the park office is required.

National Apple Museum

Adams County, of which Gettysburg is the county seat, is one of the largest apple producers in the country and the heart of Pennsylvania's fruit belt. It's home to grower-owned applesauce maker Musselman's, a Mott's plant, and the **National Apple Museum** (154 W. Hanover St., Biglerville, 717/677-4556, www.nationalapplemuseum. com, 10am-4pm Sat. and 1pm-4pm Sun. May-Oct., admission $3, seniors $2, children 6-16 $1.50). Miles and miles of orchards make for scenic drives, especially when the trees are in bloom. Visit the **Gettysburg Wine & Fruit Trail** website (www.gettysburgwineandfruittrail.com) for a map highlighting orchards, farm markets, and other agritourism attractions.

ENTERTAINMENT AND EVENTS
Performing Arts

The **Majestic Theater** (25 Carlisle St., Gettysburg, 717/337-8200, www.gettysburgmajestic.org) was the largest vaudeville and silent movie theater in south-central Pennsylvania when it opened in 1925. President Dwight D. Eisenhower and First Lady Mamie Eisenhower attended performances in the 1950s, often with world leaders in tow. In 1993 the Majestic hosted the world premiere of *Gettysburg,* one of the longest films ever released by a Hollywood studio. Today it hosts live performances by the likes of the Moscow Circus, the Temptations, and pianist Jim Brickman. Two cinemas with stadium seating were added as part of a $16 million renovation in recent years. The Majestic screens indie and critically acclaimed films seven days a week.

Festivals and Events

The Gettysburg area is apple country. It's home to apple orchards, applesauce makers, and even an apple museum. It also boasts two annual apple-themed festivals. Both feature orchard tours, pony rides, antique cars, arts and crafts vendors, live entertainment, and

an event at the National Apple Harvest Festival

more. Held the first full weekend in May, when apple trees are in bloom, the **Apple Blossom Festival** (717/677-7444, www.appleblossomfestival.info, admission $5, children under 12 free) also includes a "PA Apple Queen" contest. The reigning Apple Queen makes appearances at the **National Apple Harvest Festival** (717/677-9413, www.appleharvest.com, first two full weekends in Oct., admission $9, seniors $8, children under 12 free), the region's biggest to-do. Both festivals are held at the South Mountain Fair Grounds, 10 miles northwest of Gettysburg on Route 234.

Thousands of reenactors take part in the annual **Gettysburg Civil War Battle Reenactment** (information 717/334-6274, tickets 800/514-3849, www.gettysburgreenactment.com, early July, admission charged), firing period weapons and feigning death on farm fields just a few miles from the original battlefield. Several clashes are staged over three days. Spectators can stroll through the soldiers' camps, listen to live Civil War music and period speakers, watch period demonstrations, and shop for period wares. Arrive early to claim a spot near the front of battle viewing areas. It's a good idea to bring folding chairs, binoculars, and sunscreen. Limited bleacher seating is available but usually sells out before the event.

A host of events commemorate President Abraham Lincoln's Gettysburg Address, delivered at the dedication of the Soldiers' National Cemetery less than five months after the Battle of Gettysburg. Held on the speech's anniversary, **Dedication Day** (717/338-1243, www.gettysburgfoundation.org, Nov. 19) begins with a wreath-laying ceremony at the cemetery. Nationally renowned Lincoln actor Jim Getty recites the short speech after an oration by a person of note. Past speakers have included actor Richard Dreyfuss, newsman Tom Brokaw, astronaut Neil Armstrong, and Chief Justice William Rehnquist. Held within a few days of Dedication Day, **Remembrance Day** (717/232-7000, www.suvcw.org) features a parade of Civil War reenactors—from drummer boys to generals on horseback—that

winds through Gettysburg and ends at the National Military Park. As the day draws to a close, a luminary candle is placed on each Civil War grave in the Soldiers' National Cemetery. The cost to sponsor a candle for the **Remembrance Illumination** (717/339-2148, www.friendsofgettysburg.org) is, appropriately enough, $18.63.

SHOPPING
Downtown Gettysburg
You won't find the Gap or a Starbucks in downtown Gettysburg. Its shops are of the independent variety, and many offer things you'd be hard-pressed to find in a big city: Civil War collectibles, military artifacts from the American Revolutionary War and onward, and anything a reenactor could want, from candle lanterns to cavalry swords. Dale Gallon, one of the nation's premier historical artists, has an eponymous gallery in town: the **Gallon Historical Art Gallery** (9 Steinwehr Ave., 717/334-8666, www.gallon.com, call for hours).

Greater Gettysburg
Pennsylvania's sales tax exemption on clothing lures many a Marylander to the **Outlet Shoppes at Gettysburg** (1863 Gettysburg Village Dr., Gettysburg, 717/337-9705, www.theoutletshoppesatgettysburg.com, 10am-9pm Mon.-Sat., 10am-6pm Sun.) at Route 15 and Baltimore Street (Route 97). Stores include Jones New York, Old Navy, Tommy Hilfiger, Naturalizer, and Coach. There's a 10-screen movie theater (717/338-0101) and hotel on-site.

The quiet, tree-lined borough of **New Oxford,** 10 miles east of Gettysburg on Route 30, is an antiquing mecca with more than 500 dealers. A partial list can be found at www.newoxfordantiques.com, website of the New Oxford Antique Dealers Association.

ACCOMMODATIONS
Gettysburg has loads of lodging properties, many of which have a story to tell. There are B&Bs scarred by bullets and rooms once

occupied by generals. You can unwind in a place that once crawled with wounded soldiers. If you visit when the town is crawling with tourists, expect two- or three-night minimums at many properties. Rates are at their lowest from December through March.

Under $100

Camping is a popular and inexpensive way to stay near the battlefield during the high season. Gettysburg has half a dozen campgrounds. If your idea of camping is quietly communing with nature, you may be in for a shock. These campgrounds are fairly bustling places. Some have cottages so luxurious they make hotel rooms look rustic, and all offer a host of modern amenities. **Drummer Boy Camping Resort** (1300 Hanover St., Gettysburg, 800/293-2808, www.drummerboycampresort.com, tent site $38-57, hookup site $44-80, cabin or cottage $65-360, weekly rates available) has, in addition to more than 400 campsites and about 50 cabins and cottages, two heated pools, a 250-foot waterslide, a mini golf course, a game room, basketball and volleyball courts, and a fishing pond. Add to that a full schedule of activities and it's a wonder that campers ever leave the 95-acre resort. Drummer Boy is a few minutes east of downtown on Route 116.

A few minutes west of downtown on Route 116 is the 260-site **Gettysburg Campground** (2030 Fairfield Rd./Rte. 116 W., Gettysburg, 717/334-3304, www.gettysburgcampground.com, tent site $33-46, hookup site $37-66, cabin or cottage $65-165, weekly rates available). It too has amenities up the wazoo. Try to snag a campsite along Marsh Creek.

$100-200

Gettysburg's most iconic hotel, the ★ **Best Western Gettysburg Hotel** (1 Lincoln Square, Gettysburg, 717/337-2000, www.hotelgettysburg.com, peak season $138-390, winter $100-250), is said to have a friendly ghost. You may or may not encounter the Civil War nurse named Rachel during your

stay. You'll definitely encounter friendly staff. The hotel in the center of town, just steps from the house where President Lincoln polished his Gettysburg Address, is steeped in history. Its story begins in 1797, when a tavern opened its doors on the site. It withstood the bloody and pivotal battle of 1863 but was replaced in the 1890s by the current structure, which was christened the Hotel Gettysburg. In 1955 the hotel served as President Eisenhower's national operations center while he recuperated from a heart attack at his Gettysburg home. Eisenhower and his wife were the hotel's last guests before it closed its doors in 1964, rendered unprofitable by changes in travel habits. Ravaged by fire in 1983, the building was painstakingly restored and opened as a Best Western in 1991, grand as it ever was. The hotel has 119 guest accommodations, almost half of which are suites; a rooftop swimming pool; and a fine dining restaurant. Check the website for a list of packages that bundle accommodations with activities such as skiing and theater-going.

Also historic but considerably smaller, the **James Gettys Hotel** (27 Chambersburg St., Gettysburg, 717/337-1334, www.jamesgettyshotel.com, $145-250) is half a block from the town square. Named for the founder of Gettysburg, it dates to 1804 and looks much as it did in the 1920s. Like the Gettysburg Hotel, it closed in the 1960s and reopened as an emulation of its former self in the 1990s. The James Gettys has a dozen suites, each with a bedroom, sitting room, kitchenette, and private bath. A complimentary continental breakfast is delivered to guests daily. Housekeeping has been known to leave behind dark chocolates in the shape of the hotel.

With more than 300 guest rooms and suites, the **Eisenhower Hotel** (2634 Emmitsburg Rd., Gettysburg, 717/334-8121, www.eisenhower.com, $119-149) is the largest hotel in the area. Amenities include an indoor pool and whirlpool tub, a fitness room, dry saunas, a casual eatery, and a business center. A fun park on the hotel grounds features two go-kart tracks, 36 holes of miniature golf, a 14-acre fishing lake, and batting cages. Downtown Gettysburg is five miles to the north, and the battlefield is even closer.

B&B options in downtown Gettysburg include the impeccable ★ **Brickhouse Inn Bed & Breakfast** (452 Baltimore St., Gettysburg, 717/338-9337, www.brickhouse-inn.com, $119-189). The older of its two buildings dates to the 1830s and was occupied by Confederate sharpshooters during the Battle of Gettysburg. Its south wall still bears the scars of Union bullets. The main house is an 1898 Victorian with original wood floors and chestnut trim. Between them they have 14 guest rooms and suites, each named for a state represented in the bloody battle. Breakfast always includes a hot entrée and the B&B's signature shoofly pie. Proprietors Tessa Bardo and Brian Duncan will give you the shirts off their backs but not the secret family recipe.

A few miles south of town is a countryside oasis, the **Lightner Farmhouse Bed & Breakfast** (2350 Baltimore Pike, Gettysburg, 717/337-9508, www.lightnerfarmhouse.com, $139-195). Built shortly before the Battle of Gettysburg, the Federal-style farmhouse was used as a hospital for three weeks after the bloodshed. Nothing gory about the place today. Innkeepers Dennis and Eileen Hoover aim to provide "outrageous service," whether preparing breakfast or arranging a crash course in paranormal investigation. The B&B has five en suite rooms, a suite that sleeps up to four, and a two-floor cottage with a private wraparound deck. Quilt designs inspired the decor. Nature trails wind through the 19-acre property.

Built circa 1797, the **Cashtown Inn** (1325 Old Rte. 30, Cashtown, 717/334-9722, www.cashtowninn.com, $145-200) was the first stagecoach stop west of Gettysburg. It owes its name to its original innkeeper, who accepted only cash. These days, credit cards are welcome at the inn, which is known as much for its cuisine as its cozy accommodations. Its four rooms and three suites are named for Confederate generals, some of whom made their headquarters there during the summer of 1863. More recent (and welcome) guests have included actor Sam Elliott, who bunked there while filming the 1993 movie *Gettysburg,* and paranormal investigator Jason Hawes, who featured the Cashtown in an episode of the Syfy series *Ghost Hunters.* Room rates include breakfast.

FOOD

Gettysburg is no dining mecca, but it offers a rare opportunity for culinary time travel. A number of restaurants specialize in period fare. Best of the bunch: the **Dobbin House Tavern** (89 Steinwehr Ave., Gettysburg, 717/334-2100, www.dobbinhouse.com), offering colonial and continental cuisine in Gettysburg's oldest building. The Dobbin House was built in 1776—the same year the American colonies declared their independence from Great Britain—as a home for an Irish-born minister and his large brood. It served as a station on the Underground Railroad in the mid-1800s and as a hospital

the Dobbin House Tavern

in the immediate aftermath of the Battle of Gettysburg. Great pains have been taken to restore the house-turned-restaurant to its 18th-century appearance. Many of the antique furnishings match descriptions in the inventory of the minister's estate. The china and flatware match fragments unearthed during an excavation of the cellar. For casual dining, head to the basement Springhouse Tavern (open daily from 11:30am, $8-25). With three natural springs and two fireplaces, it's a cozy and romantic spot (that can be clammy in winter and humid in summer). Specials include spit-roasted chicken, chargrilled strip steak, and barbecued ribs, all served with a hearth-baked roll. Fine dining is available in six candlelit rooms known as the Alexander Dobbin Dining Rooms (open daily from 5pm, $17-37). The "bedroom" features a table beneath a lace bed canopy. Servers in period attire help satisfy the craving for history that brings most visitors to Gettysburg. Reservations are accepted for the dining rooms but not the tavern, where you can expect a considerable wait on summer weekends.

The **Farnsworth House Inn** (401 Baltimore St., Gettysburg, 717/334-8838, www.farnsworthhouseinn.com, dining rooms 5pm-9pm daily, call for winter hours, $17-26)

is another popular destination for period dining complete with costumed servers. Game pie, the house specialty, is a stew of turkey, pheasant, and duck topped with a golden egg crust. Built in the early 1800s, the house sheltered Confederate sharpshooters during the Battle of Gettysburg. It's believed that one of them accidentally shot Jennie Wade, the only civilian killed during the three-day struggle. Oil paintings of the commanding officers at Gettysburg and photos by famed Civil War photographer Mathew Brady decorate the bullet-scarred house, which has been restored to its 1863 appearance. Its tavern (11:30am-10pm daily, call for winter hours, $8-18), popular with reenactors, offers hot and cold sandwiches, pork and sauerkraut, meatloaf, and more. Garden dining is available in the warmer months.

Eight miles west of Gettysburg on Route 116, the **Fairfield Inn** (15 W. Main St., Gettysburg, 717/642-5410, www.thefairfield-inn.com, lunch 11am-2pm Fri.-Sat., brunch 11am-2pm Sun., dinner 5pm-7:45pm Tues.-Sat., lunch $6-12, dinner $19-32) has hosted such VIPs as Thaddeus Stevens and President Dwight D. Eisenhower since opening in 1757. The day after the Battle of Gettysburg, as the weary Confederate army retreated west

the Fairfield Inn

through Fairfield, the inn hosted their generals. Today's guests can sup on hearty ham and bean soup and chicken and biscuits, just like General Robert E. Lee, or choose from dishes like Tuscan penne, fried haddock, and roasted half duck with balsamic fig reduction.

If you're not into period dining, you're not out of luck. The Gettysburg area has some recommendable restaurants that go a different route. **Gettysburg Eddie's** (217 Steinwehr Ave., Gettysburg, 717/334-1100, www.gettysburgeddies.com, 11am-10pm Mon.-Thurs., 11am-10:30pm Fri.-Sat., 11am-9pm Sun., bar open until 11pm Mon.-Thurs., midnight Fri.-Sat., and 10pm Sun., call for winter hours, $6-27), across the street from Soldiers' National Cemetery, is a casual, welcoming spot with a stamp of approval from the sustainability-promoting Green Restaurant Association. Named for Baseball Hall of Fame pitcher Eddie Plank, born in 1875 on a farm north of Gettysburg, the restaurant has an expansive menu that includes foot-long franks, steaks, sizzling fajitas, and pasta dishes. The housemade peanut butter pie is a home run. Big LCD TVs and a full-service bar make Eddie's a popular place to watch college and pro sports.

Herr Tavern & Publick House (900 Chambersburg Rd., Gettysburg, 717/334-4332, www.herrtavern.com, lunch 11am-3pm Wed.-Sat., dinner 5pm-9pm daily, lunch $7-15, dinner $24-34) is an excellent choice for fine dining. Servers are happy to talk guests through the creative menu, which changes frequently, and extensive wine list, a winner of *Wine Enthusiast Magazine*'s Unique Distinction Award. Built in 1815, the tavern was turned into a Confederate hospital during the 1863 clash of armies. It's said that amputated limbs were thrown out of a window into a waiting wagon. Given the gruesomeness of what went down, it's no wonder the staff have some ghost stories to share. Herr Tavern is just west of downtown Gettysburg on Route 30. A few miles farther west is another historic and reportedly haunted dining destination. The ★ **Cashtown Inn** (1325 Old Rte. 30, Cashtown, 717/334-9722, www.cashtowninn.com, lunch 11:30am-2pm and dinner from 5pm Tues.-Sat., lunch $6-11, dinner $20-33) was also overrun by Confederates during the battle. The general who assumed command of the defeated army's retreat made it his headquarters. Its current owners have resisted the temptation to lure history-hungry tourists with period fare, offering New American cuisine instead. They rely on local farmers and producers for everything from eggs and apples to wine and beer.

INFORMATION

Destination Gettysburg (717/334-6274, www.destinationgettysburg.com) is a good source of information about the area. Visit its website to request a free copy of its official visitors guide or peruse a digital version. Destination Gettysburg has information desks in the Museum and Visitor Center at Gettysburg National Military Park (1195 Baltimore Pike/Rte. 97, Gettysburg, open daily) and in the historic train station in downtown Gettysburg (35 Carlisle St., open daily Mar.-Nov., closed Tues.-Wed. Dec.-Feb.).

GETTING THERE

Gettysburg is in the center of Adams County, which hugs the Pennsylvania-Maryland line just west of York County. It's about 45 miles southwest of **Harrisburg International Airport** (MDT, 888/235-9442, www.flyhia.com) via I-76 west and Route 15 south and 60 miles northwest of the larger **Baltimore/Washington International Thurgood Marshall Airport** (BWI, 800/435-9294, www.bwiairport.com). Private aircraft can fly into **Gettysburg Regional Airport** (888/235-9442, www.flyhia.com) just west of town.

There's no passenger train or commercial bus service to Gettysburg. It's very much a driving destination.

Pocono Mountains

Like New York's Catskills and the Berkshires of Massachusetts and Connecticut, Pennsylvania's Poconos are synonymous with R&R. Less than two hours by car from New York City and Philadelphia, the highlands of northeast Pennsylvania have provided respite from the rigors of urban life since the early 1800s, when people arrived by wagon to "take in the air" and scenery. For decades, the big draw was the dramatic Delaware Water Gap, a pass through the mountains carved by the Delaware River. Touted as one of the country's 15 scenic marvels in a 19th-century guidebook, the Gap gave birth to a thriving resort industry. In a 1908 *New York Times* ad, one hotel promised "commanding views for 30 miles in every direction of the grandest scenery east of the Rockies." It wasn't unusual for mom and the kids to spend whole summers at the Gap. Dads arrived by the trainful on weekends.

The Gap's popularity as a resort area waned in the years following World War I, in part because cars changed the way people vacationed. But northeast Pennsylvania was far from finished as a vacation destination. In the mid-1920s, an energy company dammed a creek near the town of Hawley, 20 miles north of the Gap. The hydroelectric project created a recreational gem: Lake Wallenpaupack. With 52 miles of shoreline, it was the largest man-made lake in Pennsylvania. (It has since slipped to third.) During World War II, many young GIs whisked their girlfriends to the Pocono Mountains before shipping overseas or while on leave. When Johnny came marching home,

he was itching to get married. The post-war surge in marriages spawned a proliferation of honeymoon resorts in the Poconos. In 1971 a photo of lovebirds smooching in the heart-shaped hot tub of one such resort appeared in *Life* magazine, sealing the region's reputation as "Honeymoon Capital of the World."

By then, northeast Pennsylvania was also enjoying a reputation as a ski destination. Pennsylvania's first commercial ski area opened in the Poconos—part of the vast Appalachians—in the 1940s and helped to pioneer snowmaking technology in the 1950s. The industry snowballed in the years that followed. Today there are about 10 major ski

---

Previous: biking in the Lehigh Gorge; snowboarding on Blue Mountain. **Above:** doe and fawn in the Poconos.
Next: wakeboarding on Lake Wallenpaupack.

Look for ★ to find recommended sights, activities, dining, and lodging.

Highlights

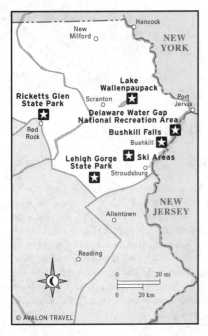

★ **Delaware Water Gap National Recreation Area:** Canoeists are cuckoo for this park, which features 40 miles of calm river. Invest in a mask and snorkel for a facedown drift down the Delaware (page 209).

★ **Bushkill Falls:** This privately owned piece of nature's artwork is hyped as "The Niagara of Pennsylvania." Hyperbole? You decide (page 212).

★ **Lake Wallenpaupack:** Boaters who feel the need for speed can satisfy it on this 13-mile-long lake, one of the few places in Pennsylvania where you can give parasailing a try (page 219).

★ **Ski Areas:** Though not terribly tall, the Pocono Mountains are an appealing destination for skiing, snowboarding, snow tubing, and even luging (page 227).

★ **Lehigh Gorge State Park:** Roiling white water and a 26-mile rail-trail make this park a must-visit for active sorts. Feeling lazy? Hop on the train that chugs through the river gorge (page 235).

★ **Ricketts Glen State Park:** Home to the 94-foot Ganoga Falls—and 21 other named water-falls—this exceptionally scenic park is hiker heaven (page 245).

areas in northeast Pennsylvania. Thanks to arsenals of snow guns, they're not completely at the mercy of Mother Nature.

Because of the concentration of ski slopes, some people think of this region as a winter destination first and foremost. That's a mistake. Indeed, winter is the off-season for many hotels and other tourism-reliant businesses in northeast Pennsylvania. There's plenty to do in the warmer months, thanks largely to the region's rivers and lakes. The water gap that captivated Victorian-era urbanites is now the centerpiece of a large national park beloved by canoeists for its 40 miles of calm river. To its west is Lehigh Gorge State Park, which offers white-water paddling. The Lackawaxen River, which flows through the quaint towns of Honesdale and Hawley on its way to the Delaware, is a magnet for fly fishers. And then there are the lakes—more than 150 in all. Still the largest in northeast Pennsylvania, Lake Wallenpaupack is alive with powerboats, Jet Skis, pontoon boats, and sailboats when it's not frozen. (The lake isn't totally useless when it is frozen. The annual Ice Tee Golf Tournament takes place atop it. Great ice fishing, too.)

The region's reputation as a honeymoon destination began to wane in the 1980s, as more and more newlyweds jetted to faraway places like Paris and Hawaii. Out of favor and out of date, several couples resorts closed in the 1990s. Three remain, so it's still possible to book a room that would make Austin Powers go "Yeah, baby!" Round beds: check. Champagne glass hot tubs: check. Heart-shaped pools: yeah, baby.

PG-rated fun can be had at any number of family resorts. The activities lists at some of these places include everything from arts and crafts to horse-drawn sleigh rides to Wii. Another family-friendly destination: Pocono Raceway. It's the only NASCAR track in Pennsylvania and one of only four in the northeastern United States, which helps explain why its marquee events attract tens of thousands of fans.

The largest cities in northeast Pennsylvania, Scranton and Wilkes-Barre, used to be nerve centers of the anthracite coal-mining industry. They're hard at work on reinventing themselves. Scranton is home to the only "Big Boy" steam locomotive in the East, which puts it on the bucket list of many a rail fan. Wilkes-Barre's Mohegan Sun at Pocono Downs was the first casino to open in Pennsylvania after lawmakers legalized electronic gaming in 2004. It's now one of two in

falls at Delaware Water Gap National Recreation Area

Pocono Mountains

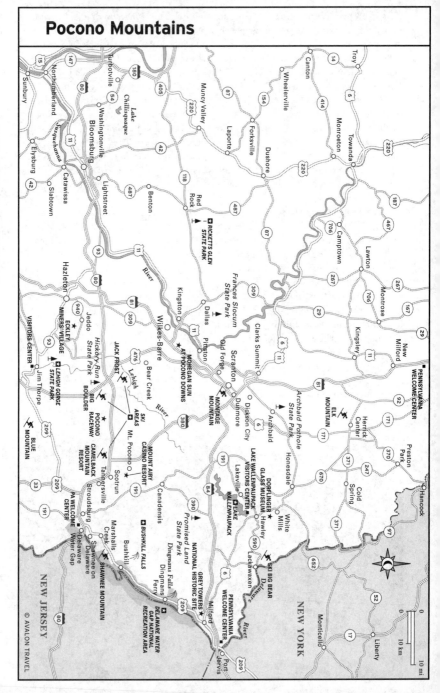

© AVALON TRAVEL

this corner of the state. The other, Mount Airy Casino Resort, was built on the site of a razed couples resort. By the looks of their parking lots, northeast Pennsylvania may soon be synonymous with R&R&R (rest and recreation and risk).

PLANNING YOUR TIME

How you organize your time depends on what brought you to this corner of Pennsylvania. If it's an outdoor activity such as skiing or snowboarding or white-water rafting, you probably live within a couple of hours' drive, and you're probably looking at a day trip. If it's reconnecting with your honey or family at an amenity-rich resort, you're probably looking to stay for as long as you can afford.

Railroad buffs should devote half a day to Scranton, home to Steamtown National Historic Site and the Electric City Trolley Museum. The truest of rail fans will also want to ride the Lehigh Gorge Scenic Railway out of Jim Thorpe. Northeast Pennsylvania was at one time a world leader in coal production, and some communities have transformed the detritus of that industry into tourist attractions. History buffs can descend into once-active mines in Scranton and Lansford, tour the company town of Eckley, and visit the jail where Irish miners fingered as murderous "Molly Maguires" were hanged.

Delaware Water Gap Area

The Delaware Water Gap, a wide chasm cut through Kittatinny Ridge by the Delaware River, attracted urbanites by the trainful in the latter half of the 1800s. Why? "From the mountain peaks on every hand open magnificent vistas, and from the river both below and above the chasm views are of marvelous extent," crowed *The New York Times* in June 1897, ticking off names of prominent New Yorkers recently arrived in the area. As one of the most popular summering spots in the eastern United States, the Gap got a lot of ink in *The Times*. Its popularity persisted into the early 20th century. Theodore Roosevelt paid a visit to the palatial Water Gap House, one of many hotels in the area, in 1910. A young Fred Astaire returned repeatedly with his family.

But the advent of automobiles expanded the realm of possibility for vacationers. In: the weekend road trip. Out: summering at large hotels near rail lines. It didn't help that the Water Gap House and the Kittatinny Hotel, grandest of the Gap's hotels, burned to the ground in 1915 and 1931, respectively. The Great Depression dealt a fatal blow to most of the remaining hotels and boarding houses.

Today the Gap is enjoying another heyday—not as a resort area but as a recreation area. Its core constituency is outdoorsy people rather than society people. The chasm in Kittatinny Ridge is the centerpiece of Delaware Water Gap National Recreation Area, one of the 10 most visited sites in the National Park System.

★ DELAWARE WATER GAP NATIONAL RECREATION AREA

Established in 1965 under President Lyndon Johnson, **Delaware Water Gap National Recreation Area** (www.nps.gov/dewa) encompasses nearly 40 miles of the Delaware River and 67,000 acres of river valley in Pennsylvania on one side and New Jersey on the other.

Getting your bearings is job one. The park is about five miles wide and 35 miles long, with the Delaware Water Gap and the Pennsylvania village named for it at its south end and the pretty town of Milford, Pennsylvania, at its north end. Route 209 is the major north-south artery on the Pennsylvania side. The exceptionally scenic Old Mine Road runs the length of the park on the New Jersey side.

There are only three bridges spanning the Delaware within the park: the I-80 bridge at the south end of the park; the privately owned Dingmans Bridge linking Pennsylvania Route 739 and New Jersey Route 560; and the Route 206 bridge at the north end of the park. Maps and brochures are available on the park website, but you can save a lot of printer ink by stopping at the ranger-staffed **Dingmans Falls Visitor Center** (Johnny Bee Rd. off Rte. 209, Dingmans Ferry, PA, 570/828-6125), open daily in the summer months and weekends through October, or **park headquarters** (River Rd. off Rte. 209, Bushkill, PA, 570/426-2452), open 8am-4:30pm weekdays year-round. Information is also available at the Pennsylvania **welcome centers** at I-80 exit 310 and I-84 exit 53.

Paddling

If you've come to paddle the river—be it for a few hours or a few days—you can get all the information and gear you need from one of the dozen or so boat liveries that operate within Delaware Water Gap National Recreation Area. They generally open in April and close at the end of October. More than 400 miles long, the Delaware is the longest undammed river east of the Mississippi. The Middle Delaware River, which flows through the park, is calm enough for even novice paddlers to navigate without a guide. On hot days it's not unusual for people to jump ship and float awhile in their life jackets. Liveries near I-80 and the south end of the park include **Adventure Sports** (Rte. 209, Marshalls Creek, PA, 570/223-0505, www.adventure-sport.com) and **Chamberlain Canoes** (River Rd., Minisink Hills, PA, 800/422-6631, www.chamberlaincanoes.com). Both rent canoes, kayaks, and rafts. Chamberlain also offers inner tubes. Most liveries near the north end of the park facilitate trips on the Upper Delaware, with its abundant white water, as well as the placid Middle Delaware. **Kittatinny Canoes** (800/356-2852, www.kittatinny.com) has multiple bases on the Upper and Middle Delaware and a huge fleet of canoes, kayaks, rafts, and tubes. It also boasts two riverfront campgrounds, a **paintball operation,** and a pair of 3,000-foot **zip lines.**

If you have your own kayak or canoe, you can take advantage of free bus service through the Pennsylvania side of the park. The Monroe County Transit Authority's **River Runner** (570/839-6282, www.gomcta.com) operates weekends from Memorial Day weekend

Delaware Water Gap

through Labor Day. Buses are equipped with a trailer that carries boats and bikes.

Swimming

The Middle Delaware is an exceptionally clean river, so don't hesitate to take a dip. There are two lifeguarded beaches on the Pennsylvania side of the park: **Smithfield Beach** (River Rd., 3.2 miles north of the village of Shawnee on Delaware) and **Milford Beach** (off Rte. 209 near Milford). The entrance fee is $7 per vehicle on weekdays and $10 on weekends and holidays. If you arrive by foot or bicycle, the fee is just $1. The beaches have restrooms and **picnic** tables. If you plan to cook, bring your own grill. Alcohol and pets aren't allowed at the beaches.

The Park Service cautions against swimming elsewhere, but plenty of folks do. If you do, be sure to wear a life jacket. Invest in a snorkel and mask to make the most of your time in the water. Trying to swim across the river is a major no-no. It's a leading cause of death on the Delaware.

Fishing

Prefer catching fish to swimming with them? Smallmouth bass, muskellunge, walleye, catfish, and panfish are found in the Delaware River. Schools of shad, which live in the ocean but migrate upstream to spawn, reach the park around May. A license from either Pennsylvania or New Jersey will do for fishing on the Delaware or from its banks. To fish in its trout-laden tributaries, you'll need the appropriate state license.

Trails

The Delaware River may be its main attraction, but DWGNRA (that's Delaware Water Gap National Recreation Area for the texting generation, LOL) has plenty to offer to landlubbers, starting with 100 miles of **hiking** trails. It contains more than 25 miles of the famed **Appalachian Trail,** which crosses the Delaware River at the Water Gap (via a walkway on the I-80 bridge). Climbing the Gap's gateposts—Mount Tammany in New Jersey and Mount Minsi in Pennsylvania—is popular with day hikers. But you don't have to climb more than 1,000 vertical feet for a visual feast. Several short trails on the Pennsylvania side of the park lead to striking waterfalls. Near the village of Dingmans Ferry, a Delaware River tributary named Dingmans Creek dives 130 feet. Dingmans Falls was privately owned from 1888 to 1975, when the federal government snapped it up, and tourists used to pay

hiking trail at Delaware Water Gap

for the privilege of seeing it. Less than half a mile long, the **Dingmans Falls Trail** is a flat, wheelchair-accessible boardwalk leading to the base of the falls. You can climb to the upper falls via some 240 steps. The trailhead is at Dingmans Falls Visitor Center (Johnny Bee Rd. off Rte. 209, Dingmans Ferry). The eponymous falls of Raymondskill Creek, which empties into the Delaware a few miles farther upstream, are only a little harder to get to. A short hike through hemlock forest puts you at the upper falls; steep, uneven stairs descend to the middle falls. Look for Raymondskill Road near milepost 18 of Rte. 209.

The 32-mile **McDade Trail,** which parallels the Delaware on the Pennsylvania side of the park, also deserves mention. Don't be put off by its length. With more than 15 trailheads, the McDade is a choose-your-own-adventure trail. Most of the trailheads are along Route 209. The unpaved trail is open to **biking** as well as hiking. In the winter, it makes for scenic **cross-country-skiing** and **snowshoeing.**

Guided hiking tours are available through **Edge of the Woods Outfitters** (110 Main St., Delaware Water Gap, PA, 570/421-6681, www.edgeofthewoodsoutfitters.com). Located two blocks from the Appalachian Trail, the outdoor gear store is a popular resupply point for backpackers. It also offers shuttle service to points on the AT, mountain bike rentals, river trips, and a pedal and paddle package.

OTHER SIGHTS
★ Bushkill Falls

A place that bills itself as "The Niagara of Pennsylvania" had better deliver, and **Bushkill Falls** (Bushkill Falls Rd., off Rte. 209, Bushkill, 570/588-6682, www.visitbushkillfalls.com, open daily Apr.-Oct. weather permitting, may be open in Nov., admission $12.50, seniors $11.50, children 4-10 $7) does not disappoint. No, you can't don a plastic raincoat and ride a steamship into a waterfall basin. But you can get close enough to a towering waterfall for a mist bath. You can marvel at the power and beauty of churning water, fill up on fudge and ice cream, and load up on souvenirs.

Unlike Niagara, Bushkill Falls is a privately owned attraction. When Charles E. Peters opened it to the public in 1904, charging 10 cents for admission, a single path and a swinging bridge brought visitors to the head of a 100-foot waterfall now known as the Main Falls. Today a series of mostly easy trails connects eight waterfalls. The original is still the

Bushkill Falls

best. A 15-minute walk yields a good view of it. For even better vantage points and access to a second waterfall, follow the popular yellow-marked trail, which takes about 45 minutes and crosses several wooden bridges strung across roaring waters. Avid hikers can take in all eight waterfalls via the two-mile **Bridal Veil Falls Trail.**

Still owned by the Peters family, Bushkill Falls has added a host of kid-friendly amenities over the years. Visitors can play a round of miniature golf ($5), ride a paddleboat ($4), race through a maze ($5 for first run, $2 for subsequent runs), fish in a pair of lakes (permit $3), mine for gemstones ($7-9), and view free exhibits on Bushkill Falls, Pennsylvania wildlife, and Native Americans. The park also has a playground and picnic areas with charcoal grills.

Shawnee Mountain

Shawnee Mountain (Hollow Rd., Shawnee on Delaware, 570/421-7231, www.shawneemt. com, all-day lift ticket $45-55, seniors and college students $36-45, children 18 and under $35-40, children under 46 inches and seniors 70 and older free, all-day equipment rental $35, snow tubing 2-hour session $20-25) offers 700 feet of vertical, 23 slopes and trails, two terrain parks, and a snow tubing park. If you've never tried skiing, it's a good place to get your feet (and butt) wet. It's an even better place to introduce kids to the sport. The ski area has an excellent reputation for its children's programs, which include ski lessons for children as young as three, snowboarding lessons for children as young as four, and mommy-and-me ski lessons. Multiday lift tickets can add up to big savings for families. Children too young or too timid to hit the slopes can chill at Shawnee's childcare facility ($5/hr, $40/day), open to children 18 months and older.

Grey Towers National Historic Site

The onetime home of Gifford Pinchot, first chief of the U.S. Forest Service, is open to the public as **Grey Towers National Historic Site** (151 Grey Towers Dr., Milford, 570/296-9630, www.fs.fed.us/gt, tour $8, seniors $7, children 12-17 $5). Under Pinchot's watch, the number of national forests climbed from 32 in 1898 to 149 in 1910. He later served two terms as Pennsylvania governor.

His son donated Grey Towers, the family's Milford estate, to the Forest Service in 1964. The mansion, which resembles a medieval

Grey Towers National Historic Site

French castle, can only be seen by guided tour. Built in the 1880s, the house originally had 43 rooms. Gifford Pinchot's wife found it rather dreary and had dividing walls knocked down to create larger rooms. She also oversaw the construction of a playhouse for their son, an archives for her husband's papers, and even a moat. The moat might have been her crowning achievement were it not for the Finger Bowl, a unique outdoor dining table consisting of a pool of water surrounded by a stone ledge wide enough for place settings. Food was floated on the water in wooden bowls.

The regular tour season runs from Memorial Day weekend through October. Tours of the first floor and several outdoor areas begin on the hour 11am-4pm daily. Special three-floor tours are offered at 10am and 4pm on Saturdays and Sundays. The mansion is reopened for about two weeks in December, when it's decorated for the holidays. Call or check the website for a schedule of holiday tours.

The Columns

A bloodstained American flag is the artifact extraordinaire at the museum of the Pike County Historical Society, aka **The Columns** (608 Broad St., Milford, 570/296-8126, www. pikehistorical.org, 1pm-4pm Wed.-Sun. July-Aug., 1pm-4pm Wed. and Sat.-Sun. Sept.-June, admission $5, students $3, children 12 and under free). The large 36-star flag was draped over a balustrade in Ford's Theatre on the night of April 14, 1865, when John Wilkes Booth shot Abraham Lincoln in the back of the head. Thomas Gourlay, a part-time stage manager at the Washington DC theater, placed the flag under the mortally wounded president's head. Gourlay kept the flag and gave it to his daughter, who moved to Pennsylvania's Pike County in 1888. Her son donated the flag to the historical society, along with stage costumes worn by his famous mother, who had a lead role in the play Lincoln was watching when he was assassinated, and other artifacts from the Civil War era. The Columns, a 1904 Neoclassical mansion, also houses Native American artifacts, early medical equipment, antique musical instruments, and an 1800s stagecoach. One of its exhibit rooms is dedicated to the brilliant logician and scientist Charles Sanders Pierce, who moved to Milford in the late 1800s. Pierce's ideas influenced the likes of Albert Einstein long after his 1914 death.

The Columns

ENTERTAINMENT AND EVENTS
Concert Venues

Jazz aficionados have been finding their way to the **Deer Head Inn** (5 Main St., Delaware Water Gap, 570/424-2000, www.deerheadinn. com) for more than 50 years. Built as a hotel in the mid-1800s, the four-story Victorian in the heart of Delaware Water Gap still offers lodging ($90-180 per night), and its proximity to the Appalachian Trail and Delaware Water Gap National Recreation Area makes it a good choice for outdoorsy types. But jazz is its raison d'être. Maestros such as saxophonists Stan Getz and Phil Woods, pianist Keith Jarrett, and guitarist Pat Metheny have played the Deer Head, which offers dinner and live music Thursday through Sunday.

Performing Arts

In 1985 arson claimed a playhouse that had stood since 1904. Thanks in part to donations from its many fans, the **Shawnee Playhouse** (552 River Rd., Shawnee on Delaware, 570/421-5093, www.theshawneeplayhouse. com) rose again. Located on the grounds of The Shawnee Inn and Golf Resort, the playhouse auditions actors in New York City for its main stage season, which runs from May through December and includes both musicals and nonmusicals. The theater's resident troupe performs in the off-season.

Festivals and Events

The **Delaware River Sojourn** (646/205-2724, www.delawareriversojourn.org, June, registration fees charged) is a weeklong paddling trip designed to heighten awareness of the ecological and recreational significance of the river, which flows through New York, New Jersey, Pennsylvania, and Delaware. It's open to both novice and experienced paddlers, who can sign up for the entire event or a portion of it. Participants catch their winks at campgrounds near the scenic river. Other notable summer happenings include the **Poconos' Wurst Festival** (Shawnee Mountain Ski Area, Shawnee on Delaware, 570/421-7231, www.shawneemt.com, July, admission charged), an homage to both Polish and German cultures. Joining wursts on the menu are kielbasa, pierogies, stuffed cabbage, sauerkraut, and more. The festival also features craft brews, ethnic crafts, and live entertainment. Count on plenty of polka music.

Shawnee Mountain Ski Area (Shawnee on Delaware, 570/421-7231, www.shawneemt. com) hosts three fun-filled fall events, starting with the **Pocono Garlic Festival** (Labor Day weekend, admission charged). Expect such unexpected foods as roasted garlic ice cream and garlic funnel cake. A few weeks later, cowboys descend on Shawnee for two days of bronc and bull riding, calf roping, steer wrestling, and other events sanctioned by the Professional Rodeo Cowboys Association. The **PRCA Rodeo & Chili Cook-Off** (late Sept., admission charged) also features barrel-racing cowgirls, live country music, line dancing, and all sorts of barbecue goodness. Lumberjacks show their stuff during the **Autumn Timber Festival** (early Oct., admission charged), held during the peak of fall foliage. Festivalgoers can board a chairlift for a bird's-eye view of hills ablaze with color. Tickets to Shawnee events are cheaper when purchased in advance.

ACCOMMODATIONS
Fernwood Resort

Fernwood Resort (Rte. 209, Bushkill, 888/337-6966, www.fernwoodresortpoconos. com, $90-250) is notable for its location and amenities. It's adjacent to Delaware Water Gap National Recreation Area and just minutes from Bushkill Falls and Shawnee Mountain. Unlike many family resorts, Fernwood isn't all-inclusive—heck, it even charges for wireless Internet access—so it's an affordable base of operations for vacationers more interested in drifting down the Delaware, hiking, waterfall hunting, or hitting the slopes than reliving sleepaway camp. Guests *can* have an action-packed day without leaving the 400-acre resort. It has an 18-hole golf course, a mini golf course, horse stables, paintball fields, indoor and outdoor pools, a bumper boat pond, a fitness center, a large arcade, and a snow tubing park. In 2013 it unveiled Blue Lightning Tubing, billed as the only all-season tubing facility in the region. It also added a ropes course and a pair of zip lines. Most of its facilities are open to the public. Fernwood's guest "villas" range from studios with a kitchenette to two-bedroom units with a full kitchen, dining room, living room, and deck.

Camping

There are plenty of camping options in and around **Delaware Water Gap National Recreation Area** (570/426-2452, www.nps. gov/dewa), including free campsites right on the river. (Those sites, however, are reserved for boaters and paddlers on overnight trips and cannot be reserved.) A list of campgrounds is available on the park's website. They include Dingmans Campground and River Beach Campsites, which boast riverfront sites and canoe and kayak rentals. **Dingmans Campground** (1006 Rte. 209, Dingmans Ferry, PA, 570/828-1551, www.dingmanscampground.com, open seasonally, $35-45) has about 20 riverfront tent sites and more than 100 tent and RV sites in wooded areas. The rustic campground is on federal property, and alcohol is prohibited. **River Beach** (378 Rte. 6/209, Milford, PA, 800/356-2852,

www.kittatinny.com, $11-18 per site, $15 per person, $7.95 for children 6-11) is one of two campgrounds owned by Kittatinny Canoes, one of the oldest and most reputable outfitters in the region. Located just north of Delaware Water Gap National Recreation Area, the campground has about 160 tent and RV sites, two modern bathhouses, laundry facilities, an arcade, and a store where you can buy everything from matches to kayaks.

Hotels and B&Bs

Start your day with yoga at **Santosha on the Ridge** (121 Santosha Ln., Shawnee on Delaware, 570/476-0203, www.santoshaontheridge.com, $145-200), a secluded B&B where worldly comforts aren't sacrificed in the name of inner peace. "Santosha" is Sanskrit for "contentment," and it's not so hard to find when cradled in a hammock on the back deck, where innkeeper Leslie Underhill offers yoga lessons when weather permits. A stone labyrinth helps guests on their inward journey. Another easy walk brings them to the lovely Delaware Water Gap.

Milford's charming downtown is home to one of only two Relais & Châteaux properties in Pennsylvania: the eminently chic ★ **Hotel Fauchère** (401 Broad St., Milford, 570/409-1212, www.hotelfauchere.com, $210-475).

breakfast at Hotel Fauchère

When the 19th-century Italianate hotel reopened in 2006 after a three-decade hibernation and five-year restoration, the *New York Post* called it "the smartest hotel to open near the city in a long time." Today's guests walk through the same marble entryway and run their hands along the same mahogany banisters as Henry Ford, Charlie Chaplin, Mae West, Babe Ruth, Franklin D. Roosevelt, and John F. Kennedy. Among the newer features: iPod docking stations, flat-panel TVs, and marble-drenched bathrooms with heated towel racks and floors. The pet-friendly boutique hotel also boasts a fine collection of mid-19th-century landscapes by Hudson River School painters. Its reputation for sumptuous lodging is matched by its culinary cachet. Tables at The Delmonico Room, the Hotel Fauchère's fine dining restaurant, and Bar Louis, its ultramodern bistro, are among the most coveted in northeast Pennsylvania. Room rates include a continental breakfast.

FOOD
Shawnee on Delaware

Located on the grounds of The Shawnee Inn and Golf Resort, ★ **The Gem and Keystone** (River Rd., 570/424-0990, www.gemandkeystone.com, 11:30am-10pm Sun.-Thurs., 11:30am-11pm Fri.-Sat., $9-26) is a tree hugger of an eatery with a snappy slogan: "Beer from here. Food from near." It's not a coincidence that the slogan puts suds before eats. Dishes are designed to pair with all-natural ShawneeCraft beers, brewed a short walk away. (Tours of the brewery are available. Call 570/213-5151 or visit www.gemandkeystone.com for details.) The Gem features hearty fare like slow-cooked ribs and pot roast, plenty of vegetarian options, and even a gluten-free menu. Rest assured that the meats are all-natural, the seafood sustainable, and the doggie bags biodegradable.

Fresh food, full-bodied flavors, and fair prices can add up to a line out the door of **Saen Thai Cuisine** (Shawnee Square, 570/476-4911, www.saenthai.com, lunch 11:30am-2pm Tues.-Fri. and noon-2pm Sat.-Sun., dinner 5:30pm-9pm Tues.-Sun., $8-21), which doesn't take reservations. It's not a bad idea to arrive about 20 minutes before the place opens for dinner on a weekend. Everything is superb, from the spring rolls to the curries to the exquisitely presented specials.

Milford

Once called "the prettiest county seat in America" by *The Atlantic* magazine, Milford can also brag of several outstanding restaurants. The chic and history-rich **Hotel Fauchère** (401 Broad St., 570/409-1212, www.hotelfauchere.com) is home to two. Its reputation as a culinary destination dates to the 1860s, when a Swiss-born chef named Louis Fauchère took over the hotel. An 1888 portrait of Fauchère presides over its fine dining restaurant, **The Delmonico Room** (breakfast 8am-11am Mon.-Sat., brunch 9am-2:30pm Sun., dinner from 6pm Thurs.-Sat. and 5pm Sun., breakfast/brunch $7-19, dinner $85 and up), which only offers a tasting menu at dinnertime. The service is superlative and the setting romantic. Though it's decorated with vintage menus from famed European restaurants, The Delmonico Room is actually named for the New York City restaurant that created the Delmonico steak. Fauchère served as master chef there before moving to Milford. **Bar Louis** (11:30am-10pm Sun.-Thurs., 11:30am-11pm Fri.-Sat., closes an hour earlier Nov.-Mar., $10-35) is named for Fauchère himself. The sleek, sexy bistro on the hotel's ground level is famous for its specialty cocktails and sushi "pizza." Also notable: the house-cured meats and olives and signature burger with truffle fries. An enormous framed photo of Andy Warhol planting a smooch on John Lennon's cheek sits behind the minimalist bar. It's all so very SoHo that you're liable to feel disoriented upon emerging onto Milford's sleepy main drag.

Something you'll never see in a New York City eatery: a working 19th-century waterwheel. Milford's ★ **Waterwheel Café, Bakery and Bar** (150 Water St., 570/296-2383, www.waterwheelcafe.com, breakfast/

lunch 8am-3:30pm daily, dinner 5:15pm-9:30pm Thurs.-Sat., breakfast/lunch $5-12, dinner $19-28, bar menu $6-13) offers diners a view of water rushing over a three-story waterwheel built in the early 1800s to power grain-grinding equipment. You can power up for your day with a house-baked scone, wholegrain pancakes, or steak and eggs. The Waterwheel spans the globe for its lunchtime options, which include Vietnamese rice noodle salad and a long list of specialty sandwiches. Dinner in the café is a fine dining affair featuring Mediterranean and modern Vietnamese cuisine.

If a picnic is in your plans, fill your basket at **Fretta's Italian Food Specialties** (223 Broad St., 570/296-7863, www.frettas.com, 8:30am-6:30pm Tues.-Sat., 9am-3pm Sun.), which bills itself as the oldest pork store in America. Established in 1906 in New York City's Little Italy neighborhood, the *salumeria* relocated to picturesque Milford in 1998. It carries all sorts of imported goodies, including cheeses, pasta, olive oil, sorbets, and tiramisu. Fourth-generation proprietor Joseph Fretta also prides himself on offering a host of house-made foods: fresh mozzarella, sopressata, capicola, pancetta, pasta sauces, and more. The takeout menu features soups, sandwiches, wraps, and pasta dishes. Don't leave without a box of Fretta's own cannoli.

INFORMATION

Maps, trail guides, and brochures on every sort of attraction can be found at area visitors centers. There are Pennsylvania **welcome centers** at I-80 exit 310, near the south end of Delaware Water Gap National Recreation Area, and at I-84 exit 53, near the north end. Personalized travel counseling is available 7am-7pm daily. The National Park Service operates the **Dingmans Falls Visitor Center** (Johnny Bee Rd. off Rte. 209, 570/828-6125, open daily in summer and weekends through Oct.) in Dingmans Ferry, Pennsylvania, a popular starting point for river trips.

The **Pocono Mountains Visitors Bureau** (1004 W. Main St., Stroudsburg, 570/421-5791, www.poconomountains.com, 8:30am-5pm Mon.-Fri.) is a good source of information about things to see and do in the region. You can request free brochures through its website.

GETTING THERE AND AROUND

Delaware Water Gap National Recreation Area is about five miles wide and 35 miles long, with the Gap at its south end and the pretty town of Milford, Pennsylvania, at its north end. It's about 70 miles northwest of New York City via I-80 and 100 miles north of Philadelphia via I-476 north, Route 22 east, and Route 33 north. Passenger airlines won't get you terribly close to the park. The nearest airports—**Lehigh Valley International Airport** (ABE, 800/359-5842, www.lvia.org), **Wilkes-Barre/Scranton International Airport** (AVP, 570/602-2000, www.flyavp.com), and **Newark Liberty International Airport** (EWR, 973/961-6000, www.panynj.gov)—are 60-70 miles away.

While the park is primarily a driving destination, you can get by without a car. **Martz Trailways** (570/421-3040, www.martztrailways.com) offers intercity bus service to Delaware Water Gap, the Pennsylvania town alongside the geologic gap. From the bus station, you can walk to the Appalachian Trail or **Edge of the Woods Outfitters** (110 Main St., Delaware Water Gap, PA, 570/421-6681, www.edgeofthewoodsoutfitters.com), which offers guided hiking tours, river trips, and mountain bike rentals. You can also catch the **River Runner** (570/839-6282, www.gomcta.com), a free bus that runs through the Pennsylvania side of Delaware Water Gap National Recreation Area. It operates weekends from Memorial Day weekend through Labor Day.

Car-less New Yorkers have another option: arrive in Port Jervis, New York, by bus (201/529-3666, www.shortlinebus.com) or rail (973/275-5555, www.njtransit.com) and get a lift from the station from **Kittatinny Canoes** (800/356-2852, www.kittatinny.com), which offers river trips, camping, and more.

Lake Region

Pennsylvania's northeast corner is home to more than 100 lakes. At 5,700 acres, Lake Wallenpaupack is the largest of them all. Created in the 1920s by an energy company, the lake provides more than hydroelectric power. It's the place to go for powerboating in the Poconos. It's also a popular destination for sailing, fishing, and camping. The countless residential and vacation homes that ring the lake are testament to its recreational appeal. In 2005 *The New York Times* observed that an increasing number of New Yorkers were weekending in the itty-bitty town of Hawley, just north of Lake Wallenpaupack, drawn by its "old-fashioned charm" and the body of water in its backyard.

The largest town in the lake region is Honesdale, about 15 minutes from Hawley. With its Victorian architecture, tall church steeples, and quaint shops, the Wayne County seat is worth a stroll. Honesdale is charming enough to have inspired the lyrics of *Winter Wonderland,* written in 1934 by Honesdale native Dick Smith and recorded by everyone from Perry Como to Ozzy Osbourne.

Flowing through the region is the Lackawaxen River, a 25-mile tributary of the Delaware that's beloved by fly fishers. Bald eagles seem to love it too, which brings out the birders.

The **Lake Wallenpaupack Visitors Center** (2512 Rte. 6, Hawley, 570/226-2141, 10am-6pm daily Memorial Day-Labor Day, 9am-5pm daily rest of year) is a good first stop for anyone new to the region. You'll find maps, brochures, exhibits, and people who know the area like the back of their hands.

★ LAKE WALLENPAUPACK
Boating

Lake Wallenpaupack, its islands, and most of its 52-mile shoreline are property of PPL Corp., which gave birth to the lake when it dammed Wallenpaupack Creek. Boat ramps and slips can be found at four PPL-owned recreation areas: **Wilsonville** (113 Ammon Dr., Hawley, 570/226-4382, www.wilsonvillecampground.com), located near the Lake Wallenpaupack Visitors Center and the only public beach on the lake; **Caffrey** (431 Lakeshore Dr., Lakeville, 570/226-4608); **Ironwood Point** (155 Burns Hill Rd., Greentown, 570/857-0880, www.ironwoodpoint.com); and **Ledgedale** (153 Ledgedale Rd., Greentown, 570/689-2181, www.ledgedalerecarea.com). Boat slip rates and reservation policies vary from one to the other. All charge a fee for boat launching. For no-fee boat launching, head to the **Pennsylvania Fish and Boat Commission access area** at Mangan Cove, located off Route 590 about a mile west of its junction with Route 6. You can find a map of the lake at www.pplpreserves.com.

If you don't have your own boat, you're not out of luck. Located at Lighthouse Harbor Marina, **Pocono Action Sports** (969 Rte. 507, Greentown, 570/857-0779, www.poconoactionsports.com) offers rental ski boats, fishing boats, pontoon boats, and sailboats. Full-day rates range from $210 for a 19-foot sailboat to $495 for a high-end pontoon boat. Tow-riffic accessories—water skis, wakeboards, kneeboards, and inner tubes—are $35 per day. Pocono Action Sports also offers Jet Skis for $70 per half hour or $120 per hour and **parasailing rides** for $70 per person. In addition to powerboats, Jet Skis, and watersports equipment, **Rubber Duckie Boat Rentals** (Rte. 507 and Rte. 390, Tafton, 570/226-3930, www.rubberduckieboatrentals.com) carries canoes and Sunfish sailboats for vacationers who don't need a motor to have a good time. Sunfish are simple enough for sailing virgins.

Perfect for anyone who wants to get on the water but leave the navigating to pros, the **Wallenpaupack Scenic Boat Tour** (2487

Rte. 6, Hawley, 570/226-3293, www.wallen-paupackboattour.com, May-mid-Oct., $14, seniors $13, children 12 and under $11) is an hour-long cruise aboard a patio boat. (Not to be confused with a party boat. There's no food, booze, or DJ on this ride.) In summer, tours depart on the hour 11am-6pm daily. Sunset cruises are offered on occasion. The tour boats also ply the lake on weekends in late spring and early fall, pushing off every hour from noon to 4pm, weather permitting. Wallenpaupack Scenic Boat Tour also offers rental pontoon boats, kayaks, and stand-up paddleboards.

Fishing

Lake Wallenpaupack is considered one of the best fishing spots in the state. The Pennsylvania Fish & Boat Commission has gone so far as to install artificial habitat structures in the lake to make it more inviting to fish—and anglers. It's home to smallmouth bass, largemouth bass, walleye, muskellunge, pickerel, yellow perch, and trout, to name a few. Call **Bill's Guide Service** (570/698-6035, www.billsguideservice.com) or **Ray's Fishing Guide Service** (570/654-5436 or 570/510-9219, www.raysguideservice.webs.com) for a helping hand.

Wallenpaupack Creek and the Lackawaxen River, which the lake drains into, offer mountain stream fishing. Both are stocked by the Fish & Boat Commission. Anglers on the Lackawaxen should watch for sudden rises in water level, which occur when water is released from PPL Corp.'s hydroelectric plant. Call 800/807-2474 or visit www.lakelevelppl.com for information on lake elevation and discharge to the river.

Fishing licenses and live bait can be purchased at **Ironwood Point** (155 Burns Hill Rd., Greentown, 570/857-0880, www.ironwoodpoint.com), one of four PPL-owned recreation areas on the lake. In 2013 the energy company installed a handicap-accessible fishing pier at Ironwood Point.

Swimming

Lake Wallenpaupack has 52 miles of shoreline but only one **public beach** (570/226-9290, 11am-7pm daily Memorial Day weekend-Labor Day weekend). It's located near the Lake Wallenpaupack Visitors Center on Route 6, about half a mile west of the Route 6 and Route 507 junction. Operated by Palmyra Township, the lifeguarded beach has picnic tables, charcoal grills, bathrooms, and a snack bar. Admission is $5 for adults, $2 for

Jet Skiing on Lake Wallenpaupack

children under 12. Seniors and infants enjoy free admission.

Swimming is not permitted at PPL Corp.'s recreation areas.

SIGHTS
Dorflinger Glass Museum

The village of White Mills lies halfway between Hawley and Honesdale on Route 6. Blink and you could miss it. There's little to suggest that White Mills was once a bustling industrial center, but that's exactly what it became after Christian Dorflinger came to town in the 1860s. Only in his 30s, the French-born glassmaker had already opened three factories in Brooklyn, New York. Sleepy little White Mills offered an escape from the rigors of city life, but Dorflinger wasn't ready to retire. He built a glass factory in the hamlet, which became home to so many workmen and craftsmen that it could no longer be called a hamlet. The White Mills plant produced some of the most exquisite cut lead crystal in the country.

In 1980 Dorflinger's White Mills estate opened to the public as the **Dorflinger-Suydam Wildlife Sanctuary** (Elizabeth St., White Mills, 570/253-1185, www.dorflinger. org, open dawn-dusk daily, free admission). Several miles of trails traverse the 600-acre sanctuary, which is home to the **Dorflinger Glass Museum** (10am-4pm Wed.-Sat. and 1pm-4pm Sun. May-Oct., Sat.-Sun. only in Nov., admission $5, seniors $4, children 6-18 $2). Opened in 1989, the museum boasts the largest collection of Dorflinger glass in the country—more than 900 pieces strong. The gift shop demands as much time as the galleries. It's filled with glass treasures, including Christmas ornaments, vases, paperweights, jewelry, and kaleidoscopes.

The wildlife sanctuary hosts the **Wildflower Music Festival,** a summer concert series that attracts touring performers. Songstress Judy Collins made an appearance in 2009. Dates, times, and ticket prices are available on the sanctuary's website. Bring lawn chairs or a blanket for the outdoor concerts.

SPORTS AND RECREATION
Winter Sports

Located about 10 miles east of Hawley, near the Pennsylvania-New York border, **Ski Big Bear** (192 Karl Hope Blvd., Lackawaxen, 570/685-1400, www.ski-bigbear.com, all-day lift ticket $45-55, seniors and children 6-12 $36-43, all-day equipment rental $30-35, snow tubing 2-hour session $25) is the northernmost ski area in the Poconos. It's relatively small, with 650 feet of vertical, 18 trails, and six lifts, which makes it a good place to learn to ski or snowboard. Group lessons for beginners age seven and up are $32. Private lessons are available for children as young as four. Ski Big Bear also offers snow tubing on weekends and select weekdays during holiday periods.

ENTERTAINMENT AND EVENTS
Festivals and Events

An end-of-summer tradition started in 2010, **Wally Lake Fest** (multiple locations, 570/226-2141, www.wallylakefest.com, late Aug., free and paid events) is three days of events and activities celebrating the lake region's recreational and cultural amenities. Past fests have featured everything from fly-casting and paddle-boarding demos to group bicycle and motorcycle rides to live music on a floating stage. The annual boat parade—with prizes for the best "dressed" boats—is open to the public. Wally Lake Fest is the only time PPL Corp. offers public tours of its dam and power plant at Lake Wallenpaupack.

If you think the lake region has nothing to offer in the frigid months, think again. Its most unique events take place in the dead of winter. In 2007 professional ice carver Mark Crouthamel used a post-holidays lull in business to create life-size sculptures of a log cabin and some critters and invited the public to come have a look. Thousands turned out for **Crystal Cabin Fever** (Sculpted Ice Works, Rte. 590, Lakeville, 570/226-6246, www.crystalcabinfever.com, Feb., admission charged), now an annual event. Playing on a different theme each year, Crouthamel and team carve an interactive display out of more than 100 tons of ice. A team of sled dogs, a giant polar bear, and caribou greeted visitors during 2009's Alaska-themed event. The bundled-up crowds got a taste of the Caribbean, coral reef and all, the following year. There's always a dual-run ice slide, so wear your waterproof pants. Ice carving competitions are among the highlights of the event, which lasts two and a half weeks.

ACCOMMODATIONS

Accommodations in the lake region run the gamut from walk-in campsites and basic motels to romantic inns and a destination spa resort. Being that boating is a main attraction, prices are generally highest in the hottest months.

Woodloch Resort

Parents, Better Homes and Gardens, Family Circle, and other national magazines have sung the praises of ★ **Woodloch Resort** (731 Welcome Lake Rd., Hawley, 570/685-8000, www.woodloch.com), an all-inclusive resort that's all about family. The lake region landmark has been owned by the same family—the Kiesendahls—since 1958. Many employees are practically family, having been with the Kiesendahls for decades. And you can guess how guests are treated: like family. Many return year after year in multigenerational posses.

On the Kiesendahls' watch, the resort on Lake Teedyuskung has grown from 12 acres with accommodations for about 40 guests to 1,000-plus acres with accommodations for more than 900. Lodging options range from endearingly outdated rooms with accordion dividers separating living and sleeping areas

Couples Only

The region once known as the "Honeymoon Capital of the World" has lost most of its couples resorts, but the species doesn't appear to be headed toward extinction. Each year, some 65,000 couples vacation at the three remaining couples resorts in the Pocono Mountains. They uncork more than 20,000 bottles of champagne, empty twice as many bottles of bubble bath, splish-splash in heart-shaped hot tubs, canoodle in private pools, and slumber on round beds under mirrored ceilings, proving that kitschy and sexy can go hand in hand.

Jointly owned by **Cove Haven Entertainment Resorts** (800/432-9932, www.covepoconoresorts.com, $340-585), the all-inclusive resorts have much in common. Each offers several suite types, all-you-can-eat breakfast and dinner (and breakfast in bed at no additional charge), a variety of indoor and outdoor activities, and live entertainment nightly. Located on the shores of Lake Wallenpaupack, **Cove Haven Resort** (194 Lakeview Dr., Lakeville, 570/226-4506) tends to draw the biggest entertainers. Comedians Howie Mandel and Sinbad, Motown legends The Temptations, and country crooner Billy Ray Cyrus have taken its stage. **Paradise Stream Resort** (6213 Carlton Rd., Mount Pocono, 570/839-8881) has the fewest amenities, but a $20 million renovation in recent years turned it into the hippest of the three. The poshest digs can be found at **Pocono Palace Resort** (206 Marquis Rd., East Stroudsburg, 570/588-6692), located just minutes from Delaware Water Gap National Recreation Area. Its multilevel Roman Tower Suites feature a king-size round bed, heart-shaped pool, dry sauna, log-burning fireplace, and seven-foot-tall champagne glass whirlpool. (All three resorts have suites with the enduringly popular champagne glass whirlpool, created in 1984 by Cove Haven founder Morris B. Wilkins.)

Guests get unlimited access to amenities at all three resorts. So couples staying at Cove Haven or Paradise Stream, which don't have a golf course, can swing to their heart's content on Pocono Palace's nine-hole course. Paradise Stream and Pocono Palace guests can journey to Cove Haven for snow tubing or ice skating. All three offer fishing, tennis, indoor and outdoor pools, mini golf, archery, and snowmobiling, among other activities.

to modern trilevel houses with five and a half baths, cathedral ceilings, and fireplaces. Rates depend on accommodation type, time of year, and children's ages (the younger, the cheaper). They include three meals a day, almost all activities, and entertainment. Not included: golfing at **Woodloch Springs** (1 Woodloch Dr., Hawley, 570/685-8102, www.woodloch.com/golf), an 18-hole par-72 course. Vacationers who want to enjoy all the amenities of the family resort but prefer cooking their meals to communal dining can rent one of the golfing community's privately owned homes.

Lake Teedyuskung is the center of resort activity in summer. Guests can lounge on a sandy beach; fish off the docks for bass, bluegill, and catfish; swim in the shimmering lake or the shamrock-shaped pool along its shore; or take to the water in a canoe, kayak, paddleboat, rowboat, or Sunfish sailboat. Waterskiing is an option for those 13 and older. Winter activities include ice fishing, ice skating, snowshoeing, and snow tubing.

Woodloch is as famous for its lavish Broadway-style revue as its array of activities. The pyrotechnics-enhanced performance is held in the resort's capacious nightclub. Entertainment of one sort or another is offered every night of the week. Ray Romano and Darrell Hammond kept Woodloch guests in stitches before starring in *Everybody Loves Raymond* and *Saturday Night Live,* respectively.

Woodloch Resort is not to be confused with The Lodge at Woodloch, an adults-only spa resort more likely to be praised by *Forbes* than *Family Circle.*

Camping

PPL Corp., the Allentown-based energy company that created Lake Wallenpaupack when it dammed Wallenpaupack Creek, maintains four public campgrounds on the lake. They're open from late April to late October. All have RV sites, boat ramps and slips, restrooms and showers, laundry facilities, and a general store. Nightly rates range from $24 to $36. With 29

sites, **Caffrey** (431 Lakeshore Dr., Lakeville, 570/226-4608) is the smallest of the four. Good prevailing westerlies make it popular with sailboaters. **Ironwood Point** (155 Burns Hill Rd., Greentown, 570/857-0880, www.ironwoodpoint.com) is situated on a wooded hill overlooking the lake. It has about 60 sites, including 13 lakefront sites for walk-in camping. Located at the southern tip of the 13-mile lake, **Ledgedale** (153 Ledgedale Rd., Greentown, 570/689-2181, www.ledgedalerecarea.com) offers 70 sites, kayak rentals, a playground, and a game room. It's adjacent to PPL's **Ledgedale Natural Area** (Kuhn Hill Rd., Greentown, open dawn to dusk), 80 forested acres with two miles of hiking trails. **Wilsonville** (113 Ammon Dr., Hawley, 570/226-4382, www.wilsonvillecampground. com) is the largest of PPL's campgrounds with 160 sites. It's just off Route 6, adjacent to the only public beach on Lake Wallenpaupack and not far from the dam.

Lake Wallenpaupack is just one of many lakes in these parts. Located off Route 6 about seven miles west of Honesdale, the 300-site **Keen Lake Camping & Cottage Resort** (155 Keen Lake Rd., Waymart, 570/488-6161, www.keenlake.com, campsite $34-56) features a privately owned lake teeming with bass, bluegill, perch, and pickerel, to name a few. Fishing licenses—and everything from bacon to board games—are available in the camp store. Campers can rent a rowboat, paddleboat, canoe, or kayak for a spin around the 90-acre lake or take a dip in the designated swim area. The well-groomed, pet-friendly campground also has a pool, several playgrounds, a game room with pool tables, and a movie lounge. A dozen unique cottages and three RVs are available for rent for $170-305 per day or $875-1,645 per week. Some are available year-round. If privacy is paramount, reserve Hermit Island, a rustic three-bedroom cottage on an island accessible only by boat.

Hotels and B&Bs
East Shore Lodging (2487 Rte. 6, Hawley, 570/226-3293, www.eastshorelodging.com,

$70-180) offers reasonably priced and majorly comfy accommodations right across Route 6 from Lake Wallenpaupack's only public beach. The motel is run by the same family behind Wallenpaupack Scenic Boat Tour—also across the street—which offers hour-long boat cruises, boat slips, and boat rentals. Most of its rooms are roomy enough for four. If you really want to feel at home, reserve the second-floor king suite, which features a spacious living room and private deck. All rooms have a microwave, refrigerator, flat-screen TV, and wireless Internet. Rates include a continental breakfast.

Since 1980 ★ **The Settlers Inn** (4 Main Ave., Hawley, 800/833-8527, www.thesettlersinn.com, $170-420) has been in the hands of Jeanne and Grant Genzlinger, whose mastery of the art of hospitality has earned the inn membership in Select Registry and its farm-to-table restaurant a AAA four-diamond rating. A handsome example of the Arts and Crafts style both inside and out, the inn is ideal for travelers who find hotels too impersonal and many B&Bs too frilly. It's also ideal for anglers: The trout-filled Lackawaxen River runs through the property. The inn has 20 guest rooms and a two-bedroom suite perfect for a family. Many feature fireplaces and

hot tubs. Eco-minded travelers will appreciate room 204 with its bamboo flooring, organic cotton bed covers, and river view. Room rates include a way-above-average breakfast. The inn's nearby sister property, **Ledges Hotel** (119 Falls Ave., Hawley, www.ledgeshotel.com, $110-330), is equally fabulous in its own unique way. It opened in 2011 in a former glass factory perched over Wallenpaupack Creek. The building isn't the only stunning example of adaptive reuse. Guest rooms feature furnishings custom-built with wood from a nearby 19th-century silk mill. In addition to single rooms, the boutique hotel offers two-story suites with 12-foot ceilings and spiral staircases. Stunning views come standard.

"Luxury" is a word used liberally in descriptions of **The Lodge at Woodloch** (109 River Birch Ln., Hawley, 570/685-8500, www.thelodgeatwoodloch.com, from $300/person). It's been named to *National Geographic Traveler*'s "Stay List" and *Condé Nast Traveler*'s "Hot List," voted one of the world's best spas by readers of *Travel + Leisure*, and even been touted as a "top man-cation destination" on ABC News. Opened in 2006, the adults-only resort on 75 sylvan acres has about 60 guest rooms and suites. Even the smallest of them have private verandas and marble bathrooms

The Lodge at Woodloch

with oversized showers. But the resort's showpiece is its spa. Soaking tubs with hydro-massaging waterfalls, an outdoor whirlpool with a radiant-heated deck for year-round enjoyment, and woodland views ensure that guests slip into a blissed-out state even before setting foot in one of the 27 treatment rooms. When they're not luxuriating in the spa, guests can unwind in other ways: kayaking on the private 15-acre lake, for example, or golfing at **Woodloch Springs** (1 Woodloch Dr., Hawley, 570/685-8102, www.woodloch.com/golf), an 18-hole championship course across the street from the resort. Overnight rates include three gourmet meals daily and any nonalcoholic beverages. The many and various group fitness classes—from "inner smile meditation" to cardio kickboxing—are included.

FOOD
Hawley

Organic farmers and producers within an hour's drive provide a great deal of what's served at **The Settlers Inn** (4 Main Ave., 800/833-8527, www.thesettlersinn.com, breakfast 7:30am-10am daily, brunch 11am-2:30pm Sat.-Sun., dinner 5:30pm-8:30pm Sun.-Thurs. and 5:30pm-9:30pm Fri.-Sat., breakfast under $10, brunch $14-24, dinner $22-42), a small hotel and immensely popular restaurant on the banks of the trout-rich Lackawaxen River. Brook trout is a favorite ingredient of innkeeper, longtime fisherman, and self-taught chef Grant Genzlinger. Pennsylvania's state fish has even found its way onto the breakfast menu in the form of a crepe-accompanying mousse. Portions are on the small side, so don't shy away from the soups and other starters. If the dinner menu doesn't fit your budget, consider dining in the inn's cozy tavern, where you can order a cheeseburger as well as more refined fare. In the warmer months, snag a table on the river-facing terrace.

Honesdale

The ★ **Trackside Grill** (734 Main St., 570/253-2462, www.tracksidegrill.net, 6am-3pm Mon., 6am-7pm Tues.-Thurs., 6am-8pm Fri., 6am-7pm Sat., 8am-2pm Sun., $4-15) is the kind of place seasoned travelers love to stumble upon. The atmosphere is welcoming, the food is satisfying, and the staff are as happy to point you to favorite spots as they are to pour you more coffee. On top of which it's a unique reflection of the town. The diner pays tribute to Honesdale's legacy as the "birthplace of the American Railroad." It's decorated

The Settlers Inn

with train memorabilia and photos of local landscapes and landmarks taken by owner Jeff Hiller. Servers wearing engineer caps and red bandanas take orders for plate-size pancakes, omelets, house-made soups, and sandwiches like the Choo Choo and the Caboose Melt. Be sure to leave room for a Conductor Sundae or the Orange Blossom Special, a Creamsicle-flavored milkshake. Open at 6am every day but Sunday, the eatery is ideal for early birds. Its children's menu and sensible prices (two bucks for a fried egg sandwich!) make it ideal for families, too.

Another great option for breakfast or lunch: **Branko's Patisserie du Jour** (501 Main St., 570/253-0311, www.brankos-patisserie.com, 7am-3pm Tues.-Sat., $5-17). Chef Branko Bozic, a silver-haired gent from Germany, worked in high-end restaurants in Europe and Las Vegas and served as personal chef to Pennsylvania governor Bob Casey before opening the café in 2005. The vibe is casual, but the soups, salads, and sandwiches are très sophisticated. Rare-grilled duck breast finds its way onto organic greens. Salami from Barcelona meets French brie on house-baked bread. Bozic is a skilled pastry chef, and his fruit tarts and Parisian chocolate domes are divine. On select Saturdays October through May, Branko's offers a prix fixe dinner in a candlelit setting. Reservations go quickly.

INFORMATION

If you're new to the lake region, make the **Lake Wallenpaupack Visitors Center** (2512 Rte. 6, Hawley, 570/226-2141, 10am-6pm daily Memorial Day-Labor Day, 9am-5pm daily rest of year) your first stop. Operated by the **Pocono Mountains Visitors Bureau** (www.poconomountains.com), the center is stocked with maps and brochures about area activities, attractions, restaurants, and lodging options. Pocono Mountains "brand ambassadors" are on hand to offer personal assistance.

The website of the **Pocono Lake Region Chamber of Commerce** (570/226-3191, www.lakeregioncc.com) is also a good resource. You can download a visitors guide or peruse a digital version.

GETTING THERE

The lake region is very much a driving destination. The town of Hawley, at the north end of the 13-mile Lake Wallenpaupack, is about 90 miles northwest of New York City and 140 miles north of Philadelphia. From New York, head west on I-280 and I-80, north on Routes 15 and 206, and finally west on Route 6. From Philadelphia, head north on I-476, east on Route 22, north on Routes 33 and 402, and finally west on Route 6. **Wilkes-Barre/Scranton International Airport** (AVP, 570/602-2000, www.flyavp.com), the nearest commercial airport, is served by United Airlines, US Airways, Delta, and the low-cost carrier Allegiant. Hawley and nearby Honesdale can be reached by bus (201/529-3666, www.shortlinebus.com) from New York City.

Ski Region

With seven major ski areas, the Pocono Mountains are Pennsylvania's number one destination for snow sports. Most of the ski areas are in the southern part of the four-county region, in Monroe and Carbon Counties. They're not the only attraction in this swath of the state. It's home to a casino, a NASCAR track, and an outlet mall. It has resorts both historic and new. Water parks are the latest rage around here. If you're looking for a winter getaway that doesn't involve snow, a resort with an indoor water park may be just the thing.

★ SKI AREAS

First off, it's worth noting that the ski mountains of northeast Pennsylvania are modest relative to those out West. Even Blue Mountain Ski Area, which boasts the greatest vertical drop in Pennsylvania (1,082 feet), is Smurf-size compared with Colorado's slopes, where verticals of more than 4,000 feet are not uncommon. So hotshots used to carving turns in places such as Colorado, Montana, and Utah won't have the thrill of their lives in Pennsylvania. That's not to say that the Pocono Mountains don't attract plenty of experienced skiers and snowboarders. After all, it's a lot easier and cheaper for Philadelphians with a passion for powder to get to Blue Mountain than to Telluride.

If you're new to skiing or snowboarding, the modest mountains of northeast Pennsylvania will do just fine. All of the major ski areas offer lessons. They also offer snow tubing, which means you can chicken out of skiing and still say you hit the slopes.

With so many ski areas in close proximity to each other, you can bet on a healthy rivalry. They're always looking for ways to distinguish themselves, often by adding amenities. One boasts the first natural luge on the East Coast. Another boasts the first mountain coaster in Pennsylvania. Visitors are the ultimate winners.

Blue Mountain Ski Area

Blue Mountain (1660 Blue Mountain Dr., Palmerton, 610/826-7700, www.skibluemt.com, all-day lift ticket $54-63, youth 6-21 $45-48, seniors 70 and older ski for free, all-day equipment rental $36, snow tubing $25 per 3-hour session) is closest to Philadelphia and Allentown, Pennsylvania's first and third most populous cities. Partly for that reason, it can get very busy on weekends and holidays. It boasts 39 trails on 164 skiable acres, 21 tubing lanes, and 14 lifts. Six terrain parks of varying degrees of trickiness make it popular with the young and the restless. Blue Mountain is the only ski area in the region with a **BigAirBag,** a colossal cushion that lets daredevils practice tricks without risking injury. In 2012 Blue Mountain unveiled the first **natural luge track** on the East Coast. It's an official recruitment site for USA Luge, which grooms Olympians, so your first run could be your first step toward appearing on a Wheaties box. If the traditional plastic sled seems intimidating, you can opt for a mini bobsled or cushy snow tube. Offered weekends only, luge runs are free with a tubing ticket and $10 for three with a ski lift ticket.

Blue Mountain has about a dozen eateries, from the enticing Waffle Cabin to the tavern-style Last Run Lounge. It also has a babysitting center for children 6 weeks to 5 years. Babysitting is $5 per hour on weekdays and $8 per hour on weekends and holidays.

In the warmer months, the mountain offers **disc golf, mountain biking,** and **laser tag.**

Camelback Mountain Resort

Camelback (Resort Dr., Tannersville, 570/629-1661, www.skicamelback.com, all-day lift ticket $51-63, seniors and children 6-18 $38-47, all-day equipment rental $37, snow tubing $25 per weekday, $20-30 per 3-hour session on weekends, $15 with ski lift ticket) has the second greatest vertical drop in the Poconos at 800 feet. It has 34 trails on 166 skiable acres, 16 lifts, and a terrain park featuring custom artwork by professional graffitists. With as many as 42 lanes, its snow tubing park is billed as the largest in the country. On weekends and holidays, tickets for three-hour sessions are sold on the hour starting at 9am. It's a good idea to arrive at least half an hour before your intended session to make sure you get a ticket.

Like Blue Mountain, Camelback can get awful crowded. Location is one of its selling points. It's about three miles from exit 299 of I-80, a major east-west artery. The Crossings Premium Outlets are also at that exit, which makes Camelback a great choice if part of your party prefers shopping to snow sports.

Come spring, waterslides replace ski slopes as Camelback transforms into **Camelbeach,** a water park billed as the largest in Pennsylvania. In recent years the resort has added a host of other between-ski-seasons attractions, including **Segway tours,** an expansive **ropes course,** a pair of 1,000-foot **zip lines,** and a pair of 4,000-foot zip lines stretching from the summit of Camelback Mountain to its base. In 2012 the resort unveiled a year-round **mountain coaster,** featuring 4,500 feet of track and two 360-degree turns. Riders can control the speed of their two-person car on their way down the mountain. Left to gravity, the cars can reach speeds of 25-30 miles per hour.

In 2013, its 50th anniversary, Camelback kicked off its biggest expansion yet. The $163 million project calls for an eight-story hotel with a massive indoor water park at the base of Camelback Mountain. It's scheduled for completion in early 2015.

Jack Frost Big Boulder

If you're a bargain hunter, you're going to like **Jack Frost Big Boulder** (570/443-8425, www.jfbb.com, all-day lift ticket $44-52, seniors and children 5-18 $33-42, seniors 70 and older $10, all-day equipment rental $28-32, snow tubing $25-47 per day, $25-27 per 3-hour session on weekends, $10 with ski lift ticket). It's actually two ski areas for the price of one. In fact, skiing both mountains is cheaper than skiing either Blue Mountain or Camelback. Dating to the 1940s, Big Boulder (1 S. Lake Dr., Lake Harmony) is the oldest commercial ski area in Pennsylvania. Its builders played a hand in the invention of snowmaking machines. Today it's best known for its terrain parks. Jack Frost (1 Jack Frost Mountain Rd., Blakeslee), which opened in

ski school at Jack Frost Big Boulder

1972, offers a greater vertical drop (600 feet), more slopes (21), and more lifts (nine) than its older sibling, but it's not equipped for night skiing and closes at 4pm. Big Boulder stays open as late as 10pm. To get the biggest bang for your buck, hit the Jack Frost slopes in the morning and migrate to Big Boulder in the afternoon. The drive takes about 20 minutes.

WATER PARKS

The region long known for its ski mountains has in recent years emerged as a major destination for splashing good times. It has three water parks, two of which opened in the 2000s. Two more are scheduled to open in 2015. Indeed, waterslides and wave pools may soon outnumber ski trails. Lest you think that water parks are a summertime attraction, the tide has turned toward indoor water parks.

Every spring, Camelback Mountain Resort undergoes an extreme makeover, transforming from a ski mountain to **Camelbeach Mountain Waterpark** (Resort Dr., Tannersville, 570/629-1662, www.camelbeach.com, admission $37.99, seniors and children under 48 inches tall $27.99, children 2 and under free). Billed as the largest water park in Pennsylvania, Camelbeach has nearly 40 rides, slides, and other attractions, from play zones for pint-size guests to the Titan, an eight-story tubing slide said to be the largest of its kind. The resort also boasts an expansive ropes course, zip lines as long as 4,000 feet, and the first mountain coaster in Pennsylvania. Most dry attractions are not included in Camelbeach admission. The water park is open daily from mid-June through Labor Day and several weekends before that period. It opens at 10am or 11am and closes at 6pm or 7pm depending on the day. Come in the late afternoon for deeply discounted admission ($20.99, seniors and children under 48 inches tall $14.99).

Just minutes from Camelbeach, **Great Wolf Lodge** (1 Great Wolf Dr., Scotrun, 800/768-9653, www.greatwolf.com) features a massive indoor water park. The resort, part of a nationwide chain, became the first new Poconos resort in three decades when it opened in 2005. Alas, its water park is reserved for registered guests. Recognizing a good thing, Split Rock Resort & Golf Club opened its own indoor water park in 2008. Its version, **H2Oooohh!** (100 Moseywood Rd., Lake Harmony, 570/722-9111, www.splitrockresort.com, admission $36-41, seniors $16, children under 42 inches tall $31-36, children 2 and under free, observer passes available), is open to the general public. It has a handful of slides, a surfing simulator, a wave pool, and play areas for little kids. Hot tubs and a tiki bar keep the grown-ups happy.

If construction goes as planned, the region will have two more resorts with water parks by the end of 2015. Camelback Mountain Resort is at work on a 453-room lodge with a 125,000-square-foot indoor water park. The African-themed **Kalahari Resort** (250 Kalahari Blvd., Pocono Manor, 877/525-2427, www.kalahariresorts.com) is expected to have 457 guest rooms and a 100,000-square-foot indoor water park when the first of two construction phases is completed. Phase two calls for adding 400 rooms and doubling the size of the water park.

OTHER SIGHTS
Mount Airy Casino Resort

If you are over 30, there's a good chance you can hum the once-ubiquitous jingle for Mount Airy Lodge, which enjoyed a decades-long reign as America's premier "honeymoon hideaway" before falling into disrepair. The resort—"Your host with the most in the Poconos: beautiful Mount Airy Lodge"—closed its doors in 2001 and was demolished several years later. Built in its place: **Mount Airy Casino Resort** (44 Woodland Rd., Mount Pocono, 877/682-4791, www.mountairycasino.com, casino open 24 hours), which boasts more than 1,800 slot machines and table games, about 190 guest rooms and suites, a championship golf course, a full-service spa, several restaurants, and a nightclub. Gone are the heart-shaped bathtubs and floor-to-ceiling mirrors that characterized its predecessor. The resort's guest accommodations were designed with a four-star rating in mind, which meant out with the kitsch, in with the elegant. A waterfall greets guests in the hotel lobby, masking the noise of the gambling floor above.

Dining options range from a 1950s-style diner to the upscale **Red Steakhouse** (dinner Mon.-Tues. and Fri.-Sun., $28-60), which specializes in prime aged beef and seafood. A casino wouldn't be complete without a buffet. Mount Airy's is best known for its $24.99 Sunday brunch, which features a seafood station stocked with oysters, snow crab, smoked white fish, and more; carving stations; and an elaborate dessert table.

Mount Airy is one of two casinos in northeast Pennsylvania. The other, Mohegan Sun at Pocono Downs, is about an hour away in Wilkes-Barre.

Pocono Raceway

NASCAR fans flock to **Pocono Raceway** (Long Pond Rd. and Andretti Rd., Blakeslee, 800/722-3929, www.poconoraceway.com) for two 500-mile Sprint Cup Series races: the Pocono 400 in June and the Gobowling.com 400 in August. The 2.5-mile track is triangular in shape with straights of varying lengths and severe turns, each with a different degree of banking. Nicknamed "The Tricky Triangle," it's unlike any other track used for NASCAR's top racing series. In 2013 IndyCar racing returned to Pocono Raceway after a hiatus of 20-plus years. The Pocono IndyCar 500, part of the IZOD IndyCar Series, is held in July.

Family owned since its inception in 1968, Pocono prides itself on its fair-like atmosphere. Its motto: "Back to the good old days." Grandstand seating starts at $45 for the NASCAR races and $25 for the IndyCar race. Premium seating options range from an open-air hospitality area ($100 for race day) to air-conditioned skyboxes ($500 for entire race weekend). Fans can pitch a tent or park an RV on the grounds for the duration of a race weekend.

Wannabe car racers can get their training wheels at Pocono. **StockCar Racing Experience** (570/643-6921, www.877stockcar.com) is a chance to suit up, strap in, and see the track from the inside of a 600-horsepower vehicle. Brave souls can either ride shotgun with an instructor or get behind the wheel. A ride-along is $139-149 for three laps, $278-298 for six laps. Four laps in the driver's seat will set you back $349-399.

Pocono Raceway

For drivers who can't get enough, there are 8-lap, 16-lap, 24-lap, and 32-lap options, plus opportunities for more advanced training. You must be at least 18 and have experience in operating a manual transmission to drive. Riders can be as young as 14, but both parents must be present for those under 18. StockCar Racing Experience, in business since 1998, also offers a team pro kart racing program. Pocono Raceway is also used by the locally based **Bertil Roos Racing School** (800/722-3669, www.racenow.com), the place to go for seat time in a Formula 2000 race car.

ENTERTAINMENT AND EVENTS
Concert Venues

The **Sherman Theater** (524 Main St., Stroudsburg, 570/420-2808, www.sherman-theater.com) in downtown Stroudsburg opened on January 7, 1929, with a live performance by Stan Laurel and Oliver Hardy. Today it's best known as a rock venue, but other music genres, theater, and dance also find their way onto the calendar.

Festivals and Events

Split Rock Resort & Golf Club (Lake Harmony, 570/722-9111, www.splitrockresort.com) hosts two popular tasting events: the **Great Tastes of Pennsylvania Wine & Food Festival** in June and the **Great Brews Classic Beer Festival** in November. The former is held outdoors and, true to its name, focuses on Pennsylvania wineries. The latter is an indoor festival that showcases breweries from around the country. Both feature live music, food and craft vendors, and a pairing dinner.

The three-day **Pennsylvania Blues Festival** (Blue Mountain Ski Area, Palmerton, 610/826-7700, www.skibluemt.com, July, admission charged) attracts some of the biggest names in blues. There's on-site camping, so you don't have to get behind the wheel after a late-night jam. VIP tickets, which include reserved seating, dinner buffets, and Sunday brunch, are worth the splurge.

SHOPPING
The Crossings Premium Outlets

With 100 stores, **The Crossings Premium Outlets** (1000 Premium Outlets Dr., Tannersville, 570/629-4650, www.premiumoutlets.com, 10am-9pm Mon.-Sat., 10am-8pm Sun.) are good reason for people who aren't fond of outdoor recreation to head to the Poconos. Pennsylvania's sales tax exemption on shoes and apparel lures many New Yorkers and New Jerseyans to the outlet mall, located off exit 299 of I-80. Stores include Kenneth Cole, Juicy Couture, and J.Crew. The Pocono Mountains Visitors Bureau has an information center in the food court.

Specialty Shops

Sweet tooths should search out **Callie's Candy Kitchen** (Rte. 390, Mountainhome, 570/595-2280, www.calliescandy.com, 11am-5pm weekends Jan.-first week of Feb., 10am-5pm daily second week of Feb.-Dec.) and **Callie's Pretzel Factory** (Rte. 390, Cresco, 570/595-3257, 11am-5pm weekends Jan.-first week of Feb., 10am-5pm weekends second week of Feb.-Apr., 10am-5pm daily May-Dec.). Owner Harry Callie was 19 when he began selling handmade candy in 1952, and shoppers can still find him hands deep in chocolate. He's known for coating just about anything with the food of the gods, including sunflower seeds, cream cheese, and Twinkies. The Pretzel Factory, which opened in the 1980s, makes hard and soft pretzels as well as flavored popcorn. A window-lined wall gives customers the opportunity to observe the pretzel-making process. Be sure to try the "everything" pretzels, inspired by everything bagels.

ACCOMMODATIONS
Great Wolf Lodge

Opened in 2005, **Great Wolf Lodge** (1 Great Wolf Dr., Scotrun, 800/768-9653, www.greatwolf.com, $290-770) kicked off the trend of indoor water parks in the Pocono Mountains. With a dozen slides, six pools, two jumbo whirlpools, a lazy river, and a 1,000-gallon soaker bucket, its weatherproof water park is one of the largest in the country. It's always a balmy 84 degrees inside, which makes it a real treat after a day on the slopes of Camelback Mountain Resort, just a few minutes away. In summer, Great Wolf's water park spills outdoors. (Incidentally, Camelback morphs into an outdoor water park, Camelbeach, after ski season.) The great thing about Great Wolf's wetlands is that long lines are as rare as lone wolves. That's because access is reserved for guests of the all-suites resort, which is part of a nationwide chain.

Great Wolf's 401 suites come in a dozen styles. A real hit with pup-size guests: themed suites with bunk beds in a walled-off space resembling a cave, tent, or log cabin. PJs are perfectly acceptable attire for nightly story time in the main lobby, where an enormous clock tower comes to life three times a day. Other resort amenities include a bowling alley with half-length lanes, a large arcade, and a glow-in-the-dark mini golf course. Great Wolf has not one but two spas: the tranquil Elements Spa Salon and an ice-cream-themed kids spa. On-site eateries include a Starbucks coffee shop and the Loose Moose Cottage, where breakfast and dinner are buffet style. Food isn't included in room rates—and it isn't cheap—so plan to dine off-site if you're on a budget.

Skytop Lodge

If the stately stone manor at the heart of this resort strikes you as an exclusive retreat for the exceptionally wealthy, that's because it used to be. Built in the 1920s, it welcomed the likes of Lucille Ball when **Skytop Lodge** (1 Skytop, Skytop, 855/345-7759, www.skytop. com, from $330) was a private resort. Celebs still check in from time to time, but these days Skytop specializes in giving regular folks the star treatment. At 5,500 acres, the resort is larger than many towns in northeast Pennsylvania. And it offers more recreational opportunities than many towns put together. Among its amenities: a spa, a championship golf course rated 4.5 stars by *Golf Digest,* a private trout stream, a 75-acre lake, 30 miles of hiking trails, a climbing wall, paint-ball fields, and an indoor laser tag course. Skytop even has its own ski hill. With a vertical drop of 295 feet and four gentle slopes, it won't knock anyone's skis off. But for novices, it's an appealing alternative to crowded

Great Wolf Lodge

ski mountains. Ski lessons for children as young as two are available. Other wintertime activities include ice skating, tobogganing, snowshoeing, and even dog sledding. (Dog sledding is in fact a year-round option. When there's no snow on the ground, Skytop's huskies pull a golf cart or off-road vehicle instead of a sled.)

The resort offers a variety of accommodations and booking options, from room-only rates to packages that include meals and activities. Perched on a high plateau, the historic Main Lodge has 125 guest rooms and suites, heavy wooden furniture and plaid accents, and a buttoned-up ambience. Golfers gravitate toward the more intimate Inn at Skytop, located on the course designed more than 80 years ago by the first president of the PGA of America. With its two-story atrium, exposed beams, and cozy cocktail lounge, the 20-room inn recalls a European ski chalet. Its 135-seat restaurant offers great views and a relatively casual dining experience. Families may prefer to stay in one of Skytop's four-bedroom cottages, which have conveniences such as washers, dryers, and small refrigerators but no common areas. The interconnecting bedrooms can be rented individually.

Hotels and B&Bs

Having opened in 2007, **Mount Airy Casino Resort** (44 Woodland Rd., Mount Pocono, 877/682-4791, www.mountairycasino.com, $120-340) offers some of the newest digs in northeast Pennsylvania. Rooms and suites feature modern furnishings, spacious bathrooms, pillow-top beds, and LCD TVs. The resort's central location—just minutes from The Crossings Premium Outlets and Camelback Mountain Resort and within half an hour of Delaware Water Gap National Recreation Area and Pocono Raceway—is a major selling point. That being said, it's entirely possible to wile away a day without leaving Mount Airy, even if you're not a gambler. In addition to a 24-hour casino, the resort has an 18-hole golf course, a first-rate

spa, and a tradition of booking well-known entertainers. Its restaurants are well above average for the region but on the pricey side.

Its hilltop setting is reason enough to splurge on a stay at ★ **The French Manor Inn and Spa** (50 Huntingdon Dr., South Sterling, 570/676-3244, www.thefrenchmanor.com, $190-385). Need more reasons? How about its fine dining restaurant, named one of Pennsylvania's best by *Gourmet* magazine? Or its green spa, where couples can enjoy side-by-side massages and facials by a crackling fire? **Le Spa Forêt,** which opened in 2009, also boasts an indoor saltwater pool and hot tub. Ron and Mary Kay Logan, owners of The French Manor since 1990, are adept at setting the stage for romance—from champagne and roses upon arrival to horseback rides and picnic lunches. The Select Registry-endorsed B&B has about 20 rooms and suites in four buildings: a stone chateau built in the 1930s, a remodeled carriage house with country-style furnishings, La Maisonneuve (French for "the new house") with its private balconies and in-room whirlpool tubs, and the even newer spa building.

INFORMATION

If you're driving to the ski region from New Jersey or New York, be sure to stop at a Pennsylvania **welcome center,** where you'll be up to your eyeballs in information. The I-80 welcome center is a half mile west of the Pennsylvania-New Jersey border at exit 310, the I-84 welcome center is a mile west of the Pennsylvania-New York border at exit 53, and the I-81 welcome center is a half mile south of the Pennsylvania-New York border. Personalized travel counseling is available 7am-7pm daily.

The **Pocono Mountains Visitors Bureau** (www.poconomountains.com) operates a visitors center in the food court of The Crossings Premium Outlets (1000 Premium Outlets Dr., Tannersville), located off exit 299 of I-80. It's open 10am to 6pm daily.

GETTING THERE

The ski region is very much a driving destination. Blue Mountain, the southernmost ski area, is about an hour and a half north of Philadelphia via I-476 and only a half hour north of Allentown via Route 145. New Yorkers can also arrive in about two hours via I-78 west. Most of the ski region's major attractions can be found along I-80, a major east-west artery.

Jim Thorpe and Vicinity

Tucked into the hills and dotted with striking Victorian buildings, the town of Jim Thorpe was known to 19th-century rail excursionists as the "Switzerland of America." Today it's better known as a gateway to outdoor adventure. Rafters, canoeists, and kayakers come for the Lehigh River, which flows through town. North of town, the Lehigh Gorge offers some of the most exciting white water in the East. South of town, the river snakes languidly toward its confluence with the Delaware River. Bikers and hikers come for the river-hugging trail between Jim Thorpe and White Haven to its north. Twenty-six miles long, it attracts cross-country skiers when conditions are right. Blue Mountain Ski Area and Jack Frost Big Boulder are just 20-30 minutes from Jim Thorpe, making it a good base of operations for alpine skiing enthusiasts. It's okay if you come unprepared for adventure. Finding an outfitter in Jim Thorpe is easier than finding a Starbucks in Seattle. In 2007 *National Geographic Adventure* magazine named the "unassuming outdoors mecca" one of the nation's best places to live and play.

That's the sentiment local officials were shooting for when they renamed the town for an extraordinarily gifted athlete. Prior to 1954, Jim Thorpe was called Mauch Chunk (pronounced mock-CHUNK). In the 19th century, Mauch Chunk thrived as a transportation hub for the anthracite coal so plentiful in the hills around it. Fortunes were made. Mansions and grand hotels rose. It's said that half of America's millionaires lived in Mauch Chunk at one time. By the 1950s, however, the town was in sorry condition. The decline of the coal and railroad industries and the

a view of Jim Thorpe

Great Depression had sapped its wealth. In the hopes that a new name would give it new life as a tourist destination, Mauch Chunk officials struck a deal with the widow of Jim Thorpe, former Olympian and pro football and basketball player. Thorpe had been born in Oklahoma and died in California and had no ties to Mauch Chunk whatsoever. No matter. In exchange for his remains, Mauch Chunk and its neighbor across the Lehigh, East Mauch Chunk, merged under the name Jim Thorpe and erected a 20-ton mausoleum for the Native American sports icon.

The town's turnaround wasn't immediate, but turn around it did. With old mansions and new galleries, ample dining and lodging options, and tourism as its lifeblood, the "Switzerland of America" could easily adopt as its tag line the title of a 1951 biopic starring Burt Lancaster: *Jim Thorpe—All American.*

★ LEHIGH GORGE STATE PARK

Lehigh Gorge State Park (570/443-0400, www.visitpaparks.com) features some of the best white water in Pennsylvania. It contains about 30 miles of the Lehigh River, from the Francis E. Walter Dam in the north to Jim Thorpe in the south. This section offers Class II and III rapids in a season that stretches from March through October and sometimes into November. Left in the hands of Mother Nature, the white-water season would be woefully short. But the U.S. Army Corps of Engineers, which manages the dam, likes to see people have a good time. It releases loads of water on select weekends, providing for rollicking rides even during the hot months of July and August.

Inexperienced paddlers should very definitely engage the services of a guide, and there's no shortage of them in or near Jim Thorpe. **Pocono Whitewater** (1519 Rte. 903, 800/944-8392, www.whitewaterrafting.com), **Jim Thorpe River Adventures** (1 Adventure Ln., 570/325-2570, www.jtraft.com), and **Whitewater Rafting Adventures** (Rte. 209 and Hunter St./Rte.

93, Nesquehoning, 570/669-9127, www.adventurerafting.com), all within 10 minutes of each other, offer **white-water rafting** through the park as well as float trips on the milder waters south of Jim Thorpe. There's also a rafting outfitter near the midsection of the park, **Whitewater Challengers** (288 N. Stagecoach Rd., Weatherly, 570/443-9532, www.whitewaterchallengers.com).

It's hard to appreciate the beauty of the deep river gorge with its cascading waterfalls and diverse wildlife when you're paddling furiously. It's easier when you're pedaling. The 26-mile **Lehigh Gorge Trail,** which follows an abandoned railroad corridor along the river, has been called one of "America's sweetest rides" by *Outside* magazine. The **biking** is especially sweet in October, at the peak of fall foliage. Start at the park's northern access area, White Haven, for an all-downhill ride to Jim Thorpe. (It's a very slight downhill grade, so you'll still break a sweat.) All of the above-mentioned outfitters offer bike rentals and shuttle service. In winter the trail is open for

rafting on the Lehigh River with Pocono Whitewater

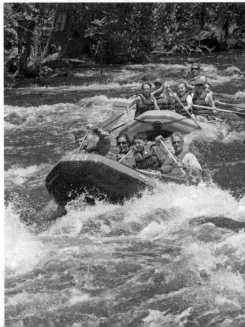

Jim Thorpe, the Man

The Pennsylvania capital of Harrisburg was named for the frontiersman who settled it in the early 1700s. British General John Forbes paid tribute to William Pitt, first Earl of Chatham, when he gave the name Pittsburgh to the settlement at the forks of the Ohio River in 1758. The city of Scranton owes its name to a family of 19th-century captains of industry. Loads of towns in the state named for founder William Penn are eponyms for a long-buried someone or other. The town of Jim Thorpe is uncommon in that it's named for a man who made his mark in the 20th century.

James Francis Thorpe was born in 1887 in a single-room cabin in what is now Oklahoma and was then known as Indian Territory. His Native American name, Wa-Tho-Huk, meant "Bright Path," which was prescient indeed. In 1904 he began attending Carlisle Indian School, a boarding school in Carlisle, Pennsylvania. It was there that Thorpe found his calling: athletics. In addition to playing football under legendary coach Glenn "Pop" Warner, he competed in track and field, baseball, lacrosse, and even ballroom dancing. In 1912 the 24-year-old sailed to Europe for the Stockholm Olympics, training aboard the ship. He won the pentathlon and the decathlon by wide margins, setting records that stood for decades. "Sir, you are the greatest athlete in the world," gushed Sweden's King Gustav V, who presented Thorpe with his medals. The greatest athlete in the world reportedly replied: "Thanks, King." He was celebrated with a ticker-tape parade in New York.

The following year, things took an ugly turn for "Bright Path." After a newspaper reported that Thorpe had played two seasons of semiprofessional baseball in North Carolina, he was stripped of his gold medals. His records were struck from the books. The ordeal didn't sour Thorpe on athletics. The six-foot-one phenom played six seasons of professional baseball for teams including the New York Giants (now the San Francisco Giants). Pro football also came calling. He played both sports for several years before retiring from baseball in 1919. His career in pro football continued for another decade and included a stint with the Chicago Cardinals (now the Arizona Cardinals). Thorpe was 41 when he finally hung up his cleats.

Over the next two decades, the father of seven struggled to make a living. He held a string of

cross-country skiing. The 15-mile section from White Haven to Penn Haven Junction is also open for **snowmobiling.** To reach the park's northern access area from I-80, take exit 273 and follow Route 940 east to the White Haven Shopping Center. Turn right on Main Street and bear right.

Experienced **hikers** may find the rail-trail a bore. Never boring: the **Glen Onoko Falls Trail,** located on state game lands adjacent to the park. The terrain is steep and sometimes treacherous—"we're always in there rescuing people," confides one park ranger—but the payoff is rich. Come in spring to see the cascading falls at their most ferocious. The trail begins at the park's southern access area, Glen Onoko, reached from Coalport Road in Jim Thorpe.

If you have a mind to raft, bike, and hike all in one day, you may be a little bit crazy, but you're not alone. Pocono Whitewater's "Big Day Out" is a chance to do just that. It starts with a hearty breakfast and ends with dinner around a bonfire. In between, participants bike the rail-trail, hike to an abandoned railroad tunnel, and raft the Lehigh. The $94.99 price tag includes all the necessary gear, shuttle service, and meals.

Lehigh Gorge Scenic Railway

Paddling the river is one way to see Lehigh Gorge State Park. Biking the rail-trail alongside the river is another. The deliciously lazy way: riding a train through the deep gorge. **Lehigh Gorge Scenic Railway** (1 Susquehanna St., Jim Thorpe, 570/325-8485, www.lgsry.com, Memorial Day weekend-Dec.) began offering train excursions in 2006, more than 40 years after railroads in the region put the brakes on passenger service. The menial jobs, including as a ditch digger and a bouncer. In 1950 Thorpe was voted greatest athlete of the first half of the century in an Associated Press poll, beating out baseball great Babe Ruth. The following year, the Associated Press reported that he was "flat broke." He died on March 28, 1953, after suffering a heart attack in his trailer home in Lomita, California.

The posthumous honors were many. In 1954 the Pennsylvania towns of Mauch Chunk and East Mauch Chunk merged and took the name of the multisport star. President Richard Nixon proclaimed April 16, 1973, as "Jim Thorpe Day," noting that "millions of young people who aspire to achievements transcending a disadvantaged background continue to take heart from Jim Thorpe's example." In 1982 his supporters won a hard-fought battle to have his Olympic titles reinstated.

Visitors to Jim Thorpe, the town, can learn about Jim Thorpe, the man, at the **Jim Thorpe Memorial,** his final resting place. Located along Route 903 on the north-east fringe of town, the memorial features a bronze statue of

Jim Thorpe in 1913 as a New York Giant

a football-toting Thorpe and an abstract sculpture, *The Spirit of Thunder and Lightning*. Flags representing America, Pennsylvania, and the Olympics stand behind his gravestone, inscribed with the words of King Gustav V. The town pays tribute to its namesake on the third weekend of every May. The **Jim Thorpe Birthday Celebration** (570/325-5810, www.jimthorpe.org, free) kicks off with a Native American ritual at the memorial, but most festivities, including a torch-lighting ceremony, take place at Josiah White Park in the heart of town.

one-hour trip begins in Jim Thorpe's historic district at a restored train station that now houses a visitors center. The train follows the curves of the Lehigh River for eight miles before returning the way it came. If it's a beautiful day, make a beeline for the open-air car or the caboose platform.

OTHER SIGHTS
Mauch Chunk Museum and Old Jail Museum

Most visitors to Jim Thorpe are more interested in outdoor adventure than local history, but the town formerly known as Mauch Chunk has a past more colorful than the Lehigh Gorge in fall. The **Mauch Chunk Museum** (41 W. Broadway, Jim Thorpe, 570/325-9190, www.mauchchunkmuseum. com, 11am-5pm daily except Tues. Memorial Day-Dec. and weekends Jan.-Memorial Day,

admission $5, children under 8 $2) does a fine job of telling its story, which is also the story of 19th-century coal mining and transportation innovations. Housed in a former church, the museum chronicles not just the town's industrial golden age but also its decline in the early 20th century, its peculiar decision to trade its name for the body and name of a sports icon, and its revitalization as Jim Thorpe.

Just down the street, a jail-turned-museum zeroes in on a grim chapter in local history. In the late 1870s, seven Irish coal miners known as "Molly Maguires" were hanged there for terrorizing and murdering mine bosses. A tour of the **Old Jail Museum** (128 W. Broadway, Jim Thorpe, 570/325-5259, www.theoldjailmuseum.com, noon-4:30pm daily except Wed. Memorial Day-Labor Day and weekends Sept.-Oct., admission $6, seniors and students $5, children 6-12 $4),

238

POCONO MOUNTAINS
JIM THORPE AND VICINITY

a fortress-like structure that served as the county jail from 1871 until 1995, is a walk on the macabre side. "Wander eerie dungeon cells," the ads beckon. "Be locked in a real jail cell." Its most irresistible selling point is a dash of the supernatural. Legend has it that on the day of his execution, one of the condemned coal miners pressed a dirty hand against the wall of his cell and swore that his handprint would remain forever as proof of his innocence. Wardens tried mightily to remove the mark, washing, painting, and even replastering the wall. But it always returned, or so it's said. See for yourself in cell 17.

No. 9 Coal Mine & Museum

For a taste of the coalminer's life, head to **No. 9 Coal Mine & Museum** (9 Dock St., Lansford, 570/645-7074, www.no9mine.com, museum admission $3, with mine tour $8, children 4 and under free), about 10 miles southwest of Jim Thorpe. A train carries visitors into the belly of the anthracite mine, a workplace from 1855 to 1972 and a tourist attraction since 2002. The guided tour continues on foot to areas including a miner's hospital and a passageway originally used by coal-hauling mules. The museum is located aboveground in a former "wash shanty,"

where miners washed up after their shift. On display are loads of tools, a tableau of a coal miner's kitchen, and life-size figures of a mine mule and a boy tasked with directing the beast of burden.

While the museum is open Wednesday-Sunday year-round, mine tours are limited to May-October. The museum is open 10am-4pm during the tour season and noon-4pm in the off-season. Tours are offered Friday-Sunday in May, Wednesday-Sunday June through August, and Saturday-Sunday in September and October.

ENTERTAINMENT AND EVENTS
Concert Venues

REO Speedwagon, Air Supply, and Kenny Rogers are among the many and various acts that have played **Penn's Peak** (325 Maury Rd., Jim Thorpe, 866/605-7325, www.penn-speak.com), a mountaintop venue with lofty ceilings and a capacity of 1,800. Its luncheon and dinner shows often sell out weeks in advance. The picturesque views from the Peak's open-air decks and patios are alone worth the price of a ticket.

Ten minutes away is the **Mauch Chunk Opera House** (14 W. Broadway, Jim Thorpe,

A tour descends into the mine at No. 9 Coal Mine & Museum.

570/325-0249, www.mauchchunkoperahouse.com), built in 1881 as a combo farmers market and concert hall. Once a regular stop on the vaudeville circuit, the Opera House became a movie theater in the 1920s and later a warehouse for a pocketbook manufacturer. Today it's once again a venue for live entertainment. Operated by the Mauch Chunk Historical Society, the acoustically superior Opera House seats 370. It's a favorite venue of Canadian folk trio The Wailin' Jennys, who recorded a live album there in 2008.

Festivals and Events

The white-water season may be winding down in October, but Jim Thorpe is more bustling than ever. People pour into town on the first three weekends of the month, known as **Fall Foliage Weekends** (throughout Jim Thorpe, 570/325-5810, www.jimthorpe.org, free and paid events), and you can bet there's more to do than leaf peep. (Though the leaf peeping *is* superb.) The festival features free music events at four venues, ticketed shows at the Mauch Chunk Opera House, train rides through the gorgeous Lehigh Gorge, and vendors selling everything from cheesesteaks and corn dogs to quilts and mittens. Organizers recommend arriving bright and early to avoid heavy traffic into town. If you're planning to spend the night, book well in advance—and brace yourself for peak rates.

ACCOMMODATIONS
Camping

If the purpose of your visit is outdoor adventure, pitch a tent at **Adventure Campground** (288 N. Stagecoach Rd., Weatherly, 570/443-9532, www.whitewaterchallengers.com, Apr.-Oct., campsite $7.50/person). It's operated by Whitewater Challengers, a rafting, kayaking, and biking outfitter whose headquarters is a short walk from the campground. Whitewater Challengers also offers zip lining, paintball programs, boxed lunches, and breakfast and dinner buffets, taking the hassle out of planning action-packed days. The campground

has bathrooms, hot showers, and volleyball and basketball courts. Don't have a tent? Tent rentals and rustic bunkhouses ($48/first night, $45/additional night, plus $7.50/person) are available. The campground occasionally admits RVs. Call for clearance.

A better choice for RV vacationers is the immaculate **StoneyBrook Estates Campground** (1435 Germans Rd., Lehighton, 570/386-4088, www.stoneybrookestates.com, campsite $40-45 for up to 4 people, $260/week), which opened in 2009. It's about 12 miles south of Jim Thorpe.

Hotels and B&Bs

During its heyday in the late 1800s, the town now known as Jim Thorpe was a tourist destination on par with Niagara Falls—so scenic that it was called the "Switzerland of America." More than half a dozen grand hotels welcomed streams of visitors. Built in 1849 and originally called the New American Hotel, ★ **The Inn at Jim Thorpe** (24 Broadway, Jim Thorpe, 800/329-2599, www.innjt.com, room $90-210, suite $150-340) invites guests to "rediscover a bygone era." The 45-room hotel in the heart of the historic district has floral carpets, tin ceilings, period furnishings, and a friendly staff. Accommodations range from generously sized standard rooms to suites with whirlpools and gas fireplaces. Amenities include a modest exercise room, a game room, and a restaurant and pub. Onsite spa services are available. Cast-iron balconies dotted with wicker rockers overlook Broadway's shops, restaurants, and galleries. In the warmer months, The Inn at Jim Thorpe is a popular base camp for adventures in nearby Lehigh Gorge State Park, so book well in advance. No luck? Look for digs in one of its sister properties: **55** (55 Broadway, 800/329-2599, www.innjt.com, $120-340), a recently restored Victorian building across the street from the inn, and **Broadway House** (44-46 W. Broadway, 800/329-2599, www.broadwayguesthouse.com, $90-250), a 13-room guesthouse a couple of blocks from the historic downtown.

FOOD

For a small town with big appeal to outdoorsy types, Jim Thorpe has a surprisingly diverse food landscape—from hoagies and pizza to handmade pasta and escargot.

With its full-service bar and laid-back atmosphere, **Molly Maguires Pub & Steakhouse** (5 Hazard Square, Jim Thorpe, 570/325-4563, www.jimthorpedining.com, kitchen 11am-10pm Sun.-Thurs., 11am-11pm Fri.-Sat., last call 1:45am, $6-22) is often the most happening spot in town. Its proprietors hail from Dublin, and the kitchen dishes out some Irish classics along with plenty of American pub grub. The half-pound burger topped with caramelized Guinness onions is a local favorite. Despite the flat-screen TVs, there's an old-timey feel to the place. It occupies the circa 1830 Hotel Switzerland, one of the oldest commercial buildings in Jim Thorpe. A large deck provides an appealing alternative to the sometimes smoky bar area.

Owned by a husband-and-wife team, ★ **Moya** (24 Race St., Jim Thorpe, 570/325-8530, www.jimthorpemoya.com, 5pm-9pm Mon.-Tues. and Thurs., 5pm-10pm Fri.-Sat., 5pm-8pm Sun., $20-28) showcases his culinary talents and her artistic talents. Chef Heriberto Yunda got his start cooking for American oil company executives in his native Ecuador and lent his talents to restaurants in New York City and Istanbul before moving to Pennsylvania in 2002. Named for his hometown, Moya is decorated with his wife's abstract paintings: riots of color against butternut squash-hued walls. The menu changes frequently, but you can expect an eclectic variety of dishes. Polenta with Gorgonzola sauce, roasted quail, seafood stew, and braised lamb shank have all made the cut. Moya draws a lot of locals and is always packed on weekends; a reservation will spare you the disappointment of being turned away. The service can be hit or miss, especially when the house is full, but the food is unassailable.

INFORMATION

The **Pocono Mountains Visitors Bureau** (www.poconomountains.com) operates a visitors center in Jim Thorpe's historic train station (2 Lehigh Ave., 570/325-3673, 9:30am-5:30pm daily).

GETTING THERE

Jim Thorpe is about 30 miles northwest of Allentown and 80 miles northwest of Philadelphia via I-476. The nearest commercial airport is **Lehigh Valley International Airport** (ABE, 800/359-5842, www.flyvia.com) in Allentown. **Wilkes-Barre/Scranton International Airport** (AVP, 570/602-2000, www.flyavp.com) is also within an hour's drive. Intercity bus service to Jim Thorpe is available through **Greyhound** (800/231-2222, www.greyhound.com) and its interline partners.

Scranton and Wilkes-Barre

Northeast Pennsylvania's largest cities are the not-so-large cities of Scranton and Wilkes-Barre. Both are county seats—a virtual guarantee of lofty architecture. Both are nestled in river valleys. Just 20 miles apart, they're often joined by a slash in references to the area. (Think Dallas/Fort Worth on a smaller scale.) They share professional sports teams, a philharmonic orchestra, and an airport. They also share an industrial heritage: both were once booming centers of the anthracite mining industry.

Anthracite is a word rarely heard these days, but for several decades, it was the most popular heating fuel in the northern United States. Sometimes referred to as hard coal or colloquially as "black diamonds," anthracite is special stuff. It has fewer impurities than any other type of coal. It burns longer. And no place in the Western Hemisphere has more of it than northeast Pennsylvania. Its discovery in the 18th century transformed the region over the course of the 19th. Immigrants poured in to meet the human capital needs of coal companies. Communities were

carved out of wilderness. Canal systems were built, and then railroads. The population of Scranton surged from less than 10,000 in 1860 to about 143,000 in 1930. Wilkes-Barre's population shot from less than 5,000 to about 87,000 in that period.

Today their populations are roughly half of what they were in 1930. Why? Because the lust for black diamonds began to wane after World War I. Oil was in; coal was out. On January 22, 1959, an anthracite mine about midway between Scranton and Wilkes-Barre collapsed under the weight of the ice-laden Susquehanna River. An estimated 10 billion gallons of river water coursed through the cavity, flooding mines throughout the area. The Knox Mine disaster, as it came to be called, killed 12 men and the nation's appetite for deep anthracite mining.

To appreciate the coal industry's enormous impact on northeast Pennsylvania, just glance at a map. Place names such as Minersville, Port Carbon, Carbondale, Coaldale, and Carbon County say it all. A deeper appreciation can be gained by visiting one or more of

Scranton is nicknamed the "Electric City."

The Office Fan's Guide to Scranton

Millions of people who've never been to Scranton know just where to get a beer if they're ever out this way. That's because they're fans of the American version of *The Office*, which was filmed in sunny California but set at the Scranton branch of a fictional paper company. References to actual places in Scranton and the surrounding area are common, which has made the city a pilgrimage site for super-fans of the hit sitcom. Shortly before the series finale aired in May 2013, the cast, crew, and thousands of fans converged on Scranton for a daylong wrap party.

The first order of business for many visiting fans is snapping a photo of the "Scranton Welcomes You" sign that appears in the opening credits. They can approach the city from every possible direction and still not find it. Until a few years ago, there were two such signs alongside inbound expressways. The bravest of fans—some might call them knuckleheads—would veer off to the side for a photo op. Now it's possible to get a pic without risking life and limb. After the city removed the signs, one was rescued from storage and placed inside **The Mall at Steamtown** (300 Lackawanna Ave., Scranton, 570/343-3400, www.themallatsteamtown.com, 10am-9pm Mon.-Sat., 11am-6pm Sun.), which itself has gotten shout-outs on the show. Rainn Wilson, who plays uber-quirky officemate Dwight Schrute, has been named an honorary mall guard.

Though Office boss Michael Scott loves Hooters, there's no Hooters in Scranton, nor is there a Beni-hana ("Asian Hooters," as Michael calls it). But the oft-mentioned **Cooper's Seafood House** (701 N. Washington Ave., Scranton, 570/346-6883, www.coopers-seafood.com, 11am-midnight Mon.-Thurs.,

the heritage attractions in the region. There's a slew of them in and around Scranton.

Like many rust belt cities, Scranton and Wilkes-Barre are working to reinvent themselves. They landed a minor league baseball team in 1989 and an American Hockey League franchise a decade later. Wilkes-Barre got a casino in 2006. Scranton has gotten loads of priceless publicity since the 2005 debut of *The Office*, a hilarious TV sitcom set in Scranton.

SIGHTS
Steamtown National Historic Site

Rail fans have a lot of love for Scranton. It's home to one of eight surviving "Big Boy" steam locomotives and the only one stored east of Wisconsin. Weighing in at 1.2 million pounds, Union Pacific No. 4012 was one of 25 Big Boys built in the 1940s to pull long freight trains over the mountains of Utah and Wyoming. Though it no longer operates, it's among the standouts in the collection of locomotives, passenger cars, freight cars, and maintenance-of-way equipment at **Steamtown** (Lackawanna Ave. and Cliff St.,

downtown Scranton, 570/340-5200, www.nps.gov/stea, regular hours 9am-5pm daily, winter hours 10am-4pm daily, admission $7, children 15 and under free).

Located on a working railroad yard that dates to 1851, the national park is dedicated to preserving the history of steam railroading in America. It's home to some 25 steam and diesel-electric locomotives. The oldest of them is a freight engine built in 1903 for the Chicago Union Transfer Railway Company. Several are in working order, and visitors can ride behind them in historic commuter cars. Short train rides ($5, children 5 and under free) are offered most days from mid-April to early December. Visitors age 16 or older can pay $30 for the privilege of riding in the locomotive cab and interacting with the crew. Only one guest is allowed in the cab. Tickets for the short train rides are sold on a first-come, first-served basis. Reservations are strongly recommended for longer excursions, which are offered on select days and range from about two hours to a full day.

Guided walking tours of the locomotive repair shop are available year-round. The 45-minute look at what it takes to maintain

11am-2am Fri.-Sat., noon-midnight Sun., $8-30) is a Scranton institution. The family-owned restaurant, famous for its beer selection and lobster hats, looks like a pirate ship complete with attacking octopus. **Poor Richard's Pub** (125 Beech St., Scranton, 570/344-4555, www.southsidebowl.com, 5pm-2am Mon.-Fri., 4pm-1am Sat.-Sun., under $10), referenced in multiple episodes, may be Scranton's most famous watering hole. Fans expecting a standalone pub will be surprised to find that Poor Richard's is actually inside the 34-lane South Side Bowl. The show has also dished out free advertising for **Alfredo's Pizza Cafe** (1040 S. Washington Ave., Scranton, 570/969-1910, www.alfredoscafe.com, 11am-11pm Sun.-Thurs., 11am-midnight Fri.-Sat., $6-20), located just around the corner from the bowling alley.

Viewers with an eye for detail spot all sorts of Scrantonalia in the Dunder Mifflin Scranton office, from University of Scranton apparel to bobbleheads of Scranton/Wilkes-Barre Red Barons players. (The minor league baseball team is now called the Scranton/Wilkes-Barre RailRiders). And those who know the area will spot all sorts of improbabilities, like Michael and Dwight's train ride to Philadelphia in one episode. (There's no passenger train service between Scranton and Philly.) In the season three episode "Beach Games," Michael takes the gang to **Lake Scranton** for a series of competitions to determine his successor. The real Lake Scranton, located southeast of downtown off Route 307, doesn't have a beach. In season two's "Booze Cruise," Michael surprises his motley crew with a January cruise on **Lake Wallenpaupack.** The real Lake Wallenpaupack, about 30 miles east of Scranton, usually freezes in winter; cruises don't resume until spring.

and repair the fire-breathing machines is included in park admission. Allot at least an hour for exploring Steamtown's two museums. One traces the history of railroading from its earliest days to the 1980s; the other focuses on the technology of steam railroading. An especially good time to visit is Labor Day weekend, when Steamtown hosts

Railfest. The celebration of railroading past and present features visiting equipment displays and special shop demos.

Electric City Trolley Museum

It's not its nightlife that earned Scranton the nickname "Electric City." It's the fact that Scranton had a commercially viable electric

Steamtown National Historic Site

streetcar system before any other U.S. city. Scranton was a booming industrial metropolis when the Scranton Suburban Electric Railway commenced operation in November 1886. By the time the railway folded in 1954, Scranton's fortunes and population had begun to diminish, and buses were supplanting streetcars across the country. The history of electric railway transit in eastern Pennsylvania is chronicled at the **Electric City Trolley Museum** (Lackawanna Ave. and Cliff St., downtown Scranton, 570/963-6590, www.ectma.org, 9am-5pm daily May-Dec., 10am-4pm Wed.-Sun. Jan.-Apr., museum admission $6, seniors $5, children 4-17 $4), located on the grounds of Steamtown National Historic Site. About a dozen trolleys are in use or on display. The museum's collection is particularly strong in trolleys of Philadelphia and its western suburbs. Most of its vehicles were in fact built in Philadelphia by the J.G. Brill Company, the world's largest trolley manufacturer in its day.

Looking at historic trolley cars is nice, but it's best to visit when you can ride one. Trolley excursions are offered Thursday-Sunday from May through October. The trolley passes through one of the longest interurban tunnels ever built as it makes its way to PNC Field, home of the Scranton/Wilkes-Barre RailRiders. The fare is $8 for adults, $7 for seniors, $6 for children 4-17. A combination ticket good for museum admission and a trolley ride is $10 for adults, $9 for seniors, $8 for children.

Everhart Museum and Nay Aug Park

When Scranton's **Everhart Museum** (1901 Mulberry St., Scranton, 570/346-7186, www.everhart-museum.org, open Feb.-Dec., noon-4pm Mon. and Thurs.-Fri., 10am-5pm Sat., noon-5pm Sun., admission $7, seniors and students $5, children 6-12 $3) opened in 1908, it housed little more than its benefactor's vast collection of mounted birds. But Dr. Isaiah Fawkes Everhart—local physician and businessman, Civil War veteran, and skilled taxidermist—did more than donate his stuffed specimens. He also created an endowment fund for his museum. Many purchases and donations later, the Everhart is the largest public museum in northeast Pennsylvania, with a focus on the visual arts as well as natural history. Its eclectic collection includes a Victorian-era wreath made with human hair, a cast of a stegosaurus skeleton, ceremonial masks from Africa, and painted coffin posts from Egypt. Among the highlights is a mural of prehistoric northeast Pennsylvania by Brooklyn-born Charles R. Knight, who became a renowned artist despite being legally blind. Painted in 1951, it was the last of his great murals.

The museum is located in Scranton's largest city-run park, **Nay Aug** (570/348-4186, www.scrantonpa.gov), boasting two playgrounds, a pool and waterslide complex, and a rose garden. But its best feature is the rock-strewn Nay Aug Gorge and its waterfalls, designated a National Natural Landmark. The best *manmade* feature is a spectacularly crafted tree house overlooking the gorge.

Anthracite Heritage Attractions

The story of coal mining in northeast Pennsylvania is not a PG one. It's a story of backbreaking work under deplorable conditions, a story of death and disfiguring injuries. It's rated R for violence. If you have the stomach for it, start with a visit to the **Pennsylvania Anthracite Heritage Museum** (McDade Park, Scranton, 570/963-4804, www.anthracitemuseum.org, 9am-5pm Mon.-Sat., noon-5pm Sun., closed Mon. Dec.-Mar., admission $7, seniors $6, children 3-11 $5), which focuses on the immigrant experience. Tens of thousands of immigrants from more than 30 nations settled in the region in the 19th and early 20th centuries to work in the iron, coal, and textile industries. The museum offers a window into their daily lives. Among its exhibits is a re-created kitchen of a typical mine worker's house, circa 1935. The museum is located in McDade Park, a county-run oasis reclaimed from coal-mining terrain.

The park is a few miles west of downtown Scranton, accessible from Keyser Avenue.

McDade Park is also home to the **Lackawanna Coal Mine Tour** (Scranton, 570/963-6463, www.lackawannacounty.org, 10am-3pm daily Apr.-Nov., admission $10, seniors $9.50, children 3-12 $7.50), where you can don a hardhat and descend 300 feet below the earth's surface to explore a once-active mine. Honest-to-goodness miners do the guiding. The descent by mine car takes several minutes; the walking portion of the tour lasts an hour and covers about half a mile. It's always 53 degrees inside the mine, so dress accordingly. Tours are scheduled on demand.

About an hour south of McDade Park is **Eckley Miners' Village** (Eckley, 570/636-2070, www.eckleyminersvillagemuseum.com, 9am-5pm Mon.-Sat., noon-5pm Sun., admission $8, seniors $7, children 3-12 $6), an example of a so-called patch town. Hundreds of "patches"—villages owned entirely by mining companies and populated by miners and their families—mushroomed across the anthracite region in the 19th century. Even the stores were company-owned, and you can bet there were no bargains to be found. Settled in 1854, Eckley had a population of more than 1,000 by 1870. Today it's property of the state and virtually uninhabited. The village-turned-museum consists of more than 50 buildings. You can't go inside buildings unless you take a guided tour ($2). The 90-minute tours are offered Memorial Day weekend through September. The "company store," which houses the museum shop, isn't original. It was built as a prop for the 1970 movie *The Molly Maguires,* based on the murderous doings of militant Irish miners. Much of the movie, starring Sean Connery, was filmed in Eckley, which had changed hardly at all in the century since the bloodshed.

Houdini Tour and Magic Show

The legendary Harry Houdini may be dead, but his legacy is alive and well in Scranton. The city's most unique attraction is the **Houdini Tour and Magic Show** (1433 N. Main Ave., Scranton, 570/383-1821, www.houdini.org, call for showtimes and prices) put on by a pair of magicians whose idolatry of the escape artist is infectious. Dorothy Dietrich, a platinum blonde famous for duplicating Houdini's escapes and sawing men in half, and Dick Brooks, aka "Bravo the Great," have been known to levitate audience members. Each magic show—complete with live animals—is complemented by a tour of their collection of Houdini memorabilia, which includes photos, posters, and props. Among the highlights: a pair of handcuffs that belonged to the escapologist himself.

Mohegan Sun at Pocono Downs

Mohegan Sun at Pocono Downs (1280 Highway 315, Wilkes-Barre, 570/831-2100, www.poconodowns.com, casino open 24 hours), a casino and harness racing track, is the younger sibling of Connecticut's Mohegan Sun. Both are property of the Mohegan Tribe of Connecticut. If you've been to the mammoth original—one of the largest casinos in the country—you'll find Wilkes-Barre's "racino" quaint by comparison. But it's impressive as Pennsylvania casinos go, boasting 2,300 slot machines, more than 80 table games, about 15 eateries and bars, and several shops.

Dining options include a buffet restaurant, a sushi bar, and chains Ruth's Chris Steak House, Wolfgang Puck Express, and Johnny Rockets. The standout: **Rustic Kitchen Bistro & Bar** (570/824-6600, 11:30am-9pm Sun.-Tues., 11:30am-11pm Wed.-Sat., bar open until midnight Wed.-Sat., $9-35), a Tuscan villa-themed restaurant with a knack for pizzas, creamy clam chowder, and seafood dishes. Its main feature is a state-of-the-art TV studio kitchen complete with tiered seating for audience members. Call or check the casino website for a schedule of live cooking shows.

★ Ricketts Glen State Park

Exceptionally scenic hiking trails make

Ricketts Glen State Park (accessible from Rtes. 487 and 118, about 30 miles west of Wilkes-Barre, 570/477-5675, www.visitpaparks.com) one of northeast Pennsylvania's main attractions. *Backpacker* magazine has for years heaped accolades on the 13,050-acre park, which boasts 22 named waterfalls. The highest of them, Ganoga Falls, is 94 feet tall. The waterfalls lie in a section of the park known as the Glens Natural Area, a registered National Natural Landmark that's also blessed with giant pines, hemlocks, and oaks. Many of the trees are more than 500 years old—too wide to wrap your arms around and dizzyingly tall. Twenty-six miles of trails crisscross the park. The one-mile Evergreen Trail is easy hiking through one of the oldest forest stands in Pennsylvania. The most talked-about trek is 7.2 miles long and passes by 21 waterfalls. It's called the Falls Trail, for obvious reasons, and it's accessible from several parking areas. The Lake Rose parking lot, at the end of a dirt road across from the park's campground, provides the closest access but fills up quickly. The less convenient options are the beach parking lots and a lot on Route 118 about two miles east of the town of Red Rock. It's a challenging trail: often rocky, sometimes slippery, and damn steep here and there. You can skip the lower section, trimming the trek to 3.2 miles, and still see most of the waterfalls.

Hiking isn't the only draw. The 245-acre Lake Jean allows for swimming and **boating** (electric motors only) in the warmer months and year-round **fishing.** Boat rentals are available in the summer. **Hunting** and trapping are allowed on more than 10,000 acres of the park, which abuts some 83,000 acres of state game lands. That adds up to a helluva lot of deer, beaver, bear, coyote, and other critters. **Horseback riding** is permitted on certain trails and roads within the park. **Braces Stables** (62 Jamison City Rd., Benton, 570/925-5253, www.bracesstables.com), just outside the park, offers one- to two-hour trail rides for a reasonable $35-50 per person. In winter Ricketts Glen attracts cross-country skiers, snowshoers, snowmobilers, and ice climbers.

The park has a modern **campground** with 120 tent and trailer sites, some of which are available year-round. More than half are on a peninsula extending into Lake Jean. Ten modern cabins can be rented year-round. Reserve online at www.pa.reserveworld.com or by calling 888/727-2757.

Ricketts Glen State Park

ENTERTAINMENT AND EVENTS

Concert Venues

Toyota Pavilion at Montage Mountain (1000 Montage Mountain Rd., Scranton, 570/961-9000, www.livenation.com), a partially covered amphitheater near the Montage Mountain ski area, is the area's largest concert venue. It has played host to Dave Matthews Band, James Taylor, Def Leppard, and Kanye West, among many others.

The **Mohegan Sun Arena at Casey Plaza** (255 Highland Park Blvd., Wilkes-Barre, 800/745-3000, www.mohegansunarenapa.com) is home to the Wilkes-Barre/Scranton Penguins, the American Hockey League affiliate of the Pittsburgh Penguins. Built in 1999, it's also used for everything from college graduation ceremonies to professional wrestling shows.

Performing Arts

The **Scranton Cultural Center at the Masonic Temple** (420 N. Washington Ave., Scranton, 570/346-7369, www.scrantonculturalcenter.org) is arguably the most architecturally impressive building in Scranton. Inaugurated in 1930 as the Masonic Temple and Scottish Rite Cathedral, the neo-Gothic and Romanesque structure was designed by Raymond M. Hood, also responsible for the *Chicago Tribune* building and New York's Rockefeller Center. It's still the hub of Freemasonry activity in the area, but these days it's also a venue for regional and touring performers, including Broadway companies. The stage has been graced by everyone from Yul Brynner in *The King and I* to Britney Spears.

Wilkes-Barre's premier theater is the **F.M. Kirby Center for the Performing Arts** (71 Public Square, Wilkes-Barre, 570/826-1100, www.kirbycenter.org), which opened in 1938 as a single-screen movie palace. The Art Deco theater is one of the few structures in the public square that predates 1972's Hurricane Agnes, when the Susquehanna River spilled into downtown. Bob Hope, Johnny Cash, Dizzy Gillespie, and Aretha Franklin are among the many entertainers who have graced its stage. Like the Scranton Cultural Center, it seats 1,800. The **Northeastern Pennsylvania Philharmonic** (570/270-4444, www.nepaphil.org), the only fully professional symphony in the region, regularly performs at both.

Festivals and Events

Like many cities across the country, Scranton and Wilkes-Barre shine a spotlight on their downtown arts scene one Friday a month. **First Friday Scranton** (570/565-9006, www.firstfridayscranton.com, 6pm-9pm) features exhibits and performances at dozens of galleries, restaurants, and other businesses. Wilkes-Barre holds its art walk on the third Friday of the month so as not to compete with Scranton. **Third Friday Wilkes-Barre** (www.thirdfridaywb.com, 5pm-8pm) is a more modest affair.

The **Clarks Summit Festival of Ice** (570/587-9045, www.theabingtons.org/

First Friday Scranton art exhibit

CSFestivalOfIce) is the hottest event around in February. Held over several days ending on Presidents' Day, the festival kicks off with a parade through the borough of Clarks Summit, about 15 minutes north of Scranton. Ice chips fly as chainsaw-wielding carvers transform blocks of ice into things of beauty. The festival also features live entertainment, children's activities, and the crowning of an ice prince and princess.

Scranton claims to have one of the largest St. Patrick's Day parades in the country, as measured by participants per population. More than 10,000 marchers and float riders take part in the **Scranton St. Patrick's Parade** (www.stpatparade.com, weekend before St. Patrick's Day), which starts in front of St. Peter's Cathedral on Wyoming Avenue after a special mass and a two-mile foot race along the parade route. St. Peter's hosts a mass in Italian during the city's other marquee ethnic celebration, **La Festa Italiana** (www.lafestaitaliana.org, Labor Day weekend). The three-day celebration features food, continuous live entertainment, and more food.

SPORTS AND RECREATION
Montage Mountain

Scranton's ski facility is much improved since coming under private ownership in 2006. Previously county-owned, **Montage Mountain** (1000 Montage Mountain Rd., Scranton, 570/969-7669, www.montagemountainresorts.com, all-day lift ticket $50-59, children 6-18 $35-45, all-day equipment rental $26-35, snow tubing $15-20 per 3-hour session) now boasts more than 20 skiing trails, two terrain parks, a snow tubing park, a new rental and retail shop, a freshly renovated food area—and an outdoor **water park.** (The water park, of course, is a summertime attraction.) It offers a variety of lift tickets, including morning and evening tickets that will save you quite a bit of money if you don't plan to spend more than a few hours on the slopes.

Montage Mountain's winter-themed water park is open Memorial Day-Labor Day.

Attractions include a wave pool, a lazy river, a funnel-shaped tube ride called Tundra Tornado, and the eight-lane Iceberg Alley Luge, which pits friends against each other in a head-first race toward the finish line. If you're not in the mood to get wet, there are batting cages, an 18-hole miniature golf course, sand volleyball courts, and a zip line.

Elk Mountain

About 30 miles north of Scranton, **Elk Mountain** (344 Elk Mountain Rd., Union Dale, 570/679-4400, www.elkskier.com, all-day lift ticket $56-68, seniors and children 6-12 $43-51, beginners lift ticket $30-35, all-day equipment rental $27-36) offers some of the most challenging terrain in Pennsylvania. Its tag line: "It's like skiing in Vermont without the drive." Because of its remoteness, Elk is generally less crowded than Montage Mountain and more southerly ski areas such as Blue Mountain and Camelback. Unlike the rest, it doesn't offer snow tubing.

In addition to all-day tickets good from 8:30am to 10pm, Elk offers a variety of cheaper tickets for narrower time frames. Skiers and snowboarders who just can't get enough can save with two-day tickets. Check Elk's website for a list of nearby hotels and inns. Best of the bunch: **Fern Hall Inn** (Rte. 247, Clifford, 570/222-3676, www.fernhallinn.com, $150-190), a handsome B&B and restaurant on 117 lakefront acres. Ask the exceedingly gracious staff to arrange for a horse-drawn carriage ride during your stay.

Spectator Sports

In 2006 the New York Yankees ended a 28-year relationship with a minor league baseball team in Ohio, naming the Scranton/Wilkes-Barre Red Barons as their new Triple-A affiliate. Sales of Red Barons tickets shot through the roof. Now known as the **Scranton/Wilkes-Barre RailRiders** (PNC Field, 235 Montage Mountain Rd., Moosic, 570/969-2255, www.swbrailriders.com), the team has advanced to the playoffs almost every year since.

The American Hockey League's **Wilkes-Barre/Scranton Penguins** (Mohegan Sun Arena at Casey Plaza, 255 Highland Park Blvd., Wilkes-Barre, 570/208-7367, www.wbspenguins.com) are the farm team to the Pittsburgh Penguins. That's why they're affectionately known as the "Baby Penguins."

ACCOMMODATIONS
Under $100

Wilkes-Barre's **Econo Lodge Arena** (1075 Wilkes-Barre Twp. Blvd., Wilkes-Barre, 570/823-0600, www.econolodge.com, $64-110) is a gem as budget hotels go. Its parent company has heaped accolades on the pet-friendly (and very people-friendly) property just off I-81. Rooms are equipped with coffeemakers, microwaves, and refrigerators. Coffee, breakfast, weekday newspapers, and wireless Internet access are complimentary.

$100-200

Scranton's most opulent hotel was once a passenger train station. Built in 1908, the Neoclassical knockout features a breathtaking lobby with a mosaic tile floor, marble walls and columns, and a barrel-vaulted stained glass ceiling. Indeed, the ★ **Radisson Lackawanna Station Hotel** (700 Lackawanna Ave., Scranton, 570/342-8300, www.radisson.com/scrantonpa, $90-250) wouldn't look out of place in a city on the world stage. It's an ideal base for exploring this one. Steamtown National Historic Site is just steps away. The Anthracite Heritage Museum, Lackawanna Coal Mine Tour, and Everhart Museum are among the attractions within a short drive. You don't need to leave the six-story hotel to enjoy a good meal. It's home to an acclaimed restaurant, **Carmen's 2.0,** and the more casual **Trax Platform Lounge** (11am-midnight daily, bar open until 2am Fri.-Sat.), where you can watch for trains as you sip a martini.

The opulent choice in the heart of Wilkes-Barre is **The Frederick Stegmaier Mansion** (304 S. Franklin St., Wilkes-Barre, 570/823-9372, www.stegmaiermansion.com,

$135-200), a brewmaster's house turned B&B and house museum. "Stegmaier" is synonymous with suds in this northeast Pennsylvania city. The Stegmaier family produced award-winning brews for more than a century before selling its eponymous brand to another local brewer in 1974. (Just about anyone in Wilkes-Barre can point you to the stately Stegmaier brewery, which has been converted into an office building.) The lavishly decorated 1870 mansion landed a 15-page spread in *Victorian Homes* magazine in 2010. It has four guest rooms and suites, each with a private bath and kitchenette.

Less than a mile from Mohegan Sun at Pocono Downs, **The Woodlands Inn** (1073 Rte. 315, Wilkes-Barre, 570/824-9831, www.thewoodlandsresort.com, $110-280) is an excellent choice if you're in town to try your luck. (It was good enough for Grammy winners LeAnn Rimes and Peter Frampton when they played the "racino.") The family-owned hotel has 150 modernly furnished rooms and suites and a host of amenities. Most famous of its amenities: a 17,000-gallon hot tub said to be one of the largest on the East Coast. Business travelers make up the bulk of the guests on weekdays, but it's a different scene on weekends. With its smoky dance club and indoor and outdoor bars, the hotel has a well-deserved reputation as party central. Other amenities include indoor and outdoor pools, two restaurants, and **Alexander's in the Woods** (570/208-1478), a salon and spa. In summer Alexander's offers alfresco massages and pedis.

FOOD
Scranton Area

The Electric City's most critically acclaimed restaurant is found in the magnificent marble-drenched lobby of the Radisson Lackawanna Station Hotel, built in 1908 as a passenger train station. ★ **Carmen's 2.0** (700 Lackawanna Ave., Scranton, 570/558-3929, www.carmensradisson.com, breakfast 6:30am-11am Mon.-Sat. and 6:30am-9:30am Sun., brunch 10am-2pm Sun., lunch

11:30am-2pm Mon.-Fri., dinner 5pm-10pm Mon.-Sat., breakfast under $10, Sun. brunch $27 for adults and $15 for children 12 and under, lunch buffet $13, dinner $19-37) attracts all-you-can-eat enthusiasts with its lunch and Sunday brunch buffets. Its dinner menu features pasta, steak, and seafood dishes—some available in half portions for lighter appetites.

Like the Neoclassical landmark that houses Carmen's, **Stirna's Restaurant & Bar** (120 W. Market St., Scranton, 570/961-9681, www.stirnas.com, 4pm-11pm Tues.-Thurs., 4pm-midnight Fri.-Sat., $7-20) has been around for more than a century. Locals of all ages come here for home-style cooking and friendly service. The "Stirnaburger," a quarter pound of ground beef cooked to order and topped with bacon, is a real crowd-pleaser, but nothing outsells the signature brownie. Whiskey sours are a house specialty.

There are a couple of dining gems a few miles north of Scranton. **Formosa** (727 S. State St., Clarks Summit, 570/585-1902, www.formosa570.com, from 5pm Mon.-Sat., $11-28) offers exquisite Asian fusion cuisine. The ingredients are fresh as can be, the curry dishes are mild and richly flavored, the waiters are quirky, and there's rarely a wait. Beloved by young professionals, **Blu Wasabi** (1008 Scranton Carbondale Hwy., Dickson City, 570/307-3282, 4:30pm-9pm Mon.-Thurs., 4:30pm-10pm Fri.-Sat., $20-50) offers "fine Japanese cuisine" and a degree of hipness uncommon in coal country. Its artfully prepared specialty rolls taste as good as they look, and its steaks are among the best in the area.

Wilkes-Barre Area

Downtown Wilkes-Barre has several recommendable restaurants. Hippest of the bunch is **Rodano's** (53 Public Square, Wilkes-Barre, 570/829-6444, www.rodanos.com, 11am-10pm Mon.-Wed., 11am-11pm Thurs., 11am-2am Fri.-Sat., 11am-9pm Sun., $7-15), a high-ceilinged space with a menu teetering between casual American and Italian fare.

Long bar tables that seat up to 12 lend to the sociable vibe of the place, which attracts families and professionals by day and college kids and other party-ready sorts by night. DJs coax revelers onto the dance floor on Friday and Saturday nights. Nearby **Cafe Toscana** (1 Public Square, Wilkes-Barre, 570/208-1252, www.cafetoscanarestaurant.com, 11:30am-10pm Mon.-Fri., 5pm-10pm Sat., $9-23) offers a more buttoned-down dining experience, white tablecloths and all. True to its name, the restaurant specializes in the light, delicate cuisine of northern Italy. The wine list is heavy on Italian reds. Save room for the ricotta cheesecake, limoncello truffle, or another house-made dessert.

For the best sushi in town—and the best hibachi in northeast Pennsylvania—head to **Katana** (41 S. Main St., Wilkes-Barre, 570/825-9080, www.katanawb.com, lunch 11:30am-2:30pm Tues.-Fri., dinner 5pm-9:30pm Tues.-Thurs., 5pm-10pm Fri.-Sat., 5pm-9pm Sun., $10-30). The owners hail from Japan and take pride in delivering an authentic Japanese experience, bento boxes and all. It's a great place for a celebration with family or friends; the hibachi tables seat 12 and can be pushed together for even larger parties. Watch chefs slice, dice, and sear your hibachi meal to perfection, or have a seat at the sushi bar for a different display of culinary artistry. The bar features one of the largest selections of single malts in the region.

Cross the Susquehanna River for home-style Greek cuisine in a whimsical setting. ★ **Theo's Metro** (596 Mercer Ave., Kingston, 570/283-2050, www.theosmetrorestaurant.com, 11am-10pm daily, lunch under $10, dinner $11-26) opened in 2001 in what used to be a popcorn factory, and it's decorated with the detritus of the corn-popping trade. Hand-painted tables, floor-to-ceiling murals, water features, and a mini golf course—yes, inside the restaurant—add to the delightfully offbeat ambience. The menu includes burgers, a chicken cheesesteak, and other American fare, but you'd be a fool to

Pizza Capital of the World

Leaving the Scranton/Wilkes-Barre region without sampling **Old Forge pizza** is like leaving Philadelphia without sampling a cheesesteak: just *wrong*. A town of about 8,300, Old Forge is the self-proclaimed "Pizza Capital of the World." That's a tall claim, but anyone who's driven down Main Street, Old Forge, is inclined to buy it. It's pizza joint after pizza joint after pizza joint. There are at least a dozen on Main Street alone and more within a few blocks — so many in such close proximity that even New Yorkers and Chicagoans wouldn't begrudge Old Forge its title.

It's not clear how pizza became the trademark of a town formerly associated with anthracite coal. Quizzing locals about causal factors is about as fruitful as pumping pizzeria owners for their cheese blend. This much we know: The anthracite industry attracted many Italians to this corner of the world. They brought their cuisine. It sells.

Old Forge pizza isn't your average pizza. Instead of round "pies," pizzerias here specialize in rectangular "trays." Servings are referred to not as "slices" but as "cuts." White pizza is also a specialty, as is double-crust pizza.

Among the veterans of the bunch is **Ghigiarelli's Restaurant** (511 S. Main St., 570/457-2652, 4pm-10pm Tues.-Thurs., 3pm-11pm Fri.-Sat.). According to local lore, Old Forge-style pizza owes its shape to a certain Mrs. Ghigiarelli, who grabbed a rectangular baking pan and made pizza to feed a bunch of card-playing coal miners many decades ago. Former Secretary of State Hillary Clinton tucked into a cut at **Revello's** (502 S. Main St., 570/457-9843, www.revellos.com, 11am-11pm Mon.-Sat., noon-10pm Sun.), which dates to the 1960s. **Arcaro & Genell** (443 S. Main St., 570/457-5555, www.arcarongenell.com, lunch from 11am daily, dinner 3pm-11pm Mon.-Sat.) serves a lot more than pizza. Start with the portobello stuffed with crabmeat and finish with an espresso. You can't go wrong with the house-made pasta or the white pizza topped with tomato slices and onions. A 1983 *USA Today* article on the nation's best pizzas hangs by the front door. "Crust eater's heaven," the writer calls Old Forge.

Given the number of pizzerias, you'd think getting a table would be easy. Not always. They tend to be crowded on Thursday, Friday, and Saturday evenings. Here's a strategy endorsed by one local: Send members of your party to different pizzerias. Have your cell phones handy. Whoever gets seated first can phone the others.

Old Forge is about five miles southwest of downtown Scranton. Scranton's Main Avenue eventually becomes Main Street, Old Forge. If traveling south on I-81, take exit 182B and turn right onto Davis Street. If traveling north on 81, take exit 182 and turn left onto Davis. Continue to Main Street in the town of Taylor and turn left. Follow Main Street for about a mile and a half to the Pizza Capital.

pass up Greek specialties like moussaka, spinach pie, stuffed grape leaves, and *youvetsi* (lamb in a clay pot with orzo pasta, tomato sauce, and parmesan cheese). Add a touch of drama to dinner by starting with the *saganaki* (imported Greek cheese dipped in batter, lightly fried, and flamed tableside with ouzo). The eatery boasts a full bar and a martini list that's as long as the River Styx.

INFORMATION

Scranton and Wilkes-Barre are the county seats of Lackawanna County and Luzerne County, respectively. The **Lackawanna County Convention & Visitors Bureau** (99 Glenmaura National Blvd., Moosic, 570/963-6363, www.visitnepa.org, 9am-5pm daily) has a large information center just a couple of minutes from Montage Mountain and PNC Field. The on-site gift shop carries merchandise made locally or related to the area's heritage—everything from locally roasted coffee to coal miners' hats. The **Luzerne County Convention & Visitors Bureau** (56 Public Square, Wilkes-Barre, 888/905-2872, www.tournepa.com, 8:30am-5pm Mon.-Fri.) has its smallish headquarters in the heart of Wilkes-Barre. Visit their websites to request free copies of their respective visitors guides.

GETTING THERE AND AROUND

Scranton and Wilkes-Barre are about 120 miles north of Philadelphia via I-476 and 120 miles west of New York City via I-80. **Wilkes-Barre/Scranton International Airport** (AVP, 570/602-2000, www.flyavp.com) is served by United Airlines, US Airways, Delta, and the low-cost carrier Allegiant. There's no passenger train service to the region. Contact **Greyhound** (800/231-2222, www.greyhound.com) for information on arriving by bus. Scranton's public transportation provider is the **County of Lackawanna Transit System** (570/346-2061, www.coltsbus.com). Wilkes-Barre's is the **Luzerne County Transportation Authority** (570/288-9356, www.lctabus.com).

Pittsburgh

Look for ★ to find recommended sights, activities, dining, and lodging.

Highlights

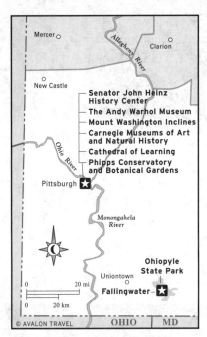

★ **The Andy Warhol Museum:** It's perhaps not surprising that a museum dedicated to one of the best-known and most provocative artists of all time could make you say "Wow!" (page 266).

★ **Mount Washington Inclines:** You just don't visit Pittsburgh without climbing aboard a cable car at the Monongahela or Duquesne Incline. You just don't (page 272).

★ **Carnegie Museums of Art and Natural History:** Born of industrialist Andrew Carnegie's largess, the conjoined museums have grown into international sensations (page 278).

★ **Cathedral of Learning:** The facade of this architectural paean to higher education is mighty impressive, but what's inside is unique in all the world (page 279).

★ **Phipps Conservatory and Botanical Gardens:** Pittsburgh's "crystal palace" is as magical as its nickname suggests (page 281).

★ **Ohiopyle State Park:** This gorgeous expanse offers some of the best white-water boating in the eastern United States, plus access to the Great Allegheny Passage rail-trail (page 318).

★ **Fallingwater:** Sure, it's an hour's drive from the city, but Frank Lloyd Wright's masterpiece is worth crossing an ocean to see. Lots of people do (page 319).

★ **Senator John Heinz History Center:** Gain a new appreciation for southwestern Pennsylvania at the state's largest history museum. Betcha didn't know the Big Mac was born here (page 264).

Ask people what they think when they hear "Pittsburgh," and they're liable to answer "steel." What they're picturing is the Pittsburgh of old, a place nicknamed "Smoky City" and described in an 1868 magazine article as "hell with the lid taken off." That image is about as current as petticoats. The city that celebrated its 250th birthday in 2008 is no longer an industrial powerhouse but rather a manicured seat of culture. Its lush parks, rehabilitated rivers, world-class museums, and magical skyline inspire accolades from even the most cosmopolitan of visitors. A writer for *The New Yorker* who visited in 1990 called it one of the three most beautiful cities in the world, along with Paris and St. Petersburg, Russia. "If Pittsburgh were situated somewhere in the heart of Europe," he wrote, "tourists would eagerly journey hundreds of miles out of their way to visit it."

Pittsburgh is a work in progress. Something is always being knocked down. Something bigger is always rising. That has led to a good amount of grumbling about high taxes and superfluous government spending, but tourism is all the better for it. The past few years have seen the addition of a riverfront casino, an African American culture center, and a spanking-new hockey arena, among other big-ticket attractions. Not everything is made from scratch. Shuttered factories, abandoned warehouses, obsolete railyards, and even churches have been repurposed. The Cork Factory doesn't cut corks these days. It's a luxury apartment complex. The opulent Grand Concourse at Station Square isn't a railroad terminal. It's a seafood restaurant. The "Burgh" will make you a believer in reincarnation.

If you're coming from the international airport, your tour begins when you emerge from the tunnels bored through Mount Washington. The feast laid out before you—rivers, bridges, and uncommonly shaped buildings—has placed Pittsburgh near the top of best-skyline lists. The city is famous for its hills, too. You need only scan the names of its 90 neighborhoods to understand the topography: Brighton Heights, Highland Park, Southside Slopes, Squirrel

---

Previous: one of Pittsburgh's inclines descending Mount Washington; The Andy Warhol Museum; Ohiopyle State Park. **Above:** Pittsburgh Pirates game.

Pittsburgh

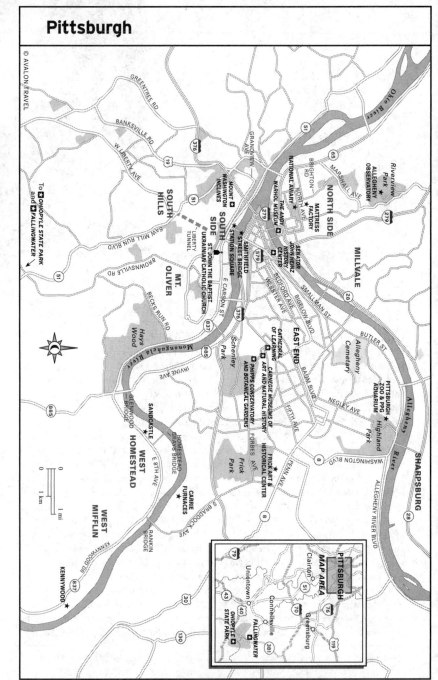

Hill. Exploring them is both anthropology and exercise.

Leave time for the countryside. You'll find Amish communities to Pittsburgh's north and a huge concentration of covered bridges to its south. In the Laurel Highlands region, southeast of the city, you'll find the state's largest ski resort, highest mountain, largest cave, and most decorated restaurant. You'll also find three houses by Frank Lloyd Wright, America's favorite architect.

Pittsburgh is working overtime to shake its outdated image. It may one day succeed in attracting large numbers of new residents and droves of tourists. In the meantime, be glad it's underrated. You can have your run of the place. You can squeeze into any hot spot save for Heinz Field, where the winningest team in Super Bowl history plays. You can dine without a reservation at just about any restaurant. You can shop without shoving. But hurry. This offer may not last for long.

PLANNING YOUR TIME

The city has enough cultural and historical attractions to keep intensely curious types busy for well over a week, but it's possible to hit the highlights in three days. Oakland, a couple of miles east of Downtown, is a good place to start. Spend a few hours exploring the Carnegie Museums of Art and Natural History before sitting down to lunch at a Craig Street eatery or, if the weather's nice, in Schenley Plaza. Afterward, take a tour around the world in the magnificent Cathedral of Learning. Its Nationality Rooms are open until 4pm. You'll still have time to marvel at the specimens at Phipps Conservatory, the "crystal palace" in Schenley Park. Cross the Hot Metal Bridge for dinner on the South Side and stick around to see why East Carson Street is considered Pittsburgh's nightlife capital.

Devote the following day to the North Side, where the Pittsburgh Steelers and Pirates play. It's home to the National Aviary, The Andy Warhol Museum, and the Mattress Factory, a renowned installation museum. If you're traveling with kids, you'll have to prioritize. The Carnegie Science Center and Children's Museum of Pittsburgh can also be found there. Drive or, better yet, walk across one of the "Three Sisters" bridges into Downtown for dinner. Try to catch a show or concert in the Cultural District. Alternatively, stay on the North Side and try to beat the odds at the Rivers Casino, one of Pittsburgh's newest attractions.

First thing in the morning, find your way

a view of downtown Pittsburgh

to the Strip District, the mile-long neighborhood adjacent to Downtown. Have breakfast at Pamela's, then wander in and out of the specialty foods markets along Penn Avenue. Load up on hard-to-find ingredients and impossible-to-resist delicacies. You can learn what's so special about Pittsburgh at the Heinz History Center, located at the western end of the Strip.

You've saved the best for last. Head toward Station Square on the south shore of the Monongahela River, climb into a cable car at the base of Mount Washington, and ascend to its crest for knock-your-socks-off views of the city. The skyline is particularly dazzling after dark, so have dinner or a cocktail at Station Square or on Mount Washington's Restaurant Row if you arrive earlier.

If you can devote more than three days to the city, get off dry land for a spell. Take a cruise on a Gateway Clipper riverboat or, during the warmer months, set off from Kayak Pittsburgh's base on the North Shore.

Pittsburgh is swell and all, but seriously consider skipping town for a day or two to explore its surrounds. First stop: Frank Lloyd Wright's Fallingwater.

Sights

DOWNTOWN AND THE STRIP DISTRICT

Downtown Pittsburgh, aka the Golden Triangle, sits at the confluence of the Allegheny and Monongahela Rivers, which join to form the Ohio River. The arrowhead-shaped neighborhood has a storied past, which visitors can explore at the Fort Pitt Museum and Senator John Heinz History Center. Today it's the city's financial center, home to corporations including H.J. Heinz Company and PNC Financial Services Group Inc. Like many business districts, it's sleepy most weekday nights. But it comes alive on weekends, when Pittsburghers and visitors flock to its performance venues and upscale eateries.

The Strip District extends from 11th Street to 33rd Street, hugging the Allegheny River the whole way. Its name implies commerce of the red-light variety, but "the Strip" was and remains a center of sanctioned trade. In

the fountain at Point State Park

the 19th century, mills and factories mushroomed along the river. In the early part of the 20th, the Strip became the hub of Pittsburgh's wholesale produce industry. These days the mile-long neighborhood is famous for its specialty foods markets. It's also home to diverse restaurants and bars.

Point State Park

It's hard to believe that the green oasis at the tip of the Pittsburgh peninsula was once a brownfield site. Completed in the mid-1970s, as the local steel industry was beginning to implode, **Point State Park** (601 Commonwealth Place, 412/565-2850, www.visitpaparks.com) is a symbol of the city's renaissance. As the only large public park in Downtown, it's a frequent site of festivals and concerts and a great place to picnic or sunbathe on a summer day. In 2013 Pittsburghers celebrated the reopening of its iconic fountain after four years of renovation. The central column of water soars to a height of 150 feet, making it visible from main entry points to the city.

The Point, as locals call it, is steeped in history. In 1753, Lieutenant George Washington of the Virginia militia advised that the British establish an outpost there to gain command of the rivers. Alas, the French also had their eye on the strategic spot. In 1754 they chased away a force of Virginians who'd built a weak stockade and proceeded to build a fort they called Duquesne. Britain's attempts to retake control failed until November 1758, when the French burned their fort and fled two days before the arrival of a massive army led by General John Forbes. Upon his arrival, Forbes ordered the construction of a new fort, naming it after British Secretary of State William Pitt. The settlement around Fort Pitt became "Pittsburgh." (The current spelling appeared in the 1816 city charter.)

A re-created bastion houses the **Fort Pitt Museum** (101 Commonwealth Place, 412/281-9284, www.heinzhistorycenter.org, 10am-5pm daily, admission $6, seniors $5, students and children 6-17 $3), which tells the story of the French and Indian War. Exhibits also speak to the ensuing hostilities between the British victors and Native Americans. Kids tend to gravitate toward the trader's cabin with its assortment of animal pelts. A costumed guide explains how Native Americans purchased everything from mirrors to muskets with buckskins and other furry currency.

The nearby **Fort Pitt Block House** (412/471-1764, 10:30am-4:30pm Wed.-Sun. Apr.-Oct., 10:30am-4:30pm Fri.-Sun. Nov.-Mar., free) is the only original fort structure and the oldest building in Pittsburgh. It was constructed in 1764 to help protect the fort from possible attacks by Native Americans. Eventually it was repurposed as a dwelling. Neville Craig, Pittsburgh's first historian, was born there in 1787. In 1894 the property was transferred to the Daughters of the American Revolution, who blocked it from destruction by the Pennsylvania Railroad and preserve it to this day. Its stone foundation, brick walls, ceiling beams, and roof rafters are original, as are the gun loops through which soldiers aimed their muskets.

Mellon Square and Vicinity

Downtown boasts a number of distinctive buildings, ranging from the old and ornate to the modern and sleek. Architecture buffs would be wise to contact the **Pittsburgh History & Landmarks Foundation** (412/471-5808, www.phlf.org), which organizes free walking tours led by guides who know their Flemish Gothic from their Georgian Classical. One good place to begin a self-guided tour is Mellon Square on Smithfield Street between Oliver and 6th Avenues. When the weather is good, Downtown workers crowd the plaza's terrazzo walks and granite benches. There's no bad seat in the house, but the best face the 1916 **Omni William Penn Hotel** (530 William Penn Place, 412/281-7100, www.omnihotels.com). The oldest hotel in the city underwent a renovation in 2004 to the tune of $22 million, and many of its original features were restored. Its

Downtown, Strip District, and North Side

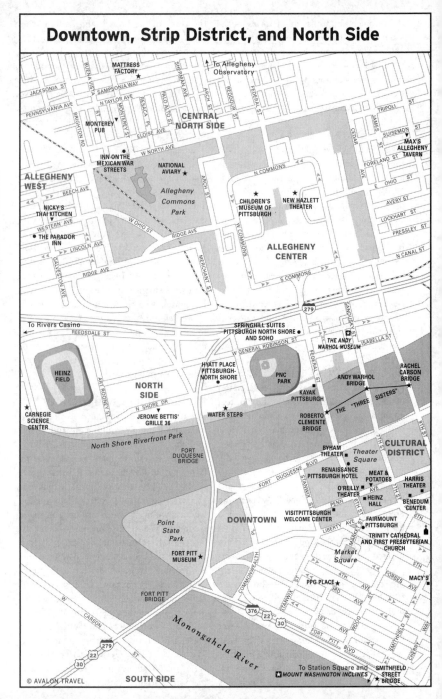

MATTRESS FACTORY ★
To Allegheny Observatory

JACKSONIA ST
BUENA VISTA
SAMPSONIA WAY
SHERMAN AVE
ARCH ST
REDDOUR ST
FEDERAL ST
JAMES ST
TRIPOLI ST

PENNSYLVANIA AVE
N TAYLOR AVE
RESACA PL
PALO ALTO ST
CEDAR AVE
SUISEMON ST

BRIGHTON RD
N MONTEREY ST
ELOISE AVE
CENTRAL NORTH SIDE
FORELAND ST
E OHIO ST

MONTEREY PUB ▼
W NORTH AVE
NATIONAL AVIARY ★
N COMMONS
MAX'S ALLEGHENY TAVERN ★

INN ON THE MEXICAN WAR STREETS ●
AVERY ST

ALLEGHENY WEST
BEECH AVE
Allegheny Commons Park
CHILDREN'S MUSEUM OF PITTSBURGH ★
NEW HAZLETT THEATER ★
LOCKHART ST

NICKY'S THAI KITCHEN ▼
WESTERN AVE
W OHIO ST
ARCH ST
RIDGE AVE
W COMMONS
ALLEGHENY CENTER
PRESSLEY ST

● THE PARADOR INN
LINCOLN AVE
GALVESTON AVE
N CANAL ST

RIDGE AVE
MERCHANT ST
S COMMONS

279

To Rivers Casino
REEDSDALE ST
SPRINGHILL SUITES PITTSBURGH NORTH SHORE AND SOHO ●
SANDUSKY ST
ISABELLA ST
THE ANDY WARHOL MUSEUM

HEINZ FIELD
ART ROONEY AVE
W GENERAL ROBINSON ST
HYATT PLACE PITTSBURGH-NORTH SHORE ●
PNC PARK
FEDERAL ST
ANDY WARHOL BRIDGE
RACHEL CARSON BRIDGE ★

NORTH SIDE
N SHORE DR
JEROME BETTIS' GRILLE 36 ▼
KAYAK PITTSBURGH ●
THE "THREE SISTERS"
9TH ST

★ CARNEGIE SCIENCE CENTER
WATER STEPS ★
ROBERTO CLEMENTE BRIDGE ★

North Shore Riverfront Park
CULTURAL DISTRICT

FORT DUQUESNE BRIDGE
BYHAM THEATER ■
Theater Square
7TH ST
HARRIS THEATER ■

RENAISSANCE PITTSBURGH HOTEL ■
MEAT & POTATOES ■
8TH ST

Point State Park
FORT DUQUESNE BLVD
O'REILLY THEATER ■
PENN AVE
HEINZ HALL ■
BENEDUM CENTER ■

STANWIX ST
VISITPITTSBURGH WELCOME CENTER ■
LIBERTY AVE
FAIRMONT PITTSBURGH ■

DOWNTOWN
6TH AVE
MARKET ST
TRINITY CATHEDRAL AND FIRST PRESBYTERIAN CHURCH ✝

FORT PITT MUSEUM ★
COMMONWEALTH PL
Market Square
MACY'S ■

PPG PLACE ★
4TH AVE
3RD AVE
FORBES AVE
SMITHFIELD ST

FORT PITT BRIDGE
STANWIX ST
WOOD ST
1ST AVE
FORT PITT BLVD
CHERRY WAY

W CARSON ST
376 22 30
22 30
279

Monongahela River

To Station Square and ✚ MOUNT WASHINGTON INCLINES
SMITHFIELD STREET BRIDGE ★

SOUTH SIDE

© AVALON TRAVEL

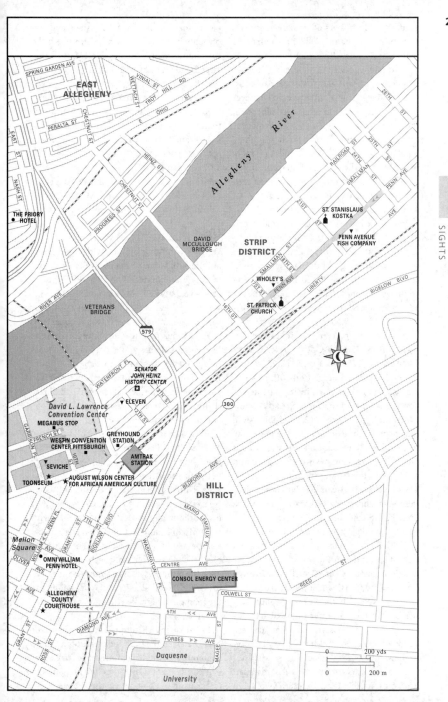

grand facade whispers of crystal chandeliers and leather armchairs. (You'll find both in the main lobby, along with a grand piano.)

Also flanking Mellon Square is a 31-story skyscraper known as the **Alcoa Building** (425 6th Ave.). Aluminum was used wherever possible when industry giant Alcoa Inc. built the slender tower in 1953. The company relocated to Pittsburgh's North Shore neighborhood in 1998, and today the building is more properly called the Regional Enterprise Tower.

Walk northwest on 6th Avenue for a gander at the **Duquesne Club** (325 6th Ave., 412/391-1500, www.duquesne.org), the Romanesque home of Pittsburgh's oldest private club. Founded in 1873, it welcomed the captains of industry whose names still grace so many Pittsburgh buildings. The current clubhouse, which opened in 1890 and didn't admit women until 1980, was dubbed "the citadel of Pittsburgh tycoonery" by *Time* magazine in 1940.

Across the street are two churches designed in the English Gothic style. **Trinity Cathedral** (328 6th Ave., 412/232-6404, www.trinitycathedralpgh.org) with its striking steeple was dedicated in 1872. Its neighbor, the twin-towered **First Presbyterian Church** (320 6th Ave., 412/471-3436, www.fpcp.org), is three decades younger and the third church to be built on this site. All but one of its nave windows were designed and produced by the Tiffany Studios in New York. The graveyard between the churches is older than both churches. Native Americans, the French, the British, and American settlers buried their dead here in the 18th century.

In the late 1800s, before skyscrapers started sprouting in Pittsburgh, the skyline was dominated by the **Allegheny County Courthouse** (436 Grant St.), located on Grant Street between 5th and Forbes Avenues. It's still one of the city's most impressive buildings. The courthouse and adjacent jail were designed by Boston architect Henry Hobson Richardson, whose style was so distinctive that it got its own name: Richardsonian Romanesque. He died in 1886, two years before the courthouse was finished, and reportedly had this to say on his deathbed: "If they honor me for the pygmy things I have already done, what will they say when they see Pittsburgh finished?" Quite a lot, in fact. The granite complex with its theatrical towers, turrets, columns, and arches has won more than a few design awards. The jail was closed in 1995 and later repurposed as a court building. A portion of a cellblock was preserved, and you can learn about prison life with a carefully timed visit. The **Jail Museum** (440 Ross St.) is open 11:30am-1pm Mondays from February through October.

PPG Place

Downtown is chockablock with impressive buildings, but none so impressive as the shimmering glass complex known as **PPG Place** (4th Ave. between Stanwix and Wood Sts., www.ppgplace.com). Finished in 1984 at a cost of $200 million, the world headquarters of PPG Industries (formerly the Pittsburgh Plate Glass Company) is a glass-skinned castle complete with neo-Gothic spires—231 of them. Some call it modern; others insist it's postmodern. Regardless, it makes Pittsburgh's skyline instantly recognizable even if you crop out the rivers and bridges.

PPG Place is composed of six buildings: the 40-story One PPG Place, the 14-story Six PPG Place, and four six-story buildings. Standing between them is an otherworldly experience. Think Superman's Fortress of Solitude. Images dance across the glass panes, making for a unique photo with every click. Nearly one million square feet of PPG-made reflective glass went into the facades. The purpose of all that glass is not only aesthetic; it helps keep the buildings cool in summer and cozy in winter. You'll also find glass paneling in the lobbies and cracked glass mirrors in the elevators.

From spring through fall, the one-acre plaza between the buildings features a granite fountain with 140 columns of water. Come winter, the plaza transforms into an outdoor ice skating rink—part of the reason why

PPG Place has been likened to New York's Rockefeller Center. **The Rink at PPG Place** (412/394-3641, admission $7, seniors $6, children 12 and under $6, skate rental $3) is open from mid-November through early March. If you're visiting between mid-November and early January, be sure to pop into the glass-enclosed **Wintergarden** (One PPG Place) for a look at the holiday exhibits.

August Wilson Center for African American Culture

Opened in 2009 after more than a decade of planning, the **August Wilson Center** (980 Liberty Ave., 412/258-2700, www.august-wilsoncenter.org, 11am-6pm Tues.-Sat., free admission) is part museum and part performing arts facility. Its core exhibition, *Pittsburgh: Reclaim Renew Remix*, features an interactive tool that allows visitors to create video collages celebrating the region's black heritage. Changing exhibits are found throughout the 65,000-square-foot building, an ultramodern composition of metal, stone, and glass on a triangular site. At the center of it all is a 486-seat theater. The August Wilson Center, which functioned as a presenting arts organization for several years before it had a home of its own, has brought the likes of filmmaker

Spike Lee, the Alvin Ailey American Dance Theater, and Grammy-winning gospel singer CeCe Winans to Pittsburgh. Its namesake, one of the 20th century's most celebrated playwrights, grew up in the Hill District, just east of Downtown. August Wilson (1945-2005) is best known for a 10-play series often referred to as the Pittsburgh Cycle. Each play depicts African American life in a different decade of the 1900s, and all but one are set in the Hill District, once known as a hotbed of jazz. Wilson won Pulitzer Prizes for *Fences* and *The Piano Lesson* and was the first African American to have two plays running on Broadway at the same time.

ToonSeum

One of only a handful of museums dedicated to the cartoon arts, the **ToonSeum** (945 Liberty Ave., 412/232-0199, www.toonseum. org, 10am-5pm daily except Tues., suggested admission $6, seniors and students $5, children 6-12 $3) relocated from its original home in the Children's Museum of Pittsburgh to a storefront across from the August Wilson Center in 2009. The move opened the door for exhibits of more provocative works. Fear not, Mickey Mouse fans. America's favorite rodent and other beloved characters such as Snoopy,

PPG Place

Superman, and SpongeBob SquarePants still have places of honor at the ToonSeum, which changes exhibits every two months. Jean Schulz, widow of Snoopy creator Charles M. Schulz, was one of its earliest supporters. Bit by the cartooning bug? The museum offers cartooning classes for kids and adults.

★ Senator John Heinz History Center

The **Senator John Heinz History Center** (1212 Smallman St., 412/454-6000, www.heinzhistorycenter.org, 10am-5pm daily, Library & Archives 10am-5pm Wed.-Sat. or by appointment, admission $15, seniors $13, students and children 6-17 $6), a six-floor former icehouse that stretches a city block in the Strip District, is the largest history museum in Pennsylvania. It tackles 250 years of Pittsburgh history, from the pre-Revolutionary period to present day. The Smithsonian-affiliated museum is anything but stuffy. It's a family-friendly medley of artifacts, artwork, audiovisual programs, and interactive exhibits. Long-term exhibitions include *Clash of Empires,* which examines the French and Indian War; *From Slavery to Freedom,* which examines the history of slavery and abolitionism; and *Heinz 57,* a tribute to the king of condiments. A two-story exhibition trumpets Pittsburgh's contributions to the world, which include the Ferris wheel and the polio vaccine.

Sports junkies can get a fix at the **Western Pennsylvania Sports Museum,** a museum within the museum that celebrates the home runs, touchdowns, goals, and other proud moments of the region's athletes. If "Immaculate Reception" means nothing to you, this is the place to go for a primer in Pittsburgh sports lore.

Saints in the Strip

Two Strip District churches warrant a respectful walkabout: **St. Patrick** (17th St. and Liberty Ave.) and **St. Stanislaus Kostka** (21st and Smallman Sts.). The former holds the distinction of being Pittsburgh's first Roman Catholic church; the latter its first ethnic Polish Catholic church. They were merged into one parish (412/471-4767, www.saintsinthestrip.org) in 1993, after decades of population shift to the suburbs.

Though St. Patrick dates to the early 1800s, the present church is relatively young, having been dedicated in 1936. Its courtyard offers calm and solitude of monastic proportions. The church vestibule features a replica of the Scala Sancta, or "Holy Stairs," in Rome. It's

Senator John Heinz History Center

believed that Jesus climbed the 28-step stairway on his way to trial. Only a handful of churches have replicas. At St. Patrick, as in Rome, the steps are ascended on one's knees.

The younger St. Stanislaus Kostka has an older church building. It was consecrated in 1892 and has withstood a variety of disasters. During the Great St. Patrick's Day Flood of 1936, water rose as high as the wainscoting, trapping the pastor on the second floor. Later that year, an explosion at the nearby Pittsburgh Banana Company weakened its twin bell towers, and their original bonnets had to be removed. The church's stained glass windows are a must-see. If you're lucky, you'll come on a day when parishioners are selling homemade pierogies to raise dough.

NORTH SIDE

Many of Pittsburgh's main attractions are located just north of Downtown in an area known, appropriately enough, as the North Side. The North Side has undergone a dramatic transformation over the past 15 years. The Pittsburgh Steelers and Pirates each got a new home there. In 2009, they got a new neighbor: the city's only casino. Two North Side institutions, the Children's Museum of Pittsburgh and the National Aviary, completed major expansions. And the makeover isn't over. Cross one of the bridges that link Downtown and the North Side and it shouldn't be long before you encounter a work crew or detour.

The North Side was once an independent municipality named Allegheny. In 1907, when it was forcibly annexed by Pittsburgh, Allegheny was a sooty city of industry with a charming park, Allegheny Commons, at its center. The residential area east of the park had become known as Deutschtown for its large population of German immigrants. Many well-to-do citizens lived north of the park in the Mexican War Streets section, where streets had been named for the battles (Buena Vista, Monterey, Resaca, Palo Alto) and leaders (Taylor, Sherman, Jackson) of the Mexican-American War. Today, both

neighborhoods are national historic districts well worth a stroll on a pleasant day.

The "Three Sisters"

Four vehicular bridges connect Downtown and the North Side, and all of them can be crossed on foot. The busiest is Fort Duquesne Bridge, a double-decker that feeds into an interstate. Its lower-deck walkway makes for a less-than-scenic stroll. For fantastic views sans deafening traffic, try one of the "Three Sisters." There's no Cinderella here; the bridges are all but identical. The yellow triplets were built between 1924 and 1928 on orders of the U.S. War Department, which feared that certain vessels wouldn't be able to pass under the variously designed bridges they replaced. The Sisters were the first self-anchored suspension bridges in the United States and remain the only trio of neighboring, nearly indistinguishable large bridges.

The bridges were originally named for the Downtown streets they adjoin: 6th Street, 7th Street, and 9th Street. Starting in 1999, they were renamed to honor local luminaries. Closest to the tip of Downtown is the **Roberto Clemente Bridge** (6th Street Bridge). Clemente, a National Baseball Hall of Famer, was drafted by the Pittsburgh Pirates in 1954. He remained with the team until 1972, when he died in a plane crash during a relief mission to earthquake-torn Nicaragua. PNC Park, where the Pirates have played since 2001, is a stone's throw from the span's northern end. The bridge is closed to vehicular traffic during Pirates home games and flooded with fans, vendors, and scalpers.

The Andy Warhol Museum sits near the northern end of the **Andy Warhol Bridge** (7th Street Bridge). The bridge was renamed in 2005 as part of the museum's 10th anniversary celebration. The **Rachel Carson Bridge** (9th Street Bridge) got its new name on Earth Day in 2006. Carson, who ignited the environmental movement with the publication of *Silent Spring,* was born in 1907 in Springdale, about 18 miles north of Pittsburgh along the Allegheny River.

the yarn-bombed Andy Warhol Bridge

★ The Andy Warhol Museum

Andy Warhol was born and buried in Pittsburgh, which might have remained a little-known fact were it not for **The Andy Warhol Museum** (117 Sandusky St., 412/237-8300, www.warhol.org, 10am-5pm Tues.-Thurs. and Sat.-Sun., 10am-10pm Fri., admission $20, students and children 3-18 $10). It opened in 1994 to celebrate the work of the influential artist whose career unfolded in New York City. The Warhol is one of the four Carnegie Museums of Pittsburgh. (As a child, Andy Warhol took free Saturday art classes at the Carnegie in Oakland, a neighborhood east of Downtown.) It's also the largest U.S. museum dedicated to a single artist. The collection includes about 900 paintings and 2,000 drawings, along with sculptures, prints, photographs, films, videos, books, and even wallpaper designed by the artist. About 500 works from the permanent collection are exhibited at any one time.

The "pope of pop" was born in 1928 to working-class immigrants from what is now Slovakia. There's another museum devoted to his work in the Slovakian town of Medzilaborce, not far from his parents' birthplace. After graduating with an art degree from the Carnegie Institute of Technology (now Carnegie Mellon University), Warhol moved to New York and gained recognition as a commercial illustrator. In the early 1960s, he shot to fame as a pop artist with paintings of consumer products such as Campbell's Soup and celebrities including Marilyn Monroe. He is buried at St. John the Baptist Cemetery in the Pittsburgh suburb of Bethel Park. Admirers still leave soup cans and other offerings at the gravesite.

If possible, visit the museum on a Friday evening, when a cash bar and special programs add a twist to the Warhol experience. The museum stays open until 10pm, and tickets are half price after 5pm.

PNC Park

PNC Park (115 Federal St., 412/323-5000, http://pittsburgh.pirates.mlb.com), home of the Pittsburgh Pirates, is the George Clooney of ballparks: handsome, classy, and alone worth your ticket price. Opened in 2001, it's a nod to early ballparks like Chicago's Wrigley Field and Boston's Fenway Park. Masonry archways, steel truss work, and a natural grass field contribute to the princely feel of the place, but PNC Park's greatest asset is its location on the Allegheny River. Many seats offer stellar views of the water, bridges, and

Extreme Makeovers

Station Square

Demolitions make good spectacles, but many Pittsburgh developers choose instead to adapt old buildings for new purposes. What looks like a church could very well be a brewpub, nightclub, or hookah bar. The building that resembles a warehouse could be gallery space. Extreme makeovers can be found throughout the city. Here's a look at a few:

THE ANDY WARHOL MUSEUM

The museum, which opened in 1994, occupies a former warehouse built in 1911. It was known as the Frick & Lindsay building when it housed mining supplies and Volkwein Music & Instruments Co. after it became a music store in the 1960s.

CHILDREN'S MUSEUM OF PITTSBURGH

This kid-centric museum occupies the former post office of Allegheny City, the municipality annexed by Pittsburgh in 1907 and now known as the North Side.

CHURCH BREW WORKS

St. John the Baptist Church closed in 1993 due to a decline in parishioners. The brewery and restaurant that took its place fills with revelers on weekends. Brewing kettles occupy the former altar.

PENN BREWERY

This brewery and restaurant opened in the 1980s in the onetime home of the Eberhardt & Ober Brewery, which operated from the 1840s to the early 1900s. A fruits and vegetables wholesaler used the building as a warehouse in the interim.

THE PRIORY HOTEL

A Catholic church called St. Mary's was built on the North Shore in 1852. A priory for the Benedictine priests and brothers who served the parish was added several decades later. Today the priory is a boutique hotel and the church a banquet hall.

SENATOR JOHN HEINZ HISTORY CENTER

The 19th-century building that houses Pennsylvania's largest history museum was once a warehouse for an ice company.

STATION SQUARE

The riverfront dining and entertainment complex was once the headquarters of the Pittsburgh & Lake Erie Railroad, which carried materials to and from the steel mills starting in the 1870s.

Downtown skyline. The home dugout was placed along the third baseline instead of the first to give the Pirates a view of Pittsburgh's skyscrapers.

Walking tours are conducted weekdays from mid-April through late September and select Saturdays. They last about 90 minutes and include the Pirates dugout, batting cages, and press box. Tour tickets are available at the main ticket window on the corner of Federal and General Robinson Streets. They're $8 for adults and $6 for seniors, students, and children 6-14.

Heinz Field

Horseshoe-shaped **Heinz Field** (100 Art Rooney Ave., 412/323-1200, www.steelers.com/heinzfield) sits at the head of the Ohio River. Its open south side features a massive scoreboard and a vista of the Downtown skyline. About 12,000 tons of steel went into the 65,050-seat stadium for the Steelers and their fans, aka Steeler Nation.

Like PNC Park, Heinz Field opened in 2001. (Before that, the Pirates and Steelers shared Three Rivers Stadium, which was imploded when each team got a home of its own.) In 2009, the Steelers became the first team in the National Football League to score six Super Bowl titles, and Pittsburgh got a new nickname: "Sixburgh." As a consequence, it's easier to get into heaven than Heinz Field when the Steelers are in the house. The University of Pittsburgh football team also calls the stadium home. Tickets to its games are considerably easier to come by.

Tours are offered weekdays from April through October and one Saturday a month from April through July. Call or check the website for details. The cost is $7 for adults and $5 for seniors, students, and children.

Water Steps in North Shore Riverfront Park

The North Side has no shortage of kid-friendly attractions, including the Carnegie Science Center, Children's Museum of Pittsburgh, and National Aviary. Admission, however, can be pricey. If you're looking for a cost-free way to entertain kids on a hot day, you can't do better than the **Water Steps** (North Shore Trail, between Mazeroski Way and Fort Duquesne Bridge, www.pgh-sea.com), a terraced wading pool with knockout views of Downtown. The creative display of water landscaping is a short walk from PNC Park by way of the paved trail that runs along the Allegheny River. If you're driving, park near the Hyatt Place Pittsburgh-North Shore (260 N. Shore Dr.). The steps are across North Shore Drive from the hotel.

Carnegie Science Center

Like The Andy Warhol Museum about a mile away, the **Carnegie Science Center** (1 Allegheny Ave., 412/237-3400, www.carnegiesciencecenter.org, 10am-5pm Sun.-Fri., 10am-7pm Sat., admission $17.95, children 3-12 $11.95, admission plus Omnimax film or laser show $22.95, children $14.95) is one of the four Carnegie Museums of Pittsburgh. It's the most kid-friendly and interactive of the four, and its store, XPLOR, is shopping nirvana for the nerdy set. Astronaut food? Check. Submarine models? Check.

The science center's permanent exhibitions include *Exploration Station*—a godsend to parents stumped by their progeny's "why" questions. Aerodynamics, embryology, magnetic forces, and dozens of other concepts and processes are explained. *SpacePlace,* one of the newest permanent exhibitions, features a two-story replica of the International Space Station and a climbing wall designed to simulate weightlessness. The Miniature Railroad & Village offers a bird's-eye view of western Pennsylvania at the turn of the 20th century. Among the 2,000 hand-built replicas is Forbes Field, Pittsburgh's beloved, bygone ballpark.

The *Highmark SportsWorks* exhibition, which explores the science of sports and the mechanics of the human body, moved into a brand-new facility in 2009. Also in 2009, the Science Center unveiled *Roboworld,* the largest permanent robotics exhibition in the country. Pittsburgh is a fitting home for the exhibition. Dubbed "Roboburgh" by *The

Wall Street Journal, the city is home to one of the leading robotics research centers in the world, Carnegie Mellon University's Robotics Institute.

Regular shows at the full-dome digital planetarium and tours of the World War II submarine moored alongside the Science Center are included in the price of admission. There is an additional charge for Omnimax movies (adults $8, children $6) and laser shows in the planetarium (adults and children $8). The Omnimax theater and planetarium stay open late into the evening on Fridays and Saturdays.

Rivers Casino

Luck rules the day at the adjacent **Rivers Casino** (777 Casino Dr., 412/231-7777, www.theriverscasino.com, open 24 hours). Pittsburgh's only casino opened in August 2009 with 3,000 slot machines, adding table games the following year. It boasts the state's first $500 slot machine, a posh lounge reserved for the highest rollers, and priceless views of the Ohio River. Even nongamblers should pay a visit, if only to marvel at what $780 million can build or to quaff a chocolate martini beneath a 70-foot-tall contemporary chandelier in the Drum Bar. (Be aware

that you have to play to park for free in the immense garage. A single round with a one-armed bandit will do ya, parking-wise.)

On-site restaurants include the upscale **Andrew's Steak and Seafood** (5pm-9:30pm Sun. and Wed.-Thurs., 5pm-11pm Fri.-Sat., $18-48), notable for its chilled seafood and selection of wines by the glass. It's named for Carnegie, Mellon, and Warhol—three Andrews who made Pittsburgh proud. Of course, a casino wouldn't be complete without an all-you-can-eat buffet. Eats at the **Grand View Buffet** (lunch 11am-3pm Mon.-Sat., champagne brunch 10:30am-3pm Sun., dinner 3pm-9pm Sun.-Thurs. and 3pm-10pm Sat., seafood buffet 4pm-10pm Fri., lunch $14.99, champagne brunch $21.99, dinner $21.99, seafood buffet $29.99) range from Italian staples to Mongolian stir-fry.

Children's Museum of Pittsburgh

Architecture and history buffs have as much reason as kiddies to visit the fabulous **Children's Museum of Pittsburgh** (10 Children's Way, 412/322-5058, www.pittsburghkids.org, 10am-5pm daily, admission $13, seniors and children 2-18 $12). It's housed in two historic landmarks. The older of the

Carnegie Science Center

two, notable for its copper dome, served as the post office for Allegheny City before its annexation by Pittsburgh in 1907. The younger opened in 1939 as a planetarium. They're linked by an eye-catching contemporary structure of polycarbonate and glass.

Inside, it's back-to-back playgrounds. There's the Studio, where budding artists can paint, sculpt, and otherwise express their creative vision; a water exhibit with opportunities to get wet from head to toe; a play area specifically for infants and toddlers; and more. In Pittsburgh, no major children's attraction would be complete without a tribute to the homegrown public television series *Mister Rogers' Neighborhood*. Set pieces can be found throughout all three floors of the museum.

If you're visiting in summer, be sure to check out **Cloud Arbor,** a mist-emitting metal sculpture that serves as the centerpiece of a community park in front of the museum. It's a good idea to bring a towel and change of clothes for your wee ones.

National Aviary

Just west of the Children's Museum is the **National Aviary** (700 Arch St., 412/323-7235, www.aviary.org, 10am-5pm daily, opens 9am Memorial Day-Labor Day, admission $13, seniors $12, children 2 and older $11), home to some 500 birds. Free-flight rooms and public feedings allow for close encounters of the bird kind. Visitors can toss fish to the pelicans, hand-feed nectar to the rainbow lorikeets, or watch the aviary's "chefs" prepare vittles for condors, macaws, and other residents. In 2009 the aviary unveiled Penguin Point, part of a multimillion-dollar expansion. The open-air exhibit features more than a dozen African penguins, also known as jackass penguins because of their donkey-like bray. They include Sidney (as in Pittsburgh Penguins captain Sidney Crosby) and Stanley (as in hockey's holy grail, the Stanley Cup). An acrylic-fronted pool and crawlspaces make it possible to observe their underwater antics.

the National Aviary

Mattress Factory

The historic Mexican War Streets is home to one of the nation's top museums for installation art. The **Mattress Factory** (500 Sampsonia Way, 412/231-3169, www.mattress.org, 10am-5pm Tues.-Sat., 1pm-5pm Sun., admission $15, seniors and students $10, children under 6 free) presents "art you can get in to"—room-size works created on-site. Its permanent installations include works by James Turrell, Bill Woodrow, and Yayoi Kusama. Each year, 8-10 new works are exhibited for several months at a time. The museum's expansion has made it an engine for community development as well as artistic expression. It has purchased nine properties since 1975, turning them into galleries, artist residences, and even an artist-created garden. The first acquisition was a former mattress warehouse built at the turn of the 20th century.

Allegheny Observatory

The heavens seem almost within reach when viewed through the 13-inch Fitz-Clark refractor at the **Allegheny Observatory** (159 Riverview Ave., 412/321-2400, www.pitt.edu/~aobsvtry). The observatory in Riverview Park, four miles north of Downtown, is a University of Pittsburgh research laboratory and only occasionally open to the public. Free tours are offered Thursdays April-August and Fridays April-October. All tours begin at 8pm with a short slide or film presentation and end about two hours later at the Fitz-Clark. On the third Friday of every month except December, local astronomers and physicists give public lectures on topics such as *The Mysteries of Quantum Mechanics*. An open house is held once a year, usually in the fall. It's the only opportunity you'll get to peer through a telescope that puts the Fitz-Clark to shame. Reservations are required for all tours, lectures, and the open house. Lectures are so popular that reservations are only accepted the Monday following the previous lecture.

SOUTH SIDE AND MOUNT WASHINGTON

It's been said that the South Side has both types of "blue hairs." One type is fond of studded collars and punk rock; the other favors sensible shoes and Dean Martin. That diversity is part of what makes the area so interesting. What's referred to as the South Side is actually several neighborhoods near the southern bank of the Monongahela River. The smallest of these is the South Shore, dominated by a dining and entertainment complex called Station Square. Overlooking it is Mount Washington, once called Coal Hill for its abundant coal seams, which supplied fuel to Pittsburgh's settlers and riverbank industries. The growth of these industries in the mid-19th century created more and more jobs—and a shortage of housing in the flatlands. So workers built houses on Pittsburgh's hillsides. For a while, they commuted on foot, trudging up steep paths after a hard day's work in the plants. The first people-moving incline opened in 1870. In the 25 years that followed, more than 15 others were built. Two remain, a mile apart on Mount Washington. The hilltop is now accessible by car, but some of its residents still use the inclines to commute to jobs in Downtown or the South Side. They're also

Step Aerobics

Pittsburgh has at least 738 outdoor staircases comprising 45,000 steps. No city in the country has more, and no neighborhood in Pittsburgh has more than the South Side Slopes. Rising from the Monongahela River, the nabe rewards those who conquer its steps with knockout views.

Driving through the Slopes is almost as challenging as hoofing it. The streets are narrow and winding and in some spots so steep that you can't see the road for the car hood. If you're working your way down and see an oncoming car, it's customary to pull to the side so the climber can have the right of way. Complicating driving is the matter of "paper" streets, so called because they appear to be streets on maps but are actually staircases. Pittsburgh has 334 of them.

During Pittsburgh's industrial heyday, the staircases linked hilltop communities with the steel mills and other workplaces on the riverbanks. The Slopes were home to Poles, Germans, and other immigrants. Their faith left an indelible mark on the neighborhood. It's dotted with churches and a larger number of former churches, rectories, and convents. Yard Way, the longest of the paper streets, climbs from a street named Pius toward a street named St. Paul, which curves its way to an avenue named Monastery.

Good to have if you're interested in exploring the staircases is Bob Regan's *The Steps of Pittsburgh: Portrait of a City* ($21.95, 866/362-0789, www.thelocalhistorycompany.com). Or mark your calendar for the South Side Slopes Neighborhood Association's **StepTrek** (412/488-0486, www.steptrek.org, Oct., registration $12, children under 12 free). Armed with maps and course descriptions, participants in the noncompetitive event climb about half of the Slopes' 5,447 steps.

popular among tourists (and lovebirds) for the vista from up top.

If Pittsburgh has a main drag, it's East Carson Street in the South Side Flats. The low-lying neighborhood was once crowded with glassmaking factories and, later, iron and steel operations. Today it's chockablock with restaurants, bars, and stores. Should gluttony get the best of you there, press on toward the South Side Slopes. The neighborhood's steep streets rival a treadmill at its highest setting.

Smithfield Street Bridge

Some years ago, the Pennsylvania Department of Transportation decided to demolish the **Smithfield Street Bridge,** which connects Downtown and the South Side, and replace it with a modern bridge. Preservationists lobbied to save it and won. Instead of being torn down, the oldest steel bridge in the United States got a new deck, a paint job, and an extra traffic lane.

Constructed in the early 1880s, the Smithfield Street Bridge is a National Historic Landmark. But what really distinguishes it from so many bridges in Pittsburgh and across the country is the foot traffic. Downtown workers who live south of the Monongahela River stream across the bridge in the morning and again come quitting time. For visitors staying in Downtown hotels, the bridge's pedestrian walkways are a great way to reach the restaurants and nightspots of Station Square and the famous Mount Washington inclines.

Station Square

A massive railroad facility turned dining and entertainment complex, **Station Square** (Carson St. at Smithfield Street Bridge, 800/859-8985, www.stationsquare.com) is one of the Burgh's most popular tourist destinations. It's the gateway to America's oldest and steepest incline, the **Monongahela Incline,** and home to the **Gateway Clipper Fleet,** which bills itself as America's largest inland riverboat fleet. Its tenants also include several other tour operators, more than a dozen eateries, a handful of nightclubs, a Sheraton

hotel, and—new in 2013—a soccer stadium. **Highmark Stadium** (510 W. Station Square Dr., 412/224-4900, www.highmarkstadium. com) is home to the Pittsburgh Riverhounds, which play in the USL Professional Division, and the Pittsburgh Passion women's football team.

Station Square hasn't shed all traces of its history as the headquarters of the Pittsburgh & Lake Erie Railroad, which thrived during Pittsburgh's steelmaking heyday. Its signature restaurant, **Grand Concourse,** looks much as it did when it served as a passenger terminal, with its stained glass cathedral ceiling and brass accents. A 1930s Bessemer converter, which was used to convert molten iron to steel, is on display in the outdoor **Bessemer Court.** The 10-ton artifact is easy to miss if you arrive when the Fountain at Bessemer Court is putting on a show. Flashy as a Vegas showgirl, the fountain features hundreds of colored water jets that jive to music by the likes of Frank Sinatra, Michael Jackson, and Christina Aguilera (who, incidentally, grew up near Pittsburgh). Shows begin every 20 minutes 9am-midnight from April through early November.

★ Mount Washington Inclines

Three 19th-century inclines remain in Pennsylvania, and two of those climb Mount Washington. (The third is in Johnstown, about 65 miles east of Pittsburgh.) They've been around for so long that you might think twice about boarding the cable cars. Board. The views more than compensate for the fear factor.

The **Monongahela Incline** (lower station Carson St. near Smithfield Street Bridge, 412/442-2000, www.portauthority.org, 5:30am-12:45am Mon.-Sat., 8:45am-midnight Sun. and holidays, one-way fare $2.50, seniors free, children 6-11 $1.25) is the oldest and steepest incline in all of America. It's also the oldest cable car operation—three years older than San Francisco's famous cable cars. The incline began operating in 1870. Its cars, which were replaced in the 1980s, ply two

Sightseeing Tours

tour bus crossing from the North Side to Downtown

Tours are a good way to learn more about Pittsburgh, whether you're a longtime resident or visiting for the first time. Many of the city's tour operators are based at Station Square, the dining and entertainment complex on the southern bank of the Monongahela River. Busiest of those is the **Gateway Clipper Fleet** (412/355-7980, gatewayclipper.com, prices vary), which offers a wide variety of cruises, from the kid-centric Good Ship Lollipop Cruise to under-21 dance parties to dinners with live oldies music. Its five riverboats explore the Monongahela, Allegheny, and Ohio Rivers year-round. They also shuttle sports fans to PNC Park and Heinz Field on game days. If the boats look up in years, it's because they're reproductions of vessels of yore.

Station Square is also home to **Just Ducky Tours** (412/402-3825, www.justduckytours.com, daily Apr.-Oct., weekends in Nov., $22, children 3-12 $15, infants $5), offering Pittsburgh's only land-and-water tours. Designed for use in WWII, its amphibious vehicles ferry passengers across the Monongahela River and through Downtown. Tours are approximately one hour.

Other Station Square-based tour operators include **Molly's Trolleys** (412/391-7433, www.mollystrolleyspittsburgh.com, $25, children 3-12 $15, infants $5), which offers two-hour sightseeing tours in a vehicle reminiscent of a 1920s-style trolley, and **Segway in Paradise** (412/337-3941, www.segwayinparadise.com, $59-97), which offers two-hour tours of Downtown and the North Side as well as a four-hour "Adventure Tour" with a stop for lunch.

Station Square is also the place to hail a horse-drawn carriage. **Mike's Carriage Service** (412/913-0664, www.caustelotfarms.com, $20 and up) can be found there most Friday and Saturday evenings from May through October.

The Pittsburgh Tour Company (445 S. 27th St., 412/381-8687, www.pghtours.com, daily Apr.-Dec., $20-25, children under 10 $10-15) makes its home at the SouthSide Works, a shopping and dining complex about 2.5 miles upriver from Station Square, but you can catch a ride on one of its double-decker buses at about 20 stops, including Station Square, Heinz Field, the Children's Museum of Pittsburgh, and Phipps Conservatory.

Whether you're hungry for local history or just plain hungry, a **'Burgh Bits and Bites Food Tour** (888/718-4253, www.burghfoodtour.com, $37) is sure to satisfy. The food-centric walking tours offer a taste of neighborhoods including the Strip District, Bloomfield, and Lawrenceville. Tickets must be purchased in advance.

parallel tracks at about six miles per hour. The creaks and groans of the machinery recall a wooden roller coaster. Rest easy; there's no plunge after the "Mon Incline" summits. The lower station is a short walk from the Smithfield Street Bridge and across the street from Station Square, where you can park for a modest fee.

The **Duquesne Incline** (lower station 1197 W. Carson St., 412/381-1665, www. duquesneincline.org, 5:30am-12:45am Mon.-Sat., 7am-12:45am Sun. and holidays, one-way fare $2.50, seniors free, children 6-11 $1.25), one mile west, opened in 1877. It joined three other Mount Washington inclines but didn't lack for passengers. In 1880, *Scientific American* magazine wrote of the Duquesne Incline: "On Sundays during the summer, 6,000 passengers are carried during the day and evening, the cars ascending and descending as rapidly as filled and emptied." Ridership shrank after the advent of the automobile, and in 1962, the company that owned the incline decided not to invest in sorely needed repairs. The incline was shut down. A group of Mount Washington residents took up its cause, raising $15,000 in six months through the sale of souvenir tickets, baked goods, and shares in the incline

company. Repairs were made, and the incline reopened. There's free parking across the street from the lower station, between West Carson Street and the Ohio River. Follow the pedestrian bridge that crosses West Carson to reach the station. You'll board one of two original Victorian cable cars and gain 400 feet of elevation in less than three minutes. At the upper station, you'll find a free museum, gift shop, and observation deck with binocular telescopes.

Grandview Avenue

Both inclines deposit passengers on Mount Washington's **Grandview Avenue,** the most stroll-worthy stretch in Pittsburgh. George Washington is said to have spotted the forks of the Ohio River from this bluff. He saw a highly strategic site for a fort. What we see today is an acclaimed cityscape. In 2003, the view from Mount Washington earned Pittsburgh the No. 2 spot on *USA Weekend* magazine's list of 10 most beautiful places in America. Pittsburghers rarely fail to bring out-of-town guests here.

The historic inclines aren't the only way to reach Grandview Avenue, which clings to the rim of the hill for about a mile and a half. PJ McArdle Roadway and Sycamore Street also

the Duquesne Incline

climb to the penthouse of Pittsburgh. Street parking is plentiful unless you arrive on the Fourth of July or another occasion for fireworks. Once on foot, make your way to one of the observation decks that jut over the hillside. You may have to bypass a wedding party or gaggle of prom-goers. This is the mother of Pittsburgh photo ops. The western (Duquesne Incline) end of Grandview is crowded with restaurants of the special occasion variety, many of which are open only for dinner. They could serve gruel and still be packed on Valentine's Day. The views from their dining areas are that romantic.

Community development types try mightily to prove that Mount Washington has more to offer than breathtaking views and "Restaurant Row." At the eastern end of Grandview, near the Monongahela Incline, signs point the way to the homey Shiloh Street business district. You'll find ATMs, several murals, and casual eateries like the aptly named **Packs-N-Dogs** (223 Shiloh St., 412/431-1855), which offers specialty beers and hot dogs (all-beef or veggie).

St. John the Baptist Ukrainian Catholic Church

The eight-domed **St. John the Baptist Ukrainian Catholic Church** (109 S. 7th St., 412/431-2531, www.stjohnspittsburgh. com) is an eye-catcher. The Byzantine-style church was built in 1895 by Ukrainian immigrants who worked in Pittsburgh's mills, factories, and mines. But there's nothing workaday about it. Its towers, stained glass windows, and domes topped with Greek crosses set it apart from the slope-roofed houses that surround it and the Victorian storefronts that line East Carson Street. It's not just the architecture that offers a taste of Eastern Europe. Every week, parishioners gather in the basement to make pierogies: dumplings stuffed with potato, cheese, or sauerkraut. Pierogi sales are held Thursdays from 10am to 3pm. A dozen of the potato or kraut varieties costs $6; cheese pierogies are $9 a dozen.

In the 19th century, pollution and overcrowding drove some Pittsburghers to the city's outskirts. Oakland, about three miles east of Downtown, started as an elite enclave. By the 1920s, thanks in no small part to its moneyed residents, Oakland had blossomed into an academic and cultural powerhouse with two major universities, a pair of world-class museums, and outstanding hospitals.

First stop for many visitors are three connected buildings that house the Carnegie Museum of Art, the Carnegie Museum of Natural History, Carnegie Music Hall, and the main branch of the Carnegie Library of Pittsburgh. Schenley Park fans out behind them, offering relaxation, recreation, and, frequently, free entertainment. Oakland's most arresting building, the 42-story Cathedral of Learning, can be seen from points near and far, guiding home coeds who wander too far from the campuses of Carnegie Mellon University or University of Pittsburgh. Central Oakland is awash in the sort of restaurants, bars, and coffee shops favored by students.

The neighborhoods east of Oakland include Squirrel Hill, Shadyside, and Bloomfield. Squirrel Hill is the center of Jewish culture in the city. Dotted with synagogues, it's the place to go for a breakfast of bagels and lox. When a Dunkin' Donuts opened on one of the neighborhood's main thoroughfares in 2009, it resolved to adhere to Jewish dietary laws. (Vegetarians can rest assured that its breakfast sandwiches are made with meatless versions of sausage and bacon.) Shadyside is among the most affluent neighborhoods in Pittsburgh. Its Walnut Street shopping district is home to high-end chains such as Williams-Sonoma and Lululemon Athletica as well as independent businesses. The parallel Ellsworth Avenue is known for its nightlife offerings, including a couple of queer-friendly joints. Bloomfield is Pittsburgh's Little Italy. On Liberty Avenue, its main drag, parking meters are painted the colors of the Italian

Oakland

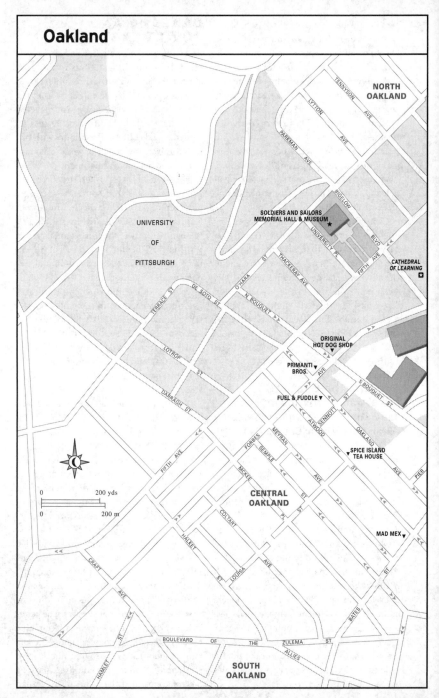

NORTH OAKLAND

TENNYSON AVE

LYTTON AVE

PARKMAN AVE

BIGELOW BLVD

UNIVERSITY OF PITTSBURGH

SOLDIERS AND SAILORS MEMORIAL HALL & MUSEUM

UNIVERSITY PL

FIFTH AVE

CATHEDRAL OF LEARNING

O'HARA ST

THACKERAY AVE

N BOUQUET ST

DE SOTO ST

TERRACE ST

LOTROP ST

DARRAGH ST

ORIGINAL HOT DOG SHOP

PRIMANTI BROS.

FUEL & FUDDLE

S BOUQUET ST

SENNOTT ST

ATWOOD ST

OAKLAND AVE

SPICE ISLAND TEA HOUSE

FIFTH AVE

FORBES

MEYRAN AVE

SEMPLE ST

MCKEE PL

CENTRAL OAKLAND

COLLART

HALKET ST

LOUISA ST

BATES ST

MAD MEX

CRAFT AVE

HAMLET ST

BOULEVARD OF THE ALLIES

ZULEMA ST

SOUTH OAKLAND

0   200 yds
0   200 m

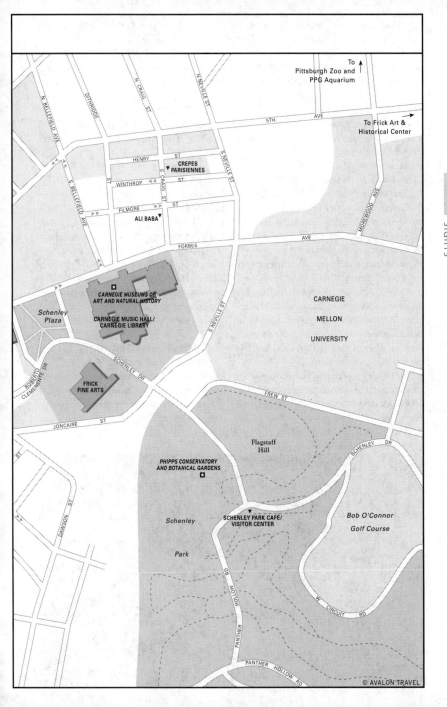

flag. These and other neighborhoods are collectively known as the East End.

★ Carnegie Museum of Art

Don't have the budget to visit the Parthenon in Greece? Head to the **Carnegie Museum of Art** (4400 Forbes Ave., 412/622-3131, www.cmoa.org, 10am-5pm Tues.-Sat., 10am-8pm Thurs., noon-5pm Sun., open Mondays in summer, admission $17.95, seniors $14.95, students and children 3-18 $11.95, includes same-day admission to Carnegie Museum of Natural History), where you'll find the Hall of Sculpture, a replica of the ancient temple's heavily columned inner sanctuary. It's made of white marble from the same quarries that provided stones for the 5th century BC Parthenon. Decorative arts objects from more recent centuries are displayed on the balcony of the hall, along with several works from the museum's celebrated architectural cast collection. Only the Victoria and Albert Museum in London and Musée National des Monuments Français in Paris have architectural cast collections that rival the Carnegie's.

The Carnegie, of course, isn't just about architecture. It has a dozen galleries devoted to art from ancient times to the 20th century and several more filled with contemporary works.

In fact, the Carnegie has been called the first museum of modern art. The industrialist and philanthropist Andrew Carnegie, who founded the museum in 1895, wished that it be filled not with the works of long-dead artists but rather with the art of "tomorrow's old masters." Early acquisitions included paintings by Winslow Homer, James A. McNeill Whistler, and other artists who were still ticking.

Every three to five years, the museum presents the Carnegie International, an exhibition of contemporary art from around the world. The exhibition draws the art world to Pittsburgh, which is exactly what Andrew Carnegie had in mind when he established the tradition in 1896. Featured artists have included Mary Cassatt, Henri Matisse, Edward Hopper, Andy Warhol, and Willem de Kooning. The museum's permanent collection includes more than 300 works purchased from its Carnegie Internationals.

★ Carnegie Museum of Natural History

Three years after opening his eponymous museums, Andrew Carnegie set his sights on bagging a dinosaur. In 1899, a bone-digging crew bankrolled by Carnegie discovered

Carnegie Museum of Natural History

the skeleton of an 84-foot sauropod in southeastern Wyoming. A longer dinosaur had never been found. Exhibiting the colossal fossil—named *Diplodocus carnegii* in recognition of its benefactor—required a $5 million expansion of the **Carnegie Museum of Natural History** (4400 Forbes Ave., 412/622-3131, www.carnegiemnh.org, 10am-5pm Tues.-Sat., 10am-8pm Thurs., noon-5pm Sun., open Mondays in summer, admission $17.95, seniors $14.95, students and children 3-18 $11.95, includes same-day admission to Carnegie Museum of Art). "Dippy" was soon joined by other dinosaur skeletons. The Carnegie boasts the third-largest display of real mounted dinosaurs in the United States, after the National Museum of Natural History in Washington DC and the American Museum of Natural History in New York City. You'll find them in dramatic poses in historically accurate environments. The exhibit of two sparring T. rex specimens is particularly striking.

Dinosaurs may be its main draw, but the Carnegie has other distinguished exhibitions. It has been building its collection of ancient Egyptian artifacts ever since Andrew Carnegie donated a mummy and its sarcophagus. The collection now includes more than 2,500 artifacts dating back to 3100 BC, about 600 of which are displayed in the Walton Hall of Ancient Egypt. For bling-bling as far as the eye can see, head to the Hillman Hall of Minerals and Gems, home to more than 1,300 specimens from around the world.

The life-size dinosaur sculpture near the museum's entrance on Forbes Avenue depicts Dippy as he would have looked with skin and flesh. It was erected in 1999 to commemorate the 100th anniversary of the museum's first dinosaur discovery. Few visitors pass up the photo op.

★ Cathedral of Learning

The 42-story **Cathedral of Learning** (4200 5th Ave., 412/624-4141, www.pitt.edu) is the second-tallest university building in the world. (It was robbed of the number one spot by a Moscow building with fewer stories and an oversized spire.) The geographic and symbolic heart of the University of Pittsburgh was designed in the early 1920s by one of the foremost neo-Gothic architects of the time and was to be the tallest building in Pittsburgh. By the time the limestone skyscraper was dedicated in 1937, the 44-story Gulf Tower had risen in Downtown. But the Cathedral didn't fail to make its point that scholarliness is next to godliness. Its three-story foyer, known as the Commons Room, is so churchlike that you half expect to find kneeling parishioners beneath the soaring arches. Instead, you find students hunched over books and laptops. Any prayers are silent.

The Cathedral houses classrooms, administrative offices, libraries, and several departments. But the main attraction is a set of classrooms gifted to the university by the city's ethnic communities. Each of the **Nationality Rooms** (412/624-6000, www.pitt.edu/~natrooms, 9am-4pm Mon.-Sat., 11am-4pm Sun., audio tour $4, children 6-18 $2) depicts a culture in a period prior to the 19th century. The first four rooms were dedicated in 1938 and the 29th in 2012. Several others are in the works. Chancellor John G. Bowman, who dreamed up the Cathedral, invited local immigrants and their descendants to create classrooms that would evoke pride in their heritage. The Chinese Classroom, inspired by a palace hall in Beijing's Forbidden City, features a round teakwood table and a slate portrait of Confucius. The Armenian Classroom with its domed ceiling emulates a 10th- to 12th-century monastery, and the Greek Classroom represents 5th-century BC Athens. Classrooms are off-limits when they're in use, so it's a good idea to visit on a weekend or during the summer break (mid-April through mid-August). Audio tours are available when school is out, with the last tour dispatched at 2:30pm. The best time to visit is from mid-November to mid-January, when the classrooms are dressed in holiday finery.

Philadelphia-born architect Charles Klauder designed two buildings to accompany his Cathedral. The university's interdenominational **Heinz Chapel** (1212 Cathedral of Learning, 412/624-4157, www.heinzchapel.pitt.edu), on the Bellefield Avenue side of the Cathedral, hosts about 1,000 events a year. A lot of those are weddings, but choral and organ concerts are held occasionally, and many of them are free. *Where's Waldo* whizzes will get a kick out of scanning the stained glass windows for 391 famous figures. At 73 feet, the transept windows are among the tallest in the world.

The **Stephen Foster Memorial** (4301 Forbes Ave., 412/624-4100) is just outside the Forbes Avenue doors of the Cathedral. It houses two theaters, a library with one of the nation's top collections of 19th-century American music, and a museum (9am-4pm Mon.-Fri.) dedicated to the Pittsburgh-born composer for whom it is named.

Schenley Plaza

Not so long ago, the verdant public park across from the Cathedral of Learning was a parking lot. Today **Schenley Plaza** (4100 Forbes Ave., 412/255-2539, www.pittsburghparks.org/schenleyplaza) is a popular sunbathing and picnicking spot and a frequent venue for free concerts, yoga classes, and other mind-expanding stuff. New Yorkers may experience a touch of déjà vu. The Schenley Plaza design team drew on the Big Apple's Bryant Park for inspiration, borrowing elements such as a carousel, a great lawn, flower gardens, and food kiosks. A full-service restaurant, **The Porch at Schenley** (221 Schenley Dr., 412/687-6724, www.theporchatschenley.com), was added in 2011.

Mosey across Schenley Drive for a peak inside the **Frick Fine Arts building,** home to the University of Pittsburgh's History of Art and Architecture Department and Studio Arts Department. What makes it of interest to nonstudents is the collection of art copies displayed in the cloister. The scale reproductions of 15th-century Italian Renaissance paintings are masterpieces in their own right. They're the work of Russian artist Nicholas Lochoff,

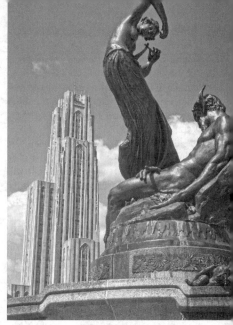

Mary Schenley Memorial Fountain in Schenley Plaza and Cathedral of Learning

commissioned in 1911 by the Moscow Museum of Fine Arts. If you can't make it to Italy to see Botticelli's *Birth of Venus,* make it to the Frick Fine Arts building.

For many years, Schenley Plaza had a neighbor nicknamed the "House of Thrills." Officially known as Forbes Field, it was the third home of the Pittsburgh Pirates and the first home of the Pittsburgh Steelers. The 1909 stadium where Babe Ruth hit his last three home runs closed in 1970, but its remnants still attract sports fans. Look for the stadium's flagpole and part of the outfield wall to the right of the Frick Fine Arts building. Baseball fans gather here every October 13 to celebrate Bill Mazeroski's ninth-inning home run in the final game of the 1960 World Series, which gave the Pirates a 10-9 win over the New York Yankees.

Schenley Park

Beauteous as it is, Schenley Plaza is but a gateway to a much larger oasis, **Schenley Park** (412/255-2539, www.pittsburghparks.org/

The Incorrigible Heiress

The woman for whom Schenley Park and Schenley Plaza are named started life as Mary Elizabeth Croghan. She gained the Schenley name—and created an international scandal—at the age of 15, when she eloped with a 43-year-old captain in the British Army. The 1842 elopement made headlines not just because of their age difference but because Mary Croghan Schenley stood to inherit large tracts of land amassed by her maternal grandfather, one of Pittsburgh's earliest captains of industry.

In 1889, Pittsburgh's director of public works learned that a real estate developer's agent planned to travel to London to persuade Mary to sell a swath of land then known as Mt. Airy Tract. The city official had another idea for the property: a grand park. He dispatched a Pittsburgh lawyer, who beat the agent to England by two days. The quick-footedness paid off. Mary gave the city 300 acres of Mt. Airy Tract, stipulating that the park be named after her and never sold. Over the next few years, the city purchased an additional 120 acres of her property and some adjoining land to complete Schenley Park.

schenley). The 456-acre park is home to an ice-skating rink, an outdoor swimming pool, the only golf course within city limits, and a sports complex, among other facilities. A good place to start is the lovely **Schenley Park Café** (Panther Hollow Rd. and Schenley Dr., 412/687-1800, 10am-4pm daily, closed Mon. in winter), which doubles as a visitors center. You'll find light lunch fare, desserts, coffee and espresso drinks, free wireless Internet access, restrooms, and trail maps. There are trailheads behind the café.

Grassy **Flagstaff Hill,** across from Phipps Conservatory and Botanical Gardens, is awash with sunbathers on summer days. On Wednesday and Sunday nights, it's packed with movie buffs and their picnic baskets. Starting at sundown, films are projected onto a large screen. (You can be assured of a kid-friendly flick on a Sunday.) Flagstaff Hill is one of several **Cinema in the Park** (www.pittsburghpa.gov/citiparks, 412/422-6426) sites in the city.

In winter, the action shifts to the **Schenley Park Skating Rink** (Overlook Dr., 412/422-6523, www.pittsburghpa.gov/citiparks, admission $4, seniors and children 17 and under $3, skate rental $2.50). The outdoor rink generally opens in early November and closes in late March. Public skating times vary from day to day.

The 18-hole **Bob O'Connor Golf Course**

(5370 Schenley Dr., 412/622-6959, www.the-bobgc.com) is open year-round. So is the **Schenley Oval Sportsplex** (Schenley Park Oval, 412/422-6523, www.pittsburghpa.gov/citiparks), which boasts a 400-meter running track, tennis courts, and a sports turf soccer field.

★ Phipps Conservatory and Botanical Gardens

The crown jewel of Schenley Park is **Phipps Conservatory and Botanical Gardens** (1 Schenley Park, GPS: 700 Frank Curto Dr., 412/622-6914, http://phipps.conservatory.org, 9:30am-5pm daily and until 10pm Fri., admission $15, seniors and students $14, children 2-18 $11). The "crystal palace," as the steel and glass structure has been called, is as wondrous as the botanical treasures inside. It opened in 1893, stocked with tropical plants from that year's Chicago World's Fair. Today the Victorian greenhouse has 19 indoor and outdoor gardens whose oxygen-producing inhabitants range from towering palm trees to rare miniature orchids. A good mix of permanent and changing displays make repeat visits a must for the horticulturally inclined. In spring and summer, you can watch butterflies emerge from chrysalises. On weekends throughout the year, Phipps offers educational programs on everything from origami to moss gardening. They're free with admission.

Phipps Conservatory and Botanical Gardens in Schenley Park

Soldiers & Sailors Memorial Hall & Museum

A grand Greco-Roman structure, **Soldiers & Sailors Memorial Hall & Museum** (4141 5th Ave., 412/621-4253, www.soldiersandsailorshall.org, museum 10am-4pm Mon.-Sat., admission $8, seniors and children 5-13 $5) opened in 1910 as a tribute to local Civil War veterans. Since then, the museum has broadened its scope to include all men and women who have served the United States in its military endeavors. Visitors can hup-two-three-four through four exhibit-filled corridors. Bronze plaques on their outer walls are engraved with the names of 25,000 men from the Pittsburgh area who served in the Union Army during the Civil War. The "Slave to Soldier" exhibit in the Gettysburg Room explores the experience of African Americans in the military. Scantily clad coeds dot the museum's expansive lawns in summer.

Frick Art & Historical Center

In December 1881, industrialist Henry Clay Frick married Adelaide Howard Childs. After their wedding trip, the couple purchased an Italianate-style house on the corner of Penn and South Homewood Avenues, about two miles east of Oakland. They named it

Clayton, and it served as the family's primary residence until 1905, when they moved to New York. Today Clayton is one of three museums on the grounds of the **Frick Art & Historical Center** (7227 Reynolds St., 412/371-0600, www.frickart.org, 10am-5pm Tues.-Sun.). More than 90 percent of the furniture and artifacts in the restored home, which opened to the public in 1990, are original. The only way to see them is via docent-led tour ($12, seniors and students $10, children 16 and under $6). Tour times vary, and reservations are strongly recommended.

There's no charge for admission to the intimate **Frick Art Museum,** which houses the personal collection of Helen Clay Frick, Henry and Adelaide's younger daughter. Helen, who inherited Clayton and its contents at her father's death in 1919, was particularly fond of early Renaissance paintings and 18th-century French paintings and decorative arts.

Henry Clay Frick's 1914 Rolls Royce Silver Ghost and an 1898 Panhard believed to be the first car in Pittsburgh are among 20-some vintage automobiles on view in the **Car and Carriage Museum.** Admission is free, as is a cell phone tour.

What used to be the Frick children's playhouse is now a visitors center and museum shop. No ordinary museum commissary, the **Café at the Frick** (11am-5pm Tues.-Sun., $11-22, reservations recommended) offers one of the loveliest lunches in Pittsburgh. Seasonal menus feature uncommon soups, salads, and sandwiches, plus several flawless entrées. The vegetables and herbs couldn't be fresher; they're grown in the on-site garden and greenhouse. Tea service is available after 2:30pm.

Pittsburgh Zoo & PPG Aquarium

More than a century old but not the least bit timeworn, the 77-acre **Pittsburgh Zoo & PPG Aquarium** (1 Wild Place, GPS: 7340 Butler St., 412/665-3640, www.pittsburghzoo.org, summer 9:30am-6pm daily, gates close at 4:30pm, fall and spring 9am-5pm daily, gates close at 4pm, winter 9am-4pm daily, gates close at 3pm, admission $14, seniors $13, children 2-13 $12 Apr.-Nov., discounted rates Dec.-Mar.) is home to thousands of animals representing more than 400 species. Thanks to extensive renovations that began in 1980,

Pittsburgh Zoo

they reside in naturalistic habitats. Highlights include the African Savanna, populated by elephants, rhinos, and giraffes, among other beasts, and the indoor Tropical Forest, which teems with primates. But nothing wows the little ones like Kids Kingdom, featuring playful sea lions, playgrounds, and a petting zoo. No wonder *Parents* magazine named this one of the top 10 children's zoos in the country.

Completed in 2000, the state-of-the-art PPG Aquarium is home to all sorts of swimmers, from ethereal seahorses to menacing sharks. Don't miss the chance to pet a stingray. Adjacent to the aquarium is Water's Edge, home to polar bears, sea otters, and more sharks. Thanks to underwater viewing tunnels, you can practically rub noses with them.

GREATER PITTSBURGH

Allegheny County has 130 municipalities, more than any other county in the state. None match Pittsburgh, the county seat, in size or sophistication. When Pittsburghers leave the city limits, it's often to shop at sprawling suburban malls. In summer, they stream across the Monongahela River to ride coasters at Kennywood and cool off at its sister water park.

Kennywood

It rarely makes headlines when the National Amusement Park Historical Association names **Kennywood** (4800 Kennywood Blvd., West Mifflin, 412/461-0500, www.kennywood.com, admission $39.99, seniors $19.99, children under 46 inches tall $26.99, rates discounted online) its favorite traditional park. The National Historic Landmark takes that prize almost every year. About 10 miles southeast of Downtown, Kennywood is virtually synonymous with summer fun for generations of Pittsburghers. Don't let its status as America's favorite traditional park fool you; this ain't no namby-pamby relic of bygone days. Founded in 1898 as a small trolley park, Kennywood has weathered everything from World War II to competition from Disneyland by enhancing its portfolio of rides. Today it's a well-balanced mix of classic and cutting-edge thrills. Its six roller coasters include two wooden beauties erected in the 1920s—Jack Rabbit and Racer—as well as Phantom's Revenge, a 21st-century steel machine. Also on tap: water rides, dark rides, and upside-down action for serious adrenaline junkies. Kiddieland caters to tots with rides such as Lil' Phantom, a pint-size coaster that maxes out at 15 mph. Famous for its fresh-cut Potato Patch fries, Kennywood is one of the few amusement parks that still permit guests to bring their own grub. Alcohol isn't allowed.

The park is open daily from mid-May to late August and some weekends before and after that period. Gates usually open at 10:30am. Quittin' time is based on weather and crowd size but usually around 10pm. The park marks the end of each season with two weeks of nightly parades. It reopens on weekend evenings in October for ghoul-themed **Phantom Fright Nights** (www.phantomfrightnights.com, admission $28.99), not recommended for children under 13, and again in late November for 12 nights of holiday-themed fun.

Sandcastle

Opened in 1989 on a former railroad yard, **Sandcastle** (1000 Sandcastle Dr., Pittsburgh, 412/462-6666, www.sandcastlewaterpark.com, admission $31.99, seniors and children under 48 inches tall $21.99) quickly became Pittsburghers' favorite place to cool off on sweltering days. The water park on the bank of the Monongahela River has more than a dozen waterslides and a 300,000-gallon wave pool. Those who prefer calmer waters can float down the quarter-mile Lazy River, wade in the Sandbar Pool, or soak in the world's biggest hot tub. Tykes get a pool and play area of their own.

Arrive by boat and dock at Sandcastle for free; drive and shell out $6 for parking. The water park is open daily from mid-June to late August and several weekends before and after that period. Gates generally open at 11am and close at 6 or 7pm.

Kennywood

Carrie Furnaces

Pittsburgh and the steel industry are inextricably linked in the public imagination. But a visitor would be hard-pressed to visualize the "Big Steel" era. In the quarter century since most of the region's steel mills closed their doors, the landscape has undergone an incredible transformation. Sprawling malls and business parks have taken the place of sprawling mills. Bicycle and pedestrian trails have replaced railways. Brownfields barely hint at the fire-belching iron furnaces that once dotted the riverbanks.

The **Carrie Furnaces** (N. Braddocksfield Ave., Rankin, 412/464-4020, www.riversofsteel.com, tour $15-25) are one of the last vestiges of southwestern Pennsylvania's industrial heyday. Towering 92 feet over the Monongahela River, the decommissioned blast furnaces look both ancient and futuristic, like something from a science fiction movie. Built in 1906, the pair were part of a complex of seven blast furnaces that produced iron for U.S. Steel's Homestead Works, which

The Carrie Furnaces produced iron for the world's largest steel works.

was one of the world's largest steelworks until it closed in 1986. Special railroad cars called torpedo cars carried the molten iron across the river, where it was converted into steel.

As part of an abandoned industrial site, the furnaces are generally closed to the public. But the nonprofit Rivers of Steel Heritage Corporation, which acquired the site in 2010, offers tours on Friday mornings from June through August and Saturday mornings from late April through October. Plans call for a multimillion-dollar rehabilitation, but for now, visitors have the rare chance to explore a largely untouched ruin of an industrial empire.

Entertainment and Events

Anybody who complains about the entertainment scene in Pittsburgh either isn't looking or hails from a much larger city. Look no further than the event listings in the weekly *Pittsburgh City Paper* (www.pghcity paper.com) for ways to unwind, whether your tastes lean toward death metal or classical dance. The pickings are particularly plenteous in summer, when many parks double as concert venues and open-air theaters, festivals abound, and the likes of Jimmy Buffett and Phish play the First Niagara Pavilion.

It's worth noting that Pittsburgh's cultural breadth has grown over the past several decades even as the population has shrunk. Theaters, galleries, artist studios, and dance companies have sprung up in both chic and rumpled sections of town. Nowhere is the phenomenon more striking than in Downtown, where a 14-square-block Cultural District has risen from the proverbial ashes. Herds of smartly dressed theatergoers roam the streets. The corner of 7th Street and Penn Avenue, once home to Doc Johnson's International House of Love Potions and Marital Aids, is now an outdoor exhibition space for temporary installations. Empty storefronts: gone. Cocktails and ceviche: check.

BARS AND LOUNGES

It shouldn't come as a surprise that a sports-obsessed city with several colleges would support numerous bars. Pittsburgh's watering holes are a diverse bunch, with sticky-floored, student-packed, Bud-and-wings joints only a slim majority. This is a town that's coming around to delicate cocktails and craft beers. Don't believe it? Witness the queue of hipsters, glass jugs in hand, at **East End Brewing Company** (147 Julius St., 412/537-2337, www. eastendbrewing.com, growler hours 4pm-8pm Tues.-Fri., noon-5pm Sat., 10am-2pm Sun.), a microbrewery that's decidedly off the beaten path. The **Steel City Big Pour** (www.con-structionjunction.org, Sept.), a craft beer festival born in 2007, sells out year after year.

Generally speaking, head Downtown for bars filled with smartly dressed professionals and theatergoers. To barhop with herds of 20-somethings, hightail it to East Carson Street on the South Side. When the Steelers or Pirates are playing, bob in a sea of black and gold on the North Side.

Downtown and the Strip District

The house drinks at **Seviche** (930 Penn Ave., 412/697-3120, www.seviche.com, 5pm-midnight Mon.-Thurs., 4pm-1am Fri., 5pm-1am Sat., tapas $8-12) are the caipirinha and pisco sour, but who can resist the mojito list? Arrive before 7pm Monday-Thursday to enjoy them at half price. The high-ceilinged, multihued bar, offspring of its French proprietor's love affair with Latin culture, also has a sweet selection of South American and Spanish wines and beers. Food-wise, Seviche specializes in—what else?—ceviche, offering an assortment of fresh seafood and seven different preparations. Be sure to sample Fire and Ice, traditional ceviche made spicier with habanero peppers and topped with homemade prickly pear granita. On Monday nights, tables are moved aside for salsa dancing.

Brick-lined and romantically lit, **Olive or Twist** (140 6th St., 412/255-0525, www.olive-twist.com, 11:30am-close Mon.-Fri., 3pm-close Sat., food $9-24) is a martini bar par excellence. The 'tini options number more than 20 and range from the classic marriage of gin and vermouth to liquid desserts like the Chocolate Covered Pretzel Martini.

Above-average appetizers, sandwiches, and entrées make Olive or Twist a fine choice for a meal. The same is true of **Tonic Bar & Grill** (971 Liberty Ave., 412/456-0460, www. tonicpittsburgh.com, 11am-midnight Mon.-Wed., 11am-2am Thurs.-Sat., food $10-22), where freshly squeezed fruit juices give extra goodness to drinks like the Goose & Juice and Lemon Drop Martini. Burgers come in your choice of Angus beef, chicken, turkey, or veggie.

Many of the Strip District's gems are along Penn Avenue. On a nice day, take in the streetscape from the deck of **Roland's Iron Landing,** upstairs neighbor to **Roland's Seafood Grill** (1904 Penn Ave., 412/261-3401, www.rolandsseafoodgrill.com, 11am-1am Sun.-Thurs., 11am-2am Fri.-Sat., food $8-40). Downstairs: 30 draft beers, game room, raw bar, and extensive menu. Upstairs: coolers packed with bottled beers and fewer food options. You can order the "famous" hot lobster roll no matter where you sit. The wood-fired pizzas are delightful and a great deal when shared.

Small-production wines and craft cocktails are the star attractions at **Bar Marco** (2216 Penn Ave., 412/471-1900, www.barmarcopgh. com, 5pm-11pm Mon., 5pm-2am Tues.-Sat., brunch 10am-3pm Sat.-Sun., food under $15), one of the most stylish spots in the Strip with its subway tile walls and handcrafted furniture. The limited menu features charcuterie, "snacks" such as lamb tartare and fried smelts, and an entrée du jour. On weekends the former firehouse opens early for brunch.

For Irish-style carousing, head to **Mullaney's Harp & Fiddle** (2329 Penn Ave., 412/642-6622, www.harpandfiddle.com, 11:30am-1am Tues.-Thurs., 11:30am-2am Fri.-Sat., food $8-17). The mostly middle-aged members of the Pittsburgh Ceili Club turn out every Tuesday evening for something akin to square dancing.

North Side

You can't swing a bat without hitting a sports bar outside PNC Park, home of the

Pittsburgh Pirates. Irish stylings are so prevalent as to warrant comparisons to Chicago's Wrigleyville. In fact, **Mullen's Bar and Grill** (200 Federal St., 412/231-1112, www.mullensbarandgrill.com, 11am-1am Sun.-Thurs., 11am-2am Fri.-Sat., food $5-15) is a younger sibling of a Wrigleyville watering hole. Neither Mullen's nor **McFadden's** (211 N. Shore Dr., 412/322-3470, www.mcfaddenspitt.com, 11am-2am Mon.-Sat., open for Sun. stadium events, food $7-15), which has its roots in New York City, offers much in the way of Irish cuisine. They're packed when the Pirates or Steelers are playing but rather cheerless otherwise.

A touch more upscale, **Atria's Restaurant and Tavern** (103 Federal St., 412/322-1850, www.atrias.com, 11am-10pm Mon.-Sat., noon-6pm Sun., food $9-27) makes a mean sherry crab bisque. It's in PNC Park but accessible from the street.

A sports bar named **SoHo** (203 Federal St., 412/321-7646, www.sohopittsburgh.com, 11am-1am daily, food $9-30) makes about as much sense as an art gallery named Sluggers. It makes more sense when you consider that SoHo doubles as the on-site restaurant of the North Shore's SpringHill Suites. The Terrible Towel crowd will find what it's looking for (13 wide-screen televisions and bottles of Iron City), as will the suit-and-tie crowd (filet mignon and a martini menu). Don't be surprised if a few Pirates belly up to the large central bar after a winning game.

There are good reasons to leave the orbit of the stadiums, namely the **Monterey Pub** and **Max's Allegheny Tavern.** The Monterey Pub (1227 Monterey St., 412/322-6535, www.montereypub.com, 3pm-midnight Mon.-Thurs., 3pm-1am Fri.-Sat., $8-14) is tucked into a residential street in the historic Mexican War Streets neighborhood, but you'll know it by its paint job: forest green with orange and white trim. If you haven't guessed already, this is an Irish-style establishment. Inside, it's cozy as can be. Slip into a mahogany booth, order a pint, and ponder the menu's unorthodox selection of nachos. If you prefer a little piece

of Germany to a little piece of Ireland, head to Max's Allegheny Tavern (537 Suismon St., Pittsburgh, 412/231-1899, www.maxsalleghenytavern.com, 11am-10pm Mon.-Thurs., 11am-11pm Fri.-Sat., 9:30am-9pm Sun., food $6-18) in the heart of the Deutschtown neighborhood. The bar and restaurant dates to the turn of the previous century. Wash down the *hasenpfeffer* (braised rabbit in spiced red wine sauce) with a Hacker-Pschorr, Spaten, or other German brew. When the Steelers have a home game, Max's offers complimentary shuttle service to Heinz Field.

South Side

No debate about it: The South Side's East Carson Street is party central. There's a bar—or two or three—on nearly every block in the business and entertainment district, roughly defined as the section between 9th and 28th Streets. It's been called the longest continuous stretch of bars in the country. Shot-n-beer joints predominate, but there's sleek sprinkled into the mix and even the occasional velvet rope. Word of caution: If you're over 25, you might feel downright geriatric as you navigate this swiftly flowing river of youth.

When it comes to beer selection and bar food, **Fat Head's Saloon** (1805 E. Carson St., 412/431-7433, www.fatheads.com, 11am-midnight Mon.-Thurs., 11am-1am Fri.-Sat., 11am-11pm Sun., food $7-30) is head and shoulders above the rest. Its 42 draft beers are mainly of the craft variety and invariably include a hand-pumped "real ale." Munchies include mussels steamed with Sierra Nevada Pale Ale and deep-fried shrimp coated in one of 13 wing sauces. Consider splitting one of the ginormous "headwiches." The Southside Slopes Headwich, an incomparable combo of kielbasa, fried pierogies, American cheese, and grilled onions, weighed in at number five when men's mag *Maxim* scoured the United States for the best "meat hog" sandwiches.

Speaking of ginormous, the specialty drinks at **Carson City Saloon** (1401 E. Carson St., 412/481-3203, www.carsoncitysaloon.com, 11:30am-1:45am Mon.-Sat., noon-midnight Sun., food $6-21) include the prophetically named Call A Cab, a 64-ounce bowl of Lord-knows-what that's meant to be shared. Some people aren't good at sharing, and those people are more than welcome at Carson City, which prides itself on "a complete lack of social morality." Draft options usually include a few fruity imports, aka girly beers. Check out the wheelchair-accessible bathroom; it was a vault when the building was a bank.

Theme bars are fairly in vogue on the South Side. The volcano-inspired **Lava Lounge** (2204 E. Carson St., 412/431-5282, www.lavaloungepgh.com, 5pm-2am Mon.-Fri., 7pm-2am Sat., 8pm-2am Sun.) attracts an artsier-than-average crowd. Its proprietors also own the Beehive coffee house, an East Carson institution, so perhaps it's not surprising that the drinks menu includes a good number of coffee cocktails and so-called coffee shots. Don't bother asking for a food menu; Lava Lounge offers meatballs on Mondays, tacos on Tuesdays, sausage sandwiches on Wednesdays, and veggie versions of all three. Nightly diversions range from DJ dance parties to spelling bees.

Lava Lounge's owners journeyed to Bali for bamboo, beads, masks, and other decorations when they decided to open a retro-style tiki bar a couple of blocks away. Buy a tropical cocktail at **Tiki Lounge** (2003 E. Carson St., 412/381-8454, www.tikilounge.biz, 4pm-2am Mon.-Sat., 8pm-2am Sun.) and you can keep the kitschy mug it comes in. DJs spin hits on weekends; a jukebox provides the tunes on school nights.

You don't have to be a bookworm to appreciate **The Library** (2302 E. Carson St., 412/381-0517, www.thelibrary-pgh.com, 11am-2am daily, food $7-28), whose food and drink menus are littered with literary references. Signature drinks include Grapes of Wrath, a combo of grape-flavored vodka, triple sec, and three fruit juices. Hungry? Try the Animal Farm sandwich: freshly sliced turkey, peppered bacon, gouda, and a fried egg on a pretzel bun baked a few doors down at

The Pretzel Shop. Let's not forget that The Library has a swell selection of craft brews and a charming rooftop patio.

Spandex never goes out of style at **OTB (Over The Bar) Bicycle Café** (2518 E. Carson St., 412/381-3698, www.otbbicyclecafe. com, 11am-2am Mon.-Sat., noon-2am Sun., food $6-12). The watering hole is a tribute to two-wheeled travel, with bicycles hanging from the ceiling, gears decorating the walls, and sconces made of spokes. Be sure to check out the toilet paper holders, also made from bike parts.

Piper's Pub (1828 E. Carson St., 412/381-3977, www.piperspub.com, 11am-midnight Mon.-Fri., 8:30am-midnight Sat.-Sun., food $8-23) promises "a taste of the British Isles," and lad does it deliver. Draft brews include Guinness, Smithwick's, and Smuttynose Old Brown Dog, but it's the scotch list that really sets Piper's apart. That and vittles rarely seen in these parts, including Scotch eggs (hard-boiled eggs wrapped in sausage meat, breaded, and deep-fried). In a city obsessed with Super Bowl wins, Piper's tunes its tellies to football matches of a different sort.

A Bavarian-style *bier* hall is one the newest additions to the South Side suds scene. The humongous **Hofbräuhaus Pittsburgh** (2705 S. Water St., 412/224-2328, www.hofbrauhauspittsburgh.com, 11am-midnight Mon.-Wed., 11am-1am Thurs., 11am-2am Fri.-Sat., noon-midnight Sun., food $9-25) couldn't be more cartoonish if Walt Disney himself had risen from the dead to design it. Picture female servers clad in dirndls. Picture men in lederhosen playing oompah music. Picture, in short, a rollicking good time. Modeled after Munich's famous Hofbräuhaus, the Pittsburgh branch employs a brew master from Germany who supervises the production of four year-round beers and a seasonal unveiled on the first Wednesday of every month. You can order a burger or fettuccine alfredo, but *come on,* this is the Hofbräuhaus. Stick to specialties you can't pronounce, like the Wurstlplatte, a sampler of three wursts. And do try the soft pretzels, imported from

Germany and served with homemade beer-infused cheese. Hofbräuhaus is two blocks north of East Carson in the SouthSide Works development. Revelers spill from the *bier* hall into a riverside *biergarten* in summertime.

East End

It's not hard to find a bar in East End neighborhoods such as Oakland, Bloomfield, East Liberty, and Shadyside. Standouts include Friendship's **Sharp Edge Beer Emporium** (302 S. Saint Clair St., 412/661-3537, www.sharpedgebeer.com, 11am-midnight Mon.-Thurs., 11am-1am Fri.-Sat., noon-9pm Sun., food $10-18), which may well have the largest beer selection in the Burgh, with 70 taps and more than 250 bottles. It's nationally recognized for its Belgians but doesn't discriminate against brews of other provenance. Bewildered by the array? You can fall back on the hops-heavy house beer, Over the Edge, or take a chance on the "mystery beer." Sharp Edge sponsors a European beer festival in June and an annual homebrew competition. The latter's winning entry is commercially brewed and added to the draft offerings. Sharp Edge has four sister establishments, including one in Downtown, but the beer list at the Friendship location is unparalleled.

The Art Deco **Kelly's Bar & Lounge** (6012 Penn Circle S., 412/363-6012) in East Liberty evokes an era when dudes called chicks "doll" and *Double Indemnity* was in theaters. Contrived? Hardly. This place has been around since the 1940s. Order a classic cocktail—a sidecar, perhaps—for maximum effect. The beer selection is quite good, and the mac and cheese worth every calorie. Wondering why so many 30-something bohos head toward the bathrooms and never return? There's a no-frills patio out back.

NIGHTCLUBS

Nightclubs tend to come and go with a rapidity that's maddening to guidebook writers. Of this you can be sure: You'll find a dance floor at Station Square (Carson St. at Smithfield Street Bridge). The dining and entertainment complex across the Monongahela River from Downtown boasts several nightclubs under one roof, so if one door closes, another will surely be open. With a capacity of 1,100 people, **Whim** (412/281-9888, www.whimpitt.com, 9pm-2am Thurs.-Sat.) bills itself as the largest nightclub in Pittsburgh. Six bars keep the masses hydrated, while guests looking for VIP treatment can choose from more than 20 bottle-service areas. DJs usually get the credit for a packed dance floor, but at Whim, the lighting technicians are partly to thank. On Thursdays the club reels in college students with an 18-and-over admission policy and $2 Yuenglings. It's strictly 21 and over on Fridays and Saturdays.

Should you tire of the Station Square scene, head east on Carson Street to **Diesel Club Lounge** (1601 E. Carson St., 412/431-8800, www.dieselclublounge.com, 9pm-2am Thurs.-Sat.). Lighting maestros from Miami had a hand in its design, which helps explain why the slick multilevel nightclub looks more South Beach than South Side.

The Strip District also has its share of nightlife options, including **Static** (1650 Smallman St., 412/315-7330, www.staticpgh.com, 9pm-2am Fri.-Sat.), notable for its devotion to electronic music. Its neighbor, **Club Zoo** (1630 Smallman St., 412/201-1100, www.clubzoo.net, 7:30pm-1am Sat.), caters to the under-21 crowd.

LIVE MUSIC

The opening of **CONSOL Energy Center** (1001 5th Ave., general information 412/642-1800, tickets 800/745-3000, www.consolenergycenter.com) in 2010 changed the city's concert landscape. The Pittsburgh Penguins' new home is not only bigger than their previous digs, but also better equipped for over-the-top stage shows, which means that big-name artists no longer have reason to bypass Pittsburgh. Paul McCartney christened the $321 million venue; Lady Gaga had committed to two shows before it even opened.

The region's largest concert venue, **First Niagara Pavilion** (665 Route 18,

Burgettstown, 724/947-7400, www.livena-tion.com), boasts pavilion and lawn seating for more than 20,000. It's about 25 miles west of Downtown.

This author's vote for most unique venue goes to **Pepsi-Cola Roadhouse** (565 Route 18, Burgettstown, 724/947-1900, www.pep-siroadhouse.com), located a stone's throw from First Niagara Pavilion. Audience members sit four to a table, feasting on roasted chicken and barbeque ribs while tapping their toes to the likes of Willie Nelson, Tim McGraw, and Keith Urban. All Roadhouse shows are open to all ages.

Mr. Small's Theatre (400 Lincoln Ave., Millvale, general information 412/821-4447, tickets 866/468-3401, www.mrsmalls.com) is runner-up in the "most unique" category. Housed in a former Catholic church, the venue boasts 40-foot-ceilings and heavenly acoustics. Most concerts are standing room only. The Mr. Small's complex also includes recording studios that count the Black Eyed Peas, 50 Cent, and Ryan Adams among their clients. What used to be the priest's living quarters is now a "rock hostel" for visiting artists. Believe it or not, Mr. Small's isn't the only church turned church of rock. So is the Strip District's **Altar Bar** (1620 Penn Ave., general information 412/263-2877, tickets 800/745-3000, www.thealtarbar.com), dedicated to "resurrecting live music in Pittsburgh," and the South Side's dueling piano bar, **Charlie Murdochs** (1005 E. Carson St., 412/431-7464, www.charliemurdochs.com).

The South Side's most revered music venue is **Club Cafe** (56-58 S. 12th St., general information 412/431-4950, tickets 866/468-3401, www.clubcafelive.com), an intimate nightclub that books biggish singer-songwriters, e.g., Jill Sobule and Marshall Crenshaw. Norah Jones made an appearance not long before collecting multiple Grammys for her debut album. Acts filed under "rock" or "blues" also take the stage. The nearby **Rex Theater** (1602 E. Carson St., 412/381-6811, www.rextheater.com) dates to 1905. Vaudeville is out, but you can still count on an eclectic lineup.

The Bloomfield neighborhood also attracts music fans. Artsy types gravitate toward **Brillobox** (4104 Penn Ave., general information 412/621-4900, tickets 866/468-3401, www.brillobox.net, 5pm-2am Tues.-Fri., noon-2am Sat.-Sun.), where local and touring indie bands dish up contemplative lyrics. The venue is perhaps better known for DJ dance parties such as "Pandemic," a global music blowout held on the first Friday of each month. More comfortable surrounded by neon beer signs than original art? Try **Howlers Coyote Cafe** (4509 Liberty Ave., 412/682-0320, www.howlerscoyotecafe.com, 4pm-2am Mon.-Fri., 6pm-2am Sat.-Sun.), neighborhood bar by day, music venue by night (or at least Wednesday through Sunday nights). Roots, rock, country, jazz, blues, metal—"the Coyote," as locals call it, doesn't discriminate. The nearby **Bloomfield Bridge Tavern** (4412 Liberty Ave., 412/682-8611, www.bloomfieldbridgetavern.com, 5pm-2am Mon.-Sat.) bills itself as "the Polish party house," but don't expect an earful of polka. Known for its pierogies and other Polish grub, the BBT offers live music on Friday and Saturday nights. The bands are predominately local and play for the door, so don't be surprised if three-quarters of the patrons know the lead singer.

Heart jazz? Head to **Little E's** (949 Liberty Ave., 2nd floor, 412/392-2217, www.littleesjazz.com) in Downtown. Blues fans should find their way to Blawnox, about 10 miles northeast of Downtown, where **Moondog's** (378 Freeport Rd., Blawnox, 412/828-2040, www.moondogs.us) has been bringing rock and blues acts to the Allegheny River burgh for nearly two decades.

PERFORMING ARTS
Cultural District

Bordered by the Allegheny River on the north, 10th Street on the east, Stanwix Street on the west, and Liberty Avenue on the south, the Cultural District boasts more than half a dozen theaters. Think of it as a miniature version of New York's Broadway theater district. Not unlike Times Square, it's the stardust-sprinkled reincarnation of a seedy section of town. The transformation can be traced to the mid-1960s, when H.J. Heinz Company Chairman Jack Heinz resolved to turn a shuttered movie palace into a new home for the Pittsburgh Symphony Orchestra. In 1971, the former Loew's Penn Theater was dedicated as **Heinz Hall** (600 Penn Ave., 412/392-4900, www.trustarts.org), a vision in red velvet, Italian marble, crystal, and 24-karat gold leaf. It's enough to give you goose bumps even before the renowned **Pittsburgh Symphony Orchestra** (pso. culturaldistrict.org) starts playing. For extra goose bumps, come on a night when the 115-voice **Mendelssohn Choir of Pittsburgh** (www.themendelssohn.org) is also under the spell of the conductor's baton. In addition to classical music performances, the orchestra offers 45-minute kid-friendly concerts and a pops series. Heinz Hall also hosts free concerts by the **Pittsburgh Youth Symphony Orchestra** (www.pittsburghyouthsymphony. org), touring Broadway shows, and other guest performances. And it's home to the annual **Pittsburgh Speakers Series** (www. pittsburghspeakersseries.org), featuring "heroes and legends" such as Madeleine Albright, Salman Rushdie, and Colin Powell.

Jack Heinz's recycling of a 1927 theater scheduled for demolition inspired further development in the "red light" district. In the mid-1980s, the newly formed Pittsburgh Cultural Trust undertook a $43 million restoration of another former movie house a block away. Billed as "Pittsburgh's Palace of Amusement" when it opened in 1928, the resplendent Stanley Theater had fallen into disrepair and into the hands of a rock concert promoter by the late 1970s. (Reggae maestro Bob Marley played his final concert there in 1980.) It reopened in 1987 as the **Benedum Center** (719 Liberty Ave., 412/456-6666, www.trustarts.org), a dead ringer for the Stanley on opening night in 1928, right down to the original 4,700-pound chandelier. The largest theater in the Cultural District, the Benedum hosts performances by

the **Pittsburgh Opera** (www.pittsburghopera.org) and **Pittsburgh Ballet Theatre** (www.pbt.org), along with musical theater productions by **Pittsburgh CLO** (www. pittsburghclo.org). Touring acts also take the stage.

The Cultural Trust's next project was the **Byham Theater** (101 6th St., 412/456-6666, www.trustarts.org), which opened in 1904 as a vaudeville house named the Gayety and became the Fulton movie theater in the 1930s. Look for its original name in the salvaged mosaic tile floor in the entry vestibule. Less ornate than Heinz Hall or the Benedum, the 1,300-seat Byham draws a more casual crowd with dance and theater performances, live music, films, and lectures. The mural on the Fort Duquesne Boulevard facade of the Byham is a tribute to Pittsburgh's steel heritage.

In 1995, the nonprofit Cultural Trust snapped up the 194-seat **Harris Theater** (809 Liberty Ave., 412/682-4111, www.pghfilmmakers.org), formerly known as the Art Cinema. What had started as Pittsburgh's first "art movie" house had morphed into a triple-X theater in the 1960s. Today the Harris is frequented by connoisseurs of classic, independent, and foreign films. It also serves as an intimate setting for live performances.

Next, the Cultural Trust undertook its first from-scratch theater project. Building the **O'Reilly Theater** (621 Penn Ave., 412/316-1600, www.trustarts.org) cost less than renovating the Benedum, even with hotshot architect Michael Graves on the job. The 650-seat theater opened in December 1999 with the world premiere of Pittsburgh-bred playwright August Wilson's *King Hedly II*. It's the only Downtown venue with a thrust stage, surrounded by seats on three sides. As the permanent home of the professional **Pittsburgh Public Theater** (www.ppt.org), good for more than 200 performances a year, the O'Reilly rarely gets a rest.

Graves also signed on to design **Theater Square** (655 Penn Ave.), completed in 2003. The nine-story complex houses a large parking garage and a box office (9am-9pm

Mon.-Sat., noon-6pm Sun.) that sells tickets to Cultural District events. It's also home to the 260-seat **Cabaret at Theater Square** (412/456-6666, www.trustarts.org), which hosts toe-tapping musical productions such as *Nunsense,* salsa dancing, wine and beer tastings, and other events.

Carnegie Music Hall

Come early if you're coming to the 1,950-seat **Carnegie Music Hall** (4400 Forbes Ave.), part of the complex that includes the Carnegie Museums of Art and Natural History. Its most magnificent feature is its anticipation-heightening foyer, 45 feet high, liberally gilded, and ringed with fat columns of green marble. The hall itself, humble by comparison, is the setting for concerts presented by the **Pittsburgh Chamber Music Society** (412/624-4129, www.pittsburghchambermusic.org), which imports the world's most celebrated ensembles. It's also one of the stomping grounds of the **River City Brass Band** (412/434-7222, www.rcbb.com), 28 brass players and percussionists with a repertoire that ranges from traditional marches to Hollywood tunes. The **Drue Heinz Lectures** (412/622-8866, www.pittsburghlectures.org) bring literary luminaries to Carnegie Music Hall on select Monday evenings. Balcony-supporting columns make for some obstructed views; steer clear of them when reserving tickets.

Carnegie Lecture Hall, a smaller venue in the same complex, is home to a lecture series for pint-size bookworms, **PA&L Kids and Teens** (412/622-8866, www.pittsburghlectures.org). Fans of traditional and contemporary roots music fill the lecture hall for concerts presented by **Calliope: The Pittsburgh Folk Music Society** (412/361-1915, www.calliopehouse.org).

City Theatre

Not content to recycle tried-and-true theatrical works, **City Theatre** (1300 Bingham St., 412/431-2489, www.citytheatrecompany.org) embraces the edgy and new. Expect a good number of world premieres in a typical season.

The 254-seat main stage and a second smaller theater are a block from the South Side's carousing corridor, East Carson Street. For $7, patrons can park at the theater for a couple of hours before and after performances and hoof it to shops, restaurants, and watering holes.

Kelly-Strayhorn Theater

The multiuse **Kelly-Strayhorn Theater** (5941 Penn Ave., 412/363-3000, www.kelly-strayhorn.org) has an ambitious agenda: support the arts *and* revitalize an urban neighborhood considered blighted at worst and transitional at best. The last of nine theaters from East Liberty's golden era, the 350-seat Kelly-Strayhorn is named for Hollywood musicals megastar Gene Kelly and jazz composer Billy "Sweet Pea" Strayhorn, two of Pittsburgh's favorite sons. Not surprisingly, it usually showcases homegrown talent.

Pittsburgh Playhouse

Point Park University's **Pittsburgh Playhouse** (222 Craft Ave., 412/392-8000, www.pittsburghplayhouse.com) is the three-theater home of four companies. The REP, the professional one in the bunch, cherry-picks plays with a Pittsburgh connection or themes that resonate here. The rest are student companies: one theater, one children's theater, and one dance. Add 'em up and you get 18 major productions and 235 performances a year.

FESTIVALS AND EVENTS
Year-Round

Missed the Pittsburgh Three Rivers Regatta or Light Up Night? You're out of luck for another year. Missed a **JazzLive** (412/456-6666, www.trustarts.org) performance? Catch next week's. The free showcase of area jazz talent takes place every Tuesday starting at 5pm in Theater Square (655 Penn Ave.) or the adjacent Katz Plaza (7th St. and Penn Ave.) in the heart of the Cultural District.

Also the work of the Pittsburgh Cultural Trust, **Gallery Crawl in the Cultural District** (412/456-6666, www.trustarts.org, free) is a quarterly roving soiree featuring live music, cheap eats, and lots and lots of art. Galleries keep their doors open until 9pm for the Friday evening crawls.

Local knitters, crocheters, potters, jewelry-makers, and other glue-gun packers peddle their wares at **I Made It! Market** (412/254-4464, www.imadeitmarket.com, free), a nomadic crafts fair. Pretty good chance you'll find your new favorite fingerless gloves there. Add your email address to the mailing list for updates about the market's whereabouts.

Summer

Pittsburghers elevate picnicking to an art form during **First Fridays at the Frick** concerts (412/371-0600, www.thefrickpittsburgh. org, first Friday June-Sept., $5 suggested donation), which signal the start and end of summer in this city. Think wine and brie. Think flickering candles. Regulars begin laying claim to sections of lawn at the Frick Art & Historical Center an hour and a half before showtime. It doesn't seem to matter what kind of music is on tap. African-inspired jazz, reggae, Celtic music—clinking glasses of chardonnay complement them all.

Several of Pittsburgh's public parks also host free concerts during the summer months. There's the **Stars at Riverview** jazz series (Sat. evenings June-Aug.) at Riverview Park, the **Reservoir of Jazz** series (Sun. evenings in Aug.) at Highland Park, and the **Bach, Beethoven and Brunch** (Sun. mornings mid-June-mid-Aug.) classical series at Mellon Park. For dates, times, and directions, consult the Citiparks website (www.pittsburghpa.gov/ citiparks) or call 412/255-2493.

The city is also sweet to movie buffs, treating them to an alfresco flick every night of the week in summer. **Cinema in the Park** locations vary from night to night, but showtime is always dusk. Check the Citiparks website (www.pittsburghpa.gov/citiparks) or call 412/422-6426 for locations and movie listings.

What started in 1960 as an effort by museum types to bring the arts to non-museum types has blossomed into the something-for-everyone **Three Rivers Arts Festival** (412/471-3191, www.3riversartsfest. org, June, free). The 10-day festival draws hundreds of thousands of people to Point State Park and other Downtown sights. Some come for the original artworks and handmade fine crafts. Some come for corn dogs, chicken on a stick, or chocolate-covered strawberries. The lineup of free performances lures everyone else.

Machines capable of speeds of 130 mph ply local waterways during the **Three Rivers Regatta** (www.threeriversregatta.net, July 4 weekend, free). But the spectacle-packed weekend isn't just about powerboat racing. Recent regattas have treated the masses to motocross and water-ski stunt shows, competitive-eating and bass-fishing contests, car-rollover simulations courtesy of the Pennsylvania State Police, and even a high-wire trek across the Allegheny River by professional daredevil Nik Wallenda—sans safety net. The regatta also presents Pittsburgh's official 4th of July pyrotechnic show.

If you find yourself driving alongside a "gullwing" Mercedes-Benz or a 1959 Ferrari, chances are it's **Pittsburgh Vintage Grand Prix** (412/299-2273, www.pvgp.org, July, free) time. The 10-day tribute to classic and exotic cars started as a one-day race in 1983 and has grown to include shows, cruises, and races in half a dozen locations. It culminates the third weekend in July with a show of some 2,000 beauts and a series of vintage sports car races at Schenley Park. Nowhere else in the nation can you see such races on city streets.

Unlike the arts festival, regatta, and many other outdoor events, the **Pittsburgh Blues Festival** (412/460-2583, www.pghblues.com, July, Saturday/Sunday admission $30-35, weekend pass $45-50, children 12 and under free) isn't free. But $50 isn't a bad deal for a weekend of first-rate blues, especially when you consider that proceeds benefit the Greater Pittsburgh Community Food Bank. (Friday admission is free with a bag of nonperishable foods.) The festival takes place at Hartwood

Acres, an Allegheny County park about 11 miles northeast of downtown Pittsburgh.

Fall

The splendid and cleverly titled **A Fair in the Park** (Mellon Park, 412/370-0695, www.afairinthepark.org, weekend after Labor Day, free) is a great opportunity to get a jump on holiday shopping. The showcase of high-quality crafts is presented by the Craftsmen's Guild of Pittsburgh.

A jolly good time, the **Pittsburgh Irish Festival** (412/422-1113, www.pghirishfest.org, weekend after Labor Day, admission $3-12) could make you fall in love with the Emerald Isle—maybe even enough to fork over 15 bucks for a bag of soil presumably gathered there. The three-day festival is heavy on music and dance but dutifully showcases other aspects of Celtic culture, including sports, crafts, cuisine, and even native dog breeds. It's set at the appropriately emerald Riverplex, a large picnic grounds adjacent to Sandcastle water park.

Winter

Downtown slips into her holiday threads on **Light Up Night** (412/566-4190, www.downtownpittsburgh.com, Nov., free) and, *girrrl*, we're talking serious bling-bling. An estimated 200,000 people turn out to see buildings and trees dripping with the electric equivalent of diamonds. Highlights include the unveiling of holiday window displays at Macy's, the lighting of towering Christmas trees, and, of course, the arrival of Santa. Across the Monongahela River, Station Square also gets its twinkle on.

First of all, **First Night Pittsburgh** (412/456-6666, www.firstnightpgh.com, Dec. 31) takes place on the last night of the year, not the first. Second of all, it's not the bacchanalia you may have come to expect from New Year celebrations. First Night is family-friendly and, like all projects of the Pittsburgh Cultural Trust, arts-focused. You

can learn to rumba, pick up puppetry, take in a magic show, sway to gospel, listen to a steel drum band, and catch a performance by Croatian folk dancers—all before counting down to midnight. The grand finale: fireworks, of course. The Cultural Trust squeezes more than a hundred programs into the six-hour party, which spans dozens of Downtown locations. A First Night button is required for indoor events; unless you're part Inuit or otherwise immune to Pittsburgh winters, shell out the $8-10. Children five and under can tag along for free.

Spring

Pittsburgh's **St. Patrick's Day Parade** (www.pittsburghirish.org/parade, mid-Mar., free) traces its history to 1869. And while the tribute to Ireland's favorite patron saint was suspended for several decades in the 1900s, it has taken a firm hold on Pittsburghers' affections in recent ones—so much so that the great blizzard of 1993, which closed airports and highways, couldn't stop it. The parade always takes place on a Saturday; if St. Patrick's Day falls on any other day, the floats, marching bands, and nimble-footed dancers snake their way through Downtown on the Saturday preceding it. Expect a fair number of inebriated spectators. Their shenanigans have prompted condemnations from parade organizers and increased police presence in recent years.

Performing arts groups from as far away as Spain and the Republic of Congo entertain at the **Pittsburgh International Children's Festival** (412/456-6666, www.pghkids.org, May). The five-day event in and around Oakland's Schenley Plaza is one of the nation's only international theater festivals for kids. All featured performances require tickets, which can be purchased in advance or at the on-site box office. Seeing as how kids are the intended audience, free "lap passes" are reserved for those under two.

Shopping

Come Black Friday, you'll find more traffic leaving Pittsburgh than coming into it. The biggest malls, not surprisingly, are outside the city limits. They're in Monroeville, Robinson Township, Ross Township, and other suburbs. But the city isn't without its shopping destinations, including the incomparable Strip District. Pittsburgh also has one of the more pleasant outdoor malls in southwestern Pennsylvania—SouthSide Works—and several shopping districts with a good number of independent, one-of-a-kind stores.

DOWNTOWN AND THE STRIP DISTRICT

Pittsburgh's business core doesn't top any lists of shopping meccas, but it is home to a massive **Macy's** (400 5th Ave., 412/232-2000, www.macys.com, open daily). It wasn't so long ago that the grand department store on the corner of 5th Avenue and Smithfield Street was known as Kaufmann's. It was, in fact, the flagship store of the home-grown chain. Locals tsk-tsked Macy's parent Federated Department Store Inc. for erasing the Kaufmann's name, but there's nary a complaint about the store's selection of clothing, jewelry, housewares, and more. Macy's curries favor by continuing a tradition started by Kaufmann's: a holiday parade held a couple of days after Thanksgiving. Its holiday window displays also draw crowds.

Downtown's neighbor to the northeast, the Strip District, is hog heaven for foodies. It's home to block after block of specialty foods purveyors, including a store wholly devoted to spices. This is where chefs go to shop. If cooking isn't your thing, go anyway, preferably on a Saturday morning. That's when the crowds are thickest and the air permeated with the smells of street foods; it's also when the Strip is more of an experience than a shopping trip.

The narrow strip of a neighborhood is bordered by the Allegheny River on the north, 11th Street on the east, and 33rd Street on the west. Most must-stops are clustered along **Penn Avenue** between 17th and 22nd Streets. At Penn and 21st, there's **Mon Aimee Chocolat** (2101 Penn Ave., 412/395-0022, www.monaimeechocolat.com, 8:30am-5pm Mon.-Fri., 7:30am-5pm Sat., 10am-3:30pm Sun.), an Elysium of specialty and artisanal chocolates. If it's a cold day, treat yourself to a swig of delectable hot chocolate.

Across Penn Avenue from Mon Aimee is **La Prima Espresso Bar** (205 21st St., 412/281-1922, www.laprima.com, 6am-4pm Mon.-Sat., 8am-2pm Sun.), run by the first certified organic coffee roaster in Pittsburgh.

A few blocks away, **Prestogeorge Fine Foods** (1719 Penn Ave., 412/471-0133, 8am-4pm Mon.-Thurs., 8am-5pm Fri., 7am-5pm Sat.) offers 400-plus varieties of coffee and loose-leaf tea. You'll be greeted by the aroma of freshly roasted beans and red-aproned specialists who can steer you toward a selection that's just right for your palate.

The legendary selection of cheeses at **Pennsylvania Macaroni Co.** (2010-2012 Penn Ave., 412/471-8330, www.pennmac.com, 6:30am-4:30pm Mon.-Sat., 9am-2:30pm Sun.) can be downright overwhelming. Try this: Say "just surprise me" to the deli staff. What you'll taste will likely become a lifelong addiction. Penn Mac, as locals call it, was founded in 1902 by three Sicilian brothers, and the family is still at the wheel. Pasta manufacturing was its first business; today it offers more than 5,000 specialty products, including all things Italian.

Five Greek brothers who landed in America in 1907 opened **Stamoolis Brothers Co.** (2020 Penn Ave., 412/471-7676, www.stamoolisbros.com, 7am-4pm Mon.-Fri., 7:30am-4pm Sat.). Olives of many shades, sizes, and tastes can be found here, along with stuffed grape leaves, spanakopita, and other Mediterranean specialties. The Strip has Asian and Mexican markets, too.

If fresh fish is what you're after, join the sea of customers at **Wholey's** (1711 Penn Ave., 412/391-3737, www.wholey.com, 8am-5:30pm Mon.-Thurs., 8am-6pm Fri., 8am-5pm Sat., 9am-4pm Sun.). It has whole fish on ice and live ones swimming in tanks, fresh fillets and steaks, smoked fish, lobster, crab, squid, and more. Wholey's (pronounced "woolies") also sells cleaned rabbit and other meats. If your hunt for the perfect cut whets your appetite, order up a fried fish sandwich or something from the on-site sushi bar, then head upstairs for seating.

Because the littlest ingredients can make the biggest difference, it's prudent to stop by **Penzeys Spices** (1729 Penn Ave., 412/434-0570, www.penzeys.com, 9am-5pm Mon.-Sat., 9am-3pm Sun.). Just try to name a spice that's not in stock. Penzeys carries everything from salt and pepper to ajwain seeds from Pakistan and whole Turkish mahlab. It also has a wide array of hand-mixed seasonings that simplify cooking. With locations across the country, Penzeys is one of the few Strip merchants that's not locally based. If you're not locally based, you'll be happy to know that many Strip favorites, including Prestogeorge, Penn Mac, and Wholey's, do a brisk business on the Internet.

Neighbors in the Strip (1212 Smallman St., mezzanine level, 412/201-4774, www.neighborsinthestrip.com, 9am-5pm Mon.-Fri.) distributes free maps that are very handy, though not comprehensive. Pick one up in the Strip or request one online. The website is a good source of information about the neighborhood's history.

SOUTH SIDE

It's easy to while away a day shopping in the **East Carson Street business district,** roughly bounded by 9th and 28th Streets. Figure 20 minutes per block, 20 blocks, and, just like that, seven hours gone. If you're an architecture buff, allow more time to admire the nation's longest Victorian-era business district. What's remarkable is that just a few decades ago, after the city's steel industry

ground to a halt, East Carson practically had tumbleweeds blowing through it.

Where once stood a massive steelmaking enterprise, now stands an open-air mall. Actually, "mall" doesn't tell the whole story. **SouthSide Works** (riverfront between 26th and Hot Metal Sts., 412/481-1750, www.southsideworks.com) is what developers call a lifestyle center. The retail/dining/entertainment/residential/office complex, complete with a tastefully landscaped "town square," officially opened in 2004 and hasn't stopped growing. It's home to a 10-screen movie theater and about 30 retailers, including H&M, Urban Outfitters, REI, Sur La Table, and American Eagle Outfitters. Independently owned stores are sprinkled into the mix. Among the dining options are Cheesecake Factory and McCormick & Schmick's Seafood Restaurant. Maps of the property and information about upcoming events are available at a guest services kiosk on the corner of East Carson and 27th Streets.

Heading west on East Carson Street from SouthSide Works, you'll find small, one-of-a-kind stores interspersed with bars and eateries, tattoo parlors, and live music venues. There's a shop that specializes in designer jeans and a shop that carries *Star Wars* figurines. East Carson even has a magic shop, **The Cuckoo's Nest** (2304 1/2 E. Carson St., 412/481-4411, www.thecuckoosnest.com, open Mon.-Sat.), where aspiring illusionists can stock up on top hats, trick coins, and much more. "Please choose carefully," read the signs. "Magic is NOT returnable."

SQUIRREL HILL

Just east of Oakland, Squirrel Hill is best known for its large Jewish population. It's home to **Pinskers Judaica Center** (2028 Murray Ave., 412/421-3033, www.judaism.com, closed Sat.), a source for Jewish books and gifts since 1954. But the shopping on its main thoroughfares, **Forbes and Murray Avenues,** is mostly of the secular variety. Just a block from Pinskers is **Jerry's Records** (2136 Murray Ave., 412/421-4533, www.jerrysrecords.com, open daily), a magnet for vinyl enthusiasts from near and far. Like its albums, which number well over a million, the expansive store is a relic of another era. *Paste* magazine crowned it the "best place to spot world-renowned crate diggers—and nab a bargain at the same time."

With its whimsical sign and obsequious staff, **Littles Shoes** (5850 Forbes Ave., 412/521-3530, www.littlesshoes.com, open daily) is also a throwback to an earlier time. But its footwear is very much in vogue. Customers range from UGG-coveting tweens to aging fashionistas who began shopping there when *they* were in their tweens.

SHADYSIDE

Just north of Squirrel Hill, Shadyside is one of Pittsburgh's most affluent nabes. It has a couple of shopping corridors. **Walnut Street** between South Negley and South Aiken Avenues is lined with big-name chain stores including Williams-Sonoma, Sephora, Ann Taylor, Gap, J.Crew, Banana Republic, Victoria's Secret, and Apple. There are independents in their midst and along the side streets. **Schiller's Pharmacy** (811 S. Aiken Ave., 412/621-5900, www.schillersrx.com, open daily) on the corner of Walnut and South Aiken has been a Shadyside institution for more than a century. It sells not just meds but also high-end fragrances, cosmetics, and bath and body products. One of the shopping district's most unusual stores is **Kards Unlimited** (5522 Walnut St., 412/622-0500, www.kardsunlimited.com, open daily). True to its curiously spelled name, it has a vast selection of greeting cards, plus stationery, books, and novelties like Jesus and Moses action figures.

Locally owned businesses predominate on Shadyside's **Ellsworth Avenue.** The street runs parallel to Walnut, but its small commercial stretch is on the opposite side of South Negley. Fans of vintage wear are especially well served here.

LAWRENCEVILLE

The riverfront neighborhood of Lawrenceville is a study in arts-driven urban revitalization. It's the larger part of the two-neighborhood **16:62 Design Zone** (www.1662designzone.com), an arts and interior design district that extends from the 16th Street Bridge in the Strip District to the 62nd Street Bridge in Lawrenceville. The zone is home to more than 100 shops, artisan studios, galleries, and professional services firms. Many are located along Lawrenceville's **Butler Street.** Shoppers should focus their energies on the stretch of Butler between 35th and 47th Streets, home to fashion boutiques such as **Pavement** (3629 Butler St., 412/621-6400, www.pavementpittsburgh.com, open daily) and **Pageboy** (3613 Butler St., 412/224-2294, www.pageboypgh.com, closed Tues.), which doubles as a salon.

For clever gifts, it doesn't get better than **Divertido** (3609 Butler St., 412/687-3701, www.divertidoshop.com, open Mon.-Sat.). The eclectic selection includes handmade bags and jewelry, original art, and unconventional baby garb.

At the other end of the shopping corridor is **Jay Design** (4603 Butler St., 412/683-1184, www.jaydesign.com, open Mon.-Sat.), a showplace for exquisite handmade soaps. You'll know it by the bathtub in the window.

GREATER PITTSBURGH

Like SouthSide Works, **The Waterfront** (149 W. Bridge St., Homestead, 412/476-8889, www.waterfrontpgh.com) is an open-air shopping center on riverfront once occupied by an immense steel producer. A line of towering smokestacks near its 22-screen movie theater pays homage to the Homestead Works, silenced in 1986 after 105 years. Far bigger than SouthSide Works, the Waterfront has room enough for Costco, Lowe's, Target, Best Buy, Petco, Office Depot, and other megastores. Clothiers including Ann Taylor Loft, Victoria's Secret, and Children's Place can also be found among its 70-plus stores, restaurants, and entertainment venues. The shopping complex is six miles from downtown Pittsburgh on the southern bank of the Monongahela River.

Sports and Recreation

Pittsburgh has a well-earned reputation as a sports town. The birthplace of football greats Johnny Unitas and Dan Marino became known as the "City of Champions" in the 1970s, when the Pirates won the last two of their five World Series titles and the Steelers claimed Super Bowl title after Super Bowl title after Super Bowl title. The Pittsburgh Penguins captured the world's attention in the early 1990s, bringing home the Stanley Cup twice in two years. If there was any doubt about Pittsburgh's eminence in pro sports, it vanished in 2009. In February, the Steelers defeated the Arizona Cardinals 27-23 in Super Bowl XLIII, becoming the first team to win six National Football League championships. Four months later, the Penguins triumphed over the Detroit Red Wings, four games to three, in the Stanley Cup Final. There's only one way to describe the elation that washed over Pittsburgh in both instances: *You had to be there.* No one was surprised later that year when *Sporting News* magazine handed Pittsburgh the title of "Best Sports City."

There are those who argue that the real heroes of Pittsburgh sports are the fans— "fans like no other," as *Sporting News* put it. "Enthusiastic" doesn't begin to describe them. "Rabid" comes close. A wardrobe without a black and gold sports jersey is something of an anomaly. (Pittsburgh is unique in that all of its major pro sports teams wear the same colors, although the Penguins occasionally don uniforms dominated by powder blue.) The citizenry's favorite accessory: the Terrible Towel, an emblem of devotion to the Steelers. Steeler Nation, as the team's fan base is called, has no geographic boundaries. Its members can be found all across the country, due in part to the team's successes and perhaps in larger part to the collapse of the city's steel industry in the early 1980s, which created a diaspora of Steelers fans.

Of course, cheering on the teams isn't the only pastime in the city of three rivers. As one

might expect, boating and fishing are among the ways to unwind. The city and its environs also afford opportunities for hiking, biking, rock climbing, cross-country skiing, snowshoeing, and more. If you're new to any of these activities or unfamiliar with the area, consider a **Venture Outdoors** (412/255-0564, www.ventureoutdoors.org) outing. The nonprofit recreation company offers a year-round calendar of group activities, from early morning paddles to sunset hikes to overnight bike tours. Instruction and gear are provided. VO folk like noshing almost as much as they like nature; a good number of excursions start or end with food and drink.

PARKS
Frick Park

Schenley Park may be Pittsburgh's most beloved green expanse, but it's not the largest. That distinction goes to **Frick Park** (412/255-2539, www.pittsburghparks.org/frick), a 561-acre sanctuary that straddles several East End neighborhoods. It's less manicured than Schenley, more woodsy. Most mountain bikers will tell you Frick has the best trails in the city. It's also popular with hikers, though the sound of vehicles on the nearby Parkway East (I-376) can really break one's reverie. Another recreational option: the medieval sport of lawn bowling. The **Frick Park Bowling Green** (7300 Reynolds St., 412/782-0848, www.lawnbowlingpittsburgh.org) is the only public lawn bowling green in Pennsylvania. You'll also find off-leash exercise areas for dogs, off-leash exercise areas for kids (aka playgrounds), and red clay tennis courts dating to 1930. Frick has a number of entrances, some marked by distinctive stone gatehouses. Families with young children flock to the playgrounds near the intersection of Forbes and South Braddock Avenues and at Beechwood Boulevard and English Lane. Both are good starting points for a walk in the woods, as is the Frick Environmental Center at 2005 Beechwood Boulevard.

Highland Park

The award for grandest entrance goes to **Highland Park** (412/255-2539, www.pittsburghparks.org/highland), located in the East End neighborhood of the same name. Follow North Highland Avenue to its northernmost point and you'll pass between sculptures atop tall pedestals, arriving at a Victorian-style entry garden complete with fountain, reflecting pool, and neatly arranged benches. Steps at the far end of the garden lead to the park's iconic feature: a 19th-century municipal reservoir circled by a three-quarter-mile promenade. You'll find walkers and joggers and, sometimes, waterfowl. Road cyclists adore Highland Park for its half-mile velodrome, formerly a driver's training course. The park is also home to the Pittsburgh Zoo & PPG Aquarium, a summer jazz series, several playgrounds, a pair of sand volleyball courts, and the city's only long-course swimming pool (151 Lake Dr., 412/665-3637, 1pm-7:45pm Mon.-Fri. and 1pm-5:45pm Sat.-Sun. during summer season, daily admission $4, children 3-15 $3).

Riverview Park

The North Side's **Riverview Park** (Riverview Ave., 412/255-2539, www.pittsburghparks.org/riverview) is popular for its wooded trails, space-themed playground, and swimming pool (400 Riverview Ave., 412/323-7223, 1pm-7:45pm Mon.-Fri. and 1pm-5:45pm Sat.-Sun. during summer season, daily admission $4, children 3-15 $3). It's particularly packed on Saturday evenings in summer, when it hosts a jazz concert followed by an outdoor movie—both free.

County Parks

City parks are a puny bunch relative to the county's collection of green spaces. **North Park** (Pearce Mill Rd., Allison Park, 724/935-1766, www.alleghenycounty.us/parks/npfac.aspx), the largest of Allegheny County's nine parks, is five times larger than Frick, the city's titan. Three county parks have wave pools, something no Pittsburgh park can boast of.

City folk rarely venture to the oases on Pittsburgh's outskirts—precisely because they're on the outskirts. The exception is **Hartwood Acres** (200 Hartwood Acres, Pittsburgh, 412/767-9200, www.allegheny-county.us/parks/hwfac.aspx), a county park so delightful and so adept at staging large events that never mind the drive. At 629 acres, the park about 11 miles northeast of Downtown is one of the smallest in the county network. Its centerpiece is a stately country estate complete with Tudor mansion, stables, and formal gardens. Billed as a window into "the life of leisure and philanthropy so fashionable in the first part of the 20th century," the 1929 mansion is filled with antiques, photographs, and personal items of the family that once called it home. Reservations are recommended for mansion tours (10am-3pm Mon.-Sat., noon-4pm Sun., admission $6, seniors and children 13-17 $4, children 6-12 $2, children 5 and under $1). For a real taste of life in the Hartwood Mansion, come for afternoon tea. Reservations are required for the intermittent tea parties, which sell out more often than not.

The park's summer concert series is hugely popular. Pittsburghers who never step foot into Downtown's Heinz Hall or Benedum Center turn out to listen to the Pittsburgh Symphony Orchestra or Pittsburgh Opera under the stars. The Hartwood Amphitheatre also welcomes reggae, blues, jazz, and country acts, popular bands such as Sun Volt and the Old 97's, and dance companies including the Pittsburgh Ballet and Duquesne Tamburitzans. In July the park hosts the **Pittsburgh Blues Festival** (412/460-2583, www.pghblues.com), a weekend of first-rate music and a fundraiser for the Greater Pittsburgh Community Food Bank. Other annual events include British Car Day and a polo match to benefit the nonprofit Family House, both held in September.

BICYCLING

Pittsburgh's steep hills and tangled streets can be intimidating to novice and new-in-town cyclists. Here to help: **Bike Pittsburgh** (188 43rd St., Suite 1, 412/325-4334, www.bikepgh. org). The advocacy group publishes the free *Pittsburgh Bike Map,* available at its office in Lawrenceville and at like-minded businesses. The map identifies car-free trails, on-street bike routes, steep hills, and *very* steep hills. The online version allows cyclists to explore routes in terrain and satellite modes.

Founded in 2002, Bike Pittsburgh presses for bike lanes and racks, bike route signage, and shared lane markings. Thanks in part to its lobbying, Pittsburgh is transforming into a bike-friendly city. In 2008, it became the first city in Pennsylvania to appoint a full-time bicycle and pedestrian czar. The following year, *Good* magazine called it one of the seven "best burgeoning bike scenes" in North America.

In 2013, local cycling enthusiasts had something else to celebrate: completion of the **Great Allegheny Passage** (www.atatrail. org), a 150-mile trail stretching from Point State Park in Downtown to Cumberland, Maryland. There it meets the 184.5-mile C&O Canal towpath, which traces the Potomac River to Washington DC. Biking to the nation's capital has become a rite of passage for Pittsburgh cyclists.

If you're more interested in a scenic excursion than a days-long journey, hit the 24-mile **Three Rivers Heritage Trail.** Rather than a continuous route, it's a set of trails along the Allegheny, Monongahela, and Ohio Rivers with names to match the areas they traverse. Maps are available from **Friends of the Riverfront** (33 Terminal Way, 412/488-0212, www.friend-softheriverfront.org, 9am-5pm Mon.-Fri.), which spearheads development of the trail.

Need wheels? **Golden Triangle Bike Rental** (600 1st Ave., 412/600-0675, www. bikepittsburgh.com, 9am-8pm daily Apr.-mid-Oct.) is conveniently located along the Eliza Furnace Trail in Downtown, part of the Three Rivers Heritage Trail and Great Allegheny Passage. It offers a wide variety of bikes, including children's bikes and tandems, plus child trailers and tag-a-longs that essentially transform an adult bike into a tandem. Adult bikes start at $8 per hour or $30 per day. Reserve at least a day in advance for a discounted day rate.

Bike enthusiasts should mark their calendars for **BikeFest** (412/325-4334, www. bikepgh.org, Aug.), Bike Pittsburgh's 17-day celebration of all things cycling, and the annual **Pedal Pittsburgh** (412/325-4334, www. pedalpgh.org, Aug.) ride. Mountain bikers will appreciate **Trail Fest** (www.ptagtrails. org), a series of organized rides, runs, and hikes showcasing Allegheny County's parks.

HIKING

If a heart-pumping, mind-quieting walk is what you're after, this famously hilly city is happy to oblige. Test your mettle on Canton Avenue in the neighborhood of Beechview, southeast of Downtown. With a grade of 37 percent, it's the steepest street in these parts and, possibly, the world. (*Guinness World Records* tips its hat to New Zealand's Baldwin Street, with a grade of 35 percent.) Of course, hiking isn't quite hiking without soil under your feet. Excellent trails can be found in many city and county parks. A standout: the 35.7-mile **Rachel Carson Trail,** which has its western terminus in North Park and its eastern terminus in Harrison Hills Park. Between the county parks, it visits woods and fields, creeks and steep bluffs, suburbia and farm country. A hiker's guide is available through the Rachel Carson Trails Conservancy (412/475-8881, www.rachelcarsontrails.org), the volunteer-based organization that maintains the trail. There are no shelters along the trail, which is intended for day hiking. It's not impossible to do the whole trail in one day. In fact, it's encouraged. Scads of brave souls attempt it every summer during the Rachel Carson Trail Challenge, a 34-mile, sunrise-to-sunset endurance hike.

BOATING

Crisscrossed as it is by three rivers, Pittsburgh offers plenty of opportunities to get off dry land. In fact, the city boasts the second-largest number of registered pleasure boats in the country. About 20 marinas dot Allegheny County's shorelines (see www.fish.state.pa.us/marinas.htm for locations). Boaters can moor at Station Square, the South Side's dining and entertainment complex, for just five bucks an hour or along the North Shore, home to the Steelers and Pirates, for free. Other attractions accessible by boat include Point State Park and Sandcastle water park.

If you're not in possession of a yacht or humbler vessel, you're not out of luck. The Station Square-based **Gateway Clipper Fleet** (412/355-7980, www.gatewayclipper.com) boasts five riverboats and an incredible array of cruises, from the kid-centric Good Ship Lollipop Cruise to under-21 dance parties to dinners with live oldies music. A humbler operation, **Pittsburgh Water Limo** (412/221-5466, www.pghwaterlimo.com) is mostly devoted to shuttling fans to PNC Park and Heinz Field on game days, but it also offers sightseeing cruises during Pittsburgh Pirates games.

Those who prefer the role of captain to passenger may wish to rent a kayak. **Kayak Pittsburgh** (www.kayakpittsburgh.org) offers flat-water kayaks, which require no experience, at three locations. Most convenient to Downtown is Kayak Pittsburgh North Shore

(412/969-9090, open daily Memorial Day-Sept. and weekends in Oct.), located under the north side of the Roberto Clemente Bridge, aka the 6th Street Bridge, a stone's throw from PNC Park. Solo kayaks are $16 for the first hour and $8 per additional half hour; tandems are $21.50 for the first hour and $10.75 per additional half hour. Bikes are also available for rent from Memorial Day through Labor Day.

If you get hooked on river boating, hook up with the **Three Rivers Rowing Association** (300 Waterfront Dr., 412/231-8772, www.threeriversrowing.org), which offers rowing, kayaking, and dragon boating programs for all skill levels. It also hosts the **Head of the Ohio Regatta** (www.headoftheohio.org, fall), a 2.8-mile race that attracts about 2,000 rowers and thousands of spectators.

SPECTATOR SPORTS

"Sixburgh," as Pittsburgh became known when the Steelers captured their sixth National Football League championship, is a sports town through and through. On game days, it seems like half the populace is clad in black and gold, colors shared by the city's professional football, hockey, and baseball teams. When the Penguins brought home the Stanley Cup, hockey's holy grail, in 2009, an estimated

pleasure boaters at Point State Park

375,000 people turned out for the victory parade in the middle of a Monday—this at a time when the city's population stood at 311,647.

Football

Founded by Art Rooney in 1933, Pittsburgh's football franchise is the fifth oldest in the National Football League. Originally called the Pittsburgh Pirates in deference to the city's much older ball club, the **Steelers** (Heinz Field, 100 Art Rooney Ave., 412/323-1200, www.steelers.com) are still property of the Rooney family. Since 2001, they've played at Heinz Field on the North Side. Tickets were terribly hard to come by even before the team captured its sixth Super Bowl title in 2009. Call or visit the website for information on (legal) ways to purchase tickets.

Pittsburgh also boasts an Arena Football League team, the **Pittsburgh Power** (412/697-7846, www.pittsburghpowerfootball. com), and not one but two women's full-tackle football teams: the **Pittsburgh Passion** (724/452-9395, www.pittsburghpassion.com) and the **Pittsburgh Force** (412/583-5774, www.pittsburghforce.net).

Hockey

Art Rooney's huge clout in the sports world proved invaluable in the mid-1960s, during Pittsburgh's successful bid for a National Hockey League franchise. When it came time to name the expansion team, inspiration came from the Downtown arena that would serve as its home, nicknamed "The Igloo" for reasons apparent to anyone who has seen it. The **Penguins** (CONSOL Energy Center, 1001 5th Ave., 800/642-PENS, http://penguins.nhl. com) played their first game in the arena in October 1967 and their last in April 2010. The three-time Stanley Cup winners moved to a brand spanking new home across the street— the $321 million CONSOL Energy Center—in time for the 2010-2011 season. There's a waiting list for season tickets, but individual game tickets can be purchased at the arena box office, at Ticketmaster outlets, online at ticketmaster.com, or by phone at 800/745-3000.

Baseball

Pittsburgh's Major League Baseball club is its oldest professional sports franchise, dating to the late 1800s. The **Pirates** (PNC Park, 115 Federal St., 412/321-2827, www.pirates.com) captured two World Series titles while the Steelers were still a twinkle in Art Rooney's eye and three more in the 1960s and '70s. Then, in the 1990s, their fortunes soured, which is

PNC Park, home of the Pittsburgh Pirates

a polite way of saying they sucked. In 2012 the "Bucs" posted their 20th consecutive losing season—a first in the history of U.S. professional sports. They finally turned things around in 2013, posting a winning season and advancing to the playoffs for the first time since 1992. Pittsburgh fell back in love with its ball team. Tickets to Pirates games can be purchased at the PNC Park box office, online at pirates.com, and by phone at 877/893-2827.

Accommodations

Pittsburgh proper has a pleasant mix of chain hotels and independently owned establishments, and capacity is rarely an issue. It lacks budget accommodations, though. Pittsburgh's only hostel closed in 2003. A movement to open another, the Pittsburgh Hostel Project (www.pittsburghhostel.org), got off the ground in 2009. But for now, budget travelers have little choice but to bunk down in chain motels on the city's outskirts.

DOWNTOWN
$100-250

Downtown is home to the city's grandest hotels, and the ★ **Omni William Penn** (530 William Penn Place, 412/281-7100, www.omnihotels.com, from $169) is the grandest of them all. With nearly 600 guest rooms and suites—beautifully appointed with cherry wood furnishings and windows that actually open—it's also one of the largest hotels in the Burgh. You don't have to be a guest to soak up the grandeur. The massive lobby has crystal chandeliers, soaring archways, and plenty of inviting couches and armchairs. Grab a drink from the on-site Starbucks and stay awhile.

The **Westin Convention Center Pittsburgh** (1000 Penn Ave., 412/281-3700, www.westinpittsburgh.com, from $165) is a great choice for anyone with business at the David L. Lawrence Convention Center because the two are connected by a skywalk. But leisure travelers needn't shy away from the massive hotel. Its location near the intersection of Downtown and the Strip District makes it convenient to numerous attractions and restaurants. The rooms are roomy, the service superb, and the rates quite reasonable for the area. The Westin also boasts an indoor pool and hot tub—invaluable amenities if you're traveling with kids.

Despite having 300 guest rooms and suites and Marriott as its overlord, the **Renaissance Pittsburgh Hotel** (107 6th St., 412/562-1200, www.renaissancepittsburghpa.com, from $199) pulls off the feel of a boutique lodging. Smack-dab in the heart of the Cultural District, the Renaissance is spitting distance to several world-class theaters. It's also so close to the Allegheny River that guests on the uppermost floors can take in a Pirates game on the opposite shore without leaving their plush rooms.

Over $250

One of the city's newest hotels, **Fairmont Pittsburgh** (510 Market St., 412/773-8800, www.fairmont.com/pittsburgh, from $250) opened in 2010 in a brand-new skyscraper named Three PNC Plaza. Its guest rooms boast floor-to-ceiling windows that make for spectacular views. The hotel is justifiably proud of its commitment to sustainability. It was the first hotel in Pittsburgh to receive LEED certification. The on-site **Habitat** restaurant makes a point of buying locally sourced and sustainable products, recycles everything from paper to cooking oil, and composts food scraps. Fairmont Pittsburgh is also notable for its 6,000-square-foot health club and day spa. Guests can exercise the old-fashioned way by taking a walk with the hotel's "canine ambassador," who can usually be found curled up near the concierge desk.

NORTH SHORE
$100-250

The quickly developing neighborhood that

includes PNC Park, Heinz Field, and the Rivers Casino has seen a surge in hotel rooms in recent years. Open since 2005, **SpringHill Suites Pittsburgh North Shore** (223 Federal St., 412/323-9005, www.marriott. com, from $169) is the oldest chain hotel in the nabe. **Hyatt Place Pittsburgh-North Shore** (260 North Shore Dr., 412/321-3000, www.pittsburghnorthshore.place.hyatt.com, from $169) is the newest. They're similar brands of hotel. Both offer guest rooms with divided living and sleeping areas, contemporary decor, complimentary breakfast and Wi-Fi, an exercise room, and an indoor pool.

Unlike Downtown, the North Shore has a smattering of unique, independently owned accommodations. Perhaps the most unusual is **The Parador Inn** (939 Western Ave., 412/231-4800, www.theparadorinn.com, $150-200), a slice of the Caribbean in the heart of Steeler Country. Owner Ed Menzer, whose long career in the hospitality industry included a stint at an oceanfront hotel in Florida, filled the B&B's enclosed courtyard with tropical plants and something akin to a beach. Built in the 1870s, the manse boasts three porches, a spectacular formal parlor, and a 2,700-square-foot ballroom with a handcrafted bar. Each of its eight guest rooms and suites has a private bathroom and working fireplace.

One of the finest B&Bs in the Pittsburgh area, the **Inn on the Mexican War Streets** (604 W. North Ave., 412/231-6544, www.innonthemexicanwarstreets.com, $129-199) has eight guest rooms and suites, each with a private bathroom. Guests are more than welcome to tickle the ivories of the baby grand piano in the gorgeous parlor.

Named one of the world's "top 10 hidden gems" by Hotels.com, ★ **The Priory Hotel** (614 Pressley St., 412/231-3338, www.thepriory. com, $99-250) is a 42-room beaut. Built in 1888 as a home for Benedictine priests, the boutique hotel is decorated with antiques and oil paintings, equipped with cable and Wi-Fi, and filled with charm. The rooms are so far from cookie cutter that rates range considerably. A suite that takes up the whole fourth floor boasts a full kitchen and a view of the Pittsburgh skyline. On the other end of the spectrum are two single-person rooms, available for as little as $99 per night.

SOUTH SIDE
$100-250

Just one block from the South Side's hard-partying main drag, the **Morning Glory Inn** (2119 Sarah St., 412/431-1707, www.gloryinn. com, $155-450) is the picture of tranquility. Many a bride's fantasy wedding has come to pass in its brick-paved, gorgeously landscaped Savannah-style courtyard. The B&B also caters to the business traveler with high-speed Internet and shuttle service to Downtown.

Over $250

A linchpin in the redevelopment of the city's South Shore, once the site of a massive railway complex, the **Sheraton Station Square Hotel** (300 W. Station Square Dr., 412/261-2000, www.starwoodhotels.com, $249-309) is a pricey but sound choice. The 399-room hotel is within walking distance of Downtown, thanks to the pedestrian-friendly Smithfield Street Bridge. The Gateway Clipper Fleet of riverboats and the famous Monongahela Incline are also within walking distance. Hotel amenities include an indoor pool, sauna, sundeck, and fitness center.

OAKLAND AND POINTS EAST

Oakland, a neighborhood dominated by universities and hospitals, is peppered with chain hotels. For digs with more character, head to Shadyside, a tony neighborhood just east of Oakland.

$100-250

Pittsburgh's only Select Registry property, ★ **The Inn on Negley** (703 Negley Ave., 412/661-0631, www.innonnegley.com, $180-300), is a short walk from Shadyside's Walnut Street and Ellsworth Avenue, both lined with shops and eateries. The restored Victorian has eight exquisitely decorated guest rooms and suites. A full-menu breakfast is prepared by a professional chef and served on fine china.

Mansions on Fifth (5105 5th Ave., 412/381-5105, www.mansionsonfifth.com, from $195) is one of Pittsburgh's newest boutique hotels. It took six years and 200 union craftsmen to restore the pair of mansions to their 20th-century grandeur. They're filled with antique and reproduction furnishings, fine European art, and the sort of architectural features that make preservationists weak in the knees. Guests also enjoy a host of modern amenities, including a fitness room, flat-screen TVs, and even iPads for use during their stay. You don't have to be a guest to enjoy a rare cognac or wine in the oak-paneled bar, which opens at 4pm daily. The hotel's elegant Sunday brunch is also open to the public.

The **Shadyside Inn** (5405 5th Ave., 412/441-4444, www.shadysideinn.com, from $145) offers an array of suites with fully equipped kitchens—perfect for an extended stay. The hotel is actually a collection of converted apartment buildings and houses scattered throughout Shadyside. Freebies include wireless Internet and shuttle service within a three-mile area.

Food

Unlike Philadelphia, which is practically synonymous with the cheesesteak, Pittsburgh doesn't have an iconic dish. Pierogies—semicircular dumplings filled with the likes of mashed potatoes and sauerkraut—may be the closest thing, thanks to an influx of Poles during the city's industrial heyday. Pittsburghers reportedly consume more pierogies than the citizenry of any other U.S. city, and Pittsburgh Pirates games feature a race between runners clad in pierogi costumes. French fries also figure prominently in local cuisine. A "Pittsburgh-style" sandwich is stuffed with fries. A "Pittsburgh-style" salad is topped with them. If you haven't figured it out already, this is a meat-and-potatoes kind of town.

If you're not a fan of meat and potatoes, don't despair. While the Burgh has a long way to go before it's considered a dining destination, you'll find everything from Ethiopian fare to vegan hot dogs if you look hard enough (or simply keep reading).

DOWNTOWN AND THE STRIP DISTRICT
American

It's not just God-fearing folk who flock to Downtown's Trinity Cathedral and First Presbyterian Church. The neighboring churches have come to be known as great lunch spots. Trinity Cathedral is home to **Franktuary** (325 Oliver Ave., www.franktuary.com, 11am-2:30pm Mon.-Fri., under $10), a hot dog shop with a sense of humor evident in its motto ("Franks be to God!"). Forget what you think about hot dog shops. Standard franks share the menu with a vegan version and the Under Dog, made with New Zealand grass-fed beef. Toppings range from classics like chili and sauerkraut to mango salsa and fresh mozzarella. Franktuary has a second location in the burgeoning neighborhood of Lawrenceville with an expanded menu and full bar.

Every day is fish day at the **Original Oyster House** (20 Market Square, 412/566-7925, www.originaloysterhousepittsburgh.com, 10am-10pm Mon.-Sat., 11am-7pm Sun., under $10), which holds the distinction of being Pittsburgh's oldest bar and restaurant. Oysters sold for a penny when it opened in 1870. Today a breaded oyster will set you back a buck ninety, and the size of the fish sandwich will blow your mind. Also popular: the Maryland-style crab cakes, the deep-fried shrimp, and the New England clam chowder, made fresh daily. Quench your thirst with a cold draft or a glass of buttermilk, which sold

Three Square Meals, Pittsburgh Style

Thanks to TV shows such as *Food Paradise* and *Man v. Food,* Primanti's sandwiches are as synonymous with Pittsburgh as steel and the Steelers, and it's not unusual for visitors to Pittsburgh to insist on Primanti Bros. for their first meal. And Primanti's isn't the only eatery offering a dining experience you're unlikely to find elsewhere:

BREAKFAST

On weekend mornings, there's often a line out the door at **Pamela's Diner** (www.pamelasdiner. com, under $10) locations. Fortunately, the line moves quickly. Pamela's is a fast-paced place. Many patrons order without so much as glancing at the menu, and the food comes sooner than you can say "eggs Benedict." That's because the local chain doesn't do eggs Benedict—or anything else in the chichi category of breakfast foods. Pamela's does scrambled eggs and cheese omelets, corned beef hash and home fries. It does what most greasy spoons do. But there's one thing it does differently: pancakes. No light and fluffy flapjacks here. Pamela's pancakes are crepe-like in their thinness, with crispy edges that defy explanation. Then-candidate Barack Obama flipped for them during a 2008 swing through the Keystone State. The following year he invited co-owners Pamela Cohen and Gail Klingensmith to the White House, where they cooked their famous pancakes for the Obamas and 80 veterans. Head to the **Strip District location** (60 21st St., 412/281-6366, 7am-3pm Mon.-Sat., 8am-3pm Sun.) to walk in the president's footsteps. Pamela's also has locations in **Oakland** (3703 Forbes Ave., 412/683-4066, 7:30am-4pm daily), **Shadyside** (5527 Walnut St., 412/683-1003, 8am-4pm Mon.-Sat., 9am-3pm Sun.), **Squirrel Hill** (1711 Murray Ave., 412/422-9457, 7:30am-3:30pm Mon.-Sat., 8am-3pm Sun.), **Millvale** (232 North Ave., 412/821-4655, 8am-4pm Mon.-Fri., 8am-3pm Sat., 8am-2pm Sun.), and the South Hills suburb of **Mt. Lebanon** (427 Washington Rd., 412/343-3344, 7:30am-3pm Mon.-Sat., 8am-3pm Sun.).

LUNCH

What makes a **Primanti Bros.** (www.primantibros.com, under $10) sandwich so special is the presence of coleslaw and fries. Coleslaw and fries are deli staples, of course, but few delis do what Primanti's does, which is place the traditional sides *inside* the sandwich. For 50 cents, it will throw a fried egg into

quite well during Prohibition. If the frozen-in-time joint looks familiar, it's probably because you've seen it in one of 20-plus movies. It's the Marlon Brando of Pittsburgh dining establishments.

Contemporary Cuisine

Downtown has no shortage of restaurants catering to professionals, theatergoers, and anyone else who expects a dining *experience* as much as a meal. Its name may suggest otherwise, but ★ **Meat & Potatoes** (649 Penn Ave., 412/325-7007, www.meatandpotatoespgh.com, lunch 11:30am-2pm Wed.-Fri., brunch 10:30am-2pm Sat.-Sun., dinner 5pm-11pm Mon.-Thurs., 5pm-midnight Fri.-Sat., 4pm-9pm Sun., lunch $12-16, brunch $8-14, dinner $11-28) delivers. With its large central

bar, eclectic decor, and high decibel level, the restaurant has been the height of cool since it opened in 2011. (Needless to say, reservations are recommended.) Its self-billing as Pittsburgh's first gastropub is disputable, but with menu items like bone marrow, pâté, and wild boar sloppy joe, there's no disputing that chef-owner Richard Deshantz raises the bar on bar food. The weekend brunch is outstanding and features a do-it-yourself Bloody Mary bar. You'll be floored by the selection of house-infused vodkas, flavorings, and garnishes.

People are invariably surprised to learn that **Six Penn Kitchen** (146 6th St., 412/566-7366, www.sixpennkitchen.com, 11am-11pm Mon.-Thurs., 11am-midnight Fri., 4:30pm-midnight Sat., Sun. brunch 10:30am-2:30pm, the mix. Primanti's, which had 17 locations in the Pittsburgh area and three in Florida at last count, dates to the 1930s, when Joe Primanti began selling sandwiches in the Strip District, then crowded with wholesale produce merchants. Many of Joe's customers were truckers on the go; they needed a meal they could eat with one hand. The rest, as they say, is history.

If possible, visit the **original location in the Strip** (46 18th St., 412/263-2142), open 24-7. You'll also find Primanti's in **Downtown** (2 S. Market Square, 412/261-1599, 10am-midnight daily), **Oakland** (3803 Forbes Ave., 412/621-4444, 10am-midnight Sun.-Wed., 10am-3am Thurs.-Sat.), and the **South Side** (1832 E. Carson St., 412/381-2583, 11am-2am Sun.-Thurs., 11am-3am Fri.-Sat.).

DINNER

Pamela's and Primanti's are easy on the wallet, if not the arteries. Come dinnertime, consider splurging on a meal on Mount Washington's "Restaurant Row." The eateries along Grandview Avenue aren't necessarily the best in town. Many locals pooh-pooh the pricey lot. But the views they serve up are so incredible that you can forgive an overcooked steak or lackluster dessert. What you'll remember, even years later, is your taste of Pittsburgh's prize-winning skyline.

LeMont (1114 Grandview Ave., 412/431-3100, www.lemontpittsburgh.com, dinner from 5pm Mon.-Sat. and 4pm Sun., $28-49), which celebrated its 50th anniversary in 2010, bills itself as "the place for special occasions." It's the picture of fancy schmancy, right down to the bow-tied servers. You can soak up the bling-bling without breaking the bank in the lounge, featuring nightly entertainment. The less ornate **Isabela on Grandview** (1318 Grandview Ave., 412/431-5882, www.isabelaongrandview.com, 5pm-10pm Mon.-Sat., à la carte $26-34, prix fixe $70) is known for its seven-course prix fixe. Seafood lovers favor **Monterey Bay Fish Grotto** (1411 Grandview Ave., 412/481-4414, www.montereybayfishgrotto.com, lunch 11am-3pm Mon.-Fri., dinner 5pm-10pm Mon.-Thurs., 5pm-11pm Fri.-Sat., 5pm-9pm Sun., lunch $10-23, dinner $23-39), located well above sea level at the top of a luxury apartment building. It offers 15 to 20 varieties of fresh fish on any given day. The **Grandview Saloon** (1212 Grandview Ave., 412/431-1400, www.thegrandviewsaloon.com, 11:30am-10pm daily, $10-35) is notable for its outdoor seating and casual grub, including buffalo chicken fingers and burgers. It's the best choice if you're on a budget.

lunch/brunch $6-14, dinner $10-34) and the Eat'n Park chain are products of the same parent company. Eat'n Park restaurants, found throughout Pennsylvania, West Virginia, and Ohio, are known for salad bars and smiley cookies. Six Penn Kitchen is the picture of casual sophistication. Its rooftop lounge is one of the city's sexiest settings for a summer dinner. Be sure to leave room for the Six Penn "Circus," a head-turning tower of cotton candy on a bed of caramel-coated popcorn and other nostalgic treats.

The **Sonoma Grille** (947 Penn Ave., 412/697-1336, www.thesonomagrille.com, lunch 11am-3pm Mon.-Sat. and 11am-4pm Sun., dinner 5pm-11pm Mon.-Sat. and 4pm-10pm Sun., lunch $8-14, dinner $19-39), ground-floor tenant of the Courtyard by Marriot, boasts a collection of more than 1,000 wines. Most are of West Coast provenance, the better to complement the California-inspired cuisine. Belly up to the bar during happy hour—5pm-7pm weekdays—for $4 glasses of wine and $5 tapas. On Sundays the restaurant offers a brunch menu and live jazz until 2pm.

Also highly regarded for its wine selection, ★ **Eleven** (1150 Smallman St., 412/201-5656, www.elevenck.com, lunch 11:30am-2pm Mon.-Fri., brunch 11am-2pm Sun., dinner 5pm-10pm Mon.-Thurs., 5pm-11pm Fri.-Sat., 5pm-9pm Sun., tavern menu 2pm-close Mon.-Fri. and 5pm-close Sat.-Sun., lunch $8-24, dinner $24-65) has been luring foodies to the Strip District since 2004, when it opened as the 11th and most ambitious restaurant by

Pittsburgh's Big Burrito Restaurant Group. It's unique among area restaurants in offering both regular and vegetarian chef's tasting menus ($65 and $45, respectively). A tavern menu ($4-18) available in the first-floor lounge and second-floor patio lets budget-minded sophisticates enjoy the modern space.

Italian

It's often said that if you can make it in New York, you can make it anywhere. TV chef and cookbook author Lidia Bastianich already had two successful restaurants in Manhattan, Felidia and Becco, when she opened **Lidia's Pittsburgh** (1400 Smallman St., 412/552-0150, www.lidias-pittsburgh. com, lunch 11:30am-2pm Mon.-Fri., brunch 11am-2:30pm Sat.-Sun., dinner 5pm-9pm Mon.-Thurs., 5pm-10pm Fri., 4:30pm-10pm Sat., 5pm-8pm Sun., lunch $10-21, dinner $10-42) in the Strip District, so it stands to reason that Pittsburghers have embraced her brand of Italian cooking. Borrowing a page from Becco's playbook, Lidia's offers unlimited servings of three pasta preparations for a fixed price ($17.95 at lunchtime and $21 at dinnertime). The lineup, which changes daily, often includes risotto or polenta dishes as well as delectable pastas. The weekend brunch is a popular gut-buster: one entrée and unlimited helpings from the antipasti and sweets tables for $24.95 per person.

Seafood

The Strip District's seafood markets are great places to grab lunch—if you don't mind the smells of fresh fish, of course. **Wholey's** (1711 Penn Ave., 412/391-3737, www.wholey.com), which has been around forever, is fantastic, offering everything from sushi to fish-and-chips in an old-school setting. But new kid on the block **Penn Avenue Fish Company** (2208 Penn Ave., 412/434-7200, www.pennavefishcompany.com) is even better. Its chalkboard menu advertises the likes of crab tacos, spicy barbecue shrimp pizza, and mussels in tomato-basil sauce—all under $10. Fish tacos, made with mahi, salmon, and tuna,

are marked down on Tuesdays: two for $4.99, three for $6.99, or all you can eat for $8.99.

NORTH SIDE
American

One of the Burgh's most beloved sports figures got into the restaurant game in 2007. **Jerome Bettis' Grille 36** (393 N. Shore Dr., 412/224-6287, www.jeromebettisgrille36.com, opens at 8am for all Pitt and Steelers home games starting before 2pm, $6-59) boasts an astonishing 50 televisions and a patio with views of the Pittsburgh skyline and Heinz Field, where Jerome "The Bus" Bettis wore the number 36 jersey for a decade. Wanna be like The Bus? Start with the cheese-smothered fries, proceed to the Soon to be Famous Deep Fried Cheeseburger, and finish with the one-pound carrot cake. Ask your server about the day's game burger—as in wild game. Bison, boar, ostrich, antelope, and even alligator have made the cut. Take your pick of 36 draft beers, 36 wines, and 36 cocktails.

Asian

★ **Nicky's Thai Kitchen** (856 Western Ave., 412/321-8424, www.nickysthaikitchen.com, lunch 11:30am-3pm Mon.-Sat., dinner 5pm-9pm Mon.-Thurs., 5pm-10pm Fri.-Sat., 4pm-9pm Sun., lunch $6-12, dinner $6-17) offers outstanding takes on familiar dishes like *tom yum* soup and pad thai, chef's specials that threaten to ruin you for other Thai eateries, and a delightful plant-filled patio. The Thai iced tea is terrific, but if you prefer something stronger, bring your own bottle. The corkage fee is a reasonable $5.

SOUTH SIDE
American

The 500-seat **Grand Concourse** (100 W. Station Square Dr., 412/261-1717, www.muer. com, 11am-10pm Mon.-Thurs., 11am-11pm Fri., 11am-11pm Sat., 10am-9pm Sun., lunch $10-15, dinner $20-56) is the largest restaurant in the city and arguably the most stunning. Set in a former train terminal, it's awash in marble, mahogany, brass, and stained glass.

Seafood is its stock-in-trade, but landlubbers can count on a few beef and chicken dishes. The popular Sunday brunch (10am-3pm, $25.99, children 4-11 $13.99) features everything from eggs and bacon to cold smoked fishes and salmon Rockefeller. Its attached sister restaurant, **Gandy Dancer Saloon** (hours same as above, $8-18), offers a more casual atmosphere and menu prices to match.

Asian

Nakama Japanese Steakhouse and Sushi Bar (1611 E. Carson St., 412/381-6000, www. eatatnakama.com, 11am-10pm Mon.-Wed., 11am-11pm Thurs.-Sat., 1pm-10pm Sun., bar open until 1am Mon.-Sat. and midnight Sun., lunch $10-16, dinner $17-70) has racked up so many accolades in so many categories—best trendy scene, best group dining, best ethnic restaurant, among others—that expectations run high round its hibachi tables. It rarely disappoints. House specialties include hibachi chateaubriand, seared scallops, and a seafood combo featuring South African lobster tail. Come 4pm-6pm Monday-Friday and mention the "early bird special" for 20 percent off a hibachi dinner. Though the sushi bar gets second billing, it's a star in its own right. Cozy up for some of the comeliest maki in all the Burgh—and great people-watching to boot.

For a steaming curry with a side of sexual innuendo, head to **Thai Me Up** (118 S. 23rd St., 412/488-8893, www.thaimeuppittsburgh. com, 11am-2:30pm and 4pm-9:30pm Mon.-Fri., noon-9:30pm Sat., $9-12), a BYOB that does a brisk takeout business. The steamed dumplings and lemongrass soup will have you begging for more.

Contemporary Cuisine

You know you're in for a gastronomic surprise when a menu features a glossary of terms. **Yo Rita** (1120 E. Carson St., 412/904-3557, www. yoritasouthside.com, à la carte tacos $6-9), which specializes in tacos, is full of surprises. For starters, it's not really a Mexican restaurant. Its glossary includes everything from Idiazabal (a Spanish cheese made from unpasteurized sheep's milk) to kimchi (Korea's national dish). If you think such ingredients have no place on a flour tortilla, you're in for another surprise. Yo Rita's couture tacos are quite simply *fabuloso.* Follow its Twitter feed for the first word on specials like turtle tacos, swordfish ceviche, and prickly pear margaritas.

A date night favorite, **17th Street Café** (75 S. 17th St., 412/381-4566, www.17thstreetcafe. com, 11am-10pm Mon.-Thurs., 11am-11pm Fri., 4pm-11pm Sat., 4pm-9pm Sun., lunch $9-14, dinner $17-29) offers a menu of mostly Italian-American dishes, along with unsurpassed service. Don't be surprised if owner Pat Joyce drops by your table as you're tucking into wild mushroom raviolis or pecan-crusted tilapia. The space is as cozy as they come, which is remarkable considering that it served as a butcher shop and a shot-and-beer joint in its first hundred years. Ask the waitstaff about ghosts in the basement, a onetime speakeasy.

Italian

Specializing in Sicilian cuisine, ★ **Dish Osteria and Bar** (128 S. 17th St., 412/390-2012, www.dishosteria.com, 5pm-midnight Mon.-Sat., bar open until 2am, appetizers and salads $5-17, entrées $18-35) is a singular choice for an after-work nibble, a special night out, or a nightcap. After work, self-soothe with house-marinated olives, beef carpaccio served with organic arugula, or mussels steamed with white wine and garlic. For a special night out, make a reservation. Dish is an intimate space, and it has a following. A tiny kitchen and keep-it-simple cooking philosophy make for a succinct selection of entrées. Finish with an exquisite dessert, a rich espresso, and a contented sigh. Dish's kitchen doesn't close until midnight, and its bar stays open as late as the law allows.

For a New York-style slice—as in very thin and very flavorful—pop into **Pizza Sola** (1417 E. Carson St., 412/481-3888, www.pizzasola. com, 11:30am-midnight Mon.-Wed., 11:30am-3am Thurs.-Sat., 12:30pm-midnight Sun., slice $1.85-5.25, pie $10-22.50). It's open until 3am on the biggest party nights of the week, and that's not the only thing it has going for it. The dough is prepared daily, and the toppings are top of the line, a fact reflected in the prices. Pizza Sola also offers wings, oven-baked sandwiches, salads, and desserts. The South Side pizzeria has siblings in **Oakland** (114 Atwood St., 412/681-7652) and **East Liberty** (6004 Penn Circle S., 412/363-7652). Alas, not one delivers.

Vegetarian

No two tables are the same at **The Zenith** (86 S. 26th St., 412/481-4833, www.zenith-pgh.com, 11:30am-8:30pm Thurs.-Sat., 11am-2:30pm Sun., $10 and under), where your seat could literally be sold out from under you. The vegetarian eatery doubles as an antiques shop, and everything from the glassware to the lamps can be yours for a price. You won't find a better deal than the $10 Sunday brunch. An entirely vegan buffet groans with more than a dozen salads (cross your fingers for crunchy mayo-less slaw and noodles in peanut sauce), breads, pies, and so many Bundt cakes that veganism could easily be confused with hedonism. The cost includes an entrée from the menu, which isn't strictly vegan, and coffee or tea. Thursdays through Saturdays, The Zenith offers a modest variety of salads, sandwiches, and entrées.

OAKLAND AND POINTS EAST
American

Pittsburgh's university district has no shortage of eateries offering affordable pub grub. Best of the bunch: **Fuel & Fuddle** (212 Oakland Ave., 412/682-3473, www.fuelandfuddle.com, 11am-2am daily, $7-18), serving everything from crispy chicken wings to thin-crusted pizzas to alligator stew. Its prominent brick oven proves handy for more than just pizzas. Try the fire-baked brie, which is billed as an appetizer but works well as a dessert.

The neon-lit **Original Hot Dog Shop** (3901 Forbes Ave., 412/621-7388, 10am-3:30am daily, under $10) is to Oakland what Pink's is to Hollywood: a landmark where hazy memories are made. The O, as it's known, has been feeding the inebriated masses since 1960. It's justly famous for its fries, cooked twice for good measure and doused with cheese if you so choose. So what if your feet stick to the floor?

Hankering for the quintessential American meal? Head to Pittsburgh's Little Italy. **Tessaro's** (4601 Liberty Ave., 412/682-6809, 11am-11pm Mon.-Sat.) has been serving what many consider to be the city's best burger for more than 20 years. Its flame-grilled patties, made with house-ground meat, weigh in at half a pound. Be prepared to wait. The Bloomfield institution has a legion of regulars.

Shadyside's **Harris Grill** (5747 Ellsworth Ave., 412/362-5273, www.harrisgrill.com, 11:30am-1am daily, bar open until 2am, $7-20) inspires similar devotion, which only grew stronger after a 2007 fire shut it down for eight months. Start with the Goat in a Boat (feta and roasted red pepper dip served with pita wedges) and finish with the Twinkiemissou, a tiramisu of sorts featuring America's favorite snack cake. In between, choose from a vegetarian-friendly selection of salads, sandwiches, and "big things," including a decadent mac and cheese prepared with lobster tail and lump crab meat. In the warmer months, Harris's outdoor tables are among the most coveted in town, especially 4:30pm-6:30pm weekdays, when drafts and the signature frozen cosmos are half price.

Asian

If backpacking Southeast Asia is on your bucket list, you can all but cross it off after a few trips to **Spice Island Tea House** (253 Atwood St., 412/687-8821, www.spiceisland-teahouse.com, 11:30am-9pm Mon.-Thurs., 11:30am-10pm Fri.-Sat., $7-14). Deep in the section of Oakland where college students live five or six to a shabby house, the eatery has provided an affordable education in the foods of Indonesia, Malaysia, Burma, Vietnam, Singapore, and their neighbors since 1995.

Chef on a Roll

menu at Station Street

No chef has done more to diversify Pittsburgh's dining landscape in recent years than Kevin Sousa. Since 2010, the Pittsburgh native has opened three restaurants and a cocktail bar in the East End. In 2014, he raised more than $300,000 through crowdfunding site Kickstarter to open another restaurant in Braddock, a run-down steel town just east of Pittsburgh. Housed in a former car dealership, **Superior Motors** is expected to open in early 2015.

Sousa's first creation, **Salt of the Earth** (5523 Penn Ave., 412/441-7258, www.saltpgh.com, 5pm-midnight Mon.-Sat., bar open until 1am, $17-29) landed him on the cover of *Pittsburgh Magazine*'s 2011 best restaurants issue. It also garnered national attention, including a spot on *Food & Wine*'s "Top 10 Restaurant Dishes of 2011" list. Sousa recently sold his stake in Salt to devote more time to Superior Motors, but Salt remains the hippest spot in the Garfield neighborhood. You won't find a familiar dish on the menu, the variability of which calls for a floor-to-ceiling chalkboard. Salt is about experimentation, uncommon ingredients, unexpected flavors, and artful presentation. You have to be somewhat of an insider—or a science nerd—to find the place. (The sign outside reads "NaCl," as in sodium chloride.)

Sousa kicked off 2012 by opening two restaurants in the East Liberty neighborhood: a hot dog shop and a barbecue joint. At **Station Street** (6290 Broad St., 412/365-2121, www.sousapgh. com, 11am-10pm Mon.-Thurs., 11am-11pm Fri.-Sat., noon-9pm Sun., under $10), the hot dog shop, standard dogs share the menu with exotic breeds like the Banh Mi Dog, topped with pork liver pâté and pickled vegetables, and the Po' Boy Dog, featuring fried oysters. Its menu also includes tacos made of such stuff as beef brisket and fried squid; *onigiri* (Japanese rice balls); and poke (Hawaiian raw fish salad). What's the common denominator? They're all street foods.

Sousa's barbecue restaurant, **Union Pig & Chicken** (220 N. Highland Ave., 412/363-7675, www.sousapgh.com, 11am-10pm Mon.-Thurs., 11am-1am Fri.-Sat., 11am-9pm Sun., bar open until 2am Mon.-Sat. and 11pm Sun., $10-20), offers brisket, ribs, pork shoulder, and chicken (available barbecued or fried), along with sides like smoked corn on the cob. Despite the sound of it, Sousa looks kindly on vegetarians, offering meatless dogs and tacos at Station Street and barbecued tofu at Union.

Before 2012 was through, Sousa opened a cocktail bar on Union's second floor. **Harvard & Highland** specializes in whiskeys and innovative concoctions with names like Backroom Agreement and Twitterpated. You can order from Union's menu at Harvard & Highland and vice versa.

The wealth of options can overwhelm first-timers. Order an appetizer—the Sumatran corn and shrimp fritters are delish—and a pot of tea, and take your time perusing the rest of the menu. Dim lighting and thrift-store decor help the imagination travel to distant lands.

Squirrel Hill, a neighborhood known for its large Jewish population, has an inordinate number of Asian restaurants. For Chinese, call **Zaw's Asian Food** (2110 Murray Ave., 412/521-3663, 11:30am-10pm Mon.-Sat., noon-9:30pm Sun., under $10) and order take-out. Dishes are made with fresh ingredients as they're ordered, which means you'll likely have to wait upwards of 25 minutes for your *chow fun*. Which is why you're going to call ahead, see?

A block away, **Chaya Japanese Cuisine** (2032 Murray Ave., 412/422-2082, www.chaya-usa.com, 5pm-9:30pm Mon.-Thurs., 5pm-9:45pm Fri.-Sat., $12-75) offers some of the best sushi in the Burgh. Owner and executive chef Fumio Yasuzawa insists on authenticity in just about every respect. Among his concessions: Americanized portion sizes and the Murray Ave. Roll, featuring salmon and cream cheese, which you'd be hard-pressed to find in his native Japan. Chaya's "special combination dinners," which feed two for $45 or less, are an affordable way to sample several traditional dishes. The BYOB charges $2 per wine or beer glass.

If it's Thai you're craving, mosey over to **Bangkok Balcony** (5846 Forbes Ave., 412/521-0728, www.bangkokbalconypgh.com, noon-10pm Sun.-Thurs., noon-11pm Fri.-Sat., $8-18) or its sister restaurant, **Silk Elephant** (1712 Murray Ave., 412/421-8801, www.silkelephant.net, 11:30am-10pm Sun.-Thurs., 11:30am-11pm Fri.-Sat., $10-21). In a city blessed with an abundance of Thai restaurants, Bangkok Balcony frequently tops polls. While seafood figures prominently in the list of house specialties, most dishes are available with your choice of chicken, beef, pork, shrimp, tofu, or vegetables. Resplendent in red and gold, the second-floor restaurant offers a full bar and Thai dance performances most Thursday and Sunday evenings. After appearing at Bangkok Balcony between 6 and 7, the talent migrates to chef Norraset Nareedokmai's newer Squirrel Hill venture. With its tapas selection ($4-9), well-rounded wine list, and specialty martinis, Silk Elephant is as suited to an after-work stopover as a lazy dinner.

Brewpubs

Some call it sacrilegious. Others call it a shining example of adaptive reuse. The **Church Brew Works** (3525 Liberty Ave., 412/688-8200, www.churchbrewworks.com, full menu 11:30am-9:30pm Mon.-Thurs., 11:30am-11pm Fri.-Sat., noon-9pm Sun., pizza served until 11pm Mon.-Thurs. and midnight Fri.-Sat., lunch $9-19, dinner $11-34, pub menu $9-17), a microbrewery and restaurant in a restored 1902 church building, has been called many things but never "typical." Guaranteed: You've never seen any place like it. Stainless steel and copper brew vessels occupy the main altar of the former St. John the Baptist Church, which closed its doors in 1993. To the right of the main aisle is the dining section, with seating made from the original pews. The oak planks of the pews were also used to build the long, curving bar to the left of the aisle. You can order from the dining or pub menu on either side, but sit on the left to take advantage of happy hour (4:30pm-6:30pm Mon.-Fri.) food specials. A courtyard between the church building and onetime rectory provides for outdoor seating in the warmer months. Try a dish as unique as the setting—buffalo and wild mushroom meatloaf, for instance—or stick to pub staples like chicken wings, onion soup, and oversized sandwiches. You can't go wrong with the pizzas, baked in a wood-fired brick oven. Service can be sluggish, so flag down a waiter before your glass is half empty.

Contemporary Cuisine

It's a darn shame that ★ **Point Brugge Café** (401 Hastings St., 412/441-3334, www.pointbrugge.com, 11am-10pm Tues.-Thurs., 11am-11pm Fri.-Sat., 11am-9pm Sun., lunch

$8-15, dinner $8-26) doesn't take reservations (except for lunch, and then only for parties of six or more). Waiting for a table as servers whiz by with steamed mussels, steak frites, and hot-out-of-the-oven macaroni gratin is downright torturous. But the torture is worth it. Tucked away in residential Point Breeze, the European-style eatery is the darling of East End foodies. The Belgian-style frites, served with basil mayo, are simply phenomenal. Golden waffles with notes of caramelized sugar make for particularly long waits during Sunday brunch (11am-3pm, $5-22). It's usually easier to snag a table at Point Brugge's newer and larger sister establishment in Highland Park, **Park Bruges Café** (5801 Bryant St., phone number, website, and hours same as above). It's no accident that their names are spelled differently. Park Bruges is more of a Francophile than its older sibling, adding tarte flambée and poutine to its offerings.

Ethiopian

Pittsburgh's only Ethiopian restaurant, **Tana** (5929 Baum Blvd., 412/665-2770, www.tanaethiopiancuisine.com, 11am-2:30pm Tues.-Sun., dinner 5pm-10pm Sun.-Thurs., 5pm-11pm Fri.-Sat., $11-20), offers a variety of authentic meat and vegetarian dishes and sampler platters for parties unfamiliar with the eat-with-your-hands cuisine. It makes its own *injera*, the spongy flatbread that doubles as food and eating utensil. It also boasts a selection of Ethiopian beers and wines, including a unique honey wine known as *tej*. Things get lively on Wednesday evenings, when the East Liberty eatery hosts a jazz jam session.

French

Devoted to "everyday French cuisine," **Paris 66** (6018 Centre Ave., 412/404-8166, www.paris66bistro.com, 11am-10pm Mon.-Thurs., 11am-11pm Fri.-Sat., 10am-3pm Sun., $10-29) offers sweet and savory crepes, escargot, quiches, mussels, and more amid framed Toulouse-Lautrec prints and a clock showing the time in France. Though inspired by the "city of love," the long, narrow restaurant is too loud to be romantic. Most tables are close enough for making new acquaintances. Patio dining is available in the warmer months.

For a crepe fix sans table service, try **Crepes Parisiennes,** with locations in Oakland (207 S. Craig St., 412/683-1912, 9am-5pm Tues.-Fri., 10am-4pm Sat.-Sun., $10) and Shadyside (732 Filbert St., 412/683-2333, 10am-4:30pm Tues.-Sat., 10am-3:30pm Sun.).

Italian

Three of the Burgh's best pizza joints are found within a two-block stretch of Murray Avenue in Squirrel Hill. Each offers hoagies and Italian staples such as ravioli and manicotti in addition to pizza by the slice or pie. In business since 1958, **Mineo's Pizza House** (2128 Murray Ave., 412/521-9864, www.mineospizza.com, 11am-1am Sun.-Thurs., 11am-2am Fri.-Sat., pie $11-29) has enough far-flung devotees that it overnights half-baked frozen pizzas anywhere in the country. Mineo's is the only one of the triumvirate to make Sicilian pizzas in addition to regular-crust red and white pies. **Aiello's Pizza** (2112 Murray Ave., 412/521-9973, www.aiellospizza.com, 11am-2am daily, pie $11-31) opened on the same block in 1978. It's the only one of the three to offer steak as a topping. The youngest of the bunch, **Napoli Pizzeria** (2006 Murray Ave., 412/521-1744, www.napolipizzasqhill.com, 11am-11pm Sun.-Thurs., 11am-midnight Fri.-Sat., pie $10-24), has been around for more than 25 years. The 70-ish mother of one of its owners makes the meatballs.

Mediterranean

Casbah (229 S. Highland Ave., 412/661-5656, www.bigburrito.com/casbah, lunch 11:30am-2:30pm Mon.-Sat., brunch 11am-2pm Sun., dinner 5pm-10pm Mon.-Thurs., 5pm-11pm Fri.-Sat., 5pm-9pm Sun., lunch $8-16, dinner $19-36) doesn't look like much from the outside. Step inside, however, and the truth is revealed: This is one of Pittsburgh's chicest dining destinations. Casbah pays homage to Mediterranean and Northern African cuisines while showcasing Pennsylvania lamb, poultry, and produce. Its wine cellar is one of the best in town. Casbah is also one of the best places in the Burgh to broaden your cheese vocabulary. Try three for $12, five for $16, or seven for $20. The prix fixe Sunday brunch ($24, children 12 and under $12) is a worthy splurge.

Mexican

With offerings like Pennsyltucky Fried Tofu and Thai Curry Burrito, **Mad Mex** (370 Atwood St., 412/681-5656, www.madmex. com, 11am-1am daily, bar open until 2am, $8-12) is a far cry from traditional Mexican. Just about every burrito and enchilada dish can be made with portobellos or marinated tofu as well as chicken, steak, or shrimp. Vegans can even request soy cheese and tofu sour cream. During happy *hora* (4:30pm-6:30pm weekdays), the small Oakland restaurant is as crowded with coeds as Cancun during spring break. Drafts and wings are half price, and 22-ounce "Big Azz" margaritas, normally $10, sell for $7. Note of warning: Parking in this student-heavy hood is a pain in the azz. Mad Mex, part of the restaurant group that includes Eleven and Casbah, has half a dozen other locations in the Pittsburgh area.

Middle Eastern

Opened in 1972 by three grad students from Syria, **Ali Baba** (404 S. Craig St.,

412/682-2829, www.alibabapittsburgh.com, lunch 11:30am-2:30pm Mon.-Fri., dinner 4pm-9:45pm daily, lunch $4-7, dinner $7-18) has never lost touch with the needs of cash-strapped scholars. Most lunch offerings are under $5, dinner specials top out at $18, and even the "premium" beers sell for less than $4. (If you prefer wine with your lamb kebabs or baked *kibbee*, bring your own.) The $17.95 "maza platter," which has enough hummus, baba ghanouj, tabouli, feta, and olives to serve as dinner for two, is a godsend to the city's vegetarians.

Squirrel Hill boasts two recommendable Middle Eastern restaurants on the same block. Local Lebanese transplants swear by the *mujaddara* at the **Mediterranean Grill** (5824 Forbes Ave., 412/521-5505, noon-8:45pm Mon.-Sat., $5-15). The basement-level restaurant is short on ambience, but its food more than compensates for the lack of natural light. **Aladdin's Eatery** (5878 Forbes Ave., 412/421-5100, www.aladdinseatery.com, 11am-10:30pm Mon.-Thurs., 11am-11:30pm Fri.-Sat., 11am-10pm Sun., $6-13), part of a chain with more than two dozen outlets in five states, serves Lebanese-inspired food and arguably the best smoothies in the Steel City. Its wrap-like rolled pitas and pita "pitzas" are good gateways for strangers to Middle Eastern cuisine. The lentil soup is heaven on a wintry day.

Information

VisitPittsburgh (800/359-0758, www.visitpittsburgh.com), the official tourism promotion agency for Pittsburgh and the rest of Allegheny County, operates several welcome centers stocked with brochures and maps and staffed by knowledgeable folk. If you're flying into Pittsburgh International Airport, look for the welcome center near baggage claim (9am-4pm Mon., 10am-5pm Tues.-Fri., 10am-4pm Sat., noon-5pm Sun.). VisitPittsburgh's main welcome center is

Downtown (120 5th Ave., 1st level, 10am-6pm Mon.-Fri., 10am-3pm Sat., seasonal Sun. hours), in a skyscraper topped with the logo of health insurer Highmark. It carries postcards, magnets, and other souvenirs, plus products from local attractions such as the Carnegie Science Center.

The VisitPittsburgh website is also a great place to gather information. You can request a copy of the agency's annual visitors guide or flip through a digital version.

Pittsburgh has two daily newspapers: the *Pittsburgh Post-Gazette* (www.post-gazette.com) and the *Pittsburgh Tribune-Review* (www.pittsburghlive.com), but when it comes to planning their leisure time, most locals reach for the free *Pittsburgh City Paper* (www.pghcitypaper.com), which comes out on Wednesdays.

Transportation

GETTING THERE

Pittsburgh is about 130 miles southeast of Cleveland via I-80 and I-76, 250 miles northwest of Baltimore via I-70, and 300 miles west of Philadelphia via the Pennsylvania Turnpike.

Roughly 18 miles from Downtown, **Pittsburgh International Airport** (PIT, 412/472-3525, www.flypittsburgh.com) is served by about a dozen carriers, including budget airlines JetBlue, AirTran, and Southwest.

At $3.75, the Port Authority's **28X Airport Flyer** (412/442-2000, www.portauthority.org) is the cheapest ride into town (unless, of course, you have a pal in Pittsburgh). You'll find the bus stop outside door #6 of the ground transportation area. The 28X operates seven days a week, including holidays, departing from the airport about every half hour from 5:30am to midnight. It takes about 40 minutes to get Downtown. The bus then makes its way to Duquesne University, Carlow University, and the University of Pittsburgh before reaching the end of its route at Carnegie Mellon University. You can transfer between the 28X and most other Port Authority buses in Downtown. A transfer costs $1 and is good for three hours. Be sure to request a transfer before paying your fare. Drivers do not carry change. **SuperShuttle** (800/258-3826, www.supershuttle.com) provides shared-van service to Downtown, Shadyside, Oakland, the North Shore, and other neighborhoods. You can book online or by phone or simply stop by the SuperShuttle counter in the airport's ground transportation area. If you're bound for Downtown, you'll pay $18-30. The same trip by cab will set you back $40-45.

It's also possible to travel to Pittsburgh by rail or intercity bus. **Amtrak** trains (local 412/471-6170, general 800/872-7245, www.amtrak.com) pull into a historic station at 1100 Liberty Avenue in Downtown, just shy of the Strip District. Constructed at the turn of the 20th century, the station building featured a spectacular waiting room that's since been converted into a lobby for well-heeled residential and office tenants. Amtrak's Pennsylvanian, which travels daily between New York City and Pittsburgh, rolls through Amish farmlands and the famous Horseshoe Curve near Altoona. The Capitol Limited route linking Washington DC and Chicago also serves Pittsburgh.

Greyhound (local 412/392-6526, general 800/231-2222, www.greyhound.com) and **Megabus** (877/462-6342, www.megabus.com) provide bus service to Pittsburgh. The Greyhound terminal is across from the Amtrak station, at the intersection of Liberty Avenue and 11th Street. The Megabus stop is beneath the David L. Lawrence Convention Center, just north of the intersection of 10th Street and Penn Avenue. When it's not possible for buses to stop beneath the convention center, you'll find them on Penn Avenue between 10th and 11th Streets. Megabus, if you're not familiar, offers intercity bus service for as little as $1.

GETTING AROUND

With its rivers, hills, and uncommon street grids, Pittsburgh is notoriously hard to navigate. ("Undoubtedly the cockeyedest city in the United States," marveled newspaper columnist Ernie Pyle in 1937. "It must have been laid out by a mountain goat. It's up and down,

a Port Authority bus

and around and around, and in betwixt.") If you're renting a car, spring for a GPS device. Fortunately, a car is not at all necessary—unless you have your heart set on exploring the hinterlands. Neighborhoods including Downtown, the Strip District, the North Shore, the South Side Flats, and Oakland are fairly walkable, and public buses can get you from one to the other.

Port Authority of Allegheny County (412/442-2000, www.portauthority.org) operates some 700 buses, a light rail system known as the T, and the Monongahela Incline. Its website has a handy "trip planner" feature that spells out how to get from point A to point B. You can also call the Authority and speak to a live trip planner. To promote transit use and

reduce boarding delays, the Port Authority declared Downtown a "free fare zone." Bus rides within Downtown are free until 7pm, after which they're $2.50. There's never a charge to ride the T within Downtown or between Downtown and the North Shore. Outside the free zone, the base fare is $2.50 or $3.75, depending on how far you're traveling. Transfers are $1. Be sure to request a transfer before paying your fare. Seniors with proper ID and children five and under ride for free. Children 6-11 pay half fare. Drivers do not carry change.

If your visit is short, getting acquainted with the public transportation system probably isn't a priority. Cabbing it is always an option. Call **Yellow Cab Co.** at 412/321-8100.

Laurel Highlands

The Laurel Highlands are to Pittsburghers what the Hamptons are to New Yorkers: respite from urban bustle. As early as the 1800s, Pittsburghers of certain means fled to this mountainous region southeast of the "Smoky City" to escape industrial pollution and summer heat. Captains of industry built

second homes; the less affluent filled boarding houses. Today the region's forests, peaks, and rivers attract not only Pittsburghers but also outdoor enthusiasts from Baltimore, Washington DC, and other cities within a half-day's drive. Its most renowned attraction, Fallingwater, draws visitors from around the world. Don't be surprised to hear a medley of languages if you visit the architectural masterpiece, which *Smithsonian* magazine named to its Life List—28 places to see before you die—along with India's Taj Mahal and Peru's Machu Picchu. What few people know is that Fallingwater is just one of *three* Frank Lloyd Wright houses in the Laurel Highlands.

"Laurel Highlands" is a label applied to the adjacent counties of Westmoreland, Fayette, and Somerset. "Laurel" is for the flowering shrubs that typically bloom in June.

"Highlands" is for the terrain. The region is home to Mount Davis, the highest peak in Pennsylvania, and the state's largest ski resort. It's a region that lends itself to travel budgets big and small. Accommodations range from trailside shelters that cost a few bucks to the five-star Falling Rock, where guests enjoy 24-hour butler service. Eateries include the Big Mac Museum Restaurant, which pays homage to the McDonalds's burger, and Lautrec, one of only 28 restaurants named to the Forbes Travel Guide five-star list for 2013.

Laurel Highlands

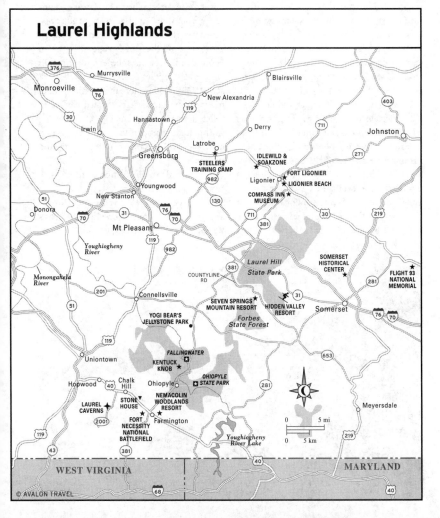

OHIOPYLE AND VICINITY
★ Ohiopyle State Park

Ohiopyle State Park (124 Main St., Ohiopyle, 724/329-8591, www.visitpaparks.com) is the Laurel Highlands' biggest tourist draw and one of Pennsylvania's most visited parks. Its star attraction is the curiously spelled **Youghiogheny ("yaw-ki-GAY-nee") River,** better known as the "Yough." The north-flowing river is a mecca for whitewater enthusiasts. The Lower Yough, which starts at the heart of the 20,500-acre park, is the busiest section of white water east of the Mississippi. Its Class III and IV rapids aren't for the faint of heart. Unless you're an experienced paddler, find yourself a guide. You don't have to look far. There's an outfitter around every bend in the wee town of Ohiopyle, nestled within the park. The tamer Middle Yough is appropriate for beginning kayakers, rafters with young children, and anglers.

You don't need a boat to experience the rushing waters of Ohiopyle. One of the park's most popular summertime attractions is a **natural waterslide** in Meadow Run, a Yough tributary. If you're up for the bumpy ride, look for the parking lot adjacent to the Route 381 bridge crossing Meadow Run, just south of Ohiopyle Borough. There's a path from the parking lot to the waterslide.

Cyclists also flock to Ohiopyle. The park is home to 27 miles of the **Great Allegheny Passage** (www.atatrail.org), a nearly level trail stretching from Pittsburgh to Cumberland, Maryland. The Ohiopyle trailhead, near the intersection of Sheridan and Sherman Streets in Ohiopyle Borough, is the most popular trailhead for the 150-mile GAP.

Ohiopyle State Park also boasts a whopping 79 miles of hiking trails (including those 27 miles of the Great Allegheny Passage). They range from short and flat to long and rocky. The 70-mile **Laurel Highlands Hiking Trail,** one of the finest rugged paths in Pennsylvania, has its southern terminus in Ohiopyle. (Contact Laurel Ridge State Park at 724/455-3744 for more information and to reserve overnight shelters, located every 8-10 miles along the trail.) Portions of Ohiopyle's trail system are open to mountain biking, horseback riding, cross-country skiing, and snowmobiling.

The park also offers fishing, hunting, rock climbing, and camping.

The itty-bitty Borough of Ohiopyle has four major outfitters: **Wilderness Voyageurs** (103 Garrett St., 800/272-4141,

Take a break from the city at Ohiopyle State Park.

the natural waterslide in Ohiopyle State Park

www.wilderness-voyageurs.com), **Laurel Highlands River Tours** (4 Sherman St., 800/472-3846, www.laurelhighlands.com), **White Water Adventurers** (6 Negley St., 800/992-7238, www.wwaraft.com), and **Ohiopyle Trading Post** (4 Negley St., 888/644-6795, www.ohiopyletradingpost. com). All offer guided rafting trips and boat and bike rentals. Between them, they provide a host of other services, including kayaking and canoeing instruction, fly-fishing clinics, guided mountain biking, guided rock climbing, and even lodging. Wilderness Voyageurs is highly regarded for its fully supported bike tours. Laurel Highlands River Tours broke from the pack in 2012 by opening a zip-lining park.

★ Fallingwater

What do you get Brad Pitt for his birthday? If you're Angelina Jolie, you spring for a private tour of **Fallingwater** (1491 Mill Run Rd.,

Fallingwater

Wright Overnight

If Fallingwater and Kentuck Knob whet your appetite for all things Wright, don't leave the Laurel Highlands without visiting—or reserving—the **Duncan House** at **Polymath Park Resort** (187 Evergreen Ln., Acme, 877/833-7829, www.polymathpark.com). It's one of only six Frank Lloyd Wright homes in the United States open to the public for lodging.

The Duncan House was built in 1957 in Lisle, Illinois. How it got to this wooded resort five miles from the Donegal exit (#91) of the Pennsylvania Turnpike is a long story. To hear it, book a tour of the resort, which also boasts two houses designed by Wright apprentice Peter Berndtson. Tours are offered daily except Saturday. They're $22 for adults, $11 for children 6-12. Children under 6 aren't permitted.

By Wright standards, the Duncan House is a modest structure. The architect envisioned mass production of such homes. But even his least expensive design was too expensive to take off. No matter. Rarity magnifies their appeal. The Duncan House has all the Wright stuff: built-in cabinetry, an oversized fireplace, clerestory windows, exposed rooflines. You'll also find stuff that belonged to its original owners, including a pastel-hued hair dryer and bathroom scale. The house, which sleeps as many six people, rents for $399-550 per night. You can also bunk at Berndtson's **Blum House** or **Balter House**—less cachet but more comforts.

Mill Run, 724/329-8501, www.fallingwater. org, regular tour $20 with advance purchase, children 6-12 $14, children under 6 not permitted), Frank Lloyd Wright's architectural masterpiece. Wright designed the house in 1935 for the Kaufmann family of Pittsburgh, owners of the now-defunct Kaufmann's department store chain. The Kaufmanns wanted a vacation home with a view of a favorite waterfall. Wright decided to cantilever the house over the 30-foot falls. The result is breathtaking—a visual and aural feast. Concrete terraces and a glass-walled living room project over the water, which provides a constant soundtrack. Fallingwater made such a splash when it was featured on the cover of *Time* magazine in 1938 that Wright, who was believed by many to be retired or dead, never wanted for work again. His last major project was Manhattan's Guggenheim Museum, which opened six months after his death in 1959. The Kaufmanns used Fallingwater until 1963, when Edgar Kaufmann Jr. entrusted it to the Western Pennsylvania Conservancy. Their artworks and furnishings, many of which were designed by Wright, still fill the house.

Tours of the National Historic Landmark are offered the first two weekends of March, every day but Wednesday from mid-March through November, and Friday-Sunday

in December, plus several days around Christmas. You'd be wise to purchase tickets in advance; it's not unusual for tours to sell out. In addition to regular tours, which last about an hour, there are a variety of specialty tours, including an in-depth tour ($65), a sunset tour ($110), and a brunch tour ($115). The house is closed in January and February. You can see the outside and explore the grounds any day of the year, weather permitting, for $8.

The visitors center has a nice café and a museum store that carries everything from postcards to jewelry to reproductions of Wright-designed furnishings.

Kentuck Knob

Six miles south of Fallingwater is a less famous but most impressive Frank Lloyd Wright creation. **Kentuck Knob** (723 Kentuck Rd., Chalk Hill, 724/329-8501, www.kentuckknob. com, regular tour $20, children 6-12 $14, children under 6 not permitted) sits high above the Youghiogheny River Gorge, wedged into the brow of a hill. Like Fallingwater, it's entwined with the terrain. Wright was 86 when ice cream magnate I. N. Hagan and his artist wife beseeched him to design a house for their 80-acre mountain property. The Uniontown couple had visited the Kaufmanns at Fallingwater and fallen in love with the architect's work. Wright was overbooked—at work on the Guggenheim in New York, Beth Sholom Synagogue in the suburbs of Philadelphia, and about a dozen residences—but took on the project anyway. He never saw the completed home, a symphony of native sandstone, tidewater red cypress, glass, and flagstone. In fact, he set foot on the site only once, when local builders were laying the foundation.

The Hagans lived in the house for 30 years, then sold it in 1986 to Peter Palumbo, a British baron, property developer, and art collector. He and his family vacationed at Kentuck Knob for a decade before opening it to the public. They still entertain there on occasion, and the house is still filled with their furniture, family photos, and artwork. A shuttle ferries guests from the visitors center to the house, about a third of a mile away. Don't pass up the opportunity to walk back. Drink in the view from the crest of the hill before meandering through fields and woods dotted with sculptures.

Tours are offered daily from March through November and Saturday-Sunday in December, plus several days after Christmas. Regular tours last about 30 minutes. In-depth tours ($55), brunch tours ($100), and sculpture garden tours ($15) are also available.

Nemacolin Woodlands Resort

Picture the Ritz Paris. Now picture a convincing knockoff of the legendary hotel in an unlikely setting: rural Pennsylvania. It's hard to imagine—until you pull into the driveway of the Chateau Lafayette, one of three hotels at the sprawling **Nemacolin Woodlands Resort** (1001 Lafayette Dr., Farmington, 724/329-8555, www.nemacolin.com). The Chateau's guest rooms feature vaulted ceilings, crystal chandeliers, and marble-slathered bathrooms with jetted tubs. And it's not even the highest-rated hotel on the property.

You don't have to be an overnight guest to enjoy the resort's astonishing array of amenities. It has a full-service spa, a separate kids spa, and a pet spa. It has two golf courses, ropes courses, a 1,060-foot zip line, one of the top sporting clays facilities in the country, tennis courts, a bowling alley, a climbing wall, and its very own ski mountain. You can climb inside a beast of a vehicle at the Jeep Off-Road Driving Academy, test your shooting skills at the Air Rifle Range or in a paintball battle, try your hand at archery, go for a horseback ride, or take a guided fly-fishing trip. The resort even offers dog sledding. In 2013 it added gambling to the long list. **Lady Luck Casino Nemacolin** (4067 National Pike, Farmington, 888/523-9582, open 24 hours) features 600 slot machines, 28 table games, and a casual dining restaurant and lounge.

Nemacolin is the brainchild of Joseph Hardy III, founder of 84 Lumber Co., and it strongly reflects his passions and whims. About $45 million in art, rare automobiles, and antique planes are scattered around the property. Free tours of the collection depart from the Chateau Lafayette lobby at 3pm daily. With 21,000 bottles, the Woodlands Wine Cellar is the largest private cellar in Pennsylvania. The resort's resident sommelier hosts weekly wine-tastings. Even more remarkable than the art and wine collections is Nemacolin's collection of animals. The resort is home to more than 100 species, including lions, tigers, bears, and zebras. Tours of their enclosures and habitats are offered daily.

No discussion of Nemacolin is complete without a mention of its restaurant collection, a mix of casual and fine dining. Pittsburghers have been known to drive 70 miles and back for a meal at Lautrec, one of only 28 restaurants named to the Forbes Travel Guide five-star list for 2013. Private jets cut the travel time; the resort has its own airstrip.

Fort Necessity National Battlefield

Just down the road from Nemacolin, **Fort Necessity National Battlefield** (1 Washington Pkwy., Farmington, 724/329-5512, www.nps.gov/fone, 9am-5pm daily,

The Whodunit That Changed History

The secluded ravine known as **Jumonville Glen** looks much as it did in May 1754, when a party of French soldiers made their camp there. There's no monument to the famous skirmish that took place when George Washington came upon them. A natural rock outcropping marks the site, and discreet signs tell the story. We know how the story ended: The leader of the French detachment, Joseph Coulon de Jumonville, lay dead. But its beginning is shrouded in mystery.

On May 24, four days before the skirmish, Washington and the frontiersmen under his command arrived at Great Meadows, a natural clearing in the woods that struck him as an ideal site for an encampment. Water was plentiful, there was grass for the animals, and the treeless terrain would make it easier to see an enemy coming. "A charming field for an encounter," he called it. Washington was 22, a newly commissioned lieutenant colonel in the Virginia militia, and he'd never come under fire.

When he learned that a group of French soldiers had been spotted several miles away, Washington left Great Meadows with about 40 men. They marched all night. On the morning of May 28, they surrounded the French, who had not posted sentries. A shot was fired, and then hundreds more. "I heard the bullets whistle, and, believe me, there is something charming in the sound," Washington would write after the clash. When it ended, all of the Frenchmen were dead or captured, save for one who escaped.

Who fired the first shot? We don't know. What were the French doing there? We don't know that either. The French survivors claimed they'd been attacked without cause. They were coming to talk, not attack, they explained. Washington felt certain they were spies rather than diplomats. Upon his return to Great Meadows, he ordered the construction of a small fort. He called it **Fort Necessity.**

The French force that attacked Fort Necessity on the morning of July 3 was 600 strong and assisted by 100 Indians. It was led by the brother of the slain Jumonville. Washington's militiamen and the regular British troops who'd joined them numbered about 400. Hours of sporadic fighting were followed by several hours of negotiations. Near midnight, Washington surrendered, signing a "capitulation" penned in French. With his signature, he unwittingly accepted responsibility for the assassination of Jumonville.

Washington and his remaining troops returned to Virginia. The following year he would retrace his steps, passing through Great Meadows as a volunteer aide to British general Edward Braddock. He would never again refer to war as "charming."

admission $5, children 15 and under free) is a must-stop for military history buffs. It was here that a young George Washington fought his first battle—on the side of the British. And it was here that he surrendered for the only time in his military career.

Start in the Interpretive and Education Center, where a film and exhibits tell the story of the July 3, 1754, battle that ignited the French and Indian War. A short path leads from the visitors center to a reconstruction of the fort built by Washington's men. The French burned the fort after their victory here, leaving few clues for historians and archaeologists. Debate over its shape raged for decades. Some experts claimed the fort was triangular, while others believed it to be diamond-shaped. The diamond camp triumphed

in 1932, when the fort was first reconstructed. But both sides ate crow in the 1950s, when archaeologists unearthed evidence of a circular fort. That's what you'll find today.

Five miles of hiking trails meander through the meadow and woods around the fort. Some trails lead to a picnic area and another to **Mount Washington Tavern,** which served as a stagecoach stop in the mid-1800s. It no longer offers food, drink, and lodging to weary travelers; instead it's a museum focusing on life along the National Road, the first federally funded highway. It's open April 15-November 1. The picnic area and tavern can also be reached by car.

Jumonville Glen, the wooded hollow where Washington confronted a band of French soldiers several weeks before the battle at Fort Necessity, is a few miles away. From the fort or tavern, follow Route 40 (aka the National Road) west for about four miles, hang a left at Jumonville Road, and continue until you reach the glen. On Route 40, you'll pass by **Braddock's Grave,** a granite monument to the British commander-in-chief killed in 1755 during a disastrous advance on the French-held Fort Duquesne in present-day Pittsburgh.

Laurel Caverns

With ceilings as high as 50 feet and an average width of more than 12 feet, **Laurel Caverns** (Skyline Dr., off Rte. 40 between Chalk Hill and Hopwood, 724/438-3003, www.laurel-caverns.com, 9am-5pm daily late Apr.-Oct., tour $12, seniors $11, youths grades 6-12 $10, children grades K-5 $9) is Pennsylvania's largest cave. It's also the state's largest natural bat hibernaculum. As soon as the bats clear out—around the end of April—the cave is opened to people. Guided tours are offered every day until the cave closes in late October. They last about an hour and require quite a bit of walking, so be sure to wear comfortable shoes. A sweater or jacket is also recommended; the cave temperature is 52 degrees year-round. In addition to the regular tour, Laurel Caverns offers caving trips ($20-25) and cave rappelling ($35). Call or check the website for caving and rappelling schedules. Leave time for a round of mini golf ($6) in Kavernputt, a large faux cave on the grounds of the real deal.

SKI REGION
Seven Springs Mountain Resort

The state's largest ski resort boasts 13 slopes, 18 trails, and consistently high marks from readers of *Ski* magazine. But snow is seasonal inventory. The average ski season lasts just four months, ending with a whimper near the end of March. That's why **Seven Springs** (777 Waterwheel Dr., Seven Springs, 800/452-2223, www.7springs.com, all-day lift ticket $58-80, children 6-11 $47-61, seniors 70-79 pay half price, seniors 80 and older ski for

free, all-day equipment rental $40-45, snow tubing $19-27 per 2-hour session) works hard to position itself as a year-round destination. There's fly-fishing. There's golf. There's paintball and bowling, horseback riding and swimming. There's a full-service spa, a sporting clays complex, a downhill bike park, two zip-line courses, a 24-foot climbing wall, and an alpine slide. In fact, Seven Springs hosts more visitors between ski seasons than during the winter months, due in large part to its conference facilities.

The resort also plays host to concerts, festivals, and other special events. Its food and booze festivals, in particular, are among the highlights of the region's social calendar. The springtime **Brewski Festival** features specialty beers from dozens of breweries and a buffet groaning with beer-basted chicken, mussels and shrimp broiled in beer, beer bread, chocolate stout cake, and more. The summertime **Wine & Food Festival** is a celebration of fine cuisine and Pennsylvania wines, complete with grape-stomping contests.

SOMERSET AREA
Flight 93 National Memorial

On Sept. 11, 2001, United Airlines Flight 93 crashed into a field near Shanksville, Pennsylvania, at 563 miles per hour. There were no survivors. Soon after, a grieving public began journeying to the remote site to pay respects to the 40 passengers and crew who perished while trying to wrest back control of the hijacked plane. They created temporary memorials: homespun collages of flowers, flags, scrawled tributes, and all manner of personal effects. In 2009, ground was broken on a permanent memorial. The **Flight 93 National Memorial** (6424 Lincoln Highway, Stoystown, 814/893-6322, www.nps.gov/flni, 9am-7pm daily May-Oct., 9am-5pm daily Oct.-Apr., free admission) is still a work in progress, but it is a powerful tribute to the men and women who thwarted a planned attack on the nation's capital. It is also their final resting place; while investigators recovered

Flight 93 National Memorial

most of the Boeing 757, including the cockpit voice recorder, less than 10 percent of the human remains were found. This is where the victims' families come to pay their respects.

Visitors walk along a low black wall that marks the edge of the crash site to a tall white wall composed of 40 marble panels, each inscribed with the name of a passenger or crew member. The Wall of Names is aligned with the plane's flight path. A boulder marks the impact point.

Forty groves have been planted in tribute to the victims. The National Park Service is now at work on a visitors center and reforestation of the land around the crash site, which was mined for coal from the 1960s to 1995. Future plans call for a 93-foot-tower containing 40 wind chimes.

Somerset Historical Center

Unlike many history museums, the **Somerset Historical Center** (10649 Somerset Pike, Somerset, 814/445-6077, www. somersethistoricalcenter.org, 9am-5pm Tues.-Sat. Apr.-Oct., 9am-5pm Tues.-Fri. Nov.-Mar., admission $6, seniors $5.50, children 3-11 $3) doesn't tell the story of great battles or important historical figures. Instead, it focuses on the farming life, showcasing the tools and

other belongings of farmers past and present. The collection includes an electric chicken plucker and a kerosene-powered slide projector. Outdoor exhibits, open April-October, include two re-created farmsteads, a maple sugar camp, and a cider press. The best time to visit is the weekend after Labor Day, when the museum hosts **Mountain Craft Days** (admission $7, children 6-17 $4). The three-day festival features demonstrations of all things country, from butter churning to barn raising.

LIGONIER AND VICINITY
Fort Ligonier

Like Fort Necessity to its south, the reconstructed **Fort Ligonier** (200 S. Market St., Ligonier, 724/238-9701, www.fortligonier. org, 9am-4:30pm Mon.-Sat. and noon-4:30pm Sun. mid-Apr.-mid-Nov., admission $10, children 6-16 $6) tells the story of the French and Indian War, the mid-1700s power struggle between Great Britain and France. The original Fort Ligonier was built in 1758 as a supply depot and staging area for British-American troops bent on ousting the French from present-day Pittsburgh. After the war ended in 1763, it served the British during the Native American uprising known as Pontiac's War.

Even more impressive than the

reconstructed fort is the museum near its entrance. Here, relics vastly outnumber reproductions. They include the mundane—canteens, coins, chamber pots, cannon balls, and gin bottles—as well as showstoppers such as a pair of pistols that belonged to George Washington.

Be aware that Fort Ligonier is closed in winter. The best time to visit is mid-October, during **Fort Ligonier Days** (724/238-4200, www.ligonier.com). The three-day festival commemorates the successful defense of the fort from a French attack on October 12, 1758. Reenactors flood the town of Ligonier, setting up camp on the grounds of the fort. Food and craft booths pop up all over town, church ladies cook up a storm, and the community puts on a parade. Best of all: twice-daily battle reenactments.

Idlewild & SoakZone

You can tell that **Idlewild & SoakZone** (Rte. 30 E., Ligonier, 724/238-3666, www.idlewild. com, admission $37.99, seniors $28.99, children 2 and under free, rates discounted online) is no ordinary amusement park by the sheer number of baby strollers. This place is as kid-friendly as kid-friendly gets. Its seven theme areas include Raccoon Lagoon, one of the largest kiddie-ride areas in the country. Mister Rogers' Neighborhood of Make-Believe, another tyke-suitable area, was designed by Fred Rogers himself. (The creator and host of *Mister Rogers' Neighborhood* was born in nearby Latrobe.) It's no wonder that Idlewild is a perennial winner of the Golden Ticket Award for Best Children's Park from *Amusement Today* magazine.

Idlewild also holds the distinction of being the oldest amusement park in Pennsylvania and one of the oldest in the country. It opened in 1878 as a picnic and camping area for city dwellers seeking a country escape. By the 1950s, Idlewild had grown into a bona fide amusement park, complete with a three-row carousel. Today that carousel is the centerpiece of Olde Idlewild, home to the park's two roller coasters and other major rides.

In recent years Idlewild has invested heavily in its water park, SoakZone. A 280,600-gallon wave pool was unveiled in 2011. Float Away Bay, a lazy river attraction, opened in 2013.

The park is open daily from early June to late August and some days before and after that period. Gates usually open at 10:30am, with rides and SoakZone opening at 11:30am. The park remains open until at

SoakZone

least 8pm, but most of its theme areas close earlier. Idlewild reopens on October weekends for **HallowBoo,** an all-ages Halloween celebration. Come in costume if you like, but steer clear of racy or gory getups. They're an Idlewild no-no, along with masks on adults.

Ligonier Beach

Less than five miles down the road from Idlewild & SoakZone is another summertime attraction with a rich history. Opened in 1925, **Ligonier Beach** (1752 Rte. 30 E., Ligonier, 724/238-9551, 11am-7pm daily Memorial Day-Labor Day, admission $8) is an astonishingly large pool—ostensibly the largest in Pennsylvania. With a capacity of 1.3 million gallons of water, it makes SoakZone's impressive wave pool look like a kiddie pool. And with admission at $8 a head, it's a relatively cheap way to pass a hot day.

Compass Inn Museum

The **Compass Inn Museum** (1382 Rte. 30, Laughlintown, 724/238-4983, www.compassinn.com, 11am-4pm Tues.-Sat. and 1pm-5pm Sun. May-Oct., admission $9, students through high school $6, children 5 and under free) is a restored 1799 stagecoach stop filled with period furnishings. Costumed docents lead 90-minute tours of the inn and three reconstructed outbuildings, all the while explaining how people lived and traveled in the early 1800s. Tours begin whenever visitors arrive. The best time to visit is during one of the museum's living history weekends, which feature craft demonstrations and hands-on activities. The Compass Inn is closed November through April except for Saturdays and Sundays from November through early December, when it's decorated for the holidays. Reservations are required for holiday tours.

LATROBE
Steelers Training Camp

Want a ticket to watch the Pittsburgh Steelers at Heinz Field? Good luck. Tickets to home games are notoriously hard to come by and cost a pretty penny. But you can catch the players in action—for free!—at their summer training camp on the campus of **Saint Vincent College** (300 Fraser Purchase Rd., Latrobe, 724/532-6600, www.stvincent.edu). *Sports Illustrated* Senior Editor Peter King called it "the best training camp in the NFL, the best venue for watching real football in the NFL, and my favorite place to soak in what sports should be." The

the Compass Inn Museum

annual training camp has been held at Saint Vincent since 1968.

The Steelers arrive in mid-July and leave about a month later. Check the team's website, www.steelers.com, for training camp dates and times. Often the schedule isn't confirmed until sometime in June or early July. The Steelers prefer privacy in the mornings, but their late afternoon practices are open to the public. After practice, fans jostle for autographs in designated areas.

Other Saint Vincent Attractions

Steelers training camp isn't the only reason to visit **Saint Vincent College** (300 Fraser Purchase Rd., Latrobe, 724/532-6600, www. stvincent.edu). The nation's first Benedictine college also has something for foodies, fans of *Mister Rogers' Neighborhood,* and nature lovers.

Built in 1854 by the Benedictine monks of Saint Vincent Archabbey, the **Saint Vincent Gristmill** (Beatty Rd., 724/537-0304, www. saintvincentgristmill.com, 9am-4pm Mon.-Sat.) is, remarkably, still in operation. Much of the original machinery is still in use, and monks are still at the controls. The gift shop carries the fruits of their labors: whole wheat flour, unbleached white flour, rye flour, buckwheat flour, and cornmeal. It also offers a variety of products made by other monastic communities. Located in what used to be the boiler room, the **Gristmill Coffeehouse** serves coffee and espresso drinks.

Saint Vincent College is also home to the **Fred Rogers Center for Early Learning and Children's Media** (724/805-2750, www. fredrogerscenter.org, 8:30am-4:30pm Mon.-Fri., free admission). Established in 2003, just months after Rogers died of cancer, the Center houses his official archive and champions high standards in children's programming. It's also home to a multimedia exhibit about the beloved creator and host of *Mister Rogers' Neighborhood,* who was born and raised in Latrobe.

The **Winnie Palmer Nature Reserve** (744 Walzer Way, 724/537-5285, www.wpnr. org) is named for the late wife of another Latrobe native, golf legend Arnold Palmer. The 50-acre reserve features more than two miles of trails, open dawn to dusk year-round, and an environmental education center open

---

"Won't You Be My Neighbor?"

Before Dora the Explorer, before Teletubbies, and even before Big Bird, there was **Mister Rogers.** *Mister Rogers' Neighborhood* began airing in 1968 and continued to captivate kids even after the death of its creator and host. Fred McFeely Rogers was an unlikely television personality. Born in Latrobe, about 40 miles southeast of Pittsburgh, Rogers was more interested in spirituality than celebrity. Several years before the public television program debuted, he graduated from Pittsburgh Theological Seminary and was ordained a Presbyterian minister. "I went into television because I hated it so," he once told CNN, "and I thought there was some way of using this fabulous instrument to be of nurture to those who would watch and listen."

Rogers taped almost 900 episodes of his eponymous show. They began the same way, with Rogers returning to his television home, slipping into more comfortable clothes, and singing: "Would you be mine, could you be mine, won't you be my neighbor?" (For many years, his mother knitted the cardigan sweaters that were his signature.) He took viewers on field trips, showing them how things like crayons are made and how things like bulldozers work. And he took them to his Neighborhood of Make-Believe, a kingdom of puppets. Rogers tackled any topic that might weigh on a child, be it war or the first day of school. He even explained, in song, that you can't be pulled down the bathroom drain. Produced in Pittsburgh, *Mister Rogers' Neighborhood* remained in syndication until September 2008, five years after its creator's death at the age of 74. Some stations still air it.

10am-4pm Tuesday-Friday and 9am-2pm the first Saturday of each month.

GREENSBURG AND VICINITY
Westmoreland Museum of American Art

It comes as a bit of a surprise to discover a first-rate museum in the foothills of southwestern Pennsylvania. The **Westmoreland Museum of American Art** (221 N. Main St., Greensburg, temporary location 4764 State Rte. 30, Greensburg, 724/837-1500, www. wmuseumaa.org, noon-7pm Wed.-Fri., 10am-5pm Sat.-Sun., free admission) is home to works by Winslow Homer, Mary Cassatt, John Singer Sargent, and other nationally recognized names. Even more impressive is its trove of art inspired by southwestern Pennsylvania.

In 2013 the museum kicked off a major renovation and expansion, moving its collection to a temporary home on Route 30 between Greensburg and Latrobe. The museum in downtown Greensburg was scheduled to reopen in spring 2015.

Colonial Sites

The Greensburg area serves up two slices of colonial history. **Bushy Run Battlefield** (1253 Bushy Run Rd., Jeannette, 724/527-5584, www.bushyrunbattlefield.com, visitors center 9am-5pm Wed.-Sun. Apr.-Oct., admission $5, seniors $4.50, children 3-12 $3) was the site of a pivotal clash in the Native American uprising known as Pontiac's War. The August 1763 battle ended in a victory for the British, opening western Pennsylvania to settlement. The site is open 8am-dusk year-round, but it's best to visit April-October, when the visitors center is open. Certified tour guides are on hand Friday-Sunday during the regular season.

Less than 10 miles away, **Historic Hanna's Town** (809 Forbes Trail Rd., Greensburg, 724/836-1800, www.starofthewest.org, 10am-4pm Wed.-Sat. and 1pm-4pm Sun. June-Aug., weekends only in May and Sept.-Oct., admission $5, seniors $4, students through high school $4) offers a glimpse of 1770s frontier life. Founded in 1773, the original Hanna's Town was a hub of political and military activity during the Revolutionary War. At the tail end of the war, it was attacked and burned by a party of Native Americans and their British allies. Today's Hanna's Town features a reconstructed Revolutionary-era fort, a reconstructed tavern/courthouse, and three 18th-century log houses.

ENTERTAINMENT AND EVENTS
Performing Arts

Located across from the Westmoreland County Courthouse in downtown Greensburg, the handsome **Palace Theatre** (21 W. Otterman St., Greensburg, 724/836-8000, www.thepalacetheatre.org) hosts a wide variety of acts, from local ballet and theater companies to internationally known entertainers like Bill Cosby and Joan Baez. The 1,369-seat theater dates to 1926 and almost had a date with a wrecking ball. Purchased in 1990 by a nonprofit organization now known as Westmoreland Cultural Trust, it has undergone more than $10 million in renovations. Many of its original features remain intact, including a candlelight chandelier in the lobby and a goldfish pond on the mezzanine level.

Festivals and Events

More than 100 locals make up the cast of *The Legend of the Magic Water*, a song-filled account of the discovery of maple syrup. The pageant has been a **Pennsylvania Maple Festival** (Meyersdale, 814/634-0213, www. pamaplefestival.com, Mar.) tradition since 1971. First held in 1948, the folksy celebration of Pennsylvania's sweetest commodity put Meyersdale on the map and gave the town its nickname: "Maple City, USA." Highlights include sugaring demonstrations, a parade, auto shows, a Maple Queen contest, and spotza making. What's spotza, you say? It's a taffy-like treat made by pouring boiled maple syrup over crushed ice. (Native Americans, who shared the recipe with settlers, used snow.) Events take place throughout Meyersdale, but the hub of activity is Festival Park. Admission to the park is $5 for adults, $1 for children 6-12.

The **Westmoreland Arts & Heritage Festival** (Twin Lakes Park, Greensburg, 724/834-7474, www.artsandheritage.com, first week of July, free), an arts-infused Fourth of July celebration, showcases the work of 200-plus craftspeople and artisans from across the country. The four-day festival also features a juried exhibition of fine art, dozens of live performances, and ethnic food aplenty.

Kilted bagpipers turn out en force for the **Ligonier Highland Games** (Idlewild & SoakZone, Rte. 30 E., Ligonier, 814/931-4714, www.ligonierhighlandgames.org, Sept., admission $20, seniors $18, children 9-15 $10), a celebration of all things Scottish. Competitions in everything from dancing to tree-tossing are a Highland Games staple.

Squeeze as many as you can into the family van. Admission to **Overly's Country Christmas** (Westmoreland Fairgrounds, Greensburg, 724/423-1400, www.overlys.com, late Nov.-Jan. 1) is $10-12 per carful. The holiday light display had its beginnings more than 50 years ago, when Harry Overly first decorated his rural home with a few strands of lights. Encouraged by his children's delight, he stepped up his game. Year after year, the lights got brighter and the crowds got bigger. After 35 years, the spectacle outgrew its creator's seven-acre property and, in 1993, found a home at the Westmoreland Fairgrounds. These days it features more than two million lights, a walk-through country-themed Christmas Village, and a life-size nativity scene complete with live animals. Visitors can roast marshmallows around the bonfire, hop in a horse-drawn wagon or sleigh, and, of course, meet Santa. Proceeds benefit at-risk families.

Some towns put fun on ice in winter. Not Ligonier. Each January it invites artists to create masterpieces from blocks of ice during the two-day **Ligonier Ice Fest** (724/238-4200, www.ligonier.com).

SHOPPING
Ligonier

Historic Ligonier is a diamond of a town, worthy of a stroll any time of year. Its epicenter, known as the Ligonier Diamond, is surrounded by specialty shops such as **Equine Chic** (100 E. Main St., 724/238-7003, open Tues.-Sat.), where you'll find horse-shaped cookie cutters, pewter napkin rings in the shape of stirrups, and other equestrian home accents. If you haven't guessed it already, this is horse-and-hound country. For almost 50 years, the famous Mellon family hosted steeplechase races on its property, Rolling Rock Farms, just east of town. Fox hunting remains a Ligonier Valley tradition. It's not unusual to see riders in breeches and boots grabbing a coffee or meal in town.

Other notable shops include **Song of Sixpence** (209 E. Main St., 919/810-2901, www.songofsixpenceligonier.com, open daily), with its delightful selection of women's clothing and accessories, and the **Post & Rail Men's Shop** (104 E. Main St., 724/238-9235, www.thepostandrail.com, open Mon.-Sat.), offering classic clothing, personal attention, and expert tailoring, plus leather armchairs for ladies in waiting.

The town's aura of chic even extends to its toy store. The six-room **Toy Box** (108 S. Market St., 724/238-6233, www.toyboxligonier.com, open daily) puts Toys "R" Us to shame with its selection of playthings. It carries everything from puzzles to plush toys—and horse collectibles, of course.

If you're visiting on a Saturday, start your day at the **Ligonier Country Market** (intersection of W. Main St. and Rte. 30, 724/858-7894, www.ligoniercountrymarket.com, 8am-noon from Sat. before Memorial Day weekend to first Sat. in Oct.) on the western end of town. In addition to an outstanding selection of fresh produce and flowers, you'll find artisan breads and other baked goods, handmade jewelry and home accessories, and more. You can munch on a piping-hot beignet as you take it all in.

ACCOMMODATIONS
Ohiopyle and Vicinity

Accommodations in the Ohiopyle area range from campgrounds to world-class hotels. Book early if you're coming in summer, when visitation is highest.

Camping in **Ohiopyle State Park** (124 Main St., Ohiopyle, 724/329-8591, www.visitpaparks.com, campsite under $35) is a great option for budget-conscious nature lovers. Open from April to mid-December, Ohiopyle's Kentuck Campground has about 200 campsites, flush toilets, and showers. Many of the sites have electric hook-ups. The campground also has a handful of yurts and rustic cottages, all of which sleep five people in bunk beds. Reserve online at www.pa.reserveworld.com or by calling 888/727-2757.

The area also has some excellent private campgrounds loaded with amenities. Kids go cuckoo for ★ **Yogi Bear's Jellystone Park** (839 Mill Run Rd., Mill Run, 724/455-2929, www.jellystonemillrun.com, campsite $55-80, cabin $115-220, campsites half price in off-season), where they can hobnob with Yogi Bear, his sidekick Boo Boo, and other costumed Hanna-Barbera characters. The "camp-resort" boasts a mini golf course, mining sluice, paintball field, game room, two playgrounds, train and wagon rides, and more. Its portfolio of pools and waterslides is especially impressive. That's part of the reason why campsites cost twice as much in summer as the rest of the year. Yogi Bear's has an array of adorable cabins in addition to tent and RV sites. Other family-friendly campgrounds include **Benner's Meadow Run** (315 Nelson Rd., Farmington, 724/329-4097, www.bennersmeadowrun.com, campsite $20-47, cabin $49-189), which is convenient to Fort Necessity National Battlefield and Nemacolin Woodlands Resort as well as Ohiopyle State Park. It's open from mid-April to mid-October. Winter stays are available by reservation.

Camping isn't the only option for budget travelers. The itty-bitty Borough of Ohiopyle, which is entirely surrounded by Ohiopyle State Park, has a motel and basic guesthouses. Built and operated by the family behind rafting company White Water Adventurers, the **Yough Plaza Motel** (28 Sherman St., Ohiopyle, 800/992-7238, www.youghplaza.com, standard room $110, suite $200) has 10 rooms that sleep up to four and five suites that sleep up to six. Another family-owned rafting company, Laurel Highlands River Tours, owns three centrally located **guesthouses** (Grant St., Ohiopyle, 800/472-3846, www.laurelhighlands.com, $45 per person based on double occupancy) that accommodate 8-12 people. You can rent a room or an entire house.

If you like the idea of renting an entire house, look into **Ohiopyle Vacation Rentals** (877/574-7829, www.ohiopylevacationrentals.com, weeknight rates $150-1,200, weekend rates $225-1,500). Its scattered properties sleep from six to 35. No two are alike, but they're all quite lovely.

The area's most luxurious accommodations can be found at ★ **Nemacolin Woodlands Resort** (1001 LaFayette Dr., Farmington, 724/329-8555, www.nemacolin.com). The humblest of its three hotels is the Tudor-style **Lodge** (room $339-395, suite $455-509), built in 1968 when the property was a Pittsburgh industrialist's private game reserve and expanded by Nemacolin founder Joseph Hardy III. It houses a good deal of the Hardy family art collection, including Tiffany lamps and Norman Rockwell prints. Room decor evokes an English country inn. **Chateau Lafayette** (regular room $455-509, regular suite $585-639, club room $679-739, club suite $809-869, presidential $2,999) is Hardy's tribute to the grand hotels of Europe. With its vaulted ceilings, crystal chandeliers, and two-story Palladian windows, the hotel built in 1997 aptly emulates the famed Ritz Paris, a century older. It's home to a cigar bar, a high-end jewelry store, and Lautrec, Nemacolin's most celebrated restaurant. Round-the-clock butler service is available to guests of the fifth-floor club level.

Butler service is available to every guest of **Falling Rock** (room $699-815, suite

Dinner and a Show (Plus Overnight Digs)

unique accommodations at Huddleson Court

If you associate fine dining and professional theater with big cities, you haven't been to the **Green Gables Restaurant** and **Mountain Playhouse.** Tucked into the woods of the Laurel Highlands, the restaurant and neighboring theater offer a night out like no other. If you're coming from a distance, might as well turn the night out into an even more memorable overnight by booking a stay at the on-site **Huddleson Court.** That's right: dining, theater, and lodging on one property in what feels like the middle of nowhere. "Unique" doesn't begin to describe it.

Founded in 1939, the **Mountain Playhouse** (7690 Somerset Pike, Boswell, 814/629-9201, www.mountainplayhouse.org) is Pennsylvania's oldest professional summer stock theater and one of only a dozen professional summer stock theaters in the country. All productions feature members of Actors' Equity Association, the union of professional actors and stage managers. The theater is housed in an 1805 gristmill that was moved, log by log, from its original site about 20 miles away. The performance season begins in June, ends in October, and includes a mix of genres. Farce is a specialty of the house.

Even older than the playhouse, the **Green Gables Restaurant** (7712 Somerset Pike, Boswell, 814/629-9201, www.greengablesrestaurant.com, lunch and brunch $8-12, dinner $23-30, reservations recommended) started life in 1927 as a roadside sandwich stand. Over the years, it was expanded room by room, and today it's an expansive space that still manages to feel cozy. The meal-and-theater experience is truly special, but Green Gables is a worthwhile destination even when the playhouse is on hiatus. Enjoy a tasty salad or sandwich at lunch for under $15 and explore the enchanting grounds in daylight. Come for dinner for artful entrées such as tomatillo-braised bison short ribs and prosciutto-wrapped pork tenderloin. Request a window-side table to enjoy a view of the stream that runs behind the restaurant. During the theater season, Green Gables is open for lunch Wednesday-Friday, brunch Saturday-Sunday, and dinner Tuesday-Sunday. In the off-season, it's open for brunch Saturday-Sunday and dinner Thursday-Sunday.

Collectively known as **Huddleson Court** (7712 Somerset Pike, Boswell, 814/629-9201, www.huddlesoncourt.com, $90-240), the rooms and cottages on the grounds of the Green Gables Restaurant and Mountain Playhouse are as quaint as they come. The Sugar Maple and Daylily rooms are an exceptional value—no more than $125 during the performance season and as low as $80 during the off-peak months (Nov.-May). Beaverdam Creek Cabin, with its wood-burning fireplace, stone staircase, and cozy loft bedroom, is the stuff of storybooks. Call or check the website for information about overnight packages that include dinner and/or a show.

$845-909), Nemacolin's most acclaimed lodging. It's as understated as the Chateau is ornate, a reverent nod to architect Frank Lloyd Wright, whose masterpiece Fallingwater is less than 20 minutes away. The hotel sits on the 18th green of the Pete Dye-designed Mystic Rock golf course, a good distance from the hub of activity at Nemacolin. It features 42 guest rooms and suites, an infinity pool reserved for hotel guests, and an upscale steakhouse. Guests can take their pick of 10 pillow types, including air pillows, buckwheat pillows, and even anti-snore pillows.

Families and groups should inquire about Nemacolin's two-bedroom townhomes and luxury homes that sleep as many as 20 people. The resort also has an RV park, **Maggie Valley** ($155-165), that's open April-October. It may be the only RV park in western Pennsylvania that offers room service.

Ski Region

If skiing is what brings you to the Laurel Highlands, there's little reason to look beyond **Seven Springs Mountain Resort** (777 Waterwheel Dr., Seven Springs, 866/437-1300, www.7springs.com, from $179) for lodging. The resort's hotel has more than 400 guest rooms and suites, making it the largest hotel in the region. Its decor is nothing remarkable, but what does that matter? There's too much to do on the 5,500-acre resort to be hanging in your room. Located at the base of the mountain, the 10-floor hotel is attached to the main lodge, which houses eateries and bars, specialty shops, a heated pool and hot tubs, a game room, and more. Families and small groups may be better off renting one of the resort's condos, townhouses, cottages, or chalets. Call for rates.

A pair of nearby state parks offer alternatives to the resort scene. **Kooser State Park** (943 Glades Pike, Somerset, 814/445-8673, www.visitpaparks.com, campsite under $35, cabin under $75) has a small campground and nine rustic cabins. The campground closes in mid-October, but the cabins can be rented year-round. They sleep up to eight people. **Laurel Hill State Park** (1454 Laurel Hill Park Rd.,

Somerset, 814/445-7725, www.visitpaparks. com, campsite under $35, lodge $171-285) boasts a five-bedroom, three-bathroom lodge that sleeps 14. It's specially equipped for winter recreation, with ski and snowboard racks, glove and boot dryers, and a large fireplace. Laurel Hill also has a campground open from early April to mid-October. State park reservations can be made online at www.pa.reserveworld. com or by calling 888/727-2757.

Somerset

An expansive marble foyer and gold leaf chandeliers greet guests at **The Georgian Inn of Somerset** (800 Georgian Inn Dr., Somerset, 814/443-1043, www.thegeorgianinnofsomerset.com, $135-175), a 22-room Georgian mansion built in 1915 for a local coal and cattle baron. Its 12 guest rooms and suites range from quaint to dignified. Guests are treated to a gourmet breakfast.

Ligonier and Vicinity

Drenched in pink and delightfully frilly, **Campbell House Bed & Breakfast** (305 E. Main St., Ligonier, 724/238-9812, www.campbellhousebnb.com, $90-165) is a stone's throw from the Ligonier Diamond and historic Fort Ligonier. Patti Campbell calls her eponymous B&B "an adult getaway," recognizing that tots could easily mistake whimsical collectibles and heirlooms for toys. Part innkeeper and part romance facilitator, Campbell offers a couples massage package and an elopement package complete with marriage ceremony and wedding cake. In addition to the B&B's six rooms and suites, she offers two efficiency motel rooms. They're a bargain at $80 per night, but you'll have to pay extra for her delectable breakfasts.

Ligonier Country Inn (1376 Rte. 30 E., Laughlintown, 724/238-3651, www.ligoniercountryinn.com, $90-189) is actually in Laughlintown, a wee little town about three miles east of Ligonier. The main house has 18 guest rooms, a restaurant known for its Sunday breakfast and brunch buffets, a pub, a charming courtyard pool, and a country feel. The adjacent Shafer House has six guest rooms with a more Victorian vibe. Innkeepers Maggie and PJ Nied also own a handful of rental cottages.

Latrobe

SpringHill Suites Pittsburgh Latrobe (115 Arnold Palmer Dr., Latrobe, 724/537-7800, www.marriott.com, $119-179) is part-owned by golf legend Arnold Palmer, who was born and raised in Latrobe. Its public areas are decorated with Palmer memorabilia, and guests have the rare opportunity to dine and golf at the private Latrobe Country Club, where he learned to play (and still plays). But there's more to its appeal than the Palmer connection. Opened in 2012, the hotel is as sleek and contemporary as it gets in these parts. Hotel amenities include an indoor saltwater pool and an outdoor patio with a large fire pit. The hotel is across the road from Saint Vincent College, where the Pittsburgh Steelers hold their summer training camp, and about 10 minutes down the road from Idlewild & SoakZone.

FOOD

This mostly rural region has quite a few recommendable restaurants, including Lautrec, one of only 28 restaurants named to the Forbes Travel Guide five-star list for 2013.

Ohiopyle and Vicinity

Smack-dab in the heart of Ohiopyle Borough, **The Firefly Grill** (25 Sherman St., Ohiopyle, 724/329-7155, www.thefireflygrill.com, 11am-8pm daily Apr.-Oct., under $10) has been feeding outdoor adventurers since 2001. Its wraps, sandwiches, and salads are fuel enough for a long bike ride or river trip, but few can pass up the fresh-cut fries. A 32-ounce hand-squeezed lemonade is just $2.50. Want something harder to quench your thirst? **Ohiopyle House Cafe** (144 Grant St., Ohiopyle, 724/329-1122, 11am-9pm Sun.-Thurs. and 11am-10pm Fri.-Sat. Memorial Day-Labor Day, $9-26) boasts a full bar, fantastic deck, and homemade potato chips.

In 2007, AAA awarded its highest honor to Nemacolin Woodlands Resort's **Lautrec** (1001 LaFayette Dr., Farmington, 866/344-6957, www.nemacolin.com, 6pm-9pm Tues.-Thurs., 6pm-10pm Fri.-Sat.), making it Pennsylvania's first new five-diamond restaurant in 13 years. Today it's also on the exclusive Forbes Travel Guide five-star list. Dining at Lautrec is an hours-long culinary adventure. Guests can choose between a four-course

the Firefly Grill in Ohiopyle

Big Mac Museum

Not long after meeting McDonald's founder Ray Kroc at a Chicago restaurant show, Jim Delligatti bought into the Golden Arches dream and began opening franchises in the Pittsburgh area. In 1967, the entrepreneur added a new hamburger to the menu of his Uniontown McDonald's. Delligatti's invention, the Big Mac, was rolled out nationally the following year, becoming such a fixture on the fast food landscape that Pittsburgh was temporarily renamed Big Mac, USA, on the sandwich's 25th anniversary. Its 40th was celebrated with the opening of the **Big Mac Museum Restaurant** (9061 Rte. 30, North Huntingdon, 724/863-9837, www.bigmacmuseum.com, lobby 5am-midnight, drive-thru open 24 hours, free admission, food under $5), a McDonald's restaurant filled with exhibits about the two-patty burger. The collection includes the world's largest Big Mac statue (the pickles alone measure two feet across), a bronze bust of the burger's inventor, Big Mac Christmas ornaments, and a Big Mac purse. Located off the Irwin exit (#67) of the Pennsylvania turnpike, the museum-restaurant also has an indoor playground.

prix fixe menu ($110 per person, $200 with wine pairings), nine-course chef's tasting menu ($145 per person, $270 with wine pairings), and the "ultimate experience" ($225 per person, $360 with wine pairings). Vegetarian and vegan tasting menus are also available. Needless to say, the service is impeccable. Waitstaff are not only well versed in the food and the placement of forks but are also remarkably friendly. So while men are urged to wear jackets and denim is verboten, the atmosphere in the rounded, richly hued dining room is entirely unstuffy.

Just minutes down the historic National Road from Nemacolin, the ★ **Stone House** (3023 National Pike, Farmington, 724/329-8876, www.stonehouseinn.com, 11:30am-9pm Tues.-Sun., $10-30) first opened its doors in 1822. The inn has attracted renewed interest since 2012, when Jeremy Critchfield took over its kitchen. Critchfield's resume reads like a list of luxury resorts. He joined the Stone House as co-owner and chef after stints as executive chef at Nemacolin and vice president of food and beverage at The Greenbrier in West Virginia. Don't let his high-end credentials scare you off from the Stone House. The atmosphere is historic-casual, the prices reasonable, and the food approachable. A quick scan reveals Critchfield's fondness for barbecue and from-scratch Italian. During the warmer months, he fires up a smoker

and serves ribs, beef brisket, pulled pork, and other barbecue classics in the parking lot.

Ski Region

Out of the Fire Café (3784 State Rte. 31, Donegal, 724/593-4200, www.outofthefire-cafe.com, 11am-3pm and 5pm-9pm daily, closed Mon.-Tues. in fall and winter, lunch $9-14, dinner $24-35) opened in 2007, but its roots go back to 1974, when owner Jeff Fryer got his first taste of smoked salmon. It was love at first bite, and in the years that followed, Fryer perfected his own recipe. Out of the Fire makes ample use of that recipe, offering a smoked salmon appetizer, smoked salmon salad, and smoked salmon sandwich. But the stylish BYOB isn't a one-note operation. Its seafood entrées and steaks are also top-notch, and its dessert menu deserves attention. The roasted mushroom soup has such a following that it's available to go (as is the signature smoked salmon). Out of the Fire is just off the Donegal exit (#91) of the Pennsylvania Turnpike, western gateway to the Laurel Highlands' ski resorts.

Seven Springs Mountain Resort has a diverse portfolio of eateries. One, **Helen's** (777 Waterwheel Dr., Seven Springs, 800/452-2223 ext. 7827, www.7springs.com, dinner service Tues.-Sun., $25-40), is worth going out of your way for. Formerly the home of Seven Springs' founders, the upscale restaurant favors locally sourced and sustainably raised ingredients, showcasing them in dishes like puree of corn soup, whole roasted trout, and duck prepared two ways. It's known for its tableside preparation of Caesar salad, warm service, and sylvan views. Helen's is particularly romantic when there's snow piled outside and frosting the trees.

Somerset

Crazy Alice's Café (Glades Court Mall, 101 W. Main St., Somerset, 814/443-6370, www. crazyalicescafe.com, 7am-4pm Mon.-Thurs., 7am-9pm Fri., 8am-9pm Sat., breakfast and lunch under $10, dinner $14-20) opens nice and early, serving reasonably priced omelets, pancakes, and other breakfast foods until 11am. It's a good place to fuel up for a visit to the Flight 93 National Memorial, about 20 minutes away. Crazy Alice's shares a small indoor mall with Young Heart Books, a great children's bookstore that also carries a variety of toys and children's clothes.

Ligonier and Vicinity

Ligonier is arguably the most fetching hamlet in the Laurel Highlands, with a gazebo at its center and an array of boutique shops. It also boasts a high concentration of recommendable eateries.

Built for the town's first mayor, the large Victorian now known as the **Ligonier Tavern** (137 W. Main St., Ligonier, 724/238-4831, www.ligoniertavern.com, 11:30am-9pm Mon.-Thurs., 11:30am-10pm Fri.-Sat., noon-8pm Sun., bar open late, $6-23) was the first home in Ligonier with indoor plumbing. Today it's many locals' first choice for a casual, high-quality meal. Homemade is the name of the game here. The tavern even has an in-house bakery. Its creamy artichoke dip caught the attention of *Bon Appetit* magazine some years ago. The burgers, pasta dishes, and crab cakes are also popular.

The Kitchen on Main (136 E. Main St., Ligonier, 724/238-4199, www.thekitchenonmain.com, breakfast 8am-3pm Sat.-Sun., lunch 11am-3pm Wed.-Sun., dinner 5pm-8pm Wed.-Thurs. and Sun. and 5pm-9pm Fri.-Sat., breakfast $6-14, lunch $9-16, dinner $10-32) opened in 2012 to high expectations. Chef-owner Josh Fryer is the son of Jeff Fryer, owner of Donegal's acclaimed Out of the Fire Café. The younger Fryer didn't disappoint. Offerings like pepper-crusted rib-eye steak sandwich, crispy shrimp and corn fritters, and sweet potato risotto quickly earned him a following. His father's famed smoked salmon shows up at breakfast, which, sadly, is only served on weekends. Like Out of the Fire, The Kitchen is a BYOB establishment. Bloody Mary fans need only bring vodka; the restaurant supplies the rest.

By day, **Flavors Café** (138 W. Main St., Ligonier, 724/238-3284, www.theflavorscafe. com, lunch 11am-3pm Tues.-Sat., dinner 6pm-9pm Fri.-Sat., lunch $8-14, dinner $24-32) is a casual spot, with customers lining up at the counter to order salads, sandwiches, and colossal burgers. Before dinner, however, the BYOB slips out of blue jeans and into a ball gown. Guests are greeted with crisp linens, flickering candles, smooth jazz, and the owner herself. Personalized attention is a point of pride at Flavors, which has fewer than 10 tables.

Brasserie du Soleil (201 E. Main St., Ligonier, 724/995-8057, www.brasseriedusoleil.net, noon-9pm Tues.-Thurs. and Sun., noon-10pm Fri.-Sat., lunch $9-13, dinner $16-25) is another excellent option. Chef-owner William Csikesz set out to transport guests to the south of France, and to that end, Du Soleil offers outdoor seating when weather permits. The menu of authentic French fare does the rest.

Don't leave Ligonier without a visit to **Joe's Bar** (202 W. Main St., Ligonier, 724/238-4877, 11am-2am Mon.-Sat., noon-2am Sun.). To the naked eye, Joe's is a smoky beer-and-shot joint. But walk beyond the bar and you'll enter a taxidermy museum that's at once ghastly and impressive. If you've never seen a rhinoceros, red lechwe, or blue wildebeest up close, here's your chance. Globetrotting hunter Joe Snyder couldn't keep all his trophies at home, so he displayed them in his bar. They take up four rooms on two floors. A massive elephant head, trunk raised and ears flared, hangs from the ceiling.

Nearby Laughlintown is so small that it makes Ligonier look like a metropolis, but it has a huge reputation among dessert lovers thanks to **The Original Pie Shoppe** (1379 Rte. 30, Laughlintown, 724/238-6621, www.theoriginalpieshoppe.com, 6am-5pm Mon.-Tues., 6am-9pm Wed.-Sun., under $10). Established in 1947, the bakery is best known for its cinnamon rolls. In addition to sweets, sweets, and more sweets, it offers picnic-style foods like hot dogs, chili, and potato salad.

INFORMATION

Before your visit, visit the website of the **Laurel Highlands Visitors Bureau** (800/333-5661, www.laurelhighlands.org) to request a free destination guide or view a digital version. The visitors bureau has its headquarters in Ligonier Town Hall (120 E. Main St., Ligonier), but it's only open weekdays. It also has a visitors center in Ohiopyle's defunct train station (7 Sheridan St., Ohiopyle),

adjacent to the Great Allegheny Passage. The center is open from dawn to dusk year-round. Information specialists are on hand 10am-4:30pm daily from late May to mid-October. On Fridays, Saturdays, and Sundays from Memorial Day to Labor Day, they stick around until 6pm.

GETTING THERE AND AROUND

Most visitors to the three-county Laurel Highlands region arrive by car. Donegal, its approximate center, is about 50 miles southeast of Pittsburgh via the Pennsylvania Turnpike (I-76).

Arriving by plane, train, or bus isn't out of the question. Latrobe's **Arnold Palmer Regional Airport** (LBE, 724/539-8100, http://www.palmerairport.com), named for the golf legend who grew up less than a mile from its runway, is served by Spirit Airlines. **Amtrak** (800/872-7245, www.amtrak.com) provides train service to Latrobe, Greensburg, and Connellsville. You can also get to Latrobe and Greensburg via **Greyhound** (800/231-2222, www.greyhound.com) bus. However you get there, you'll want a car to get around.

Vicinity of Pittsburgh

Pittsburgh's environs boast quite a few distinctions. Lawrence County is the self-proclaimed Fireworks Capital of America. Indiana County, which lays claim to the title of Christmas Tree Capital of the World, gave us Hollywood legend Jimmy Stewart. Armstrong County was once home to Nellie Bly, the crusading journalist who circled the globe in 72 days in the late 1800s. Indiana County has a town with the unique name of Home; Armstrong County has Parker, the smallest city in the country; and Washington County has 80 buildings constructed almost entirely of poured-in-place concrete—one of Thomas Edison's not-so-bright ideas. But you're interested in destinations, not distinctions, so let me cut to the chase. In the parlance of tourism promoters, these counties are Pittsburgh's "countryside." There are, indeed, bucolic settings. There are even Amish communities. But there are also highways, drab malls, unsightly industry, and generally depressed areas. That's not to discourage you from leaving the city. By all means, take a daycation. If you know where to go (and you will, if you continue reading), you won't be disappointed.

SOUTH OF PITTSBURGH: WASHINGTON AND GREENE COUNTIES

Washington County boasts a burgeoning hotel and shopping district centered on a harness race track and casino. It has family-friendly attractions, too, including the state's largest and oldest trolley museum. What Greene County lacks in attractions it makes up for in events. Among them: a professional bull riding competition, a festival devoted to a species of swallows, and the **Sheep and Fiber Fest** (724/627-8119, www.sheepandfiber.com, third weekend in May), which celebrates the county's heritage as a wool producer. Between them they have almost 30 covered bridges—cause for an annual festival that's not to be missed.

Meadowcroft

In 1973, University of Pittsburgh archeologists began excavation at a farm in northern Washington County. Over the course of six years, they unearthed evidence that humans have been in the Americas for at least 16,000 years. Now known as **Meadowcroft Rockshelter** (401 Meadowcroft Rd., Avella, 724/587-3412, www.heinzhistorycenter.org, noon-5pm Wed.-Sat. and 1pm-5pm Sun. Memorial Day-Labor Day, open weekends in May and Sept.-Oct., closed Nov.-Apr., admission $12, seniors $11, students and children 6-17 $6), the site was credited with revolutionizing "how archeologists view the peopling of the New World" upon its designation as a National Historic Landmark in 2005. Visitors learn about the hunter-gatherers who camped here thousands of years ago. Two re-created villages illustrate how later Americans lived. The **Indian Village** offers a glimpse of life in Western Pennsylvania some 400 years ago, before the arrival of Europeans, while **Meadowcroft Village** re-creates a 19th-century rural community. Meadowcroft is operated by Pittsburgh's Heinz History Center, an affiliate of the Smithsonian Institution.

Pennsylvania Trolley Museum

Home to nearly 50 streetcars, the **Pennsylvania Trolley Museum** (1 Museum Rd., Washington, 724/228-9256, www.patrolley.org, 10am-4pm Mon.-Fri. and 10am-5pm Sat.-Sun. Memorial Day-Labor Day, call for fall and spring hours, admission $9, seniors $8, children 3-15 $6) transports visitors to an earlier era. The price of admission includes unlimited trolley rides and a tour of the trolley display building. An extended tour of the display building is offered Friday-Sunday at 1pm. It costs $4 and is not recommended for children under 15 years old. There's a shaded picnic area on the museum grounds, so pack a lunch if you'd like to stay a while.

The Meadows Racetrack & Casino

Just half an hour from downtown Pittsburgh, **The Meadows Racetrack & Casino** (210 Racetrack Rd., Washington, 724/503-1200, www.meadowsgaming.com, open 24 hours) is Disney World for grown-ups, a thrill-a-minute environment where dreams come true—albeit very occasionally. Harness racing at The Meadows dates to the 1960s. The track hosts live races more than 200 days a year, year-round. It's home to the Delvin Miller Adios, which is to harness racing what the Kentucky Derby or Belmont Stakes are to thoroughbred racing.

Gaming enthusiasts can take their pick of more than 3,500 slot machines and about 60 table games. An on-site bowling center offers 24 lanes, wait service, and a club-like atmosphere on weekends.

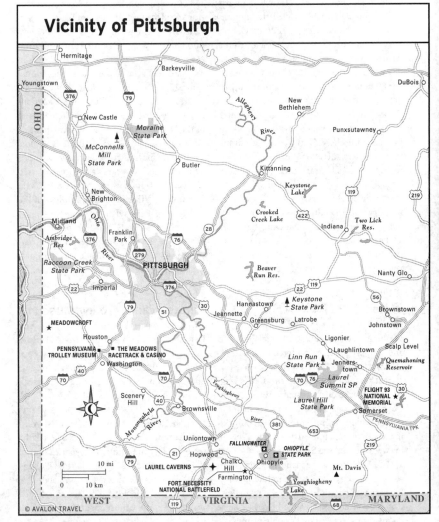

Vicinity of Pittsburgh

© AVALON TRAVEL

Covered Bridges

Washington County is home to 23 covered bridges—one of the largest concentrations in the country. Seven dot the hills of Greene County. Their jointly hosted **Covered Bridge Festival** (724/228-5520, www.visitwashingtoncountypa.com, third weekend in Sept.) tends to be the busiest weekend of the year, a testament to the allure of so-called kissing bridges. Festivities take place at 10 bridges and include live music, horse-drawn wagon rides, crafting demonstrations, and clashing Civil War reenactors. Most other times of year, the covered bridges of Washington and Greene Counties are quiet idylls. Visit the website of the Washington County Tourism Promotion Agency, provided above, to request a free driving guide or download a digital version.

Accommodations

One look at the **Montgomery Mansion** (1274 National Pike Hwy., Claysville, 724/663-7767, www.montgomerymansion.net, $129-159) and you'll know why locals call it the gingerbread house. The extra-ornate Victorian was built in the 1870s and owned, at one point, by the Catholic church next door. Converting it into a B&B with modern-day amenities was a 12-year project. Period furniture and Persian carpets make the inside as fetching as the outside. Problem is, do you choose the Holly room with its solid copper tub and surround shower or the Heather room with its stained glass doors and private sauna?

Rooms at **Grammy Rose's Bed & Breakfast** (405 E. Maiden St., Washington, 724/228-1508, www.grammyroses.com, $95-125), another stunning Victorian, are named for the four granddaughters of proprietors Tim and Rose, whose hospitality makes guests feel like family. In-room HBO is a nice touch but hardly necessary with The Meadows Racetrack & Casino, Tanger Outlets, and other attractions just a few miles away.

Built in 1923, **The George Washington** (60 S. Main St., Washington, 724/225-3200, www.thegeorgewashington.com, $99-380)

played host to Harry S. Truman, Al Capone, Marilyn Monroe, and John F. Kennedy before falling into disrepair in the latter part of the century. Several years of renovations by current owner Kyrk Pyros culminated in its reopening as a hotel in 2008. Accommodations range from 600-square-foot rooms to 1,800-square-foot suites complete with whirlpool tubs. Amenities include meeting and banquet facilities, two restaurants, and a lounge named for David Bradford, the Whiskey Rebellion leader who lived a stone's throw away. The Pioneer Grill, open for dinner, is notable for its massive murals by the late Malcolm Parcell, a Washington native. Painted in the 1930s and valued at millions, they portray the settling of Washington and the anti-tax uprising that put it on the map.

Chores are part of the fun at kid-friendly ★ **Weatherbury Farm** (1061 Sugar Run Rd., Avella, 724/587-3763, www.weatherburyfarm.com, two-night stay starts at $394), where guests can help "Farmer Dale" pump the water, feed the animals, and gather the eggs. Doing nothing at all is also encouraged. Guests stay in two-story suites in what used to be a horse stable.

A getaway geared toward grown-ups, **So'Journey Farm** (1841 Bristoria Rd., Holbrook, 724/499-5680, www.sojourneyfarm.com, $130) serves up gourmet meals and a generous helping of serenity. The 45-acre farm is home to grass-fed Scottish Highland cattle, pastured chickens, and one rug-hooking ace happy to share her expertise. Catfish are an easy catch in the spring-fed pond and cooked to order.

Overlooking the bank of the Monongahela River, **The Captain's Watch Inn** (105 County St., Greensboro, 724/943-3131, www.thecaptainswatch.net, $90-185) makes an excellent base camp for hiking and other outdoor recreation. A few hundred yards downstream from the B&B is the eastern terminus of the **Warrior Trail,** a path worn by Native Americans that stretches more than 60 miles to the Ohio River in West Virginia. Guests can take in the Mon from a wicker rocker on the wraparound verandah or paddle across it in one of the Captain's canoes. Bicycles are also free for the borrowing.

Food

Born in Frank Sarris's basement, **Sarris Candies** (511 Adams Ave., Canonsburg, 724/745-4042, www.sarriscandies.com, 9am-9pm Mon.-Sat., 10am-9pm Sun.) has grown into an operation the size of a football field. The factory store is a sweet tooth's fantasyland, complete with 1,500-pound chocolate castle. Slide into a red and brass booth in the connected Ice Cream Parlour, designed to evoke an old-fashioned soda fountain, and devour a sundae made with Sarris's ice cream and toppings.

"Farm to table" takes on new meaning at ★ **The SpringHouse** (1531 Rte. 136, Washington, 724/228-3339, www.springhousemarket.com, 9am-9pm Mon.-Sat., noon-9pm Sun., winter hours 9am-7pm Mon.-Thurs., 9am-8pm Fri.-Sat., noon-9pm Sun., $7-12), located on a 420-acre family farm. Part creamery, part country store, and part restaurant, the SpringHouse offers lunch and dinner buffets all week and a breakfast buffet on Saturdays. Wash down a from-scratch dessert with a glass of milk courtesy of the Holstein and Jersey cows grazing out back. Got kids? Check the farm's schedule of special events, which include an Easter egg hunt, hayrides, hog roasts, and breakfast with Santa.

Proving that love is blind, locals pack the timeworn **Shorty's Lunch** (34 W. Chestnut St., Washington, 724/228-9919, 8am-5pm Mon.-Sat., $5), which has been serving chili dogs, gravy fries, and other greasy goodies for more than 70 years. Another favorite of locals, **Old Mexico of Washington** (125 Murtland Ave., Washington, 724/250-7899, 11am-10pm Mon.-Sat., 11am-9pm Sun., $5-13) specializes in strong margaritas and sizzling fajitas. Servers who *no habla ingles* boost the authenticity quotient.

Fall-off-the-bone ribs flavored with brown sugar and soy sauce have graced the menu of **The Back Porch** (114 Speers St., Belle Vernon, 724/483-4500, www.backporchrestaurant.com, 11:30am-9pm Tues.-Sat., 4pm-9pm Sun., $10-29, reservations recommended) since it opened on Valentine's Day in 1975. Also known for its beef, duck, lamb, and seafood dishes, the fine dining restaurant near the bank of the Monongahela River occupies an 1806 landmark said to have served as a stop on the Underground Railroad. Original brickwork is still visible in the dining rooms. A bistro menu is available in the bar area, open 4pm-9pm Tuesday-Sunday.

The even older **Century Inn** (2175 National Rd. E., Scenery Hill, 724/945-6600, www.centuryinn.com, lunch noon-3pm daily, dinner 4:30pm-8pm Mon.-Thurs., 4:30pm-9pm Fri.-Sat., 4pm-7pm Sun., limited hours in winter, $11-26, reservations recommended) has played host to the likes of George Washington, Andrew Jackson, and James Polk. Its menu changes as often as the chef goes shopping, which is to say it changes daily. Cross your fingers for creamy peanut soup the way Thomas Jefferson liked it. Libations include international microbrews, domestic and imported wines, and some 20 types of single malt Scotch whiskey. In operation since 1794, the antiques-filled inn closes for a couple of weeks in January, then serves on Fridays and Saturdays only until April.

Information

The **Washington County Tourism Promotion Agency** (724/228-5520, www.visitwashingtoncountypa.com) has offices at 273 South Main Street in downtown Washington and in the food court at Tanger Outlets (Exit 41 off I-79, 724/225-8435, www.tangeroutlet.com/washington). The former is open 9am-4:30pm weekdays and the latter 10am-6pm Monday-Saturday and noon-4pm Sunday. The website of the **Greene County Tourist Promotion Agency** (417 E. Roy Furman Hwy., Waynesburg, 724/627-8687, www.greenecountytourism.org) is also a good source of information and includes a printable calendar of events.

NORTH OF PITTSBURGH: BEAVER, BUTLER, AND LAWRENCE COUNTIES

The counties to Pittsburgh's north and northwest are blessed with spectacular state parks. Recreational opportunities run the gamut, from barbecuing on a pontoon boat to rappelling down a rock face. The area also affords visitors a glimpse of two uncommon cultures, including one that's now extinct. When you see how the Harmonists lived in the 19th century or how the Amish live now, you might see your own life in a new light.

Moraine State Park

Dedicated in 1970, **Moraine State Park** (park office 225 Pleasant Valley Rd., Portersville, 724/368-8811, www.visitpaparks.com, sunrise-sunset daily), which offers year-round recreation, is Butler County's biggest attraction. Its greatest asset is the sprawling Lake Arthur, the 3,225-acre product of a dam built on Muddy Creek. Here's a recipe for summertime fun: Pack a cooler with your favorite cookout foods, rent a pontoon boat and gas grill from **Crescent Bay Marina** (south shore, 724/368-9955, www.moraineboatrentals.com), and spend the rest of the day on the lake. The boat rental also offers kayaks, canoes, and motorboats.

Another way to cruise the lake is aboard ***Nautical Nature*** (McDanel's Launch, north shore, 724/368-9185, www.morainepreservationfund.org), a 37-passenger enclosed pontoon boat operated by the Moraine Preservation Fund. The group offers boat tours (advance tickets $11, seniors $9, children 2-12 $5) on Saturday and Sunday afternoons throughout the summer, dinner cruises ($30) on select Saturdays, and brunch cruises ($25) on select Sundays. Be sure to make reservations at least seven days in advance for dinner and brunch cruises.

Boating isn't the only way to enjoy the lake. There's also swimming, sunbathing, and picnicking at one of two **beaches,** which are open from Memorial Day weekend to Labor Day. Pleasant Valley Beach on the south shore of Lake Arthur is a better choice if you have small children because it has a playground. It also has sand volleyball courts. Both beaches have bathrooms, shower facilities, and snack shops. Watch your step when taking a stroll because the shores serve as bathrooms for waterfowl.

Lake Arthur in Moraine State Park

Other popular warm-weather activities include **hiking** and **biking.** The park's 28 miles of hiking trails run the gamut from short and easy to rough and rocky. Stop at the park office near the entrance to the south shore for trail maps. Cyclists have a choice between seven miles of paved trail or six miles of rugged off-roading. The bike trails are on the north shore, where you'll also find a **bike rental** (North Shore Drive, about 1.5 miles from Route 422, 724/368-9011 or 724/944-3239, open daily Memorial Day weekend-Labor Day and weekends Apr.-May and Sept.-Oct.) with a wide selection, including tandem bikes and children's bikes.

Cold weather brings other recreational opportunities: cross-country skiing, snowmobiling, sledding, iceboating, ice fishing, and ice skating.

What Moraine State Park lacks are overnight facilities. There are 11 modern cabins on its 16,725 acres, which can be reserved online at www.pa.reserveworld.com or by calling 888/PA-PARKS (888/727-2757). An overnight shelter is available to backpackers, and tent camping areas are available to organized groups, but anyone else with a yen to sleep under the stars should head to a nearby private campground. Best of the bunch: **Bear Run Campground** (184 Badger Hill Rd., Portersville, 724/368-3564, www.bearrun-campground.com, mid-Apr.-late Oct., tent sites $25-43, RV sites $35-57, cabins $79-169). The "full-service family vacation center" has more than 300 tent and RV sites, a variety of cabins, free Wi-Fi, a heated swimming pool, a game room, and more.

McConnells Mill State Park

Just a few miles west of Moraine State Park and much smaller, **McConnells Mill State Park** (2697 McConnells Mill Rd., Portersville, 724/368-8091, www.visitpaparks.com, sunrise-sunset daily) is the adrenaline junkie's first choice. Its central feature is a steep-sided gorge created by the draining of glacial lakes thousands of years ago. Rocky outcrops, huge boulders, and the swift-flowing Slippery Rock Creek make for challenging hiking, climbing, and white-water paddling. The park has nine miles of hiking trails and two climbing and rappelling areas. One climbing spot is across the creek from the 1800s gristmill that gave the park its name. The other, near Breakneck Bridge, is for more advanced climbers. Rafters, canoeists, and kayakers generally start near a Route 422 bridge upstream of the park. (There's no boat rental facility in the park.) Depending on water level, Slippery Rock Creek can provide a mild to wild ride; helmets are strongly recommended. Don't even think about going for a swim. More than a few people have drowned in the creek. Fishing is fine.

Guided tours of the aforementioned gristmill, which was retired in 1928, are offered Memorial Day through Labor Day. It can still do its water-powered thing. Corn grinding demonstrations are part of the fun at the **McConnells Mill Heritage Festival,** held the last full weekend in September. Festivalgoers can try their hand at old-time games and crafts and enjoy a Civil War encampment. Best of all, they get to see the forested park in its fall splendor.

Harmony Society Sights

Two towns a half hour's drive from downtown Pittsburgh offer a window into the curious way of life of the Harmonists, a Christian communal society that gained riches and fame but died out anyway. Adherence to celibacy will do that. Their story begins in southern Germany, where in the late 1700s, a peasant-turned-preacher named George Rapp and his followers split from the Lutheran Church. Life wasn't easy for the separatists. They were harassed and imprisoned; their books, confiscated. In 1803, Rapp made the journey to the United States. He bought a tract of land in Butler County and summoned his followers. There, they formally organized themselves as the Harmony Society. Membership required relinquishment of all possessions to Rapp and the Society. The band of pietists swiftly carved a town, Harmony, out of the wilderness.

Convinced that the Second Coming of Christ was around the corner, they adopted celibacy to purify themselves. They channeled their energy into agriculture and industry, earning a reputation for excellent textiles and woolens, wines, and whiskey.

The Harmonists didn't stay for long, relocating to Indiana after 10 years, but Harmony hasn't forgotten them. In 1974, the area that includes their surviving buildings was designated a National Historic Landmark District. What used to be a Harmonist warehouse is now the main building of the **Harmony Museum** (218 Mercer St., Harmony, 724/452-7341, www.harmonymuseum.org, 1pm-4pm Tues.-Sun., admission $5, seniors $4, children 6-17 $3), which houses a modest collection of Harmonist furniture and other artifacts. Visitors can descend into a vaulted stone cellar where wines were fermented. The museum isn't devoted solely to the Society. It also tells the story of those who came before, including Native Americans and a young George Washington, and those who followed, including the Mennonites who purchased the Harmonists' holdings.

The Harmonists moved back to Pennsylvania in 1824, this time settling along the Ohio River in Beaver County, less than 20 miles northwest of Pittsburgh. They called their third and final commune Economy. A National Historic Landmark, **Old Economy Village** (270 16th St., Ambridge, 724/266-4500, www.oldeconomyvillage.org, 10am-5pm Tues.-Sat. and noon-5pm Sun. Mar.-Dec., admission $10, seniors $9, children 3-11 $6) comprises 17 buildings filled with thousands of Harmonist artifacts. Among them is Rapp's impressive house, flanked by a formal garden. The visitors center features an exhibit and video that trace the history of the Harmonists, whose economic achievements captured the world's attention. Their diverse business ventures included silk manufacturing, railroad construction, and oil production. By the end of the 19th century, however, only a few Harmonists remained. The Society was dissolved in 1905, and Economy was renamed Ambridge by its new industrial heavyweight, the American Bridge Company.

Lawrence County Amish Country

Say "Pennsylvania Amish" and people think Lancaster County, several hours to the east of here. But Lawrence County has an Amish community of about 3,300, including the third-largest Old Order Amish sect in the United States. The largest concentration lives around the villages of New Wilmington and Volant, connected by Route 208. How do you experience Amish country? You get behind the wheel and drive—well below the speed limit if you happen to find yourself behind a horse-drawn buggy—and keep a lookout for hand-painted signs advertising goods for sale. The **Lawrence County Tourist Promotion Agency** (229 S. Jefferson St., New Castle, 888/284-7599, www.visitlawrencecounty.com) publishes a map that indicates the location of one-room schoolhouses, a covered bridge, and **Teena's Quilt Shop** (43 Quilt Shop Ln., Volant, 8am-5pm Mon.-Sat.), an Amish purveyor of furniture and rugs as well as quilts. The shop, a favorite of bus groups, is on a farm about a mile and a half west of Volant on Route 208.

In Volant itself, Route 208 is an old-fashioned Main Street lined with homes converted to darling shops (www.volantshops.com). One specializes in miniatures, another in nostalgic candies and gums, a third in premium teas. **Native and Nature** (808 Main St., 724/533-5054, www.nativeandnature.com) sells jewelry and decorative items with a Native American flavor, while **James Creek Galleries** (425 Main St., 724/533-2313, www.jamescreekgalleries.com) offers reasonably priced reproductions of classic American furniture and decor. Both are open 10am-5pm Monday-Saturday and noon-5pm Sunday. Leave time for a tasting at **Volant Mill Winery** (1229 Main St., 724/533-2500, www.volantmillwinery.com, 11am-5pm Mon.-Thurs., 11am-6pm Fri.-Sat., noon-5pm Sun.).

A must-stop while cruising the Amish

countryside: the **Apple Castle** (277 Rte. 18, New Wilmington, 724/652-3221, www.apple-castle.com, 9am-5:30pm Dec.-July, 9am-8pm Aug.-Nov.), a sixth-generation family farm that grows about 50 varieties of apples. The farm market sells apples year-round and a variety of other fruits and vegetables when they ripen. Its inventory also includes cheese, local eggs, apple butter, honey, and, often, baked goods made by Amish neighbors. But the Apple Castle is most famous for its honey wheat and apple spice donuts. Wash one down with a glass of fresh cider. The market is a good landmark if you're searching for Poverty Point Road, part of the driving route recommended by the tourism agency. Pranksters love to steal the street sign. Poverty Point is the first left after the Apple Castle if you're driving north on Route 18.

Food

Not far from Moraine and McConnells Mill State Parks, ★ **North Country Brewing Co.** (141 S. Main St., Slippery Rock, 724/794-2337, www.northcountrybrewing.com, 11am-11pm Mon.-Thurs., 11am-midnight Fri.-Sat., 11am-10pm Sun., $8-23) is not what you'd expect from a bar in a college town. No Coors or wine coolers here. The beers are handcrafted on site, the wines are made in Pennsylvania, and the grub ain't boring. Start with a beer sampler and an order of pub pretzels, then choose from a wide selection of main courses that's plenty mindful of herbivores. Dinner selections come with a delicious beer bread baked and served in a terra-cot pot. What really sets North Country apart from other eateries is the decor. It's a multilevel wonderland of whimsical wood carvings, rustic beams, and dining nooks. Owners Bob and Jodi McCafferty are environmental stewards, organizing community cleanups and helping to maintain the North Country Trail, which stretches across seven states and comes within a couple of miles of its eponymous brewpub.

Up in Amish country, **Tavern on the Square** (108 N. Market St., New Wilmington, 724/946-2020, www.thetavernonthesquare. blogspot.com, 11am-8pm Mon.-Thurs., 11am-9pm Fri.-Sat., noon-8pm Sun., $8-15) serves deep-fried green beans, sandwiches made with fresh-baked croissants, and homemade pierogies, among other things. Once a stop on the Underground Railroad, the tavern is now famous for its sticky buns.

Information

You'll find the latest visitors guides to Beaver,

North Country Brewing Co.

Butler, and Lawrence Counties on the websites of their respective tourism bureaus: the **Beaver County Recreation & Tourism Department** (Bradys Run Park Recreation Facility, 121 Bradys Run Rd., Beaver Falls, 724/770-2062, www.visitbeavercounty.com), the **Butler County Tourism & Convention Bureau** (310 E. Grandview Ave., Zelienople, 724/234-4619, www.visitbutlercounty.com), and the **Lawrence County Tourist Promotion Agency** (229 S. Jefferson St., New Castle, 888/284-7599, www.visitlawrencecounty.com).

NORTHEAST OF PITTSBURGH: ARMSTRONG AND INDIANA COUNTIES

Crisscrossed by waterways, Armstrong County beckons boaters and anglers. Neighboring Indiana County offers miles and miles of rail-trails, the lovely Yellow Creek State Park with its 720-acre lake, an Amish community, and a museum dedicated to one very beloved screen legend.

Jimmy Stewart Museum

The star of *It's a Wonderful Life* got his start in life in the town of Indiana, about 60 miles northeast of Pittsburgh. Fans can learn about his roots and rise to fame at the **Jimmy Stewart Museum** (835 Philadelphia St., Indiana, 800/835-4669, www.jimmy.org, 10am-4pm Mon.-Sat., noon-4pm Sun., admission $7, seniors $6, children 7-17 $5) on the third floor of the public library. Dedicated in 1995 in celebration of Stewart's 87th birthday, the museum has several galleries and a 50-seat theater. Its collection includes something from each of Stewart's 81 films, including a propeller blade autographed by the cast of *Flight of the Phoenix*. A gallery devoted to *It's a Wonderful Life* features photos of cast members, posters, and a note from director Frank Capra. Visitors can watch film clips and career retrospectives in the theater with its velvet drapes and wine-colored seats. Full-length films are shown Saturdays and Sundays at 1pm.

The museum isn't Indiana's only tribute to its favorite son, who died in 1997. The county airport, northeast of town, is named for him. A bronze statue of the screen legend stands on the lawn of the Indiana County Courthouse, next door to the museum. Every November, Indiana marks the beginning of the holiday season with the *It's a Wonderful Life* **Festival and Parade** (724/463-6110, www.downtownindiana.org). A large decorated Christmas tree joins Jimmy on the courthouse lawn.

Smicksburg Amish Country

Like Volant and New Wilmington in Lawrence County, Indiana's County's Smicksburg is a place where cars share the roads with horse-drawn buggies. The area is home to more than 280 Old Order Amish families. Where there's a community of Amish, there's usually good shopping, and Smicksburg is no exception. The town has about 20 specialty shops—not counting Amish home-based businesses. For locally crafted furniture, head to **Downtown Smicksburg Amish Country** (21875 Indiana Rd., 814/257-8696, www.smicksburgfurniture.com, 10am-5pm Mon.-Sat., noon-5pm Sun.). You'll find everything from gun cabinets to cradles, plus a wide variety of specialty foods and Amish-made goods such as baskets and doilies.

Just north of town, **Smicksburg Community Cheese** (24062 Rte. 954, 814/257-8972, www.smicksburgcheese.com, 8am-5pm Mon.-Sat., noon-5pm Sun.) is a locavore's delight. Amish farmers supply about 80,000 pounds of milk a week to the factory, which makes more than 30 varieties of cheese. Stop in to sample uncommon creations like chocolate cherry cheddar and chicken soup cheese. Locally made cheese deserves a locally made wine. No problem. Smicksburg's **Windgate Vineyards & Winery** (1998 Hemlock Acres Rd., 814/257-8797, www.windgatevineyards.com, noon-5pm daily) has collected more than a hundred awards at regional and national competitions since opening its doors in 1987.

Accommodations

John Truett was living in Tampa, Florida, when an eBay real estate listing caught his eye. For sale: a century-old church and the house beside it, formerly a rectory for Episcopal clergy, in a Pennsylvania town he'd never of. Truett clicked "place bid." In October 2009, three and a half years after quitting his job with the Walt Disney Company, he opened the ★ **The Old Parsonage B&B** (156 Siberian Ave., Leechburg, 724/236-0061, www.oldparsonagebandb.com, $65-85) in the onetime rectory. Truett, a nondenominational minister, is quite catholic in his decorating tastes. There's an Egyptian-themed guest room complete with sarcophagus and a Victorian-themed guest room. There's also a suite with two beds—perfect for a family of three. The B&B is just a few minutes' walk from Leechburg's riverfront and unique shops such as Books and Beans and Graff Gourmet & Specialty Foods. The River's Edge Canoe & Kayak is less than two miles upstream.

Just two blocks from the campus of Indiana University of Pennsylvania, **Heritage House** (209 S. 6th St., Indiana, 724/463-3430, www.heritagehousesuites.com, $100-200) was among the grandest homes east of Pittsburgh when it was built in 1870. In the 1940s, the three-story brick house was divided into eight apartments, several of which have now been converted to spacious suites for nightly, weekly, or extended stays. Amenities include private bathrooms, full kitchens, Wi-Fi, cable TV, and laundry access.

Food

Renowned for its fresh seafood, flown in weekly from Hawaii, ★ **1844 Restaurant** (690 Rte. 66, Leechburg, 724/845-1844, www.1844restaurant.com, 5pm-10pm Thurs.-Sat. and daily to private parties, $12-36) is reason alone for Pittsburghers to make the 45-minute trip to southern Armstrong County.

1844 opened in 1974 in a nine-room brick farmhouse built in the 1830s. Bob Gorelli, its proprietor then and now, does the produce and meat shopping. He's handyman, gardener, and bartender, too. Son Brandon, who washed dishes in his teens, now presides over the kitchen, serving an ambitious menu that includes both sashimi and linguini. Ask for a table in the Keeping Room when making a reservation. Elegant and rustic with its fieldstone walls and ceiling-high fireplace, it once served as a root cellar.

It's absolutely criminal to pass by **Dean's Diner** (2175 Rte. 22 Hwy. W., Blairsville, 724/459-9600, $5-20) without stopping for a slice of pie. The 24-hour diner offers 15-20 varieties daily, including coconut cream with sky-high meringue, banana cream, peanut butter cream, peanut butter and chocolate, peanut butter and chocolate *and* banana, apple, cherry, peach, apricot, and blueberry. For Boston cream, come on a Sunday. The pie baker, who slips in every evening, also makes cake donuts. Dean's is good for more than dessert. Hot roast beef sandwiches, hamburgers, meatloaf, and fried chicken are hot sellers.

For well-executed Italian in a homey setting, try **Pie Cucina Ristorante** (181 E. Brown St., Blairsville, 724/459-7145, www.piecucinaristorante.com, 11am-9pm Mon.-Fri., 4pm-9:30pm Sat., $8-22). It's got the usual: pizza, pasta, eggplant parmesan, steaks, veal, chicken, and seafood. It's also got a great patio.

Information

You'll find the latest visitors guides to Armstrong and Indiana Counties on the websites of their respective tourism bureaus: the **Armstrong County Tourist Bureau** (125 Market St., Kittanning, 724-543/4003, www.armstrongcounty.com) and the **Indiana County Tourist Bureau** (2334 Oakland Ave., Suite 7, Indiana, 724/463-7505, www.visitindianacountypa.org).

The Alleghenies

Look for ★ to find recommended sights, activities, dining, and lodging.

Highlights

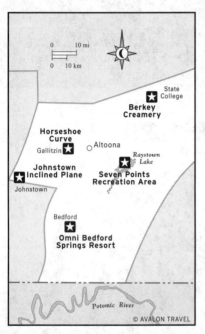

★ **Johnstown Inclined Plane:** The world's steepest vehicular funicular (try saying that three times) carried people to safety during two deadly floods in the 20th century. Hop on for killer views of "Flood City" (page 352).

★ **Horseshoe Curve:** The 1854 feat of engineering that allowed trains to traverse the Alleghenies is still awe-inspiring after all these years (page 358).

★ **Berkey Creamery:** Best. Ice cream. Ever (page 364).

★ **Seven Points Recreation Area:** Take a dip, hit the trails, or rent a houseboat for a few days of peaceful, easy living (page 374).

★ **Omni Bedford Springs Resort:** The mineral-rich springs at this luxury resort were believed by Native Americans to have curative powers. "Take the waters" and decide for yourself (page 385).

These mountains we call the Alleghenies used to be a real headache. They didn't make it easy on settlers traveling west, where land and opportunity awaited them. Traversing the mountains by wagon took ages and not a little bit of gumption. They stymied canal systems. They baffled railroad builders. In time, of course, engineers tamed this section of the Appalachian range. They threaded a rail line right through the Alleghenies and, later, highways. What made the region so challenging two centuries ago—peaks and valleys, wide rivers and dense woods—is what makes it appealing today. It calls to hikers, cyclists, boaters, anglers, and wildlife watchers. The scenery makes getting from point A to point B so pleasant that the region's image-makers promote motor touring more zealously than they do most destinations.

That's not to say that the destinations are ho-hum. They include towns rich in history, the state's largest inland lake, its highest skiable peak, and a premier mountain biking trail. Towns like Johnstown, Altoona, and Bedford are so diligent about preserving their heritage that visitors can virtually taste life as a steelmaker, railroader, or frontiersman. State College is home to Pennsylvania State University and the mega parties that are Nittany Lions football games. Countless villages offer quaint bed-and-breakfasts and quietude. The region is especially quiet in winter, when amusement parks, show caverns, and even some museums are closed, boats are in storage, and the open road is less welcoming.

PLANNING YOUR TIME

It's possible to digest Johnstown's heritage sights in a day. Plan on catching the sunset and a nightcap at the top of the famous inclined plane. Altoona is also doable in a day—unless you're a diehard rail fan. If that's the case, book a room at a B&B where you can watch the choo-choos go by and take a few days to explore the various railroad-related

---

Previous: the golf course at Omni Bedford Springs; the Allegheny Mountains; Seven Points Marina. **Above:** view from observation deck of Johnstown Inclined Plane.

sights. Be aware that most of them, including the Railroaders Memorial Museum and Horseshoe Curve National Historic Landmark, are closed during the chilliest months.

If you're visiting State College, chances are you're the parent of a Penn Stater, a prospective student, or a nostalgic alumnus. I wouldn't presume to tell you how long to stay. Raystown Lake and the Bedford area are vacation destinations. The former attracts boaters, mountain bikers, and other outdoorsy types. The latter, with its historic "springs resort," attracts a well-heeled crowd. Suggested stay length: as long as possible.

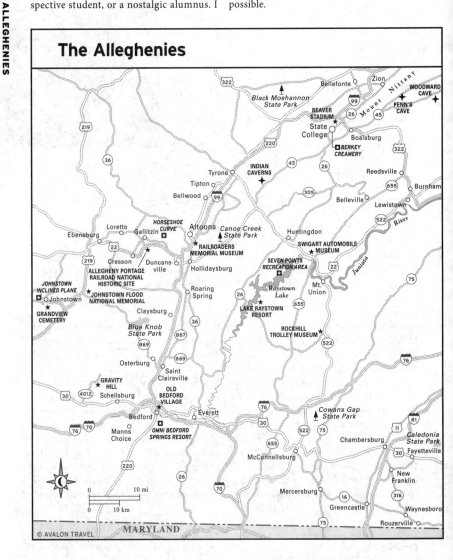

The Alleghenies

© AVALON TRAVEL

Johnstown and Vicinity

Johnstown was once an unrivaled steel producer, a magnet for the industry's innovators and working-class immigrants. Its industrial base disintegrated, and its immigrants assimilated, but the city hasn't paved over its past. Johnstown's rivers are still lined with former mills, some of which have found new tenants. Its cityscape is still ornamented with ethnic churches, though many no longer house parishes. In a sense, the city is a museum of its former self, and that serves it well. One of its newer industries is tourism, driven largely by heritage attractions. Steelmaking is only part of its story. The better-known part is the Great Flood of 1889, which razed large swaths of the city and killed about 2,200 people—the largest single-day loss of life in the United States before September 11, 2001. There are two museums dedicated to the tragedy: one in the downtown area and another about 10 miles northeast of Johnstown, at the site of the dam break that caused the flood. The catastrophe was the biggest news story of the latter 19th century after the assassination of Abraham Lincoln. It's a riveting tale of rich and poor, rated R violence, and rebirth.

Flood City, as Johnstown was dubbed after two more deadly floods, has more recently become known as a motorcycle town. Bikers are fond of the scenic routes on all sides of the

The 40-Foot Wave

In Hollywood's hands, the story of the Johnstown Flood of 1889 would probably begin like many thrillers: with an idyllic scene. The camera would pan the South Fork Fishing and Hunting Club, a summer retreat for Pittsburgh's wealthiest industrialists and financiers. It would zoom in on the likes of Andrew Carnegie and Henry Clay Frick fishing on the club's private Lake Conemaugh, their wives strolling with parasols, their children sailing. Then the camera would dive beneath the surface to take in the expensive game fish and, finally, the dam holding back the lake. The dam, we'd discover, is in dire need of repair.

A night of torrential rain found the lake swollen on the morning of May 31, 1889. In Johnstown, 14 miles downstream, there was water in the streets. Residents weren't terribly concerned, even as they lugged belongings to the upper stories of their homes and businesses. Johnstown's position in a river valley meant that flooding was a fact of life.

At Lake Conemaugh, club officials rounded up laborers to fortify the dam and relieve pressure from its breast. Despite their furious efforts, the dam crumpled shortly after 3pm, unleashing 20 million tons of water. Witnesses would later describe a 40-foot wave of water and debris rushing toward Johnstown. The wave was so powerful that bodies of victims were found as far away as Cincinnati. Some people swept up by the wave were deposited on a massive pile of wreckage that accumulated at the Pennsylvania Railroad Company's stone bridge in Johnstown. About 80 who survived the wild ride perished when the debris caught fire.

In the weeks and months after the disaster, the death toll climbed to 2,209. More than 750 of the victims were never identified, their bodies so badly mangled. Journalists, photographers, doctors, and relief workers, including American Red Cross founder Clara Barton, rushed to Johnstown. Donations of money, food, clothing, medical supplies, furniture, and even lumber for rebuilding arrived from all over the world. The South Fork Fishing and Hunting Club contributed 1,000 blankets.

Lawsuits against the club proved fruitless, the courts ruling that the flood was an act of God. But its elite members were condemned in the court of public opinion. One newspaper cartoon depicted them sipping champagne on the clubhouse porch as the flood leveled Johnstown. In fact, only a handful of members were on premises that deadly day. It was spring yet; most of them were still in their city manses. And they would never return.

valley in which Johnstown is cradled. Every June, they descend upon the city in great numbers for a motorcycle rally that may be the largest in the state. Johnstown holds another distinction, one recognized by *Guinness World Records.* The Johnstown Inclined Plane, which climbs 900 feet from the river valley, is the world's steepest vehicular inclined plane. No visit is complete without a trip to the top.

SIGHTS
Johnstown Flood Museum

The 26-minute documentary shown hourly at the **Johnstown Flood Museum** (304 Washington St., Johnstown, 814/539-1889, www.jaha.org, 10am-5pm daily Apr.-Dec., 10am-5pm Tues.-Sun. Jan.-Mar., admission $8, seniors $7, children 3-18 $6) is a first-rate primer on the 1889 disaster. It won an Academy Award for best documentary, short subject. The museum also features a large relief map that illustrates the flood's path and an original "Oklahoma house," which served as temporary housing for people left homeless by the flood.

Tickets to the museum include admission to other attractions operated by the Johnstown Area Heritage Association: the Frank & Sylvia Pasquerilla Heritage Discovery Center and the Wagner-Ritter House & Garden. No need to rush through them; tickets are good for five days.

Frank & Sylvia Pasquerilla Heritage Discovery Center

The **Heritage Discovery Center** (201 6th Ave., Johnstown, 814/539-1889, www.jaha.org, 10am-5pm daily Apr.-Dec., 10am-5pm Tues.-Sun. Jan.-Mar., admission $8, seniors $7, children 3-18 $6) occupies a former brewery in the Cambria City section of Johnstown, where thousands of European immigrants settled in the 19th and early 20th centuries. In 1880, 85 percent of the neighborhood's residents were foreign-born. Appropriately enough, the center's main exhibit is the interactive *America: Through Immigrant Eyes.* Upon entry, visitors choose a card with a photo of an immigrant

character—a 12-year-old peasant from Poland, for instance—and follow their character's path from the old country to Johnstown's ethnic neighborhoods.

The Discovery Center also houses the **Iron & Steel Gallery** and **Johnstown Children's Museum.** The centerpiece of the former is a film that tells the story of the Cambria Iron Company, whose rise and fall ushered Johnstown's. The theater is equipped with infrared heaters to give viewers a sense of the heat in a working steel mill. The Children's Museum, located on the third floor of the Discovery Center, is geared toward children 3-10.

Discovery Center tickets include admission to other attractions operated by the Johnstown Area Heritage Association: the Johnstown Flood Museum and the Wagner-Ritter House & Garden. Tickets are good for five days.

Wagner-Ritter House & Garden

A house museum two blocks from the Heritage Discovery Center tells the story of the German immigrants who once occupied it. Three generations of a working-class family lived in the **Wagner-Ritter House** (418 Broad St., Johnstown, 814/539-1889, www.jaha.org, noon-5pm Sat.-Sun. Apr.-May, noon-5pm Wed.-Sun. June-Oct., closed Nov.-Mar., admission $8, seniors $7, children 3-18 $6, includes admission to Johnstown Flood Museum and Frank & Sylvia Pasquerilla Heritage Discovery Center) from the time it was built in the 1860s through 1990. The house withstood the 1889 flood, even though water rose so high that family members were able to pull a woman to safety from a second-floor window.

★ Johnstown Inclined Plane

In the aftermath of the Great Flood, communities sprang up in higher elevations. One of those was Westmont, which sits atop Yoder Hill. The hill, with its 70.9 percent grade, was too steep for a road. So an inclined railway

way, seniors free) began operating in June 1891 and hauled about a million passengers a year in its heyday. It was both commuter line and lifeline. During the deadly floods of 1936 and 1977, the world's steepest vehicular inclined plane carried people out of the valley to safety.

The lower station is accessible from downtown by a footbridge that crosses Route 56. If driving east on Route 56, pull onto the ramp that leads to the incline and either park there or continue across a bridge that spans Stonycreek River and drive right onto a cable car. The fare for automobiles is $6 one-way. Motorcycles ride for $4 and bicycles for free.

There's a visitors center up top, where you can learn more about Johnstown's various floods and pick up information about area attractions. An observation deck affords a bird's-eye view of greater Johnstown and insight into the path of the 1889 floodwaters, which crashed into Yoder Hill. Ice cream and other refreshments are sold on the deck during the warmer months.

Cable cars aren't the only way to climb Yoder Hill. The **James Wolfe Sculpture Trail** takes hikers past large steel sculptures made with remnants from local plants.

Grandview Cemetery

Many of the 2,209 victims of the 1889 flood

Johnstown Inclined Plane

was built to carry people, horses, and wagons to the tony neighborhood 900 feet above the river valley. The **Johnstown Inclined Plane** (upper station 711 Edgehill Dr., Johnstown, 814/536-1816, www.inclinedplane.org, hours vary by season, fare $4 round-trip, $2.25 one way, children 2-12 $2.50 round-trip, $1.50 one

---

Recommended Reading

If Johnstown's attractions leave you hungry for more information about the cataclysm of 1889, pick up David McCullough's ***The Johnstown Flood.*** The page-turning account of America's worst inland flood, first published in 1968, was McCullough's first book. The social historian researched the disaster while the last survivors were still alive. Later books earned him two Pulitzer Prizes and two National Book Awards. Here's a nibble:

> Johnstown of 1889 was not a pretty place. But the land around it was magnificent. From Main Street, a man standing among the holiday crowds could see green hills, small mountains, really, hunching in close on every side, dwarfing the tops of the houses and smokestacks.

> The city was built on a nearly level flood plain at the confluence of two rivers, down at the bottom of an enormous hole in the Alleghenies. A visitor from the Middle West once commented, "Your sun rises at ten and sets at two," and it was not too great an exaggeration.

are interred at **Grandview Cemetery** (801 Millcreek Rd., Johnstown, 814/535-2652, www.grandviewjohnstownpa.com, gates open at 7:30am daily, close at dusk May-Oct. and 5pm Nov.-Apr.) on Yoder Hill, a mile south of the inclined plane's upper station. A monument dedicated in 1892 overlooks the Unknown Plot, where 777 unidentified victims are buried.

Johnstown Flood National Memorial

Operated by the National Park Service, the **Johnstown Flood National Memorial** (733 Lake Rd., South Fork, 814/495-4643, www.nps.gov/jofl, 9am-5pm daily, admission $4, children 15 and under free) marks the site of the infamous South Fork Dam, whose collapse on May 31, 1889, caused the hellish Great Flood. The visitors center features a 35-minute film, shown at 15 minutes past the hour, and exhibits designed to convey the flood's magnitude. In addition to the dam ruins, the Park Service preserves several buildings that were part of the South Fork Fishing and Hunting Club, which owned the dam and the lake it created. In summer, rangers lead tours of the vast clubhouse where Pittsburgh's elite swilled brandy and smoked cigars.

ENTERTAINMENT AND EVENTS
Bars

Tulune's Southside Saloon (36 Bridge St./Rte. 403, Johnstown, 814/536-1001, www.southsidesaloon.com, 4pm-close Tues.-Sat., food under $10) boasts the area's largest selection of imported and craft beers—large enough to fill an eight-page menu—and a strict "no jerks allowed" policy. The kitchen, open until 10pm on weeknights and 11pm Friday and Saturday, dishes up burgers, Bavarian soft pretzels, and other beer-friendly grub.

Performing Arts

The **Pasquerilla Performing Arts Center** at the University of Pittsburgh at Johnstown (450 Schoolhouse Rd., Johnstown, 814/269-7200, www.upjarts.pitt.edu) hosts a wide variety of touring acts, including Broadway companies, dance troupes, comedians, and tribute bands. It's home to the **Johnstown Symphony Orchestra** (814/535-6738, www.johnstownsymphony.org), founded in 1929. Homegrown dance and theater groups also take the stage on occasion.

The **Band of Brothers Shakespeare Company** (814/539-9500, www.bandofbrothers

Johnstown Flood National Memorial

shakespeare.org) has raised more than $200,000 for Johnstown's Stackhouse Park, where it has performed every summer since 1991.

Festivals and Events

A throwback to the years when Johnstown teemed with immigrants from Central and Eastern Europe, **PolkaFest** (St. Mary's Byzantine Catholic Church, 411 Power St., Johnstown, 814/536-7993, www.visitjohnstownpa.com/polkafest, weekend after Memorial Day, free) features nationally known polka bands, an outdoor dance floor, and plenty of ethnic eats. Jazz may be an American-born art form, but **Jazz Along the River** (St. Mary's Byzantine Catholic Church, 411 Power St., Johnstown, 814/539-5875, fourth Fri. May-Sept., free) concerts are another opportunity to fill up on kielbasa, pierogies, and haluski. The parish kitchen opens about an hour before the music starts at 6pm.

For four days in June, Johnstown becomes biker heaven. The streets fill with all manner of motorcycles: pimped-out choppers, dirt bikes, drag-racing machines—you name it. **Thunder in the Valley** (814/536-7993, www.visitjohnstownpa.com/thunderinthevalley) doesn't discriminate. The rally attracted about 3,500 motorcycling enthusiasts in 1998, its first year. Now, more than 200,000 pour into Johnstown and surrounding communities during the fourth weekend in June. The city's hotels burst at the seams; Altoona, Bedford, Ligonier, Indiana, and other towns absorb the overflow. Thunder isn't a leather-clad bacchanalia. It's a family-friendly event that attracts plenty of nonriders. Motorcycle manufacturers show off their latest models. Vendors peddle chaps, helmets, jewelry, and other biker accoutrements. There's also live music, a children's play area, charity rides, stunt shows, and a parade.

The **AmeriServ Flood City Music Festival** (Peoples Natural Gas Park, 90 Johns St., Johnstown, 814/539-1889, www.floodcitymusic.com, first weekend in Aug., single-day admission $10-20) boasts multiple stages and acts from across the country. Consider buying a three-day pass ($40-100) and camping nearby. A list of camping options can be found on the festival website.

Today's **Cambria County Fair** (883 N. Julian St., Ebensburg, 814/472-7491, www.cambriacofair.com, begins Sun. before Labor Day, admission $8) is held on the same grounds as the original fair in 1891. It's a weeklong celebration of the rural life, complete with livestock exhibits, amusement rides, tractor and truck pulls, square dancing, and the crowning of a fair queen. Cambria County is the second largest producer of potatoes in Pennsylvania, which is cause for another annual celebration, **PotatoFest** (downtown Ebensburg, 814/472-8780, www.potatofest.com, last Sat. in Sept., free). Food vendors serve up potato soup, homemade potato chips, sweet potato fries, potato pancakes, potato pizza, and even potato candy.

ACCOMMODATIONS

National chains dominate the lodging scene in downtown Johnstown, but independent establishments can be found in the hills and valleys around it.

Under $100

Once the homestead of Johnstown founder Joseph Schantz, **Schantz Haus** (687 E. Campus Ave., Davidsville, 814/479-2494, www.schantzhaus.com, $65-80) offers three guest rooms, two of which share a bath. It's located on a working dairy farm; guests can try their hand at milking a cow or bottle-feeding a calf. The Swiss-born Schantz, whose surname was anglicized to Johns, is buried on the property along with several generations of descendants.

The ★ **Collins Inn Bed and Breakfast** (114 E. High St., Ebensburg, 814/472-4311, www.nooncollins.com, $90) is so replete with antique furnishings that it has the feel of a house museum. The Red Room's grand bed with decorative scrollwork once belonged to railroad builder Philip Collins, who lived in the 1834 Federal-style stone mansion more than a century ago. During World War I, the local draft board occupied the parlor. Pittsburgh native Gene Kelly ran a dance studio on the property in the 1930s. Today the historic home has six guest rooms, each with a private bathroom, and modern amenities such as air-conditioning, cable TV, and wireless Internet access.

The garden-themed **Dillweed Bed & Breakfast** (7453 Rte. 403 S., Dilltown, 814/446-6465, www.dillweedinc.com, $85-125) has four flower-festooned guest rooms that share two bathrooms, plus a suite with a small kitchen and full private bathroom. It's adjacent to the 36-mile Ghost Town Trail, and its two-floor Trailside Shop offers snacks and beverages for weary hikers along with country gifts such as scented candles and homemade soaps.

$100-150

The owners of the **King's Springs Farm Bed and Breakfast** (3044 Ben Franklin Hwy., Ebensburg, 814/749-9168, www.kingsspringsbb.com, $135) raise hay, organic beef, flowers, herbs, fruits, and vegetables on their hundred-acre property, so you can bet that breakfast is made with fresh, local ingredients. Guests are free to explore the gardens, pastures, orchard, wooded paths, and two ponds. Rooms boast remote-controlled gas fireplaces, but many guests prefer to relax on the farmhouse's wraparound porch.

Majestic World Lodge & Retreat (679 Memory Ln., Portage, 814/693-0189, www.majesticworldlodge.com, $110-120) specializes in guided hunts for elk, red deer stags, buffalo, and other beasts, but nonhunters are more than welcome at the mountaintop getaway. The main lodge has seven rustic guest rooms, each with its own bath. Larger parties can book a four-bedroom, four-bath house next to the main lodge.

FOOD

Johnstown eateries eschew pomp in favor of a laid-back vibe. The city likes its sub sandwiches and hot dogs, and local establishments do a fine job with both. Skip Subway and try a torpedo from **Em's Original Sub Shop** (345 Main St., 814/535-5919, 7am-8pm Mon.-Fri., 9am-7pm Sat., 11am-4pm Sun.; 612 Goucher St., 814/255-6421, 6am-9pm daily; 1111 Scalp Ave., 814/269-3493, 8am-9pm daily, under $10), which has three locations in Johnstown. To look at the menu behind the register is to broadcast your out-of-town-ness. Locals know exactly what they like between their 12 inches of Italian bread.

Coney Island may be in Brooklyn, New York, but **Coney Island Lunch** (127 Clinton St., 814/535-2885, www.coneyislandjohnstownpa.com, 6am-4am Mon.-Sat., $2-6) is a Johnstown landmark. It's been around and owned by the same family since 1916. Locals pile into the joint after bars close to ward off hangovers with hot dogs smothered in homemade chili sauce—just $1.70 a pop. A more exotic choice is the Sundowner, a cheeseburger topped with a fried egg, mustard, chili sauce, and chopped onions. Just two hours after it closes, Coney Island reopens to serve up eggs and hotcakes.

"If it swims we have it," promises **The Fish Boat** (544 Main St., 814/536-7403, 10am-5:30pm Mon.-Thurs., 9am-6:30pm Fri., 10am-5pm Sat., $4-15), an otherwise humble seafood market and restaurant. The Fisherman's Delight platter offers a bit of everything: haddock, scallops, clams, shrimp, oysters, and a crab cake, plus your choice of sides.

Nyko's Restaurant on Scalp (935 Scalp Ave., 814/254-4099, www.nykosrestaurant.com, 3pm-10pm Mon., 11am-10pm Tues.-Sat., $8-29) is best known for its sushi, but there are options aplenty for diners who don't walk on the raw side, including Korean-style dishes and Italian staples like penne pasta and chicken parmesan.

"Comfort food" and "health conscious" are an improbable duo of restaurant descriptors. The romantic ★ **Back Door Café** (402 Chestnut St., 814/539-5084, www.thebackdoorcafe.com, 4pm-9pm Tues.-Thurs., 4pm-10pm Fri.-Sat., $13-20) proves it's possible with dishes loaded with fresh seasonal ingredients, many of them local.

The ever-changing menu always includes a variety of flatbread pizzas with toppings such as sautéed Hungarian hot peppers or wild mushrooms handpicked by chef Tom Chulick.

Ambience reaches new heights at **Asiago's** (709 Edgehill Dr., 814/266-5071, www.asiagostuscanitalian.com, 11:30am-9:30pm Tues.-Thurs., 11:30am-10:30pm Fri.-Sat., 11:30am-8pm Sun., $9-19), located atop the Johnstown Inclined Plane. In addition to fantastic views, the restaurant offers Tuscan Italian cuisine, more than 50 wines, and an intriguing array of martinis.

INFORMATION

The **Greater Johnstown/Cambria County Convention & Visitors Bureau** (111 Roosevelt Blvd., Johnstown, 814/536-7993, www.visitjohnstownpa.com, 8am-5pm Mon.-Fri., 11am-3pm Sat.) is a good source of information about area attractions and events.

GETTING THERE

Johnstown is about 70 miles east of Pittsburgh, a drive of about an hour and a half. From Pittsburgh, follow Route 22 east for about an hour, exit at Route 403 south, and follow the road into Johnstown.

Johnstown has an airport, the **John Murtha Johnstown-Cambria County Airport** (JST, 814/536-0002, http://www.flyjohnstownairport.com), but you can only fly there from Washington Dulles International Airport (IAD) in Virginia. **Pittsburgh International Airport** (PIT, 412/472-3525, www.flypittsburgh.com) is the nearest major airport to Johnstown.

Amtrak (800/872-7245, www.amtrak.com) provides train service between Johnstown and New York City, Philadelphia, Harrisburg, Pittsburgh, and other cities on its Pennsylvanian line. Johnstown's Amtrak station (47 Walnut St.) is across the Little Conemaugh River from downtown. Local transit provider **CamTran** (814/535-5526, www.camtranbus.com) offers a 25-cent shuttle (Route 18) between the station and its downtown transit center. The shuttle also makes stops at the Johnstown Flood Museum and Johnstown Inclined Plane.

Greyhound (800/231-2222, www.greyhound.com) offers bus service to Johnstown, discharging passengers near a donut shop at 126 Clinton Street in downtown.

GETTING AROUND

Driving is the easiest way to get around Johnstown and the surrounding area, but it's not the only way. **CamTran** (814/535-5526, www.camtranbus.com) provides bus service in and around the city. The base fare is $1.50 and transfers 30 cents. One-day passes are available ($4.15 adults, $2.10 students) at the Bus Stop Shop (551 Main St., Johnstown, 814/535-4720, 7am-3pm Mon.-Fri.), a convenience store in CamTran's downtown transit center.

For door-to-door service, call **Greater Johnstown Yellow Cab** (814/535-4584).

Altoona and Vicinity

Altoona is a product of the railroad industry, the demise of which hasn't diminished the city's appeal to rail fans. For the first half of the 19th century, what's now Altoona was farmland and wilderness. The tract's location at the eastern foot of the Allegheny Mountains—a formidable obstacle as railroads moved west across America—made it attractive to the Pennsylvania Railroad. The PRR, or "Pennsy," transformed it into a base camp, and thousands of workers arrived to help design, build, test, and repair trains. By 1945, the Altoona Works had become the world's largest rail shop complex. The area was so important to the nation's transportation infrastructure that it was a Nazi target during World War II. (Six saboteurs deposited by submarines off the shores of Florida and Long Island were executed. Two more were returned to Germany after serving prison sentences.)

Peacetime brought a decline in the demand for rail services, and the subsequent construction of a nationwide highway system marked the end of the railroading era. The Altoona Works were largely dismantled. The roundhouse, one of the largest in the country, was torn down in the 1960s. But there are traces of bygone days. A railroad museum occupies the 1882 building that housed the Pennsy's testing labs. Some 50 trains a day still snake around the Horseshoe Curve, the railroad's ingenious answer to the problem posed by the mountain range. Steam engines were retired more than 50 years ago, but the soot they produced still necessitates frequent dusting in the city built for railroaders.

SIGHTS
Railroaders Memorial Museum
A life-size replica of a steam locomotive dominates the lobby of the impressive **Railroaders Memorial Museum** (1300 9th Ave., Altoona, 814/946-0834, www.railroadcity.com,

10am-4pm Mon.-Sat. and 11am-4pm Sun. early Apr.-early May, 9am-5pm Mon.-Sat. and 11am-5pm Sun. early May-late Oct., 10am-4pm Fri.-Sat. and 11am-4pm Sun. late Oct.-late Dec., admission $10, seniors $9, children 2-11 $8), located in the former Pennsylvania Railroad master mechanics building in downtown Altoona. Three floors of interactive exhibits tell the story of the Pennsy, the enormous task of crossing the Allegheny Mountains, and the rail barons and laborers who made it happen. Regularly shown films help visitors make sense of the engineering marvel that is Horseshoe Curve, which is about 20 minutes away by car. Museum ticket prices include same-day access to the trackside viewing area at the Curve.

★ Horseshoe Curve
How do you solve a problem like the Allegheny Mountains? The answer came from a young civil engineer named J. Edgar Thompson, who designed a way for trains to ascend gradually—about 90 feet per mile—along the mountain contour. The **Horseshoe Curve** (1500 Glenwhite Rd., Altoona, 814/946-0834, www.railroadcity.com, 10am-4pm Mon.-Sat. and 11am-4pm Sun. early Apr.-early May, 9am-6pm Mon.-Sat. and 11am-6pm Sun. early May-late Oct., 10am-4pm Fri.-Sat. and 11am-4pm Sun. late Oct.-late Nov., admission $6, combo package that includes admission to Railroaders Memorial Museum available) opened for rail traffic in 1854, revolutionizing east-west transport of people and the raw materials essential to industry. Today the Curve is owned by the Norfolk Southern Railway, which hauls everything from ethanol to appliances over the Alleghenies. It's rare for an hour to pass without at least one train making an appearance. You can ride a funicular or climb roughly 200 steps to reach a trackside viewing area, dotted with benches and picnic tables. Turn your back to the tracks for

a striking panorama of the mountain landscape, which has changed hardly at all since the Curve's earliest days.

Allegheny Portage Railroad National Historic Site

Before the railroads revolutionized travel and trade, canals were America's "highways." To overcome the Allegheny Mountains, Pennsylvania's canal builders designed a railroad system of 10 inclined planes, five on each side of a mountain. Stationary steam engines moved thick ropes that pulled barges up the mountain. Completed in 1834, the Allegheny Portage Railroad cut travel time between Philadelphia and Pittsburgh to three to five days—versus three or more weeks by horse and wagon. It remained in operation until 1854, when the Pennsylvania Railroad completed the Horseshoe Curve, cutting travel time between the two cities to less than a day.

The **Allegheny Portage Railroad National Historic Site** (110 Federal Park Rd., Gallitzin, 814/886-6150, www.nps.gov/alpo, 9am-5pm daily, admission $4, free for children under 16), about 12 miles west of Altoona, features a historic tavern and a replica of an engine house. Exhibits and models tell the story of the ingenious—and dangerous—mode of transport. Deadly accidents were common because the ropes that pulled barges up from Johnstown on the west side of the Alleghenies or Hollidaysburg on the east side were wont to break.

"The Portage" boasted the first railroad tunnel in the United States. Today the 900-foot **Staple Bend Tunnel** is an outlying part of the National Historic Site and can be reached via a two-mile hiking and biking trail.

Other Railroading Sights

One mile from the Allegheny Portage site, **Gallitzin Tunnels Park & Museum** (411 Convent St., Gallitzin, 814/886-8871, www.gallitzin.info, park open dawn-dusk daily year-round, museum open 11am-4pm Tues.-Sun. May-Sept., free admission) boasts a restored 1942 Pennsylvania Railroad N5C caboose and killer views of trains entering and exiting the 3,605-foot Allegheny Tunnel, built in the early 1850s. A bridge overlooking the tracks has camera ports so photographers can get unobstructed shots.

The **Portage Station Museum** (400 Lee St., Portage, 814/736-9223, www.portagepa.us, noon-4pm Tues.-Sat., free admission) occupies a restored 1926 railroad depot building about 25 miles southwest of Altoona.

Horseshoe Curve

A 173-square-foot model train display features area railroad attractions, including the Horseshoe Curve and the depot itself, which was used by the Pennsylvania Railroad until 1954. On the first Saturday of each month, engines from different time periods pull as many as 40 cars around the miniature tracks. A documentary chronicles the 1940 Sonman Mine explosion, which killed 63 miners near Portage.

Canal Basin Park (101 Canal St., Hollidaysburg, 814/696-4601, www.blairco.org, park open dawn-dusk daily, visitors center 11am-5pm Tues.-Fri., 9am-3pm Sat., 1pm-5pm Sun., closed in winter, free admission) in Hollidaysburg, a quaint county seat just south of Altoona, gives visitors a window into canal culture. Hollidaysburg once had two large water basins connected by a canal lock. Boats were pulled out of the lower basin and onto the Allegheny Portage Railroad. The park features a replica of the lock mechanisms and other displays about the canal system.

Amusement Parks

The Altoona area has not one but two amusement parks. **Lakemont Park & The Island Waterpark** (700 Park Ave., Altoona, 800/434-8006, www.lakemontparkfun.com, open Wed.-Sun. late May-early Sept., hours vary, all-day pass $5 Wed.-Fri., $9.95 Sat.-Sun.) boasts the world's oldest roller coaster, Leap-the-Dips. It costs an additional $2.50 to ride the antique coaster, which was built at the park in 1902 and named a National Historic Landmark in 1996. The seen-better-days amusement park has about 30 rides and attractions, including go-kart tracks, an 18-hole mini golf course, paddle boats, and an arcade. Its regular season ends in September, but Lakemont reopens in late November for **Holiday Lights on the Lake** (6pm-10pm daily, $10 per car), which runs through early January.

Most amusement parks make a name for themselves with thrilling rides. **DelGrosso's Amusement Park** (4352 E. Pleasant Valley Blvd., Tipton, 814/684-3538, www.delgrossos.

com, open daily June-late Aug. and weekends in May and Sept., picnic grounds open 8am, rides and attractions open 11am, all-day pass $13.95 May and Sept., $17.95 June-Aug.) is famous for its food. When Altoona railroader Fred DelGrosso bought the park in 1946, he set up a special kitchen in its restaurant to experiment with his mother-in-law's pasta sauce recipe. At first his sauce was used only in the park's restaurant. In time it gave birth to DelGrosso Foods Inc., which today produces pizza sauce, meatballs, and other Italian specialty items in addition to pasta sauces. Park-goers feast on family recipes during **Spaghetti Wednesday,** celebrated weekly during the summer. The park's potato salad is something of a legend. It's available daily, along with freshly made pizza. An Italian food festival is held in September. The rides, by the way, are also tempting.

The Wall That Heals

The Wall That Heals (James E. Van Zandt VA Medical Center, 2907 Pleasant Valley Blvd., Altoona, 814/940-7759, open year-round, free), a half-scale replica of the Vietnam Veterans Memorial in Washington DC, came to Altoona in 1999 and was supposed to leave after four days. But locals were so reluctant to see it go that they raised enough money to keep it there for good. Located on the grounds of Altoona's VA medical center, the powerful memorial is inscribed with the names of more than 58,000 U.S. service members who were killed or classified as missing during the Vietnam War.

Historic Loretto

In the final years of the 18th century, a young priest named Demetrius Gallitzin arrived at a small, isolated settlement in the Allegheny Mountains. Gallitzin, who'd given up a life of luxury as part of Russia's aristocracy, renamed the settlement Loretto in honor of Loreto, Italy, a Catholic pilgrimage site. Under his guidance—and thanks in no small part to his wealth—Loretto became a hub of Catholicism. His parish, St. Michael's, was the first Catholic church between Lancaster, Pennsylvania, and St. Louis, Missouri. By the time of his death in 1840, Loretto required three priests to minister to its thousands of Catholics. Today, the tiny town about 20 miles west of Altoona is home to a university founded by Franciscan friars, a Franciscan monastery, and a Carmelite monastery.

Father Gallitzin's original log church is long gone. In its place is the **Basilica of Saint Michael the Archangel** (321 St. Mary's St., 814/472-8551). The impressive stone structure, shaped like a Latin cross, was financed by Loretto native and steel magnate Charles M. Schwab. It has three bells, four Italian marble altars, and a communion railing of Mexican onyx. The nearby **Prince Gallitzin Chapel House** (357 St. Mary's St., 814/472-5441, 9am-4pm Mon.-Fri. year-round, 1pm-5pm Sun. during summer) was Gallitzin's home for the last few years of his life. A set of vestments, a chalice, glasses, books, and other artifacts once used by the "Apostle of the Alleghenies" are displayed.

The church wasn't Schwab's only investment in his hometown. He also built an opulent summer estate he called Immergrun (German for "evergreen"). Wanton spending and the stock market crash of 1929 cost Schwab his fortune and his thousand-acre retreat. A portion of the estate became a Franciscan monastery. Schwab's palatial limestone mansion, now the **St. Francis Friary** (141 St. Francis Dr., 814/693-2890), is not open to the public. But its lavish sunken gardens are accessible from sunrise to sunset. Religious and classical sculptures, reflecting pools, and waterfalls operated on Sundays in the summer make the gardens worthy of pilgrimage even for atheists.

ENTERTAINMENT AND EVENTS
Performing Arts
The grand **Mishler Theatre** (1212 12th Ave., Altoona, 814/944-9434, www.mishler-theatre.org), more than a century old, is home to **Altoona Community Theatre** (814/943-4357, www.altoonacommunity-theatre.com), **Allegheny Ballet Company** (814/941-9944, www.alleghenyballet.org), and the **Altoona Symphony Orchestra** (814/943-2500, www.altoonasymphony. org). It also plays host to touring artists and companies.

Festivals and Events
The **Blair County Arts Festival** (Penn State Altoona, 814/949-2787, www.blaircounty-artsfestival.org, mid-May), which benefits Altoona's historic Mishler Theatre, features a juried fine arts exhibit, a fine crafts market, a children's village, and oodles of live entertainment.

The Greater Altoona Economic Development Corp. sponsors free concerts by regional artists on select Friday evenings from June through August. The **SummerSounds** concerts are held along 11th Avenue in downtown Altoona. The Blair County Historical Society hosts free **Summer Concerts on the Lawn** at Baker Mansion (3419 Oak Ln., Altoona, 814/942-3916, www.blairhistory. org) on Sunday afternoons in August and September.

SPORTS AND RECREATION
Canoe Creek State Park
Not long ago, **Canoe Creek State Park** (205 Canoe Creek Rd., Hollidaysburg, 814/695-6807, www.visitpaparks.com) was best known for having one of the largest bat colonies in Pennsylvania. Sadly, the disease known as white-nose syndrome has all but wiped out the bat population, making bat watching a thing of the past. There's still good reason to visit the 955-acre park—several good reasons, actually. Not the least of them is Canoe Lake, which is popular for fishing year-round. The 155-acre lake is stocked with walleye, muskellunge, bass, trout, crappies, and other fish. The lake also boasts a sand beach, open 8am to sunset May-September. A boat rental adjacent to the swimming area offers rowboats, paddleboats, kayaks, and canoes.

Eight miles of hiking trails explore the lakeshore, wetlands, forests, and fields, which provide habitat for more than 200 species of birds and mammals. Biking is limited to a one-mile trail that passes through the historic site. Cross-country skiing is permitted on all hiking trails.

The park doesn't have a campground, but eight modern cabins are available year-round. The cabins have two bedrooms, a living/dining room, a bathroom, and a kitchen. Reserve online at www.pa.reserveworld.com or by calling 888/727-2757. A one-week minimum applies during the summer months.

Lower Trail

The 16.5-mile **Lower Trail** (814/832-2400, www.rttcpa.org), which runs along the Frankstown Branch of the Juniata River, has seen all sorts of traffic. Before it was a recreational trail—open for **hiking, biking, horseback riding, cross-country skiing,** and any other nonmotorized activity—much of the Lower was a rail corridor. And before that, it was a towpath for the Pennsylvania Canal. Remnants of the canal era can still be seen along the trail, which is extremely flat. The Lower (pronounced like "flower") has six trailheads, all of which are located at or near former railroad stations and can be reached from Route 22. The westernmost trailhead, near Canoe Creek State Park, is about a quarter of a mile south of Route 22 and reachable by Flowing Springs Road. Map boxes can be found at each trailhead.

Prince Gallitzin State Park

With its 1,635-acre lake and large campground, **Prince Gallitzin** (966 Marina Rd., Patton, 814/674-1000, www.visitpaparks.com) is popular with boaters, anglers, and campers. The picturesque park about half an hour northwest of Altoona also boasts many miles of trails for hiking, mountain biking, snowmobiling, and cross-country skiing.

Boats with motors of 20 horsepower or less are permitted on Glendale Lake, the recreational heart of the park. The lake has multiple boat launches, mooring facilities, and marinas. It also has a public beach open from late May to mid-September.

Open from early April to late October, the park's modern campground features a beach of its own, a boat rental, playgrounds, and a camp store. In addition to nearly 400 campsites, the campground has a handful of camping cottages that overlook the lake. For a touch more luxury, book one of 10 modern cabins on the other side of the lake. The two- and three-bedroom cabins are available year-round. Campsites, camping cottages, and cabins can be reserved online at www.pa.reserveworld. com or by calling 888/727-2757.

ACCOMMODATIONS

Altoona's lodging scene is dominated by chains like the **Courtyard Altoona** (2 Convention Center Dr., Altoona, 814/312-1800, www.marriott.com), conveniently connected to the Blair County Convention Center. Bed-and-breakfasts near the city offer an alternative.

Under $100

Just north of Altoona, **Elizabeth Rest Bed & Breakfast** (Sabbath Rest Rd., Altoona, 814/940-1842, www.elizabethrest.com, $65-130) offers simple accommodations at affordable rates. Built in 1830, the brick colonial is outfitted with wireless Internet, air-conditioning, and satellite TV. The Chimney Suite is a good choice for a longish stay because it has a private kitchen and living room.

The Blue Lantern (327 High St., Williamsburg, 814/937-1823, www.thebluelanternbandb.com, $90), about half an hour east of Altoona, is a great choice for outdoor enthusiasts because it's a few blocks from the Lower Trail and a few miles from Canoe Creek State Park. The B&B has three guest rooms and spacious porches overlooking a trout pond.

Nothing says "away from it all" like a dirt lane, so don't be surprised if you feel your worries melting away as you approach **Sunhearth Trails Bed & Breakfast** (204

Sunhearth Ln., Roaring Spring, 814/227-5558, www.sunhearth.org, $75-95). The rural escape less than half an hour south of Altoona has four guest rooms, two of which share a bath. Feel free to bring your furry friends; the 5.5-acre property has a fenced area for pets.

$100-150

Location, location, location—and historic flair—make the ★ **Mimosa Courtyard Inn** (418 N. Montgomery St., Hollidaysburg, 814/330-9917, www.mimosainn.com, $140-225) a fine choice. The 16-room mansion, which dates to the 1830s, is half a block from the main drag in Hollidaysburg, a darling little town just south of Altoona. Enjoy a country breakfast in the formal dining room before taking a short walk to unique shops or a short drive to attractions such as the Railroaders Memorial Museum and Canoe Creek State Park. The B&B's newest addition, the Toys in the Attic Suite, has a bedroom, living room, kitchen, and bath, making it a good choice if you're traveling with children or staying a while. Its nightly rate includes breakfast for four.

FOOD

There's no shortage of national chains in the Altoona area. Thoroughfares are lined with the likes of TGI Friday's, Olive Garden, Red Lobster, and Chili's. Locally owned restaurants are a rare breed and most often found in town centers.

Altoona

★ **Tom and Joe's Diner** (1201 13th Ave., 814/943-3423, www.tomandjoes.com, 7am-2pm Mon.-Fri., 7am-1pm Sat., 7am-noon Sun., under $10), across from City Hall in downtown Altoona, was founded in 1933 by brothers named—you guessed it—Tom and Joe. Tom's grandson runs the place today. Like the retro decor (checkered floors, red counter stools, and knotty pine walls), the specials hark back to an era before cholesterol checks. Cap a meal of ham potpie or liver and onions with a malted shake.

If you're more in the mood for a margarita than a malted shake, give the regional chain **El Campesino** (206 E. Plank Rd., 814/944-3121, www.elcampesino.net, 11:30am-10pm Mon.-Thurs., 11:30am-10:30pm Fri.-Sat., noon-9pm Sun., $6-20) a chance. The Altoona location is one of seven. El Campesino is as good as Mexican gets in these parts.

Hollidaysburg and Duncansville

Fresh crepes are reason enough to visit **Allegheny Creamery and Crepes** (505 Allegheny St., Hollidaysburg, 814/696-5055, 7am-8pm Mon.-Thurs., 7am-9pm Fri., 9am-9pm Sat., 9am-3pm Sun., under $10) in Hollidaysburg, about seven miles south of Altoona, but you'll also find excellent soups, salads, and panini. The ice cream served here hails from Ritchey's Dairy, a family-owned affair in nearby Martinsburg, Pennsylvania.

In the diminutive town of Duncansville, just a few minutes west of Hollidaysburg, you'll find **Marzoni's Brick Oven & Brewing Co.** (165 Patchway Rd., Duncansville, 814/695-2931, www.marzonis.com, 11am-11pm daily, $6-23), which features exactly what its name suggests: pizza cooked in brick-lined ovens and hand-crafted beers. Ask for a tour of the brewery if you're curious about the process. In addition to pizza, the restaurant offers sandwiches, pasta dishes, and meat and seafood selections.

INFORMATION

For brochures, maps, discount cards, and answers to any and all questions about the area, contact **Explore Altoona** (814/943-4183, www.explorealtoona.com).

GETTING THERE AND AROUND

Altoona is about 95 miles east of Pittsburgh, a drive of about two hours. From Pittsburgh, take Route 22 east to I-99/Route 220 north. Exit 33 (17th Street) will put you in the center of town.

You can fly to **Altoona-Blair County Airport** (AOO, 814/793-2027, www.altoonablaircountyairport.com), about 20 miles south of Altoona in Martinsburg, from Washington Dulles International Airport (IAD) in Virginia. **Pittsburgh International Airport** (PIT, 412/472-3525, www.flypittsburgh.com) is the nearest major airport to Altoona.

Amtrak (800/872-7245, www.amtrak.com) trains and **Greyhound** (800/231-2222, www.greyhound.com) buses serve the **Altoona Transportation Center** (1231 11th Ave.), which is the primary hub for Altoona's public transit provider, **AMTRAN** (814/944-4074, www.amtran.org). Local taxi services include **Blue & White Taxi** (814/941-2711) and **Yellow Cab Co.** (814/944-6105).

State College and Vicinity

Steelmaking built Johnstown, and railroading built Altoona. Their neighbor State College is the product of a different industry: education. The town is home to Pennsylvania State University, better known as Penn State, which was founded in 1855 as a publicly supported agricultural college. Town and gown have grown in tandem. In 1875, the school had only 64 undergraduates. In 2012, enrollment at its 24 campuses exceeded 96,000. Almost half of Penn State students are enrolled at the flagship campus, University Park. Their numbers make State College a lively, culturally rich, and commercially robust town.

Penn State long ago expanded its curriculum beyond the agricultural sciences, but farming is still the way of life for many in this region. Farmlands radiate from State College. They're interrupted by mountains and forests and the occasional town, including the particularly quaint Boalsburg and Bellefonte. When Penn State's Nittany Lions play football at home, State College and its neighbors swell with fans. If that's when you visit, you'll see why Penn State was ranked the nation's number one party school. Tranquility awaits you most other times of year.

SIGHTS
★ Berkey Creamery

This ain't no ordinary ice cream joint. Penn State's **Berkey Creamery** (corner of Bigler and Curtin Roads, University Park, 814/865-7535, www.creamery.psu.edu, 7am-10pm Mon.-Thurs., 7am-11pm Fri., 8am-11pm Sat., 9am-10pm Sun.) is a pilgrimage site. People come from near and not so near to indulge in fresh ice cream produced by the country's largest and most sophisticated university creamery. How fresh? How does four days from cow to cone sound? The school's own cowherd can't supply enough milk to meet demand, so the creamery relies on local producers. Don't be deterred by the snaking line to the counter. Most patrons know what they like, and there's no agonizing over one scoop or two. There's only one serving size: generous. Quarts and half-gallons of the rich stuff are such popular souvenirs that Berkey sells travel bags and dry ice for the road.

The creamery, which occupies the first floor of the Food Science Building, is a laboratory for students in the College of Agricultural Sciences. They learn the dairy business by working in it, producing milk, cheeses, yogurt, sour cream, frozen yogurt, and sherbet along with the famous ice cream. Want a taste of life in the ice cream trenches? The university's Ice Cream Short Course covers every aspect of production. It's how Ben and Jerry got their start.

Mount Nittany

That tree-covered hump on the horizon? It's probably **Mount Nittany** (www.mtnittany.org), and you should definitely hike it. The mountain is part of a ridge separating two valleys; on a clear day, the crest affords postcard-quality views of both. Its name is derived from the Algonquin "nit-a-nee," which means either "single mountain" or "barrier against the wind," depending on who you ask. Penn State borrowed the mountain's name for its mascot, the Nittany Lion.

Finding the trailhead is arguably the trickiest part of the hike. It's at the dead end of Mount Nittany Road, which begins in the quaint village of Lemont. From State College, take South Atherton Street (Business Rte. 322) east to the traffic light at Branch Road. Turn left onto Branch and follow to Mount Nittany Road. Turn right, drive one mile, and—voilà!—there it is. Take your pick of two blazed loop trails: the four-mile white trail or 5.5-mile blue trail. Both start out rocky and steep. For a view of campus from 1,940 feet, you needn't go farther than the Mike Lynch Overlook, 0.75 mile up the white trail. You can hike Mount Nittany any time of year, but spring and fall are particularly good for wildlife viewing. Winter's leafless trees make for exceptional valley views. Hunting is permitted, so it's wise to wear orange.

If you're short on time or shy of the climb, you can take in Mount Nittany from an observation area between Beaver Stadium and the Bryce Jordan Center on campus. There's no charge to use the high-powered binoculars.

Beaver Stadium

The best way to experience **Beaver Stadium** (University Dr. and Park Ave., University Park), den of the Nittany Lions football team, is to go to a home game. Alas, tickets are so prized that even students have to scramble for them. Don't let the lack of a ticket keep you away on game day. Penn State has a tailgating tradition par excellence. Fans with motor homes arrive as early as Thursday to set up camp. On Saturday, the parking lots and fields around Beaver Stadium fill with revelers. There's music. There's food. There's even a good chance you'll find fans (and the occasional scalper) selling extra tickets. "If you haven't been to [State College] in the fall, you're missing out on one of the great happenings in all of sports," ESPN's Kirk Herbstreit gushed in 2008.

Beaver Stadium is impressive even when empty. With a seating capacity of 107,282, it's the second largest stadium in the country after Michigan Stadium. Tours that include the Nittany Lions locker room are offered by the **Penn State All-Sports Museum** (814/865-0044, www.gopsusports.com/museum, 10am-4pm Tues.-Sat., noon-4pm Sun., hours vary in winter and on home game weekends, suggested donation $5, children/students/

Berkey Creamery

Anatomy of a Mascot

What's a **Nittany Lion** anyway? The question will brand you an outsider in State College, where the Penn State mascot is revered. Fear not. Here's the lowdown on the region's favorite feline.

Until 1904, Penn State didn't have a mascot. That year, the school's baseball team visited Princeton University, home of the Tigers. When Penn State's Harrison "Joe" Mason was shown a statue of the fearsome mascot, the ballplayer pulled a fast one: He crowed that the Nittany Lion, "fiercest beast of them all," would take down the Tiger. And, indeed, Penn State defeated Princeton that day.

Mason's fabrication had roots in reality. Mountain lions roamed central Pennsylvania when Penn State was founded. A mountain named Nittany was and remains the most prominent natural landmark near campus. Mason put the two together to create a unique symbol of might. A branding whiz couldn't have done it better. Back at Penn State, support for Mason's brainchild was so widespread that the mascot was adopted without so much as a vote.

seniors $3). The 10,000-square-foot museum in the southwest corner of the stadium celebrates the achievements of Penn State athletes and coaches. Its collection includes the 1973 Heisman Trophy of running back John Cappelletti and the 1952 Olympics gold medal of steeplechaser Horace Ashenfelter.

Beaver Stadium, by the way, is named not for the dam-building rodent but for James A. Beaver, a former governor of Pennsylvania and president of the university's board of trustees.

Nittany Lion Shrine

Said to be the most photographed site on campus, the **Nittany Lion Shrine** resides near the Recreation Building at the west end of Curtin Road. Sculptor Heinz Warneke and stonecutter Joseph Garatti coaxed the crouching lion out of a 13-ton block of Indiana limestone. It was dedicated during homecoming weekend in 1942. In 1966, fans of homecoming rival Syracuse University doused the lion with hard-to-remove paint. Penn State students, faculty, and alumni have guarded (read: partied at) the shrine during homecoming weekend ever since.

Historic Boalsburg

On an October day in 1864, three women decorated the graves of fallen Civil War soldiers in a small Boalsburg cemetery. Their respectful gesture would later become an American tradition, giving Boalsburg bragging rights as the birthplace of Memorial Day. Few towns do it up like Boalsburg come the last Monday in May. The village along Business Route 322, just several minutes east of State College, hosts a daylong festival that culminates in a ceremony at the same cemetery where the three paid their respects. A life-size statue of the ladies in ground-sweeping skirts stands there today. Boalsburg's reverence for history makes it worth a visit any day of the year. It has three museums, diligently maintained 19th-century homes, and a tavern that opened its doors in 1819. To boot, the quaint village boasts several boutiques worthy of a big city.

Boalsburg was settled in 1808 but called Springfield until 1820, when it was renamed to honor its most distinguished residents, the Boals. The **Boal Mansion Museum** (163 Boal Estate Dr., 814/466-6210, www.boalmuseum.com, 1:30pm-5pm Tues.-Sun. in spring and fall, 10am-5pm Tues.-Sat. and noon-5pm Sun. in summer, by appointment Nov.-Apr., admission $10, children 7-11 $6) displays the family's many treasures, including original furnishings and military artifacts from the Revolutionary War to World War I. In 1909, a Boal and his French-Spanish wife, a descendant of Christopher Columbus, imported a centuries-old chapel from the Columbus Castle in Spain. The **Columbus Chapel** is preserved in a structure of Pennsylvania stone adjacent to the mansion. It contains an admiral's desk said to have belonged to the explorer himself and religious statues from the 15th century.

The **Boalsburg Heritage Museum** (304 E. Main St., 814/466-3035, www.boalsburgheritagemuseum.org, 2pm-4pm Tues. and Sat. and by appointment, closed mid-Dec.-Apr., free admission) is an example of a more modest early home, filled with historical and community artifacts.

The site of the **Pennsylvania Military Museum** (51 Boal Ave., 814/466-6263, www.pamilmuseum.org, 10am-4pm Wed.-Sat. and noon-4pm Sun. mid-Mar.-Nov., admission $6, seniors $5.50, children 3-11 $4) was once part of the Boal estate. In 1916, with war raging in Europe, Theodore Davis Boal organized a horse-mounted machine gun troop on his property. The museum honors them and other Pennsylvania military men and women. It also showcases the tools of war, including the massive gun barrels of a battleship that survived the 1941 Japanese attack on Pearl Harbor. Military service ribbons inspired the cubistic mural on the front facade of the museum.

If you're hungry for more history or just plain hungry, head to **Duffy's Tavern** (113 E. Main St., Boalsburg, 814/466-6241, www.duffystavernpa.com, 11:30am-10pm Mon.-Sat., 11:30am-9pm Sun., hours subject to change in winter, $7-33), a watering hole since 1819. Boalsburg was a busy stop on a stagecoach route in the early 19th century—busy enough to keep three taverns in business at one point. This one, with its 22-inch stone walls, is believed to have served the gentry.

Victorian Bellefonte

The very Victorian town of Bellefonte, 15 miles north of State College, is the seat of Centre County. It owes its (somewhat faded) grandeur to the prosperous and powerful men who called it home in the 19th century: iron and limestone barons, bankers, lawyers, judges, and seven U.S. governors. Much of their real estate is lovingly preserved,

which makes Bellefonte attractive to architecture and history buffs, romantics, and the tea-and-scone crowd. It's also popular with anglers. Spring Creek, famous for its large trout, meanders through the storybook town. Bellefonte is never more magical than in winter, when homes, businesses, and county buildings are dressed in holiday finery. The annual **Bellefonte Victorian Christmas** (814/355-2917, www.bellefontevictorianchristmas.com, second weekend in Dec.) is a town-wide trip back in time, complete with horse-drawn buggy rides, a gingerbread house contest, tours of historic homes, concerts, and, of course, a Victorian tea party.

Start your visit at pretty **Talleyrand Park** along Spring Creek. Bring breadcrumbs for a closer gander at the waterfowl and trout. Talleyrand's 1889 train station is home to the Bellefonte Intervalley Area Chamber of Commerce (320 W. High St., 814/355-2917, www.bellefontechamber.org) and a satellite office of the Central Pennsylvania Convention & Visitors Bureau. You can pick up free maps, information about area attractions, and a Wi-Fi signal.

A former match factory at the edge of Talleyrand Park is now the **American Philatelic Center** (100 Match Factory Place, 814/933-3803, www.stamps.org, 8am-4:30pm Mon.-Fri., free admission), headquarters for a society of more than 44,000 stamp collectors. Visitors can learn the ABCs of stamp collecting, browse exhibits of stamp collections and stamp-related memorabilia, and learn about Bellefonte's important role in the early days of airmail. Pilots refueled in the town on their way from New York City to Chicago. A monument honors those who lost their lives en route.

Follow High Street east to the very center of town, where the **county courthouse** stands. The 1810 Georgian-style house at 133 N. Allegheny Street, two blocks north of the courthouse, was once home to former Governor James A. Beaver. Today it's the **Bellefonte Art Museum** (814/355-4280, www.bellefontemuseum.org, 1pm-4:30pm Fri.-Sun., free admission).

For an ivy-clad Victorian gem, continue to the intersection of North Allegheny and Linn Streets. The **Reynolds Mansion** (101 W. Linn St., 814/353-8407, www.reynolds-mansion.com, $135-205) is so fetching that it graced the cover of a *Select Registry* guide-book to distinguished inns. Built in 1885 by a wealthy businessman, the B&B is a blend of Gothic, Italianate, and Queen Anne styles. You don't have to book a room to explore the ornate interior. The Reynolds Mansion is open to the public 11am-4pm. A guided tour of the common areas, including a snuggery where men retired after dinner to sip brandy and smoke cigars, is $5 per adult. (These days, women are welcome in the snuggery, but smoking isn't.) For more Victorian splendor, continue east on **Linn Street.** The three-block stretch of elegant residences between North Allegheny and Armour Streets includes no fewer than four bed-and-breakfasts.

Show Caves

An all-water limestone cavern 17 miles northeast of State College wows the Wii generation like it did 19th-century tourists. **Penn's Cave** (222 Penns Cave Rd., Centre Hall, 814/364-1664, www.pennscave.com, open daily Mar.-Nov. and weekends in Dec. and Feb., cavern tour $16.95, seniors $15.95, children 2-12 $8.95) is a half-mile wonder-land of stalactites and stalagmites, columns and curtains. Tours by motorboat depart on the hour. Joke-cracking guides dole out geol-ogy factoids and point out curiously shaped formations (and the occasional beaver). Bring a sweater or jacket even in summer because the temperature inside is a constant 52 degrees. Boats emerge from the tunnel-like cave into the man-made Lake Nitanee, where they linger for wildlife viewing before the return trip.

Ninety-minute **wildlife tours** ($19.95, se-niors $18.95, children 2-12 $11.95) of the for-ests and fields around Penn's Cave are offered April-November. The 1,600-acre property is home to longhorn cattle, bison, gray wolves, black bears, and bobcats, among other ani-mals. A cavern and wildlife tour package is available. Penn's Cave also offers two-and-a-half-hour **off-road tours** ($44.95, children 8-12 $24.95, reservations required) over man-made obstacles, up steep cliffs, and through mountain ravines.

When local cave enthusiasts say "the big one," they're talking about **Woodward Cave** (Woodward Cave Dr., Woodward, 814/349-9800, www.woodwardcave.com, open daily late May-late Aug. and weekends late Aug.-mid-Oct. and mid-Apr.-late May, tour $11, children 4-12 $5.50), about 30 miles east of State College. Its spacious rooms include the 200-foot-long Hall of Statues, which features a 14-foot stalagmite known as the Tower of Babel. Woodward Cave is extra chilly—48 degrees year-round—so dress accordingly for the 50-minute, five-room tour. There's no menagerie here, but there is a campground. The **Woodward Cave Campground** has hot showers, a snack stand, a game room, and other amenities, plus a packed calendar of events including pig roasts and horseshoe tournaments. Rates start at $18.

ENTERTAINMENT AND EVENTS
Nightlife

Bank on a good time and outstanding brews at **Zeno's Pub** (100 W. College Ave., State College, 814/237-4350, www.zenospub.com, noon-2am Mon.-Fri., 1pm-2am Sat.-Sun.), which *BeerAdvocate* called one of the top beer bars on the planet.

Don't go to **Bar Bleu** (114 S. Garner St., State College, 814/237-0374, www.dantesinc.com, 5:30pm-2am Mon.-Fri., noon-2am Sat., 4pm-2am Sun.) expecting live jazz or blues. That was several incarnations ago. Today Bar Bleu is a sports bar with 22 flat-screen moni-tors, 16 draft beers, and 43-ounce "fishbowl" cocktails. It serves up live music Thursday through Saturday.

The Saloon (101 Hiester St., State College, 814/234-1344, www.dantesinc.com, 8pm-2am daily) fancies itself an English pub, but its famous "Monkey Boy" drink is a State College original. The concoction of clear alcohols emboldens many a student on karaoke Mondays. Bands make the noise most other nights.

Performing Arts

The likes of Carrie Underwood and Keith Urban perform at Penn State's **Bryce Jordan Center** (corner of University Dr. and Curtin Rd., University Park, 814/863-5500, www.bjc.psu.edu), home of Nittany Lions basketball. Word has it that Tim McGraw borrowed a jeep from a Jordan Center employee some years ago to take another performer, Faith Hill, for a spin. Thus began their romance.

Penn State's **Center for the Performing Arts** (corner of Shortlidge and Eisenhower Roads, University Park, 814/863-0255, www.cpa.psu.edu) hosts some 200 events a year. Wynton Marsalis, David Copperfield, and the Martha Graham and Alvin Ailey dance companies have graced its stage. The **Nittany Valley Symphony** (814/231-8224, www.nvs.org) is a regular user.

The State Theatre (130 W. College Ave., State College, 814/272-0606, www.thestatetheatre.org) in downtown State College opened as a cinema in 1938. Today the renovated venue offers movies and a whole lot more, including musical theater, stand-up comedy, opera, and rock 'n' roll.

Festivals and Events

More than 125,000 people flood downtown State College and the Penn State campus during the **Central Pennsylvania Festival of the Arts** (814/237-3682, www.arts-festival.com, starts Wed. after July 4), a tradition since 1967. Artists and craftspeople from around the country exhibit and peddle their work. Musicians, dancers, and puppeteers entertain. All the while, a massive sand sculpture takes shape in Central Parklet. Admission to some performances requires a $10 button.

You don't have to go home when the exhibits and amusement rides at the **Centre County Grange Fair** (Grange Fairgrounds, Centre Hall, 814/364-9212, www.grangefair.net, late Aug., one-day admission $6) close for the night. The weeklong farm-centric fete is one of the largest encampment fairs in the country, with more than 2,000 tent and RV sites. Funnel cake for breakfast, anyone? Penn State hosts the more scholarly **Ag Progress Days** (Russell E. Larson Agricultural Research Center, Rock Springs, 814/865-2081, www.apd.psu.edu, Aug., free), a showcase of the latest farm machinery, management practices, and research.

First Night State College (814/237-3682, www.firstnightstatecollege.com) is an alcohol-free, arts-focused New Year's Eve celebration known for jaw-dropping ice sculptures. Admission to many performances and crafts workshops requires a $10 button.

SPORTS AND RECREATION

Though best known for college football, the State College region offers much more in the way of sports and recreation, including world-class fishing and glider flying.

Black Moshannon State Park

Don't be daunted by the tea-colored waters at **Black Moshannon State Park** (4216 Beaver Rd., Philipsburg, 814/342-5960, www.visitpaparks.com). They're darkened by plant tannins, not pollution. The bog that hugs Black Moshannon Lake is crowded with sphagnum moss and other wetland plants, including species rarely seen in Pennsylvania. Three carnivorous plants and 17 species of orchids thrive in or near the bog. Thanks to trails and boardwalks that wind through the bog area and surrounding forests, it's possible to get up close to the wildlife. (But don't get too close. The carnivorous plants probably won't catch you, but rangers could.) The 0.3-mile Bog Trail is the easiest of the bunch. If you're more adventurous and not afraid to get your feet wet, try the 7.7-mile Moss-Hanne Trail. Hike it between late July and September if you're fond of blueberries. In winter, all trails are open to cross-country skiers. The park is surrounded by more than 43,000 acres of state forest, which attracts mountain bikers and snowmobilers.

Boating and fishing are permitted on the lake, and rental boats are available during the summer. A sand beach is open from late May to mid-September. When the lake freezes, you can ice skate on a maintained section or ice fish on the rest.

The park's campground is open from the second Friday in April to mid-December. Rustic cabins with wood-burning stoves and bunk beds provide another seasonal lodging option. Six modern cabins with electric heat are available year-round. Reserve online at www.pa.reserveworld.com or by calling 888/727-2757.

Fishing and Paddling

The State College area is known for superb angling. In 2009, members of PaFlyFish.com named Bellefonte the best fly-fishing town in the state, citing its proximity to Spring Creek, Penns Creek, Spruce Creek, and other premier fly-fishing waters. Spring Creek, which runs through the town on its way to Bald Eagle Creek, is among the best wild trout streams in the East and even has a section called Fisherman's Paradise.

Part outfitter and part B&B, **Riffles and Runs** (217 N. Spring St., Bellefonte, 814/353-8109, www.rifflesandruns.com) offers fly-fishing instruction and guiding along with two guest rooms with a shared bath.

State College has two specialty stores for fly anglers. **Flyfisher's Paradise** (2603 E. College Ave., State College, 814/234-4189, www.flyfishersparadise.com, 10am-6pm Mon.-Fri., 10am-5pm Sat.) has been in business for nearly 40 years. Walk in on any given day and you're liable to find a pair of staff members with 80 years of fly-fishing experience between them. New kid on the block **TCO Fly Shop** (2030 E. College Ave., State College, 814/689-3654, www.tcoflyfishing.com, 9am-6pm Mon.-Sat., 10am-4pm Sun.) offers a website with loads of information about area waters along with a wide selection of products, instruction, and guide services.

You can explore the waterways that so many fish call home by canoe or kayak. **Tussey Mountain Outfitters** (308 W. Linn St., Bellefonte, 814/355-5690, www.tusseymountainoutfitters.com, hours vary by season) rents and sells both. Its paddle pros are happy to provide shuttle services.

Outdoors Gear

Appalachian Outdoors (123 S. Allen St., State College, 814/234-3000, www.appoutdoors.com, 9:30am-8:30pm Mon.-Thurs., 9:30am-9pm Fri., 9am-8pm Sat., 10am-6pm Sun.) sells all manner of outdoor clothing and equipment, and its blog offers reviews and tales of adventure.

Flying

At **Ridge Soaring Glidersport** (3523 S. Eagle Valley Rd., Julian, 814/355-2483, www.eglider.org, glider ride $100-220), you can take flight in an aircraft with no engine. Seriously.

Sky's The Limit Ballooning (814/234-5986, www.paballoonrides.com, flight $200/person) offers a different way to soar over the State College area. The hot air balloon lifts off twice a day year-round, barring rain, fog, snow, or strong winds.

Winter Sports

The Alps it's not, but **Tussey Mountain** (341 Bear Meadows Rd., Boalsburg, 814/466-6266, www.tusseymountain.com, lift ticket $20-41, ski/snowboard rental $24-35, snow tubing 2-hour session $18) attracts Penn Staters in need of a quick skiing fix. It offers several trails for skiing and snowboarding, plus a snow tubing park. Tussey does its best to stay relevant in warmer months with a zip line, mini golf course, go-kart track, batting cages, nine-hole golf course, driving range, skate park, fishing pond, and the occasional concert.

ACCOMMODATIONS

The State College area has a wide array of lodging options, from mom-and-pop motels to exclusive boutiques. Rates tend to skyrocket during Penn State football games, parents weekend, graduation, the Central Pennsylvania Festival of the Arts, and other busy periods. Not surprisingly, you'll get the best rates when campus is closed.

Under $100

Get your fill of fresh air at **Bellefonte/ State College KOA** (2481 Jacksonville Rd., Bellefonte, 814/355-7912, www.bellefontekoa. com, campsite $22-85, one-room cabin $40-85, deluxe cabin $85-187). The campground four miles northeast of Bellefonte has 18 rental cabins in addition to tent and RV campsites. It also has a swimming pool, a stocked fishing pond, and a snack bar. Summertime freebies include nightly hayrides, Friday night movies, and Sunday morning pancakes.

You don't have to go to the countryside for accommodations in this price range. **The Stevens Motel** (1275 N. Atherton St., State College, 814/238-2438, www.thestevensmotel. com, $42-58) offers clean rooms, courteous service, and proximity to Penn State.

When the **Autoport** (1405 S. Atherton St., State College, 814/237-7666, www.the-autoport.com, $75-115) opened in 1936, it provided travelers with lodging, food, and car repair services. The garage is long gone, but the 87-room motel still offers an array of amenities, including a heated pool, restaurant, bar, smoking lounge, and live entertainment at least three times a week.

$100-200

The Penn Stater Conference Center Hotel (215 Innovation Blvd., State College, 800/233-7505, www.thepennstaterhotel.psu. edu, $115-225) is the humbler of two hotels operated by the university's Hospitality Services Department. It looks rather like a dormitory from the outside, but you won't find bunk beds or lava lamps in its 300 guest rooms and suites. The Penn Stater knows well the needs of the PowerPoint crowd. Leisure travelers are also welcome.

Penn State's picture-perfect ★ **Nittany**

Lion Inn (200 W. Park Ave., State College, 800/233-7505, www.nittanylioninn.psu.edu, $135-285) is the only hotel on campus. An inviting facade and lobby bespeak a boutique lodging, but in fact the hotel has 223 guest rooms and suites, not to mention meeting facilities and ballrooms. How it manages to feel so intimate may have something to do with the white-glove service.

The eminently elegant **Atherton Hotel** (125 S. Atherton St., State College, 814/231-2100, www.athertonhotel.net, $99-158) will shine your shoes while you sleep—for free— but it's doubtful you'll need the service. A complimentary shuttle virtually ensures scuff-free footwear.

Bellefonte is the area's B&B capital. The kingly ★ **Reynolds Mansion** (101 W. Linn St., Bellefonte, 814/353-8407, www.reynolds-mansion.com, $135-205) has eight uniquely decorated guest rooms. Ladies gravitate toward Grace's Garden Room with its turret sitting area and ornate inlaid floor or Louisa's Cherub Room, remarkable for its ceiling mural. Men feel like men in the Colonel's Green Room, which has a king-size bed, a working fireplace, and a large black whirlpool tub.

The Queen, A Victorian Bed & Breakfast (176 E. Linn St., Bellefonte, 814/355-7946, www.thequeenbnb.com, $99-229) is preened to perfection. Its tireless owner, Nancy Noll, was named Innkeeper of the Year in 2008 by the Pennsylvania Tourism & Lodging Association. Victorian clothes and accessories decorate one room, hunting and fishing collectibles another, and vintage toys a third. The Maid's Quarters, an apartment with a full kitchen and views of Noll's perennial gardens, sleeps up to four. Noll also rents out a three-bedroom house ($229-339) on an adjoining property. Among the other Bellefonte beauties is **Judge Walker's House** (337 E. Linn St., Bellefonte, 814/355-0591, www.judgewalkershouse.com, $95-195), an artist-owned Queen Anne Victorian with four cozy guest rooms.

FOOD

A town packed with students is by necessity a town packed with eateries. But State College delivers more than typical student grub. There's inventive cuisine among the subs, pizza, and wings. You won't find this volume or variety of restaurants anywhere else in the Alleghenies. College and Beaver Avenues and their cross streets in downtown State College are particularly crowded with dining options.

American

The Diner (126 W. College Ave., State College, 814/238-5590, www.thedineronline. com, 7am-10pm Mon.-Thurs., open 24 hours from 7am Fri.-8pm Sun., under $10) is almost as legendary as Penn State football, thanks to a sticky bun slathered with butter and cooked until golden brown. "Grilled stickies" have gained so many fans over the decades that the restaurant now ships them anywhere in the country.

Don't get too attached to an entrée at **Harrison's Wine Grill** (1221 E. College Ave., inside Hilton Garden Inn, State College, 814/237-4422, www.harrisonsmenu.com, 11am-9pm Mon.-Fri., 11:30am-9pm Sat.-Sun., $6-29), because it might not be there next month. Chef Harrison Schailey's specialty is farm-to-table fare. If it's not in season, he's not interested.

Communities around State College offer more fine options. A onetime stagecoach stop, **Duffy's Tavern** (113 E. Main St., Boalsburg, 814/466-6241, www.duffystavernpa.com, 11:30am-10pm Mon.-Sat., 11:30am-9pm Sun., hours subject to change in winter, $7-33) serves elegant dishes like pork tenderloin with warm fruit in its dining room and more casual fare in the adjacent tavern. You can't miss **Kelly's Steak and Seafood** (316 Boal Ave., Boalsburg, 814/466-6251, www.kellys-steak. com, 11am-midnight Mon.-Sat., 2pm-midnight Sun., late-night menu after 9pm Sun.-Thurs. and 10pm Fri.-Sat., $7-45). There's a giant bovine on its roof. The kitschiness belies the kitchen's sophistication. Husband-and-wife chefs Sean and Tien Kelly, who met in

Seattle, bring a Pacific Northwest sensibility to dishes such as grilled fish tacos and cedar-plank-roasted salmon.

The unique **Gamble Mill** (160 Dunlap St., Bellefonte, 814/355-7764, www.gamblemill. com, 11:30am-9pm Mon.-Sat., 4pm-8pm Sun., $9-38) is reason enough to visit lovely Bellefonte. The restaurant and microbrewery is housed in a former gristmill that was condemned and slated for destruction several decades ago. A local group rallied to its cause, and it became the first building in Bellefonte to be placed on the National Register of Historic Places. Celebrate its preservation with a selection from the 1,600-bottle wine room or a pint of house-brewed beer. You'll find the same menu in the bar and main dining room. It's short and sweet, with about a dozen sandwiches, burgers, and entrées. The market fish and chips are always a good bet.

They won't take your fare at the old train station in Centre Hall. Instead, they'll serve you comfort fare like seafood lasagna and slow-roasted prime rib. Passenger service to Centre Hall ended in the 1950s, and the 1885 station eventually became the **Whistle Stop Restaurant** (104 E. Wilson St., Centre Hall, 814/364-2544, www.whistlestopcentrehall. com, 11am-8pm Wed.-Thurs., 11am-8:30pm Fri.-Sat., 11am-7pm Sun., $4-22). Look for the original ticket window inside and a restored passenger car outside.

Asian

Cozy Thai Bistro (232 S. Allen St., State College, 814/237-0139, www.cozythaibistro. com, lunch 11am-3pm Mon.-Fri. and noon-4pm Sat., dinner 5pm-9pm Mon.-Thurs., 5pm-9:30pm Fri., 4pm-9:30pm Sat., $8-16) pairs fresh herbs with imported seasonings for flavorful renditions of common dishes like pad thai and uncommon creations like Cozy Thai canapés—wedges of wheat bread topped with a mixture of deep-fried shrimp and pork.

If you don't like your stir-fry or soup at **Green Bowl** (131 W. Beaver Ave., State College, 814/238-0600, www.thegreen-bowl.com, 11am-9pm Mon.-Fri., noon-9pm

Sat.-Sun., $9-13), you've got only yourself to blame. That's because you get to pick the ingredients and sauces that go into your meal. Fortunately, an error in judgment won't leave you hungry. This is an all-you-can-eat establishment. Simply grab another bowl and start over.

Brewpubs

Beer lovers just love **Otto's Pub & Brewery** (2235 N. Atherton St., State College, 814/867-6886, www.ottospubandbrewery.com, 11am-10pm Sun.-Thurs., 11am-11pm Fri.-Sat., bar closes 2 hours later, $9-24), which offers about a dozen brews daily and taps a firkin every Friday. The food more than holds its own, thanks to a chef who's partial to fresh ingredients from local producers. Otto's beers even find their way into the entrées.

Elk Creek Café + Aleworks (100 W. Main St., Millheim, 814/349-8850, www.elkcreek-cafe.net, 4pm-10pm Wed.-Thurs., noon-11pm Fri.-Sat., 11am-2pm Sun., $4-23) is 20-some miles from State College, but its craft beers, from-scratch cuisine, and music hall bring in the crowds. The proprietors strive for a zero-waste operation, so no need to feel guilty about that plateful of Belgian-style fries. The fryer oil powers a diesel Mercedes.

Cajun and Creole

★ **Spats Cafe & Speakeasy** (142 E. College Ave., State College, 814/238-7010, www. spatscafe.com, 11:30am-9pm Mon.-Thurs., 11:30am-9:30pm Fri.-Sat., $8-35) does New Orleans proud with flawlessly executed Cajun and Creole cuisine. Lazily spinning fans and deep red walls evoke the sensuality of the southern seaport, while dishes like jambalaya, pan-fried gator, and chicken and andouille gumbo make a po'boy out of anyone who passes up this State College gem.

Indian

The popular lunch buffet at **India Pavilion** (222 E. Calder Way, State College, 814/237-3400, www.indiapavilion.net, lunch 11:30am-2:30pm daily, dinner 5pm-10pm daily, $9-20) delights vegetarians and omnivores alike. South Indian specialties like *uttapam* and *idli* make an appearance during weekend buffets. *Thalis*—platters laden with a little bit of a lot of dishes—are a good dinner choice for the uninitiated. Bring your own booze if you like. There's no corkage fee.

INFORMATION

For information on everything from birdwatching to brewpubs, stop by the headquarters of the **Central Pennsylvania Convention & Visitors Bureau** (800 E. Park Ave., State College, 814/231-1400, www.visitpennstate.org, 7:30am-6pm Mon.-Fri., 9am-6pm Sat.-Sun.) across from Beaver Stadium.

GETTING THERE AND AROUND

State College is in Centre County, so named because it's smack-dab in the center of Pennsylvania. It's about 140 miles northeast of Pittsburgh via Route 22 east and I-99 north, 165 miles northwest of Baltimore via I-83 north and Routes 22 and 322 west, and 190 miles northwest of Philadelphia via I-76 west and Routes 22 and 322 west.

University Park Airport (SCE, 814/865-5511, www.universityparkairport.com), just a couple of miles from Beaver Stadium, offers daily flights from Detroit, Philadelphia, and Washington Dulles International Airport (IAD) in Virginia. **Greyhound** (800/231-2222, www.greyhound.com) and **Megabus** (877/462-6342, www.megabus.com) offer intercity bus service to State College.

Local bus service is provided by the Centre Area Transportation Authority, or **CATA** (814/238-2282, www.catabus.com). One-way adult cash fare is $1.50, and transfers are free. Bus drivers don't carry change. CATA provides fare-free transportation around the Penn State campus and between campus and downtown State College.

Local taxi services include **AA Taxi Inc.** (814/231-8294, www.statecollegetaxi.com) and **Handy Delivery** (814/355-5555, www. handydelivery.com).

Raystown Lake Region

At 8,300 acres, Raystown Lake is the largest lake entirely within Pennsylvania. Search for it on a map and you won't find a big blue blob. Raystown is a corkscrew of a waterway, 28 miles of zig and zag. The lake in Huntingdon County owes its existence to a dam on the Raystown Branch of the Juniata River, built in the early 1970s to reduce flood damage. The dam wasn't yet completed when Hurricane Agnes dumped as much as 19 inches of rain in parts of Pennsylvania, killing dozens. Still, the lake stored so much floodwater that communities along the Juniata and Susquehanna Rivers were spared an estimated $60 million of damage. To boot, the lake has made tourism the second largest industry after agriculture in Huntingdon County. Raystown attracts about two million visitors a year. The U.S. Army Corps of Engineers, which manages the lake and surrounding land, places no limits on boat size or horsepower, making Raystown a mecca for boating, Jet Skiing, and waterskiing enthusiasts. Thanks to no-wake areas, it's also popular with anglers, bird-watchers, and other connoisseurs of quietude. The island-riddled lake is home to stripers, walleye, musky, crappie, and other game fish. (Bring high-quality tackle. The lake creatures are fighters.) Bald eagles nest in the tree-covered hills that give the lake its snakelike shape.

You might expect a lake of such beauty to be ringed with homes and resorts, but the federal government and many locals frown on development here. Only about 2 percent of the 118-mile shoreline is developed. There are accommodations aplenty in the hills and valleys surrounding the lake, but it isn't impossible to find waterfront digs, especially if your idea of a good time includes a tent. If the shore isn't close enough, you can stay *on* the lake. Raystown Lake is one of the few places in Pennsylvania where you can rent a houseboat—complete with hot tub.

★ SEVEN POINTS RECREATION AREA

There's no better place to kick off your "Raycation" than **Seven Points Recreation Area** (Seven Points Rd., Hesston, 814/658-3405, http://raystown.nab.usace.army.mil), located in the central region of the 28-mile-long lake. It's the largest developed area at Raystown and, along with Lake Raystown Resort, one of two hubs of activity. The recreation options include boating, swimming, hiking, and camping. Start your visit at the **Raystown Lake Region Visitor Center** (6993 Seven Points Rd., Hesston, 9am-5pm daily Memorial Day-Labor Day, hours vary in off-season), where you can pick up information about everything from boat launching at Raystown to rock concerts in nearby Huntington. The two-story facility also offers exhibits about area history and wildlife, a gift shop, and stunning views of the lake.

Boating

Seven Points is home to one of eight public

Don't Tempt the Teddy

What do you do if you're boating on Raystown Lake and see a black bear taking a dip? Take a picture, of course. Besides that? Steer clear. Avoid the temptation to speed toward the teddy for a closer look. Bears can grab hold of a boat and come aboard faster than you can say "ahoy." Many of the bears at Raystown Lake were brought there because they did naughty things like pillage trash cans or bird-feeders in residential areas, which is to say that they're not shy of humans.

boat launches at Raystown. It's unique in that it has overflow trailer parking. That makes it a wise choice on summer weekends and holidays, when launches can fill to capacity. There's no fee for parking or boat launching. For more information on boating at Raystown or to check parking status, call the U.S. Army Corps of Engineers at 814/658-3405.

Seven Points is also home to one of two full-service marinas at Raystown. With roughly 950 slips, **Seven Points Marina** (5922 Seven Points Marina Dr., Hesston, 814/658-3074, www.7pointsmarina.com) is Pennsylvania's largest marina. It's one of the few places where you can rent a live-aboard houseboat. Don't think you could live on a boat? You probably haven't seen a boat with a wet bar, sun deck, sliding board, and hot tub. Check the marina website for photos and descriptions of the rental houseboats, which sleep anywhere from four to 10 people. They can be rented from Monday afternoon to Friday morning (four nights) or Friday afternoon to Monday morning (three nights), with prices starting at $945 during peak season (mid-June through August). Off-season discounts are available.

The marina's rental fleet also includes ski pontoon boats and fishing skiffs, which are available by the hour or day. Eight-person pontoon boats, which come with everything you need for waterskiing or tubing, are $125 per hour or $400-450 per day during peak season. Four-person fishing skiffs start at $50 per hour or $100 per day during peak season.

For those who prefer manpower to horsepower, Huntingdon-based **Rothrock Outfitters** (814/643-7226, www.rothrockoutfitters.com) offers rental kayaks and canoes at the marina noon-6pm Monday-Thursday and 10am-6pm Friday-Sunday during the warmer months.

If you'd rather leave the navigating to pros, hop aboard the marina's 75-foot touring boat, the **Princess.** Sightseeing cruises are offered weekends from mid-May to mid-October and daily from mid-June to late August. The two-hour tours cost $15 for adults, $14 for seniors, and $7.50 for children 4-12. For a schedule of dinner cruises or information on private charters, visit the marina website.

Hiking and Biking

The forests, meadows, and rocky outcrops surrounding Raystown Lake are threaded with more than 65 miles of trail. Seven Points Recreation Area affords opportunities for short nature walks, long mountain bike excursions, and everything in between.

Raystown Lake Region Visitor Center

The **Hillside Nature Trail,** a 0.5-mile loop behind the Raystown Lake Region Visitor Center, snakes through songbird habitats and serves up a scrumptious view of Seven Points Marina. The **Old Loggers Trail,** a 4.5-mile loop connecting Seven Points Campground and the primitive Susquehannock Campground, offers moderate hiking. Exhibits along the trail explain how proper forest management improves food and cover for wildlife.

The 33-mile **Allegrippis Trail System** (www.allegrippistrails.com), which attracts mountain bike enthusiasts from as far as Hawaii and Scotland, has two trailheads at Seven Points. Designed for mountain bikers, the network of single-track trails is also beloved by hikers, cross-country skiers, and snowshoers. Huntingdon-based **Rothrock Outfitters** (814/643-7226, www.rothrock-outfitters.com) offers rental bikes at Seven Points Marina noon-6pm Monday-Thursday and 10am-6pm Friday-Sunday during the warmer months.

Trail maps are available at the Raystown Lake Region Visitor Center or online at http://raystown.nab.usace.army.mil.

Swimming

Though swimming is allowed in most parts of Raystown Lake, the U.S. Army Corps of Engineers encourages visitors to use one of two public beaches, which are inspected to ensure safety. Open daily from Memorial Day weekend through Labor Day weekend, **Seven Points Beach** boasts an array of amenities, including water trampolines, a playground, showers, flush toilets, and a food concession.

Picknicking

Picnic tables and pedestal charcoal grills can be found near Seven Points Beach (open daily Memorial Day weekend-Labor Day weekend) and in other parts of Seven Points. The good news: There's no fee to use them. The bad news: They're available on a first-come, first-served basis and cannot be reserved. It's best to arrive early, especially on a holiday weekend. If worse comes to worst, you can always find a grassy spot and roll out a picnic blanket.

Seven Points also has several picnic shelters that accommodate as many as 80 people. Shelter reservations are $50 and can be made by calling the Corps at 814/658-3405. Unreserved shelters are available on a first-come, first-served basis for no charge.

Camping

With more than 260 campsites, **Seven Points**

Seven Points Marina

Campground is the largest campground in the Raystown region. Reservations are a must during the peak season of Memorial Day weekend through Labor Day weekend and can only be made through Recreation.gov (877/444-6777, www.recreation.gov). In the off-season, sites are available on a first-come, first-served basis. Camping fees start at $23 per night. Waterfront sites are the priciest at $30 per night.

Other Activities

Countless carp congregate at Seven Points Marina, so bring a loaf of bread or pick up a 50-cent bag of fish food at the marina store.

Bring a lawn chair or blanket, too, because Seven Points Recreation Area is home to an **amphitheater** that hosts concerts and other programs on Friday and Saturday evenings throughout the summer.

LAKE RAYSTOWN RESORT

Along with Seven Points Recreation Area, **Lake Raystown Resort, Lodge & Conference Center** (3101 Chipmunk Crossing, Entriken, 814/658-3500, www.raystownresort.com) is one of two hubs of activity at Raystown. Located at the southern end of the lake, the family-owned resort offers a wider array of lodging options than Seven Points—from campsites with cable hookups to beachfront bungalows to log cabins perched on cliffs overlooking the lake. You don't have to be a resort guest to enjoy its amenities, which include a 650-slip **marina;** a **mini golf** course; and a **water park** featuring twisting slides, an inner tube ride, and a spray park with a 500-gallon dumping bucket.

Like Seven Points Marina, Lake Raystown Resort boasts a **rental boat** fleet that includes live-aboard houseboats. The four-bedroom, two-bath houseboats sleep as many as 10 people and can be rented Monday-Friday or Friday-Monday for $2,200. For $3,600, the boat is yours for an entire week. The rental fleet also includes ski pontoon boats, 15-horsepower fishing boats, and canoes.

Pontoon boats, which come with everything you need for waterskiing or tubing, can be rented 8:30am-5pm or 5:30pm-7:30pm for $200-460 per period. Fishing boats are $30 per hour or $150 per day. Canoes go for $10 per hour or $75 per day.

Lake Raystown Resort is home to the **Proud Mary Showboat,** used for public cruises from late May through October as well as private events. Ninety-minute sightseeing cruises, which are offered at 2:15pm daily until Labor Day and weekends thereafter, are $9.50 per person. Check the resort website for a schedule of breakfast, karaoke, dinner, and late-night cruises.

The resort is also home to **Angry Musky Outfitters** (814/280-1344), a fishing guide service with the motto "Forget Fishing, Let's Go Catching!" Captain Kirk Reynolds, who has been fishing the lake since childhood, offers four-, six-, and eight-hour trips on a boat that accommodates up to six passengers. Charter rates start at $225. On Wednesday mornings, Angry Musky offers a four-hour public fishing trip for $50 per person. Reservations are required.

OTHER SIGHTS
Historic Huntingdon

The "big town" in Raystown country is the small town of Huntingdon. It's one of the oldest continuously inhabited settlements in Pennsylvania and the seat of Huntingdon County. It's also home to **Juniata College,** a liberal arts school founded in 1876 by members of the Church of the Brethren. The **Juniata College Museum of Art** (17th and Moore Streets, 814/641-3505, www.juniata.edu/museum, 10am-4pm Mon.-Fri. and noon-4pm Sat. Sept.-Apr., noon-4pm Wed.-Fri. May-Aug., free admission) is worth a visit. It occupies Carnegie Hall, which was built in 1907 as the college library and features a grand rotunda and stained glass oculus. The permanent collection includes paintings by key members of the Hudson River School and dozens of portrait miniatures by American and European artists.

In 1988 the college commissioned Maya Lin to create an open-air chapel within a nature preserve near campus. The architect responsible for the Vietnam Veterans Memorial in Washington DC planted a large circle of rough granite stones on a hilltop and a smooth granite disk on a slightly higher neighboring hill. To reach the *Peace Chapel* from the museum, follow Moore Street north to Cold Springs Road, turn right, continue to Warm Springs Avenue, and take another right. Drive four blocks and turn left onto Peace Chapel Road. The site is open from dawn to dusk. It's not the only example of environmental art in Huntingdon. Look for murals on the corner of Penn and 8th Streets and on the concrete pillars of an abandoned railroad trestle that runs through Portstown Park. Both celebrate the region's history.

History goes 3-D during **Mayfest** (814/386-2638, www.mayfestofhuntingdon. org, free), held on the last Saturday in April. (That's no typo. Huntingdon's Mayfest does indeed take place in April.) The event offers a "stroll through history," with five different eras represented in a five-block area. Costumed performers and vendors help the Renaissance, the tie-dyed days of Woodstock, and other themes come alive. It's the only festival of its kind in the state.

Swigart Automobile Museum

You might recognize one of the mint-condition machines at the **Swigart Automobile Museum** (12031 William Penn Hwy./Rte. 22, Huntingdon, 814/643-0885, www.swigartmuseum.com, 10am-5pm daily Memorial Day-Oct., open until 6pm Fri., admission $7, seniors $6.50, children 6-12 $3). Its 1948 blue Tucker was used in the 1988 film *Tucker: The Man and His Dream,* starring Jeff Bridges. Another celebrity on permanent display: the 1960 Volkswagen named Herbie, aka "The Love Bug." What started as a private collection in the 1920s now includes about 150 cars, some of which are one of a kind. Antique bicycles, toys, and automobile artwork round out the collection. The museum's lawn comes alive with candy-colored antiques during the annual auto meet in August.

Rockhill Trolley Museum

About half an hour southeast of Huntington, the rural village of Rockhill has long been a mecca for rail fans thanks to the **East Broad Top Railroad** (421 Meadow St., Rockhill, 814/447-3011, www.ebtrr.com), the only original narrow-gauge railroad east of the Rockies. In 2012, the EBT ceased operating as a tourist railroad, but tours of the rail yard and 1882 roundhouse are available by prearrangement. There's still good reason to make a trip to Rockhill. Next door to the East Broad Top, the **Rockhill Trolley Museum** (430 Meadow St., Rockhill, 814/447-9576, www.rockhilltrolley.org, 11am-4:20pm Sat.-Sun. Memorial Day weekend-Oct., admission $7, children 3-12 $4) is home to about 15 city, suburban, and interurban trolley cars that operated in places near (e.g., Philadelphia) and far (e.g., Portugal). The collection includes several operational trolleys, giving visitors a chance to experience an all-but-extinct mode of transportation. Trolleys depart about once an hour.

Rockhill's fleet includes the only open car operating in Pennsylvania. Assembled in balmy Rio de Janeiro in 1912, it was acquired by the museum in 1965, brought to New York aboard a coffee bean ship, and transported to rural Rockhill Furnace by railroad and highway. In addition to trolley cars, the museum owns a handful of cars used to maintain track, remove snow, and move freight cars.

The museum's regular season runs through October, but cars are called into service in late November and early December, when the trolley line is flanked with lighted decorations. Check the museum's website for information about Polar Bear Express Trolley, Santa's Trolley, and other special events.

Rail fans, consider bunking at the **Iron Rail Bed & Breakfast** (371 Meadow St., Rockhill Furnace, 814/447-3984, www.ironrailbandb. com, $70-110). Once home to the East Broad Top's superintendent, the 1885 Victorian was completely renovated in 2007. It has four guest

Come Wednesday, Go to the Big Valley

You won't find Big Valley on a Pennsylvania map, and that's fine by the Amish and Mennonite communities that call it home. Unlike their brethren in the Lancaster region, the "plain people" of the bucolic Big Valley have managed to stay out of the limelight for more than 200 years. The wide valley nestled between two long ridges is more properly known as Kishacoquillas Valley, in honor of a Shawnee chief who warned settlers of attacks by other tribes, but "Kishacoquillas" doesn't roll off the tongue like "big." The valley floor is a tapestry of more than 1,000 farms. Wednesday is a good day to visit the largest of its five towns and villages: wee little Belleville. From daybreak to midafternoon, Amish and Mennonites mingle with worldlier folk at the **Belleville Livestock Market** (Sale Barn Ln., Belleville, 717/935-2146), where everything from pies to piglets trades hands. Vendors peddle produce and flowers, new junk and old treasures. Chickens squawk and children romp. To find the action from Belleville's Main Street (Route 655), simply follow the parade of horse-drawn buggies. White-topped buggies belong to the most conservative of the valley's Amish. Black tops and yellow tops signify membership in more progressive congregations. Big Valley is believed to be the only place where the three coexist.

The drive from either State College or Huntingdon takes about 40 minutes. Since an early arrival ensures the best selection, consider spending Tuesday night at **Brookmere Winery** (5369 Rte. 655, Belleville, 717/935-2195, www.brookmerewine.com, tasting and store hours 10am-5pm Mon.-Sat., 1pm-4pm Sun.). That's right, at a winery. In 2008, winemakers Ed and Cheryl Glick transformed an 1866 mansion into a B&B with four guest rooms, all with private baths. Rates at the **Vineyard Inn** range $95-175.

Of course, the Belleville market isn't the only opportunity to witness a way of life that's little changed since the 18th century. Follow any road branching from Route 655 and you're liable to find Amish farms. It shouldn't be long before you see a sign at the bottom of a lane advertising carrots or cabbage or rabbits or pine furniture. Drive down the lane for the goods and a closer gander. Be aware that the Amish don't do business on Sundays. If you spot dozens of buggies outside a home, chances are they're worshiping inside.

---

bedrooms and a sitting room with an antique piano. A tree-shaded side porch affords views of the EBT complex.

Show Caves

The Raystown region boasts Pennsylvania's largest concentration of caves, including two that are open to the public for tours. **Lincoln Caverns** (7703 William Penn Hwy./Rte. 22, Huntingdon, 814/643-0268, www.lincolncaverns.com, open daily Mar.-Nov. and weekends in Dec., tour $12.98, seniors $11.98, children 4-12 $7.48), three miles west of Huntingdon, was discovered in 1930 during the construction of Route 22. Hour-long tours of its winding passageways and otherworldly rooms depart every few minutes during the summer and every half hour in spring and fall. The temperature is a constant 52 degrees, so bring a sweatshirt or jacket even in summer. For a modest fee, you can stay overnight at

the primitive Warrior Ridge Campgrounds at Lincoln Caverns. There's no charge to use the picnic pavilions, nature trails, or meditation chapel.

Pennsylvania's largest limestone cave can be found on the banks of Spruce Creek about 18 miles northwest of Huntingdon. **Indian Caverns** (5374 Indian Trail, Spruce Creek, 814/632-7578, www.indiancaverns.com, open weekends Apr.-May, daily Memorial Day weekend-Labor Day, and weekends Sept.-Oct., tour $13, seniors $12, children 4-12 $11) opened to the public in 1929, but it has been visited by humans for eons. Arrowheads and other artifacts found in the cave indicate that Native Americans used the cave more than 400 years ago. In the early 19th century, it served as a hideout for the outlaw David "Robber" Lewis and his entourage. Tours depart on the hour from 10am to 5pm and cover almost a mile of cavern, including a naturally phosphorescent room. The temperature is a constant 56 degrees.

ENTERTAINMENT AND EVENTS
Festivals and Events

Folk musicians flock to Huntingdon County twice a year: first for **Folk College** (Juniata College, 814/643-6220, www.folkcollege.com, May, registration fee charged) and later for the **Greenwood Furnace Folk Gathering** (Greenwood Furnace State Park, 814/643-6220, www.folkgathering.com, Sept., registration fee charged). Both feature workshops, jam sessions, and concerts.

Thousands of Christian music fans turn out for **Creation** (Agape Farm, Shirleysburg, 800/327-6921, www.creationfest.com, late June, admission charged), a four-day festival on 400 acres. There's music from morning to night, worship services, water baptisms, and a whole lot more. Revelers hike "Jesus Mountain" behind the main stage for heavenly views.

The **Huntingdon County Fair** (10455 Fairgrounds Access Rd., Huntingdon, 814/643-4452, www.huntingdoncountyfair.com, early Aug., admission charged) is an agricultural expo extraordinaire, complete with midway rides, live music, a fair queen contest, and a demolition derby. A museum dedicated to agricultural history, normally open by appointment only, is open throughout the week.

SPORTS AND RECREATION

Raystown Lake isn't the only recreational amenity in these parts. Huntingdon County is chockablock with creeks, parks, forests, hiking trails, and wildlife. It's long been known for world-class fishing. In 2009, with the opening of the Allegrippis Trail System, it also became a mecca for mountain bikers.

Allegrippis Trail System

Designed by the International Mountain Bicycling Association, the 33-mile **Allegrippis Trail System** (www.allegrippistrails.com) attracts **mountain bikers** from far and wide. It's a stacked-loop system consisting of numerous single-track trails, which means that users can customize the length and difficulty of their trip. The trails, which traverse ridges, woods, and the shores of Raystown Lake, also make for excellent **hiking, bird-watching, cross-country skiing,** and **snowshoeing.** A detailed map can be purchased at the Raystown Lake Region Visitor Center (6993 Seven Points Rd., Hesston, 9am-5pm daily Memorial Day-Labor Day, hours vary in off-season).

There are two main public trailheads: one at the visitors center and another along Baker's Hollow Road near the Susquehannock Campground. To reach the Baker's Hollow trailhead from southbound Route 26 at Route 22, continue south eight miles to the blinking light, and turn left toward Seven Points (marked by sign). Continue 2.7 miles, and turn left onto Baker's Hollow Road. Continue 1.5 miles to the trailhead (marked by sign). There's a third trailhead along Seven Points Road between the Seven Points entrance station and the visitors center, but parking is very limited.

Rothrock Outfitters (418 Penn St., Huntingdon, 814/643-7226, www.rothrockoutfitters.com, 11am-5pm Mon.-Tues., 11am-4pm Wed., 11am-6pm Thurs.-Fri., 9am-5pm Sat., 9am-noon Sun.) offers rental bikes and a whole lot of expertise. In summer, you can save yourself a trip to downtown Huntingdon and rent a bike from Rothrock's seasonal outpost at Seven Points Marina (5922 Seven Points Marina Dr., Hesston).

Bird-Watching

Raystown Lake boasted four active bald eagle nests as of 2013—and that's not the only thing that brings birders to the region. In spring, shorebirds are a sure thing at the man-made **Old Crow Wetland** off Route 22 near Hoss's Steak and Sea House (9016 William Penn Hwy./Rte. 22, Huntingdon). More than 150 avian species have been inventoried in **Whipple Dam State Park** (20 miles northeast of Huntingdon off Rte. 26, 814/667-1800, www.visitpaparks.com).

For guaranteed sightings of golden and bald eagles, owls, and other birds of prey, head to Penn State's **Shavers Creek Environmental Center** (3400 Discovery Rd., Petersburg, 814/863-2000, www.shaverscreek.org, 10am-5pm daily mid-Feb.-mid-Dec., free admission). It's home to injured raptors that can't fend for themselves in the wild. The center's annual Birding Cup, held the first weekend in May, challenges teams to identify as many species as possible in a 24-hour period.

Fishing

Raystown Lake. Juniata River. Spruce Creek. Standing Stone Creek. Aughwick Creek. Shavers Creek. Great Trough Creek. The list of waterways goes on and on, and so does the fishing season. Pros have been casting their lines in this region for decades. Hobbyists unfamiliar with the area may wish to hire a guide.

Lake Raystown is well stocked with boat charter services. Sparky Price is the record-shattering angler behind **Trophy Guide Service** (814/627-5231, www.trophyguide.com). The 53-pound striper he pulled out of the lake is the largest the state has seen. Lake Raystown Resort's **Angry Musky Outfitters** (814/280-1344, www.raystownresort.com) has as its motto "Forget Fishing, Let's Go Catching!"

Open since 1986, **Spruce Creek Outfitters** (4910 Spruce Creek Rd., Spruce Creek, 814/632-3071, www.sprucecreekoutfitters.org, hours vary by season) specializes in fly-fishing on the Little Juniata River, which is thick with wild brown trout.

Hiking

The Raystown region is a hiker's paradise, with trails for every skill level. **Seven Points Recreation Area** (Seven Points Rd., Hesston, 814/658-3405, http://raystown.nab.usace.army.mil) is a good starting point for easy or moderate hiking. It's home to the **Hillside**

Nature Trail, a 0.5-mile loop through songbird habitats, and trailheads for the 4.5-mile **Old Loggers Trail** and 33-mile **Allegrippis Trail System**. Designed for mountain bikers, the Allegrippis Trails are no less appealing to joggers and hikers. Maps of these and other trails are available at the visitors center at Seven Points (6993 Seven Points Rd., Hesston, 9am-5pm daily Memorial Day-Labor Day, hours vary in off-season).

For serious trekkers, there's the **Terrace Mountain Trail,** which spans the eastern side of Raystown Lake. The 30-mile route has five access points, so you can tackle it all at once or in segments. Overnight camping with potable water is available at two access points, and primitive camping is permitted at designated spots along the trail. For trail conditions and more information, contact the U.S. Army Corps of Engineers (814/658-3405, http://raystown.nab.usace.army.mil).

Twelve miles of trails traverse **Trough Creek State Park** (16362 Little Valley Rd., James Creek, 814/658-3847, www.visitpaparks.com), a gorge formed as Great Trough Creek cuts through Terrace Mountain and empties into Raystown Lake. Among the wondrous sights: the large boulder known as Balanced Rock because it clings to the edge of a cliff, beautiful Rainbow Falls, mountain laurel blooms in June, rhododendron blooms in July, and an occasional copperhead.

Hunting

It's not called Huntingdon County for nothing. The home of Raystown Lake is also home to a plethora of wild game: whitetail deer, rabbit, turkey, grouse, pheasant, fox, duck, goose, and bobcat, to name a few. A Pennsylvania hunting license is required. Check the website of the Pennsylvania Game Commission (www.pgc.state.pa.us) for hunting seasons and regulations. Hunting and fishing licenses are available at **Jaydens Outdoors** (11559 William Penn Hwy./Rte. 22, Huntingdon, 814/506-8340, 9am-8pm Mon.-Fri., 9am-5pm Sat.-Sun.). The store specializes in hunting, fishing, and archery supplies, and its staff is impressively knowledgeable.

ACCOMMODATIONS

The Raystown region is notable as one of the few places in Pennsylvania where you can rent a houseboat, but its overnight options don't end there.

Under $100

With roughly 2,000 campsites, the Raystown region calls to nature-loving budget travelers. There are several campgrounds on federal property ringing Raystown Lake, including the amenity-rich **Seven Points Campground** (open seasonally, $23-30), the primitive **Susquehannock Campground** (open seasonally, $12-17), and the remote **Nancy's Camp** (open year-round, $10), which is accessible only by boat. You can reserve a site at Seven Points or Susquehannock through the federal recreation portal Recreation.gov (877/444-6777, www.recreation.gov). Sites at Nancy's Camp cannot be reserved. For information on site availability, call the U.S. Army Corps of Engineers ranger station at 814/658-6809.

The waterfront **Lake Raystown Resort, Lodge & Conference Center** (3101 Chipmunk Crossing, Entriken, 814/658-3500, www.raystownresort.com, campground open seasonally, campsite $32-75) has a variety of lodging options, including more than 200 campsites. Campground amenities include water, electricity, cable hookups, and wireless Internet service. But it's the list of resort amenities—mini golf, water park, rental boats, and more—that makes campers come back again and again.

The smaller **Heritage Cove Resort** (1172 River Rd., Saxton, 814/635-3386, www.heritagecoveresort.com, open seasonally, campsite $45-55) has about 200 campsites with water, electricity, sewage hookups, picnic tables, and fire rings. The retreat at the southern end of Raystown Lake also offers two- and three-bedroom cottages starting at $179. Resort amenities include a pool, playground,

volleyball court, and camp store. Canoes, kayaks, a pontoon boat, and bicycles are available for rent.

$100-200

★ **The Inn at Solvang** (10611 Standing Stone Rd., Huntingdon, 814/643-3035, www.solvang.com, $105-145) looks like something out of *Gone with the Wind*. The three-story brick mansion with four massive columns sits at the end of a tree-lined lane off Route 26 about four miles north of Huntingdon. (It's easy to miss the turnoff. Look for an ornate *S* between two white posts.) Gourmet breakfasts are served on fine china, but the atmosphere is far from prim. Guests are welcome to fish on the stream that runs through the property.

The menu of accommodations at **Lake Raystown Resort, Lodge & Conference Center** (3101 Chipmunk Crossing, Entriken, 814/658-3500, www.raystownresort.com) is as diverse as the menu of activities. The lodge ($106-209 during peak season) has 50 guest rooms and two suites, each with a private balcony overlooking the lake. You could also opt for a one-bedroom log cabin ($115-153), a cottage ($145-175) complete with master bedroom and full kitchen, a two-bedroom beachfront bungalow ($1,400 per week during peak season, $139-159 in off-season), or a villa ($815-880 per 3-night weekend stay or 4-night weekday stay, $1,500-1,600 per week) nestled in the woods.

Over $200

For a romantic getaway à la Tarzan and Jane, swing over to **Junglewood** (2553 Timberlake Dr., James Creek, 800/673-9211, www.shybeaverlakeviewwest.com, $240-255), perched high above Raystown Lake. The vacation home feels like a treehouse—a treehouse with satellite TV and a large hot tub.

FOOD

Like many recreation areas, Raystown Lake is blessed with homespun eateries that you can walk into water-soaked or mud-splattered and still be greeted with a smile. Burgers, hoagies, pizza, ice cream, and other foods that don't call for utensils are the norm. But exceptions can be found.

Huntingdon

Start your day at **Standing Stone Coffee** (1229 Mifflin St., Huntingdon, 814/643-4545, www.standingstonecoffeecompany.com, 7am-9:30pm Mon.-Thurs., 7am-11pm Fri., 7:30am-11pm Sat., 10am-9pm Sun.), which roasts its own java. Pair your drip-brewed or French-pressed coffee with a mini quiche, baked oatmeal, or other breakfast item. Standing Stone has free Wi-Fi and—get this—a self-service laundry.

The husband and wife behind **Boxer's Café** (418 Penn St., 814/643-5013, 11am-9pm Mon.-Thurs., 11am-10pm Fri.-Sat., under $10) refuel their modified vehicles with oil used in the kitchen's fryers. With wings, Cajun fries, and breaded mushrooms on the menu, there's nary a shortage. Named for the dog breed, not the fighting sport, Boxer's is known for its large selection of import beers and microbrews.

For an upscale dinner, there's ★ **Mimi's** (312 Penn St., Huntingdon, 814/643-7200, www.mimisrestaurant.net, 4:30pm-10pm Mon.-Sat., bar open as late as 2am, $8-28). The restaurant and martini bar offers sandwiches and burgers along with entrées like veal Oscar and chicken piccata. Its lengthy cocktail menu takes a while to digest.

There's more than one way to satisfy a sweet tooth during your stay in Raystown country. **Sweethearts Confectionery** (723 Washington St., 814/643-3785, 8am-6pm Mon.-Sat.) in downtown Huntingdon specializes in scratch-baked cupcakes. It also carries a wide selection of candies, including nostalgic varieties and Jelly Belly products. Just outside of town along Route 22, **Gardners Candies** (9154 William Penn Hwy./Rte. 22, 814/643-5302, www.gardnerscandies.com, 10am-8pm Mon.-Sat., noon-5pm Sun.) offers ice cream and a fantastic variety of locally made chocolates. Founded in 1897 by a 16-year-old boy, Gardners is famous for its Original Peanut Butter Meltaways.

Vicinity of Huntingdon

Four miles east of Huntingdon along Route 22, **Top's Diner** (12151 William Penn Hwy./Rte. 22, Mill Creek, 814/643-4169, www.topsdiner.net, 6am-8pm Mon.-Thurs., 6am-9pm Fri.-Sat., 7am-8pm Sun., $3-15) is known for its signature burger and daily specials. The decades-old diner also boasts outdoor seating, so you can have a side of sunshine with your meal.

INFORMATION

The hilltop **Raystown Lake Region Visitor Center** (6993 Seven Points Rd., Hesston, 9am-5pm daily Memorial Day-Labor Day, hours vary in off-season) is a good place to start your "Raycation," as the folks who market the lake like to say. It houses the Huntingdon County Visitors Bureau (814/658-0060, www.raystown.org) and offices of the U.S. Army Corps of Engineers (814/658-3405, http://raystown.nab.usace.army.mil). You'll find bushels of free brochures, a gift shop, and exhibits on the region's history, geology, and wildlife. A deck affords majestic views of the lake and Seven Points Marina.

GETTING THERE AND AROUND

Huntingdon, the Raystown region's commercial center, is about 30 miles east of Altoona via Route 22 and 30 miles south of State College via Route 26. If you're flying commercial, you can't get closer than **Altoona-Blair County Airport** (AOO, 814/793-2027, www.altoonablaircountyairport.com) or **University Park Airport** (SCE, 814/865-5511, www.universityparkairport.com) in State College. The larger **Harrisburg International Airport** (MDT, 888/235-9442, www.flyhia.com) is about 100 miles east of Huntingdon. **Amtrak** (800/872-7245, www.amtrak.com) provides train service to Huntingdon from New York City, Philadelphia, Harrisburg, Pittsburgh, and other cities on its Pennsylvanian line. Huntingdon's train station (4th and Allegheny Streets) is less than 500 feet from **Rothrock Outfitters** (418 Penn St., 814/643-7226, www.rothrockoutfitters.com), where you can rent a bicycle, and a short walk from **Enterprise Rent-A-Car** (100 S. 4th St., 814/643-5778, www.enterprise.

com). There's no bus service in Huntingdon. **Maidens Taxi Service** (814/644-9999) is your best bet if you don't have wheels.

To get to Raystown Lake from Huntingdon, take Route 26 south and watch for brown lake access signs.

Bedford and Vicinity

As British troops carved a wagon road over the Allegheny Mountains in 1758, they stopped to construct fortifications along the way. One of these, Fort Bedford, sat on a bluff overlooking the Raystown Branch of the Juniata River. The supply fort built to support Britain's campaign against the French had the side effect of transforming a backwoods into a bona fide town. Bedford homesteads became hot property because the fort provided protection from Indian attacks.

Bedford got even hotter in the 1800s, when word spread of mineral-rich springs with curative powers. People traveled great distances to "take the waters." The luxe Bedford Springs Hotel attracted a bevy of politicians and other upper-echelon types during the 19th and early 20th centuries. In 1858, President James Buchanan received the first transatlantic telegram at the resort, which had come to be known as his "summer White House." It closed in the 1980s but reopened in 2007 after a $120 million restoration and expansion. Thanks to

its rebirth and relatively low property costs, the Bedford area is once again gaining popularity as an idyllic retreat for city folk.

SIGHTS
Historic Bedford

Fort Bedford deteriorated in the 1770s, but a museum suggestive of a blockhouse stands near the site. The **Fort Bedford Museum** (110 Fort Bedford Dr., 814/623-8891, www.fortbedfordmuseum.org, 11am-5pm Wed.-Sun. May-Oct., admission $5, seniors $4.50, students 6-18 $3.50) houses a model of the irregularly shaped fort and a variety of military and civilian artifacts. The jewel of its collection is a 1758 flag that hung in the officers' quarters. It was a gift from England's fourth Duke of Bedford, for whom the fort was named.

The **Espy House** (123 East Pitt St.) served as President George Washington's headquarters during the Whiskey Rebellion. Snap a few pictures, but don't expect its

Washington Slept Here

Farmers in western Pennsylvania didn't take kindly to a federal excise tax imposed on whiskey producers in 1791. They took out their irritation on tax collectors and other government representatives (think tar and feathers). When their bullying turned to outright insurrection in 1794, President George Washington invoked martial law to summon a force of nearly 13,000. He led the militia army as far west as Bedford. While his men camped in open fields, Washington slept in the home of Colonel David Espy—the nicest digs in town. It was the first and only time a U.S. president would command troops in the field.

By the time troops reached the Pittsburgh area, the epicenter of the so-called Whiskey Rebellion, most of the rebels had fled into the hills. The federal government had proven its might. The whiskey tax remained in force until 1801. In 1984, the **Espy House** was named a National Historic Landmark.

current occupants to invite you inside. For a warm welcome, try the **Golden Eagle Inn** (131 E. Pitt St., 814/624-0800, www. bedfordpainn.com). Travelers have been stopping here for a bite to eat and a bed to sleep in since the late 1700s. (Bedford's Pitt Street was once part of the Forbes Trail, the route cut by British troops in 1758 and followed by many a stagecoach driver.) The house next door was built in 1814 for Dr. John Anderson, who saw patients in the front and operated Bedford's first bank in the back. Today it's home to **Anderson House Antiques** (137 E. Pitt St., 814/623-8999, open from 10am daily except Wed.).

The architect responsible for Dr. Anderson's house built the **Bedford County Courthouse** (200 S. Juliana St.) in the late 1820s. Two self-supported circular stairways lead to a second-floor courtroom bedecked with portraits of judges.

The **Bedford County Visitors Bureau** (131 S. Juliana St., 800/765-3331, www.visit-bedfordcounty.com, 9am-5pm Mon.-Sat. and noon-5pm Sun. May-Oct., 9am-5pm Mon.-Fri. Nov.-Apr.) offers free guided tours of downtown's historic sites on Fridays May-October. Tours start at 3:30pm and last about 90 minutes. Smartphone users can download a 75-minute video tour from the bureau's website.

Old Bedford Village

A "living history village" two miles north of downtown leaves nothing to the imagination. When **Old Bedford Village** (220 Sawblade Rd., Bedford, 814/623-1156, www.oldbedfordvillage.com, 9am-5pm daily except Wed. Memorial Day-Labor Day, Thurs.-Sun. after Labor Day-Oct., admission $10, seniors $9, students 6-18 $5) isn't staging reenactments of pre-21st-century battles, its costumed artisans are demonstrating coopering, quilting, candle making, and other early American crafts. The village has more than 40 original and reconstructed structures, including a two-story log farmhouse from the 1700s and an octagonal schoolhouse built in 1851.

★ Omni Bedford Springs Resort

Bedford doctor John Anderson wasted no time when Native Americans led him to mineral-rich springs on the southern outskirts of town. In 1796 he bought a 2,200-acre swath of countryside that included the springs. Soon, patients were arriving from near and far to bathe in and drink the reputedly curative waters. At first the savvy doctor housed them in tents. In 1806 he built a hotel with stone quarried from a nearby mountain. The resort grew along with its popularity, opening one of America's first golf courses in 1895 and an indoor pool fed by spring waters a decade later. Musicians serenaded the swimmers from a balcony overlooking the pool. By the time it closed in 1986—timeworn and cash-strapped—the Bedford Springs Hotel had hosted 11 presidents and a long list of captains of industry, celebrities, and other bigwigs.

Reopened in 2007 after a restoration and expansion to the tune of $120 million, the resort offers the luxuries they enjoyed and then some. Now known as the **Omni Bedford Springs Resort** (2138 Business Rte. 220, Bedford, 814/623-8100, www.omnihotels.com, $249-409), it boasts a 30,000-square-foot spa that uses water from a spring discovered during the makeover. The restored golf course was named the top playable classic course in Pennsylvania by *Golfweek* magazine. New Italian marble flooring surrounds the lavish indoor pool, and private cabanas ring the outdoor pool.

You don't have to be a guest of the resort to enjoy the 18-hole golf course or the **Springs Eternal Spa.** And you don't have to spend an arm and a leg to have a fantastically soothing spa experience. Book any service—from a $20 eyebrow wax to a $185 mud wrap—and you can spend all the time you like sipping tea in the coed lounge, strolling in the adjacent garden, or moving between steam room, hot-water pool, and cold-water pool as part of the spa's signature self-guided bathing ritual.

Dining options include the **1796 Room,** an upscale steak and chop house, and the casual **Frontier Tavern,** where you can wash down

Omni Bedford Springs Resort lobby

a tempeh sandwich or bacon-topped burger with a Pennsylvania microbrew. S'mores lovers set up camp at the resort's fire pit.

Gravity Hill

There's a spot in suburban New Paris, about 15 miles from Bedford, where a car in neutral will roll uphill—or so it's said. From Route 30, drive to the town of Schellsburg, which is about eight miles west of Bedford. At Schellsburg's only traffic light, turn north onto Route 96, drive about four miles, and turn left onto Bethel Hollow Road. Drive about two miles to an intersection with a stop sign for oncoming traffic, and bear right. Within a quarter of a mile, you'll see "GH" spray-painted on the road. Continue past the first "GH" and stop before you reach the second "GH." Put your car in neutral. Take your foot off the break pedal. Defy gravity.

Wise men say that **Gravity Hill** (800/765-3331, www.gravityhill.com) is an example of an optical illusion, not of supernatural forces. It's a trip either way.

Covered Bridges

Bedford County boasts 14 covered bridges.

Most were built in the 1800s in the Burr-truss style, named for designer Theodore Burr, and are still drivable. A covered-bridge driving tour is available on the website of the **Bedford County Visitors Bureau** (800/765-3331, www.visitbedfordcounty.com). You can also call the visitors bureau and request a free brochure on the bridges.

ENTERTAINMENT AND EVENTS
Festivals and Events

The weeklong **Bedford County Fair** (just west of downtown Bedford on Business Rte. 30/W. Pitt St., 814/623-9011, www.bedford-fair.com, late July, admission charged) offers the usual: animal exhibitions, live music, midway rides, and a queen competition. Be sure to check out the unusually large **Coffee Pot** at the entrance to the fairgrounds. The 1920s structure was once a lunch stand along the Lincoln Highway, America's first coast-to-coast road. It was moved to its present location in 2003.

The **Fall Foliage Festival** (800/765-3331, www.bedfordfallfestival.com, first two weekends of Oct., free) brings hundreds of

one of Bedford's covered bridges

craft vendors and tens of thousands of visitors to Bedford. Live music, an antique car parade, and children's activities are festival staples.

the 1920s Coffee Pot at the entrance to the Bedford County Fairgrounds

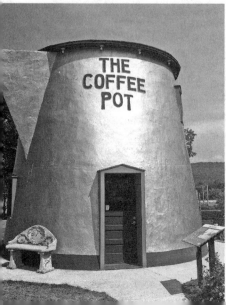

SPORTS AND RECREATION
State Parks

Blue Knob State Park (124 Park Rd., Imler, 814/276-3576, www.visitpaparks.com) in northwestern Bedford County is home to Blue Knob, Pennsylvania's second-highest mountain after Mount Davis. The mountain makes for breathtaking views and challenging hikes. Mountain biking, horseback riding, snowmobiling, cross-country skiing, hunting, and fishing are all permitted in the park. **Blue Knob All Seasons Resort** (1424 Overland Pass, Claysburg, 800/458-3403, www.blueknob.com, all-day lift ticket $38-60, children and seniors $28-40, all-day ski rental $30, snow tubing $20 per 2-hour session) offers skiing, snowboarding, and tubing on land leased from the state. The resort also has an 18-hole golf course.

Boaters may prefer the smaller **Shawnee State Park** (132 State Park Rd., Schellsburg, 814/733-4218, www.visitpaparks.com) with its 451-acre lake stocked with warm-water game fish. Paddleboats, canoes, and rowboats can be rented during the summer. A swimming beach is open 8am-sunset from late May to mid-September.

Both parks offer modern campsites starting the second Friday in April. Blue Knob's 50 tent and trailer sites close in late October. Shawnee has almost 300 sites and a camping season that stretches to late December. Reserve online at www.pa.reserveworld.com or by calling 888/727-2757.

Biking

Bedford County is home to Cannondale Bicycle Corp.'s U.S. factory, but that's not the only reason it's beloved by cyclists. They also dig its lightly traveled roads and scenic vistas. Turn-by-turn directions for about 20 rides, including an easy 12.2-mile loop that takes in four covered bridges, are available at www.visitbedfordcounty.com/bikeloops.

If you don't have wheels, head to **Fat Jimmy's Outfitters** (109 Railroad St., Bedford, 814/624-3415, www.fatjimmys. com, 10am-6pm Mon. and Wed., 10am-5pm Thurs., 9am-8pm Fri., 9am-5pm Sat.). Bicycle rentals start at $20 per day.

Grouseland Tours (467 Robinsonville Rd., Clearville, 814/784-5000, www.grouseland.com), about 25 miles southeast of Bedford, not only rents and sells Cannondales but also offers fully supported bike tours. It's especially known for its tours of the Pike 2 Bike, an abandoned highway turned bike trail.

Boating

Novice paddlers will appreciate the slow-moving Raystown Branch of the Juniata River, which flows through Bedford. Canoe and kayak rentals start at $30 per day at **Fat Jimmy's Outfitters** (109 Railroad St., Bedford, 814/624-3415, www.fatjimmys. com, 10am-6pm Mon. and Wed., 10am-5pm Thurs., 9am-8pm Fri., 9am-5pm Sat.).

Horseback Riding

Greenridge Horse Ranch (130 Horse Ranch Rd., Artemas, 814/784-5223, www.greenridgehorseranch.com) promises to have you riding "the cowboy way" in no time. Trail rides

start at $50 for a 90-minute trip. Pony rides are $35 per half hour. The ranch is closed from Thanksgiving through December, when deer hunters roam the woods.

ACCOMMODATIONS
Under $100

Clean rooms, low rates, and gracious hosts of Pennsylvania Dutch stock greet guests at **Judy's Motel** (3521 Business Rte. 220, Bedford, 814/623-9118, www.judysmotel. com, $40-50), 1.5 miles south of Pennsylvania Turnpike exit 146.

The full-service **Friendship Village Campground** (348 Friendship Village Rd., Bedford, 814/623-1677, www.friendshipvillagecampground.com, campsite $25-43, cabin $60-125, weekly rates available) has campsites, rustic cabins, and cottages complete with air-conditioning and cable TV. Amenities include two swimming pools, a miniature golf course, and an arcade room. From Memorial Day to Labor Day, the campground hosts Saturday evening "gospel sings" and Sunday morning church services.

$100-200

The impeccable **Chancellor's House Bed and Breakfast** (341 S. Juliana St., Bedford, 814/624-0374, www.thechancellorshouse. com, $130-175) in Bedford's historic district has three guest rooms with private bathrooms and a wide front porch complete with rocking chairs. Another great option in the heart of Bedford: the **Golden Eagle Inn** (131 E. Pitt St., 814/624-0800, www.bedfordpainn.com, $99-165), built in 1794 as the first brick building in town.

Nature lovers can explore miles of trails through privately owned wetlands and woods at **Whitetail Wetlands** (967 Dunnings Creek Rd., New Paris, 814/839-2622, www.whitetailwetlands.com, $75-200). The lodge has three guest rooms, a kitchenette for self-prepared meals, a baby grand piano, and working fireplaces. Primitive camping sites are also available.

An idyllic vacation on a working sheep

farm? That's right. Guests aren't asked to lend a hand at **Monsour Sheep Farm** (120 Oppenheimer Rd., Bedford, 814/623-8243, www.monsourvacationhomes.com), which has four vacation homes along with a flock of more than 1,000 ewes. Accommodations range from the two-bedroom Shepherd's Chalet ($150), a renovated granary with a large deck, to a five-bedroom farmhouse ($299) that sleeps as many as 15. A two-night minimum stay is required. Come in May for a chance to bottle-feed a newborn lamb.

Over $200

Fronted by columns of solid white pine and rows of balconies, the ★ **Omni Bedford Springs Resort** (2138 Business Rte. 220, Bedford, 814/623-8100, www.omnihotels. com, $249-409) offers more than 200 luxuriously appointed guest rooms and a handful of suites. They're divided between a historic building and a modern spa wing. The latter is advisable if you plan to spend much time luxuriating in the fabulous spa, swimming in the indoor or outdoor pools, or exercising in the fitness center. Guests can pass the time fishing on a private lake or stocked trout stream (kids can have the chef cook their fresh catch), hiking or biking 25 miles of trails (knobby walking sticks provided), or playing a game of golf, tennis, bocce ball, or badminton. Roasting marshmallows around the fire pit is an evening tradition. The resort's cooking workshops are also quite popular.

FOOD
Downtown Bedford

There are a good number of recommendable eateries in the heart of Bedford. **The Green Harvest Co.** (110 E. Pitt St., Bedford, 814/623-3465, 7am-4pm Mon.-Fri., 7:30am-4pm Sat., under $10) takes the peanut butter and jelly concept to new heights. Try the Apple PB sandwich, made with all-natural peanut butter, apples, bacon, and cheddar, or the PB Starter with its local jam and sliced bananas.

Bird's Nest Farm Café (113a S. Richard St., Bedford, 814/623-6378, breakfast and lunch 8am-3pm daily, dinner 5pm-9pm Thurs.-Sat., breakfast and lunch under $10, dinner $10-18) is another great choice for breakfast or lunch. The salmon-ginger cake sandwich is a hot seller. Owner Michael Stipanovic's pumpkin blondies are reason enough to visit Bedford in the fall.

For fresh-brewed iced tea and a slice of fresh-baked pie, you can't beat **The Eatery** (100 S. Juliana St., Bedford, 814/623-9120, 11:30am-3pm daily, under $10). The café tucked inside the mammoth Founders Crossing crafts and antiques co-op also offers soups, salads, and sandwiches.

The **Bedford Tavern** (224 E. Pitt St., Bedford, 814/623-9021, www.bedford-tavern. com, 5pm-2am Mon.-Sat., 4pm-9pm Sun., $4-34) is known for its seafood—from frog legs to lobster tail—and "all you care to eat" dinners. You'll find the same menu in the downstairs sports bar as the upstairs dining room.

For fine cuisine in a historic setting, head to the **Golden Eagle Inn** (131 E. Pitt St., 814/624-0800, www.bedfordpainn.com, lunch 11am-2pm Mon.-Fri., brunch 10am-2pm Sat.-Sun., dinner 5pm-9pm Mon.-Sat., lunch and brunch $7-14, dinner $11-32). The menu is hardly traditional, featuring dishes like bison tartare, pulled pork eggrolls, and soba noodles in coconut curry. Even a grilled cheese sandwich gets the gourmet treatment here. (Think artisan cheeses, roasted tomatoes, and house-baked bread.)

Vicinity of Bedford

A few miles west of town, the ★ **Jean Bonnet Tavern** (6048 Lincoln Hwy., Bedford, 814/623-2250, www.jeanbonnettavern.com, 11am-9pm Sun.-Thurs., 11am-10pm Sat.-Sun., $7-35) offers lamb stew, roasted duck with raspberry liqueur sauce, and dry-aged strip loin steak, and a selection of draft beers that's heavy on Pennsylvania microbrews. If the thick fieldstone walls of the 1760s landmark could talk, they'd tell of farmers meeting in opposition to a federal whiskey tax and the troops sent to quell their insurrection in 1794. Diners can warm up by old hearth fireplaces in winter or catch a breeze on the outdoor dining porch (a newer amenity) in summer. Tired travelers can stay in one of four guest rooms ($120-140).

INFORMATION

The **Bedford County Visitors Bureau** (131 S. Juliana St., 800/765-3331, www.visit-bedfordcounty.com, 9am-5pm Mon.-Sat. and noon-5pm Sun. May-Oct., 9am-5pm Mon.-Fri. Nov.-Apr.) in downtown Bedford has brochures devoted to everything from covered bridges to birding hot spots. Brochure racks can also be found at **HeBrews Coffee Company** (103 S. Richard St., Bedford, 814/623-8600, 7am-5pm Mon.-Thurs., 7am-6pm Fri., 8am-5pm Sat.) and the 24-hour **Gateway Travel Plaza** (16563 Lincoln Hwy., Breezewood, 814/735-4011, www.gatewaytravelplaza.com), located off exit 161 of the Pennsylvania Turnpike near the intersection of I-76 and I-70.

GETTING THERE

Bedford is about 100 miles east of Pittsburgh via the Pennsylvania Turnpike (I-76) and 140 miles northwest of Baltimore and Washington DC via I-70. The east-west Pennsylvania Turnpike (I-76) and Route 30 pass through Bedford County, as does the north-south Route 220/I-99. To reach downtown Bedford from the turnpike, take exit 146 and turn right onto Business Route 220.

There are no commercial flights into Bedford County Airport.

Lake Region

Look for ★ to find recommended
sights, activities, dining, and lodging.

Highlights

★ **Presque Isle State Park:** A National Natural Landmark, this sandy peninsula is sheer bliss for beach lovers and birders (page 396).

★ **Erie Maritime Museum and Flagship** *Niagara:* The airy museum brings to life the Battle of Lake Erie, a major American victory during the War of 1812. It's doubly interesting when Pennsylvania's official flagship is docked behind it (page 400).

★ **Wine Country:** With its proliferation of wineries, the town of North East is a first-rate day-trip destination, especially during the harvest months of September and October, when the air is heavy with the scent of grapes (page 403).

★ **The Spillway:** At this heavily visited spot on man-made Pymatuning Lake, ducks walk on the backs of fish. Seriously (page 414).

★ **Oil Creek & Titusville Railroad:** Soak up Pennsylvania's oil heritage during a 27-mile round-trip journey through "the valley that changed the world." Better yet, bike in one direction and take the train in the other (page 421).

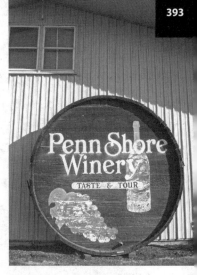

When Pennsylvanians say they're taking a beach vacation, odds are they're going out of state. Maybe they're driving to the Jersey Shore or the Outer Banks of North Carolina. Maybe they're flying to Florida or The Bahamas or even farther.

Ask them about the seashore in their backyard, and many will answer with blank stares. *A seashore? In Pennsylvania?*

That's to be expected. People who know their geography think of the United States as having three coastlines: the East Coast, the West Coast, and the Gulf Coast. Pennsylvania borders none of those. But it does border the "Fourth Seacoast," as Congress dubbed the Great Lakes in 1970. The five freshwater lakes on the nation's border with Canada are ocean-like in more ways than one. They offer sandy beaches, sloping dunes, and surfable waves. And they're vast. At more than 4,500 miles, the U.S. Great Lakes shoreline is longer than the East and Gulf Coasts combined.

The northwest corner of the Commonwealth abuts Lake Erie, shallowest and warmest of the Great Lakes. Pennsylvania's share of the shoreline is small—less than 80 miles—but of note. Presque Isle, a peninsula attached to the mainland just west of the city of Erie, is a natural wonderland. Just seven miles long, it boasts six distinct ecological zones and an incredible diversity of plants and animals. *Birder's World* magazine named it one of the best places in the country for bird-watching. It's one of the best—if not *the* best—place in Pennsylvania to watch the sun set. And its beaches are hands down the best in the state.

While Presque Isle is the number one reason to visit the lake region, it's certainly not the only one. Erie County is a major grape grower, and you can guess what that means: wineries. Erie, its county seat and largest city, is home port to Pennsylvania's official state ship, a faithful reconstruction of an 1813 brig that sealed one of the most important naval victories in American history. She's a sight to behold, especially when she's sailing, and the opportunity to live on board as part of her crew is truly unique. Another

Previous: kayaking near Presque Isle; Erie's Bayfront District; the flagship *Niagara*. **Above:** Penn Shore Winery.

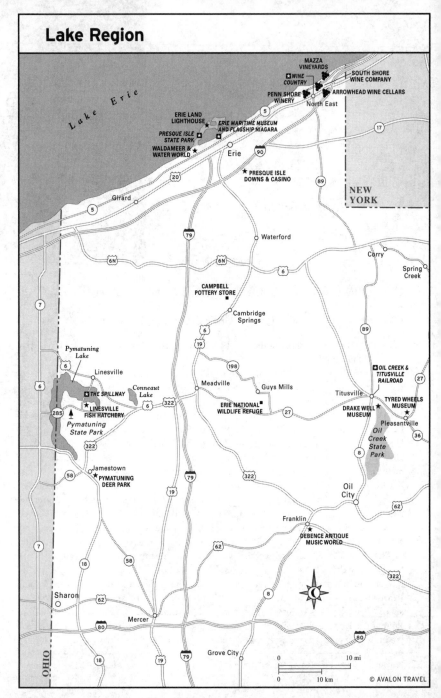

Lake Region

Lake Erie

MAZZA VINEYARDS
WINE COUNTRY
SOUTH SHORE WINE COMPANY
PENN SHORE WINERY
North East
ARROWHEAD WINE CELLARS

ERIE LAND LIGHTHOUSE
ERIE MARITIME MUSEUM AND FLAGSHIP NIAGARA
PRESQUE ISLE STATE PARK
WALDAMEER & WATER WORLD
Erie

NEW YORK

PRESQUE ISLE DOWNS & CASINO

Girard

Waterford

Corry

Spring Creek

CAMPBELL POTTERY STORE

Cambridge Springs

Pymatuning Lake

Linesville

Conneaut Lake

THE SPILLWAY
LINESVILLE FISH HATCHERY

Pymatuning State Park

Meadville

Guys Mills

OIL CREEK & TITUSVILLE RAILROAD

Titusville

TYRED WHEELS MUSEUM

DRAKE WELL MUSEUM

Pleasantville

ERIE NATIONAL WILDLIFE REFUGE

Oil Creek State Park

Jamestown
PYMATUNING DEER PARK

Oil City

Franklin

DEBENCE ANTIQUE MUSIC WORLD

Sharon

Mercer

Grove City

OHIO

0   10 mi
0   10 km

© AVALON TRAVEL

unique opportunity awaits at man-made Pymatuning Lake, within an hour's drive of Erie. There, the simple pleasure of tossing crumbs to chubby carp and ducks is punctuated by the "holy crap!" sight of a duck scrambling over a fish's back. Nowhere else does the state sanction feeding of wildlife. Like Presque Isle, Pymatuning is a magnet for birders. You can bet money that you'll spot a bald eagle there. Nearby Erie National Wildlife Refuge rounds out the region's birdwatching triple bill. As the birthplace of the modern oil industry, northwest Pennsylvania also has special appeal to history buffs. Their triple bill: the former boomtowns of Titusville, Oil City, and Franklin.

PLANNING YOUR TIME

There are good times to visit northwest Pennsylvania, and there are bad times to visit. Winter is a bad time. Why? Three words: lake-effect snow. Lake-effect snow is what happens "when a mass of sufficiently cold air moves over a body of warmer water, creating an unstable temperature profile in the atmosphere," according to weather.com. To put it in plain terms, Erie and its surrounds get buckets and buckets of snow. With an average annual snowfall of nearly 90 inches, Erie is one of the 15 snowiest cities in the country. That would be great if the attractions in this corner of the state included ski resorts, but when locals want to hit the slopes, they head to New York's Peek'n Peak. Among the very few reasons to visit in winter is to gaze at the otherworldly ice dunes along the shore of Lake Erie. Holing up in a B&B with your honey is another.

If you're going to visit Presque Isle in summer, which, of course, is the most popular time to visit the beach-lined peninsula, plan well ahead. Accommodations fill quickly. Do the same if you're planning on wine-tasting during the harvest months of September and October.

Erie and Vicinity

With a population of roughly 102,000, Erie is Pennsylvania's fourth largest city after Philadelphia, Pittsburgh, and Allentown. Its relative largeness has much to do with its location on Presque Isle Bay, a natural harbor formed and sheltered by the peninsula for which it's named. Erie was a speckle of a town when the United States declared war on Great Britain in 1812. With Canada under British control, the Great Lakes became a theater of war. As one of the few American settlements on Lake Erie and the only one with a good harbor, Erie was a natural staging ground. Virtually overnight, it transformed into a naval shipbuilding center. In August 1813, a fleet of warships left Presque Isle Bay and headed west to meet the enemy. The engagement on September 10 opened with several hours of intense cannon fire and ended with a victory for the Americans. The Battle of Lake Erie marked the first time in history that an entire British naval squadron was defeated and captured.

Erie's reputation as a maritime center was sealed, and Presque Isle Bay quickly became a major stop on the Great Lakes. Completed in 1844, the Erie Extension Canal moved passengers and freight from the port city to the Pittsburgh region. Railroads came to Erie less than a decade later. Its impressive transportation systems made it appealing to industry, and by the end of the 19th century, the city was renowned for its metalworking factories. Its contribution to the World War I effort included more than 1,400 cannons. In the early 1900s Erie was also regarded as the freshwater fishing capital of the world. At one point in the 1920s, a record 144 commercial fish tugs operated out of the city. The bayfront was crowded with fish-processing houses, icehouses, shipbuilders and chandlers, and restaurants, hotels, and boardinghouses serving the men who worked the fishing fleet. Erie's commercial fishing industry eventually fell victim to overfishing and pollution. By the turn of the 21st century, only one commercial fisherman was still in business. The not-so-crowded bayfront is now home to a museum devoted to Erie's maritime heritage, including its great fishing past. Local waters continue to attract sports and recreational anglers.

Erie remains an industrial city. Locomotive manufacturer GE Transportation has its world headquarters here and tops the list of largest employers. The plastics industry also has a significant presence in Erie. The heyday of lake trade is long past, but Erie's harbor is still in the business of import and export. It's now able to handle the large vessels that carry cargos between the Atlantic Ocean and the Great Lakes via the St. Lawrence Seaway, a system of locks and canals completed in 1959.

★ PRESQUE ISLE STATE PARK

If **Presque Isle** (301 Peninsula Dr., Erie, 814/833-7424, www.visitpaparks.com) weren't property of the state, the sandy peninsula would almost certainly be crowded with million-dollar vacation homes. It's that stunning. Just seven miles long, the spit jutting into Lake Erie boasts sandy beaches, a 19th-century lighthouse, and a remarkable diversity of plant and animal life. This National Natural Landmark is unlike any other place in Pennsylvania. Indeed, it's more like Southern California than the rest of the Commonwealth. (More precisely, in *summer*, it bears some resemblance to SoCal—inline skaters, kite flyers, and all. In winter, there's nothing California-ish about it. California doesn't have ice dunes, for one thing.)

The claw-shaped peninsula juts out from the mainland four miles west of downtown Erie and widens as it stretches northeastward. It forms and protects Presque Isle Bay, the deep harbor that put Erie on the maritime map. The peninsula refuses to stay put. It's been creeping eastward ever since it formed thousands of years ago. Wind and water are forever pushing sand from the peninsula's neck toward its eastern end, known as Gull Point. That's a problem the U.S. Army Corps of Engineers has been battling since the early 1800s. Today the agency's anti-erosion arsenal includes dozens of breakwaters, which are aligned parallel to the beaches and partially block the waves. The Corps also steps in when

Presque Isle lighthouse

storms cause breaches in the neck of Presque Isle—French for "almost an island"—and turn it into a bona fide island. It's happened at least four times since 1819.

Presque Isle is reached via Peninsula Drive (Route 832) or by boat. If you're driving, stop at the **Tom Ridge Environmental Center** (301 Peninsula Dr., Erie, 814/833-7424, www. trecpi.org, 10am-6pm daily, free admission), or TREC for short, to learn about Presque Isle's history and ecosystems and grab a map of the 3,200-acre park. Named for a former Pennsylvania governor who served as the nation's first secretary of homeland security, the airy and ecofriendly facility houses 7,000 square feet of interactive exhibits, a small orientation theater showing a free 15-minute movie, and the **Big Green Screen Theater** (814/838-4123, 45-minute films shown on the hour 11am-5pm daily, ticket $7.50, seniors $6, children 3-12 $5.50) with its four-story, 45-foot-wide screen. It also has a café and a lovely shop full of whimsical gifts, including model sailboats, miniature lighthouses, wind chimes, and beach glass jewelry. Be sure to climb (or take the elevator) to the top of TREC's 75-foot observation tower for views of Lake Erie. You can spot Canada on a clear day.

Presque Isle is strictly a day-use park, so if you're planning to spend the night, you'll have to do it on the mainland. Book accommodations well in advance if visiting in the summer.

Beaches

Plenty of Pennsylvania's interior lakes advertise sandy beaches (that Mother Nature had *nothing* to do with), but none can deliver surf swimming or a water horizon. Lake Erie is so large that Presque Isle beachgoers see nothing but water and sky when they gaze northward. It's almost like being at the ocean. In at least one way, it's better than being at the ocean: There's no risk of being stung by jellyfish. Presque Isle's beaches are open 10am-7:30pm daily from Memorial Day weekend to Labor Day unless otherwise posted.

If you're toting a cooler, take your pick of beaches. If not, you may want to choose a beach with a food and beverage concession: Beach 6, Beach 8 (Pettinato Beach), Beach 10 (Budny Beach), or Beach 11. Beach 6 has the added benefit of sand volleyball courts, which attract a lot of teens. Families with small children may prefer Beach 11, a sheltered beach with shallow water, a bathhouse with changing areas, and a playground. Beach 7, also

playing at one of many beaches in Presque Isle State Park

known as Waterworks Beach, is the only other beach with playground equipment. It's notable in that its restrooms and picnic tables and even the water's edge are ADA accessible. If you're looking for a deserted beach, you've come to the wrong place. The Mill Road Beaches, a group of adjacent beaches with shaded picnic areas, are your best bet for a quiet and romantic experience.

Trails

There's no better way to take in Presque Isle than by biking the **Karl Boyes Multi-purpose National Recreation Trail,** which makes a 13.5-mile circuit of the park. Named for a late state legislator, the paved trail is popular with inline skaters and joggers as well as cyclists. No wheels? No worries. **Yellow Bike Rental** (814/835-8900, 8am-8pm daily Memorial Day-Labor Day and 10am-6pm weekends weather permitting) offers bicycles, tricycles, inline skates, and even four-wheeled surreys. It's about 2.5 miles from the park entrance in what's known as the Waterworks area. In winter, part of the Karl Boyes trail is left snow-covered for cross-country skiers.

Maritime history buffs can retrace the steps of lighthouse keepers on the 1.25-mile **Sidewalk Trail.** At its north end is the **Presque Isle Lighthouse.** The brick tower was built in 1873 and raised to 68 feet in the 1890s. Before electric bulbs came into use, keepers climbed to the top every four hours to refill an oil lamp. Today the light is automated, and the attached dwelling, home to nine keepers until 1944, is a residence for park staff. At the south end of the trail is Misery Bay, named such because of the hardships endured by sailors based there during the War of 1812. Lighthouse keepers followed the Sidewalk Trail to their boathouse in the bay when they needed supplies from the mainland. Once a wooden boardwalk, the trail was resurfaced with concrete in 1925.

Hikers can take their pick of about a dozen unpaved trails. Popular with bird lovers, the 1.5-mile **Gull Point Trail** begins at the east end of Beach 10 (Budny Beach) and makes a loop through Gull Point, a resting spot for migrating shorebirds. It's one of the longer trails and requires walking through sand traps, so don't bother if you're looking for an easy hike.

The easier **North Pier Trail** (0.7 mile) follows the shoreline from Beach 11 to North Pier, a popular fishing spot and home to the **North Pier Light,** which has been guiding ships into Erie's harbor since 1858.

Boat Tours and Taxi

It would be a shame to leave Pennsylvania's Great Lakes port without logging some boat time. Various watercraft can be rented on Presque Isle and in Erie's Bayfront District, but you also have the option to leave the navigating to pros. **Presque Isle Boat Tours** (814/836-0201, www.tinytimsfishing.com, fare $16, children 5-12 $9) offers 90-minute voyages aboard the *Lady Kate* on weekends from mid-May through mid-June, daily from mid-June through Labor Day, and on weekends through the remainder of September. The 110-passenger vessel docks near Presque Isle's Perry Monument, a tribute to the sailors who fought under Commodore Oliver Hazard Perry during the War of 1812. Knowledgeable guides describe points of interest, including historic lighthouses and the nature preserve at the eastern end of the isle, as she cuts through the water. Reservations are recommended.

A water taxi plies Presque Isle Bay from Memorial Day weekend until the weather takes a nasty turn in September or October, stopping at Presque Isle's Waterworks ferry dock once an hour. Known as the **Presque Isle Aquabus** (814/881-2502, noon-6pm Mon. and 10am-6pm Tues.-Sun., all-day fare $9 for adults, $7 for children under 12, one-way fare $4 for adults and children), the taxi leaves Dobbins Landing on Erie's waterfront on the hour, heads west to Liberty Park, and then crosses the bay, arriving at Presque Isle on the half hour. From there it returns to Dobbins Landing.

Presque Isle's interior lagoons, home to herons, beavers, turtles, and a host of other critters, also beg to be explored by boat. Free pontoon tours are offered Thursday-Sunday from Memorial Day weekend through June and daily from July until early September. Call or check the website of the Tom Ridge Environmental Center (814/833-7424, www.trecpi.org) for a departure schedule. Be sure to preregister for sunset rides, which fill quickly.

Water Sports

Just about anything you can do at the ocean, you can do here, including waterskiing, surfing, windsurfing, paddleboarding, kayaking, fishing, and scuba diving. For boaters, Presque Isle offers four launching areas and a marina with almost 500 slips. All of the boat launches are on the bay side of the peninsula. Vista Launch, closest to the park entrance, is only recommended for small boats and Jet Skis. Niagara and Lagoon Launches can accommodate small- and medium-size watercraft. The four-lane West Pier Launch, located near the marina, is recommended for larger vessels. Open May through October, the marina (814/833-0176) can accommodate boats as long as 42 feet. Slips are highly coveted, so call ahead to determine availability. During the off-season, call the main park office rather than the marina. Beaching of boats along the shoreline is permitted except at the easternmost portion of Gull Point from April through November and within 100 feet of designated swimming areas.

Presque Isle Canoe & Boat Livery (814/838-3938, 10am-6pm daily May-Oct.), located on Graveyard Pond across from Misery Bay, rents watercraft by the hour. Its inventory includes canoes, kayaks, rowboats, paddleboats, small motorboats, and pontoon boats, plus fish finders and rods and reels.

Famous for its walleye fishing, Lake Erie also yields perch, bass, trout, and steelhead. Presque Isle Bay teems with panfish, muskellunge, northern pike, crappie, and smelt. The peninsula's piers, boat landings, and interior lagoons are popular shore-fishing areas.

Snorkeling is prohibited, but certified scuba divers can swim with the fishes. Divers must register at the ranger station on the bay side of the peninsula, about two miles from the park entrance.

Segway Tours

Introduced in 2013, Segway tours are a fun way to soak in the beauty of Presque Isle. **Presque Isle Touring Co.** (814/833-7347, www.presqueisletouringcompany.com) offers morning, afternoon, and sunset tours throughout the summer. The tours cost $45-55 and last about 90 minutes, including 20-30 minutes of training. Be sure to bring a pair of closed-toe athletic shoes.

Winter Activities

Presque Isle is quite a magical place in the dead of winter. Lake ice, wave surge, and freezing spray conspire to create otherworldly ice dunes. Look for them on the lake side of the peninsula. Wintertime activities include ice skating, ice fishing, iceboating, cross-country skiing, and snowshoeing. A concession in the Waterworks area offers rental skis and snowshoes on weekends from mid-November through March, provided there's snow.

Bird-Watching

Presque Isle is an ecological wonderland, home to a whopping array of plants and animals. Its birds get the most press. More than 320 species have been spotted on the peninsula, named one of the country's top birding spots by *Birder's World* magazine. Part of the reason for the incredible diversity of birdlife is Presque Isle's location along the Atlantic Flyway, a major bird-migration route. The peninsula is to migrating birds what a turnpike service plaza is to motorists: a place to eat and rest. Shorebirds that migrate from beyond the Arctic Circle to South America and back again "pull over" at Presque Isle in April and September. Waterfowl migration can be observed in March and from late November through December. Come in mid-May or September to commune with warblers.

Shorebirds can be viewed from an observation platform at the edge of the Gull Point

Natural Area. The protected area at the east end of the isle is closed to the public from April through November, but the platform can be reached by hiking the Gull Point Trail. For an eyeful of wetland birds, kayak or canoe the interior lagoons. In the hot summer months, morning and early evening are the best times for birding.

The **Presque Isle Audubon Society** (814/860-4091, www.presqueisleaudubon. org), a chapter of the National Audubon Society, offers field trips and workshops throughout the year.

BAYFRONT DISTRICT

Once crowded with shipyards and criss-crossed by railroad tracks, Erie's Bayfront District is slowly transforming into a recreational destination. It's home to the fantastic Erie Maritime Museum, which opened in 1998. Local and intercity buses deliver passengers to a sprawling transportation center, built a few years later, just east of the museum. West of the museum is the $44 million Bayfront Convention Center, which opened in 2007 after seven years in the making. It's connected by a glass-walled pedestrian bridge to the Sheraton Erie Bayfront Hotel, which opened in 2008. Recreational marinas, boat launches, and an amphitheater also dot the evolving waterfront.

Bicentennial Tower

First stop for many visitors is the **Bicentennial Tower** (814/454-8723, www. porterie.org/bicentennial, call for hours, admission $3, children 7-12 $2, free admission first Sun. of each month), which sits on a pier at the foot of State Street, Erie's main drag. Built for the 1995 celebration of the city's 200th birthday, the tower measures 187 feet to the top of its flagpole. Its two observation decks, both reachable by stairs or elevator, afford views of Presque Isle, the natural harbor it forms, and downtown.

★ Erie Maritime Museum and Flagship *Niagara*

America's attempts to seize Canada from the British during the oft-forgotten War of 1812 did not go well. The initial three-pronged offensive was a full-out failure, with Detroit falling to the British in August of 1812. An elaborate attempt to attack Montreal the following year was also unsuccessful. But 1813 wasn't without a bright spot for the United States. On September 10, nine U.S. ships under Commodore Oliver Hazard Perry

Erie Maritime Museum

defeated a British squadron of six vessels on Lake Erie. The victory forced the British to retreat from Detroit and lifted the nation's morale, at least temporarily. (A year later the British would march into Washington DC and torch public buildings, doing serious damage to morale.) The **Erie Maritime Museum** (150 E. Front St., Erie, 814/452-2744, www. flagshipniagara.org, 9am-5pm Mon.-Sat. and noon-5pm Sun. Apr.-Oct., 9am-5pm Thurs.-Sat. Nov.-Mar., admission $10, seniors $8, children 3-11 $5) brings to life the dramatic events of the Battle of Lake Erie. One exhibit features a replica of the battered hull of the *Lawrence,* Perry's original flagship. After the 20-gun brig was disabled and most of its crew wounded or killed, Perry transferred to her undamaged sister ship, the *Niagara,* hoisted his battle flag, and sailed to victory.

The Battle of Lake Erie didn't unfold near Erie's shores. It was fought near Put-in-Bay, Ohio. But Erie is rightfully proud of its role in the American victory. Six of the nine U.S. ships that sailed into battle, including the *Niagara,* were built in Erie. If that sounds unremarkable, consider that Erie had roughly 500 residents at the outbreak of the war. It had oak trees but not a single sawmill. Turning the remote town into a warship-building center required the recruitment of shipwrights, blacksmiths, and laborers from other parts. Pittsburgh sent rigging and anchors. Philadelphia contributed canvas for the sails. Cannons arrived from the nation's capital. The fleet was completed in a matter of months.

The museum on Erie's waterfront is home port to the **Flagship *Niagara,*** a reconstruction of Perry's relief flagship. When the square-rigged wooden vessel is in port, museum visitors are treated to guided tours. She sails during the warmer months, visiting other Great Lakes ports. If you're 16 or older, in good health, and crave a taste of the seafarer's life, you can apply to be a live-aboard trainee for a minimum of two weeks. An appetite for spartan conditions is required. Though the present *Niagara,* completed in

1990, has auxiliary propulsion engines and modern navigation equipment, she emulates the original in just about every other way. That means no showers, no hot water, and no privacy. Sailing excursions of just a few hours are offered when the ship isn't en route to another port. A day sail from the Erie Maritime Museum is $60 for Pennsylvania residents, $70 for out-of-state visitors. Visit the museum website for a training program application or schedule of day sails.

The museum, housed in a former electricity generating plant, isn't solely devoted to the Battle of Lake Erie. Visitors can learn about Erie's lighthouses, its once-booming fishing industry, and its rich shipbuilding heritage.

Boat Tours and Taxi

Like Presque Isle, the Bayfront District is a good place to catch a ride on a boat. The ***Victorian Princess*** (814/459-9696, www. victorianprincess.com, sightseeing cruise $13, happy hour cruise $14.95, meal cruises $17.95-34.95), a pretty paddle-wheeler that docks beside the Bicentennial Tower, plies the bay from May through October. It offers lunch cruises on Tuesdays and Thursdays; a happy hour cruise on Wednesdays; dinner cruises on Tuesdays, Thursdays, and Fridays; and brunch and early dinner cruises on Sundays. Call or check the website for a schedule of shorter sightseeing cruises. Reservations are required.

You can also cruise the bay in a water taxi. **Presque Isle Aquabus** (814/881-2502, noon-6pm Mon. and 10am-6pm Tues.-Sun., all-day fare $9 for adults, $7 for children under 12, one-way fare $4 for adults and children) operates from Memorial Day weekend until the weather takes a nasty turn in September or October. It leaves from the pier at the foot of State Street, aka Dobbins Landing, on the hour and arrives at Liberty Park, a popular picnicking spot, about a quarter past. Five minutes later it departs for Presque Isle. Typically the water taxi returns to Dobbins Landing after visiting the peninsula, but on weekends from early July through Labor Day, it first stops at South Pier, near Lampe Marina and its popular campground.

Water Sports

The Bayfront District is a popular starting point for boating and fishing expeditions. Boat owners should peruse the website of the Erie-Western Pennsylvania Port Authority (814/455-7557, www.porterie.org) for information on marinas and boat launches on Presque Isle Bay and adjacent waters. The port authority operates the popular **Lampe Marina,** located just outside the entrance to Presque Isle Bay. Lampe has 252 slips that accommodate boats as long as 30 feet, public launch ramps, and 24-hour security. **Perry's Landing Marina** (W. Bayfront Parkway, 814/455-1313, www.perryslandingmarina.com), just west of Liberty Park, is also commendable. It has a clubhouse with a heated swimming pool and two-tiered sundeck.

To rent a boat, head to **Port Erie Sports** (Chestnut Street Boathouse, 402 W. Bayfront Parkway, Erie, 814/452-2628, www.porteriesports.com, 7am-sundown weather permitting). The selection includes kayaks, canoes, small motorboats, and Jet Skis. Water skis, tubes, and fishing equipment and bait are also available.

Anglers unfamiliar with Erie's waters can up their big-catch odds by heading out in a party fishing boat. The **Edward John** (814/881-7611, www.edwardjohnperchfishing.com), a 52-foot perch-pursuing party boat, departs at 7am and 4pm daily from its slip near the Bicentennial Tower. Captain John Nekoloff is a 20-year veteran of the U.S. Coast Guard. Each trip is several hours long and costs $32 for adults, $27 for seniors, and $22 for children under 16. It's also possible to reserve the whole boat, which can accommodate as many as 40 passengers.

Scuba divers and sailing enthusiasts can also find a friend in the Bayfront District. **Lakeshore Towing** (814/453-6387, www.lakeshoretowing.com) offers diving charters from Wolverine Park Marina, a transient facility at the corner of State Street and the

the *Victorian Princess*

Bayfront Parkway. Lake Erie is strewn with shipwrecks at various depths. Lakeshore Towing charges $75-95 for wreck dives depending on the depth. Night dives and custom training dives are also available. Also operating out of Wolverine Park Marina, **Lake Effect Sailing** (814/434-0600, www.lakeeffectsailing.com, $50 per hour for group of up to 6, 2-hour minimum) offers private charters on a 32-foot cutter named *Namaste*.

Other Activities

You don't have to leave dry land to have a good time. Erie's bayfront offers plenty of land-based recreation, including easy biking. You can rent bikes from **Port Erie Sports** (Chestnut Street Boathouse, 402 W. Bayfront Parkway, Erie, 814/452-2628, www.porteriesports.com, 7am-sundown weather permitting). The bayfront also boasts an 18-hole mini golf course, **Harbor View Miniature Golf** (36 State St., Erie, 814/874-3536, www.harborviewminigolf.com, open May-Sept., game $6, seniors $4.50, children 3-12 $4).

Pack a picnic basket and head to **Liberty Park** in time to watch the sun set. The waterfront park is about a quarter mile west of the Bicentennial Tower and adjacent to Bay Harbor Marina. It features a large children's play area and an outdoor amphitheater that's host to a free summer concert series, **8 Great Tuesdays** (814/455-7557, www.porterie.org).

★ WINE COUNTRY

The massive ice sheet that covered part of the northern United States tens of thousands of years ago left lovely gifts on its way out, among them the Great Lakes. On the southern shores of Lake Erie, it left ridges of soil and gravel that proved splendid for grape growing. How splendid? The Lake Erie grape belt is North America's largest grape-growing region outside of California and the largest Concord grape-growing region in the world.

Concord grapes aren't the only variety cultivated in this prolific region. Recent decades have seen a profusion of small wineries, and a good deal of land has been replanted with premium wine grapes. The town of North East, located 15 miles northeast of downtown Erie on the New York border, is home to about 10 wineries. North East milks its viticulture heritage for all it's worth. Grapes festoon the website of its chamber of commerce, its high school athletes are known as the Grapepickers (their fans are filled with "Picker Pride"), and its charming lodgings include the Grape Arbor B&B and Vineyard B&B. The social highlight of the year is the three-day **Wine Country Harvest Festival** (3 locations, 814/725-4262, www.lakeeriewinecountry.org, last full weekend of Sept., wine-tasting $20 in advance, $25 at gate). WineFest traditions include a cruise-in, an arts and crafts show, a champagne breakfast featuring local bubbly, and, of course, grape stomping.

If you catch the winemaking bug, head to **Presque Isle Wine Cellars** (9440 W. Main Rd./Rte. 20, North East, 814/725-1314, www.piwine.com, 9am-5pm Mon.-Fri., 9am-noon Sat.), which sells all manner of equipment and raw materials. And if North East's wineries leave you wanting more, drive east along Lake Erie's shore into New York. You'll find more than a dozen wineries between the border and Silver Creek, New York. Visit the website of **Lake Erie Wine Country** (877/326-6561, www.lakeeriewinecountry.org) for a map and more information.

Mazza Vineyards

Established in 1972 by Italian-born brothers, **Mazza Vineyards** (11815 E. Lake Rd./Rte. 5, North East, 814/725-8695, www.mazzawines.com, 9am-8pm Mon.-Sat. and 11am-4:30pm Sun. July-Aug., 9am-5:30pm Mon.-Sat. and noon-4:30pm Sun. Sept.-June, tasting fee $3) has a distinctly Mediterranean look. But don't expect to sample chianti and montepulciano d'abruzzo inside. The Mazza brothers thought the land better suited for Germanic varieties and became known for riesling in the early years. Mazza Vineyards still offers riesling, but today it's better known for sweet, fruity wines made from niagara, concord, and catawba grapes—varieties born in the United States. It's also known as a pioneer of Pennsylvania ice wines. Producing an ice wine can be tricky business. At Mazza, vidal blanc grapes are left on the vine for two or three months after they ripen, getting ever sweeter but losing their looks. When the temperature dips below 15 degrees and the shriveled buggers freeze, they're picked by hand (sometimes in two or three feet of snow) and pressed immediately. The result is a honeylike dessert wine that sells for upwards of $40 a bottle. Mazza also produces a couple of faux ice wines, made by harvesting grapes and then freezing them artificially. They sell for about $25 apiece. Just about everything else on the menu is under $15, including oak-aged dry reds such as cabernet sauvignon and chambourcin.

South Shore Wine Company

In 2007, the family behind Mazza Vineyards restored and reopened Erie County's first commercial winery, which had fallen victim to Prohibition in the 1920s. The **South**

Shore Wine Company (1120 Freeport Rd./ Rte. 89, North East, 814/725-1585, www. ss.mazzawines.com, 10am-5:30pm Mon.-Sat. and noon-4:30pm Sun. May-Oct. with extended hours Mon.-Sat. in July and Aug., noon-5:30pm Mon.-Fri., 10am-5:30pm Sat., and noon-4:30pm Sun. Nov.-Apr., tasting fee $3) boasts a stone wine cavern built in the 1860s, one of very few of its kind in the United States. Don't pass up a tasting if you've already visited Mazza Vineyards; their wine selections are different. In the warmer months, buy a bottle and enjoy it with a cheese plate, sandwich, or salad in the patio café.

Penn Shore Winery

Penn Shore Winery (10225 E. Lake Rd./Rte. 5, North East, 814/725-8688, www.pennshore. com, 9am-5:30pm Mon.-Thurs., 9am-8pm Fri.-Sat., and 11am-4:30pm Sun. July-Aug., 9am-5:30pm Mon.-Sat. and 11am-4:30pm Sun. Sept.-June, tasting fee $1) snagged one of the first two "limited winery" licenses issued after passage of the Pennsylvania Limited Winery Act of 1968, which allowed grape farms to break into the wine biz, and opened its doors in 1970. It claims the distinction of offering the first Pennsylvania champagne. Tours of the facility, including the champagne cellar, are offered daily from June through August; large parties can take a look-see any time of year. Head to the open-air patio to drink in the view of row upon row of grapevines.

Arrowhead Wine Cellars

Nick and Kathy Mobilia opened **Arrowhead Wine Cellars** (12073 E. Main Rd./Rte. 20, North East, 814/725-5509, www.arrowhead-wine.com, 10am-6pm Mon.-Sat. and noon-4pm in summer and fall, winter and spring hours vary, no tasting fee) on their 250-acre fruit farm in 1998, making them relative newcomers to the winemaking scene. But their wines are perennial medalists at the Pennsylvania Farm Show and other competitions. Their peaches, sweet and sour cherries, frozen sour cherries, and freshly pressed grape juice for home winemaking are also held in high esteem and sold seasonally at the farm stand adjacent to the winery.

Courtyard Wineries

Even newer than Arrowhead, **Courtyard Wineries** (10021 W. Main Rd., North East, 814/725-0236, www.courtyardwineries.com, 10am-6pm Mon.-Sat., noon-5pm Sun., tasting fee $2) was opened in 2010 by seven wine enthusiasts. The winery has two tasting bars, one for its LaCourette line of dry and semidry wines and another for its Barjo Bons ("crazy friends") line of sweet and semisweet blends. For a special occasion, reserve a VIP tasting in the barrel room. Led by the winemaker himself, the tasting features a flight of wines paired with chocolates, artisan cheeses, or other foods.

Lakeview Wine Cellars

A retirement dream turned reality for Sam and Becky Best, **Lakeview Wine Cellars** (8440 Singer Rd., North East, 814/725-4440, www.lakeviewwinecellars.com, 10am-5pm Mon.-Sat. and noon-5pm Sun. June-Nov., 10am-5pm Mon. and Sat., 11am-5pm Thurs. and Fri., and noon-5pm Sun. Dec.-May, tasting fee $1-2) specializes in oak-aged wines. The hilltop winery also serves up spectacular views.

OTHER SIGHTS
Waldameer & Water World

Located just short of the entrance to Presque Isle State Park, **Waldameer** (3100 W. Lake Rd., Erie, 814/838-3591, www.waldameer.com, open weekends in May, Tues.-Sun. Labor Day weekend-Memorial Day, free admission) is the 10th oldest amusement park in the country. It celebrated its 100th anniversary in 1996 with an ambitious expansion and continues to add new attractions almost yearly. The Ravine Flyer II, a wooden coaster unveiled in 2008, garnered the Best New Ride award from *Amusement Today*, a trade newspaper. The family-owned amusement park has 30-some rides in all, including a 140-foot drop tower and a Ferris wheel that affords fantastic views of Presque Isle and Lake Erie. **Water World** (call for hours), a water park added in 1986, features a variety of tube and body slides, a lazy river attraction, a massive hot tub, and kiddie pools.

There's no charge for parking or admission. To ride or slide, you'll need to purchase a wristband or rechargeable Wally Card, which works like a debit card. Wristbands for unlimited rides at Waldameer are $25 for adults, $16.50 for children under 48 inches tall. Wristbands for unlimited slides at Water World are $18 for adults, $13.50 for children. One- and two-day combo passes are also available. Wally Cards can be used for midway games, food, and souvenirs as well as rides, which range from $1.50 to $4.50.

Erie Land Lighthouse

Scuba divers love Lake Erie for its abundance of shipwrecks. The number of sunken ships would undoubtedly be much higher were it not for Presque Isle Bay's historic lighthouses. One, the **Erie Land Lighthouse,** sits high on a bluff at the foot of Lighthouse Street, overlooking the harbor entrance. Built in 1867, it's the third lighthouse at this site. The first,

erected in 1818 about 200 feet west of the present tower, was one of the first lighthouses on the Great Lakes. It was demolished after it began to sink. A second lighthouse was built in 1857 but also proved unstable, lasting just 10 years. The 49-foot conical tower that stands today is no longer operational but still a magnet for lighthouse enthusiasts. It's normally closed to the public, but the **Erie Playhouse** (814/454-2852, www.erieplayhouse.org) offers occasional tours to raise money for its youth theater program. The tours, which are conducted by costumed actors, cost $5 per person.

Erie County Historical Society Museums

The **Erie County Historical Society** (419 State St., Erie, 814/454-1813, www.eriecountyhistory.org) operates several museums in and around the city. Most impressive is the **Watson-Curtze Mansion** (356 W. 6th St., Erie, 814/871-5790, 11am-4pm Wed.-Sat., 1pm-4pm Sun., admission $5, children 12 and under $3), a house museum that provides a glimpse into life during Erie's industrial heyday—life as the upper crust knew it. The 24-room mansion, built in the Richardsonian Romanesque tradition in 1891, is one of the

fun at Waldameer

few manses on the section of West 6th Street known as "Millionaire's Row" that have retained their original integrity. Open for self-guided tours, the three-story museum is filled with decorative woodwork, stained glass windows, and 12 elaborate fireplaces.

In 1959 the mansion's carriage house was transformed into the **Erie Planetarium** (814/871-5790, admission $5, seniors and students $4, children 12 and under $3). Primarily used by Boy Scout troops and other organized groups, the small planetarium offers public shows on Thursdays and Saturdays. Call the planetarium or check the historical society's website for a schedule.

The historical society's headquarters on State Street, just half a mile from the Watson-Curtze Mansion and planetarium, houses the **Museum of Erie County History** (11am-4pm Tues.-Sat., admission $5, children 12 and under $3). Its main exhibit gallery presents a timeline of events from presettlement to recent times. Next door at 417 State Street is the 1839 **Cashier's House** (11am-4pm Tues.-Sat., included in admission to Museum of Erie County History), so called because it was built for the chief executive officer of Erie's branch of the Bank of the United States. The interior of the three-story townhouse is CEO-worthy with its marble flooring, coffered ceilings, keyhole-shaped doorways, and egg-and-dart molding.

The historical society also operates the **Battles Museums of Rural Life** (436 Walnut St., Girard, open by appointment) in the town of Girard, about 16 miles southwest of downtown Erie. Situated on 130 acres of farmlands and woods, the pair of house museums interpret two centuries of agricultural life in Erie County.

Erie Art Museum

It's easy to mistake the **Erie Art Museum** (411 State St., Erie, 814/459-5477, www.erieartmuseum.org, 11am-5pm Tues.-Sat., 1pm-5pm Sun., admission $7, seniors and students $5, children under 5 free, free admission every Wed. and second Sun.) for a bank or government building. The stately Greek Revival-style structure, completed in 1839, has served as both. As northwest Pennsylvania's only art museum, it provides a showcase for local artists and an opportunity for local residents to experience art from around the world. The museum's 6,000-object permanent collection includes religious paintings from Tibet, photographs from 19th-century Japan, and European prints. Its pride and joy is a collection of about 100 bronze and stone sculptures from ancient India. The annual **Erie Art Museum Blues & Jazz Festival** (Frontier Park, first full weekend of Aug., free) is the largest blues and jazz festival in the region, featuring local, regional, and national acts.

Erie Zoo

Erie Zoo (423 W. 38th St., Erie, 814/864-4091, www.eriezoo.org, 10am-5pm Mon.-Sat. and 10am-6pm Sun. Mar.-Nov., peak season admission $8.50, seniors $6, children 2-12 $5) is home to some 500 animals representing 100 species, including the warthog, the red panda, the white-cheeked gibbon, the black-footed penguin, and the gray kangaroo. It's as much botanical garden as it is menagerie, boasting more than 600 species of plants. Compact enough to see in two or three hours, the zoo is next door to Glenwood Park, one of Erie's largest municipal parks. Allow extra time for a picnic in the park or a little orangutan action on its playground.

Splash Lagoon Indoor Waterpark Resort

Long after Erie's harbor freezes over and ice dunes form on the lakeshore, the city remains a destination for splish-splashing fun. Lake-effect snowstorms have no effect on **Splash Lagoon** (8091 Peach St., Erie, 814/217-1111, www.splashlagoon.com, call or check website for hours, admission $39.95-44.95, children under 42 inches $29.95-34.95, children 2 and under free). It's always a balmy 84 degrees at the indoor water park, located south of downtown at exit 24 of I-90. Splash Lagoon's attractions range from toddler-friendly play areas to slides dope enough for teenage adrenaline junkies. The "Hurricane Hole," dopest of them all, involves shooting through a tube at 40 miles per hour and circling a funnel before plunging into six feet of water. Other attractions include a 200,000-gallon wave pool—said to be the largest indoor wave pool in the eastern United States—and a lazy river lined with larger-than-life fish statues decorated by local artists.

If you don't feel like getting wet, you can hang out in the arcade, which features more than 100 games; test your balance on the ropes course ($6.95 per climb, $9.95 for all-day pass, admission to water park not required); or play laser tag (814/864-9463, $12 per 20-minute session, admission to water park not required).

Call or check the website for information on overnight packages. Walkways connect the water park to three hotels: Comfort Inn (8051 Peach St.), Residence Inn by Marriott (8061 Peach St.), and Holiday Inn Express (8101 Peach St.). Free shuttle service is available to several off-site hotels.

Presque Isle Downs & Casino

Presque Isle Downs & Casino (8199 Perry Hwy., Erie, 866/374-3386, www.casinoinerie.com, open 24 hours) isn't on Presque Isle or even nestled on Lake Erie. But that didn't stop the "racino," which opened in 2007, from adopting the name of Erie's main attraction. Located at exit 27 of I-90, the casino and thoroughbred racing track are major attractions in their own right. The atmosphere is particularly electric when the thunder of hooves competes with the ding-ding-ding of slot machines. Live racing begins in early May and continues until late September. The **Downs Clubhouse & Lounge** (814/866-8363, opens at 11am Wed.-Sun., 4pm Mon.-Tues. $8-22), a three-tiered casual dining restaurant, is a popular gathering spot for both live racing and simulcast racing because it overlooks the track and has a plethora of plasma TVs. It serves up live entertainment on Friday and Saturday nights. The racino's eateries also include the upscale **Sensory 3 Steakhouse** (814/866-8361, 5pm-10pm Wed.-Sat., 3pm-10pm Sun., $20-45) and a buffet restaurant.

ENTERTAINMENT AND EVENTS
Concert Venues

Elton John, Rod Stewart, and Barry Manilow have rocked the **Erie Insurance Arena** (809 French St., Erie, 814/452-4857, www.erieevents.com), which is home to the city's professional basketball, ice hockey, and indoor football teams.

Boats drop anchor within listening distance when bands perform at the **Burger King Amphitheater at Liberty Park** (W. Bayfront Parkway, 814/455-7557, www.porterie.org). Bring a blanket or chair to listen from dry land; the waterfront venue doesn't have seating. On Tuesdays in July and August, the amphitheater hosts a free concert series, **8 Great Tuesdays** (814/455-7557, www.porterie.org), that attracts acts as diverse as folk singer Arlo Guthrie and pop band Sixpence None the Richer.

Performing Arts

Erie's lavish **Warner Theater** (811 State St., Erie, 814/452-4857, www.erieevents.com) was built, surprisingly enough, during the Great Depression. Within months of opening its doors in 1931, the movie palace initiated a vaudeville season, and Bob Hope made an appearance soon thereafter. Today the theater hosts the **Erie Broadway series** (814/452-4857, www.eriebroadwayseries.com) and concerts by touring musicians. It's also home to the **Erie Philharmonic** (814/455-1375, www.eriephil.org), which predates the Warner, and the younger **Lake Erie Ballet** (814/871-4356, www.lakeerieballet.org).

Founded in 1916, the **Erie Playhouse** (13 W. 10th St., Erie, 814/454-2852, www.erieplayhouse.org) is one of the oldest community theaters in the country. Homeless at times in its history, the theater is now ensconced in a 1940s movie house that seats about 440.

The Station Dinner Theatre (4940 Peach

St., Erie, 814/864-2022, www.canterburyfeast. com) is best known for *A Canterbury Feast*, a long-running musical comedy set in medieval times. Performers do double duty, serving the victuals while staying in character. The dinner theater also cooks up farces and musical tributes.

Festivals and Events

Thousands of motorcyclists roll into Erie for **Roar on the Shore** (814/833-3200, www. roarontheshore.com, mid-July, free), which kicks off with a celebrity-led bike parade. Past grand marshals have included rocker and reality TV star Bret Michaels, professional daredevil Robbie Knievel, and 1990s hip-hop sensation Vanilla Ice. Bikers ride en masse through Presque Isle State Park and other parts of Erie County during the three-day bike rally.

Another major event in July is **Discover Presque Isle** (Presque Isle State Park, 814/838-5138, www.discoverpi.com, last weekend of July, free), a celebration of the superb state park and a fundraiser for the nonprofit organization devoted to making it even better. It has all the fixings of an arts festival, plus an emphasis on sporty fun. Festivalgoers can try their hand at rock climbing, archery, and kayaking; compete in beach volleyball and sand sculpting; and explore the peninsula alongside professional naturalists.

Downtown Erie gets its turn in the spotlight during **Celebrate Erie** (814/870-1234, www.celebrateerie.com, mid- or late Aug., free). The four-day extravaganza highlights the city's culinary and cultural offerings. Fireworks over the bayfront serve as grand finale.

Stars of such films as the original *Texas Chain Saw Massacre* and *Dawn of the Dead* turn out for the cleverly named **Eerie Horror Fest** (Warner Theatre, Erie, 814/452-4857, www.eeriehorrorfilmfestival.com, Oct., admission charged, free for children 12 and under). Started in 2004, the four-day event is part indie film festival and part fan convention. Horror, science fiction, and suspense films culled from hundreds of submissions are shown on the big screen. Fans can have a bloody good time among celebs, film company reps, and merchandise vendors at the Carnival of Carnage Expo. Bring cash if you're keen on collecting autographs.

ACCOMMODATIONS
Waterfront

Not surprisingly, many people who come to Erie when it's best to come to Erie—in summer—want to be near the water. Surprisingly, waterfront accommodations are scarce in this waterfront city. There's no lodging on Presque Isle and just one hotel on Erie's bayfront. A seashore-style vacation requires advance planning—or a good deal of luck.

You'll increase your odds of scoring waterfront digs if you're open to camping. At **Sara's Campground** (50 Peninsula Dr., Erie, 814/833-4560, www.sarascampground.com, $25-35), a stone's throw from the entrance to Presque Isle State Park, you can pitch a tent on a private beach. But Sara's doesn't accept reservations. Its 100-some campsites are doled out on a first-come, first-served basis, ostensibly because they're worth the gamble.

Lampe Marina Campground (foot of Port Access Rd., Erie, 814/454-5830, www. porterie.org, $30 Sun.-Thurs., $35 weekends and holidays), open May through October, accepts reservations up to six months in advance. Operated by the Erie-Western Pennsylvania Port Authority, the campground near the entrance to Erie's natural harbor has 42 campsites with water and electric hookups, a dump station, and fantastic views. All sites have picnic tables; some also have fire rings. On one side of the campground is the popular Lampe Marina with its free public boat launch. (Boat slips are an additional $20 per day when available.) On the other is a pier popular with anglers and anyone who likes to watch boats go by. Erie's water taxi makes stops at the pier on weekends during peak tourist season, whisking campers to the Bayfront District and Presque Isle State Park. The water taxi also docks near the

Sheraton Erie Bayfront Hotel (55 W. Bay Dr., Erie, 814/454-2005, www.sheraton.com/erie, $109-209), which opened in 2008 near the Bicentennial Tower. It's connected to the Bayfront Convention Center by a water-spanning walking bridge and has all the amenities you'd expect from a hotel that caters to conference-goers, including complimentary Wi-Fi and a business center open round-the-clock. All 200 guest rooms are nonsmoking. Many feature bay or marina views to match the nautical color scheme. Bring a swimsuit for the indoor pool and sunscreen for the adjacent deck. And bring your pooch if you like; the hotel provides dog beds. There's one restaurant on-site, the classy but casual Bayfront Grille, and several more within spitting distance.

About 15 minutes east of downtown Erie is an altogether different waterfront option: the family-owned ★ **LakeView on the Lake** (8696 E. Lake Rd./Rte. 5, Erie, 814/899-6948, www.lakeviewerie.com, $109-235). This is the sort of place to bring that stack of books you've been meaning to work your way through. Adirondack chairs dot the charming mini-resort, which sits atop a 120-foot bluff overlooking Lake Erie. Guests can reach the water via a wooden staircase. Many return year after year for the spectacular sunsets and laid-back vibe. LakeView has several types of accommodations, including a six-room motel, one- and two-bedroom cottages, and "Annie's Retreat," a one-bedroom home-away-from-home with a living room, dining room, full kitchen, two bathrooms, and private deck. Amenities include a swimming pool and lawn enough for bocce, badminton, and horseshoes.

Inland Erie

That's it for waterfront accommodations, but there are plenty of places to bed down within a few minutes of Presque Isle State Park and its sandy beaches. The **Glass House Inn** (3202 W. 26th St., Erie, 814/833-7751, www.glasshouseinn.com, $104-124) is a very pleasant motel owned by a very pleasant couple. Its 30 rooms are equipped with refrigerators, microwaves, coffeemakers, and wireless Internet. The small outdoor pool is open for hours after Presque Isle's beaches close for the day. Another good option is the 131-room **Bel-Aire Clarion Hotel and Conference Center** (2800 W. 8th St., Erie, 814/833-1116, www.belaireclarion.com, $80-270), offering complimentary airport transportation, an exercise room, an indoor pool and hot tub, and a restaurant and bar. Breakfast is a bargain at $4 per person.

If romance is on the agenda, consider a bed-and-breakfast in Erie or wine country to its east. With no room over $100, the Queen Anne-style **George Carroll House** (401 Peach St., Erie, 814/459-2021, www.georgecarrollhouse.com, $75-90) in downtown Erie is a great choice. Breakfast is a continental affair. Another good choice: **The Spencer House** (519 W. 6th St., Erie, 814/464-0419, www.spencerhousebandb.com, $90-175), a Victorian manse on "Millionaire's Row." Once home to manufacturing, shipping, and banking magnates, the historic district is now home to a good deal of college students.

Wine Country

Wine lovers should make a base camp in North East, a town known for vineyards and Victorian architecture. The **Grape Arbor Bed & Breakfast** (51 E. Main St., North East, 814/725-0048, www.grapearborbandb.com, $125-200) consists of two side-by-side mansions in the center of town. Built as private homes in the 1830s, they housed a stagecoach tavern, professional offices, and a primary school before their rebirth as a B&B. Grape Arbor's eight guest rooms and suites are traditionally furnished, outfitted with wireless Internet, and named for varieties of grapes grown in the region. The Cabernet Suite boasts a private entrance through a side porch, a built-in gas fireplace, and a two-person whirlpool tub. Also grape-themed, **Vineyard Bed & Breakfast** (10757 Sidehill Rd., North East, 888/725-8998, www.vineyardbb.com, $80-105) offers cheaper, country-style accommodations. Innkeepers Clyde and Judy Burnham have lived in the turn-of-the-20th-century farmhouse since 1953. Breakfast includes their homemade grape juice.

FOOD
Presque Isle

Presque Isle's dining scene consists of a few concession stands, but one of the region's most adored eateries is just outside its entrance. You can't miss **Sara's** (25 Peninsula Dr., Erie, 814/833-1957, www.sarasandsallys.com, open Apr.-Sept., 10:30am-9pm Apr.-Memorial Day and Labor Day-Sept., 10:30am-10pm Memorial Day-Labor Day, under $10) with its red-and-white striped awning, bustling picnic tables, and six-foot hot dog statue. Its menu, like its decor, pays tribute to 1950s malt shops. Even its prices are on the retro side. Five bucks gets you a foot-long hot dog smothered with homemade chili and a Coke in an old-fashioned glass bottle. (The hot dogs are Smith's brand, produced locally by a fourth-generation family business.) Save room for soft-serve ice cream; Sara's is famous for its Creamsicle-like "orange vanilla twist." From Memorial Day through Labor Day its owner opens a 1957 stainless steel diner parked nearby for customers who want to eat in air-conditioned comfort.

Another place to grab a bite near Presque Isle is **Waldameer** (3100 W. Lake Rd., Erie, 814/838-3591, www.waldameer.com, open weekends in May, Tues.-Sun. Labor Day weekend-Memorial Day). The amusement park doesn't charge for parking or admission, and it's dotted with concession stands offering the likes of fresh-cut fries and funnel cake.

Bayfront District

Erie's Bayfront District is not yet a bona fide dining and entertainment hub, but it's edging toward that goal. There's now a small cluster of restaurants at the foot of State Street, near the Bicentennial Tower. They have just the recipe for a summer day: outdoor tables and cold drinks. The most casual of the bunch is ★ **Rum Runners** (133 E. Dobbins Landing, Erie, 814/455-4292, 11am-2am daily Apr.-Oct., kitchen closes between 10pm and midnight, under $10), named for the bootleggers who braved the unpredictable waters of Lake Erie to bring Canadian booze into Prohibition-era America. Boats can dock right beside its large waterfront patio, which hosts live bands on Fridays and Saturdays throughout the summer. Rum Runners isn't much to look at (think Dairy Queen), and its fare is nothing fancy, but the bay view and the potent signature drink—a frozen blend of rum, liqueurs, and fruit punch—make the seasonal eatery a favorite among locals and tourists. Its all-seasons sister restaurant, **Rum Runners Cove** (2 State St., Erie, 814/454-7160, www.rumrunnerscove.com, 11am-2am Mon.-Sat. and 11am-10pm Sun. in summer, kitchen closes at 10pm Mon.-Thurs., 11pm Fri.-Sat., and 9pm Sun., hours vary in off-season, $7-19), features a seafood-heavy menu and a thatch-roofed outdoor bar. Food options are limited to starters, soups, salads, and sandwiches until 4pm, when they expand to include entrées such as coconut-crusted Hawaiian sunfish and the ever-popular seafood fettuccine.

The **Bayfront Grille** (55 W. Bay Dr., Erie, 814/454-2005, www.sheraton.com/erie, 6:30am-10pm Sun.-Thurs., 6:30am-11pm Fri.-Sat., $8-33) is the most upscale option in the area but hardly hoity-toity. Part of the Sheraton Erie Bayfront Hotel, it offers something none of the others do: breakfast. It's also notable for its spicy clam chowder and griddle cakes of crabmeat and roasted corn.

Downtown Erie

State Street, Erie's main drag, boasts a good number of restaurants and bars. But judging an establishment by the size of the crowd inside could lead you astray. That's because the city has a couple of colleges, and students generally gravitate toward cheap grub and suds. Colm McWilliams came to Erie from Ireland to attend one of those colleges and stayed to open **Molly Brannigans** (506 State St., Erie, 814/453-7800, www.mollybrannigans.com, 11am-11pm Mon.-Wed., 11am-midnight

And for Dessert . . .

Listen up, chocolate lovers: Pass on dessert when dining in Erie. Pay the bill, get in the car, and drive straight to **Romolo Chocolates** (1525 W. 8th St., Erie, 814/452-1933, www.romolochocolates.com, 8am-8pm Mon.-Fri., 9am-8pm Sat., 10am-5pm Sun., open until 10pm daily June-Aug.), showplace of master chocolatier Tony Stefanelli. At one end of the building, modeled on an Italian villa, is an airy café. Sink into a couch with a cup of the signature cocoa, made with dark chocolate, cream, and milk. If it's warm outside, order the iced version and have a seat on the patio. The strawberry cocoa—imagine chocolate-covered strawberries in liquid form—is especially delightful. Romolo's Cocoa Café also serves coffees and teas, espresso drinks, and ice cream and baked goods made on site. At the other end of the building is a theater-style chocolate shop, where you can observe the last stages of the candy-making process as you browse shelves lined with truffles, caramels, nougats, and other confections. Between them is Mercato, a gift shop geared toward sweet tooths.

The sweets emporium is named for Stefanelli's Italian-born grandfather, who immigrated to New York City around the turn of the 20th century and learned the candy-making trade there. The Great Depression brought sugar rationing and drove many candy makers out of the city. Romolo Stefanelli settled in his wife's hometown of Erie, where he began making candy in the basement of his father-in-law's house. By the mid-1950s the operation had outgrown the basement and the backyard. He opened a store on West 8th Street and shortly after passed the reins to his two sons. The business thrived. Today there are four **Stefanelli's Candies** (www.stefanelliscandies.com) stores in Erie, including the original (2054 W. 8th St., Erie, 814/459-2451, 9am-6pm Mon.-Sat.), but there hasn't been a Stefanelli at the helm since the early 1990s. Tony Stefanelli, who studied the art of candy making under his grandfather, father, and uncle, opened Romolo Chocolates in 1994, shortly after Stefanelli's was sold out of the family.

Erie has not two, but three homegrown chocolatiers. Established in 1903, **Pulakos 926 Chocolates** (www.pulakoschocolates.com) has three locations. Its flagship store (2530 Parade St., Erie, 814/452-4026, 9am-5:30pm Mon.-Fri., 9am-3pm Sat.) and manufacturing facility are at 26th and Parade Streets in downtown Erie.

Ask a group of locals if they prefer Romolo, Stefanelli's, or Pulakos, and you'll likely get a heated debate. Pulakos has long been known for its chocolate-covered strawberries (far-flung fans pay upwards of $80 to have them overnighted) and Stefanelli's for its "sponge candy," a melt-in-your-mouth confection with an airy, crispy center and a coat of chocolate. But Romolo does a brisk business in both, and the youngest brand on the block may well be the most traditional. "We do things like my grandfather wanted us to," says Tony Stefanelli, whose grandfather introduced sponge candy to Erie. "We use older style machines. We don't use any kind of enzyme or thinner when we're working with our chocolate. We don't use preservatives." That doesn't mean there's no room for new ideas. "When my father was alive, he would let my kids coat anything they wanted to coat with chocolate," he recalls. "My daughter was a grape freak, so we coated some red seedless grapes. When I opened Romolo, she was in her early 20s, but that was the first thing she asked for." He made a batch and put some on a tray for customers. The rest, as they say, is history. Today the shop sells upwards of 10 pounds of chocolate-covered grapes a day.

Thurs., 11am-1am Fri., noon-1am Sat., noon-9pm Sun., $8-15), one of the State Street standouts. The Irish pub is furnished from floor to ceiling with items imported from the Emerald Isle, including a bar salvaged from a hotel. A large fireplace lends a cozy feel to the high-ceilinged space. The menu includes burgers, wraps, and other standard American fare, but the big movers here are shepherd's pie and the fish and chips platter. Wash it all down with a Guinness combo—a pint consisting of the quintessentially Irish stout and another draft beer.

Beer lovers also gravitate toward **Erie Ale House** (1033 State St., Erie, 814/454-4500, 11am-2am Mon.-Fri., 4pm-2am Sat., $6-10), where beer cans are displayed like artworks and $4 buys a four-beer sampler paddle. The fare is familiar stuff—chicken fingers, cheese-burgers, and the like—with one exception: beef on weck, a regional favorite consisting of thinly sliced roast beef on a roll topped with coarse salt and caraway.

State Street offers more than pub grub. The upscale **1201 Kitchen** (1201 State St., Erie, 814/464-8989, www.1201restaurant.com, 5pm-10pm Mon.-Sat., $19-28) serves "Latin/Asian inspired food," including the best sushi in town. Named for its address, the chic chef-owned restaurant changes its menu every few weeks, giving understated names like "fried chicken" and "land & sea" to entrées as original as the artwork on its walls. Kobe beef and scallops almost always make the cut. Reservations are encouraged but not required.

Not every recommendable restaurant in downtown Erie has a State Street address. There's fine French food just off the main drag at **Bertrand's Bistro** (18 N. Park Row, Erie, 814/871-6477, www.bertrandsbistro.com, 5pm-9pm Tues.-Thurs., 5pm-10pm Fri.-Sat., 11am-2pm Sun., $16-34), named for its French-born chef, Bertrand Artigues. The menu is heavy on veal and steak, but even vegetarians will find something to "ooh la la!" over. For $19 you can start your Sunday with Nutella-filled crepes, eggs Benedict, bourbon raisin bread, and more.

The Pufferbelly (414 French St., Erie, 814/454-1557, www.thepufferbelly.com, 11:30am-8pm Mon.-Thurs., 11:30am-10:30pm Fri.-Sat., 11am-8pm Sun., $7-23) is also known for its all-you-can-eat Sunday brunch (11am-3pm, $16.99), featuring made-to-order omelets and decadent desserts, among other things. The firehouse-turned-restaurant is no less impressive as a lunch or dinner destination. If you think you're not a salad person, you may reconsider after sampling the sirloin steak salad or honey-dill glazed salmon salad. The decor pays homage to the building's eight-decade history as a firehouse.

There's no shortage of historic atmosphere at **The Brewerie at Union Station** (123 W. 14th St., Erie, 814/454-2200, www.brewerie.com, 11:30am-10pm Mon.-Thurs.,

11:30am-midnight Fri.-Sat., $7-19), which is housed in Erie's 1927 train station. Its menu is heavy on comfort foods: beer-battered pickles, pulled-pork nachos, fried bologna and grilled cheese sandwiches, and even a burger topped with bacon, chorizo, and a fried egg. The Brewerie isn't too proud to offer bottled beer from other Pennsylvania microbreweries along with drafts of its own creations. It hosts the **Erie Micro Brew Festival** (www.wqln.org/beer) in April and live music most Friday and Saturday nights.

INFORMATION

If you're driving to Erie from New York via I-90 west, look for the Pennsylvania **welcome center** near the state line. It's stocked with brochures about attractions in the region and throughout the state. Personalized travel counseling is available 7am-7pm daily; the restrooms are always open. If you're driving from Ohio via I-90 east, you can load up on brochures at a rest stop about a mile past the state line. **VisitErie** (208 E. Bayfront Parkway Ste. 103, Erie, 814/454-1000, www.visiterie.com, 8:30am-5pm Mon.-Fri.), Erie County's tourism promotion agency, staffs an information desk inside the rest stop from late May through September. Once in Erie, head to VisitErie headquarters or the **Tom Ridge Environmental Center** (301 Peninsula Dr., Erie, 814/833-7424, www.trecpi.org, 10am-6pm daily) for answers to any questions about where to go and how to get there.

GETTING THERE AND AROUND

Erie is in Pennsylvania's northwest corner, about 130 miles north of Pittsburgh via I-79, 100 miles northeast of Cleveland via I-90, and 90 miles southwest of Buffalo, New York, via I-90. If you're coming from Pittsburgh or other points south, you'll arrive via I-79. I-90 is the major east-west thoroughfare, but if you value scenery over speed, follow the coastal Route 5 into town. The **Great Lakes Seaway Trail,** one of the first roads in America to be designated a National Scenic Byway, runs along Route 5 for most of its course in Pennsylvania.

Erie International Airport, Tom Ridge Field (ERI, 814/833-4258, www.erieairport. org) is served by three major airlines offering service from Cleveland, Detroit, and Philadelphia. **Amtrak** (800/872-7245, www. amtrak.com) provides train service to the city via its Lake Shore Limited line. Erie's train station (W. 14th and Peach Sts.) boasts an onsite brewpub. **Greyhound** (800/231-2222, www.greyhound.com) buses pull into the **Intermodal Transportation Center** (208 E. Bayfront Parkway, Erie) in the Bayfront District.

Local bus service is provided by the **Erie Metropolitan Transportation Authority** (814/452-3515, www.ride-the-e.com). A good way to get the lay of the land is to hop on the free **BayLiner Trolley,** which runs between the bayfront and downtown's 14th Street every day but Sunday.

You'll find taxis at the airport and the Intermodal Transportation Center. Call **Erie Yellow Cab** (814/461-8294, www.erieyellow-cab.com) if you need a lift from elsewhere in the area.

A water taxi plies Presque Isle Bay from Memorial Day weekend until the weather takes a nasty turn in September or October. Known as the **Presque Isle Aquabus** (814/881-2502, noon-6pm Mon. and 10am-6pm Tues.-Sun., all-day fare $9 for adults, $7 for children under 12, one-way fare $4 for adults and children), it leaves from the foot of State Street on the hour, heads west to Liberty Park, and then crosses the bay, arriving at Presque Isle on the half hour.

Pymatuning and Vicinity

Lake Erie isn't the only body of water luring boaters, anglers, and bird-watchers to Pennsylvania's northwest corner. Less than an hour south of the Great Lake's shoreline is a great lake named Pymatuning. Unlike Lake Erie, a thousands-year-old product of geologic forces, Pymatuning is relatively young and the product of a man-made dam. It's Pennsylvania's largest lake and the centerpiece of its largest state park, Pymatuning State Park. (The lake spills into Ohio, which has a Pymatuning State Park of its own.) Man-made though it is, Pymatuning has long been a destination for ardent observers of the natural world. The state's first migratory waterfowl refuge was established there in 1935, shortly after the dam was constructed. A few years later, Pymatuning became the site of the state's first wildlife education center. From 1968 to 1980, only three pairs of bald eagles were known to nest in Pennsylvania, and all of them were in the Pymatuning area. The raptors can now be found in many areas of the state, but the frequency of sightings at Pymatuning brings birders back again and again. There's something else that brings people back again and again—something delightfully freakish. At Pymatuning, ducks walk on the backs of fish. That's right, *on their backs.* Read on.

Just a few miles east of the state's largest lake is its largest natural lake, Conneaut Lake, which is popular with the speedboating set. East of Conneaut is the city of Meadville, home to a very old market house and the very unusual Johnson-Shaw Stereoscopic Museum. And east of Meadville is the Erie National Wildlife Refuge, a federally managed haven for waterfowl and, like Pymatuning, a paradise for bird-watching enthusiasts.

PYMATUNING STATE PARK

At 21,122 acres, **Pymatuning State Park** (2660 Williamsfield Rd., Jamestown, 724/932-3142, www.visitpaparks.com) is the largest of Pennsylvania's 120 state parks. Its distinctions don't end there. The park is home

pier at Pymatuning Lake

to Pennsylvania's largest lake. It has more campsites than any other Pennsylvania state park. It's one of the most visited state parks in Pennsylvania. And it's the only state park where feeding of (certain) wildlife is not seriously frowned upon.

You can rent a boat, take a swim, and stay the night on the south or north shore of Pymatuning Lake. The south shore, near the town of Jamestown, can be reached from Route 322. The north shore, near the town of Linesville, can be reached from Route 6. Head to the north shore for the region's main attraction: a reservoir spillway where feeding of ducks and fish results in the phenomenon that made Linesville famous as the place "Where the Ducks Walk on the Fish."

Pymatuning Lake spills into Ohio, which has its own Pymatuning State Park. For information about recreation on the west shore, call 440/293-6030 or visit www.dnr.state.oh.us/parks.

★ The Spillway

Want to see a monkey atop an elephant? Buy a ticket to a circus. Want to see a duck atop a fish? Buy a loaf of bread and head to the Pymatuning spillway, located two miles south of Lineville on Hartstown Road. Each

year, hundreds of thousands of people visit the spillway to hurl bread crumbs (or whole loaves) at the fish and waterfowl that congregate there. The fish—big, mean-looking carp—are so thick that they form a writhing carpet on the water's surface. A carp with its sights set on a saltine or slice of Wonder bread will sometimes leap out of the water and somersault over its brethren. To say that ducks walk the carp carpet is a bit of an overstatement. Once in a while, a duck in hot pursuit of baked goods will scramble over a fish or two. It's a magical moment that keeps many families coming back year after year.

In 2008 state conservation officials tried to put a stop to the decades-old bread-tossing tradition, arguing that the carp were eating too many carbs (or something like that). Visitors could still feed the fish special pellets sold at a state-run concession stand, they said. The "let them eat pellets" proclamation incited a public outcry, attracting the attention of state legislators. Attacked like a hamburger bun in the heart of the spillway, the Department of Conservation and Natural Resources backed down.

The bread hurling begins with the spring thaw and continues through late fall. Refreshments, souvenirs, and fish food are available at the spillway concession stand, which is generally open weekends mid-April to Memorial Day, daily through Labor Day, and weekends for the remainder of September.

The road to the spillway takes you past a large fish hatchery and then Ford Island, a renowned bird-watching site.

Linesville Fish Hatchery

Anglers and anyone who's owned an aquarium will enjoy a visit to the state-run **fish hatchery** (13300 Hartstown Rd., Linesville, 814/683-4451, www.fish.state.pa.us/images/fisheries/fcs/linesville/fcs.htm, 8am-3:30pm daily, free admission) about a mile north of the spillway. Built in 1939, the hatchery raises millions of gilled swimmers each year: about a dozen warm-water species as well as trout destined for Lake Erie's tributaries. Its visitors center features a two-story aquarium filled with walleye, crappie, perch, catfish, bass, and other warm-water fish; a collection of vintage fishing equipment and boat motors; and plenty of mounted trophy fish, including the state record muskellunge—a 54-pounder pulled from nearby Conneaut Lake in 1924. Kids get a kick out of an interactive exhibit that tests their fish identification skills.

A platform overlooking the hatch house gives visitors a chance to observe workers bringing in adult fish, stripping the eggs out, fertilizing them, and otherwise going about their day. Though fish rearing is a year-round business at Linesville, there's less to see during the coldest months. Sometime in October or early November, hatchery workers drain the 10,000-gallon aquarium, releasing the fish into Pymatuning. Production ponds are also drained. They remain empty until the ice comes off the lake in March or early April.

The hatchery grounds are popular with bird-watchers. Bring binoculars or a spotting scope to scan the skies and trees for bald eagles. Bring a picnic basket if you plan to stay awhile; there are tables and benches on the property but no concession stand.

Boating and Fishing

Pymatuning Lake isn't a destination for adrenaline junkies. A 20-horsepower limit rules out Jet-Skiing, waterskiing, wakeboarding, and the like. (Head to nearby Conneaut Lake if that's what floats your boat.) If you enjoy peace and quiet and pretty scenery, you'll enjoy Pymatuning. Ditto if you enjoy sailing or canoeing.

The lake's Pennsylvania shores are dotted with boat ramps and three public marinas: the

ducks near the Pymatuning spillway

203-slip Jamestown Marina (724/932-3267) on the south shore, the 170-slip Linesville Marina (814/683-4339) on the north shore, and the 184-slip Espyville Marina (724/927-2003) on the east shore. Generally open from late March or early April through October, the marinas rent a variety of watercraft, including motorboats, pontoons, and canoes. Fishing tackle, bait, and snacks are available.

Common species in the warm-water fishery include walleye, muskellunge, crappie, bluegill, and largemouth and smallmouth bass. Anglers can cast anywhere on the lake with a fishing license from either Pennsylvania or Ohio, but shore fishing requires a license from the appropriate state. Popular fishing spots include an 850-foot breakwater at Espyville Marina and a 280-foot fishing pier adjacent to Linesville Marina.

Serious anglers can be found on Pymatuning even in the dead of winter. Iceboating is permitted everywhere on the lake.

Swimming

The state park has several swimming beaches, which are open the weekend before Memorial Day through Labor Day, weather permitting. There's one public beach on the north shore, near Linesville Campground and Marina. The southern/Jamestown end of the park has two public beaches, and Jamestown Campground has its own beach for campers.

Campgrounds and Cabins

The state park has two camping areas: **Jamestown Campground** (716 Williamsfield Rd., Jamestown) on the south shore of Pymatuning Lake and the smaller **Linesville Campground** (3388 W. Erie St. Extension, Linesville) on the north shore. Open April-October, the campgrounds have showers, flush toilets, and a mix of electric and nonelectric campsites. Both are convenient to swimming, boating, and fishing.

Not a camper? There are modern **cabins** near both campgrounds. The two- and three-bedroom cabins have a furnished living area, kitchen/dining area, and bathroom. Bring your own linens, towels, cookware, and tableware. There are 20 cabins at the southern/Jamestown end of the park, and they're available year-round. The five cabins at the northern/Linesville end are available from mid-April to late October. Reserve campsites and cabins online at www.pa.reserveworld. com or by calling 888/727-2757.

OTHER SIGHTS
Pymatuning Deer Park

Known for its bald eagles and other native wildlife, the Pymatuning area is also home to some not-so-native animals, including African lions, Siberian tigers, and various primates. You'll find them at **Pymatuning Deer Park** (804 E. Jamestown Rd., Jamestown, 724/932-3200, www.pymatuningdeerpark. com, 10am-5pm Mon.-Fri. and 10am-6pm Sat.-Sun. Memorial Day weekend-Labor Day, 10am-5pm certain weekends in May and Sept., admission $8, seniors $7, children 2-12 $6), a family-owned attraction near the southern end of Pymatuning Lake. Established in 1953, the menagerie has grown to more than 250 animals and birds, both domestic and exotic. Its petting zoo, miniature train ($2), and pony rides ($2) are hugely popular with pint-size visitors. The animal park encourages feeding of many animals, including bears, primates, emus, and deer. Don't bring yesterday's leftovers; only park-sold animal food is permitted.

Conneaut Lake

Less than 10 minutes from Pymatuning's shores, Conneaut Lake is the largest natural lake in Pennsylvania. Let's get this clear: It's not very large. At 934 acres, it's a puddle relative to the 17,088-acre Pymatuning. But the glacial lake near the town that shares its name has a certain appeal, as evidenced by the vacation homes along its shores. Pymatuning is no deeper than 35 feet, and the state imposes a 20-horsepower limit on the man-made lake. Conneaut is almost 70 feet deep, and there's no horsepower limit. So speedboating, water-skiing, Jet-Skiing, and the like—prohibited on Pymatuning—are kosher on Conneaut. You'll need your own watercraft, however. Rentals are hard to come by.

For generations of Pennsylvanians, Conneaut Lake calls to mind **Conneaut Lake Park** (12382 Center St., Conneaut Lake, 814/382-5115, www.conneautlakepark. com, hours vary, free admission, rides $1-3), an amusement park that traces its history to 1892. The park is best known for its classic Blue Streak coaster, which opened in 1938. In recent years it's become known for financial woes and some lousy luck. Its rides stood idle in 2007 due to lack of funds. In early 2008 an arson fire destroyed its century-old Dreamland Ballroom, where Perry Como and Doris Day once sang. Just two months later, its old bowling alley collapsed. But the debt-laden park limps on, touting $3 Blue Streak rides and a trip back in time.

Meadville

About 15 minutes from Conneaut Lake and 25 from Pymatuning, the city of Meadville offers quaint B&Bs and cultural attractions. It's a college town—about 2,100 of its roughly 13,000 residents are students of Allegheny College, a liberal arts institution founded in 1815—and the county seat of Crawford County. (It's also the birthplace of actress Sharon Stone. Years before famously uncrossing her legs in *Basic Instinct*, she enjoyed local fame as Miss Crawford County.) The **Meadville Market House** (910 Market St., Meadville, 814/336-2056, 10am-6pm Mon.-Fri., 8am-4pm Sat.), a community gathering spot since 1870, is a good place to start the day. It's home to a greasy spoon known for its breakfasts. It's also a destination for locally made crafts and specialty foods, including baked goods and homemade pasta. During the growing season, farmers sell their produce outside.

The **Baldwin-Reynolds House Museum** (639 Terrace St., Meadville, 814/333-9882, www.baldwinreynolds.org, tours on the hour noon-3pm Wed.-Sun. mid-May-Aug., admission $5, children 6-18 $3) is another of Meadville's cultural attractions. The Greek Revival mansion was built in the 1840s for U.S. Supreme Court Justice Henry Baldwin. He died within a year of moving in, and for a few years his dream home served as a finishing school for girls. In 1847 his widow deeded the property to her nephew, William Reynolds, a young Pittsburgh attorney and graduate of Allegheny College. Reynolds moved his family to Meadville, became one of its most influential businessmen, and served as its first mayor. The house stayed in the Reynolds family until 1963, when it was purchased by the Crawford County Historical Society. Tours take visitors through more than 20 antiques-filled rooms.

Meadville also has a museum devoted to stereoscopy, a parlor pastime in the days before television and Nintendo. The **Johnson-Shaw Stereoscopic Museum** (423 Chestnut St., Meadville, 814/333-4326, www. johnsonshawmuseum.org, 10am-4pm Wed.-Fri. and 10am-5pm second Sat. of the month Apr.-Dec., other times by appointment, admission $5, seniors and students $3) houses a collection of stereoviews—photographs that appear three-dimensional when viewed through a binocular-like device—made by the Keystone View Company. Founded in Meadville in 1892, the company was the nation's leading manufacturer of stereoviews by the early 20th century. Another unusual attraction is the **Greendale Cemetery** (700 Randolph St., Meadville, 814/336-3545, www.greendalecemetery.org). More than 150 years old, Greendale has so many stories to tell that there's an iPhone app, iGreendale, to guide visitors to points of interest. The parklike cemetery is absolutely enchanting in springtime, when more than 1,500 rhododendrons bloom.

Erie National Wildlife Refuge

About 30 miles east of Pymatuning Lake is another bird-watching mecca. Established in 1959 as a haven for migratory birds, **Erie National Wildlife Refuge** (11296 Wood Duck Ln., Guys Mills, 814/789-3585, www.fws.gov/refuge/erie, headquarters 8am-4:30pm Mon.-Fri., outdoor facilities open daily from 30 minutes before sunrise to sunset, unless otherwise posted) consists of two expanses of federal land. It attracts some 240 species of birds, including waterfowl, bald eagles and other raptors, shorebirds, and marsh birds. A detailed bird brochure is available at the refuge headquarters, located on the larger and more intensely managed tract. The 5,206-acre Sugar Lake Division, as it's called, lies in a narrow valley on the outskirts of Guys Mills, about 10 miles from Meadville. A two-loop trail near the headquarters offers a 1.2- or 1.6-mile jaunt through wetlands, meadows of upland grasses, and mixed forests. In winter it's popular with cross-country skiers and snowshoers. It's possible to spot a variety of birds without stepping foot outside the headquarters. An indoor bird observation area with seating, binoculars, and bird identification materials overlooks feeding stations installed outside. Thanks to microphones placed under the stations, visitors can even listen to the banter of the feasting birds.

The 3,594-acre Seneca Division is about 10 miles north of Sugar Lake Division, or four miles southeast of the town of Cambridge Springs.

ENTERTAINMENT AND EVENTS
Performing Arts

Opened in 1885, the **Academy Theatre** (275 Chestnut St., Meadville, 814/337-8000, www.theacademytheatre.org) welcomed more than its fair share of traveling troupes thanks to Meadville's location along railroad lines between New York City and Chicago. These days the performers who take its stage are mostly local (and there's no passenger train service to Meadville). The theater began showing films in the early 1900s and still does. They're mostly of the artsy or foreign persuasion.

The **Riverside Inn** (1 Fountain Ave., Cambridge Springs, 814/398-4645, www.theriversideinn.com), which also dates to 1885, is a hotel-cum-dinner theater open from April through December. It squeezes about a dozen shows—lighthearted productions like *Love, Sex, and the IRS; Drinking Habits;* and *Hot Flashes*—into its season.

Festivals and Events

More than two dozen hot air balloons take flight over Meadville every Father's Day weekend. The **Thurston Classic Hot Air Balloon Event** (185 Park Ave., Meadville, 814/336-4000, www.thurstonclassic.com, late June, free) pays tribute to Samuel Sylvester Thurston, a Meadville hotel operator who took up ballooning in 1860, and the son who followed in his footsteps. The younger Thurston launched his balloon from the roof of the still-standing Meadville Market House on at least one occasion.

The likes of Abraham Lincoln and Daniel Boone—or men who look a lot like them—turn out for the **Pymatuning Pioneer & Arts Festival** (Pymatuning State Park, 724/927-9473, www.pymatuningpioneerdays.com, last full weekend of July, admission $1), featuring a Civil War encampment and an Indian encampment. Festivalgoers can count on demonstrations of old-school skills like butter churning and cow milking, a pie-eating contest, and live entertainment.

The **Crawford County Fair** (Rte. 77, Meadville, 814/333-7400, www.crawfordcountyfairpa.com, Aug., admission charged) is billed as the largest agricultural fair in Pennsylvania. It's got all the hallmarks of an ag fair: lots of livestock, lots of food, live entertainment, amusement rides, truck and tractor pulls, and a pageant. Actress Sharon Stone won the coveted Miss Crawford County crown in 1975.

SHOPPING

Bill Campbell's pottery is sold in some 600 galleries in the United States and Virgin Islands, but opening his own store a few miles from his production facility was a gamble. The big question: Would people come to the country for his elegant, richly colored porcelain? They did. The **Campbell Pottery Store** (25579 Plank Rd., Cambridge Springs, 814/734-8800, www.campbellpotterystore.com, 10am-5pm daily Mar.-Dec.), about 20 minutes north of Meadville and half an hour south of Erie, is well worth a detour. Heck, it's a destination in its own right. There are three floors to explore. The basement level, once a dirt-floored milking area, is now a gallery used for group or solo shows, demos, workshops, and other special events. Exquisite creations in a variety of mediums and price ranges fill the ground level and loft area, where massive hand-hewn beams and other original architectural features compete for the eye's attention. In addition to the largest selection of Campbell Pottery in the world, including experimental pieces available nowhere else, you'll find handcrafted soaps, baby goods, decorative items for home and garden, and sophisticated jewelry.

ACCOMMODATIONS

If you're a camper, you won't have trouble finding a place to lay your head near Pymatuning Lake. Pymatuning State Park has hundreds of campsites—more than any other state park in Pennsylvania, in fact—and 25 cabins. Should you encounter a No Vacancy sign, take your business to **Pineview Camplands** (15075 Shermanville Rd., Linesville, 814/683-5561, www.pineviewcamplands.com, open Apr. 15-Oct. 15, $20-30). It's extremely well situated: Pymatuning is a few minutes away in one direction, and Conneaut Lake is a few minutes away in another.

There are no hotels on Pymatuning's shores. Conneaut Lake had quite a few during its heyday as a resort area in the late 19th and early 20th centuries. **Hotel Conneaut** (12382 Center St., Conneaut Lake, 814/213-0120, www.clphotelconneaut.com, $80-300) is the lone survivor. Room rates were $1 per day when it opened on the grounds of Conneaut Lake Park, the amusement park on the western shore, in 1903. Its longevity is rather remarkable for a wooden structure. In 1943 it was struck by lightning, and the resulting blaze destroyed more than half of its roof. The hotel is still seasonal, operating only during the summer months.

Like Hotel Conneaut, the ★ **Riverside Inn** (1 Fountain Ave., Cambridge Springs, 814/398-4645, www.theriversideinn.com, $89-240) is the lone survivor of a once-booming resort industry. In the late 1900s, the rural village of Cambridgeboro, about 25 miles northeast of Conneaut Lake, gained renown for its mineral springs. Dozens of hotels and rooming houses sprang up to accommodate believers in the water's healing powers, and by the end of the century, Cambridgeboro had been renamed Cambridge Springs. The mineral water craze didn't last long. While other grand hotels closed, the 1885 Riverside Inn adapted. Instead of therapeutic baths and electrical treatments, it now offers golf packages, artist workshops, a dinner theater, fine dining, and a taste of a bygone era. The Victorian beauty on the banks of French Creek is open from April through December.

Year-round accommodations can be found in Meadville. The college town has a mix of budget hotels and B&Bs. **Mayor Lord's House** (654 Park Ave., Meadville, 814/720-8907, www.mayorlords.com, $65-120), best of the B&Bs, is in the heart of Meadville, just two blocks from Allegheny College. The beautifully restored house was built in the 1920s for a former mayor of Meadville.

FOOD

If you work up an appetite feeding the fish and fowl at the Pymatuning spillway, head to **Rebecca's Family Restaurant** (144 W. Erie St., Linesville, 814/683-4484, www.goodfoodlinesville.com, 6am-2:30pm Sun.-Tues.,

6am-9:30pm Wed.-Sat., $5-20). Delightfully cozy with its hand-hewn log furniture, river rock fireplace, and an expansive brick wall uncovered during a gut renovation in 2007, the casual eatery in the heart of Linesville is known for phenomenal pies and its "cinnamon roll sundae." Named for the owners' daughter, Rebecca's does everything from eggs to meatloaf sandwiches to steak dinners just right. It offers a breakfast buffet on Saturdays and Sundays. Come 4pm-6pm for a hearty dinner at a price that matches your arrival time.

As the largest town in the area, Meadville has the widest selection of recommendable restaurants. For a quick bite, **The Pampered Palate** (748 N. Main St., Meadville, 814/337-2100, www.pamperedpalate.net, 6am-6pm Mon.-Fri., 7am-5pm Sat., under $10) can't be beat. Start with a crock of French onion soup topped with three bubbling cheeses or save your appetite for an oversized sandwich on your choice of breads. The pressed sandwiches are especially satisfying and include a vegetarian version stuffed with portobello mushrooms and roasted peppers.

Ten miles north of Meadville and very definitely worth the drive is ★ **Sprague Farm & Brew Works** (22113 Rte. 6/Rte. 19, Venango, 814/398-2885, www.sleepingchainsaw.com, 3pm-9pm Thurs., noon-9pm Fri.-Sat., under $10), a brewpub in a refurbished dairy barn. Fresh beer and joviality are the main attractions, but the Brew Works also offers a selection of Pennsylvania wines and a menu that includes soft pretzels, made-in-Erie Smith's hot dogs, sandwiches and wraps, and mini kebabs. Don't have a designated driver? Rent the Sprague's Sleeping Leaf Lodge ($300), a five-bedroom farmhouse within stumbling distance of the pub.

INFORMATION

The **Crawford County Convention and Visitors Bureau** (16709 Conneaut Lake Rd., Meadville, 814/333-1258, www.visitcrawford. org, 8:30am-4:30pm Mon.-Fri.) is a good source of information about the Pymatuning region. It's usually closed on weekends, but you'll find brochures outside its doors.

GETTING THERE

The town of Linesville, gateway to the northern end of Pymatuning State Park, is an hour southwest of Erie and nearly two hours north of Pittsburgh. From Erie, head south on I-79 for about 35 miles and then west on Route 6, which will take you past Conneaut Lake on your way to Linesville. If you're coming from Pittsburgh, head north on I-79 for about 70 miles, then west on Route 285 to Conneaut Lake. From there, follow Route 6 west into Linesville.

Greyhound (800/231-2222, www.greyhound.com) provides bus service to Meadville, which is 15 miles east of Linesville. Private jets can land at Port Meadville Airport (GKJ), but passenger aircraft can't get any closer than **Erie International Airport, Tom Ridge Field** (ERI, 814/833-4258, www.erieairport.org). It's served by three major airlines offering service from Cleveland, Detroit, and Philadelphia.

Oil Region

In 1857, a New York native named Edwin Drake arrived in the northwest Pennsylvania town of Titusville with a mission: Bore a hole in the planet and bring up petroleum. Most people thought he was off his rocker. To be sure, there was crude oil in this corner of the world. It oozed from the banks and bed of the creek flowing through Titusville, giving the Allegheny River tributary a rainbow sheen and its name, Oil Creek. Hundreds of years before Drake's arrival, Native Americans had dug pits along the creek, waited for oil to rise to the surface of the water that collected in them, and then skimmed off the oil, which they prized for medicinal purposes. White settlers had also gotten the hang of gathering oil from natural seeps.

But Drake wasn't interested in a gallon here, a gallon there, and it was his method that struck locals as ludicrous. No one in Titusville had ever attempted to drill for oil. Drake's mission was ridiculed as "Drake's folly." Boy, were the locals wrong. In August 1859, Drake struck pay dirt. What happened next has drawn comparisons to the California Gold Rush. Drillers, speculators, and others poured into the Oil Creek valley in search of "black gold." Trees were felled. Derricks were raised. Boomtowns sprang up virtually overnight. By the end of 1860, there were more than 70 producing oil wells in and around Oil Creek. U.S. oil production that year totaled 509,000 barrels, up from about 2,000 barrels in 1859. "Drake's folly" had given birth to the modern oil industry.

The local oil rush didn't last long. Today the valley looks much as it did before Drake's history-making mission, which is to say, beautiful. A large state park encompasses 13 miles of Oil Creek below the site of Drake's well. Once coated with oil, the creek teems with trout.

But the oil boom certainly hasn't been forgotten. It's the basis for the region's tourism industry. A full-scale replica of Drake's engine house and derrick stands on the site of the original. An excursion train chugs through the state park in summer and fall, its passengers taken back in time by guides whose forbears witnessed oil fever. Titusville and nearby Oil City celebrate their oil heritage with yearly festivals. The latter has a daily newspaper named *The Derrick*. Graceful Victorian buildings throughout the region bear testimony to the great wealth born of oil. The most vibrant city in the oil region, Franklin, has such an abundance of them that it's been dubbed "Victorian City."

SIGHTS
★ Oil Creek & Titusville Railroad

There's no better way to experience the Oil Creek Valley—"the valley that changed the world," as local boosters call it—than aboard a vintage train. The **OC & T** (home station 409 S. Perry St., Titusville, 814/676-1733, www. octrr.org, runs weekends June-Oct. and select weekdays July-Aug. and Oct., ticket $19, seniors $17, children 3-12 $13) snakes along Oil Creek from Titusville to Rynd Farm Station at the southern tip of Oil Creek State Park, crossing multiple bridges on its 27-mile round-trip journey. Guides regale riders with colorful stories of the oil boom days, when the banks of the creek were thick with derricks. Today they're thick with trees, which is why OC & T tickets are in hot demand in October. Be sure to make a reservation during leaf-peeping season.

Rail fans will find plenty to ooh and aah over on the train. Its most unique car is a railway post office—the only operating one in the country. RPOs were used on thousands of routes during the salad days of passenger train service. Mail was sorted while in transport to speed up delivery. Today riders can buy and mail postcards on the restored 1927 car, a substation of the Oil City post office.

Sitting on tracks next to the home station is the **Caboose Motel** (800/827-0690, www.octrr.org/caboosemotel.htm, open May-late Oct., $90). Each of its 21 caboose cars has a king-size bed or two double beds, a heat and air-conditioning unit, and a television. Overnight packages with reduced train fares are available.

Drake Well Museum

In 1876 the engine house and derrick over Edwin Drake's history-making oil well were dismantled and sent to Philadelphia, where they were reassembled and displayed at the Centennial Exhibition, the first major World's Fair held in the United States. Millions of people got a look at the simple drilling tools that launched a giant industry. The tools found their way back to Titusville and now are part of the collection at the **Drake Well Museum** (202 Museum Ln., Titusville, 814/827-2797, www.drakewell.org, 9am-5pm Wed.-Sat. and noon-5pm Sun. Jan.-Mar., 9am-5pm Tues.-Sat. and noon-5pm Sun. Apr.-Dec., admission $10, seniors $8, children 3-11 $5), whose doors are spitting distance from the hole Drake drilled in 1859. The museum

does more than tell the tale of Drake's innovation and the ensuing oil mania. Operated by the Pennsylvania Historical and Museum Commission, it illustrates how oil has seeped into the very fabric of our lives. It's best to visit May through October, when the steam engine and other oil field machinery on the museum grounds are running.

Oil Creek State Park

The creek banks that attracted so many fortune seekers after Edwin Drake struck oil in 1859 now attract bicyclists, hikers, history buffs, and fly-fishing enthusiasts. Stretching from the site of Drake's well in the north to just outside Rouseville in the south, **Oil Creek State Park** (main entrance off Rte. 8, 1 mile north of Rouseville, park office 1080 Petroleum Centre Rd., Oil City, 814/676-5915, www.visitpaparks.com) is threaded with more than 50 miles of trails. The most popular is a 9.7-mile paved trail along Oil Creek. Custom-made for leisurely bike rides, it's dotted with historical markers, picnic tables, benches, and restrooms. **Rental bicycles** (8am-4pm weekdays and 10am-6pm weekends Memorial Day-Labor Day, some weekdays earlier in May and later in Sept., $5 per hour, $10 per day, $25 family special) are available

Drake Well Museum

at the park office, located near the southern trailhead. The northern trailhead is near Drake Well Museum. The park also boasts a **backpacking trail.** Thirty-seven miles long and named for the volunteer who created it in the 1980s, the Gerard Trail winds through the whole park, passing scenic vistas, waterfalls, and historic sites. Yellow blazes identify the main trail. Connecting loops blazed in white allow for shorter day hikes.

Vestiges of the oil rush are so few that a full-scale tableau was erected at the southern end of the park, on the site of a farm that was overrun by oil opportunists in the mid-1860s. The farmer, a certain Mr. Benninghoff, pocketed some $6,000 a day during the madness. The **Benninghoff Farm** tableau features six 35-foot oil derricks and an oil barge. At the northern end of the park is the **Hunt Farm** tableau, reflective of mom-and-pop oil operations of the mid-1900s. Like movie sets, the tableaus are all form and no function. The buildings are empty, and the machinery doesn't work.

Oil Creek, which joins the Allegheny River in Oil City, is known for bass and trout **fishing.** Boughton Run, Toy Run, and Jones Run, which empty into the creek at the northern end of the park, provide brook trout fishing. Oil Creek also offers scenic **canoeing and kayaking.** Because water levels can change on a dime, boaters should call the park office for conditions. March, April, and May are usually the best months for paddling.

Camping isn't permitted in the park except in two hike-in areas along the Gerard Trail. Both have tent sites and Adirondack-style shelters with fireplaces. Reservations are required.

Tyred Wheels Museum

If you like antique automobiles, you'll like Gene Burt. His collection grew so large that he opened a museum. In addition to about 25 antique cars, **Tyred Wheels** (1164 Russell Corners Rd., Pleasantville, 814/676-0756, 1pm-5pm Sat.-Mon. Memorial Day weekend-Labor Day, admission $3.50, children 8-16 $2)

displays more than 5,000 miniature vehicles. Burt's collecting interests extend to old radios, dollhouses, tin toys, bicycles, pedal cars, and even spark plugs. When the weather's nice, he's easily coaxed into taking museum visitors for a spin in one of his antique cars. Tyred Wheels is off Route 227 between Pleasantville and Plumer, about 20 minutes from either Titusville or Oil City.

Venango Museum

As its name suggests, Oil City is a product of the petroleum industry. The city played such a significant role in the oil industry that it earned the nickname "Hub of Oildom." So it's fitting that the **Venango Museum of Art, Science & Industry** (270 Seneca St., Oil City, 814/676-2007, www.venangomuseum.org, 10am-4pm Tues.-Fri., 11am-4pm Sat., 2pm-5pm Sun., closed Jan.-early Apr., admission $4, seniors $2, children 12 and up $2, children under 12 $1.50) in Oil City's seen-better-days downtown devotes much space to petroleum. Its collections include more than 800 Pennzoil artifacts and a 1937 convertible by Cord, a brand of automobiles manufactured for just a decade.

National Transit Building

On the same block as the Venango Museum is the 1890 National Transit Building, named for the oil pipeline company for which it was built. Today it's an arts center with classrooms, studio and performance spaces, and a gallery that sells works by regional painters, photographers, potters, weavers, and other artists. The **Transit Fine Arts Gallery** (206 Seneca St., Oil City, 814/676-1509, www.oc-artscouncil.com, 10am-4pm Tues. and Thurs.-Sat.) also has a growing collection of books by area writers and CDs by area musicians. The building's artist tenants open their studios to the public on the second Saturday of every month, noon-5pm. Many are happy to entertain visitors on other days.

DeBence Antique Music World

Prepare for an aural feast at **DeBence** (1261

Liberty St., Franklin, 814/432-8350, www.de-bencemusicworld.com, 11am-4pm Tues.-Sat. and 12:30pm-4pm Sun. Apr.-Oct., by appointment Nov.-Mar., admission $8, seniors $7, high school and college students $5, children 3-14 $3), home to more than 100 player pianos, nickelodeons, calliopes, and other old-time automatic musical instruments. The tinkling of music boxes, the tunes of Irving Berlin and John Philip Sousa, and the nostalgia-inducing strains of merry-go-round organs punctuate tours of the incredible collection, which was started in the 1940s by Jake and Elizabeth DeBence. In 1965 the couple retired to a farm in the Franklin area, filling a barn with these iPods of yesteryear. After Jake's death, area residents formed a nonprofit and raised more than $1 million to purchase the collection and a place to display it. It now resides in a former five-and-dime in downtown Franklin.

The mechanical marvels date from the mid-1800s to the 1940s. Many are very rare. The museum's Berry-Wood A.O.W. orchestrion, which was designed for use in moving picture houses and does the work of a 10-piece orchestra, is the last of its kind.

ENTERTAINMENT AND EVENTS
Performing Arts

Fans of whodunits have a killer time aboard the **Oil Creek & Titusville Railroad's Mystery Train** (409 S. Perry St., Titusville, 814/676-1733, www.octrr.org, ticket $62). The evening begins with a buffet dinner at the Perry Street Station and, naturally, a murder. Dessert is served—and the crime is solved—after a train ride along Oil Creek. The OC & T offers half a dozen murder mystery train rides during its June-October operating season.

The **Barrow-Civic Theatre** (1223 Liberty St., Franklin, 814/437-3440, www.barrow-theatre.com) in downtown Franklin boasts a year-round season. Dedicated in 1993, the venue sometimes attracts touring performers but primarily showcases local talent. Shows by its Old Time Radio Troupe, dedicated to the art of the audio play, are a particular treat.

Festivals and Events

The region's oil heritage is celebrated not once but twice a year. Both the **Oil Heritage Festival** (814/676-8521, www.oilheritagefestival.com, late July, free) in Oil City and the **Oil Festival** (814/827-2941, www.titusville-chamber.com, early Aug., free) in Titusville feature an arts and crafts show, a parade, concerts, and fireworks. But the region's biggest fete isn't about oil. It's about a fruit. Franklin's **Applefest** (814/432-5823, www.franklinapplefest.com, first weekend of Oct., free) started as a pie-baking contest in 1983 and has grown into a three-day affair that attracts more than 100,000 people. The apple dumplings, apple cider, and other festival fare are big draws. So is the enormous antique and classic car cruise. The abundance of apple trees in the Franklin area is owed in part to the fabled Johnny Appleseed, who lived there in the opening years of the 19th century.

ACCOMMODATIONS
Titusville

There isn't *that* much to do in the mostly rural oil region, so there's a lot to be said for amenity-rich lodging. ★ **Oil Creek Family Campground** (340 Shreve Rd., Titusville, 814/827-1023 or 800/395-2045, www.oilcreekcampground.com, campsite $25-29, cabin $30-55, camper $70-75) fits the bill. It has a heated swimming pool, an 18-hole disc golf course, a fishing pond stocked with smallmouth bass and bluegill, a playground, a miniature train, a softball field, basketball and volleyball courts, and horseshoe pits. And that's not all. This place has a llama petting pen. The long-necked critters enjoy apples, pears, and grapes, so shop accordingly. Situated within walking distance of Oil Creek State Park, the campground has a variety of campsites, from secluded tent sites to full hook-up sites. A handful of cabins and 30-foot campers are available for rent.

What **Bromley's Hillhurst Bed & Breakfast** (701 N. Perry St., Titusville, 814/827-1101, www.bromleys-hillhurst.com, $95) lacks in llamas it makes up for in on-site massages. The turn-of-the-last-century manse boasts a grand staircase, fireplaces galore, and a great room with a player piano. It's packed with antiques and old-fashioned dolls, and guests who love that sort of thing will love its gift shop. The guest suites are spacious and the breakfasts sumptuous.

Titusville's other notable accommodations are the **Caboose Motel** (409 S. Perry St., Titusville, 800/827-0690, www.octrr.org/caboosemotel.htm, open May-late Oct., $90) and the **Knapp Farm** (43776 Thompson Run Rd., Titusville, 814/827-1092, www.theknappfarm.com, $90). Geared toward rail fans, the former sits on train tracks next to the home station of the Oil Creek & Titusville Railroad and consists of 21 caboose cars furnished with beds, heat and air-conditioning units, and televisions. Geared toward horse lovers and hunters, the latter offers B&B accommodations, guided trail rides, and hunts for pheasant, partridge, quail, wild turkey, and deer.

Oil City and Vicinity

Oil City's lodging options are few, which is good for business at the **Days Inn Oil City Conference Center** (1 Seneca St., Oil City, 814/677-1221, www.oilcityhotel.com, $69-99). Formerly known as The Arlington Hotel, it's centrally located near the confluence of Oil Creek and the Allegheny River, walking distance from the Venango Museum and National Transit Building. Amenities include a restaurant and lounge, an outdoor pool overlooking the Allegheny, and a guest laundry. Wireless Internet, continental breakfast, and access to a nearby YMCA are complimentary.

Franklin

Franklin's heart-of-it-all hotel is the **Quality Inn & Conference Center** (1411 Liberty St., Franklin, 814/437-3031, www.qualityinn.com, $90-200), offering rooms with refrigerators and microwaves, whirlpool suites, free Wi-Fi and breakfast, an exercise facility, and privileges at the local YMCA to boot.

For a charming bed-and-breakfast experience, book a room at the **The Witherup House** (828 Liberty St., Franklin, 814/437-7203, www.thewitheruphouse.com, $80). Owners Ann and Marty Rudegeair offer workshops on green building and living, and they walk the walk. Breakfast is a lesson in sustainable eating, with seasonal fruits and berries, locally made breads, and eggs from local grass-fed chickens.

FOOD
Titusville

If you're new to the **Blue Canoe Brewery** (113 S. Franklin St., Titusville, 814/827-7181, www.thebluecanoebrewery.com, 3pm-midnight Tues.-Fri., 12:30pm-midnight Sat., 12:30pm-9pm Sun., $8-20) start with a sampler paddle of seven beers. The food doesn't play second fiddle to the house-brewed suds, which find their way into the peel-and-eat shrimp, the bratwurst platter, and the char-grilled steaks. The brewpub also offers vegetarian tacos, portobello pasta, and hand-tossed pizza.

Oil City

The **Mosaic Café** (237 Seneca St., Oil City, 814/676-4773, www.mosaiccafeoilcity.com, 10am-3pm Tues., 10am-9pm Wed.-Thurs., 10am-8pm Fri., 11am-8pm Sat., kitchen opens 1 hour after café, under $10) bills itself as "the freshest place in town" but also shines in the creativity department. The salad and sandwich selection is impressive, and the beignets—executive chef David Gundrum trained in New Orleans—are not to be missed. The café is BYOB, but with drinks like housemade hot white chocolate and caramel apple smoothie on the menu, you may not want to bother.

Franklin

The lousy thing about the **AmaZing Foods Café** (1327 Elk St., Franklin, 814/437-3663, www.amazingfoodscatering.com, 8am-2pm Mon.-Fri., $4-9), the public face of a catering operation in downtown Franklin, is that it's not open on weekends. Boo to that. Yay to its delectable pancakes, piping hot oatmeal, and other morning starters. There's a Mediterranean tinge to the lunch menu of sandwiches and sides. AmaZing is all about fresh, sustainable ingredients, so it changes its menus often but is always true to its name.

★ **Bella Cucina** (1234 Liberty St., Franklin, 814/432-4955, www.bellacucinapa. com, lunch 11am-2pm Tues.-Sat., dinner 5pm-9:30pm Tues.-Sat., lunch $9-12, dinner $19-34) promises a "divine dining" experience and delivers. Its Italian name belies the eclecticism of its cuisine. The appetizers alone run the gamut from fried calamari to duck egg rolls.

INFORMATION

The **Oil Region Alliance** (217 Elm St., Oil City, 814/677-3152, www.oilregion.org, 8am-5pm Mon.-Fri.) promotes tourism in Titusville, Oil City, Franklin, and other municipalities within a 708-square-mile area known as the Oil Heritage Region. Its website is a good source of information about the region, which was designated a Pennsylvania Heritage Area in 1994 and a National Heritage Area a decade later. Stop by its office in downtown Oil City or the home station of the **Oil Creek & Titusville Railroad** (409 S. Perry St., Titusville, 9:30am-5pm Sat.-Sun. in June and Sept., Wed.-Sun. in July, Aug., and Oct.) to load up on brochures.

GETTING THERE

The cities of Titusville, Oil City, and Franklin lie along Route 8, a north-south route stretching from Erie to Pittsburgh. Titusville, the northernmost of the cities, is about 45 miles southeast of Erie via Routes 19, 97, and 8 south.

Franklin has an airport, **Venango Regional Airport** (FKL, 814/432-5333, www.flyfranklin.org), but you can only fly there from Cleveland. The larger **Erie International Airport, Tom Ridge Field** (ERI, 814/833-4258, www.erieairport.org) is served by three major airlines offering service from Cleveland, Detroit, and Philadelphia.

Pennsylvania Wilds

Look for ★ to find recommended
sights, activities, dining, and lodging.

Highlights

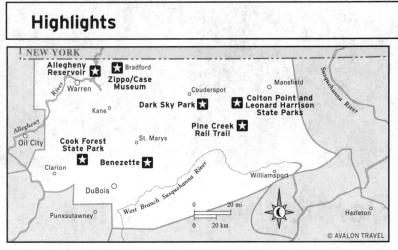

★ **Allegheny Reservoir:** The lake born of a 1960s anti-flooding project is a stunner whether you're gazing at it from a perch in Pennsylvania's only national forest or racing across it in a motorboat (page 432).

★ **Zippo/Case Museum:** Dedicated to the handsome lighter that has appeared in more movies than John Wayne (who himself carried a Zippo), this museum speaks volumes about American culture (page 435).

★ **Cook Forest State Park:** Wrap your arms around a 350-year-old tree, take a horse ride, and race a go-kart all in one day. Now that's recreation (page 437).

★ **Colton Point and Leonard Harrison State Parks:** Both afford breathtaking views of the gorge known as Pennsylvania's Grand Canyon (page 444).

★ **Pine Creek Rail Trail:** Get high on nature and some low-impact exercise on the 60-mile trail that winds through wondrous Pine Creek Gorge, open to hikers, bikers, snowshoers, skiers, and even covered wagons (page 445).

★ **Dark Sky Park:** Good-bye, light pollution. Helloooo, heavenly bodies! Cherry Springs State Park offers some of the best stargazing on the eastern seaboard (page 446).

★ **Benezette:** This itty-bitty town is ground zero for communing with the largest herd of free-roaming elk east of the Rockies (page 461).

May as well leave your cell phone at home when you visit the Pennsylvania Wilds. It won't work in many parts of the vast and lightly populated region. To say that north-central Pennsylvania has more trees than people is a colossal un-

derstatement. More than 80 percent of the Wilds—a brand the state cooked up—is forestland. Perhaps that's why one county in the region advertises itself as "God's Country." Philadelphia has more than twice as many residents as the 12 counties that make up the Wilds.

Almost a third of the region—about two million acres—is public land, open to anyone with an itch to explore. There's room for just about every form of outdoor recreation, from hunting to hang gliding. Anglers and boaters will find thousands of miles of streams and waterways, including more than 2,000 wild trout streams. Hikers will find trails at every turn. The region isn't just for rugged types. It's for berry pickers, leaf peepers, and stargazers. It's for anyone with a yen for nature. Pennsylvania's only national forest, the river gorge known as the "Grand Canyon of Pennsylvania," and the largest free-roaming elk herd in the northeastern United States can all be seen without so much as leaving your car.

The wealth of natural resources that makes the region so attractive to outdoorspeople made it irresistible to 19th-century oil and lumber barons. The industries created boomtowns like Bradford ("High-Grade Oil Metropolis of the World") and Williamsport ("Lumber Capital of the World") and scarred the landscape. A century ago, the breathtaking Pine Creek Gorge was a smoldering wasteland of tree stumps, sawdust, and ash. Pennsylvania elk were unheard of. But the earth healed, thanks in part to government conservation efforts. As for the towns, they faded from the limelight. Their populations dwindled, and their mansions fell into disrepair. Today many Pennsylvanians from other parts would be hard-pressed to name a town in the Wilds (though Punxsutawney, made famous by a groundhog and a Bill Murray movie, might come to mind eventually). That may change if the region continues to attract nature lovers

Previous: Kinzua Bridge Skywalk; elk in Benezette; Pine Creek Rail Trail. **Above:** covered wagon tour of Pine Creek Gorge.

Pennsylvania Wilds

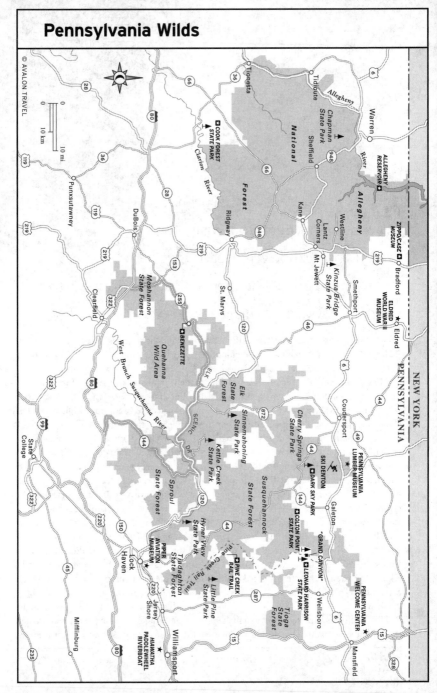

and families grateful for low-cost recreation. In recent years it has attracted another demographic: natural gas explorers. If their bullish predictions prove accurate, the Wilds may very well snag a new "capital" crown.

PLANNING YOUR TIME

The largest region in Pennsylvania is bigger than some states—and more than twice the size of Connecticut. That means you'll be doing a lot of driving if you want to take in the major sights. Fortunately, the region is made for road trips. Its east-west thoroughfares are Route 6 across the upper half and I-80 across the bottom. The former is a favorite of motorcyclists and other aficionados of the open road. Contact the **PA Route 6 Tourist Association** (877/276-8836, www.paroute6. com) for a free guide to the highway's historic and scenic attractions. If you're visiting the region for just two or three days, take in Kinzua Dam in the Allegheny National Forest and Pine Creek Gorge in Tioga County, traveling Route 6 between the two. If you have more time, head south via Route 15, Route 219, or any number of meandering roads, and pay a visit to Pennsylvania's wild elk herd or the birthplace of Little League Baseball.

National Forest Region

The river valleys and steep hillsides of Pennsylvania's only national forest are blanketed with black cherry, red maple, and other hardwoods. They didn't always look like this. Two hundred years ago, the woods of northern Pennsylvania were thick with shade-tolerant eastern hemlock and American beech and laced with white pine and oak. When European settlers arrived in the early 1800s, they cut trees to make cabins and barns and to clear land for farming. As the nation grew, so did the demand for timber. Sawmills, tanneries reliant on hemlock bark for turning hides into leather, and railroads sprouted across the state's northern tier. The wood chemical industry, born near the end of the century, provided a market for virtually every accessible tree. By the time the **Allegheny National Forest** (814/723-5150, www.fs.usda.gov/allegheny) was established in 1923, the land was

Allegheny National Forest

so barren and so prone to wildfires that residents jokingly referred to it as the "Allegheny brush patch."

Worries that the forest would never recover proved unfounded. A new and different forest arose, dominated by sun-loving hardwoods. They make motor touring a popular pastime in the fall, when the hills are ablaze with crimson and gold. (The best leaf peeping is in late September and early October.) In the 1940s, timber harvesting resumed under the strict guidelines of the U.S. Forest Service. It continues to this day, so don't be surprised if you find yourself driving behind a trailer loaded with timber. The biggest change to the national forest came in 1965, with the completion of Kinzua Dam on the Allegheny River. The resultant reservoir is the hub of recreational activity in the forest, which spans more than half a million acres in four counties. Warren, Bradford, and other towns on the forest's fringes offer a range of lodging and dining options, plus cultural attractions including a museum dedicated to Zippo lighters.

★ ALLEGHENY RESERVOIR

The construction of Kinzua Dam was not without controversy. It forced the relocation of Pennsylvania's only remaining Native American community and its sacred burial ground, inspiring a federal lawsuit and a song recorded by country legend Johnny Cash. But the U.S. government saw the dam as necessary armament in its war against flooding. The Army Corps of Engineers estimates that Kinzua Dam (pronounced "KIN-zoo") has prevented flood damages in excess of $1.2 billion since its completion in 1965. Its contribution to the recreational appeal of the Allegheny National Forest is priceless.

The dam created the **Allegheny Reservoir** (814/726-0661, www.corpslakes. us), also known as Kinzua Lake. More than 24 miles long, the lake straddles the Pennsylvania-New York border. In Pennsylvania, it's completely surrounded by the Allegheny National Forest. In New York,

it's bordered by Allegany State Park and the Allegany Indian Reservation of the Seneca Nation. (Yep, the spelling varies.) Its largely undeveloped shoreline is dotted with picnic areas, boat launches, and campgrounds.

Kinzua Dam itself is in Warren County, nine miles east of the city of Warren. From Warren, head east on Route 6 for about two miles and turn left (east) on Route 59, which leads to a parking lot at the top of the dam. Check out the giant carp that congregate on one side of the dam and the hydroelectric facilities on the other. Displays at the Army Corps' **Big Bend Visitor Center** (Rte. 59, 814/726-0678, 10am-3:45pm weekends Memorial Day weekend-Labor Day), just downstream of the dam, illustrate the hydroelectric process. The outflow area is a popular fishing spot.

Two nearby overlooks offer bird's-eye views of the river valley (and attract rock climbers). Leaving the dam, drive east on Route 59 for about three miles. Just before reaching a bridge that crosses the reservoir, turn right onto Longhouse Scenic Drive (Forest Road 262). Make the first right off Longhouse to reach **Jakes Rock Overlook.** The access road to **Rimrock Overlook,** Forest Road 454, is about three miles farther east on Route 59. Follow the forest road until it ends at a parking lot. A short hike leads to the viewing area atop a large rock face. There are picnic areas at both overlooks.

Between the overlooks is the 250-slip **Kinzua Wolf Run Marina** (Rte. 59, 3 miles east of Kinzua Dam, 814/726-1650, www. kinzuamarina.com, mid-May-mid-Sept.), which rents houseboats, pontoon boats, motorboats, canoes, and kayaks. The entrance to **Kinzua Beach** is across Route 59 from the marina. The beach features a roped-off swimming area, a sandbox, picnic tables and grills, and restrooms.

Camping

You can pitch a tent just about anywhere in the Allegheny National Forest (814/723-5150, www.fs.usda.gov/allegheny), but nothing

"As Long as the Grass Shall Grow"

Kinzua Dam

The construction of Kinzua Dam on the Allegheny River flooded lands that had been promised to the Seneca Nation by President George Washington. Native American folksinger Peter La Farge wrote a song about the plight of the Senecas, which Johnny Cash recorded in 1964. "As Long as the Grass Shall Grow" is the first song on Cash's *Bitter Tears* album.

> ...On the Seneca reservation there is much sadness now
> Washington's treaty has been broken, and there is no hope no how
> All across the Allegheny River, they're throwing up a dam
> It will flood the Indian country, a proud day for Uncle Sam ...
> As long as the moon shall rise
> As long as the rivers flow
> As long as the sun will shine
> As long as the grass shall grow

beats lakeside camping. There are several modern campgrounds on the shores of the Allegheny Reservoir in Pennsylvania. **Willow Bay** is on the eastern shore along Route 346, about 15 miles west of Bradford. It has more than 100 campsites and about a dozen rustic cabins with electricity. Amenities include a concrete boat launch and a large picnic area overlooking the reservoir. Canoes and kayaks are available for rent.

There are two modern campgrounds, **Dewdrop** and **Kiasutha,** along Longhouse Scenic Drive (Forest Road 262) on the western shore of Kinzua Bay, a southern branch

of the Allegheny Reservoir. Both have concrete boat launches. The latter also boasts a large swimming beach and picnic area. **Red Bridge** campground, located along Route 321 on the eastern shore of Kinzua Bay, doesn't have a boat launch, beach, or picnic area, but it is adjacent to a popular bank fishing area.

Willow Bay is open year-round. Dewdrop and Kiasutha are open from Memorial Day weekend through Labor Day. Red Bridge is open April to mid-December. Campsite fees are $17-30. The four- and six-person cabins at Willow Bay rent for $50-65 per night. Peak-season reservations can be made through www.recreation.gov or by calling 877/444-6777. Off-season reservations can be made through Allegheny Site Management (814/368-4158, www.alleghenysite.com), a private company that operates recreation facilities in the national forest.

There are also several primitive campgrounds on the shores of the Allegheny Reservoir in Pennsylvania: Handsome Lake, Hooks Brook, Hopewell, Morrison, and Pine Grove. They can only be reached by foot or boat. Campsites are available on a first-come, first-served basis. Visit the website of the Allegheny National Forest or Allegheny Site Management for more information.

The Forest Service prohibits camping on the shores of the reservoir except in these designated areas.

Fishing

The Allegheny Reservoir has produced record-setting walleye, northern pike, and channel catfish. Keep in mind that a Pennsylvania fishing license doesn't fly in New York's share of the reservoir, where jurisdiction is divided between the state and the Seneca Nation. Be sure to have a license from the appropriate agency for the portion of lake you're fishing. Want to maximize your odds of catching a trophy fish? Call Red Childress of **Allegheny Guide Service** (814/723-5912 or 814/688-2309, www.alleghenyguideservice.com). He offers fishing trips on the Allegheny River, Allegheny Reservoir, and Tionesta Lake, an Army Corps project at the southwest corner of the national forest.

OTHER SIGHTS
Historic Warren

The city of Warren, just west of the Allegheny Reservoir, boasts a 28-block National Historic District. Ask for a walking tour brochure at the **Warren County Historical Society** (210 4th Ave., 814/723-1795, www.warrenhistory.org, 8:30am-4:30pm Mon.-Fri. year-round and 9am-noon Sat. in summer). The society's headquarters is itself a historic property: an 1870s Second Empire-style house that's especially enchanting come Christmastime. The tour ends at the **Warren County Courthouse** (204 4th Ave., 8:30am-4:30pm Mon.-Fri.), site of a 1954 courtroom shooting that left a judge dead and captured the nation's attention. You can still find bullet holes in the woodwork.

Vicinity of Warren

The hodgepodge of artifacts at the **Wilder**

the city of Warren, on the Allegheny River

Museum (51 Erie Ave., Irvine, 814/563-7773, www.warrenhistory.org/wilder_museum.htm, 1pm-5pm Tues. and Fri.-Sat. mid-May-early Oct., by donation) includes a one-handed clock invented in Warren and a two-person vacuum. With 14 exhibit rooms, the museum operated by the Warren County Historical Society even has space for a 1963 Mercedes-Benz. Tiny Irvine is about eight miles west of Warren along Route 6.

Call ahead to make sure someone is in at the **Simpler Times Museum** (111 Simpler Times Ln., Tidioute, 814/484-3483, www.warrenhistory.org/SimplerTimesMuseum.html, open by chance or appointment), an oversize collection of equipment related to the oil and farming industries. Bruce Ziegler and his wife began collecting vestiges of the oil boom and farming equipment in the mid-1990s. In 15 years they amassed more than 90 gasoline pumps, hundreds of gasoline signs and globes, 100 tractors, and more than a dozen antique cars, among other things. The Simpler Times collection is housed in five buildings on their property, located five miles north of Tidioute on Route 62.

Historic Bradford

The city of Bradford, east of the Allegheny Reservoir on Route 219, was once a small lumber town named Littleton. Its population exploded in the late 1800s with the discovery of a prolific oil field. In 1881, at the height of production, the field produced three-fourths of the world's oil output, and Bradford reigned as the "High-Grade Oil Metropolis of the World."

Bradford is still a hub of oil-related activity. The world's first billion-dollar field is still in business, though on a much smaller scale. Bradford's Minard Run Oil Company, owned by the same family since its establishment in 1875, is still prospecting. American Refining Group's Bradford refinery, established in 1881, is the world's oldest continuously operating crude oil refinery. The McDonald's in downtown Bradford has the usual—Big Macs, McNuggets, fries—and a working oil well in

its parking lot. Drilled in the 1870s, the well produces about a barrel a day.

Downtown Bradford deserves a stroll for its historic architecture and smattering of specialty shops. Start at the **Allegheny National Forest Visitors Bureau** (80 E. Corydon St., Bradford, 800/473-9370, www.visitanf.com, 9am-5pm Mon.-Fri.), where you can grab a map and brochures about area attractions. The visitors bureau is housed in one of Bradford's most impressive buildings, a former post office fronted by six large pillars.

Don't miss **Main Street Mercantile** (45 Main St., Bradford, 814/368-2206, www.bradfordmsm.com, 10am-6pm Mon.-Thurs., 10am-7pm Fri., 10am-6pm Sat., noon-4pm Sun.), a sprawling store with more than 75 vendors. You'll find antiques, local art, alpaca products, pottery, maple syrup, and more.

★ Zippo/Case Museum

The most visited museum in the region isn't dedicated to art or history but a little bit of both: the Zippo lighter. The Zippo was born in the early 1930s, after Bradford native George G. Blaisdell noticed a friend fumbling with an Austrian-made lighter. Blaisdell decided to make a lighter that was easier to use and handsome to boot. The first lighter he produced is one of hundreds of models and prototypes displayed at the museum within the **Zippo/Case Visitors Center** (1932 Zippo Dr., Bradford, 814/368-1932, www.zippo.com, 9am-5pm Mon.-Sat., 11am-4pm Sun., open until 7pm Thurs., free). The museum tells the uncommonly compelling story of how a lighter became a cultural icon with more than 1,000 movie, TV, and stage credits under its belt. Its collection includes contemporary artworks created with Zippos and examples of "trench art"—lighters decorated by servicemen during wartime. Knives made by W.R. Case & Sons Cutlery, a subsidiary of Zippo Manufacturing Company since 1993, are also exhibited.

Visitors can watch technicians at work in the Zippo Repair Clinic. The company fixes or replaces any broken Zippo, no matter how mangled, free of charge. (Tours of the factory, elsewhere in Bradford, are not available.) The store adjacent to the museum sells the complete line of Zippo and Case products, including collectors' items not found anywhere else.

Penn Brad Oil Museum

Located three miles south of Bradford on Route 219, the **Penn Brad Oil Museum** (901 South Ave., Bradford, 814/362-1955, 9am-4pm Mon.-Fri., 9am-2pm Sat., admission $5, seniors $4.50, children under 12 free) takes visitors back to oil boom times. Its large collection of oil field artifacts includes a 72-foot-tall drilling rig. Tours led by oil industry veterans heighten the experience.

Eldred World War II Museum

Even before the United States entered World War II, the town of Eldred was contributing to the Allied effort. A munitions plant serving British armed forces began operating in the Eldred area in mid-1941. The plant has since been dismantled, but Eldred hasn't forgotten its role in the global conflict. The **Eldred World War II Museum** (201 Main St., Eldred, 814/225-2220, www.eldredwwiimuseum.net, 10am-4pm Tues.-Sat., 1pm-4pm Sun., admission $5, children free) tells the story of the home front and the war abroad through artifacts, automated dioramas, and videos. An extensive library boasts rare and out-of-print books. Eldred is about 17 miles east of Bradford at the junction of Routes 346 and 446.

Kinzua Bridge Skywalk

When the Kinzua Bridge was built in 1882, it was the highest and longest railroad bridge in the world. At 301 feet high and 2,053 feet long, the bridge spanning the Kinzua Creek Valley was heralded as a work of engineering genius. Originally built of iron, it was reconstructed of steel less than 20 years later to handle heavier trains loaded with coal, timber, and oil. Long after it was outranked by other bridges and discarded by the Erie Railroad in 1959, sightseers packed excursion trains to cross it. A *New York Times* writer described soaring over the valley as "more akin to ballooning than railroading." But after more than a century of service, the man-made marvel was no match for Mother Nature. In July 2003, a tornado ripped 11 of the bridge's 20

The Kinzua Bridge Skywalk has a partial glass floor.

towers from their concrete bases, tossing them on the valley floor.

Instead of rebuilding the bridge, the state transformed its remains into a unique tourist attraction. Built on six surviving towers, the **Kinzua Bridge Skywalk** (Kinzua Bridge State Park, 1721 Lindholm Rd., Mount Jewett, 814/965-2646, www.visitpaparks.com) is a 600-foot walkway ending in an observation deck with a partial glass floor. Those who brave it are rewarded with spectacular views, especially at the height of fall foliage.

★ Cook Forest State Park

The Cook Forest literature talks a lot about old trees. No doubt, the trees are something to talk about. Many of the pines and hemlocks in the forest's old-growth areas are about 350 years old. Some are pushing 450. But old-growth timber isn't what brings most people to **Cook Forest State Park** (Rte. 36, Cooksburg, 814/744-8407, www.visitpaparks.com). The sprawling park just south of Allegheny National Forest offers some of the most scenic hiking and paddling in Pennsylvania. And unlike many wilderness areas, it has spawned a small tourist industry. The area is peppered with rental cabins, canoe liveries, horse rentals, and family fun parks. It's one of those rare places where you can hike to a National Natural Landmark—the old-growth area known as the Forest Cathedral—and race a go-kart in the same day.

If **hiking** is on your agenda, it's best to start at the park office, just right of the main entrance, where you can pick up a park guide and a brochure describing the trails. Several trailheads are a short walk from the office. In addition to 29 miles of hiking trails, the park boasts a 13-mile **biking** route composed of lightly traveled roads and part of a short hiking trail. Biking on all other hiking trails is prohibited. A description of the bike route is available at the park office.

The Clarion River is another of the park's main attractions. It's a beginner river, which means you don't need **paddling** experience—or even a paddle—to take it on. Plenty of visitors forgo canoes and kayaks in favor of an inner tube. Area liveries include **The Pale Whale Canoe Fleet** (6 River Rd., Cooksburg, 814/744-8300, www.canoecookforest.com, Apr.-Oct.), which rents canoes, kayaks, single and double tubes, and even floating coolers. The river also provides good **fishing.** Tom's Run, which runs through Cook Forest and joins the Clarion River near the park office, is popular for trout fishing. There's also a fishing pond stocked with trout near the park office. It's reserved for children 12 and under and people with disabilities.

Horseback riding is permitted in parts of the park. Horse rentals are available through **Cook Forest Scenic Trail Ride** (1661 Scott Dr., Clarion, 814/226-5985 May-Oct., 814/856-2081 Nov.-Apr., www.patrailride.com) and **Silver Stallion Stables** (83 Meadow Ln., Cooksburg, 814/927-6636).

There are plenty of places to **spend the night** in and near the park. Open from mid-April to mid-December, the park's Ridge Campground has more than 200 campsites. The park also offers rustic cabins. Some are perched on a hill overlooking the Clarion River. Campsites and cabins can be reserved online at www.pa.reserveworld.com or by calling 888/727-2757.

Another overnight option: **The Inn at Cook Forest** (105 River Rd., Cooksburg, 814/744-8590, www.theinnatcookforest.com, $115-150). The bed-and-breakfast was once home to the Cook family, for whom the park is named. The Cooks, who began logging the area in the early 1800s, had the foresight to spare some of its oldest, tallest trees. The state purchased the circa 1870 homestead in 2008, spent three years renovating it, and opened it as The Inn at Cook Forest in 2012.

The website of the Cook Forest Vacation Bureau (www.cookforest.org) is a good resource on privately owned campgrounds, cabins, and lodging properties in the Cook Forest area. It can also point you to attractions like the **Cook Forest Fun Park** (2952

rustic cabins in Cook Forest State Park

Rte. 36, Leeper, 814/744-9404, www.cookforestfunpark.com, 10am-10pm Mar.-Nov.), featuring go-karts, bumper boats, miniature golf, and a large waterslide.

ENTERTAINMENT AND EVENTS
Performing Arts

The **Struthers Library Theatre** (302 W. 3rd Ave., Warren, 814/723-7231, www.strutherslibrarytheatre.com) in the heart of Warren's Historic District was built in 1883. It's home to the **Warren Players** (www.warrenplayers.com), an amateur theater company organized in 1930, and an annual film series. The **Warren Concert Association** (814/723-2348, www.warrenconcertassociation.com) brings everything from bluegrass to baroque to the Struthers.

The **Bradford Creative & Performing Arts Center** (814/362-2522, www.bcpac.com) presents music, theater, and dance by talented Bradfordians as well as professional artists and troupes from around the country.

The hexagon-shaped **Verna Leith Sawmill Theatre** at the Cook Forest Sawmill Center for the Arts (140-170 Theatre Ln., Cooksburg, 814/927-6655, www.sawmill.org) hosts performances by area theater groups from May to September.

Festivals and Events

There's no better time to visit the forest region than late September and early October, when the leaves are changing color. And there's no better place to take in the majesty than Kinzua Bridge State Park with its 225-foot-high observation deck. May as well time your visit with the **Kinzua Bridge Fall Festival** (814/887-2754, www.kinzuabridgefoundation.com, 3rd weekend of Sept., free), featuring live music, food and craft vendors, and a Bigfoot calling contest.

Competitions between professional lumberjacks from as far away as New Zealand are a highlight of the **Johnny Appleseed Festival** (814/968-3906, www.johnnyappleseedfest.net, early Oct., free). Held in the forest town of Sheffield, the three-day affair also features chainsaw carving, an antique tractor pull, a wine-tasting, a pie-baking contest, and fireworks.

Perfectly sane people plunge into insanely cold water during **Warren County Winterfest** (814/726-1222, www.warrencountywinterfest.com, Jan., free) at Chapman State Park. In addition to the "polar bear plunge," the weekend festival includes ice fishing and snow-sculpting contests, sled dog races, and sleigh rides.

SPORTS AND RECREATION

The Allegheny Reservoir and Cook Forest State Park are popular hubs of recreation in the national forest region, but they're hardly the whole story. The region is crisscrossed with trails and rivers, peppered with state parks and game lands, and blessed with the sort of scenery that makes driving a pleasure. What follows is a mere sampling of recreation opportunities.

ATV Trails

The national forest has more than 100 miles of trails for all-terrain vehicles and dirt bikes. For directions to trailheads, trail maps and descriptions, condition reports, and other information, visit the forest website (www. fs.usda.gov/allegheny) or call 814/362-4613 or 814/927-6628.

All ATV trails are marked with yellow diamonds. Riding on unmarked routes is a major no-no, as is riding without a permit. Daily permits ($10) and season permits ($35) are available at a number of locations, including the forest supervisor's office (4 Farm Colony Dr., Warren, 814/723-5150), the Bradford Ranger District office (29 Forest Service Dr., Bradford, 814/362-4613), and the Marienville Ranger District office (131 Smokey Ln., Marienville, 814/927-6628).

If you're new to off-roading or bringing along children, head to **Majestic Trails** (Rte. 46, 9 miles south of Bradford, 814/465-9979, www.majestictrails.com), an ATV park on privately owned property just east of the national forest. Majestic offers guided ATV and dirt bike tours, dirt bike lessons, and kid-friendly trails, along with plenty of challenging terrain for experienced riders. It also offers cabin rentals and "wilderness-style" camping.

Biking

Mountain bikers are welcome on ATV and snowmobile trails, select hiking trails, and gated roads in the national forest (814/723-5150, www.fs.usda.gov/allegheny). Road cyclists can pedal through the forest on Route 6.

The state-endorsed BicyclePA Route Y generally follows Route 6 from one end of the state to the other.

Boating

The national forest region is beloved by powerboaters and paddlers alike. The former make waves on the **Allegheny Reservoir** and **Tionesta Lake** (Rte. 36, just south of Tionesta, 814/755-3512, www.corpslakes.us), an Army Corps project on the western fringe of the national forest. The latter are welcome on these lakes but also have their pick of rivers and streams.

The **Allegheny River** below Kinzua Dam sees a good number of professional canoe and kayak races, but it's calm enough for paddling novices. **Allegheny Outfitters** (2101 Pennsylvania Ave. E., Warren, 814/723-1203, www.alleghenyoutfitters.com, Apr.-Oct.) offers rental canoes and kayaks and facilitates paddling trips on the river. Its most popular trip starts at Kinzua Dam and ends seven miles later at the livery.

Tionesta-based **Outback Adventures** (Rte. 62, just south of Tionesta Bridge, 814/755-3658, www.outbackadventure-spa.com, Apr.-Oct.) specializes in trips on **Tionesta Creek** as well as the Allegheny River. The creek makes for a magical float in early spring; by June, water levels are generally too low for paddling. Outback Adventures also operates a riverfront campground.

The **Clarion River,** one of the major tributaries of the Allegheny, was once believed to be the most polluted river in Pennsylvania (think acid mine drainage). You wouldn't know it from the recovered section that snakes through Cook Forest State Park and along the southern border of the national forest. There are several liveries in the Cook Forest area, including **The Pale Whale Canoe Fleet** (6 River Rd., Cooksburg, 814/744-8300, www. canoecookforest.com, Apr.-Oct.).

Fishing

The region's lakes, ponds, rivers, and streams are home to many species of fish. Directions to more than two dozen fishing spots are available on the national forest website (www.fs.usda.gov/allegheny). The **Allegheny Reservoir** and **Allegheny River** below Kinzua Dam are particularly popular with anglers because they yield some of the largest freshwater fish in the state. For help getting in on the action, call Red Childress of **Allegheny Guide Service** (814/723-5912 or 814/688-2309, www.alleghenyguideservice.com), who leads fishing trips on the Allegheny River, Allegheny Reservoir, and **Tionesta Lake.**

If you're confident in your skills, consider visiting the region in late September, during the **Pennsylvania State Championship Fishing Tournament** (814/484-3585). It's open to anyone with a valid Pennsylvania fishing license, including children as young as three. The tournament has been held in the itty-bitty town of Tidioute, which sits at a sharp bend in the Allegheny River, for more than 50 years.

Information on fishing licenses and seasons can be found on the website of the Pennsylvania Fish & Boat Commission (814/337-0444, www.fishandboat.com).

Hiking

Hundreds of miles of hiking trails snake through the national forest region.

Trails near the Allegheny Reservoir include the **Morrison Trail,** an 11.4-mile loop that can be broken into two shorter loops. The trailhead parking lot is off Route 59, seven miles east of Kinzua Dam. The trail leads to the primitive Morrison campground on the shores of the reservoir.

Trails in the southern part of the forest include the 9.6-mile **Buzzard Swamp** system, near the town of Marienville. Buzzard Swamp—a string of 15 man-made ponds—offers some of the best wildlife viewing in the forest, especially during the spring waterfowl migration. From Marienville, follow Lamonaville Road 2.5 miles east to reach the northern trailhead.

The **North Country National Scenic Trail** (616/897-5987, www.northcountrytrail.org), which stretches from New York to North Dakota, traverses the length of the national forest.

Guides to these and other trails are available on the national forest website (www.fs.usda.gov/allegheny) and at Forest Service and tourism promotion offices.

Horseback Riding

Riding is permitted in most parts of the Allegheny National Forest. A number of ranches on its borders supply well-mannered horses. **Hickory Creek Wilderness Ranch** (2516 Economite Rd., Tidioute, 814/484-7520, www.hickorycreekranch.com) offers trail rides, camping, and cabin rentals. In July it offers a chance to see professional bull riders in action at the **Battle on Bull Mountain.**

The 600-acre **Flying W Ranch** (685 Flying W Ranch Rd., Tionesta, 814/463-7663, www.theflyingwranch.com) also offers trail rides, camping, and cabin rentals. Its overnight pack trips, which include a night on the ranch, a night on the trail, and a cook, are a great way for city slickers to sample the cowboy life. In July the ranch hosts the **Allegheny Mountain Championship Rodeo,** featuring steer wrestling, bronco riding, and other man-versus-wild spectacles.

Skydiving

The **Freefall OZ Skydiving Center** (Ceres Township, PA, 716/378-2211, www.freefallozskydiving.com) offers tandem jumps and free-fall instruction—and killer breakfasts. Owners Ash and Celeine Easdon-Smith turned a century-old barn into a rustic-chic B&B, **Oz's Homestay** (www.ozhomestayhuntinglodge.com, 716/378-2211, $119-139). Ash, who hails from Australia, crafted much of the furniture from trees from their 122-acre property.

Winter Sports

The Allegheny National Forest has more than 300 miles of groomed snowmobile trails and about 50 miles of trails designated for cross-country skiing. Visit the national forest website (www.fs.usda.gov/allegheny) for trail maps and information on snow conditions.

ACCOMMODATIONS

Campgrounds and cabins abound in the national forest region, but it also offers unique lodging options like The Lodge at Glendorn, a member of the uber-exclusive Relais & Châteaux group.

Under $100

Kane Manor (230 Clay St., Kane, 814/837-6522, www.kanemanor.com, $59-69) was built in the final years of the 19th century for Elizabeth Kane, widow of the abolitionist and Civil War general for whom the town of Kane is named. Today it's a B&B with 11 guest rooms, period furnishings, Kane family mementos, and an impressive portico overlooking the lush grounds.

Hand-crocheted afghans and homemade baked goods await at **The Inn on Maple Street Bed & Breakfast** (115 E. Maple St., Port Allegany, 814/642-5171, www.theinnonmaplestreet.com, $89-169), one block off Route 6 in picturesque Port Allegany.

$100-200

Horton House Bed & Breakfast (504 Market St., Warren, 814/723-7472, www.hortonhousebb.com, from $134) is named for Isaac Horton, the lumber magnate who built the 7,500-square-foot house (of wood, naturally) in the late 1800s. Its rooms are so lovingly decorated that it's hard to tell which were the servants' quarters. Guests can soak in the outdoor hot tub year-round.

Built in 1934 at the "gateway" to Cook Forest State Park, ★ **Gateway Lodge** (14870 Rte. 36, Cooksburg, 814/744-8017, www.gatewaylodge.com, rooms $150-200, suites $225-250, cabins $135-215, weekly rates available for cabins) has morphed into the picture of rustic elegance in the hands of Deb Adams, its owner since 2006. It boasts fireside whirlpool tubs, private balconies, an on-site spa, and fabulous food and wine. Gateway's farm-to-table

restaurant, which is open to the public, serves breakfast ($10) and dinner ($15-35) daily.

Over $200

Pull up to ★ **The Lodge at Glendorn** (1000 Glendorn Dr., Bradford, 814/362-6511, www.glendorn.com, rooms from $450, suites from $735, cabins from $750) and a staff member or two will be waiting outside to greet you. Sink into a velvety couch in the all-redwood main lodge and another will offer you a drink. Come dinnertime, a seasoned server will produce a menu written just for you. Prefer to have the executive chef cook for you in the privacy of a hilltop cabin? Just ask. The effect is rare and priceless: you'll feel like you own the place. Indeed, for almost 70 years, Glendorn was a private estate, an idyllic retreat for the oil-rich Dorn family. They opened it to the public in 1995, and it quickly earned a reputation as one of the nation's premier hideaways. The property is so secluded that many area residents don't know what or where it is—all the better for guests like Denzel Washington, who stayed there during filming of 2009's runaway-train thriller *Unstoppable*. One of only three Orvis-endorsed fly-fishing lodges in Pennsylvania, Glendorn offers the fly fisher nearly three miles of privately managed trout angling. Other amenities include three trout-filled ponds, a 60-foot pool, tennis courts, a trap and skeet shooting range, and a vast trail system.

FOOD
Bradford

True to its name, **Beefeaters** (27 Congress St., Bradford, 814/362-9717, www.thebeefeatersrestaurant.com, 4pm-10pm Mon.-Sat., $9-24) specializes in beef. Guests can eye the goods at the "beef bar," where beef roast after beef roast is carved into slices for dishes like beef on weck, a sandwich distinguished by its seasoned roll. Chicken, seafood, and pasta dishes are also on offer. The restaurant is housed in a stately building that served as Bradford's library for nine decades.

For breakfast or lunch, you can't beat **John**

William's European Pastry Shop (20 Mechanic St., Bradford, 814/362-6637, 6am-5pm Mon.-Fri., 6am-3pm Sat.-Sun., under $10). In addition to delectable baked goods, the old-fashioned scratch bakery serves up omelets, panini, croissant sandwiches, salads, and more.

Kane

You can swirl, sniff, sip, and go—or stay a while—at **Flickerwood Wine Cellars** (309 Flickerwood Rd., Kane, 814/837-7566, www.flickerwood.com, 11am-7pm Mon.-Thurs., 10am-9pm Fri.-Sat., noon-6pm Sun.). The award-winning winery features a lounge where guests can savor a glass of wine while noshing on cheese and pepperoni, chicken skewers, mini quiches, and other hors d'oeuvres. Flickerwood's reds, whites, and blushes are the creations of Ron Zampogna, who served the red, white, and blue as a Forest Service employee for 36 years.

Warren

The ★ **Plaza Restaurant** (328 Pennsylvania Ave. W., Warren, 814/723-5660, 7am-8pm Mon.-Sat., under $10) is "still doing things the hard way," according to its owner, whose Greek-born father opened the diner in 1959. In other words, it still makes just about everything from scratch—from mashed potatoes to heavenly pies. Skip the standard diner grub and order a Greek specialty like souvlaki or spinach pie. Finish with a slice of cream pie.

Legends (809 Jackson Ave. Ext., 814/723-9170, www.dinerz.com/legends, 5pm-9pm Wed.-Sat., $8-18) is known as much for its decor as its steaks, seafood, and massive sandwiches. A 1953 Santa Fe caboose serves as one of its dining rooms, an ice-filled bathtub serves as the salad bar, and desserts are laid out in the open trunk of a 1949 pink Cadillac. Crank telephones, vintage gas pumps, pump organs, and other antiques decorate every corner.

Westline

The town of Westline is a speckle on forest maps. Find it and you'll be rewarded with fine French cuisine. **The Westline Inn** (Westline Rd., 814/778-5103, www.westlineinn.com, dinner 5:30pm-9pm Tues.-Thurs., 5:30pm-10pm Fri.-Sat., 3pm-7pm Sun., bar open from 3pm Mon.-Thurs., noon Fri.-Sat., 3pm Sun., $9-30) offers escargot, crepes stuffed with seafood, bouillabaisse, and the like. Prefer an American-style burger? Ask for the pub menu. First, though, you have to find the place. From the intersection of Routes 6 and 219, head north on 219 for five miles to a sign pointing left to Westline. Follow the narrow road for three miles.

INFORMATION AND SERVICES

The headquarters of the **Allegheny National Forest** (4 Farm Colony Dr., Warren, 814/723-5150, www.fs.usda.gov/allegheny, 8am-4:30pm Mon.-Fri.) is about five miles north of downtown Warren on Route 62. In addition to reams of free literature on forest recreation, you'll find T-shirts, topographical maps, books on plants and birds, and other merchandise. You can also load up on information at the **Bradford Ranger District** office (29 Forest Service Dr., Bradford, 814/362-4613), responsible for the upper part of the forest, or the **Marienville Ranger District** office (131 Smokey Ln., Marienville, 814/927-6628), responsible for the lower part.

The Army Corps of Engineers operates the seasonal **Big Bend Visitor Center** (Rte. 59, 9 miles east of Warren, 814/726-0678, 10am-4pm daily Memorial Day weekend-Labor Day and weekends through Oct.), just downriver of Kinzua Dam. For a daily summary of water conditions, call 814/726-0164.

The national forest stretches across four counties represented by three tourism promotion agencies, each of which can supply a plethora of information about the region. The **Allegheny National Forest Visitors Bureau** (80 E. Corydon St., Bradford, 800/473-9370, www.visitanf.com, 9am-5pm Mon.-Fri.), which represents McKean County, is headquartered in downtown Bradford. The **Warren County Visitors Bureau** (22045

Rte. 6, Warren, 814/726-1222, www.wcvb. net, 9am-4:30pm Mon.-Fri., 11am-4pm Sat.) is about six miles west of downtown Warren. The lower part of the forest lies in Forest and Elk Counties, which are represented by the **PA Great Outdoors Visitors Bureau** (2801 Maplevale Rd., Brookville, 814/849-5197, www. visitpago.com, 8:30am-4:30pm Mon.-Fri.).

GETTING THERE AND AROUND

The forest region, like the rest of the Wilds, is driving country. The national forest is roughly framed by Route 62 on the west and Route 219 on the east. Route 6 wriggles across it. Another east-west road, Route 59, crosses the Allegheny Reservoir, the recreational heart of the forest.

Bradford Regional Airport (BFD), just east of the Allegheny Reservoir, is served by United Airlines. **DuBois Regional Airport** (DUJ) to the forest's south and **Chautauqua County Airport-Jamestown** (JHW) to its north also offer commercial service. The larger **Erie International Airport** (ERI, 814/833-4258, www.erieairport.org) and **Buffalo Niagara International Airport** (BUF) are within a two-hour drive of the forest.

Pine Creek Gorge and Vicinity

Often referred to as the "Grand Canyon of Pennsylvania," Pine Creek Gorge deserves an identity all its own. It's less imposing than the real Grand Canyon, less masculine angles and more womanly curves. With its thick blanket of trees—the kind that change color—Pine Creek Gorge has no comparison in the arid southwest. It's Pennsylvania through and through.

The glacially carved gorge starts near the Route 6 village of Ansonia and continues south for 47 miles. Most visitors take in its majesty from one of two state parks near its northern end, where the canyon is about 800 feet deep. Near its southern end, Pine Creek Gorge is as deep as 1,450 feet and a whopping mile wide. Whopping is a relative term, of course. The real Grand Canyon, in Arizona, is as deep as 6,000 feet and 10 miles wide on average. Still, Pine Creek Gorge is "one of the

Pine Creek Gorge, the "Grand Canyon of Pennsylvania"

Pine Creek Gorge

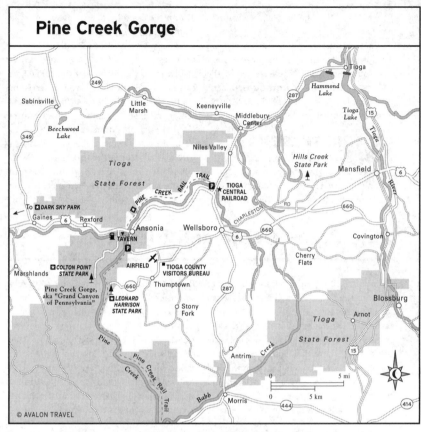

© AVALON TRAVEL

finest examples of a deep gorge in the eastern United States," according to the National Park Service, which has seen them all.

The 60-mile Pine Creek Rail Trail brings hikers, bikers, horseback riders, cross-country skiers, and snowshoers to the region, while the swift waters of Pine Creek call to anglers and paddlers.

★ COLTON POINT AND LEONARD HARRISON STATE PARKS

On the west rim of the gorge, there's Colton Point State Park. On the east, there's Leonard Harrison. The former is accessible from Route 6 at Ansonia, though the road leading to it is easily missed. You'll find Colton Road between a small gas station and the Burnin'

Barrel Bar. Follow it for five miles to the state park and its series of scenic overlooks.

The better-groomed Leonard Harrison offers superior views of the canyon (and bathrooms with plumbing). From the town of Wellsboro, follow Route 660 west for 10 miles to the park. You can stop at the **Tioga County Visitors Center** (2053 Rte. 660, Wellsboro, 570/724-0635, www.visittiogapa.com, 8am-4:30pm Mon.-Fri. year-round, 9am-1pm Sat. May-Oct., 9am-1pm Sun. Oct.) along the way. The state park office at the entrance to **Leonard Harrison** (4797 Rte. 660, Wellsboro, 570/724-3061, www.visitpaparks.com, 8am-4pm Mon.-Fri. spring-fall or as staffing allows) handles queries about both parks. The main overlook and an environmental interpretive center are a quarter of a mile up the road.

Both parks have picnic tables and pavilions, several miles of hiking trails, and seasonal campgrounds. Sites at Colton Point, which has rustic toilets, are first-come, first-served. The Leonard Harrison campground has modern facilities, including flush toilets and some electric hookups. Sites can be reserved online at www.pa.reserveworld.com or by calling 888/727-2757.

Hiking

While short, the steep rim-to-creek trails at Colton Point and Leonard Harrison State Parks can challenge even experienced hikers. The highlight of **Colton Point's Turkey Path,** a three-mile down-and-back trail, is a 70-foot cascading waterfall less than half a mile from the trailhead. **Leonard Harrison's Turkey Path** is two miles down and back, leading to a vista and waterfall before reaching the canyon floor. There's no bridge across Pine Creek, so hikers can't waddle down one Turkey Path and up the other.

★ PINE CREEK RAIL TRAIL

To traverse the 60-mile Pine Creek Rail Trail is to experience unspoiled wilderness. Dramatic outcrops, gushing waterfalls, and diverse flora greet today's visitor. The woods are home to coyote, deer, wild turkey, and black bear, among other creatures. River otters were reintroduced to the canyon in the 1980s and fishers in the 1990s. Even bald eagles have returned to the area.

Maps of the Pine Creek Rail Trail are available at state park, forestry, and tourism promotion offices. The gently graded gravel path starts at Wellsboro Junction, a defunct railway junction at Routes 6 and 287, about three miles north of downtown Wellsboro. Darling Run, about nine trail miles from Wellsboro Junction, is a popular point of entry for hikers and bikers. It's located along Route 362, a mile and a half south of Route 6 at Ansonia and about seven miles west of Wellsboro.

The horseback trailhead is along Marsh Creek Road near the junction of Routes 6 and 362 at Ansonia. Horses are restricted to the dirt access road that runs alongside the trail for nine miles. Thanks to **Ole Covered Wagon Tours** (1538 Marsh Creek Rd., Wellsboro, 570/724-7443 or 607/857-5256, www.olecoveredwagon.com), even non-equestrians can have a giddy-up experience of the gorge. Pulled by teams of Percheron draft horses, the covered wagons are larger and cushier than the Conestogas of yore. Call or check the website for departure times. Walk-ins are welcome, but be sure to make a reservation from late September to mid-October, when the gorge is awash with autumn colors and demand is highest. Ole Covered Wagon is about 12 miles west of Wellsboro on Route 6. Look for the covered wagon sign at the intersection of Route 6 and Marsh Creek Road.

If you're looking for more than a daytrip, you're in luck. There are camping areas on public forestlands and private property along the trail.

DOWNTOWN WELLSBORO

The gateway to the Grand Canyon of Pennsylvania is the exceedingly charming town of Wellsboro, where gaslights burn 24/7. It's small enough to see in one day, and that's exactly why some visitors stay a few. Wellsboro's manicured town square, tree-lined streets, and general absence of hustle and bustle are almost as soothing as a spa getaway.

Let the calming begin at the town square, better known as "the green," across from the county courthouse on Main Street. The fountain statue at its center, *Wynken, Blynken, and Nod,* was inspired by an 1889 lullaby of the same name and depicts three children sailing across the sky in a wooden shoe. The bronze sculpture is a replica of the marble original in Denver. Wellsboro has another Denver connection. Its **Gmeiner Art and Cultural Center** (134 Main St., 570/724-1917, www.gmeinerartscenter.com, 2pm-5pm daily, by donation) was a gift of the late Arthur Gmeiner, a Denver entrepreneur and philanthropist who was born not far from Wellsboro. Exhibits change frequently.

Information about local events, attractions, and businesses is available at the **Wellsboro Area Chamber of Commerce** (114 Main St., 570/724-1926, www.wellsboropa.com, 8:30am-4:30pm Mon.-Fri.). You'll find brochures on the porch even when the chamber is closed. Pause in the front yard to meet Wellsboro's oldest resident: a massive elm tree that's been growing since the 1700s.

OTHER SIGHTS
Tioga Central Railroad
The passenger trains that once served this region are long gone, but it's still possible to ride the rails. The **Tioga Central Railroad** (Rte. 287, 3 miles north of downtown Wellsboro, 570/724-0990, www.tiogacentral.com) operates excursion and charter trains on a 34-mile railroad extending from Wellsboro to just south of Corning, New York. It offers a variety of excursions, including dinner and Sunday brunch excursions, from Memorial Day weekend to late October. The Santa Express, offered in late November and December, ferries pajama-clad children to the "North Pole."

Pennsylvania Lumber Museum
It's hard to imagine what north-central Pennsylvania looked like when work, not play, attracted people to its woods. The **Pennsylvania Lumber Museum** (5660 Rte. 6 West, Galeton, 814/435-2652, www.lumbermuseum.org, 9am-5pm Wed.-Sun., closed Nov.-Mar., admission $6, seniors $5, children 3-11 $3) makes it a little easier. Thousands of artifacts, including a 1912 logging locomotive, tell the story of the state's forest industries. Visitors can tour an operational steam-powered sawmill and a re-created logging camp complete with blacksmith shop, horse barn, and mess hall.

★ Dark Sky Park
To feast your eyes on heavenly bodies, head to **Cherry Springs State Park** (4639 Cherry Springs Rd., Coudersport, 814/435-5010, www.visitpaparks.com), located on Route 44 about 15 miles southeast of Coudersport. Thanks to its exceptionally dark night sky, the tiny park is one of the best places in the eastern seaboard for stargazing. In 2008, Cherry Springs was designated as the second International Dark Sky Park by the International Dark-Sky Association, an Arizona-based nonprofit that agitates against light pollution.

The park's stargazing field offers a 360-degree view of the sky. If you plan to stay for just a few hours, park at the defunct Cherry Springs Airport and walk to the field. You can drive onto the field if you're staying overnight. If you arrive after dark, you have to enter the field sans headlights. On a dark-moon weekend, some 200 amateur astronomers and their equipment could be scattered across the field. Four small observatories can be reserved online at www.pa.reserveworld.com or by calling 888/727-2757.

The park's location affords an excellent view of the nucleus of the Milky Way. If you can't tell Sagittarius from Scorpius, check the park's schedule of free public stargazing programs. For a personal sky tour, contact local star guru Stash Nawrocki of **Crystal Spheres: Adventures in Stargazing** (814/848-5037, crystalspheres@gmail.com).

ENTERTAINMENT AND EVENTS
Performing Arts
The Art Deco **Arcadia Theatre** (50 Main St., Wellsboro, 570/724-4957, www.arcadiawellsboro.com) in downtown Wellsboro was built in 1921 for silent pictures. These days it shows the fruits of Hollywood's labors and art house films on four screens. Since 2002, the Arcadia has also presented live theater productions.

Opened in 2012, Wellsboro's **Deane Center for the Performing Arts** (104 Main St., Wellsboro, 570/724-6220, www.deanecenter.com) boasts five performance venues, including a state-of-the-art black box theater that seats 190. It's also home to shops and an art gallery.

A Dimly Lit Tussle

The world's first night football game was played on September 28, 1892, on a field in Mansfield, Pennsylvania. Electric lights and the game of football were both novelties, so organizers weren't surprised that a crowd of thousands gathered to watch it. The players wore little padding and no helmets, and the lighting was so minimal that it was hard to tell which team had the ball. Before either squad could score, the referee deemed it too dangerous to continue.

A reenactment of the anticlimactic but historic game is the highlight of Mansfield's **Fabulous 1890s Weekend** (570/662-3442, www.1890sweekend.com, last weekend in Sept.). Mansfield University students and area residents play by the rules of 1892 in uniforms created 100 years later for a commercial for General Electric, which supplied the lights for the first night game. The game is followed by fireworks, just as it was in 1892. The Fabulous 1890s parade also strives for historical accuracy, which means no motors and a whole lot of horses.

Festivals and Events

The blooming of Pennsylvania's state flower is cause for much merrymaking in Wellsboro. The **Pennsylvania State Laurel Festival** (570/724-1926, www.wellsboropa.com) starts the second weekend in June and continues through the third. Events include a road cycling race, a 10K foot race, a crafts fair, and not one but two parades.

The parade of renowned musicians who perform at the **Endless Mountain Music Festival** (570/662-5030, box office 570/787-7800, www.endlessmountain.net, summer, admission charged) makes it one of Pennsylvania's premier classical music events. The international festival was born in 2006, after a vacation in Wellsboro convinced acclaimed conductor Stephen Gunzenhauser that mountain scenery and world-class music would be a potent combination. The festival features solo recitals, chamber music concerts, and an orchestra of musicians from around the world—conducted, of course, by the maestro who fell in love with the mountains.

The hills are alive with the buzz of chainsaws during the **Woodsmen's Show** (814/435-6855, www.woodsmenshow.com, early Aug., admission charged) at Cherry Springs State Park. ESPN watchers may recognize the pro lumberjacks who face off in events like two-man logrolling, ax throwing, and tree felling. Amateurs can also test their skills. Chainsaw artists create masterpieces on-site over the course of the weekend.

The three-day **Hickory Fest** (570/439-1549, www.hickoryfest.com, mid-Aug., admission charged) brings the finest in bluegrass and acoustic music to canyon country.

True nostalgics should visit Wellsboro the first full weekend in December, when Main Street is transformed into an early Victorian marketplace for the **Dickens of a Christmas** celebration. Costumed food and craft vendors, carolers, and street-corner thespians help turn back the clock.

SHOPPING
Wellsboro

The bulk of Wellsboro's shops line Main Street. No national chains here. Wellsboro's answer to Barnes & Noble is **From My Shelf Books** (25 Main St., 570/724-5793, www.wellsborobookstore.com, open daily). The ever-changing stock of new and gently used books includes out-of-print treasures. **Dunham's** (45 Main St., 570/724-1905, www.dunhamswellsboro.com, open daily), one of the oldest family-owned department stores in the country, has called Wellsboro home since 1905.

Adventurers can stock up on gear and apparel by the likes of Marmot, Kelty, and SIGG at **Wild Asaph Outfitters** (71 Main St., 570/724-5155, www.wildasaphoutfitters.com, open daily). Its staff are a good source of information about area trails and rock-climbing spots. **Country Ski & Sports** (81 Main St., 570/724-3858, www.countryskiandsports.com, open Mon.-Sat.) offers kayaks in the warmer months, skiing and snowboarding equipment in the colder ones, and bikes year-round.

SPORTS AND RECREATION
Biking

Bikers who want a bumpier ride than the Pine Creek Rail Trail provides can find any number of backcountry routes in and around the gorge. The Asaph section of Tioga State Forest, site of the **Laurel Classic Mountain Bike Challenge** (www.twistedspokes.org, Sept.), boasts a course with quad-busting climbs and creek and log crossings. Longtime biker Bill Yacovissi recommends more than a dozen loops, mostly on unpaved state forest roads, on his Pine Creek Canyon Bike Rides website (www.pinecreekbikerides.com).

Paddling and Fishing

Paddlers can sightsee and fish for hours or days on Pine Creek. Sadly, the window of opportunity is small. With no dams, Pine Creek relies on snowmelt and rainfall for its flow-jo.

As spring turns to summer, water levels begin to drop. Paddlers must find other waters—or pray for thunderstorms heavy enough to swell the creek again.

Maps of the Pine Creek Rail Trail indicate creek access areas. The 54-mile state-designated Pine Creek Water Trail begins at the Big Meadows access area at Ansonia. The road leading to it is on the south side of Route 6, opposite a church. Don't put in at Big Meadows if you're looking for a quickie float. The first advisable take-out is 17 miles downstream, at the village of Blackwell. It takes about six hours to get there, though vigorous paddlers can do it much faster and an unhurried angler can take much longer. A few sections approach Class III (difficult) water, so novice paddlers would be wise to hire a guide. **Pine Creek Outfitters** (5142 Rte. 6, Wellsboro, 570/724-3003, www.pinecrk.com, 9am-6pm daily, closed late Dec.-Jan.) offers daily raft tours from March to late May. Guided trips may continue into June if water levels allow. The outfitter also rents rafts, canoes, kayaks, and wetsuits, along with bikes for cycling the Pine Creek Rail Trail. Shuttle service and sage advice are available for anyone paddling the creek, biking the rail-trail, or hiking the West Rim Trail.

bicyclists on the Pine Creek Rail Trail

The upper stretches of Pine Creek and its many tributaries offer some of the finest trout fishing in the Northeast. The lower part of the creek (downstream of Waterville) is better known for warm-water species. Vehicles can access the western riverbank from Ansonia by turning onto Colton Road and then left onto Owasee Road, which traces the creek for about four miles. There are ample pull-offs along Route 414, which hugs the creek from Blackwell to just north of Waterville. **Slate Run Tackle Shop** (Rte. 414, Slate Run, 570/753-8551, www.slaterun.com, 8am-6pm Sun.-Thurs., 8am-8pm Fri.-Sat., reduced hours in winter) is a full-line Orvis dealer with an impressive inventory (thousand-dollar fly rods included) and an equally impressive acquaintance with local waters. Staff gladly dispense directions to sections of stream and can tag along to provide on-stream instruction.

Hiking

The Pine Creek Rail Trail and the rim-to-creek trails at Colton Point and Leonard Harrison State Parks are popular with day-trippers. Backpackers will find even more to love in canyon country. The 30-mile **West Rim Trail** traverses the western rim of Pine Creek Gorge, affording spectacular views of the valley. Its northern terminus is on Colton Road one mile south of Route 6 at Ansonia. The southern terminus is on Route 414 at the Rattlesnake Rock access area, two miles south of the village of Blackwell. Contact Tioga State Forest (570/724-2868, www.dcnr.state.pa.us/forestry) for more information about the trail. It connects with Pennsylvania's longest hiking trail, the **Mid State Trail** (www.hike-mst.org), at Blackwell.

As if that weren't enough, backpackers can reach the 42-mile **Black Forest Trail** from the southern end of the West Rim Trail by following the Pine Creek Rail Trail to Slate Run. The Black Forest trailhead on Slate Run Road can also be reached via Route 414. The very difficult loop trail darts into and out of the gorge several times. Contact Tiadaghton State Forest (570/753-5409, www.dcnr.state.pa.us/forestry) for information.

Skiing

The Pine Creek Rail Trail and state forestlands offer hundreds of miles of cross-country skiing. Downhill skiers and snowboarders will find Pennsylvania's steepest slopes and plenty of natural snow at **Ski Denton** (5661 Rte. 6, Coudersport, 814/435-2115, www.skidenton.com, 8-hour lift ticket $25-39, children 6-11 and seniors 65-69 $19-26, seniors 70 and over

cross-country skiing on the Pine Creek Rail Trail

ski for free, Monday lift ticket $10, all-day ski rental $27, snow tubing 2-hour session $10), 34 miles west of Wellsboro between Galeton and Coudersport. Its trails are open to mountain bikers in the warmer months. **Ski Sawmill** (383 Oregon Hill Rd., Morris, 570/353-7521, www.skisawmill.com, all-day lift ticket $26-37, children 6-11 $22-30, all-day ski rental $25, snow tubing 1-hour session $6), 18 miles south of Wellsboro, has 12 slopes, a terrain park, and a tube slide. Both ski areas offer limited and rather spartan accommodations.

Snowmobiling

There are hundreds of miles of snowmobile trails on public lands surrounding Pine Creek Gorge. The **PA Grand Canyon Snowmobile Club** (4814 Rte. 6, Wellsboro, 570/724-2888, www.pagrandcanyonsnowmobileclub.com) is a good source of information about trails at the northern end of the gorge. Trails from the clubhouse lead everywhere from the west rim of the canyon to local watering holes.

ACCOMMODATIONS
Camping

It doesn't cost a cent to camp on state forestlands within the spectacular Pine Creek Gorge, but it does require a permit. Contact **Tioga State Forest** (570/724-2868, www.dcnr.state.pa.us/forestry) about camping in the Tioga County portion of the gorge and **Tiadaghton State Forest** (570/753-5409, www.dcnr.state.pa.us/forestry) about the lower portion in Lycoming County. The county line is between the villages of Blackwell and Cedar Run, about 20 miles from the northern mouth of the gorge. Some state forest camping areas have amenities like potable water and vault-style bathrooms.

For those who prefer a touch more luxury, there are modern campgrounds and other accommodations on private property in the canyon. You'll find them at Blackwell and points farther south. One such campground is **Pettecote Junction** (400 Beach Rd., Cedar Run, 570/353-7183, www.pettecotejunction.

com, campsite $25-35, cabin $100). The proprietors aren't exaggerating when they advertise "direct access." The campground is wedged between Pine Creek and the rail-trail. Not surprisingly, it offers rental canoes, tubes, and bikes. In addition to tent and RV sites, Pettecote Junction has several cabins that sleep four to six people.

Canyon Country Campground (130 Wilson Rd., Wellsboro, 570/724-3818, www.campinpa.com, Apr. 15-Oct., campsite $25-36, cabin $49-68) isn't in the gorge but has an enviable location near its eastern rim. A walking trail leads from the campground to Leonard Harrison State Park and its acclaimed overlooks.

$50-100

It's not hard to imagine former guest Groucho Marx striding through the **Penn Wells Hotel** (62 Main St., Wellsboro, 570/724-2111, www.pennwells.com, $75-140, winter $50-100). Built in 1869 on the site of Wellsboro's first inn, the hotel pulses with history. Soak in the vibe of bygone days in the lobby or adjacent bar, but stay in one of the more recently renovated rooms if you can. The hotel's restaurant is open to the public and particularly hopping during Friday night fish fry and Sunday brunch. The hotel's younger sister, the **Penn Wells Lodge** (4 Main St., Wellsboro, 570/724-3463, www.pennwells.com, $80-95, winter $60-70), boasts larger rooms and an indoor pool.

The streamside **Hotel Manor** (392 Slate Run Rd., Slate Run, 570/753-8414, www.hotelmanor.com, $90) was rebuilt in the summer of 2004 after a fire destroyed the logging-era original. The speed at which it was rebuilt—five months—speaks to its popularity with anglers and others. The hotel has 10 guest rooms and a restaurant featuring meaty fare and an expansive deck.

$100-200

A B&B-cum-sheep farm, **Arvgården** (5159 Arnot Rd., Wellsboro, 570/724-4337, www.arvgarden.com, $105) offers solitude in a rural setting within easy reach of Wellsboro. Guests of the Swedish-style B&B can visit with the New Zealand-style sheep, check out the looms used to turn their wool into woven items, or explore the farm's bird habitats. Owners Keith and Hilma Cooper share the bounty of their garden during breakfast.

The three rooms at **Wellsboro Inn on the Green** (3 Charles St., Wellsboro, 800/661-3581, www.wellsboroinnonthegreen.com, $115-185, winter $99) take their names from the *Wynken, Blynken, and Nod* statue in the town square, which the B&B overlooks. Nod, a garage-turned-guesthouse, is a page out of a Pottery Barn catalog, while Wynken and Blynken take a more flouncy approach to elegance. Music by the likes of Dean Martin accompanies divine breakfasts served at private tables. Innkeepers Cindy and Rob Fitzgerald also own the aptly named **Crossroads Bed & Breakfast** (131 S. Main St., Mansfield, 800/661-3581, www.crossroadsbb.com, $115-165, winter $99-125) at the corner of Routes 6 and 15 in nearby Mansfield.

It's easy to reach the Pine Creek Rail Trail from **Bear Mountain Lodge** (8010 Rte. 6, Wellsboro, 570/724-2428, www.bearmountainbb.com, $109-249). Just walk or bike half a mile down a country road. What's hard is leaving the den of creature comforts. Two of the four guest rooms have private decks complete with hot tubs, and the other two have whirlpool baths. All have natural-gas fireplaces, flat-screen TVs, and queen beds of hickory, white cedar, or black cherry—crafted locally.

FOOD
Wellsboro

Ask for the Grand Canyon at **The Native Bagel** (1 Central Ave., 570/724-0900, www.nativebagel.com, 6am-4pm Mon.-Fri., 7am-3pm Sat., 7am-2pm Sun., under $10) and you won't get directions to the Pine Creek Gorge. You'll get a triple-decker sandwich with ham, turkey, bacon, and barbecue sauce. Sandwiches are named for local attractions and made with breads that couldn't be more

local. Loaves, bagels, and pastries are made on-site.

A local institution, the **Wellsboro Diner** (19 Main St., 570/724-3992, 6am-8pm Mon.-Sat., 7am-8pm Sun., $5-15) serves up meatloaf, mashed potatoes, and the like in a deliciously authentic setting. The 1938 Sterling diner car was placed at the corner of Main Street and East Avenue in 1939 and hasn't budged since.

With 16 draft beers behind its 150-year-old bar, the ★ **Wellsboro House** (34 Charleston St., 570/723-4687, www.wellsborohouse.com, lunch noon-5pm Fri.-Sat., dinner 5pm-9pm Mon.-Sat., bar closing time varies, $8-25) could draw a crowd if it served a little more than hot wings. But convivial owners Chris and Laura Kozuhowski wouldn't hear of that. Their take on hot wings is a buffalo chicken sandwich dressed with crumbly bleu cheese and diced celery. The restaurant is generally closed on Sunday, but not during football season. Look no further than the menu's South Philly cheesesteak to guess which team the Kozuhowskis root for.

South of Wellsboro

Cedar Run Inn (281 Beulah Land Rd., Cedar Run, 570/353-6241, www.cedarruninnpa.com, dinner only, reservations recommended, $17-25) is home to one of the finest restaurants in the region. Anglers and hunters can wash up at an old marble sink beneath a mounted buck before digging into the house pâté, a medley of clams and herbs baked with parmesan cheese. Be sure to call ahead for restaurant hours; they vary throughout the year.

Mansfield

In the Route 6 town of Mansfield, 13 miles east of Wellsboro, mornings find locals lined up at **Gramma's Kitchen** (1080 S. Main St., 570/662-2350, 7am-3pm Mon.-Sat., under $10) for freshly baked bread. The pies and cookies at the friendly-as-grandma's breakfast and lunch spot are also homemade. You can order breakfast right up to closing time.

The chef-owned **Wren's Nest** (102 W. Wellsboro St., 570/662-1093, www.

wrensnestpa.com, 5pm-9pm Tues.-Sat., $11-29) offers fine dining in an 1856 cottage and the occasional live jazz night.

INFORMATION

If you're arriving via Route 15 south, look for the state-run **welcome center** seven miles south of the Pennsylvania-New York line. Personalized travel counseling is available 7am-7pm daily; the restrooms are always open.

The **Tioga County Visitors Center** (2053 Rte. 660, Wellsboro, 570/724-0635, www.visittiogapa.com, 8am-4:30pm Mon.-Fri. year-round, 9am-1pm Sat. May-Oct., 9am-1pm Sun. Oct.) is conveniently located just a few miles east of the entrance to Leonard Harrison State Park and its glorious views of Pennsylvania's Grand Canyon. The visitors center has loads of information about the gorge and other area attractions. The county seat, Wellsboro, also has an advocate in the **Wellsboro Area Chamber of Commerce** (114 Main St., 570/724-1926, www.wellsboropa.com, 8:30am-4:30pm Mon.-Fri.).

The **Potter County Visitors Association** (118 N. Main St., Coudersport, 814/274-3365, www.pottercountypa.org, open by chance) can be counted on for information about westerly attractions like the Pennsylvania Lumber Museum and Cherry Springs State Park. If no one is in, brochures can be found across the street at the Hotel Crittenden (133 N. Main St., Coudersport).

South of Blackwell, Pine Creek and its eponymous rail-trail cross from Tioga County into Lycoming County, represented by the **Lycoming County Visitors Bureau** (210 William St., Williamsport, 800/358-9900, www.vacationpa.com, 8:30am-5pm Mon.-Fri., 8am-3pm Sat., 11am-3pm Sun.).

GETTING THERE

The town of Wellsboro, gateway to Pennsylvania's Grand Canyon, is about 50 miles north of Williamsport. It lies along the east-west Route 6. Leonard Harrison State Park, on the east rim of the canyon, is 10 miles west of Wellsboro via Route 660. Colton Point State Park, on the west rim of the canyon, is five miles south of Route 6 at Ansonia.

The nearest commercial airport is New York's **Elmira Corning Regional Airport** (ELM, 607/739-5621, www.ecairport.com), 55 miles northeast of Wellsboro.

Williamsport and Vicinity

The largest city in the Wilds region is the not-so-large city of Williamsport, population roughly 30,000. It's situated on the West Branch of the Susquehanna River. In the latter half of the 19th century, so many logs were floated down tributary streams and captured by a log boom at Williamsport that the city became known as the "Lumber Capital of the World." Its riverfront was crowded with sawmills—more than 30 at the peak of logging activity in Pennsylvania. Its West Fourth Street was crowded with the opulent residences of lumber barons. They moved to (literally) greener pastures as the lumbering era waned, but their showplaces still stand on the street known as Millionaires Row. The local high school's sports teams go by Williamsport Millionaires.

The city that once claimed to have more millionaires per capita than any place in the world now prides itself on a different distinction: birthplace of Little League Baseball. Every August, 16 teams of preteen ballplayers and tens of thousands of fans converge on the Williamsport area for the Little League Baseball World Series. A museum dedicated to Little League serves as a year-round pilgrimage site for little kids with big dreams.

LITTLE LEAGUE SIGHTS

In 1938, an oil company clerk named Carl Stotz decided to start a baseball program for boys in his hometown of Williamsport. He rounded up neighborhood children and began experimenting with different equipment and field dimensions. By the summer of 1939, Stotz had found sponsors for three teams of 10 and a name for his program: Little League. To learn how Williamsport's three-team league grew into the world's largest organized youth sports program, visit the **World of Little League: Peter J. McGovern Museum** (525 Rte. 15 Hwy., South Williamsport, 570/326-3607, www.littleleague.org/museum,

9am-5pm daily, admission $5, seniors $3, children 5-12 $2). The collection includes balls signed by U.S. presidents and professional players, photographs of major leaguers with their Little League teams, and the uniform Williamsport native and baseball great Mike "Moose" Mussina wore when he represented local restaurant Johnny Z's as a Little Leaguer.

The museum is part of Little League International's 66-acre complex in the borough of South Williamsport, across the Susquehanna River from Williamsport. It overlooks two stadiums used during the annual **Little League Baseball World Series** (571/326-1921, www.littleleague.org, Aug.). First held in 1947, the World Series wasn't always played in South Williamsport. Before 1959, the action unfolded on a field across the street from Williamsport's minor league ballpark, Bowman Field. The original field, now named the **Carl E. Stotz Field** (1741 W. 4th St., Williamsport, 570/323-1308, www.leaguelineup.com/originalleagueinc), is still in active use. It's operated by Original League Inc., a youth baseball organization born of a rift between Stotz and Little League International in the 1950s. Surviving members of Little League's original teams gather at the field during World Series week and give tours of the memorabilia-filled clubhouse.

MILLIONAIRES ROW HISTORIC DISTRICT

A drive down West 4th Street in Williamsport belies the wealth that once flowed into the city in the form of tens of millions of logs. The moneyed have moved elsewhere. Their erstwhile homes show their age. More than a few house students from the nearby Pennsylvania College of Technology. But a stop here and there reveals Williamsport's rich history.

First stop is the Lycoming County Historical Society's **Thomas T. Taber Museum** (858 W. 4th St., Williamsport,

570/326-3326, www.tabermuseum.org, 9:30am-4pm Tues.-Fri., 11am-4pm Sat., 1pm-4pm Sun., closed Sun. Nov.-Apr., admission $7.50, seniors $6, children $5), a modern building amid the Victorian-style structures of West 4th, aka Millionaires Row. The museum skillfully chronicles the history of the region, which didn't start with the arrival of loggers. Visitors can explore a gallery devoted to Native Americans as well as a string of period rooms that illustrate the lifestyles of subsequent inhabitants. The Taber is also home to more than 300 toy trains, one of the finest collections in the country.

A real train car sits outside the **Peter Herdic Transportation Museum** (810 Nichols Place, Williamsport, 570/601-3455, www.phtm.org, 10am-3pm Tues.-Sat., admission $5, seniors $4, children under 12 $3), a stone's throw from the Taber. Named for Williamsport's most prominent lumber baron and the inventor of a horse-drawn taxi, the museum celebrates transportation achievements as wide-ranging as the birch bark canoe and the public bus. As the hub of the 19th-century lumber industry and the home of so many millionaires, Williamsport was first in line for transportation innovations. Herdic himself oversaw the construction of a streetcar railway that went into service in 1865.

To learn more about Williamsport's rich history, take a **Williamsport Trolley Tour** (570/326-2500, www.ridetrolleys.com, June-Aug., fare $5, seniors $4, children under 12 $3). The trolley tours and Peter Herdic Transportation Museum are operated by River Valley Transit, Williamsport's public transit agency, and tickets are interchangeable. In addition to the transportation museum, trolleys stop at the riverfront Susquehanna State Park, where the *Hiawatha* riverboat docks, and River Valley's 3rd Street parking garage. You can hop on or off at any of the three stops. The tour takes about an hour and a half.

OTHER SIGHTS
Hiawatha Paddlewheel Riverboat

The ***Hiawatha*** (2205 Hiawatha Blvd., Williamsport, 570/326-2500, www.ridehiawatha.com) is a gaily painted excursion boat that cruises the Susquehanna River from May through October. A variety of cruises, including dinner cruises, late-night karaoke cruises, and concert cruises, are offered throughout the season. You can learn about the river and its role in Williamsport's lumber era during

the *Hiawatha* paddlewheel riverboat

a narrated "public cruise" ($7.50, seniors $7, children 3-12 $3.50). The hour-long cruise is offered several times a day Tuesday-Sunday from June through Labor Day.

The *Hiawatha* docks in Susquehanna State Park, accessible via the Reach Road exit of Route 220. The park has restroom facilities, riverside picnic tables, and a public boat launch.

Piper Aviation Museum

In 1937, a fire destroyed the Bradford, Pennsylvania, factory of aircraft manufacturer William T. Piper. The man who would come to be known as the "Henry Ford of Aviation" relocated to an abandoned silk mill in Lock Haven, a river city about 25 miles west of Williamsport. It was there that his company, Piper Aircraft, produced the legendary J-3 Cub, the low-cost, easy-to-fly airplane that "taught the world to fly." Lock Haven is no longer home to Piper Aviation (new owners consolidated manufacturing in Florida in the 1980s), but it is home to the **Piper Aviation Museum** (1 Piper Way, Lock Haven, 570/748-8283, www.pipermuseum.com, 9am-4pm Mon.-Fri., 10am-4pm Sat., noon-4pm Sun., closed Sun. Dec.-Mar., admission $6, seniors $5, children 7-15 $3, family rate $12). The museum, which occupies a former Piper engineering building, preserves all things Piper, from vintage aircraft to flight journals.

ENTERTAINMENT AND EVENTS
Bars

Located a beer pong toss from the Pennsylvania College of Technology campus, **Kimball's** (972 2nd St., Williamsport, 570/322-1115, www.kimballspub.com, 11am-2am Mon.-Fri., 5pm-2am Sat.-Sun., kitchen closes at 10pm, food $5-9) is steadfast in its support of craft brewers, including Pennsylvania's own Sly Fox, Troegs, Victory, and Weyerbacher.

More of a rum-swiller? The Caribbean-themed **Rumrunners Pub & Eatery** (241 Market St., Williamsport, 570/322-0303, www.rumrunnerspub.com, 4pm-1:30am daily, food $7-22) stocks more than a hundred varieties. Yah, mon. The kitchen sends out island-style and Italian dishes and hybrids like a pizza topped with pineapple, sweet red peppers, and jerk chicken.

Performing Arts

Williamsport's cultural hub is the **Community Arts Center** (220 W. 4th St., Williamsport, 570/326-2424, www.caclive.com), a 1920s vaudeville theater turned modern performance venue. The acoustically exemplary theater seats just over 2,100 people for concerts, dance performances, plays, comedy acts, and movies. The likes of Jerry Seinfeld, Ray Charles, Barry Manilow, and B. B. King have brought down the house. Local performing arts organizations, including the **Williamsport Symphony Orchestra** (570/322-0227, www.williamsportsymphony.org), also take the stage.

All about local talent, the **Community Theatre League** (100 W. 3rd St., Williamsport, 570/327-1777, www.ctlnet.org) produces about 10 plays a year and hosts concerts that run the gamut from bluegrass to barbershop. Its intimate theater-in-the-round can be found in the McDade Trade and Transit Centre, Williamsport's bus hub.

Professional summer stock theater can be found in a barn that once housed registered Holstein cattle. Founded in 1963, the tireless **Millbrook Playhouse** (258 Country Club Ln., Mill Hall, 570/748-8083, www.millbrookplayhouse.com, tickets $18, students $10, children under 12 $8) generally squeezes four main stage productions, an equal number of cabaret performances, and a couple of children's musicals into a two-month season. Theater alumni include *Twin Peaks* star Kyle MacLachlan and Michael Tucker of *L.A. Law* fame. Come fall, Millbrook raises funds with Brews in the Barn, a beer-tasting extravaganza complete with live entertainment and a picnic-style dinner. The town of Mill Hall is about 30 miles east of Williamsport, near Lock Haven.

Founded in 1831, Williamsport's **Repasz Band** (www.lycoming.org/repaszband) is one of the oldest community bands in the country. It played at Appomattox Court House in Virginia when General Robert E. Lee surrendered to General Ulysses S. Grant. Today the band plays pieces from its lengthy repertoire at free indoor and outdoor concerts throughout the area.

Festivals and Events

Live music, meet-the-artist events, and extended store hours enliven downtown Williamsport on the **First Friday** (570/326-1971, www.williamsport.org) of every month.

Live music is all the rage in Lock Haven. The city (570/893-5900, www.lockhavencity.org) sponsors free concerts not once but twice a week from June through August, dishing out classic rock, country, swing, polka, and more. On Friday evenings, bands perform at Triangle Park at Bellefonte Avenue and West Main Street. The Sunday evening venue is the uniquely charming **J. Doyle Corman Amphitheater** at Jay and Water Streets. The amphitheater is built into the levee that guards Lock Haven from flooding by the Susquehanna River, and the stage floats on the water.

Fans of bluegrass and blues look forward to June, when the **Smoked Country Jam Bluegrass Festival** (Loganton, 570/753-8878, www.smokedcountryjam.com, admission charged) and **Billtown Blues Festival** (Lycoming County Fairgrounds, 300 E. Lycoming St., Hughesville, 570/584-4480, www.billtownblues.org, admission charged) are held.

SPORTS AND RECREATION
Pine Creek Rail Trail

The southern trailhead of the 60-mile Pine Creek Rail Trail is in the town of Jersey Shore, a 20-minute drive from Williamsport. The trail shortly meets Pine Creek and follows it into the deepest section of Pennsylvania's Grand Canyon. It's beloved by hikers, bikers, cross-country skiers, and snowshoers.

State Parks

Nestled in Tiadaghton State Forest, **Little Pine State Park** (4205 Little Pine Creek Rd., Waterville, 570/753-6000, www.visitpaparks.com) offers big fun for hikers. The **Mid State Trail** (www.hike-mst.org), Pennsylvania's longest hiking trail, passes through the 2,158-acre park, which has several trails of its own. The park is also home to a 94-acre lake and 4.2 miles of Little Pine Creek, making it popular with anglers. Its modern campground, open from the first weekend in April to mid-December, has 99 campsites and a handful of yurts and cottages. Reserve online at www.pa.reserveworld.com or by calling 888/727-2757.

Hyner View State Park (Hyner View Rd., North Bend, 570/923-6000, www.visitpaparks.com) is pretty much in the middle of nowhere and measures a measly six acres. It doesn't offer hiking or biking, boating or fishing. What it does offer is a spectacular view of the Susquehanna River. Some come for the view alone, but even more come to watch hang gliders sprint off the scenic overlook and sail over the river. Hyner View is one of the highest hang-gliding sites in the state and one of the oldest on the East Coast. The best times to visit are around Easter, Memorial Day, Fourth of July, Labor Day, and the second full weekend of October, when the **Hyner Hang Gliding Club** (www.hynerclub.com) hosts multiday "fly-in" events. Pilots land on a grassy expanse near the river. Come nightfall, it's aglow with their campfires.

Boating and Paddling

Susquehanna State Park (Arch St., Williamsport, 570/988-5557, www.visitpaparks.com) in Williamsport has a boat launch that provides access to the Susquehanna River and to a 652-acre dam that's deep enough for waterskiing. The park is also home to the *Hiawatha* (570/326-2500, www.ridehiawatha.

com), an old-style riverboat offering public cruises from May through October.

A few miles east of Williamsport, **Country Ski & Sports** (836 Broad St., Montoursville, 570/368-1718, www.countryskiandsports. com, 10am-8pm Mon. and Fri., 10am-6pm Tues. and Thurs., 10am-5pm Wed. and Sat.) offers canoes, kayaks, and paddling clinics.

Fishing

Pine Creek and Loyalsock Creek, tributaries of the West Branch of the Susquehanna ("Suskie" to in-the-know anglers), are among the more popular fishing streams in the Williamsport area. The former empties into the West Branch near Jersey Shore, about 15 miles west of Williamsport, and the latter at Montoursville, about eight miles east of the city.

Fly fishers will find a selection of more than 350 hand-tied flies at **McConnell's Country Store & Fly Shop** (10853 Rte. 44 N., Waterville, 570/753-8241, www.mcconnellscountrystore.com, 7am-7pm Sun.-Thurs., 7am-9pm Fri.-Sat., winter hours 7am-5:30pm Sun.-Thurs., 7am-9pm Fri., 7am-7pm Sat.), 12 miles north of Jersey Shore in the village of Waterville, where Little Pine Creek meets the "Big Pine." McConnell's offers guides as well as gear.

Hiking

The 59-mile **Loyalsock Trail** runs roughly parallel to Loyalsock Creek, which empties into the West Branch of the Susquehanna River at Montoursville, just east of Williamsport. It's a strenuous trail that rewards hikers with spectacular vistas. The western terminus is on Route 87, about nine miles north of I-180/Route 220 at Montoursville. The Alpine Club of Williamsport (570/322-5878, www.lycoming.org/alpine), which maintains the trail, sells a detailed guide with full-color maps. The trail also appears on the free public-use map for Loyalsock State Forest (570/946-4049, www.dcnr.state.pa.us/forestry). For gear, backpackers need look no further than **Lyon Camping & Supply** (361 Broad St.,

Montoursville, 877/368-5966, www.lyon-camping.com, 10am-5pm Mon.-Tues. and Thurs., 10am-3pm Wed. and Sat., 10am-5:30pm Fri.).

Scuba Diving

For the lowdown on local dive sites and gear galore, hunt for **Sunken Treasure Scuba Center** (664 Geiler Hollow Rd., Jersey Shore, 570/398-1458, www.divestsc.com, summer hours noon-9pm Mon. and Fri., 10am-5pm Tues. and Thurs., 9:30am-1pm Sat.).

ACCOMMODATIONS
Under $100

The house Pennsylvania governor John Andrew Schulze built after his 1823-1829 term didn't stay in his family. It was seized and sold to pay a legal debt. In 2007, it opened as the **Governor Schulze House Bed and Breakfast** (748 Broad St., Montoursville, 570/368-8966, www.govshulzehouse.com, $80-120), a tastefully decorated retreat that caters to business travelers and honeymooners alike. The latter are best off in the Eck Suite with its corner whirlpool tub and curtained four-poster bed.

$100-200

The ★ **Genetti Hotel** (200 W. 4th St., Williamsport, 570/326-6600, www.genetti-hotel.com, $90-295) has welcomed the likes of Gene Kelly, Rita Hayworth, and Robert Kennedy since opening in 1922. Thanks to a major renovation in 2006, the Williamsport landmark offers the comforts and amenities of a modern hotel along with a heaping of historic charm. Amenities include an outdoor pool and an American restaurant. It's as centrally located as it gets, next door to the Community Arts Center.

The **Peter Herdic Inn** (411 W. 4th St., Williamsport, 570/326-0411, www.herdichouse.com, $95-200), a beautifully restored mansion on Williamsport's Millionaires Row, has six guest rooms, including a two-room suite with a whirlpool tub. Expect great things at breakfast, which is included in weekend rates and may be available on weekdays for an extra charge. The innkeepers also own the Peter Herdic House Restaurant, one of the city's finest restaurants, next door.

As remote and tranquil as its name suggests, the **Serene View Farm Bed & Breakfast** (80 Engle Mill Ln., Williamsport, 570/478-2477, www.sereneviewfarm.com, $100-140) sits on 128 acres of critter-filled woodlands and meadows about 20 miles northeast of Williamsport. The 1890s farmhouse has a wraparound porch complete with rocking chairs, a family room with an original, working cookstove, and three homey guest rooms.

FOOD
Williamsport

Award-winning microbrews and frequent live entertainment are reason enough to hop to the **Bullfrog Brewery** (229 W. 4th St., Williamsport, 570/326-4700, www.bullfrog-brewery.com, 11am-11pm Mon.-Wed., 11am-midnight Thurs.-Sat., 9am-10pm Sun., bar open until 2am, $5-23), but the food is also something to croak about. The Bullfrog buys its baked goods from local bakeries and its beef from a free-range co-op. On Sundays, the Bullfrog opens early for brunch and serves up free jazz starting at noon. Call or check the online calendar for information about performances throughout the week.

Built in 1854 for Williamsport's most extravagant lumber baron, the ★ **Peter Herdic House** (407 W. 4th St., Williamsport, 570/322-0165, www.herdichouse.com, dinner from 5pm Wed.-Sat., lunch offered on select days in Dec., dinner $24-33) now serves meals befitting a millionaire. Appetizers include such delicacies as escargot, chicken and duck livers sautéed with onion and bacon, and locally smoked shad. Be sure to explore the ornate property before or after your meal. There's a wisteria-covered patio for outdoor dining and a lounge with its own menu (think free-range chicken wings).

Founded in 1984 as a maker of fine pastas and sauces, **DiSalvo's** (341 E. 4th St., Williamsport, 570/327-1200, www.disalvo-pasta.com, lunch 11:30am-2pm Wed.-Fri., dinner 5pm-9:30pm Mon.-Thurs. and 5pm-10pm Fri.-Sat., lunch $9-14, dinner $16-28) now enjoys a reputation as Williamsport's finest Italian restaurant. Offerings range from simple wood-fired pizzas to roasted rack of lamb. The house gnocchi is creamy heaven.

The **Barrel 135 Wine Bar & Bistro** (135 W. 3rd St., Williamsport, 570/322-7131, www.barrel135.net, lunch 11:30am-2pm Mon.-Fri., brunch 10:30am-2pm Sun., dinner 5pm-10pm Mon.-Sat., bar open until 2am Mon.-Sat., lunch $8-13, brunch $7-17, dinner $9-32) is one of the trendier spots in Williamsport, offering sushi and small plates along with soups, salads, sandwiches, and dinner entrées.

Don't let memories of school cafeterias keep you from **Le Jeune Chef** (1098 Hagan Way, Williamsport, 570/320-2433, www.pct.edu/lejeunechef, lunch 11:30am-1:30pm Mon.-Fri., dinner 5:30pm-8pm Wed.-Sat., lunch $7-13, dinner $8-30) on the Pennsylvania College of Technology campus. The restaurant offers real-world training for students in the college's School of Hospitality and a fine-dining experience for patrons. Call or check the website to see if Le Jeune Chef—French for "the young chef"—is offering an à la carte menu or multicourse meal.

Freshly baked, unapologetically addictive sticky buns make **Mr. Sticky's** (1948 E. 3rd St., Williamsport, 570/567-1166, www.mrsticky.net, 6am-7pm Mon.-Wed., 6am-9pm Thurs.-Sat., under $10) a good choice for sweet tooths. Phil Poorman and his family opened the restaurant in 2003 after several years of peddling their buns from concession trailers. Now they serve soups, salads, and sandwiches on homemade rolls along with four varieties of gooey buns.

Lock Haven

It's not much to look at, but the **Old Corner** (205 N. Grove St., 570/748-4124, www.theoldcorner.com, 11am-midnight daily, bar closes at 2am, $3-8) is revered for its burgers cooked to order at budget prices. Its sandwiches, flatbread pizzas, and salads (mixed greens!) are also commendable. The neighborhood hang has but a handful of tables; don't be shy to cozy up to the bar.

Dutch Haven Restaurant (201 E. Bald Eagle St., 570/748-7444, www.dutchhaven-restaurant.com, 11am-8:30pm Wed.-Thurs., 11am-9pm Fri., 5pm-9pm Sat., 10am-2pm Sun., $6-18) is a happy marriage of German and American cuisines. Whether your tastes run toward schnitzel and spaetzle or steak and fries, you'll almost surely leave stuffed. Come Sunday, Dutch Haven puts on a buffet of eggs, pancakes, ham, turkey, homemade sticky buns, and a whole lot more.

INFORMATION

You can download a visitors guide to Williamsport and other Lycoming County communities from the website of the **Lycoming County Visitors Bureau** (210 William St., Williamsport, 800/358-9900, www.vacationpa.com, 8:30am-5pm Mon.-Fri., 8am-3pm Sat., 11am-3pm Sun.), or pop by its headquarters in downtown Williamsport for brochures.

For information about the Piper Aviation Museum and other attractions in Clinton County, Lycoming's neighbor to the west, visit the website of the **Clinton County Economic Partnership** (212 N. Jay St., Lock Haven, 570/748-5782, www.clintoncounty-info.com, 8am-5pm Mon.-Fri.).

GETTING THERE AND AROUND

Williamsport is about 85 miles north of the state capital of Harrisburg via Route 22 west and Routes 11 and 15 north. **Williamsport Regional Airport** (IPT, www.flyipt.com) is served by US Airways. **Susquehanna Trailways** (800/692-6314, www.susquehan-nabus.com) provides intercity bus service to Williamsport and Lock Haven to its west.

Local bus service is available through **River Valley Transit** (570/326-2500, www.ridervt.com). For door-to-door service, call **Billtown Cab Co.** (570/322-2222).

Elk Country

Majestic elk once roamed throughout Pennsylvania. But as the human population increased in the mid-1800s, the elk population dwindled. By the end of the century, every last elk had fallen victim to unregulated hunting and habitat loss. Which is why it's no small matter that north-central Pennsylvania is today home to the largest herd of free-roaming elk east of the Rockies. The animals we see today are descendants of 177 Rocky Mountain elk from Yellowstone National Park and other parts that were released in Pennsylvania between 1913 and 1926. In 2013, 900-1,000 elk prospered in an 835-square-mile range stretching across Elk, Cameron, and Clearfield Counties. The heart of the elk region is the remote village of Benezette, so tiny that elk-viewing visitors outnumber residents at times.

The best time to visit is during elk mating season, aka the rut. It starts in September and winds down in October. During the rut, elk country reverberates with the bugling of mature bulls. The piercing call is an invitation to cows and a challenge to rival bulls. Bulls battle for control of cow harems, locking antlers until the weaker of the two retreats. Much of the action takes place in the open, where it's easier for harem masters to stand guard. Bring binoculars and a camera with ample zoom capabilities; stay well clear of the frays.

In winter, snow and ice make the country roads riskier and some areas inaccessible. The upside: If you find elk, you'll probably find a large number. The animals congregate in lower elevations, where they're more likely to find food. A good bet is to travel Route 555, which connects the villages of Weedville and Driftwood and passes through Benezette.

Elk FAQs

What exactly are elk?

The elk is the second largest member of the deer family in North America. The moose is larger. Good luck finding one of those in Pennsylvania.

How do I distinguish elk from white-tailed deer?

For one thing, white-tailed deer are common throughout the Commonwealth. Free-roaming elk can be found only in a handful of counties in the Wilds region. Elk are much larger than white-tailed deer. A mature male elk, aka a bull, weighs 600-1,000 pounds. His female counterpart, aka a cow, is a relative featherweight at 500-600 pounds. Elk have the barest hint of a tail; white-tailed deer have longer tails with white undersides. Elk have darkish necks; white-tailed deer have a white throat patch. The antlers of bulls sweep backward; those of bucks (male deer) curve forward.

Why can't bulls just get along?

Normally they do. For the bulk of the year, bulls roam on their own or in small "bachelor groups." It's not until mating season that they butt heads—literally. Their battles over the ladies rarely end in serious injury.

Can I feed the elk?

Absolutely not. In fact, Pennsylvania law prohibits it. Elk that are habituated to humans generally have shorter life spans than elk that steer clear of them. Think poachers. Think car-elk collisions.

How close can I come to the elk?

Elk will let you know how close is too close. When they sense danger, they raise their heads, cock their ears forward, and move stiffly. They sometimes bark to warn their comrades. Or they simply flee. Try not to make the elk flee. It ruins things for other viewers, and it stresses the elk. They're particularly vulnerable in wintertime, when they need every ounce of energy just to survive.

If elk are so precious, why are elk burgers on the menu?

The elk on the menu wasn't part of Pennsylvania's free-roaming herd. It was raised on a farm.

Elk continue to feed near streams in the spring, gradually moving out of the valleys as higher elevations green up. (If you have a mantel just begging for a pair of elk antlers, this is the time to go scavenger hunting. Bulls drop their antlers in late winter or early spring—finders keepers.)

Come summer, when food is plentiful throughout the range, it's unusual to see large groups of elk. The hottest months are the worst for elk viewing because the beasts skulk in the relative coolness of dense forest. No matter when you visit, the best times to view elk are the first hour or two of daylight and just before dusk. That's when they're most likely to be grazing on legumes, grasses, and forbs in open fields.

★ BENEZETTE

The capital of elk country is the Route 555 village of Benezette. Elk can often be found near town (and occasionally in town) in large part because the state and conservationists roll out the green carpet. Area forest openings are planted with alfalfa, clovers, and other food crops irresistible to elk. By attracting elk and other animals to clearings on public land, these buffets also serve human visitors hungry for wildlife sightings.

The **Elk Country Visitor Center** (950 Winslow Hill Rd., Benezette, 814/787-5167, www.experienceelkcountry.com, 8am-8pm daily June-Oct., 9am-5pm Thurs.-Mon. Nov.-Dec., 9am-5pm Sat.-Sun. Jan.-Mar., 9am-5pm Thurs.-Mon. Apr.-May), located just north of town off Winslow Hill Road, is a good place to start an elk-spotting adventure. Opened in 2010, it features exhibits about elk and wildlife conservation, a "4-D" theater (admission $3, children under 5 free) presenting a 22-minute show every half hour, and panoramic windows that look out at elk feeding areas. A series of trails and wildlife viewing areas are accessible from the center.

If you continue along Winslow Hill, heading away from Benezette, you'll soon arrive at another popular elk viewing area, **Dent's Run** (Winslow Hill Rd., 3.5 miles from Route 555 in Benezette). The vantage point overlooks fields where many a bull have locked antlers to win the affections of cows. The fields are also visited by white-tailed deer, wild turkeys, foxes, and even bobcats and black bears. Scan the skies for hawks and other birds of prey.

Another premier viewing area, **Hicks Run,** is 8.5 miles east of Benezette on the north side of Route 555. The blind affords a front-row

elk viewing by horse-drawn wagon at the Elk Country Visitor Center

view of elk and other animals in a wide clearing planted with succulent snacks.

Driving in circles is rather effective as elk spotting goes. Try the following loop: From Benezette, follow Winslow Hill Road for 2.2 miles, turn right to stay on Winslow Hill Road, continue for 0.7 mile, and bear right at Summerson Road. Continue on Summerson to Route 555, and turn right to return to Benezette. Repeat as necessary.

If you spot elk while driving, don't stop in the middle of the road. Find a place to pull off, being careful to avoid shoulders near sharp bends and private driveways. (If you see cars parked along a road, it's safe to assume that elk are nearby.) Keep in mind that people who live in places like Benezette value peace and quiet; they don't necessarily appreciate the growing wave of ecotourism. Don't go traipsing through private lands without permission. Certainly don't honk if you find yourself in traffic.

ELK SCENIC DRIVE

Elk Scenic Drive is a 127-mile route peppered with 23 sites of interest to nature lovers, including the viewing areas near Benezette. It winds through three state forests and three state game lands, starting and ending at points on I-80. From the west, leave I-80 at Penfield exit 111 at Route 153. From the east, take Snow Shoe exit 147 at Route 144. Look for distinctive signage.

All but a few of the sites require diverging from the main route. The journey can take a few hours or a few days, depending on your level of interest in sites such as Kettle Creek State Park, with its 167-acre stocked trout lake. It's not unusual for animals to amble across roads, so drive carefully. Be especially alert when you see an "elk crossing" sign.

GUIDED ELK VIEWING

Spotting elk is never a sure thing, but you can stack the odds by hiring an experienced guide. Few know elk habits better than the husband-and-wife team behind **Hicks Run Outfitters** (814/787-4287, hicksrunoutfitters@yahoo.

com). Jeff and Janet Coldwell, along with Janet's daughter, Cody, happily lead photographers, hunters, and anyone else seeking a close encounter of the elk kind off the beaten track. Call **PA Elk Range Adventures** (814/486-0305, http://paelkrangeadventures.tripod. com) to explore the range alongside nature photographer and writer and self-described hunting "addict" Phil Burkhouse.

BEYOND ELK
Straub Brewery

Elk aren't the only attraction in these parts. The city of St. Marys, a 20-mile drive from Benezette, is not only Pennsylvania's second largest city by land area after Philadelphia but also the home of **Straub Brewery** (303 Sorg St., St. Marys, 814/834-2875, www.straubbeer. com). The award-winning brewery, family owned since 1872, has a fiercely loyal following in places where its beers can be found. The beer is free of sugar, salt, and preservatives and just plain free to brewery visitors age 21 and older. Come between 9am and 4:30pm on a weekday or before 1pm on a Saturday to drink from the keg known as the "eternal tap." Tours are also free and open to anyone 12 or older. They're conducted 9am-noon weekdays. Call in advance if you want to make sure you visit when bottles are rolling off the line. The brewery's drive-up store is open 8:30am-8pm Monday-Thursday and 8:30am-9pm Friday and Saturday.

Ridgway

The seat of Elk County was founded as a lumbering town in the 1820s. Lest you forget Ridgway's long association with wood, streets and parks are decorated with chainsaw carvings 5-6 feet high. Pop by the **Ridgway-Elk County Chamber of Commerce** (300 Main St., Ridgway, 814/776-1424, www.ridgwaychamber.com, 10am-4pm Mon.-Fri., brochures always accessible) for a guide to these so-called Enchanted Woodlins. While you're there, grab a walking tour map of the "Lily of the Valley" National Register Historic District. More than 700 buildings reflect

Face Time with Phil

Groundhog Day in Punxsutawney

The resurrection of Pennsylvania's elk herd is a good story, but it's a different animal that grabs headlines year after year. That would be Punxsutawney Phil, the world's most famous weather forecaster (apologies to Al Roker). His hometown of Punxsutawney is a bit southwest of the elk range and more than a bit enamored of its renowned resident. Six-foot fiberglass effigies of the furry seer are scattered throughout town.

Unless you've been in a burrow for the last couple of decades, you probably know that Phil comes out of his hole every February 2, aka Groundhog Day, to predict if spring weather is around the bend or still weeks away. You may have seen him portrayed in *Groundhog Day*, the 1993 comedy starring Bill Murray. Maybe you caught him on *Oprah*. But the groundhog who inspired a Beanie Baby isn't so famous that you can't see him in person. Most days of the year, you'll find him at his pad in downtown Punxsy, **Phil's Burrow** at Punxsutawney Memorial Library (301 E. Mahoning St., 814/938-5020, www.punxsutawneylibrary.org). He and his groundhog entourage are visible from inside or outside.

The best time to visit, of course, is **Groundhog Day** (814/618-5591, www.groundhog.org). In the dark of night, thousands of people gather at **Gobbler's Knob** (1548 Woodland Ave. Ext.), a clearing just south of town, to await Phil's prognostication. He delivers it at daybreak. (Sadly, Phil himself does not address the crowd. That's left to men in top hats and bow ties who call themselves the Inner Circle.) The annual prediction is occasion for several days of festivities and activities, including The Groundhog Ball, a catered picnic, musical performances, and hayrides.

Punxsutawney also honors its favorite citizen in the summer with the weeklong **Punxsutawney Groundhog Festival** (814/938-2947, www.groundhogfestival.com, week of July 4), featuring free concerts, a craft show, and fireworks. The **Punxsutawney Area Chamber of Commerce** (102 W. Mahoning St., 800/752-7445, www.punxsutawney.com) hawks all things groundhog, from a fuzzy groundhog golf club cover to the official Groundhog Day Habanero Hot Sauce.

Are Phil's predictive abilities good enough to merit all the fuss? Members of the Inner Circle will tell you he's never wrong. They'll also tell you there's been only one Phil since the Knob tradition began in 1887. You can explore the science and lore of weather forecasting at the kid-centric **Punxsutawney Weather Discovery Center** (201 N. Findley St., 814/938-1000, www.weatherdiscovery.org, 10am-4pm Mon.-Tues. and Thurs.-Sat., admission $4, children under 2 free). As for their second claim, you'll have to make up your own mind.

Ridgway's century of significance in the lumber industry.

There's a real buzz in town in late February, during the **Ridgway Chainsaw Carvers Rendezvous** (814/772-0400, www.chainsawrendezvous.org). The noncompetitive showcase of ear-splitting sculpting attracts hundreds of wood and ice carvers from around the world and thousands of spectators. Feel inspired to take chainsaw to wood? Learn how at **Appalachian Arts Studio** (17245 Boot Jack Hill, Ridgway, 814/772-0400, www.appalachian-arts.com), owned by the couple responsible for the Rendezvous. Classes in pottery, painting, photography, and other arts are also available. Those who prefer collecting to creating can find works by local and regional artists at the gallery of the **Elk County Council on the Arts** (237 Main St., Ridgway, 814/772-7051, www.eccota.com, 10am-5pm Tues.-Fri., 10am-2pm Sat.).

One of the loveliest things to do in Ridgway is to leave it by way of the **Clarion/ Little Toby Trail** (www.tricountyrailstotrails.org). The rail-trail extends 18 miles to Brockway, following first the Clarion River and then Little Toby Creek. The Ridgway trailhead is on Water Street, one block off Main Street. Nearby **Country Squirrel Outfitters** (3 Main St., Ridgway, 814/776-6285, www.countrysquirreloutfitters.com, summer hours 8:30am-6pm daily, winter hours noon-6pm Tues.-Fri., 9am-6pm Sat., 10am-3pm Sun.) rents bicycles, cross-country skis, and snowshoes, plus canoes and kayaks for those who'd rather paddle the river than cruise alongside it.

ACCOMMODATIONS
Under $100

A stay at the **Bennett House Bed and Breakfast** (14019 Rte. 555, Benezette, 814/787-4842, www.bennetthousepa.com, $90) is rather like visiting Grandma. Innkeeper Ginger McCoy is liable to greet you with a hug and send you on your way with Christian literature. The three guest rooms are small and plain and the bathrooms shared, but the location is hard to beat. Hicks Run, one of the most prolific elk-viewing areas, is just two miles from the homestead that once belonged to Ginger's great-great-grandfather. Eggs served for breakfast are courtesy of her hens.

$100-200

A stone's throw from the Elk Country Visitor Center, the three-bedroom **Elk Mountain Homestead** (950 Winslow Hill Rd., Benezette, 814/787-5168, www.experienceelkcountry.com, $132-288, weekly $989-1,265, rates good for up to 6 people, $40 per night for each additional person) offers sweeping views of fields, woods, and the critters that inhabit them. Proceeds from the rental of the state-owned farmhouse benefit conservation efforts. The house, which sleeps as many as 10 people, has a fully equipped kitchen, two showers, and a covered viewing platform. Light sleepers should consider shutting their windows in the fall, when bulls bugle all night long.

The six modern cabins at ★ **Wapiti Woods** (5186 River Rd., Weedville, 814/787-7525, www.wapitiwoods.com, $175, weekly $1,100) boast wood-burning fireplaces, creek-facing porch entryways, and off-the-charts coziness. Two of the knotty pine masterpieces also have whirlpool tubs. The 34-acre retreat along the Bennett Branch of Sinnemahoning Creek has its very own wildlife-wooing feed plot.

The cheery Jerome Powell Suite at the ★ **Towers Victorian Inn** (330 South St., Ridgway, 814/772-7657, www.towersinn.com, $85-149) pays tribute to the lumber baron who built the Italianate mansion in 1865. But the most stately of guest accommodations is named for town founder Jacob Ridgway. The inn has a two-bedroom carriage house that sleeps as many as seven in addition to six rooms and suites in the main house. Hikers, bikers, and boaters can arrange for drop-off and pick-up service.

The third-floor suite at the elegant **Victorian Loft Bed and Breakfast** (216

S. Front St., Clearfield, 814/765-4805, www. pawildsvacation.com, $100-130), big enough for two or three couples, boasts a whirlpool tub overlooking the West Branch of the Susquehanna River. Antique silver and china place settings greet breakfasters in the formal Victorian dining room. Innkeepers Tim and Peggy Durant also offer a one-bedroom pad in downtown Clearfield and a divinely secluded three-bedroom cabin in Moshannon State Forest.

Over $200

The three-bedroom **Elk Terrace Lodge** (Elk Terrace Dr., Benezette, 814/772-4854, www. elkterracelodge.com, $250 for 2 adults) boasts a hot tub, satellite TV, and a gas fireplace. Best of all, elk have a habit of visiting the property.

Your majesty may enjoy a stay at **MacDarvey Castle** (153 Elk Terrace Dr., Benezette, 814/546-2043, www.macdarvey-castle.com, $491 for 2 nights, 2-night minimum), undoubtedly the most unusual lodging in elk country. Guests can gaze upon grazing elk from 67 windows, shoot pool in the "dungeon," or feast in the dining room. You'll be king or queen of the castle whether you rent one bedchamber or all five; it's rented to just one group at a time. Dragon not included.

FOOD

When it comes to high-quality grazing, elk have it somewhat better than humans in these parts. Restaurants are few and far between and tend toward pub grub. But the pub grub is rather good in some cases and downright colossal in one.

Benezette

The **Benezette Hotel** (95 Winslow Hill Rd., 814/787-4240, www.benezettehotel.com, 11am-9pm daily, late-night menu 9pm-midnight daily, $5-18) is so centrally located that it's frequently referenced in directions to elk viewing areas. It serves everything from wings to "wedgies" (grilled steak or ham, cheese, and vegetables enfolded in a 12-inch pizza shell),

along with beer and other beverages. Wrangle a table on the patio and you may spot a live one as you bite into an elk burger.

St. Marys

Gunners (33 S. St. Marys St., 814/834-2161, www.gunners.biz, 4pm-10pm Mon.-Sat., bar open until midnight Mon.-Thurs. and 1am Fri.-Sat., $7-24) hits the mark with a jovial atmosphere and just-right steaks.

Clearfield

Clearfield is a good 45 minutes from Benezette, but meat lovers gladly go out of their way for ★ **Denny's Beer Barrel Pub** (1452 Woodland Rd., 814/765-7190, www.dennysbeerbarrelpub.com, 10am-midnight Mon.-Sat., 11am-11pm Sun., $7-29). With 72 hours' notice, the restaurant can cook up a burger that weighs more than 100 pounds. Two or three pounds of beef is more than enough for most guests. Finish a two-pounder in an hour and you get a free T-shirt, half off the $19.99 price, and a place in the Hall of Fame. The $28.99 three-pound burger is free if you finish it in 90 minutes. In addition to 30-plus burgers, Denny's Beer Barrel Pub offers wings in dozens of flavors, pizzas, steak and seafood dishes, Irish fare, Mexican *comida,* and more.

INFORMATION

The **PA Great Outdoors Visitors Bureau** (2801 Maplevale Rd., Brookville, 814/849-5197, www.visitpago.com, 8:30am-4:30pm Mon.-Fri.) is a fount of elk-viewing tips and other information about the region.

GETTING THERE

The main corridor through elk country is the east-west I-80. Benezette, its unofficial capital, is about 130 miles northeast of Pittsburgh via Route 28 north, I-80 east, and Routes 255 north and 555 east.

The closest airport with commercial service is DuBois Regional Airport (DUJ), about 40 miles southwest of Benezette. It's served by United Express.

Background

The Landscape

If you look at a map of the original 13 American colonies you will see that Pennsylvania is located right in the middle. The "Keystone State" was so-named since Pennsylvania is geographically in the center of the arch formed by the other colonies, similar to the keystone that stonemasons put in the middle of an arch to hold the rest of the stones together. Today Pennsylvania is surrounded by the states of New York, New Jersey, Delaware, Maryland, West Virginia, and Ohio. It has a land area of 44,820 square miles, ranking 33rd in area among the 50 states, and has 1,239 square miles of water surface. The elevation in the state ranges from its highest peak of Mount Davis in Somerset County (3,213 feet above sea level) to its lowest point at sea level, on the banks of the Delaware River outside Philadelphia.

It was for good reason that King Charles II of England in 1681 coined the name Pennsylvania, translated from Latin to mean "Penn's woods." When early Europeans first explored the eastern shores of North America they were awed by the vastness and density of the forest as trees covered more than 90 percent of Pennsylvania's territory. Its moderate climate, abundant rainfall, and rich soils gave rise to dense forests with plants and animals unknown to European settlers. A famed natural scientist named John Bartram was traveling up the Susquehanna River in 1743 and found forests so thick that "it seems almost as if the sun had never shown on the ground since the creation." Today, more than 17 million acres, almost 60 percent of the state, are covered by a quality hardwood forest, and Pennsylvania is the nation's largest producer of hardwood lumber (over a billion board feet per year). The State Forest system, comprising 2.1 million acres, is one of the largest public forest ownerships in the eastern United States.

GEOGRAPHY

The variety of natural landscapes in Pennsylvania is the result of millions of years of continents shifting and crashing into one another, creating the state's mountains and valleys. The Appalachian mountain range, which bisects present-day Pennsylvania, was formed some 480 million years ago and marks the first of several mountain-building plate collisions that culminated in the construction of the supercontinent Pangea, with the Appalachians near the center. Compared to the modern-day Himalayas in Asia, the Appalachians once stood as tall and were covered under large glaciations and vast oceans. Weathering and erosion prevailed as Pangea broke apart and the mountains began to wear away. By the end of the Mesozoic era (65 million years ago), the Appalachian Mountains had been eroded to an almost flat plain. It was not until the region was uplifted during the most recent geologic era that the distinctive present topography formed. Broad-topped mountains, called plateaus, include the Allegheny and Pocono ranges of the Appalachian Mountains.

From the Appalachian Mountains, the landscape slopes downward to the east and west forming rolling hills and lowlands that make up the five major land regions. The largest of these land regions is the Appalachian Plateau, which covers most of western and northern Pennsylvania. This region, which includes the regions south and north of Pittsburgh, holds a big share of the state's natural resources; it was the location of the world's first successful oil well and a source

Previous: a deer on the lawn at Valley Forge National Historical Park; Gettysburg National Military Park.

of rich veins of coal. East of the Appalachian Plateau is the Appalachian Ridge and Valley, a region of narrow and steep mountain peaks and numerous valleys that resemble parallel arcs if viewed from space. Grouping the valleys of Cumberland, Lebanon, and Lehigh together makes up the Great Appalachian Valley, an area that stretches from the south-central border with Maryland to the eastern border with New Jersey. Farther southeast is the region called the Piedmont Plateau, an area of low hills, ridges, and valleys that has some of the richest farmland in the state and, some say, of the country. Due to the soil conservation techniques practiced by the Amish since the early colonial days, the area has remained agriculturally productive even through the industrial pillaging of the 19th and 20th centuries. The remaining two regions are close to water and the smallest regions of the five—the Atlantic Coastal Plain and the Erie Lowland or Erie Plain. The Atlantic Coastal Plain covers the extreme southeastern corner of the state while the Erie Plain covers the extreme northwestern corner of Pennsylvania.

The River Valleys

Three major river systems in Pennsylvania drain more than 90 percent of the state's land: the Delaware, Susquehanna, and the combined Allegheny, Ohio, and Monongahela Rivers. These river systems were important in the development of the state's transportation systems and industries such as steel and lumber. The Delaware River is the main river of the eastern part of the state and actually defines the jagged eastern border of the state. The river separates Pennsylvania from New York and New Jersey as it serpentines through narrow rapids and wide regions from New York to the Delaware Bay. This is the same river of the famous "Delaware Crossing," which involved an improvised boat crossing undertaken by George Washington's army during the American Revolution on Christmas Day 1776.

Due to its access to the Atlantic Ocean, the Delaware is a major shipping lane that is second only to the Mississippi River in the amount of commerce it carries each year. The Upper Delaware offers some of the finest recreational opportunities in the northeastern United States. In particular, sightseeing, boating, camping, hunting, fishing, hiking, and bird-watching are popular activities in the river area.

Running north to south through the

the Susquehanna River

central part of the state is the Susquehanna (sus-ka-HAN-na) River, renowned for its fantastic fishing and recreation. Anglers can fish for muskies, walleye, smallmouth bass, panfish, catfish, and carp. The river meanders 444 miles from its origin near Cooperstown, New York, until it empties into the Chesapeake Bay at Havre de Grace, Maryland. In a similar north-to-south manner, the Allegheny River flows down the western portion of the state. This river begins as a spring in a farmer's field off of Route 49, a couple of miles east of the little town of Colesburg and nine miles from Coudersport in the upper Appalachian Mountains of northern Pennsylvania. The Allegheny River joins the Monongahela (monon-ga-HAY-la) River in Pittsburgh to form the westward-pointing Ohio River, which eventually flows into the Mississippi. The Ohio provides 35 percent of all of the water that empties out into the Gulf of Mexico.

CLIMATE

In spite of its proximity to the ocean, Pennsylvania has a humid continental climate that is due to the prevailing winds from the west. These prevailing westerly winds carry most of the weather disturbances from the interior of the continent into the state, so that the Atlantic Ocean has only a limited influence upon the climate. Pennsylvania is also situated in the conflict zone between polar air masses from the north and tropical air masses from the south. These air masses create large annual, daily, and day-to-day temperature ranges that Pennsylvanians experience in four distinct seasons. In addition, local elevation and geological features can drastically vary the climate.

Winters usually bring snow to most of the state (more to the mountainous areas), with temperatures ranging from below zero Fahrenheit to the high 30s. The coldest time of the year is usually January, with northern latitudes recording colder temperatures and southeastern locations with milder temperatures. In summer the temperature rarely breaks 100 degrees, yet the humidity is often high, especially in August and September. Evenings during the summer months cool down from their daytime highs, which average in the 80s in July. Spring and autumn are the best times to travel to Pennsylvania as the temperatures are moderate and the state is covered in greenery in the spring and is blanketed in brilliant colors in the autumn. The spring months of March through May see the temperatures slowly ramping up from

a winter day in Adams County

an average of 40s to 70s, while the autumn months of September through November see the reverse.

The state averages 41 inches of precipitation each year, which helps trees and other plants grow abundantly. The greatest amount of precipitation usually occurs in spring and summer months, while February is the driest month, having about two inches less than the wettest months. Thunderstorms, which average between 30 and 35 occurrences per year, are concentrated in the warm months and are responsible for most of the summertime rainfall. Sometimes tropical systems from the south (or their remnants) affect the state by causing flooding rains, especially in the eastern portion of the state. Tornadoes can and do occur, but they usually cause minor damage. Yet in May 31, 1985, a total of 21 tornadoes killed 65 people, injured 707, destroyed over 1,000 homes, and caused $380 million (1985 figure) in damage. A rare F-5, the strongest tornado, nearly leveled the town of Wheatland in Mercer County.

Among the major population centers, Philadelphia and Pittsburgh have similar temperatures with annual mean temperatures of 54 and 50 degrees, respectively, and similar precipitation amounts of 42 inches and 37.8 inches, respectively. However, Pittsburgh usually has more snow (44 inches) as compared with 21 inches for Philadelphia. The greatest weather extremes usually occur in the northeastern and north-central part of the state. The average number of cloudy days increases from the southeast corner of the state near Philadelphia (average of 160 cloudy days) to the northwest corner of the state near Erie (average of 205 cloudy days).

ENVIRONMENTAL ISSUES

When the first Europeans settled in Pennsylvania, the horizon-to-horizon forest had many 400-year-old trees. Trees that densely covered the state were cut down by early settlers who viewed them as obstacles to agriculture and timber for cabins and barns.

Since 1682, the advancing human population has conquered the vast forests that covered the state. The last bison was shot in 1801, and the last native elk in 1867.

As the Industrial Revolution progressed in the 19th century, Pennsylvanians cut, mined, quarried, hunted, harvested, and in other ways extracted nature's bounty with unrelenting enthusiasm and voraciousness. By 1900, Pennsylvania had lost more than 60 percent of its forests. Its polluted waterways, denuded landscapes, impoverished soils, extinct and disappearing plant and animal life, and foul air motivated many to embrace new conservation and preservation ethics. Fears of a "timber famine" gave birth to a national conservation movement for the protection and rejuvenation of forests for future use. In the early 20th century, Pennsylvania passed a broad network of laws to restrict the pollution of its waters and air, protect wildlife, and regulate extraction of natural resources. It established fish, game, and forest commissions to conserve and manage these resources. In addition, the state acquired more than four million acres of land and established 20 state forests for timber conservation, plant and wildlife preservation, and recreation. Unfortunately, most of the damage was done and is irreversible: Pennsylvania has lost as many as 156 species of native vascular plants and vertebrates in the past 300 years. An additional 351 species have become endangered or threatened. Moreover, 56 percent of Pennsylvania's wetlands have been lost since 1780.

Yet old challenges endured and new threats emerged during the 20th century. Leaded gasoline, acid rain, DDT, PCBs, and other carcinogens polluted the water and the air, wreaking havoc on the flora and fauna of the state (the Fish and Boat Commission issues an annual advisory on which areas and fish to avoid). By 1999, Pennsylvania led the nation in toxic discharges into its surface water, had the worst acid rain problem in the nation, and was the nation's largest importer of municipal waste. The state was second in the number of Superfund toxic waste sites, rate of suburban sprawl, and toxic air emissions from coal mining and processing; third in toxic air emissions from coal, oil, and electrical utilities; and fourth in the release of toxic chemicals from manufacturing. Pennsylvania has the distinction of being the home to the town of Centralia, where an exposed seam of coal caught fire in 1961, forcing the entire community to flee the area as the underground fire continues to this day and is expected to burn for decades more. No single event drove home the potential costs of industry more than the accident at Three Mile Island, which in 1979 ended the American romance with nuclear energy. Yet the greatest danger to Pennsylvania's remaining wildlife is the risk of habitat destruction by sprawl: the building of parking lots, shopping malls, and houses.

The introduction of nonnative insects, plants, and diseases has caused millions of dollars in damage and altered the forest ecosystem. Certain parts of the state have been overrun by Norway maple, Japanese knotwood, autumn olive, and other plants imported from abroad. A popular plant with home gardeners called the purple loosestrife escaped into the wild and rapidly displaced native plants, choked wetlands, and caused millions of dollars of economic damage. The Asian long-horned beetle, which entered the country in wooden pallets from China, threatens to cause billions of dollars in damage by attacking a wide range of American trees. Multiagency surveys are in place to detect threats before they become established in the state.

One native threat to the state, unbeknownst to the average tourist, has been the white-tailed deer. All but gone from Penn's woods at the beginning of the 20th century, deer now exist in unprecedented numbers, averaging 60 deer per square mile. They overgraze the native plants of the forest while leaving the nonnative plants untouched, contribute to the spread of Lyme disease, and cause thousands of motor vehicle accidents each year. By eating and killing off the seedlings and saplings that regenerate woodlands they have radically altered the state's forests.

Conservation efforts by the state and private organizations have made great strides in turning back the clock to the pre-European settlement days. By the 20th century, the state passed stricter wildlife-protection laws and enforced those that were already on the books. Over the last century the Pennsylvania Game Commission has reintroduced beaver from Canada, elk from Wyoming, white-tailed deer from Michigan, cottontail rabbits from Kansas and Missouri, and quail from Mexico. Using the fees paid each year by hunters and fishers, the state has set up hatcheries and nurseries to restock streams and forests with shad, trout, ruffled grouse, pheasant, and other species. River otters, once ubiquitous across Pennsylvania before over-trapping and poor water quality, are thriving after being reintroduced throughout the state starting in the mid-1990s. Likewise, several bird species, such as the osprey, peregrine falcon, and bald eagle, are slowly increasing in population.

Flora and Fauna

FLORA

Pennsylvania is situated in the middle of the transitional zone between the great northern and southern forests of eastern North America. The mixed hardwoods of the southern forests—the broadleaf oak, hickory, chestnut, and walnut—merged into mixed softwood and hardwood forests of the north—the great white pine, hemlock, sugar maple, beech, and birch. The forest that you see today is largely the result of two things: the exploitation of timber at the turn of the 20th century, which devastated the old-growth variety of trees, and 87 years of Mother Nature's forces and management by the Forest Service. Various disturbances such as wind, fire, insects, disease, deer, and human intervention worked together to create the unique conditions for hardwood trees to become established and flourish (over 108 species of native trees and many others introduced from Europe and Asia). Pennsylvania's forests contain more hardwood growing stock than those of any other state, providing raw material for a forest-products industry that earns $5 billion per year while employing nearly 100,000 people.

Located primarily in the north-central part of Pennsylvania are 20 sites that are designated "old-growth" or virgin forests. These forests contain trees that have attained great age (usually 300 to 400 years old) and exhibit characteristic features such as large trunk diameters. Most of the sites are within what is known as the Lumber Heritage Region, the 15 counties from which most of the timber resources were extracted in the 19th and early 20th centuries. Although industrialization removed the majority of these trees, those that are left from that era are usually in areas that were inaccessible, such as steep slopes, or accidents of boundary overlaps. Within Cook Forest State Park, nine different old-growth forest areas—covering over 2,200 acres—can be found within the boundaries of the park. Every fall, the deciduous trees in the state put on an unrivaled blaze of glory along its highways, country roads, and coastline with rich and vibrant hues of red, orange, yellow, and brown.

Spring in Pennsylvania brings abundant

pine trees in Dutch country

rainfall and glorious blooms of native wildflowers and flowering shrubs. Throughout spring, yellow forsythia, azaleas, rhododendrons, trilliums, elderberries, honeysuckles, and mountain laurels bring splashes of color to the state's forests, fields, and roadsides. This colorful display brings thousands of tourists from the Commonwealth and surrounding states each spring. Mountain laurels, the state flower of Pennsylvania, normally begin to bloom late in May, and their pink and white blossoms are in evidence well into June. They are particularly abundant in the mountainous sections of the state, particularly the Laurel Highlands in the south and the Allegheny Mountains in the northeast. The distinctive plant, with its three- to five-inch lustrous, dark green leaves, is used extensively as ornamental shrubbery. Pennsylvania's climate also ensures wild berries such as cranberries, blackberries, thimbleberries, strawberries, and elderberries throughout the early spring and into the fall season. Wild strawberries, noticeable by their smaller size compared to their cultivated cousins, can be seen in early May through June throughout the state. High-bush cranberries grow in northern Pennsylvania and can be recognized by their three-lobed leaves and large seeds.

FAUNA

The white-tailed deer, the icon for the state animal, is undoubtedly one of the most influential species of wildlife in Pennsylvania. Deer provide the greatest wildlife value to the citizens of this state as watchable wildlife, a huntable resource, and venison for countless families. Much of Pennsylvania's rural cultural heritage is closely linked to this species. Around 1900, the Game Commission estimated that only about 500 white-tailed deer remained in the state. The commission began bringing deer from Michigan and Kentucky in 1906 and continued through the 1920s. Seeing a deer in the forest (or in the headlights) is no longer a rare event in much of Pennsylvania. Since development has dramatically reduced their habitat they are frequently sighted,

therefore keep a lookout along roads. Along with deer, the garden variety of forest critters are commonly seen in Pennsylvania, including: wild rabbits, black and gray squirrels, raccoons, foxes, minks, opossums, skunks, and woodchucks. Beavers, nearly extinct due to over-trapping (prime pelts netted $65 each in colonial times), are now abundant in each state county. Less common, but still found around campsites and cabins, are black bears, which are mostly found in the north-central and northeastern counties of the state. Black bear attacks in the eastern United States are rare, yet bears dependent on eating human food can become slightly aggressive when people get between them and food. Rarer still are wildcats, which live in northern mountain habitats.

Between 1913 and 1926, the Pennsylvania Game Commission attempted to restore an elk herd by releasing 177 western elk from Wyoming. A recent survey indicated the herd size to be more than 600 animals, typically found in southwestern Cameron and southeastern Elk Counties. Elk are much larger than white-tailed deer, weighing 700-1,000 pounds with a height of about five feet. Males are usually sporting a set of backward-curving antlers that can have as many as 16 points, while females are somewhat smaller and antlerless. The elks' coat can vary from dark brown to reddish, depending on the season, yet a large buff-colored patch covering the rump is its characteristic signature. Elk are best observed at dawn and dusk, in September and October during the mating season, and from a safe distance. They can be very dangerous, especially bulls during the mating season.

Snakes

Hikers and campers should be aware that most snakes in Pennsylvania are harmless, although there are three native poisonous snake species that inhabit the state (northern copperheads, timber rattlesnakes, and the eastern massasauga rattlesnake). All these venomous snakes possess an indentation or pit on each side of the head between the eye and nostril, a vertically elliptical eye pupil resembling that of a cat, and a single row of scales on the underside of the tail. Reports of venomous snakebites in the state are rare, with bites usually occurring while a person is trying to catch or carelessly handle one of these snakes. All of these species are usually nonaggressive and prefer to avoid confrontation, usually moving away from an approaching human or remaining completely still as a threat passes by.

Birds

Bird-watching, or birding, has become a popular activity in Pennsylvania thanks to the 373 species of birds. The largest number and species of birds may be found during May when migration for most long-distance migrants is well under way. In some locations more than 150 species have been recorded in 24 hours; these include flycatchers, wrens, thrushes, and orioles. Bird song all but ends in August as the nesting season is usually over for most species. The ruffed grouse, known as the state game bird and sometimes called the partridge or pheasant, is easily recognized by its territorial drumming and the roar of its wings when it takes flight. Distinguishable characteristics include a plump body, feathered legs, and mottled reddish-brown color. Great horned owls, the largest and most widely distributed resident owl in Pennsylvania, are powerful birds of prey that feed on a wide variety of mammals and birds. They are most often detected when vocalizing during the mating and breeding season in fall through winter. A nesting female may sit on eggs through the worst of weather and sometimes is seen covered with snow.

In the Water

With 83,184 miles of stream and rivers and more than 4,000 lakes and ponds, Pennsylvania has no shortage of game fish, including trout, bass, muskie, walleye, steelhead, and panfish. The Susquehanna River and its tributaries, Roaring Creek and Hemlock Creek, feature wild and stocked trout and smallmouth bass. Potter County boasts a huge collection of Class A wild trout streams, while Oil Creek State Park offers excellent fly-fishing for walleye and smallmouth bass. Many streams are stocked to ensure good fishing and regulated with minimum size and daily limits by the Fish and Boat Commission. Lake Erie is sometimes called the freshwater fishing capital of the world thanks to trout, perch, walleye, smallmouth bass, northern pike, and muskie. In recent years, more attention has been given to the threat of nonnative species and the impact these species have on native wildlife within the Lake. Nonnative fish (e.g., round goby) and invertebrates such as the zebra mussel or rusty crayfish are currently occurring in high densities in Lake Erie drainage and may be seriously impacting native fauna by eliminating them from their former ranges.

One positive trend in wetland wildlife is the increase in river otters, which had drastically declined in the state because of fur trapping and destruction of river water quality. Through a state reintroduction program that started in 1982, more than 110 river otters have been released in Pennsylvanian rivers and streams. Otters were reintroduced in several watersheds across northern Pennsylvania and as far south as the lower Susquehanna River and Youghiogheny River. You might notice a river otter due to its playful antics, particularly its practice of repeatedly sliding down stream banks into the water. Amphibians such as frogs, salamanders, and turtles can also be seen throughout the state. One turtle in particular, the bog turtle, is a 3- to 4.5-inch-long turtle species usually found in southeastern and eastern Pennsylvania. Development and selfish collectors who find them irresistibly cute have decimated their population, and as a result they have received federal threatened status. Eastern hellbenders, large and wondrously ugly amphibians, are usually found in the western part of the state and can live to be 30 to 50 years old. They are a superb indicator of the health of the environment and can provide an early warning of when an ecosystem is in trouble since they prefer clean and clear-flowing rivers and streams.

History

ANCIENT CIVILIZATION

The first people to live in Pennsylvania were part of the earliest waves of human migration that came during the end of the last Ice Age (about 30,000 to 10,000 years ago), when lower ocean levels exposed the Bering Land Bridge between Siberia and Alaska. These Paleo-Indians, as archaeologists call them, were a nomadic hunter-gatherer tribe that fashioned tools from stone, bone, and wood in order to hunt mammoths, elk, and moose but did not plant crops or build permanent dwellings. A Paleo-Indian archaeological site in Pennsylvania, the Meadowcroft Rockshelter, which is 30 miles southwest of Pittsburgh, shows evidence of human occupation possibly as early as 16,000 years ago, meaning it may be the earliest documented site of human occupation in North America. About 13,000 years ago ice glaciers located in the northeastern and northwestern parts of the state began to recede. During the Archaic Period (8000-1000 BC), as the climate slowly got warmer, Indian hunter-gatherers continued to seek shelter at Meadowcroft, but their technology diversified and they began to hunt deer, elk, bear, and turkey in deciduous forests with a rich understory of berries and other plant foods.

Several sites have yielded arrowheads, stone axes, sinkers for fishing nets, and other Archaic Period artifacts. By the Late Woodland Period (AD 1000-1500), there were two major Indian tribe population centers that congregated along the major river systems of the Delaware and the Susquehanna. The northern and southern parts of the Delaware Valley were inhabited by the Lenapes or Delawares. To the west, close to modern-day Lancaster County, the northern Susquehanna Valley was home to Iroquoian-speaking peoples called the Susquehannocks. Numerous tribes, which can't be identified with certainty, inhabited western Pennsylvania before the Europeans arrived but were eliminated by wars and diseases in the 17th century. The Iroquois Nation, a confederacy of numerous tribes joined together, lived mostly in present-day New York yet traveled to present-day northern Pennsylvania to hunt.

EUROPEAN EXPLORATION AND SETTLEMENT

The age of discovery in Europe brought a desire for territorial gains beyond the seas, first by Spain and Portugal and later by England, France, the Netherlands, and Sweden. Captain John Smith, famous for later establishing the Jamestown settlement, journeyed from Virginia up the Susquehanna River in 1608, visiting the Susquehannock people. Later in 1609 Henry Hudson, an Englishman in the Dutch service, sailed the *Half Moon* into Delaware Bay and made contact with the Lenape, thus giving the Dutch a claim to the area. Not until 1640, however, did the Dutch establish their first trading post at Fort Nassau (near present-day New Jersey), which soon developed a fairly prosperous exchange of Dutch items for Indian beaver pelts. Surprisingly, the Swedes were the first to establish a settlement in the Delaware Bay area, called New Sweden, beginning with the expedition of 1637-1638, which established a small colony of Swedes near the current site of Wilmington, Delaware. Governor Johann Printz of New Sweden relocated the capital to Tinicum Island in 1643, which was 20 miles south of present-day Philadelphia. There he directed a rough band of conscripts, army deserters, and debtors to build new blockhouses and log cabins as well as a new fort that aimed four cannons at a Dutch trading station. In the 1640s, Holland and Sweden were at peace, yet competition in the fur trade created ongoing tensions between Printz and his Dutch counterpart, Peter Stuyvesant, governor of New

Netherlands. After some skirmishes between the two groups, the settlers lived and worked together peaceably and established an effective legal system that punished crimes based on fines rather than imprisonment.

In 1664 King Charles II of England decided to give all the land between Connecticut and Maryland to his brother, James, Duke of York. As a result of this declaration, the Dutch decided to seize the Hudson and Delaware Valleys, in spite of English claims to these regions. During the war that followed, the British captured New Amsterdam, whose name they changed to New York, and English laws and civil government were introduced to the region in 1676. By 1680, Pennsylvania included Swedes (the largest nationality in the region) along with lesser numbers of Dutch, Finnish, German, French, Welsh, and English settlers.

WILLIAM PENN AND THE QUAKERS

an engraving of William Penn

During the late 17th century, England was undergoing religious upheaval as Protestants persecuted Catholics, Catholics persecuted Protestants, and both persecuted other religious beliefs. A new Protestant sect called the Religious Society of Friends came in the spotlight due to its rejection of rituals and oaths, its opposition to war, and its simplicity of speech and dress. Outsiders tended to call the followers of this sect Quakers because they were said to quake and tremble when they rose to speak during their religious services. George Fox, the radical preacher credited with founding the Quakers, was decried a heretic, and his followers were widely persecuted and imprisoned. William Penn, a charismatic young aristocrat who frequented the king's court and was trusted by the Duke of York (later known as King James II), embraced Fox's teachings. Despite high social rank and an excellent education, Penn shocked his upper-class associates by his conversion to Quaker beliefs that insisted that God valued each individual equally—a drastic change to the British class system. King

Charles II of England owed a large sum of money to Penn's father, a deceased admiral in the British Navy. Seeking a haven in the New World for persecuted Quakers, Penn asked the king to grant him land in the territory between Lord Baltimore's province of Maryland and the Duke of York's province of New York. With the duke's support, Penn's petition was granted. By giving Penn a colony, the king managed to pay off an outstanding debt and at the same time get rid of people that constantly challenged English laws and the legitimacy of the Anglican Church, the nation's established church. On March 4, 1681, King Charles II of England granted 45,000 square miles of land, an area almost as large as England itself. King Charles named the new colony "Penn's woods" (in Latin, Pennsylvania) in honor of the admiral.

The old manorial system in Europe was breaking down, creating a large class of landless people ready to seek new homes. In addition, wars in southern Germany caused many Germans to migrate eventually to

Pennsylvania. The Reformation led to religious ferment and division, not only with Quakers, Puritans, and Catholics from England, but with Pietists, Mennonites, and Lutherans from the Rhineland, Scotch Calvinists via Ireland, Amish from Switzerland, and Huguenots from France. Penn guaranteed the settlers of his new "Holy Experiment" freedom of religious worship, yet Pennsylvania's charter restricted the right to vote and to hold political office only to Protestants. In addition, Penn's Holy Experiment did not extend the protections of his charter to enslaved Africans and African Americans.

CITY OF BROTHERLY LOVE

Penn's first visit to Pennsylvania in 1682 brought 100 prospective colonists, one-third of whom would die after smallpox broke out during the voyage. His ship, the *Welcome,* was the first of a fleet of 23 ships that carried more than 2,000 men, women, and children to Pennsylvania in the next year. Penn's agents recommended that the capital be established on a sparsely settled peninsula at the confluence of the Schuylkill and Delaware Rivers, far from the Dutch and Swedish settlements that were previously established. Named Philadelphia, or City of Brotherly Love, the peninsula was also one of Penn's original three counties, along with Bucks and Chester. Rather than simply occupy the land without consent of the Lenape people, Penn wrote letters and met with Lenape chiefs, asking permission to "enjoy the land with your love and consent."

The capital city of Philadelphia laid claim to most of Penn's attention during his first months. He appointed a surveyor general and immediately directed him to lay out "a greene country town where every house be placed in the middle of the plot, so that there may be ground on each side, for gardens, or orchards or fields and so that it will never be burnt, and always be wholesome." Penn also called for the creation of parks by directing that "four

squares be set aside for physical recreation" and that a "ten-acre Center square be reserved for a House of Public Affairs." In addition, he mandated that land for "Publick Houses" be set aside on every block as community gathering places. A city grid pattern was developed that set precedent for future American towns; streets running east-west were to be named after trees, and those running north-south were to be numbered. During his second visit in 1699-1701, Penn lived at a country estate he had built north of Philadelphia on the Delaware River that was known as Pennsbury Manor. Forced to return to England in 1700 to protect his control of the colony from the government and forced to remain there because of poor health, Penn spent only five years in Pennsylvania over his two visits. Penn's colony paved the path for the future of the young American republic by providing a democratic form of government and a legacy of toleration, which can still be seen in the First Amendment's protection of religious liberty. Thanks to its central position in the colonies and its wealth, Philadelphia became the largest and most important city in the colonies by the time of the American Revolution.

EXPANSION AND THE COLONIAL WARS

As immigrants arrived in waves to North America, many were drawn to Pennsylvania by its reputation as "the best poor man's country," since the land was cheap and plentiful, taxes were low, and no state church hounded religious dissenters. The vast majority of these immigrants stepped ashore in the Delaware River ports of Philadelphia or New Castle, yet they did not stay there for long. The quickest way to acquire property and independent livelihood was to move west, into the frontier region of the lower Susquehanna Valley. This westward expansion intruded on Native Americans who had only recently settled in the area, already displaced by expanding colonial populations elsewhere. In diplomatic councils with colonial leaders, these Indians often reminded their counterparts of William

Penn's pledge to always deal peacefully and fairly with them; unfortunately, Penn's successors were not so principled. In the Walking Purchase of 1737, the Lenape agreed to give away the amount of land a person could walk in a one day. The shrewd colonists cheated by hiring athletes to run in relays, covering much more land than the Lenape thought they were giving away.

In the years 1753 and 1754, the French sent troops south from their Canadian territory to occupy and claim the Ohio Valley. For the French, the Allegheny-Ohio watershed was part of a highway that linked their imperial dominions in Canada and Louisiana, and securing it would make the continent's interior their own. George Washington of Virginia failed to persuade the French to leave, and in 1754 they defeated his militia company at Fort Necessity, about 10 miles southeast of present-day Uniontown. Washington's humiliating defeat touched off an international crisis that became the French and Indian War in North America, which pitted the British versus French and Indian forces. The decade of warfare involved European armies that cut roads through the wilderness to build forts on strategic waterways, Native Americans who conducted raids against colonial homesteads for scalps and captives, and colonial militias and vigilantes who attacked and in some cases murdered Indians regardless of their political sympathies. While this war had many theaters around the globe, much of its blood and treasure were spilled in western Pennsylvania along French forts at Erie (Fort Presque Isle), Waterford (Fort LeBoeuf), Pittsburgh (Fort Duquesne), and Franklin (Fort Machault). In 1755, General Edward Braddock led a British army into the Pennsylvania wilderness to take Fort Duquesne, only to be decimated by French and Indian forces. British might returned in force in 1758 when General John Forbes cut his own route across southern Pennsylvania from Carlisle to the Forks of the Ohio, forcing the French to abandon Fort Duquesne and making possible the construction of Fort Pitt, a fortress designed to cement British supremacy in the region. After the war, the Native Americans were disillusioned with the British, and Ottawa war chief Pontiac sparked a widespread native resistance movement known as Pontiac's Rebellion. Pennsylvania, a state celebrated by colonists and Native Americans alike for its peaceful intercultural relations, had become a killing ground in which each side became convinced that its future rested on extirpating the other. Two military campaigns in 1763 and 1764 by Colonel Henry Bouquet brought the hostilities to an end at the Battle of Bushy Run and a subsequent punitive expedition against the Delawares and Shawnee in the Ohio Country. As the 1760s gave way to the Revolutionary Era, the British would find that governing an American empire was more difficult than conquering one.

THE REVOLUTIONARY WAR

On the eve of the American Revolution, Pennsylvania was a multiethnic colony of about 250,000 inhabitants, with an ethnic mixture of mainly English, Germans, and Scots-Irish. Pennsylvania's role as a supplier of raw materials for British manufacturers as well as consumers of their products was in stark contrast to colonies like Massachusetts and Virginia, where resistance to imperial measures was common, especially after 1765 when the British Parliament began to impose a series of revenue-raising taxes. The First Continental Congress met in Philadelphia in 1774 with delegates from each of the colonies except Georgia to protest the commerce restrictions and taxes. By the time the Second Continental Congress convened in May 1775, the opening salvo of the War for American Independence had already been fired in Massachusetts, and Pennsylvania joined the 12 other colonies in a war for national liberation against Great Britain. During the American Revolution, the Pennsylvania State House—today known as Philadelphia's Independence Hall—became the center for the wartime business of the new United

States government, except when the British threat caused the capital to be moved successively. While Congress was sitting in York, Pennsylvania (October 1777 to June 1778), it approved the Articles of Confederation, the first step toward a national government. The final military victory at Yorktown, Virginia, in 1781 assured political independence, greater social equality, and more economic freedom. But at the end of the war, Pennsylvanians, like the rest of American people, still had to determine how to govern themselves and how to adapt to the new, more egalitarian society that was taking shape in the new nation.

By the end of the war, Pennsylvania had won control of the disputed areas in the northeast and received title to most of the disputed lands in western Pennsylvania, extinguishing all Indian claims to their lands within the state. Pennsylvania became the first state to begin the gradual abolition of slavery; by 1800, all but 55 of Philadelphia's more than 6,400 blacks were free. Philadelphia grew in importance as the nation's financial and cultural center as well as its temporary capital while Washington DC was being constructed. The city boasted the nation's first museum (1786), first stock exchange (1791), first paved road and turnpike (1792), the largest public building (the State House), and largest market.

INDUSTRIALIZATION AND THE CIVIL WAR

Into the 1790s large areas of the northern and western parts of the state were undistributed or undeveloped. The state adopted generous land policies and distributed free "Donation Lands" to Revolutionary veterans. The immigrant tide into the state increased as Irish fled the potato famine of the late 1840s and Germans fled the political turbulence of their homeland. In 1820 more than 90 percent of the working population was involved in agriculture, and by 1840 more than 77 percent of the 4.8 million employed persons in Pennsylvania were in agriculture. As agriculture began to decline into the 1860s, there was increased industrialization as Pennsylvania

became the leading iron manufacturer in the nation. The state was blessed with iron ore deposits, vast forests that provided charcoal, abundant coal beds that also supplied fuel, limestone used as flux, and streams for water power. By 1861, the factory system became the foundation of the state's industrial greatness as noted by the shift to machinery in the textile industry. Leather-making, lumbering, shipbuilding, publishing, and tobacco and paper manufacture all prospered throughout the 1800s.

The expression "underground railroad" may have originated in Pennsylvania, where numerous citizens, especially Quakers, aided the escape of slaves to freedom in Canada. During the Civil War, Pennsylvania played an important role in preserving the Union as Confederate forces invaded Pennsylvania three times by way of the Cumberland Valley, a natural highway from Virginia to the North. Pennsylvania's multifaceted resources with its railroad system, iron and steel industry, and agricultural wealth were essential factors in the economic strength of

Gettysburg

Union cause. In June 1863, General Robert E. Lee turned his 75,000 men northward on a major invasion across the Mason-Dixon line into Pennsylvania. Confederate forces captured Carlisle, Pennsylvania, and advanced to within three miles of Harrisburg. In a bitterly fought engagement in Gettysburg, the Union army threw back the Confederate forces in the war's bloodiest battle, with 51,000 casualties, marking the major turning point in the struggle to save the Union.

With the end of the war came an era of industrialization led by entrepreneurs who built the mills, mines, and factories of the late 19th century. Businessmen like Henry Clay Frick, Andrew Carnegie, Joseph Wharton, and William Scranton saw fortunes to be made as the coming of mass-produced steel in the 1870s created a modern industrial society in Pennsylvania. These new mills, mines, and factories created a labor shortage. While most of the state's pre-1861 population was composed of ethnic groups from northern Europe, the later period brought increased numbers of Slavic, Italian, Scandinavian, and Jewish immigrants. Between 1900 and 1910, during the height of this "new immigration," Pennsylvania witnessed the largest population increase of any decade in its history. Several important labor struggles took place in the state, such as the Homestead Steel Strike of 1892, igniting the birth of the modern labor union movement.

THE WORLD WARS

As an industrial state, Pennsylvania followed a predictable course that involved devastating economic slumps and financially invigorating wars throughout the 20th century. Although the state continued to be an industrial powerhouse, its national prominence began to subside as economic development became more widespread into the western and the southern parts of the country. Pennsylvania's resources and manpower were of great value in World War I as shipyards in Philadelphia and Chester were decisive in maintaining maritime transport. African American migration

from the South intensified after 1917, when World War I restricted European immigration, and again during World War II.

The effects of the Great Depression were drastic, as 24 percent of the state's workforce was unemployed in 1931, and later in 1933 unemployment reached 37 percent. Only the war-related production demands of World War II, which began in Europe in 1939, restored vitality to the state's economy. Tagged as the "Arsenal of America," factories poured out planes, tanks, armored cars, fuel, and guns. A steady stream of war goods flowed over its railroads and highways. Pennsylvania was second only to New York in the number who served, and it can be said that one out of every seven members of the armed forces in World War II was a Pennsylvanian. In 1940 the Commonwealth was the second largest state in the nation with a population two-thirds that of New York.

Pennsylvania played a key role in the development of major technologies from the late 19th century into the 20th century. George Westinghouse, an American entrepreneur and engineer based in Pittsburgh, invented the railway air brake and was a pioneer in the electrical industry. Westinghouse's electrical distribution system, which used alternating current based on the extensive research by Nikola Tesla, made it possible to provide electricity to the nation's homes and factories. The state became a center for electronics during World War II, when the first computer, ENIAC, was constructed at the University of Pennsylvania in Philadelphia. The first all-motion-picture theater in the world was opened on Smithfield Street in Pittsburgh on June 19, 1905, where the term "nickelodeon" was coined. The first commercial radio broadcast station in the world was KDKA in Pittsburgh, which started daily schedule broadcasting on November 2, 1920.

CONTEMPORARY TIMES

After World War II the coal, steel, and railroad industries declined considerably in

Pennsylvania. Oil and natural gas were by then regarded as so much more convenient to use than coal for heating buildings, while the railroads were losing ground to the growing trucking industry. The state's steel production began to contract in 1963, although the nation's output, stimulated by the Vietnam War, rose to its all-time maximum in 1969 of 141 million tons. The decline in manufacturing jobs has been followed with an increase in education and health services as well as high-tech industry jobs.

Although the state continues to be one of the largest coal-producing states in the nation, a natural gas boom with the Marcellus Shale that covers two-thirds of the state will create new economic opportunities. Both Philadelphia and Pittsburgh, along with numerous other Pennsylvanian cities,

are undergoing revitalization efforts to reclaim abandoned or underused industrial and commercial facilities and are trying to reverse the "brain drain" of talented people moving out of the state. Newly constructed sports stadiums, convention centers, and art centers have attracted new businesses, which in turn have brought hotels, restaurants, and housing to previously blighted sections. This transformation is also seen in the landscape as once-polluted rivers become viable for fishing and recreation and unused railways are converted to trails. In fact, recognition to the state has come from *Forbes* magazine in its 2010 "America's Most Livable Cities" listings: The Pittsburgh metropolitan area received the number one ranking and the Harrisburg-Carlisle metropolitan area received the number five ranking.

Government and Economy

GOVERNMENT

Pennsylvania uses the designation of "Commonwealth" instead of "State," just like Virginia, Kentucky, and Massachusetts. The designation is a remnant from the founding days of William Penn, when to be a commonwealth meant power was derived from equally free and independent people rather than a hierarchical and/or feudal system under a king. When the United States separated from Great Britain and its monarchy and became part of a democratically governed nation, the term commonwealth lost its meaning. The State Seal does not use the term, but it is a traditional, official designation used in referring to the state, and legal processes are in the name of the Commonwealth. In 1776, the state's first constitution referred to Pennsylvania as both "State" and "Commonwealth" (either term can be used correctly today). In Pennsylvania, all legal processes are carried out in the name of the Commonwealth. The Capitol and center of the state government has been located in Harrisburg since 1812, by authority of an act

of February 21, 1810. Philadelphia and then Lancaster were earlier capital cities. The present Capitol building was dedicated in 1906, after an earlier building was destroyed by fire in 1897.

At the federal level, Pennsylvania is represented by two members of the United States Senate and 19 members of the United States House of Representatives. Like the United States, Pennsylvania's state government is defined by a constitution, which was originally drafted in the State Constitutional Convention of 1776 with amended constitutions in 1790, 1838, 1874, and 1968. And, like that of the United States, Pennsylvania's government comprises three equal and independent branches: the executive, legislative, and judicial. The legislative branch makes commonwealth laws, a responsibility carried out by the General Assembly. The General Assembly is made up of 253 members—a Senate with 50 members and a House of Representatives with 203 members. The executive branch administers commonwealth laws and is overseen by the governor. The governor serves a term of four years and, if reelected, may serve a maximum of two terms in succession. And the judicial branch preserves the rule of law and guarantees citizens' rights by resolving disputes through the courts. The judicial branch consists of the Supreme Court, the Superior Court, the Commonwealth Court, courts of common pleas, community courts, and municipal/traffic courts in Philadelphia. Justices and judges are elected statewide and their regular term is 10 years, with judges in the magisterial district and municipal/traffic courts in Philadelphia serving a term of six years.

At the local level there are four general types of municipalities in Pennsylvania (counties, cities, boroughs, and townships) along with active authorities and school districts. With 67 counties, 56 cities, and over 4,000 boroughs, townships, and active authorities, Pennsylvania local government is quite the mosaic. All operate under the laws of the Commonwealth yet each is distinct and independent of other local units and may operate under its own code of laws, although they may overlap geographically and may act together to serve the public.

The state has swung from being a Republican-leaning state during much of the 20th century to a more Democratic-leaning state in the 21st century, as it has backed the Democratic presidential candidate in every election since 1992. Both Philadelphia and Pittsburgh are Democratic strongholds in the state, often delivering huge margins for Democrats in statewide elections, while rural areas tend to be more conservative and support Republicans. City suburbs tend to be the swing areas that can change political views based on a candidate's social and fiscal positions. Overall, the state tends to support officials that have a more pro-life and gun-supporting stance. On the state government level, the senate and representative seats are usually evenly divided between both major parties. The governorship has been frequently held by Republicans since 1861 with

Harrisburg is Pennsylvania's capital.

Democratic governors recently gaining a foothold in the office.

ECONOMY

At different times in history Pennsylvania was the worldwide leader in the production of leather, lumber, steel, zinc, pig iron, coal, coke, glass, cement, and aluminum. Ironically, Pennsylvania's earlier domination in industrial development created a major liability within factories and mills. The enormous capital investment, past and present, left a complex now less efficient than newer industrial centers elsewhere. In steel, Pennsylvania's integrated mills have been less efficient than the South's minimills and the new steel complexes abroad in Japan and China. Yet Pennsylvania is still a national leader in specialty steel products.

Agriculture is concentrated in the fertile counties of the southeast, and prized farmlands lie in the Great Appalachian Valley, where the best agricultural soil can be found.

A cow grazes in a field in Dutch country.

In 2012, the state had 59,309 farms, down from 63,163 five years earlier. Milk is the top agricultural commodity by market value. Tourism is also important to Pennsylvania's economy, with traveler spending rising to $38.4 billion in 2012 from $37 billion in 2011. Heavy industry has declined in general, but the state still manufactures metal products, transportation equipment, chemicals, and other products. The number of manufacturing jobs has fallen to about 560,000 from 960,000 in the 1990s. The number of jobs in education and health services, in contrast, has risen to 1.2 million from 750,000 jobs in 1990.

People and Culture

DEMOGRAPHY

Pennsylvania's 2013 population was estimated at 12.8 million, up from 12.3 million in 2000, making it the sixth most populous state in the country. Pennsylvania had long been the second-most populous state, behind New York, but fell behind California in 1950, Texas in 1980, Florida in 1987, and Illinois in 1990. Eighty percent of Pennsylvania's current population growth comes from international immigration, and 20 percent from the excess of births over deaths among residents. The number of people leaving Pennsylvania each year is larger than the number moving here from other states, so domestic migration is not a positive factor in the state's population growth.

Although most of Pennsylvania is rural, about 70 percent of the population lives in urban areas.

Pennsylvania's population has been growing older. The median age has increased to 40.1 years from 38 years in 2000, and 15.5 percent of the population is 65 or older. Its senior citizen population is one of the five highest in the country.

RACE AND ETHNICITY

Based on the 2010 census, the racial composition of the state is about 82 percent white, 11 percent black or African American, and 3 percent Asian. About 6 percent of Pennsylvanians identify as Hispanic or Latino. The percentage of black or African American residents is

Roughly 70 percent of Pennsylvania's population lives in urban areas, such as Philadelphia.

slightly below the national average of 13 percent, and the percentage of Hispanic or Latino residents is considerably lower than the national average of 16 percent. Philadelphia County has the state's highest concentrations of black or African American and Hispanic or Latino residents. (Black or African American residents represent about 44 percent of the county's population. About 13 percent of residents identify themselves as Hispanic or Latino.)

The largest number of Pennsylvanians identify their ancestry as German, followed by Irish, Italian, English, and Polish. The late 19th and early 20th centuries brought increased numbers of Slavic, Scandinavian, and Jewish immigrants from the eastern Mediterranean and Balkan regions. Many of the new immigrants settled in the east-central and Ohio Valley regions, where coal-mining jobs were plentiful. You can still find ethnic enclaves throughout the state. Pennsylvania's foreign-born population is about 738,000, or 6 percent of the total population, which is less than the national average of 13 percent.

RELIGION

Religion played the major role that led to the founding of Penn's colony. In a Declaration of Rights issued in 1682 by William Penn, the idea that individuals have a natural right to worship according to the dictates of their own conscience was a radical, even subversive notion. At the time, no nation in Europe embraced it. Pennsylvania's religious composition at the beginning of the 21st century can be judged by statistics compiled by the Association of Religion Data Archives. A total of 8,448,193 individual religious adherents are believed to presently exist, amounting to 68.8 percent of Pennsylvania's population according to the Association of Religion Data Archives; 1,331,835 (or 15.8 percent) of that total figure is estimated because numerous congregations are known to exist but have no record of their total adherents. These unaccounted faiths include the Church of Christ, Scientist, and various African American denominations. The archives identified 115 different faiths in Pennsylvania with the breakdown showing Catholics as the largest religious group, followed by Methodists, Lutherans, Presbyterians, and Jewish denominations. Other smaller faiths include Baha'i, Buddhism, Church of Jesus Christ of Latter-day Saints, Hindu, Jain, Jewish, Muslim, Tao, Unitarian Universalism, and Zoroastrian. Although Quakers (Society of Friends) were part of the majority religious denomination in Pennsylvania's early years, the number of adherents to the faith is only 11,800.

Pennsylvania Germans belonged largely to the Lutheran and Reformed churches, but there were also several smaller sects, such as German Baptist Brethren or "Dunkers," Schwenkfelders, and Moravians, the largest groups of which are the Amish and Mennonites, who number 99,500 followers. Pennsylvania has the second largest Amish settlement in the country, which is located in the Lancaster County area (Holmes County in Ohio is first). Other Amish settlements can be found in Mifflin, Indiana, and New Wilmington Counties.

LANGUAGE

As in other states in the United States, English is the dominant language in Pennsylvania. The 2000 census figure shows that 10,583,054 Pennsylvanians—91.6 percent of the population five years old or older—speak only English at home. Two distinctive dialects are noticeable when listening to native Pennsylvanians. One of these is the Midland dialect, which is significant as foundation for speech across the Midwest and Western United States. In the northern counties of the state you hear predominantly the Northern dialect, which has its origins in upstate New York State. In much of south-central Pennsylvania, descendants of the colonial Palatinate German population retain their speech as Deutsch, often misnamed Pennsylvania Dutch. Travels around the state will show that names of numerous rivers and towns have Native American origins, such as Punxsutawney, Aliquippa, Pocono, Towanda, Susquehanna, and Shamokin.

Essentials

Transportation

AIR

Philadelphia International Airport (PHL, 215/937-6937, www.phl.org), the only major airport serving Pennsylvania's largest city, is by far the busiest airport in the state. More than 30 million passengers passed through it in 2012. But seasoned travelers will find it quaint in comparison to airports in Atlanta, Chicago, Los Angeles, Miami, and other major cities. It's served by about 30 passenger airlines, including low-cost airlines AirTran, Frontier, JetBlue, Southwest, Spirit, and Virgin America, and it's a primary hub for US Airways. You'll want to price flights to Philadelphia even if your ultimate destination is Pennsylvania Dutch country or the Pocono Mountains because your savings could be significant. Smaller airports in the eastern half of the state include **Harrisburg International Airport** (MDT), **Lehigh Valley International Airport** (ABE, 800/359-5842, www.lvia.org) in Allentown, and **Wilkes-Barre/Scranton International Airport** (AVP, 570/602-2000, www.flyavp. com).

Pittsburgh International Airport (PIT, 412/472-3525, www.flypittsburgh.com) is Pennsylvania's second busiest airport. It's what the Federal Aviation Administration calls a "medium hub," meaning it's rarely a madhouse. It's served by about a dozen passenger airlines, including low-cost airlines AirTran, Frontier, JetBlue, and Southwest. It's a good idea to price flights to Pittsburgh even if you're bound for the Alleghenies or the Lake Region. Smaller airports in the western half of Pennsylvania include **University Park Airport** (SCE) in State College and **Erie International Airport** (ERI, 814/833-4258, www.erieairport.org).

CAR

Pennsylvania is an easy drive from cities including New York, Baltimore, and the U.S. capital of Washington DC. Its major north-south highways are **I-81** in the eastern part of the state and **I-79** in the western part. I-81 enters Pennsylvania from Maryland and passes through or by the cities of Carlisle, Harrisburg, Wilkes-Barre, and Scranton before continuing north into New York State. I-79 enters Pennsylvania from West Virginia, passes by Pittsburgh, and ends in Erie.

Pennsylvania's main east-west highway is the 359-mile **Pennsylvania Turnpike** mainline (I-76/I-70/I-276), which connects the Pittsburgh, Harrisburg, and Philadelphia areas. It's about five hours from Philadelphia to Pittsburgh via the turnpike, which is is a toll highway. When you enter the turnpike, you pick up a ticket listing the toll for each exit. Be sure not to misplace the ticket; if you do, you'll have to pay the maximum toll at your exit. You'll save money and a bit of time if you have an E-ZPass transponder. E-ZPass is an electronic toll-collection system used on most tolled roads in the northeastern United States. The transponder allows you to enter the turnpike without stopping for a ticket and exit without stopping to pay. Any tolls you incur will be deducted from your pre-paid E-ZPass account. You can sign up for E-ZPass at www.paturnpike.com, by phone at 877/736-6727, at all Pennsylvania Turnpike service plazas, and at select retail locations across the state. As of early 2014, it cost $38 cash to drive the length of the mainline westbound versus $27.24 using E-ZPass—a savings of nearly 30 percent. Pennsylvania Turnpike tolls are increased each year. If you don't have an E-ZPass transponder, be sure to have some

ESSENTIALS
TRANSPORTATION

Previous: a bus in Philadelphia; an Amish buggy in Lancaster County.

cash in your wallet, and steer clear of lanes marked "E-ZPass Only." You don't have to exit the turnpike to grab a bite. There are 15 service plazas along the mainline and two more on the turnpike's Northeast Extension (I-476), which connects the Philadelphia, Lehigh Valley, and Scranton/Wilkes-Barre areas. In addition to dining options, plazas offer fuel and restrooms. Many have gift shops and picnic areas; a few even boast seasonal farmers markets. All plazas are open 24 hours.

It is possible to travel across the southern part of Pennsylvania without paying any tolls. **U.S. Route 30** passes through Pittsburgh, the Laurel Highlands, Bedford, Gettysburg, York County, Lancaster County, and Philadelphia on its way from the West Virginia line east to New Jersey.

I-80 is the major east-west roadway across northern Pennsylvania. It doesn't serve any major cities in Pennsylvania. **U.S. Route 6** is the choice for an exceptionally scenic drive across northern Pennsylvania. Visit www.paroute6.com for trip ideas.

In 2010 the American Society of Civil Engineers (ASCE) gave Pennsylvania's roads a grade of D-, down from a D four years earlier, warning that "many of the state's roads are at or have exceeded their design capacity." Pennsylvania has some of the oldest highways in the country, and truck traffic on its interstates is more than double the national average. ASCE's Report Card for Pennsylvania's Infrastructure also noted that Pennsylvania has more road miles than nearly any other state that contends with severe winters, which take a heavy toll on pavements. Maintaining the extensive road system is a costly and Sisyphean endeavor.

Traffic can be severely hampered by snow and ice in the coldest months and road construction in the warmer ones. Motorists should take extreme care in winter, especially on steep or winding roads. Heavy snow can render minor roads impassable. Road crews are one of the first signs of spring in Pennsylvania. Where there are crews, there are often road or lane closures, decreased speed limits, and increased police presence.

Safety Laws

Nothing ruins a perfectly good day like a traffic ticket—or worse yet, an accident—so pay close attention to posted speed limits and other traffic signs. It's especially important in areas with road construction. If you're caught speeding or violating other traffic laws in an active work zone, you'll face doubled fines and could lose your license temporarily.

In addition to posted signs, heed the following Pennsylvania safety laws:

- **Cell phones:** Pennsylvania law allows talking on the phone while driving, but texting and emailing are forbidden. The fine for using a mobile device to send or receive messages is $50. Just because it's legal to talk on the phone doesn't mean it's sensible. Use a hands-free device or pull off the road when possible, especially when driving in an unfamiliar area.

- **Seat belts:** Pennsylvania law requires drivers and front-seat passengers to wear a seat belt. Passengers under 18 years old must buckle up even when seated in the back.

- **Child car seats:** Pennsylvania law requires a federally approved child car seat for children under four years old and a booster seat for children four to eight years old.

- **Motorcycle helmets:** Motorcyclists under 21 years old must wear protective headgear. Pennsylvania law allows motorcyclists 21 or older to go without a helmet if they have at least two years of riding experience or have passed a motorcycle safety course approved by the Pennsylvania Department of Transportation or Motorcycle Safety Foundation. The fine for riding without a helmet is $25.

Welcome Centers

State-run welcome centers are located along many major roads into Pennsylvania. Don't pass one up. Welcome centers are stocked with free maps and brochures and staffed by travel specialists. They're generally open 7am-7pm.

From Delaware:

- I-95 north, 0.5 mile north of the PA border

From Maryland:

- I-70 west, 0.5 mile west of the PA border
- I-81 north, 1.5 miles north of the PA border
- I-83 north, 2.5 miles north of the PA border

From New Jersey:

- I-276 west, King of Prussia service plaza of PA Turnpike
- I-78 west, 0.5 mile west of the PA border
- I-80 exit 310, 0.5 mile west of the PA border

From New York:

- I-84 exit 53, 1 mile west of the PA border
- I-81 south, 0.5 mile south of the PA border
- Route 15 south, 7 miles south of the PA border
- I-90 west, 0.5 mile west of the PA border

From Ohio:

- I-80 east, 0.5 mile east of the PA border

From West Virginia:

- I-70 east, 5 miles east of the PA border
- I-79 north, 5 miles north of the PA border

BUS

Greyhound (800/231-2222, www.greyhound.com), the largest intercity bus company in North America, offers service to about 130 locations in Pennsylvania, including Philadelphia, Pittsburgh, Allentown, Altoona, Bethlehem, Erie, Harrisburg, Lancaster, Reading, Scranton, State College, Wilkes-Barre, Williamsport, and York. Traveling by Greyhound is generally more time-consuming than driving because buses make frequent stops, and many trips require transfers. But it is economical, especially if you're traveling alone. As of early 2014, service between Philadelphia and Pittsburgh cost as little as $25 with advance purchase. The trip from Philadelphia to Pittsburgh takes anywhere from five hours and forty five minutes to more than nine hours, depending on the route as well as the number of stops, layovers, and transfers. Competition from **Megabus** (877/462-6342, www.megabus.com), which offers express service and fares as low as $1, has helped keep prices down. In Pennsylvania, Megabus provides service to Philadelphia, Pittsburgh, Erie, Harrisburg, and State College. **YO! Bus** (855/669-6287, www.yobus.com), a discount bus service operated by Greyhound and Peter Pan Bus Lines, provides nonstop service between Philadelphia and New York City (2 hours, from $10).

RAIL

Pennsylvania has a rich train heritage—witness the number of tourist railroads, train museums, and rail-trails across the state—but today there's only one choice for passenger service: the National Railroad Passenger Corporation, better known as **Amtrak** (800/872-7245, www.amtrak.com). About a dozen Amtrak routes serve Philadelphia's 30th Street Station, making it one of the busiest intercity passenger rail stations in the country. Rail travel is generally pricier than bus travel, and it's not necessarily faster. The following Amtrak routes include stops in Pennsylvania:

- **Acela Express:** Boston to Washington DC by way of Philadelphia

- **Capitol Limited:** Washington DC to Chicago by way of Pittsburgh

- **Cardinal:** New York to Chicago by way of Philadelphia

- **Carolinian:** New York to Charlotte, North Carolina, by way of Philadelphia

- **Crescent:** New York to New Orleans by way of Philadelphia

- **Keystone:** New York to Harrisburg, with stops including Philadelphia and Lancaster

- **Lake Shore Limited:** New York/Boston to Chicago by way of Erie

- **Northeast Regional:** Boston to points in Virginia by way of Philadelphia

- **Palmetto:** New York to Savannah, Georgia, by way of Philadelphia

- **Pennsylvanian:** New York to Pittsburgh, with stops including Philadelphia, Lancaster, Harrisburg, Altoona, Johnstown, and Latrobe

- **Silver Service:** New York to Miami by way of Philadelphia

- **Vermonter:** northern Vermont to Washington DC by way of Philadelphia

Travel Tips

CONDUCT AND CUSTOMS
Photo Etiquette in Amish Country

It's tempting to take pictures at every turn when visiting Pennsylvania's Amish communities, whose way of dress and way of life are in stark contrast to the mainstream. Please exercise self-restraint. Most Amish believe that posing for photographs violates the biblical commandment against graven images. They also see it as a sign of pride—a dirty word in a society that cherishes humility and community. You don't need to agree with their reasons to see the case for restraint. Imagine tourists cruising through your neighborhood, snapping pictures of your house, your vehicles, and your children. Disconcerting, to say the least.

That's not to say that you can't take any photos of their picturesque farmlands, horse-pulled buggies, and one-room schoolhouses. Just be discreet, and don't aim your camera at anyone's face.

Liquor Laws

If you live in a place where wine and beer are readily available at supermarkets and convenience stores, you'll be shocked by what it takes to stock up in Pennsylvania. The state's alcohol laws are among the strictest and most befuddling in the country. Wine, vodka, gin, rum, and other spirits can only be sold at stores operated by the Pennsylvania Liquor Control Board (PLCB), whose monopoly has made it the largest purchaser of wine and spirits in the United States. While the PLCB claims that its volume-purchase discounts are passed on to consumers, prices tend to be higher than in many parts of the country. (The state liquor tax of 18 percent is included in shelf prices.) The PLCB operates about 600 stores, including a small number of "one-stop shops" conveniently located in supermarkets. Its online store, finewineandgoodspirits.com, has a store locator feature. The PLCB chooses which products it sells, and some may find the selection limited. (Pennsylvanians who have lived in California and other states with more liberal alcohol laws speak longingly of bargain-priced Charles Shaw wines, better known as "Two-Buck Chuck.") Be aware that many wine and spirits stores are closed on Sunday, and they're all closed on most major holidays. So if you run out of Chardonnay while celebrating Independence Day, you're out of luck.

Thirsting for beer? You won't find it in the state-operated stores. Beer can be purchased from licensed bars, restaurants, and distributors. Distributors generally have better prices, but they're required to sell beer by the case or keg. For a six-pack or two, head to the nearest bar. Some Pennsylvania supermarkets now sell beer in on-premises "restaurants," but they are few and far between. Per state law, bars and restaurants cannot sell alcohol after 2am, and beer distributors are closed on Sundays.

With limited exceptions, it's illegal to bring alcohol into the state. (But between you and me, there's not much chance of getting caught.)

SENIOR TRAVELERS

Pennsylvania has a large elderly population—only three U.S. states have a higher percentage of citizens age 65 and over—so senior travelers will find it quite welcoming. Many attractions offer senior discounts, which can be significant. Seven Springs Mountain Resort, for example, offers half-price lift tickets to skiers age 70-79 and free tickets to anyone older. Seniors also enjoy free or discounted public transportation in cities including Philadelphia and Pittsburgh. Discounts aren't necessarily posted, so make a habit of inquiring before paying.

TRAVELERS WITH DISABILITIES

Federal laws protecting the rights of people with disabilities are generally adhered to throughout Pennsylvania, but the historic nature of some attractions makes them inaccessible to wheelchairs. For example, wheelchair users cannot ascend to the cupola of the 1832 building that houses the Seminary Ridge Museum in Gettysburg. In some parts of Pennsylvania, sidewalks are in such terrible disrepair that they're impassable to wheelchair users. The state and some municipalities have also been slow to install or improve curb ramps at pedestrian intersections.

GAY AND LESBIAN TRAVELERS

Gay and lesbian travelers flock to parts of Pennsylvania, most notably its largest city, Philadelphia, and in May of 2014, Pennsylvania joined the growing number of states that allow same-sex marriage when a federal judge ruled the state's same-sex marriage ban unconstitutional. The City of Brotherly Love, as Philadelphia is known, was one of the first cities in the country to prohibit discrimination based on sexual orientation. It's the site of multiple annual events for the lesbian, gay, bisexual, and transgender (LGBT) community, including the largest LGBT film festival on the East Coast and the largest National Coming Out Day event in the world. Street signs in the city's "Gayborhood" sport the colors of the rainbow flag. The publisher of *Philadelphia Gay News*, one of the nation's oldest and most respected LGBT newspapers, has argued that Philadelphia is the nation's most gay-friendly city "by a long shot." And in 2013, Philadelphia earned a score of 100 out of 100 on the Human Rights Campaign's Municipal Equality Index, which rates U.S. cities on their inclusivity of LGBT people. Only 25 of the 291 cities rated received perfect scores.

The town of New Hope in Bucks County, about an hour north of Philadelphia, is also known as a gay-friendly destination. In most other parts of Pennsylvania, including Pittsburgh, rainbow flags and public displays of affection among gays and lesbians are usually reserved for pride parades and other LGBT-focused events.

Health and Safety

MEDICAL SERVICES

Pennsylvania has high-quality health care, but it usually comes at a high price. Visitors from other countries would be wise to purchase international health insurance. Domestic travelers who have health insurance should be aware that some plans will not cover care provided by "out of network" doctors and hospitals.

If you have a medical emergency, dial 911 from any phone. You'll be connected to an operator who can dispatch an ambulance. U.S. law requires hospitals to treat emergency cases regardless of the patient's ability to pay.

EXTREME TEMPERATURES

Pennsylvania can be very hot and humid in summer and very cold in winter. Extremes of temperature are potentially dangerous. Heat-related dangers include heat exhaustion, which is characterized by weakness and dizziness, and heatstroke, which can be deadly. The elderly and those in poor health are particularly vulnerable. The best defense is to drink plenty of water and take it easy. Even healthy young people can suffer heat disorders, often from exercising outside. Seek medical aid if you notice signs of heatstroke, which include lethargy, confusion, and unconsciousness.

In winter, temperatures can dip below 0 degrees Fahrenheit (-18 degrees Celsius). Cold-weather dangers include frostbite, falls on icy sidewalks, and car accidents on icy or snow-covered roads. Protect yourself by dressing appropriately—a coat, hat, gloves, and shoes with good traction are must-haves—and limiting your time outside. If you're going to drive, make sure your vehicle is in good condition and has plenty of gas. Breakdowns are downright scary when the weather is frigid. It's a good idea to invest in all-season tires or winter tires. Clear snow and ice from your vehicle before hitting the road, and drive with caution.

TICKS AND LYME DISEASE

Pennsylvania has one of the highest incidences of Lyme disease in the United States. The disease is transmitted to humans through the bite of infected ticks. Early symptoms include fever, headache, fatigue, and a red rash that resembles a bull's eye. If left untreated, Lyme disease can affect joints, the heart, and the nervous system. The best defense is to reduce your exposure to ticks, which are most active in the warmer months. The U.S. Centers for Disease Control and Prevention advises avoiding wooded and bushy areas; walking in the center of trails; applying an insect repellent with 20-30 percent DEET to clothing and exposed skin; treating clothing and gear with products that contain permethrin; and checking your body, clothing, and gear for ticks. For more information and instructions for tick removal, visit www.cdc.gov/lyme.

Information and Services

MONEY

The U.S. dollar ($) is the only currency accepted in Pennsylvania. Visitors from other countries may be able to purchase U.S. dollars from their bank. Most international airports, including Philadelphia International Airport and Pittsburgh International Airport, have currency exchange counters. Don't wait until you're settled in to exchange currency; exchange companies can be hard to find in U.S. cities. If you have an Automated Teller Machine (ATM) card, you can withdraw U.S. dollars from any ATM in the country. ATMs are ubiquitous in Pennsylvania's larger cities, and you shouldn't have much trouble finding one even in small towns or rural areas. When using an ATM that's not owned by your bank, you may be charged a service fee by both the ATM's bank and your bank.

CELL PHONES

Cell phone reception is generally strong in urban areas of the state. In rural or mountainous areas, expect some dead zones. Reception is particularly shaky in north-central Pennsylvania. It's a good idea to check your cell phone carrier's coverage in and around areas you plan to visit. You can find coverage maps on most carriers' websites.

Pennsylvania law prohibits texting or emailing while driving.

INTERNET ACCESS

If you want Internet access while traveling, it's best to have a data-enabled mobile device.

Internet cafés are virtually unheard of in Pennsylvania, and while wireless networks are numerous, many are password-protected. Hotels and coffee shops are your best bet for finding a public wireless network, though some charge for access. Free wireless access is available at Philadelphia International Airport and Pittsburgh International Airport, on most Greyhound and Megabus trips, and in select Amtrak stations and trains.

MAPS AND TOURIST INFORMATION

Road maps are sold at most gas stations, but if you're not planning to do a lot of driving, they're hardly necessary. Pennsylvania's visitors centers are well stocked with tourist maps, many of which are free. Maps focused on hiking, biking, fishing, boating, or other recreational opportunities are also available at many visitors centers. There are more than a dozen state-run welcome centers near Pennsylvania's borders, and visitors centers operated by local or regional tourism promotion agencies can be found in many popular destinations. In addition to maps, they usually carry a large selection of brochures on area attractions and accommodations. Some offer free wireless Internet access. If you're heading to a national or state park, there's little need to stop at a visitors center en route; you'll find maps on arrival.

Resources

Suggested Reading

HISTORY

Ellis, Joseph J. *Founding Brothers: The Revolutionary Generation.* Winner of the 2001 Pulitzer Prize for History, this book explores the oft-contentious relationships between America's founding fathers. Read it en route to Philadelphia, where so many of their squabbles played out.

Kraybill, Donald B. *The Amish of Lancaster County.* Donald Kraybill, a professor at Lancaster County's Elizabethtown College and a nationally recognized authority on Anabaptist groups, has authored or edited more than 20 books. This 2008 book is an easily digestible explanation of the lifestyle of the Lancaster County Amish, complete with full-color photographs.

McCullough, David. *The Johnstown Flood.* First published in 1968, this riveting account of the 1889 flood that killed more than 2,000 people in a Pennsylvania steel town was David McCullough's first book. The Pittsburgh-born historian has since won two Pulitzer Prizes and the Presidential Medal of Freedom.

McIlnay, Dennis P. *The Horseshoe Curve: Sabotage and Subversion in the Railroad City.* This is the gripping story of the Nazi plot to destroy the Pennsylvania Railroad's Horseshoe Curve during World War II. Published in 2007, the book includes eyewitness accounts of the execution of six saboteurs convicted of the failed plot. Author Dennis McIlnay, who lives within a few miles of the targeted section of rail track, delves into the history of the Pennsylvania Railroad and the construction of the Curve.

FICTION

Chabon, Michael. *The Mysteries of Pittsburgh* and *Wonder Boys.* Michael Chabon's first two novels are set in Pittsburgh, where the Pulitzer Prize-winning author went to college. The main character in *Wonder Boys* was inspired by one of his professors at the University of Pittsburgh. Both books were adapted into films.

Dillard, Annie. *An American Childhood.* Annie Dillard's enchanting memoir paints a vivid picture of Pittsburgh in the 1950s.

Shaara, Michael. *The Killer Angels.* Winner of the 1975 Pulitzer Prize for Fiction, this superbly crafted historical novel tells the story of the Battle of Gettysburg. The page-turner was adapted into the 1993 film *Gettysburg,* another excellent treatment of the Civil War's bloodiest battle.

OUTDOORS

Carson, Rachel. *Silent Spring.* Pennsylvania-born biologist and nature writer Rachel Carson has been called the mother of the modern environmental movement—largely because of this 1962 book on the harmful effects of pesticides.

Egan, Timothy. *The Big Burn: Teddy Roosevelt and the Fire that Saved America.* This is the story of a devastating blaze that killed more than 100 firefighters. It's also the story of Gifford Pinchot, America's first forester and one of Pennsylvania's favorite sons.

MAGAZINES

Pennsylvania Heritage. Historians, curators, and archivists contribute to this liberally illustrated magazine, co-published by the Pennsylvania Historical and Museum Commission and the Pennsylvania Heritage Foundation. To receive the quarterly magazine, become a member of the Heritage Foundation at www.paheritage.org or by calling 866/823-6539.

Pennsylvania Magazine. Showcasing the state's places, people, and events since 1981, *Pennsylvania Magazine* is published six times a year. Request a free issue or subscribe at www.pa-mag.com or by calling 800/537-2624.

Internet Resources

TRAVEL

Pennsylvania Tourism Office
www.visitpa.com
Pennsylvania's official tourism website provides information on countless attractions, plus trip ideas for those not sure where to start.

HISTORY

Pennsylvania Historical & Museum Commission
www.phmc.state.pa.us
The website of Pennsylvania's official history agency is a good starting point for information on the people and events that shaped the Commonwealth.

www.explorepahistory.com
WITF, Harrisburg's PBS and NPR affiliate, organizes this website in conjunction with the Pennsylvania Historical and Museum Commission. You could spend days engrossed in the stories behind the 2,000-odd historical markers that dot the state.

CULTURE

Amish Studies
www2.etown.edu/amishstudies
This site, maintained by the Young Center for Anabaptist & Pietist Studies at Lancaster County's Elizabethtown College, answers frequently asked questions about the Amish.

OUTDOORS

Pennsylvania Bureau of State Parks
www.visitpaparks.com
This site provides detailed descriptions of Pennsylvania's state parks, which numbered 117 at last count. The companion reservation site, www.pa.reserveworld.com, allows you to search for parks by region and amenities such as white-water boating and beach swimming.

National Parks in Pennsylvania
www.nps.gov
About 30 of Pennsylvania's historic sites, scenic trails, and river corridors are part of the National Park System. Visit this site for a comprehensive listing.

Pennsylvania Trails
www.explorepatrails.com

Launched by the state Department of Conservation and Natural Resources in late 2009, ExplorePAtrails.com allows outdoorsy types to find and share information on thousands of miles of land and water trails.

Pennsylvania Fish & Boat Commission
www.fish.state.pa.us

Purchase a fishing license, register a boat, read up on regulations, or submit a request for the state agency's free publications. The site boasts a number of interactive maps designed for anglers and boaters.

Pennsylvania Game Commission
www.pgc.state.pa.us

Hunters can find information on seasons, bag limits, and everything else they need to know on the website of Pennsylvania's wildlife management agency.

LODGING

Pennsylvania Campground Owners Association
www.pacamping.com

This trade association represents more than 200 individually owned and operated campgrounds. Search its online directory or request a free copy of the printed version.

PA Tourism & Lodging Association
www.painns.com

This is a handy directory of bed-and-breakfasts, inns, boutique hotels, and other unique accommodations represented by the PA Tourism & Lodging Association.

Index

Drake Well Museum: 422
Dream Garden: 33
drive-in theaters: 107
driving: 487–489
ducks: 414
Duffy's Tavern: 367
Duncan House: 320
Duncansville: 363
du Pont, Alfred I.: 93
du Pont, E.I.: 93
du Pont, Henry Francis: 93
du Pont, Pierre S.: 92
DuPont chemicals: 92, 93
Duquesne and Monongahela Inclines: 24, 254, 272, 274
Duquesne Club: 262
Dutch Eating Place: 54
Dutch Springs: 111
Dutch Wonderland: 20, 130

E

Eakins Oval: 46
East Broad Top Railroad: 378
East Carson Street: 15
East End Pittsburgh: 289
Eastern State Penitentiary: 14, 26, 46
Eckley Miners' Village: 245
economy: 482–483
Eerie Horror Fest: 408
8 Great Tuesdays: 403
Eisenhower, President Dwight D.: 195
Eisenhower National Historic Site: 195
Eldred World War II Museum: 436
Electric City Trolley Museum: 24, 243
Elfreth's Alley: 38
Elfreth's Alley Museum: 39
elk country: 11, 19, 459–465
Elk Country Visitor Center: 461
Elk Mountain: 248
emergency services: 492
Endless Mountain Music Festival: 447
environmental issues: 470–471
Ephrata Cloister: 136
Equality Forum: 66
equestrian events: Brandywine Polo Club 96; Devon Horse Show and Country Fair 96; Ludwig's Corner Horse Show and Country Fair 96; Meadows Racetrack & Casino 338; Mohegan Sun at Pocono Downs 245; Point-to-Point 95; Presque Isle Downs & Casino 407; Radnor Hunt Races 95
Erie: 16, 395–400
Erie Art Museum: 406
Erie Art Museum Blues & Jazz Festival: 406
Erie County Historical Society Museums: 405
Erie Land Lighthouse: 405

Erie Maritime Museum and Flagship *Niagara*: 392, 400–401
Erie National Wildlife Refuge: 418
Erie Planetarium: 406
Erie Playhouse: 405
Erie Zoo: 406
Espy House: 384
ethnic groups: 483
European settlers: 475–476
Everhart Museum: 244

F

Fabric Row: 68
Fabulous 1890s Weekend: 447
Factory Tour Capital of the World: 182
Fairmount Park: accommodations 78–79; performing arts 65; sights 43–48
fairs, agricultural: *see* agricultural fairs
fall: 12
Fall Carlisle: 177
fall foliage: general discussion 12; Autumn Timber Festival 215; Fall Foliage Festival 386; Fall Foliage Weekends 239; Kinzua Bridge Fall Festival 438; Lehigh Gorge Trail 18, 235; Pine Creek Gorge 445; Wissahickon Valley Park 72
Fall Harvest Festival: 95
Fallingwater: 11, 15, 21, 254, 319
Fallsington: 103
farmers markets: Apple Castle 345; Broad Street Market 175; Central Market (York) 183; Central Market, Lancaster 126; Ligonier 329; Meadville Market House 417; Reading Terminal Market 54
farms: Amish Farm and House 123; Arrowhead Wine Cellars 404; Big Valley 379; Cherry Crest Adventure Farm 20; Kuerner Farm 17, 94; Landis Valley Village & Farm Museum 132; Plain & Fancy Farm 122; Somerset Historical Center 324
Farm Show: 176
fauna: 473–474
Fernwood Resort: 215
Fete Day: 40
film festival: 408
firefighting: 175, 184
Fire Museum: 184
First Continental Congress: 36
First Fridays at the Frick: 293
First Friday Scranton: 247
First Fridays in Old City: 30
First Fridays Lancaster: 125
First Friday Williamsport: 456
First Night Pittsburgh: 294
First Night State College: 369
First Presbyterian Church: 262
fish: 414
fishing: Allegheny National Forest 439; Allegheny Reservoir 434; Bayfront District, Erie 402;

QR

XYZ

List of Maps

Photo Credits

page 4 Amish buggies © www.padutchcountry.com/Terry Ross; page 5 Pittsburgh's skyline at night © Sean Pavone/123rf.com; page 6 (top left) © Cristalli Simone/123rf.com, (top right) © Sean Pavone/123rf.com, (bottom) © Visions Of America LLC/123rf.com; page 7 (top) © Jon Bilous/123rf.com, (bottom left) York County Convention & Visitors Bureau, (bottom right) © Delmas Lehman/123rf.com; page 8 © David Fulmer; page 9 (top) © Jon Bilous/123rf.com, (bottom left) © Jon Bilous/123rf.com, (bottom right) © Kiya/123rf.com; page 11 © James Dugan/123rf.com; page 12 (top) © Jon Bilous/123rf.com, (bottom) © snehit/123rf.com; page 13 (top) © Kiya/123rf.com, (bottom) © Jon Bilous/123rf.com; page 14 (left) © Natalia Bratslavsky/123rf.com, (right) © Anna Dubrovsky; page 15 © Longwood Gardens; page 16 (top) poconomountains.com, (bottom) © Anna Dubrovsky; page 17 © Anna Dubrovsky; page 18 © Anton Foltin/123rf.com; page 19 © Mary Linkevich/Hawk Mountain Sanctuary/GoGreaterReading.com; page 20 © Hershey Entertainment & Resorts; page 21 © Anna Dubrovsky; page 22 © Anna Dubrovsky; page 23 © Paul Witt/www.DestinationGettysburg.com; page 24 © Michele Schaffer; page 25 both photos © Wasin Pummarin/123rf.com; page 26 © 123rf.com; page 27 © Visions Of America LLC/123rf.com; page 29 © Andrew Kazmierski/123rf.com; page 33 © Wallace Weeks/123rf.com; pages 35 - 40 © Visions Of America LLC/123rf.com; page 43 © Jon Bilous/123rf.com; page 45 © Marco Rubino/123rf.com; page 46 © tupungato/123rf.com; page 47 © 123rf.com; page 48 © Florence McGinn/123rf.com; page 49 © 1999 & 2013 City of Philadelphia Mural Arts Program/Meg Saligman/Photo by Steve Weinik © 2013. Reprinted by permission; page 51 © Jon Bilous/123rf.com; page 53 © Visions Of America LLC/123rf.com; page 55 © Wasin Pummarin/123rf.com; page 56 © Olivier Le Queinec/123rf.com; page 83 © Anna Dubrovsky; page 87 © Visions Of America LLC/123rf.com; page 90 © tupungato/123rf.com; page 92 © Longwood Gardens; page 99 courtesy of the Bucks County Playhouse; page 102 © Washington Crossing Historic Park; page 104 courtesy of Inn at Bowman's Hill; pages 107 - 111 © Discover Lehigh Valley; page 112 © Anna Dubrovsky; page 115 © (top) Liane Harrold/123rf.com, (bottom) © Delmas Lehman/123rf.com; page 116 The Hershey Story Museum; page 117 © Visions Of America LLC/123rf.com; page 119 © Jon Bilous/123rf.com; page 120 © www.padutchcountry.com/Coy Butler; page 122 © Anna Dubrovsky; page 124 © Anna Dubrovsky; page 126 © Jon Bilous/123rf.com; page 128 Strasburg Railroad Company/RR Tennison; pages 130 - 139 www.padutchcountry.com; page 146 © Anna Dubrovsky; page 150 © Jon Bilous/123rf.com; page 152 © Visions Of America LLC/123rf.com; page 154 © Mary Linkevich/Hawk Mountain Sanctuary/GoGreaterReading.com; page 160 www.VisitHersheyHarrisburg.org; page 161 The Hershey Story Museum; page 162 The Hershey Story Museum; page 165 www.VisitHersheyHarrisburg.org; page 172 © Jon Bilous/123rf.com; page 173 www.VisitHersheyHarrisburg.org; page 174 © Henryk Sadura/123rf.com; page 179 www.VisitHersheyHarrisburg.org; pages 183 - 188 York County Convention & Visitors Bureau; page 191 © Jeremy Hess/www.DestinationGettysburg.com; page 193 © Liane Harrold/123rf.com; pages 194 - 202 www.DestinationGettysburg.com; page 204 both photos poconomountains.com; page 205 © Mike Klemme/poconomountains.com; page 206 poconomountains.com; page 207 © Jay Mudaliar/123rf.com; page 210 © Songquan Deng/123rf.com; page 211 poconomountains.com; page 212 © Lou Perez/123rf.com; page 213 poconomountains.com; page 214 © Jeff Greenberg/poconomountains.com; page 216 © Bruce Buck/poconomountains.com; page 220 © Jeff Greenberg/poconomountains.com; page 224 poconomountains.com; page 225 © Rare Brick Photography/poconomountains.com; pages 228 - 234 poconomountains.com; page 235 © Pocono Whitewater/poconomountains.com; page 237 Wikimedia Commons/public domain; page 238 poconomountains.com; page 241 © Francisco Antunes; page 243 © Michele Schaffer; page 246 © Delmas Lehman/123rf.com; page 247 courtesy FirstFridayScranton.com; page 253 (top) © Gino Santa Maria/123rf.com, (bottom) © Dustin Lee; page 254 © Steven Heap/123rf.com; page 255 © Richard Kane/123rf.com; pages 257 - 258 © Anna Dubrovsky; page 263 www.visitpittsburgh.com; page 264 © Senator John Heinz History Center/www.visitpittsburgh.com; page 266 © Anna Dubrovsky; page 267 © Jeff

Acknowledgments

In the short time since the last edition of this book, I have become a mother to two delightful children. I hope to someday dedicate a book to them. This book, however, is dedicated to my mother, who makes it possible for me to be both mother and writer. Having traveled far and wide, I can say with reasonable certainty that there is no better grandmother in all the world.

I also owe a debt of gratitude to the folks at Avalon Travel, who entrusted me with this project and tolerated my tardiness. I learned my lesson: book deadlines and baby due dates do not mix. Thank you to acquisitions director Grace Fujimoto; editors Nikki Ioakimedes, Elizabeth Hollis Hansen, and Kevin McLain; production coordinator Elizabeth Jang; and cartographic editor Kat Bennett.

When faced with the daunting task of updating this guide, I went looking for a whipsmart intern from Pittsburgh's Chatham University. I was fortunate to find three: Meaghan Clohessy, Marguerite Sargent, and Maggie Yankovich. Thank you, ladies, for your enthusiasm and diligence.

I'm grateful to Pennsylvania's dedicated tourism promoters, who led me in interesting directions and answered my incessant questions. Thanks to Quinn Bryner, Donna Schorr, Nina Kelly, Kim Lilly, George Wacker, Joel Cliff, Lisa Haggerty, Rick Dunlap, Allison Freeman, Carl Whitehill, Alicia Quinn, Kristin Mitchell, Lisa Rager, Olivia Bragdon, Jennifer Fleck, Christie Black, Ed Stoddard, Christine Pennsy, Linda Devlin, Lori Copp, Allison Senchur, Carla Wehler, and especially Julie Donovan.

As I traveled around this unique state, I picked the brains of everyone from barflies to museum curators. I'm grateful to them for sharing their time and the sort of juicy tidbits that set this book apart from so much travel content.

Finally, I wish to thank my friends, particularly the Lady Council and Ashley Lee. To borrow the words of Billy Joel, you come to me when I'm feeling down and inspire me without a sound. For a writer, there is no greater gift than inspiration—except perhaps a sleek and powerful MacBook, for which I thank my ever so practical husband.

MAP SYMBOLS

Symbol	Name	Symbol	Name	Symbol	Name	Symbol	Name
▭▭▭	Expressway	★	Highlight	✗	Airfield	⚓	Golf Course
▭▭▭	Primary Road	○	City/Town	✈	Airport	🅿	Parking Area
▭▭▭	Secondary Road	◉	State Capital	▲	Mountain	▱	Archaeological Site
-------	Unpaved Road	⊛	National Capital	✚	Unique Natural Feature	⛪	Church
- - - -	Trail	★	Point of Interest	🥦	Waterfall	⛽	Gas Station
··········	Ferry	●	Accommodation	▲	Park	〰	Glacier
-··-··-	Railroad	▼	Restaurant/Bar	🚩	Trailhead	⬚	Mangrove
▭▭▭	Pedestrian Walkway	■	Other Location	🎿	Skiing Area	▱	Reef
⊞⊞⊞	Stairs	⅄	Campground			▱	Swamp

CONVERSION TABLES

°C = (°F - 32) / 1.8
°F = (°C x 1.8) + 32
1 inch = 2.54 centimeters (cm)
1 foot = 0.304 meters (m)
1 yard = 0.914 meters
1 mile = 1.6093 kilometers (km)
1 km = 0.6214 miles
1 fathom = 1.8288 m
1 chain = 20.1168 m
1 furlong = 201.168 m
1 acre = 0.4047 hectares
1 sq km = 100 hectares
1 sq mile = 2.59 square km
1 ounce = 28.35 grams
1 pound = 0.4536 kilograms
1 short ton = 0.90718 metric ton
1 short ton = 2,000 pounds
1 long ton = 1.016 metric tons
1 long ton = 2,240 pounds
1 metric ton = 1,000 kilograms
1 quart = 0.94635 liters
1 US gallon = 3.7854 liters
1 Imperial gallon = 4.5459 liters
1 nautical mile = 1.852 km

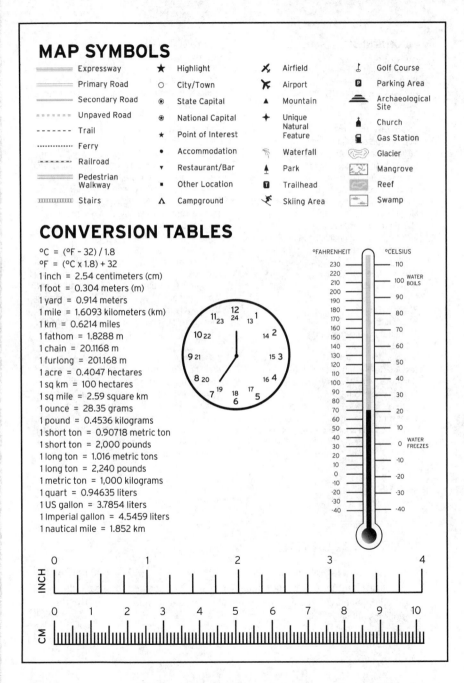

MOON PENNSYLVANIA
Avalon Travel
a member of the Perseus Books Group
1700 Fourth Street
Berkeley, CA 94710, USA
www.moon.com

Editor: Nikki Ioakimedes
Contributor: Dan Eldridge
Series Manager: Kathryn Ettinger
Copy Editor: Alissa Cyphers
Graphics Coordinator: Elizabeth Jang
Production Coordinator: Elizabeth Jang
Cover Design: Faceout Studios, Charles Brock
Moon Logo: Tim McGrath
Map Editor: Kat Bennett
Cartographer: Stephanie Poulain
Indexer: Rachel Kuhn

ISBN-13: 978-1-61238-770-3
ISSN: 1096-9543

Printing History
1st Edition – 1998
5th Edition – December 2014
5 4 3 2 1

Front cover photo: fall foliage on a rural Pennsylvania road © Russell Kord/Alamy

Title page photo: the *LOVE* sculpture, by Robert Indiana, in Philadelphia's Love Park, photo © Sean Pavone/123rf.com

Printed in Canada by Friesens

KEEPING CURRENT

If you have a favorite gem you'd like to see included in the next edition, or see anything that needs updating, clarification, or correction, please drop us a line. Send your comments via email to feedback@moon.com, or use the address above.